A social history of GERMANY 1648–1914

Eda Sagarra

HOLMES & MEIER PUBLISHERS
NEW YORK

First published in the United States of America 1977 by
Holmes & Meier Publishing Company, Inc.
101 Fifth Avenue
New York, New York 10003

Library of Congress Cataloging in Publication Data

Sagarra, Eda.
A social history of Germany, 1648–1914.

Bibliography: p.
Includes index.
1. Germany—Social conditions. 2. Social classes—Germany—History. 3. Germany—Economic conditions. I. Title.
HN445.S23 1977 301.1′43 77-24201
ISBN 0-8419-0332-8

PRINTED IN GREAT BRITAIN

Contents

Part I: 1648–1806

From the end of the Thirty Years War to the fall of the Holy Roman Empire

Introduction to Part I
Germany and the Thirty Years War

In the last, most barbarous phase of the war (1618–48), the Swedish ambassador to the Netherlands, German-born Ludwig Camerarius, wrote to a friend in Nuremberg: 'Happy are they who in this wretched time are already asleep in the Lord.'[1] It was a sentiment expressed frequently by his countrymen in those years, in poetry and letters, in diary entries and funeral orations. For unlike the wars of the twentieth century (apart from 1944–5), the Thirty Years War was fought almost wholly on the territory of the Holy Roman Empire. As a result, in the war theatres along the main transit routes, a whole generation of Germans had grown to manhood knowing nothing else but fighting, pillaging and burning. The damage done to life and property made this war the most destructive in Germany's history before the mid twentieth century. Thus a traveller making his way from Pomerania in the north-east during the late 1640s, across Mecklenburg, turning southwards through Brandenburg, Magdeburg and Thuringia, and then on to the Palatinate and Swabia in the south, would have found countless numbers of devastated villages, seen towns which had been sacked not once, but three and four times, the surviving inhabitants reduced in some cases to cannibalism.[2] In all these areas the total loss in population has been estimated as at least 40–60 per cent, and in some districts to have been as high as 70 per cent. Yet it would have been possible in the same years to travel north-west from Vienna, avoiding central Bohemia, through Upper and Lower Saxony, across Bremen into Holstein, and see little evidence of the war apart from the region around Leipzig and Magdeburg. For the war had been selective in its targets. The populations of neutral Switzerland, and of Austria, the Tyrol, Holstein and Frisia, had changed little between 1618 and 1648. It was said that during these years not a single foreign soldier had crossed the frontiers of the territory of Oldenburg, in the north-west, where the ruler, Count Anton Günther, was able to increase the prosperity and revenues of his realm from his famous stud farm. Hamburg too went unscathed, a fact it owed to the wise foresight of the city fathers in preparing adequate defences. Further east, the thriving corn markets in mid century Danzig, Königsberg and Thorn contrasted sharply with conditions elsewhere in the Empire, where fighting and plague threatened to turn the land, in Camerarius's phrase, into 'an Arabian desert'.[3]

In general it was the same areas which bore the brunt of the war, of battle and marauding soldiers, the burghers being pillaged if they refused, getting into hopeless debt if they complied with the invaders' demands. As if to emphasize the injustice of life, those areas around the main transit routes which suffered most in the war also experienced the worst of the plague epidemics in the 1630s and 1640s. It was the plague, and the starvation in its wake, which was the real cause of drastic population loss. Thus in Leutkirch, a free imperial town in Württemberg, the parson reported the deaths of 413 adults and 269 children; in the Lutheran community only thirty-seven couples and nineteen children survived among his parishioners; in the Catholic parish of Leutkirch barely 100 survived out of a former total of 1500.[4] Such figures are not uncommon for the worst-affected areas.

Population statistics from this period are of course only approximate. In the seventeenth century it was usual but not obligatory to keep parish registers. However, it was common in wartime for the parish priest or vicar to lead his flock to the safety of the forest for weeks or even months in face of danger, and in such cases records were not kept up. Tax returns, such as the *Reichstürkensteuer*, levied since the sixteenth century for the defence of the Empire against the Turk, are helpful, but fragmentary. Some princes, such as the Austrian ruler, did take a census of their subjects in the years after the war; others, notably the ecclesiastical princes, were mindful of the Lord's disapproval of King David's efforts to record the number of his subjects and refrained from the attempt.[5] How unreliable a local census could be is illustrated by the reaction of the Zwickau town council in 1655 to an enquiry from Dresden for tax purposes: 'It ought to be borne in mind, that if we return the rolls and the numbers of men as high, it might turn out as it did with the poll tax; but if we return too few, His Highness the Elector might populate this place with strangers.' The vicar of Langhennersdorf in 1658 was more succinct: 'were more for certain reasons not returned.'[6]

Modern scholars are more or less in agreement that Germany lost some 40 per cent of its rural and 33 per cent of its urban population in consequence of war and epidemics. Although such figures are substantially lower than those given by earlier historians, and although we no longer share their view that the war and its consequences impoverished the German people economically and culturally for the next 150 years, it remains true that the years 1618–48 brought about far-reaching changes in the political and social structure of the country. Politically, the most significant effect of the peace settlement of Westphalia, the treaties which finally ended the war, was the emergence of over 300 states, owing little more than nominal allegiance to the Holy Roman Emperor. None was strong enough to provide political or economic leadership, while the archaic framework within which the member states operated made the conduct of business on a national scale, such as the levying of taxes for defence, slow and wearisome. German states in the subsequent hundred years or so were often not more than a negative factor in the calculations of foreign powers: thus the French paid subsidies to Bavaria and other states to prevent the establishment of Austrian hegemony in south Germany. Yet although cumbersome and often ineffective in its working, the conglomeration of member states known as the Holy Roman Empire was a genuine federation. Certainly, the war and its consequences greatly strengthened the power of the territorial princes and led directly to absolutist forms of government in most German states, but it nevertheless remains true that some provincial and even municipal liberties survived longer in Germany than in countries such as France or England.

Germany recovered slowly from the war, remaining a poor country until the nineteenth century. The basis of life remained agricultural, and despite some revival of trade, the land provided the chief source of princely revenue. It was on the land too that the privileged status of the aristocracy in the political and social organization of the territories in post-war Germany was based. Its position of eminence was to be consolidated in the course of the second half of the seventeenth century and contrasted sharply with the general symptoms of decay which many observers had regarded as characteristic of that class in the century before the outbreak of the Thirty Years War. Fortune, so frequently evoked in baroque literature, thus demonstrated yet again her fickle nature. For the privileged status of the landed nobility in the service of the prince in seventeenth and eighteenth century Germany was won at the cost of the very social group which in the sixteenth century had appeared likely to succeed as the new governing class, that of the educated and prosperous burghers. It was on the basis of the decay of the commercial classes, the decline of the towns, on the poverty and political defeat of the old estates by a number of able princes that the political and social order characteristic of the age of absolutism was consolidated.

The devastation wrought by the war years led to far-reaching changes in the social structure of Germany generally. The decay of large areas of farmland, much of which had not been cultivated for years, caused changes in the social stratification of the peasantry, and in certain areas, notably the north and east, in the system of land tenure. A diminished demand for food after the war, due to a decline in urban population, caused the bottom to fall out of the grain market and placed an intolerable burden on farmers. In Munich, Augsburg and Würzburg in 1669–73 the price of rye was barely a quarter of what it had been at the beginning of the war. Unable to pay debts incurred in the war or to meet current dues, peasants still had to find wages for hired hands. 'Now indeed it is better to be a farmhand than a master', complained a peasant in a pamphlet entitled *The Golden Age* (1652): 'The poor sorry farmer can no longer make sense of his accounts, except to know that while the work and the cost involved entitle him to 6 *gulden* a measure of corn, he is often forced to throw it away for but three and a half, simply to pay the threshers.'[7] Many farmers were forced to acknowledge their declining position in the social scale by marrying their daughters to farmhands and day labourers, or even to sell out and seek work themselves as hired hands.

In south and west Germany the war years accelerated a development already well advanced by the early seventeenth century, namely the disintegration of the old manorial system. However, immigration to the devastated regions from Switzerland, Austria and other lands unaffected by fighting, kept the ratio of peasant to noble ownership much as it had been before the war. Moreover, in Bavaria, by contrast with Prussia, neither the largest landowner, the church, nor the Elector was interested in giving the local nobility the kind of tacit support in subduing the peasantry which the *Junkers* received from their ruler. In the very different conditions prevailing along the Baltic littoral, the Thirty Years War greatly accelerated changes in the social structure of the landed population, which had been in train since late medieval times. The economic basis of the East Elbian landowners was the grain export trade, and for some time past, enterprising noblemen had been trying to increase their holdings at the cost of the peasant farmer, and to extend their powers over the peasants living in their lands. The sharp fall in grain prices in mid seventeenth century Germany provided an incentive to those who could do so both to increase the services and rents of the peasantry and to counteract the acute shortage of labour by tying the actual cultivator of the land as close as possible to the soil. The landlords either seized deserted peasant property or offered impoverished farmers protection and stock in return for part surrender of their land. In subsequent decades the numbers of peasant farmers declined all over the north-east, while the number of day labourers grew. By 1746 in Beeskow-Storkow in the Mark Brandenburg there were 429 peasants where there had been 814 before the Thirty Years War, but 828 landless labourers where formerly there had been only 172.[8] The prince often gave tacit support to the landowners in their measures. Thus in the Neumark (Brandenburg) robot or servile labour dues became obligatory for the whole life of the individual peasant: in 1685 it was laid down that if subjects ran away and did not return within four weeks, their names were to be written on the gallows: if caught they would be executed or condemned to life imprisonment. The landlords here, as in Lusatia and Mecklenburg, were able to extend their power over the peasantry because the territorial rulers required their nobility's aid in the restoration of the region, and were prepared to concede them patrimonial rights in return for this support. In name these peasants were not serfs; unlike their fellows in Pomerania they could marry and make wills but they could not leave without permission of the lord, and in fact were or became his bondsmen. With increasing obligations the peasants had too little time to cultivate what land still remained to them and were rarely in a position to sell corn; hence their dependence, particularly in bad years, on their landlord.

This development had social and economic (as well as political) consequences which were very enduring. In large areas of northern and eastern Germany urban life was insignificant; even villages were rare in parts of East Elbia. The social system of a dominant landowning class and a depressed peasantry, once established, was difficult to modify. The lack of alternative sources of wealth from commerce reinforced the determination of the ruling stratum to preserve long into the modern age the social organization created under absolutism. Moreover, when demand for food increased with the rise of the east German rural population in the eighteenth century, the rigidity of outlook characteristic of the way of life and the lack of investment capital proved hostile to innovation on the land and ultimately to increased production. However, before about the early nineteenth century, opposition to change was less the product of conscious conservatism on the part of the ruling class than the provinciality of their way of life, the lack of cosmopolitan culture in the region and the lack of facilities for travel and education in the outside world: neither the rulers nor the ruled could envisage as possible an economic and social system or a way of life different from that which they and their fathers and grandfathers had known. In East Elbia, in marked contrast with certain regions of Austria, Bavaria and Switzerland in the early modern period, peasant unrest was rare.

Turning from the land to urban life in mid seventeenth century Germany, it is clear that, by comparison with the peasants, town dwellers suffered less in the war. However, all over Germany, with some few exceptions, the period between the end of the Thirty Years War and the end of the Holy Roman Empire is characterized by the stagnation of urban life and culture. The toll taken by epidemics, especially the plague, was very high indeed in many towns. But the war did not actually cause the decline; since the last decades of the sixteenth century, the so-called price revolution and the continued devaluation of currency, coupled with the gradual movement of trade routes away from central Europe to the west, had already had a serious effect on urban life in Germany. The Hanseatic League, despite efforts to revive it, and despite the prosperity of individual members, was moribund; the Netherlands had supplanted it in political influence and economic power long before 1648. The long-term effects of the Great War and the peace settlement were to destroy finally the political power of the urban bourgeoisie in all but isolated cases.

Yet although the depredations of the war had been far greater on the land than in the towns, land recovered in time in a way trade and commerce did not. If commerce, crafts and manufacture flourished at all in subsequent decades, it was – apart from Hamburg and one or two more towns – in the princely residences or through the active encouragement of the territorial ruler. The two most impressive urban centres of the late seventeenth century, Karlsruhe and Mannheim, were princely foundations, created in the minds of architects engaged by the ruler for that purpose, and built to specification for the further glory of the prince. The political and economic power of the towns had rested on their gold; now the majority of them were bankrupt. Towns which had been the glory of late medieval Germany – Augsburg, Lübeck and Nuremberg, Cologne and Magdeburg – never recovered their former status, though the work of physical restoration, as in the case of

Magdeburg which had been razed in a famous siege in 1631, was already completed within a generation and a half after the peace; some remained in provincial obscurity until the nineteenth century. A well-connected young burgher, contemplating his future career in 1650, would therefore have been much less likely to consider seeking his fortune in commerce than he would have been half a century earlier. Instead he might study law, often at university in Italy or the Netherlands, and then enter the service of a prince.

In subsequent decades his example would be followed by many noblemen's sons. Gradually the privileged status of the nobility was demonstrated in this sphere also, as the senior posts in government service of both major and minor German states became the exclusive provenance of scions of the nobility – and seemed likely to remain so. The enthusiastic response, among burgher circles, to Schiller's *Kabale und Liebe* (1782) owed much to the way in which he made the effective debarring of middle class talents from responsible posts the object of criticism and ridicule. In the seventeenth century and early eighteenth century it was unusual to remain at one court for all one's life. The mobility of princely servants was dictated by the fact that payment, usually in kind, was uncertain and pensions were arbitrary. This was to change in the course of the eighteenth century; they were then paid salaries and gradually became the officials of their own sovereign prince. The growing power of the executive which took place between the mid seventeenth century and late eighteenth century, and the consequent bureaucratization of life, created a hierarchy of official posts. Although the positions of influence in the state became virtually closed to burgher talent, in contrast with sixteenth century practice, opportunity arose for the educated man with or without means in government service. Thus the administration of fiscal policies designed to strengthen the ruler and make him independent of the estates – such as urban excise in Prussia and Saxony – required a large number of civil servants. In the late eighteenth century there were 8000 customs and excise officials in Prussia alone, poorly paid but enjoying a certain status. Even clergymen and teachers generally fell into the category of civil servants by this time; their status and authority derived less from the nature of their work than from the sovereign's delegation to them of part of his own authority.

In one respect Germany was singularly successful in recovering from the war: in her population growth. In a Europe which between 1650 and 1750 saw the population of several states decline or stagnate, Germany's alone grew significantly. That of France, according to Fr. Quesnay's estimate, declined between 1650 and 1750 from about 24 million to 19 million; Montesquieu mused gloomily that this was 'un vice intérieur, un vénin secret et caché, une maladie de langueur' which in 1000 years would turn Europe into desert.[9] Yet Germany's population, about 18 million in 1618, 10–11 million in 1650, was by the mid eighteenth century once more almost back to 18 million again. Barely ten years after the war travellers remarked on the large number of children to be seen everywhere. Parish records give evidence of the many marriages, the high fertility, and the short space of time between the death of a partner and the remarriage of a survivor. It will be seen in subsequent chapters that in certain walks of life a young man frequently married his predecessor's widow in order to establish himself and on her decease married someone his own age. G. Franz noted a somewhat bizarre illustration from seventeenth century Bischoffingen in Baden: of the four daughters of a couple, one married four times, and the husbands of her three sisters married two, three and four times respectively; all the marriages were fertile.[10] It is thought probable that, as a general rule, Germans did not try to limit their families, although Abraham a Sancta Clara's *Abrahamisches Gehab dich wohl* (1729) and J. G. Schnabel's *Der im Irrgarten der Liebe herumtaumelnde Cavalier* (1746) suggest that methods of birth control were known, and practised.[11] Apart from natural increase, a vital source of Germany's manpower in the years after the war came from outside, in the form of religious refugees. The most important gains, doubly valuable for their skills and enterprise, were made by Brandenburg, where successive Hohenzollern rulers offered to Protestants, Catholics and Jews tolerance and tax concessions. The revocation of the Edict of Nantes in 1685 brought 30 000 French Huguenots to Germany, 20 000 of them to Brandenburg; the Austrian Counter-Reformation drove 150 000 Bohemians into Saxony, most of them members of Protestant sects. Fifty Jewish families came in 1670 from Vienna to Brandenburg, paving the way for many more. Twenty thousand Protestant peasants were expelled from Salzburg in 1731 and settled in the north. Mennonites settled in East Prussia and other remote regions, self-contained, but the most industrious and least troublesome of all settlers. Italians came into south Germany, and Swiss in large numbers from their own overcrowded homeland, which had been neutral in the war, some to escape the consequences of peasant uprisings in which they had taken part. The internal immigration was important too, the largest numbers coming from Austria and settling mainly in Franconia; a century later, under the aegis of Maria Theresa's colonization policies for her Balkan territories, many Franconian and Swabian settlers made their way via Vienna to farm in the lower Danube basin.

In the fifty years after the end of the war, Germany's population and her economy effected a slow recovery. In the eighteenth century, however, the pace of change in her price and wage structure became less favourable. Already in the first decades of the new century prices began to rise; wages, however, remained generally stagnant. The imbalance between the two grew more serious as the century advanced, especially when, in the last decades, a sudden and sustained rise in the population occurred. The increase was not a nationwide phenomenon, but was concentrated in certain, mainly agricultural, areas. Food began to be scarce. The years 1771–2 brought famine to many regions; in Bohemia it was estimated that one tenth of the population perished. Traditional methods of cultivation could not increase yields to meet the greater demand, and the hostility to new methods was ingrained. The Germans, it was often observed by visitors, were among the most conservative of peoples, and were suspicious of change, however enlightened the motives. Thus the agriculturalist Schubart, from Saxony, later ennobled as von Kleefeld ('of the clover field', for his pioneering work in its cultivation), reported how in 1778 he had tried to introduce beetroot to his estate in place of cabbage; it was both more nutritious and more labour saving. His workmen refused to handle the plant; he took the matter to court but the judge ruled against him: traditional methods, he said, were best. Yet at this time high society was showing a passionate interest in agriculture. Joseph II had himself painted standing beside a plough, Frederick II declared agriculture to be the first of the arts, without which neither merchants, poets nor philosophers could exist. However, even Frederick, for all his energetic and practical schemes for drainage, improved stock breeding, bee keeping etc., was not able to do much to change the complex system of land tenure and cultivation, and the attitudes of mind which they bred. Most regions of Germany remained poor, or became poorer still, the standard of living of professional people as well as that of the working classes modest. Countless memoirs written by those growing up in the last decades of the eighteenth century contain accounts of the experiences of need, even privation in the childhood and adolescence of their authors. At the lowest levels of society, the problem of pauperism was beginning to make itself felt. This phenomenon and the new developments in manufacturing in many areas belong, however, to a later section.

Modern historical research with its greater concentration on regional studies and on social development has modified our picture of Germany in the aftermath of the Thirty Years War. It is no longer a uniformly gloomy one. Certainly the shortage of consumer goods and capital lasted for a long time, but the needs created by destruction and depopulation stimulated greater administrative skills in a number of German states which benefited the population. Princely absolutism, as it emerged in Prussia, Austria, Saxony, the ecclesiastical states and many more, might seem a lamentable development to a nineteenth or twentieth century observer thinking in terms of the liberty of the individual. In the special circumstances of Germany between 1648 and the French Revolution, a period in which a divided country continued to be the battleground of Europe, and where the political settlement of Westphalia (1648) stood in the way of economic advance, the absolute rulers in general provided a level of existence for their subjects which another kind of government might not have been able to offer. Conditions prevailing in Mecklenburg well into the nineteenth century give some indication of what the alternative was. Here the feudal nobility successfully resisted the power of the Grand Duke; the lower orders of society remained the most oppressed and the whole region one of the most backward in Germany. Much remains to be investigated at regional level, but it is clear that there was greater variation in the standard of living and the quality of life in the different areas of Germany than earlier historians supposed. The regions themselves, often individual towns and villages within a comparatively small compass, could vary greatly in prosperity, and over the period as a whole their fortunes could alter considerably. The case of the rural community of Hirschberg in Lower Silesia is a good example. The initiative of an imaginative mayor and a few enterprising families developed the linen industry there in the late seventeenth century; between 1680 and 1740 Hirschberg became a sophisticated and agreeable place to live in. In parts of south Germany and Saxony the more well-to-do ecclesiastical princes (notably the Schönborns) and some secular princes employed their subjects, trained by skilled foreigners, to create magnificent residences for themselves, as well as churches and abbeys, and they fostered local industry to maintain their courts. The burghers of seventeenth century Danzig were as wealthy and self-confident as any shrewd Amsterdam banker, as a number of contemporary paintings show; yet further east along the Baltic their former equals in Reval had become timorous and xenophobic after a long period of declining trade. In time Danzig's fortunes also began to fluctuate; when the eighteenth century Polish Partitions robbed it of control of the grain trade, it also lost the self-confident republicanism which had been the characteristic expression of its singular prosperity.

In some ways the effects of the Thirty Years War seem less uniformly disastrous than earlier historians alleged, but the political, social and economic changes it brought were nonetheless profound. The fragmentation of its territory, the proliferation of internal tariffs imposed by individual rulers to safeguard their economy, the failure of any state to become strong enough to provide gifted men with a focus and outlet for their talents, all this tended to cut Germany off from the mainstream of European life. Only exceptional individuals were able to share the wider horizons of commercial and intellectual circles in more fortunate states.

In other ways Germany failed to share in the dominant trends of European development. While the war had demonstrated the inability of popular forces in Germany to organize their own religious life and institutions, and had greatly increased the personal power and authority of the territorial ruler, the secularization of politics was very much less in evidence in Germany in the late seventeenth and early eighteenth centuries than it was in France or even in Britain. The ruler's concept of his own authority, and the subject's relationship with the secular power was rooted in a religious ethic, and indeed religion played a far more dominant role in the lives of German people generally, even of the educated, than elsewhere in western Europe. The reverence expected towards a traditional order sanctified by custom and religion was compounded by the lack of knowledge of other modes of living and divergent attitudes in consequence of Germany's limited contacts with the outside world. Accordingly conservative and acquiescent attitudes were characteristic of Germans and generally approved of by society as a whole. Communications actually deteriorated in the post-war period by comparison with the sixteenth century. The position of Germany in these years has been aptly described as that of a country 'where politics and war had added artificial to natural obstructions hampering economic progress and where the dearth of private economic agents could only be supplied by the state'.[12] The essential feature of German life from the late seventeenth century to the age of Napoleon or, some might argue, to the mid nineteenth century, is a turning in on itself, an excessive preoccupation with local, even parochial, concerns. Nor should this surprise us, when we learn something of the actual conditions of life in the various states: in Baden-Durlach, for instance, the higher state officials in the early eighteenth century were actually bondsmen of the margrave. A few princes in this period showed interest in world affairs: the count of Hanau attempted to gain a foothold in Guinea, while the great mercantilist, J. J. Becher, tried to interest Austria and Bavaria in colonies overseas. All of them failed. There was nothing in the programme or the achievements of German governments in these decades which could be remotely compared with the colonial settlements of western nations, with the great trading companies or the seventeenth century colonization of Siberia by the Russians. Germans participated as soldiers, sailors, miners, geographers and merchants in various projects around the world, but always under a foreign flag or foreign leadership. The concept of Empire and the office of the Emperor remained real enough for most Germans, especially those not subject to one of the more forceful territorial princes, yet by contrast with Englishmen, Frenchmen, Swedes or Spaniards, Germans could not feel that the *Reich* in which they lived was a larger extension of themselves, that it provided a commitment or something approaching a patriotic ideal. Although there are a number of outstanding exceptions, in general the character of the German in the century and a half after 1648 was 'not proud and free, not cosmopolitan, but narrow and timorous, his mentality formed by his status as a subject, lacking in personal judgement or opportunity'.[13]

Chapter 1
The Holy Roman Empire

Almost a century of German historiography, up to the end of the Second World War, based on the virtually uncontested assumption that the nation state was the only desirable form of government, has prejudiced many generations in their view of the Holy Roman Empire. According to this line of argument, the Empire inhibited Germany's political development, delayed unification and generally placed her at a disadvantage by comparison with France, England or Holland. From the time of the founding of the Second Empire in 1871 – whose very title sought to exploit the traditions of the previous Empire while denying its authority – national unification under Prussia was presented as a kind of apotheosis of German history. It is not surprising that institutions and governments which had stood in the way of this end should have been open to misrepresentation. This certainly has been the fate of the Holy Roman Empire, particularly with regard to its later years. Indeed for the period 1648–1806 many German historians chose to ignore it altogether, preferring in their researches to concentrate on the history of the different states, and quoting with evident relish Pufendorf's dictum that the Empire was an 'irregulare aliquod corpus et monstro simile'.

Irregular it certainly was. The multiplicity of sovereignties, and the variety of legal relationships within its borders was, to say the least, confusing, though not senseless, to those who formed part of it and enjoyed its protection. Nineteenth and twentieth century historians have been excessively concerned with the state's power, often judging individual regimes according to their ability to impose their authority on the state's frontiers. In the preceding centuries, the subject of this part of the present book, individuals and social groups in Germany looked to the state not for its power, but for protection against natural disasters or the predatory instincts of others. Seen from this point of view, the political and social entity known as the Holy Roman Empire can be seen as a highly complex but also highly articulated system of checks and balances, like one of those intricate and lovely clocks in which connoisseurs of that time so delighted, and in which the Emperor, in Franz Grillparzer's famous image, was the crown wheel, regulating the movement of the whole.[1]

From 1438 to 1806, apart from a brief period in the 1740s, the imperial crown was worn by a member of the Habsburg dynasty, archdukes of Austria and, from the early sixteenth century, kings of Bohemia and of Hungary. The geographical location of the Habsburg lands on the south-east of Germany, the centuries-old charge thrust on Habsburg rulers of defending Christendom against the Turk, made them believe in and indeed cherish the medieval universalist concept of the Holy Roman Empire far longer than did other German territorial princes, particularly those in the north. The Reformation in the sixteenth century had fostered German self-awareness – already in the fifteenth century the title of the Empire had been changed to the somewhat eccentric one of 'the Holy Roman Empire of the German Nation', which was retained until Napoleon abolished the ancient edifice in 1806. However, despite this and despite the lack of dynamism of Germany by contrast with the national states of France, Sweden, the Netherlands or England, the ideal or the myth of a Christian universal Empire continued to have meaning to Germans, particularly when, as in the time of Louis XIV, the 'nation' was threatened from without. Yet, in contrast with medieval times, German territories from the fifteenth to the eighteenth centuries gradually developed a new sense of state identity, based on their individual assemblies, administrations and legal and tax procedures.[2]

The Emperor did not succeed according to primogeniture, despite the Habsburg tenacity in retaining the office over so many centuries. He was elected by seven leading princes, the so-called College of Electors, comprising the three ecclesiastical princes, archbishops of Mainz, Trier and Cologne, the King of Bohemia, Count Palatine, and the Electors of Saxony and Brandenburg. Their number was increased to nine in the seventeenth century, by the addition of Bavaria and Hanover. They formed the first chamber of the imperial assembly (*Reichstag*) which met in Regensburg (Ratisbon), the second being composed of all territorial rulers below the rank of Elector and known as the Council of Ruling Princes or *Fürstenrat.* The third was made up of representatives of the towns which owed direct allegiance to the Emperor, the so-called free imperial towns (*freie Reichsstädte*); by the late fifteenth century these were the chief centres of population and wealth and were therefore an important source of imperial revenue. Thus on the eve of the Reformation, German political life was developing at both federal and state level, for the imperial assembly concerned itself with the internal and external welfare of the Empire, while the presence of the state rulers there helped to strengthen the lines of communication between the two areas.

The Reformation checked the progress of federal institutions and introduced a new and complicating factor into imperial politics. However, the course of the Thirty Years War alone clearly demonstrates how fallacious it would be to think in terms of imperial and Catholic, Protestant and national. On the other hand, the Reformation settlement certainly encouraged territorial rulers, including Catholic ones, to extend their power over their subjects. State law gradually ousted the old feudal contractual law. Individual rulers began to employ state officials to augment their personal authority within their lands. Yet the sense of a federal dimension of politics and of the Emperor as the ultimate authority in such matters, remained with Germans in this period, over and above the loyalty they might feel as citizens of Hamburg or Nuremberg to their city, or as subjects of a secular or ecclesiastical prince who governed their lives. And the case of the Tyrolean pedlar Peter Prosch, who walked to Vienna to see the Empress, suggests that the concept of Emperor meant something to the vast mass of countryfolk, even if they invested him with the awe and remoteness of God in His Heaven (see p.26).

What makes the political organization of Germany difficult to understand in this period is that the two elements, the federal and the territorial, existed side by side, and that, furthermore, innumerable authorities and jurisdictions overlapped in many areas of Germany, making it impossible for clearly defined frontiers to emerge. As the author of a recently published authoritative study puts it: 'Early modern Germany was not a nation state, yet it was still a working political reality. ... "Germany" includes the concept of some kind of native grass-roots federalism synonymous with the German term, *Reich*, ... which developed in the fifteenth century and remained into the eighteenth century.'[3]

The weaker members of the *Reich* benefited more than the stronger from their membership. Their support of the Emperor was one of the factors which enabled him to exercise restraint on the larger states. When the Emperor in his capacity as territorial ruler of Austria began to allow these interests to dictate his imperial policy, the authority and stability of the whole *Reich* institution was seriously weakened. The most significant case of this was the religious policy of Ferdinand II which helped to realign the parties in the Thirty Years War, but there were cases in the eighteenth century too – notably Charles VI's policies in the early decades of the century and Joseph II's attempt to win Bavaria. Joseph II's ambitions enhanced the reputation of Frederick II of Prussia, allowing him to appear in the role of 'defender of the liberties of the imperial estates', as well as stimulating the Austro-Prussian rivalry which was bound in the long run to destroy the Empire. For Joseph II the Holy Roman Empire was already an anachronism. Most Habsburg rulers distinguished precisely between their offices of Emperor and territorial sovereign. Thus the Counter-Reformation policies, which eradicated Lutheranism so ruthlessly in seventeenth century Austria, could not be applied in the Empire after 1648. The constitution of the Holy Roman Empire was enshrined in the Treaties of Westphalia, and provided sufficient restraints on any prince who might attempt such divisive action.

The most important function of the main institutions of the Empire was to maintain the *status quo* undisturbed. These institutions were: the three estates represented in the imperial assembly (*Reichstag*) at Regensburg, the slow-moving Supreme Court (*Reichskammergericht*) at Speyer until 1684, and thereafter at Wetzlar, and the relatively efficient Imperial Tribunal (*Reichshofrat*) at Vienna. For this they needed to have an Emperor respectful of their 'liberties', yet strong enough to defend their interests. Charles VI (1711–40), father of Maria Theresa, tried to extend the Habsburg power in the Empire; on his death, therefore, the electors chose, for the first time in 300 years, a non-Habsburg to succeed him, the Wittelsbach Charles VII of Bavaria. However, he proved too weak, and on his death Maria Theresa's husband, known as Francis Stephen of Habsburg-Lorraine, from then on the official title of the house, was chosen in his place.

The imperial assembly, the *Reichstag*, met at Regensburg in 1654 and again in 1658; a permanent conference at the imperial assembly was instituted there in 1663.[4] It has been the object of much patronizing comment from nationalist historians, but has now begun to benefit from the reassessment of German history since the end of the Second World War. It is no longer condemned for failing to be what it was never intended to be, a parliamentary assembly. In this period it was a conference of ambassadors, and the fact that the larger states felt it necessary to be represented there showed that they regarded it as a place where policy could be initiated and even implemented. One person might represent a number of states, but the importance of Regensburg is proved even in the late eighteenth century by the calibre of the men appointed to look after the interests of the major states, for example those of Austria and Prussia, Hanover and Saxony. The intricacies of the *Reich* constitution demanded that an ambassador, to be effective, must have a wide knowledge of the law. Several highly intelligent and able men filled these requirements in the *Reichstag*: outstanding figures at Regensburg in the last decades of the Holy Roman Empire were the representatives of Saxony, Count Peter von Hohenthal, of Austria, Count Borié, and of Hanover, Count Ompteda, a pupil of the master of imperial constitutional law at Göttingen, Professor J. Pütter, and himself no mean scholar. The most genial figure was one Count Görtz, to whom Prussia owed much of its growing authority. Johann Eustach, Count von Schlitz, known as Görtz, was quite unlike the stereotype Prussian; he was a man of charm, the soul of the debates, which he rarely missed; his tact won him a position of responsibility, which his tolerance enhanced, and he was often asked to act as mediator in disputes fought out in the sessions of the assembly. Regensburg had a significance which is easily overlooked if we forget that Germany had no capital. It served as a meeting place, and as a listening post. An ambassador could put out feelers to the representatives of other states without being seen to do so at official level. Here he and his colleagues could inform themselves about political and military matters in other parts, and about prominent individuals. The social centre of Regensburg lay in the home of the imperial Princes of Thurn and Taxis, concessionaries of the postal service. At gatherings in their elegant residence at the heart of the city a discreet word, a delicately conveyed hint of financial or other reward, could pay rich dividends.

It was in indirect ways that the less powerful estates could make themselves useful to the greater and so help to protect their own interests. The ecclesiastical princes and the knights are a case in point. Militarily speaking, eighteenth century Hesse-Kassel was far more important than Mainz, Trier or Bamberg, but the family connections between holders of such ecclesiastical office gave them considerable influence. Nephew very frequently followed uncle as bishop, as for instance in Bamberg, Würzburg or Mainz, where the Schönborn family was especially prominent. The bishops could combine in the assembly or in the imperial circles of the Empire, which were still effective in south Germany, and they could get through a vote for military supplies in wartime, of great value to the Emperor. The imperial knights (*Reichsritter*) had no vote at Regensburg, but they had a strong sense of group loyalty and a very real potential importance in that they had a virtual monopoly of the seats in cathedral chapters, and elected candidates to the episcopacy, or even – as in Mainz, Trier and Cologne – the elector.

The bishops, abbots and imperial counts (*Reichsgrafen*) were nominally members of the high nobility, but in their style of life they were actually closer to the lower nobility. These and the imperial towns have been described by a leading historian in this field, Baron Aretin, as the 'Mörtel des Reichs zwischen den Quadern der grossen Stände' ['mortar of the Empire between the blocks of the great estates'].[5] Their function and significance lay in their ability to check the efforts of the greater estates to pursue their own sovereign interests at the expense of the *Reich*. Many of the smaller elements were extremely effective at local level, as is illustrated in the case of the imperial circles not dominated by a great power. Besides being intended as administrative units, these circles were a kind of federal system of peace keeping and were under obligation to provide military contingents for the defence of the Empire. In the south and south-west they functioned well into the eighteenth century, as well as acting as a kind of cooperative of political units too small to be effective on their own. In the north and central parts of Germany local rulers, or two or more princes in combination, had managed to dominate at least seven of the ten circles, and the circles had ceased to function in the capacity for which they had been created. The active elements of the remaining three were to be found in the Upper Rhine, the Franconian, and, most energetic of all, in the Swabian circle.

The Emperor saw fit to send an ambassador each year to the Swabian *Kreistag*, or regional assembly, which met at Ulm in May; there he witnessed the formulation and implementation of plans to improve the economic life of the area. The representatives' careful management of local interests in Swabia offset the disadvantages of particularism, while at the same time maintaining that personal voice in affairs which south Germans especially valued. Thus the Swabian circle built highroads in the eighteenth century which were far superior to those of many more powerful states; in 1761 their representatives combined with those of the Bavarian circle to accept the *gulden* as a unit of currency, also valid in parts of the Upper Rhine and the Austrian possessions in south-west Germany (*Vorderoesterreich*).

Contrary to commonly held opinion, the later centuries of the Empire were not characterized by greater fragmentation of territory. From the late fifteenth century onwards, primogeniture was the rule for the dynasties in the territories. Of 405 named in the Worms Register for 1521, only 314 were still in existence in 1780.[6] From the early eighteenth century it became usual for only one member of knightly families to inherit the estate, though this would not necessarily be the eldest; it was also common practice for only one son to marry in the family – thus for example Baron von Stein, the liberal reformer in Prussia, was the fortunate one chosen among five brothers by the family council to enjoy this privilege.

In the last decades of the eighteenth century Emperor Joseph II's impatient handling of *Reich* business, and his ill-considered thrift in stopping pensions to those sympathetic to Austria at Regensburg and at individual courts, cut off essential sources of information about personalities and policies in Germany, as well as losing him support to Prussia. Austro-Prussian rivalry, and the strains and stresses of the French revolutionary wars, submitted the Holy Roman Empire to pressures it was unable to resist, making it easy for later generations to believe that Goethe's or Görres's sardonic references did justice to its antiquated structure. In its last days, as Voltaire had observed, the Empire may have been neither holy nor Roman nor empire. For the greater part of the period 1648–1806, however, it provided a framework of authority to those who lived within its borders, dispensing protection and justice in a manner which seems inefficient to later generations, whose time scale is so much shorter, but which was meaningful and relatively effective to those under its canopy.[7]

Chapter 2
Court life

'We shall set Germany afire and we shall so manage things, that we shall reap the fruits of its death when God ordains it', wrote Duplessis-Mornay, intellectual friend of King Henry IV of France a decade before the Thirty Years War broke out.[1] Germany did not in fact die at the hands of France and her allies, although they devastated vast tracts of her territories in the subsequent war, and in the many other wars which followed at irregular intervals for a hundred years or more. However. the hegemony of France in seventeenth and early eighteenth century Europe had profound consequences for Germany, helping to perpetuate the divisions of the German nation, and keeping alive the particularist traditions of life, government and social structure. The French threat to Germany culminated in 1683 in an event which had symbolic significance for contemporaries – namely, the fall of Strasburg to Louis XIV. Strasburg, according to a widely believed, but possibly apocryphal precept of the great Emperor Charles V, must always be defended, at whatever cost. In September of the same year, 1683, Vienna successfully repulsed the two-month-old siege of the city by the Turks, for over a century allies of France. The military commanders of the Habsburgs now began the conquest of Turkish-held lands in Hungary and the adjoining territories, which would eventually establish Austria as a Balkan as well as a German power. The decision taken in the summer of 1683 by the Emperor Leopold I and his advisers, to accept the fate of

Strasburg but to defend Vienna, was a radical one by that least radical of men and monarchs. It epitomized a development which was a direct consequence of France's 'setting fire' to Germany – namely that the nerve centre of the Holy Roman Empire had by this time moved away from the old cultural and commercial lands along the Rhine, to the lands in the east. The important German states in the last century and a half of the Holy Roman Empire's life, in the years between the Treaties of Westphalia and the Napoleonic conquest of Germany, lay in the eastern half of the country: Austria, Saxony, Brandenburg and Bavaria. Among the rulers of these territories, the Habsburg monarchy proved resilient enough, despite innumerable reverses, to contain the military threat to its borders and to exert a powerful cultural influence on German society, particularly on the upper classes.

It is widely assumed, and still frequently reiterated in general and literary histories, that the German courts of this age were but a pale imitation of Versailles. It is of course true that France under Louis XIV and his successors exercised great influence over German princes, over ones as different as the extravagant Elector of Saxony, Augustus the Strong, and Frederick II of Prussia, and that many minor territorial princes, who drew important subsidies from France, invested these in the erection of castles, opera houses and theatres, hunting lodges and parks, in emulation of the Sun King. A number of ecclesiastical rulers, such as the Elector of Cologne or the Bishop of Würzburg, built country seats (e.g. Brühl in the Rhineland and Pommersfelden in Franconia) modelled on the French examples. However, to see the German courts purely in terms of French influence is to ignore the variety of influences at work; indeed, to do so is to fail to appreciate the particular character of baroque art and culture in Germany, which extends from the end of the Great War to about the year 1740, when both Maria Theresa of Austria and Frederick II of Prussia ascended the throne. French cultural influence was not paramount in Germany until the late seventeenth century onwards, and even then it did not extend over the whole territory of the *Reich*. Vienna, despite the French circle around the military commander, Prince Eugene of Savoy, remained aware of its character as an alternative culture in Europe, drawing on the rich resources of Spain and Italy, as well as embellishing daily life in all sorts of significant details, with tastes and habits learned from the ancient enemy, the Turk. Leopold I spoke Latin and German, Spanish and Italian, but not French. The tutor of his eldest son, Joseph I, one Wagner von Wagenfels, wrote a work entitled *Ehren-Ruf Teutschlands, der Teutschen und ihres Reiches* (1697), in which he warned his clever young charge, then just thirteen, against the craven imitation of all things French to which many German princes seemed to be becoming addicted.

Among the diverse influences on the character and ceremonial of German court life, one of the most important was the Burgundian tradition, which came to Vienna by way of Spain and remained dominant there until the late eighteenth century. Humanism also helped to form the character of a number of major courts, such as that of Rudolph II at Prague, which became an intellectual and cultural centre of the first magnitude in the decades before the great war, as well as that of Albrecht V, Duke of Bavaria, at Munich, and of his grandson Maximilian I, and from there spread to several of the minor courts. Nor should the influence of the traditional pageantry and festivities of the ancient free imperial towns, such as Frankfurt, seat of the coronation of the King of the Romans, heir designate to the Emperor, or Nuremberg, be forgotten. Royal consorts were a further source of cultural fertilization, not least because of the retinue which generally accompanied a foreign bride to her new home, including, as in the case of the Spanish infantas, a host of clerical and diplomatic figures, who gravitated to the court in their suite. This was especially characteristic of Vienna and of Munich, since as Catholics the rulers had little choice in Germany for brides for their sons, and were generally forced to look to Spain, to the Italian states, and to Lorraine, still part of the Empire even after it was conquered by Louis XIV. However, in the early years of the seventeenth century, the foreign visitor to the German courts was more likely to have been impressed by the general addiction to food and drink than by the cultural tone of court life. Accounts of princely weddings from those years rarely fail to chronicle the quantities of refreshment consumed, nor contemporary illustrations to record their well-born guests (or hosts) dealing with the effects of excess. Even at a court known for its general cultivation, that of the Calvinist Frederick IV, father-in-law of the Winter Queen, it was recommended to the courtiers not to consume more than seven litres of wine per day.

Indeed it would not be exaggerated to compare life in some of the smaller and poorer 'courts' of German territorial princes untouched by humanist influences to that of the peasants, who formed the bulk of the population.

The most impressive German court at the end of the Thirty Years War was that of Munich, the 'German Rome', as the Jesuit poet Jakob Balde apostrophized it in an elegant Latin sonnet. The war had given its Duke, Maximilian, who reigned for over half a century, the opportunity to develop his most salient characteristic: judiciousness. He had long anticipated the outbreak of hostilities and prepared himself accordingly. The coveted prize for his support of the Emperor against the Calvinist Elector Palatine was the latter's electoral title, which he received, along with the Upper Palatinate, in northern Bavaria. He also gained the famed Palatine library, which he sold to the Vatican, where it is still housed. Culture meant much to him, but money meant more: it meant power and the opportunity to indulge his particular tastes. With his army he protected suppliants – at a price. Nuremberg paid in kind for his protection against the Swedes: Dürer's painting of the four Evangelists.[2] The Nuremberg lawyer Ludwig Behaim, Camerarius's friend and correspondent, negotiated the affair. In consequence of the Elector's wise foresight, Bavaria rapidly recovered from the war. For all his famed thrift, Maximilian believed that money spent on representation, in the form of rich apparel, banquets and entertainments, and above all on a setting commensurate with the role of the prince, was money wisely invested. The Munich residences were extended, and palaces were built in the surrounding countryside, at Nymphenburg and Schleissheim; the brides of the electoral family attracted numbers of Italian craftsmen to accompany them to their new home, and these men executed work, not only for the ruler, but for monasteries, noble mansions and provincial towns in the territory.

Two features were characteristic of the German court in the baroque age: on the one hand there was the desire, common to most European courts of the time, to project the authority of the ruler by means of an impressive setting, enhancing it on special occasions by spectacle and pageantry; on the other hand there was a patriarchal quality in German princely rule, which stressed the duties of the prince to his subjects, and was reflected by a host of ordinances governing their lives, regulating attendance at church and school, overseeing police matters, etc. The concern of the absolute prince for those whose lives were in his care could be tyrannical, particularly with regard to their propensity for war, and it could be niggling, as in the case of Frederick William I of Prussia. On the whole, despite notorious exceptions, a German ruler felt genuine concern for 'his' people. The ecclesiastical rulers, such as the Schönborns, one of whom, Johann Philipp, the greatest gardener of his age, was Elector of Mainz and had four nephews prince bishops, spent enormous sums on palaces, parks and on the not so very spiritual glories of the chase. However, many of them showed careful concern for the physical well-being of their subjects, even down to the minutest details. Wolf-Dietrich of Salzburg built isolation barracks for the victims of fevers, in Würzburg Bishop Lothar Franz von Schönborn went as far as to organize measures to extirpate caterpillars and other pests.[3] It was this combination of princely grandeur and paternal care, combined with the relatively small size of the majority of German territories, that made state authority seem such a personal thing to the subjects. Even in the case of powerful princes, the person of the ruler was much more accessible to the public than is the case with most modern statesmen. The elusive Emperor, Rudolph II, was prepared to take his meals in public and listen to the grievances of the humble. The accessibility of their princes helped Germans to identify abstract state authority with the person of the ruler right up to the nineteenth century. An apt illustration of how this worked in practice is to be found in the memoirs of a Tyrolean pedlar, named Peter Prosch, who journeyed on foot not once but twice to see the Empress Maria Theresa about a legal matter weighing on his mind, and on each occasion was graciously received by her: she even ordered three dozen pairs of the gloves he peddled.[4]

The rise of Vienna in the second half of the seventeenth century to be the leading German court was largely a consequence of the great war. Although the institution of the Holy Roman Empire was weakened by its outcome, the personal power of the Emperor as ruler of Austria was greatly increased. The creation of a court nobility beholden to him personally, to whom he had granted estates confiscated from rebellious lords, provided him with the opportunity to establish a permanent court, commensurate with his position and power. Hitherto the Habsburg court had favoured sometimes Innsbruck, sometimes Prague as its residence; under Ferdinand III Vienna was chosen as the permanent seat of the imperial court. Burgundian ceremonial and Spanish etiquette demanded an extravagant number of persons to be in attendance at court; these were presided over by the four most important office-holders, Lord Chamberlain, Lord Steward, Master of the Imperial Household and Master of the Horse. At the Prague court of Rudolph II in 1576, there were 531 such persons, whereas under Charles VI, perhaps the most extravagant of Habsburg princes, there were 2175.[5]

The inherited sense of imperial dignity, so eloquently captured by Grillparzer in his *Ein Bruderzwist im Hause Habsburg*, was a true Habsburg trait, even in those not specially favoured by nature. Leopold I never lost his impressiveness, despite his small stature and the family characteristic, the protruding lower lip, exaggerated to a point of 'monumental ugliness', as one commentator put it. He favoured a long curling wig, which in its raven hue seemed to pay no attention to the passing of the years, the death of two consorts, including his 'mia Margarita unica' of Spain, and thirteen of his nineteen children. As the Austrian historian Hugo Hantsch once put it: 'es gibt eine Sphäre der

Unnahbarkeit um den Monarchen, in die niemand einzudringen wagt' ['an aura of remoteness encompasses the monarch, which none may dare to penetrate'].[6] On Leopold's younger son, Charles VI, the imperial dignity weighed more heavily. Charles had been brought up in the expectation that he would succeed to the throne of his cousin, Carlos II of Spain. The death of his brother, Joseph I, in 1711 and the outcome of the War of the Spanish Succession decreed otherwise, but Charles remained excessively conscious of the demands of protocol, as he had imbibed it in his youth at the Spanish court, even to the point of embittering relations with important neighbours. In 1732, for example, the King of Prussia stated a wish to make his acquaintance and discuss matters of mutual importance. The Emperor, who needed Frederick William's support to further the claim of his daughter Maria Theresa to succeed him, for he had no living son, informed his advisers that 'bey solcher zusammenkunfft die Hand Ihme umb so weniger geben könnten, alss ein solches res Summa consequentia und dero allerhöchsten Kayserl. Authorität nachtheillig ...' ['At such a meeting it would be out of the question for me to offer him my hand, since such an act would be of great consequence and detract from the all-highest imperial authority'].[7] The visit was not a success. Yet in their private lives Habsburg princes were almost always warm and natural. Leopold could write, gently mocking of his consort's homeland: 'La fiesta de toros müess schön gewest sein, allein scheint es ein paradoxum zue sein, dass ein Ochs ein Ross sammt dem Esel, so vielleicht darauf gesessen, fliegen gelernt' ['The bullfight must have been fine, though it is somewhat of a paradox that an ox should teach a horse, and the donkey seated on its back, how to fly'].[8] Maria Theresa, brought up by her Spanish governess to observe the rigid forms of etiquette, managed to slip in undetected terms of endearment into her letters to her future husband, Francis Stephen of Lorraine. A gouache drawing by Archduchess Maria Christina, one of Maria Theresa's sixteen children – twelve of them born when she was reigning monarch – gives an intimate glimpse of their family life: it is St Nicholaus Day 1762, in the palace of Schönbrunn outside Vienna, the Emperor is reading a newspaper, while his consort brings him a cup of chocolate, and the children open their presents around the room. The sense of the dignity of their high office was not, as in the case of the French ruler, an exaltation of the person of the monarch, but was derived from a religious concept of imperium, and it was to sustain the dynasty through many reversals of fortune.

Religious observances in fact took up a singularly large amount of time at the devout Viennese court, as at that of Madrid. Yet the high masses, benedictions and processions were also a kind of sublime recreation, the harmony of form and colour in the great baroque churches, the uplifting music, the intoxicating smell of incense and wax candles, gratifying the senses of the participants. The Viennese court under Leopold, and many other German courts as well, were places where learning too was both admired and pursued. Leopold spent many hours with his court librarian, Peter Lambeck from Hamburg, and was grievously distressed when he learned of the fire which destroyed the fine library of the Escurial in 1667. Many Protestant princes, educated in the humanist tradition, were connoisseurs of art and authorities on antiquities of many kinds; the coin collections and items of natural history were often the feature of their court of which they were most proud. Well-connected visitors were allowed to inspect and use the facilities of the library and collections, but not, initially, the general public. The great bibliophile Duke Anton-Ulrich of Brunswick-Wolfenbüttel, founder of the still famous library, was one of the first princes to allow the public into it. Charles VI followed suit in 1726, allowing all but 'Idioten, Bedienstete, Faulenzer, Plappermäuler' ['idiots, servants, layabouts and gossips'] into perhaps the most glorious of all baroque profane buildings, Fischer von Erlach's court library in the Burg at Vienna.[9]

Music was a feature of everyday life at court, as well as a vital element on all great occasions. The numbers of composers and performers among German princes is astonishingly high. Frederick II of Prussia and his grandnephew Prince Louis Ferdinand are among the best known; Leopold and Charles preferred music making to virtually anything else and, in the view of their advisers, spent far too much time in practice. The Landgrave of Hesse-Darmstadt at the turn of the eighteenth century devoted four evenings a week to conducting his own orchestra; indeed, so jealous was he of his reputation in this regard that he would only assign the poorly attended Sunday afternoon concerts to his director of music, Carl Maria von Weber. Music played a specially important role in the smaller German courts, since their princes could not afford to indulge in the building mania of the wealthy, but might emulate their reputation in this less costly art. Where funds were limited, players had to be versatile. Bach's employers, the Hanoverian dukes, Ernest Augustus and his brother, and his later patron Prince Leopold of Anhalt-Köthen, played several instruments, as did members of court orchestras generally. Improvisation was called for, actors had to be employed as opera singers – hence the origin of the *Singspiel*, forerunner of the operetta, with its spoken dialogue and arias with musical accompaniment. The Elector of Mainz shared a troupe of actors with the neighbouring imperial city of Frankfurt in the late eighteenth century. Musicians did duty as secretaries, butlers and even lackeys at small courts; in fact servants were not infrequently chosen for their musical talents, their masters proving generous in providing them with musical training. Opera could only be put on in carnival time in the minor courts, but it had such status value that princes of moderate substance showed themselves willing to spend a disproportionate amount of their revenue in providing it. Thus Duke Anton-Ulrich built a four-tiered opera house in his residence in 1685, followed by a five-tiered theatre in 1690. Charles Theodore, Count Palatine, spent 20 000 *gulden* annually on his opera and theatre at the new capital of his state at Mannheim. Princely patronage provided a unique opportunity for talented musicians – such as Mozart at Mannheim – to study and perform.[10] Wealthy noblemen imitated the example of their princes – thus the owners of the great Bohemian *latifundia*, whose country houses resembled miniature courts, sent talented peasant boys as far away as Paris for their musical training in the eighteenth century. The Hungarian Esterházys discovered and paid for the education of Joseph Haydn.

It was above all at Vienna that the function of court opera was most fully realized. Through the magnificence of its presentation the regal state of the prince was proclaimed, and his pleasure indulged, and he also fulfilled the duty of the absolute ruler to patronize talent and provide entertainment for his subjects. Charles VI, who was married to the granddaughter of the highly cultivated Anton-Ulrich, paid his musical director, the well-known composer J. J. Fux, the truly princely salary of 3100 *gulden* in 1715; his court orchestra numbered 134 musicians in 1723.[11] In the latter year Charles was crowned King of Bohemia; Fux composed an opera for the occasion, entitled *La Constantia e la Forteza*, constancy referring to the motto of the Emperor, which, just about the same time, the court architect Fischer von Erlach was representing symbolically in the twin pillars of the mighty baroque church of St Charles in Vienna, and *Forteza* (power) being an allusion to the might of the Holy Roman Emperor. Fux, who suffered from gout, was carried, at the Emperor's express wish, in a litter from Vienna to Prague to attend the solemn performance. In conformity with contemporary fashion and the tastes of the Habsburgs, opera at that time, and for many decades to come, was exclusively Italian. Hesse, the director of music at the Saxon court of Dresden for many years, composed over one hundred Italian operas, while at Berlin Frederick II's *Capellmeister* or musical director, Graun, composed thirty. The great Metastasio, whose name became a password for opera *libretti* and whose works were used over and over again by ambitious composers, came to Vienna in 1730 and remained there for over half a century. One of his tasks was to compose Italian arias for the young Archduchess Maria Theresa to sing. The reputation of the Viennese court opera was deservedly high. Glück was its director for ten years from 1754, Saliere from 1774 to 1792. Open-air performances were especially popular. In the gardens of the same royal palace, the *Favoriten*, not far from the present-day opera house, which had once witnessed one of the most lavish baroque court spectacles, the cosmic drama *The Battle of the Elements*, in connection with Leopold's marriage to the Spanish Infanta in 1667, Lady Mary Wortley Montagu attended a performance of *Alcina* by J. J. Fux. She wrote:

> Nothing of that kind was ever more magnificent; and I can easily believe what I am told, that the decoration and the habits cost the Emperor thirty thousand pounds sterling. The stage was built over a very large canal, and, at the beginning of the second act, divided into two parts, discovering the water, on which there immediately came, from different parts, two fleets of little gilded vessels, that gave the representation of a naval fight....
>
> The theatre is so large, that it is hard to carry the eye to the end of it; and the habits in the utmost magnificence, to the number of one hundred and eight.[12]

The budget had to sustain the staggering demands of a social round, whose purpose was to impress on the world the might and magnificence of the prince in an age when 'state' and 'dynasty' were virtually identical. Increasingly magnificent festivities gradually became an end in themselves, distracting the courtiers in their artificial world, where the enemy was boredom, and where a host of talent, which gravitated to princely residences, had to be employed. An inexhaustible attention to detail and a lavishness designed to gain the maximum effect, with no thought of accountability, was characteristic of these occasions. On one occasion, the Elector of Saxony, August the Strong, saw fit to have 2000 loads of snow conveyed to his capital at Dresden, in order to simulate a sledge ride. In Salzburg the Prince Archbishop ran up a little castle in a few weeks for a particular occasion, the building being aptly known as the 'Monatsschlössl'. Despite their transient nature, many of the festivals of that time are legendary, though few could compete with the sumptuous scale offered at the court of Versailles. One such occasion was part of the celebrations in connection with Leopold's first marriage, to the Infanta Margarita of Spain, whose portrait by Velasquez hangs in the Viennese Art Gallery. On the lake of the *Favoriten* palace, the Italian

Burnacini staged his magnificent drama, *La contesa dell' aria e dell'aqua.* Floats, for which Burnacini was famous, bore representations of the four elements, and the whole thing was a spectacular glorification of the power of the prince.[13] Fire and water played a leading role in most baroque spectacles. If open-air opera, theatres, concerts and ballets, including (in Vienna) equestrian ballet, were favourites with court and crowd alike, firework displays most aptly epitomized the function of such occasions. These had been part of the traditional festivities of the wealthy German towns in the sixteenth century, such as that put on by Frankfurt for Ferdinand I's coronation in 1558 or by Nuremberg for the Kaiser's visit in 1612. In Düsseldorf on the occasion of a display of fireworks in 1585, a chronicler named Graminäus attributed to them an aesthetic and a moral influence, similar to that of the theatre: 'nicht allein das Gesicht v. Sinnlichkeit damit zuergetzen u zuerfrewen/sondern auch zu nützlicher Lehr/geheimniss und zonderer bedeutnuss zugericht/wie bey den Alten die Comedien/Tragedien/als kurtzweilige Lehrspil den grossen Herrn und gemeinen hauffen vorgetragen worden' ['Not alone to appeal to and delight the sense, but to act as a useful and meaningful lesson, as in the ancient world, comedies and tragedies were played to entertain and to edify great lords and the common people'].[14] Seventy years later fireworks were widely favoured at court, because the displays inspired, by means of fire, sudden noise, smoke and general magnificence the sentiments thought fitting for the subject to entertain of his sovereign: awe, fear, and a vicarious sense of glory in his might. Birthdays, namedays, weddings and anniversaries provided the occasion for celebration. A visit by the Margrave of Ansbach to his neighbour, the Prince Bishop of Würzburg, scarcely a day's journey away, was seen by his host as an opportunity to show what he could do. Upwards of 3000 people, according to the Berlin newspaper *Dienstagischer Mercurius* (*Tuesday Mercury*), a diligent spreader of court gossip and fashion, greeted the margrave, 'die Cavalliere und andere sich auf das herrlichste ausgeputztt, wie des Herrn Margraffen seine auch' ['the cavaliers and others splendidly attired as were those accompanying the margrave'], only to be surprised by a sudden thunder-storm with the result that 'die schönen Baruquen so vorhin auff das schöneste gepudert waren possirlich aussahen, wie auch die Federn auff den Hüten, im übrigen keinen trockenen Faden am Leibe' ['the fine wigs up to a moment ago beautifully powdered, looked very odd, as did the plumes on their hats; indeed there was not a single dry thread on all their persons'].[15] The correspondent, reporting from Würzburg, gives the impression that the whole thing still managed to be a highly diverting spectacle, although some cursed and swore enough to make 'der grösseste Schlossthurn' ['the mightiest castle turret'] collapse.

Splendid festivals took their toll. One glimpses something of the underlying barbarity of many such occasions in the coarse humour of August the Strong, who entertained his guests on his birthday in May with a display of fountains and fireworks, followed by a drinking and feasting orgy: when his guests sought to retire to rid themselves of their excess carousing, they found the palace guard barring the exit – with disastrous consequences for their gold-braided and jewelled attire. In the country seat of the Prince Archbishop of Salzburg, at Hellabrunn, water jets concealed under the seats at the banqueting table, pits and ditches designed to catch the unwary guest, and many more crude practical jokes were specially designed by the host for his amusement.

Yet side by side with drunkenness and greed went a general refinement of the palate among the upper classes. The wine trade was remarkably buoyant, despite the frequency of wars. Vienna imported wines from Franconia and the Neckar, from Spain and Hungary; the Portuguese wine trade had several contacts in Germany. Tokay enjoyed especial popularity at court; a Berlin wine dealer in Frederick William I's reign lists as many as four different kinds of Tokay, as well as claret, burgundy, and wine from Alicante which, alas, 'machet dick Geblüthe, und Verstopfungen der Eingeweide' ['makes the blood thick, and blocks the entrails'].[16] It was above all in the art of cooking that the baroque age and above all the baroque court was unique in German history. In this respect French influence was already paramount by the latter half of the seventeenth century, penetrating even to Vienna which enjoyed a high culinary reputation but was ready to learn from French chefs. In his biography of Eugene of Savoy, Nicholas Henderson quotes from the Duc de Saint-Simon's memoirs an account of the olive salad, created by the chef of Olympia de Soissons, Mazarin's niece and Eugene's mother: the olives were stuffed one by one into quails, the quails into partridges, the partridges into pigeons, the pigeons into chickens, the chickens into sucking pigs and they into calves, roasted on the spit until the olives were succulent with juice and fit for so elevated a palate as that of the King of France.[17] It hardly needs to be added that an army of kitchen staff was necessary to create, not just one supreme dish, but that host of courses which were obligatory for solemn occasions. For just as ceremonious greeting, use of full title, the proper raiment and accompanying gestures were regarded by the recipient (and the bystander) as a measure of his worth in the eyes of the person receiving him, so too the food set before a guest, its quality and its quantity, reflected what the host thought of him. It was thus fitting that the banquet, given after conclusion of the peace negotiations between the imperial forces and the Swedes in 1648, should have been on a scale commensurate with the event it was celebrating. A full account has been preserved of the occasion: on the tables stood two decorative dishes of monumental proportions, a triumphal arch and a six-sided mountain, adorned with allegorical and mythological figures, Latin and German symbols. There were four 'courses', each consisting of 150 dishes, after which the guests were offered fruit on silver dishes and suspended from miniature trees, and candied flowers were strewn on the tables. The final dish was one greatly beloved by Germans, then and now, although the capacity of contemporaries seems seriously diminished by comparison: 'Marzipan auf zwei Silberschalen, von denen jede zehn Pfund schwere waren' ['Marzipan on two silver dishes, each weighing ten pounds']. Outside, the poor were fed on two oxen, while red wine and white flowed from the mouth of a stone lion for fully six hours.[18]

It is hardly surprising that those whose social functions obliged them to participate in heavy eating and drinking should have been preoccupied with the process of digestion and with matters of health generally. Memoirs and diaries give intimate details of the bodily functions, recording with scarcely concealed satisfaction the proper workings of the body, and carefully noting beverages, foods and herbs likely to assist in the process. The salubrious effect on the constitution of exercises in the open air was therefore an important recommendation for its pursuit, and one of the reasons for the general addiction of court and nobility to the chase. Many of the new residences built from the late seventeenth century to the late eighteenth were sited in areas expressly suited for hunting, Pommersfelden, already mentioned, Laxemburg near Vienna, Ludwigsburg near Stuttgart, which was built as a hunting lodge and only later, under Charles Eugene, extended as a princely castle. The lure of the golf course for American and Japanese business magnates today, not to speak of lesser mortals, is but a pale imitation of the passion for the chase in those days. Emperor Charles VI, no athlete, killed twenty-two bears in the 1717 season; boars, wild cats and stags roamed the estates around his capital. In 1732 he shot his Master of the Horse, Adam Prince Schwarzenberg, who died twelve hours later but not before assuring his stricken master, according to a report in the Viennese '*Diarium*' or gazette, 'Es seye ein Schicksal, dass ich von I.M. habe müssen geschossen werden. ... Er seye jederzeit schuldig gewesen, sein Leben für Se. Majestät zu sacrificiren' ['It was fate that I should have been shot by Your Majesty. ... It was his duty to be ready to sacrifice his life for his Emperor'].[19] Even the hunt was capable of being stylized into a court spectacle: in Nymphenburg outside Munich a 'masked stag hunt' was put on during the carnival season. Men and women attended, attired in various costumes, including characters from the popular *commedia dell'arte,* Pulcinello, Harlequin, the doctor and the Austro-Bavarian comic figure, Hanswurst. On another occasion a model of the *Bucintoro,* the Venetian ship of state, was erected on the Starnberger lake not far away: the court waited armed on board, while the beaters fired cannons, blew horns and rallied the hounds to drive the game into the lake, where they swam to their death at the hands of the hunters. It was not until the middle of the eighteenth century that voices were aroused in protest at the enormous damage done to crops by the huntsmen, damage for which the farmer got little more than abuse if he sought recompense. However, from the number of anecdotes and legends, telling of conversations between the prince and his more humble subjects on the occasion of a hunt, when the ruler gets detached from the main body of the riders, it may be that there was a positive side to the matter, that hunting gave both rulers and courtiers a glimpse into the lives of the masses, on whose labour their way of life depended.

A noble and impressive setting was demanded of the German court in the age of the baroque. Impressiveness was all important. It did not matter that the imposing marble pillars in the great hall of some princely residence turned out on closer inspection to be made, not of marble, but of a kind of papier mâché; the illusion of power and majesty was undeniably there. It is important to visit baroque buildings when they are illuminated, just as one should see a church of that age when a service is in progress, when the addition of light and music brings the senses into play, in the manner envisaged by the builders. Impressions were paramount in people's lives, at every social level. Not what one was as a person mattered, but what one represented, which caste and which social élite one belonged to. Anyone who was anyone played a role and dressed accordingly; hence the fashion for the full-bottomed wig, the magnificent feathered hat, the sweeping gesture, the extravagant obeisance, the grave demeanour. Hence too the popularity of the dance, particularly the minuet and all stylized forms of movement and communication. The opera was perhaps the art form most adequate to express the character of contemporary society, both in the stylization of performance, the splendid staging and spectacle, and also in its setting, the many-tiered house reflecting the strictly segregated strata of court and burgher society (commoners were allowed into the court opera houses in the eighteenth century, though they had to pay for their seats and 'keep their place'). The same concept of society was mirrored in church architecture too, most notably in the Dresden *Frauenkirche,* which had a royal 'box' for the ruler, smaller ones for the courtiers, as well as the equivalent of a dress circle for the quality, and galleries for the common people.

The baroque court exaggerated, though it did not invent, a hierarchical view of society in which social differences were preordained. Luther had wholeheartedly identified himself with such a view, declaring: 'Im eusserlichen, weltlichen Leben da soll die ungleyheyt bleyben, wenn denn die Stende ungleych sein. Ein Bauer füret ein ander leben und Stand denn ein Bürger, Ein Fürst ein ander Stand denn ein Edelmann. Da ist alles ungleych und soll ungleych bleyben.... Das will Gott also haben, der hat die Stend also geordnet und geschaffen' ['In the external, worldly life, inequality shall be retained, since the estates are unequal. A peasant has a different kind of life and belongs to a different estate than a burgher, a prince of a different estate than a nobleman. All are unequal and shall remain so... This is the will of God, who ordained and created the estates'].[20] The hierarchy of unequals was to contemporaries the pledge of order in a transient world.

'Nichts ist schöner, nichts ist fruchtbarer als die Ordnung' ['Nothing is more lovely, nothing more fruitful than order'], wrote the Westphalian theologian J. H. Alsted, a century later, in the introduction to his *Enzyklopädie,* published at Herborn in 1630: 'Die Ordnung verschafft auf dem riesigen Theater dieser Welt allen Dingen Wert und Rang. Die Ordnung ist in der Kirche Gottes der Nerv des Corpus mysticum. Die Ordnung ist die stärkste Hand im Staats-und Familienleben' ['Order gives worth and rank to everything in the mighty theatre of this world. Order in the Church of God is the nerve of the *corpus mysticum.* Order is the strong hand in the life of the state and the family'].[21]

In court festivals and processions, in banquets and dances, everyone had his appointed place and function, thus mirroring society at large. The baroque court witnessed that most characteristic social development of Germany between the Treaties of Westphalia and the French Revolution: the establishment of an exclusive nobility, whose privileges derived, not from their capacity as feudal landowners, owing military service to the ruler, but from their role as members of the court, daily companions, advisers and servants of the prince. Their position was won by excluding the burghers as far as possible from the nerve centre of the state. This process, whereby the prince singled out for special favour members of the nobility, brought them to join him in his palace, and associated himself with their lives, can be illustrated by the case of electoral Saxony. In the late sixteenth century the Elector, August I, had begun to invite the landed nobility to attend feasts at court in their capacity as members of the estates of the realm. In 1638 Elector John George I used the occasion of his heir's wedding to start a custom of gracing the weddings of well-born men and women with his presence; his successor sent the court orchestra to play at ceremonial occasions in the houses of his nobility – in two years alone John George II attended or was represented at 120 such functions. He acted as godfather to noble princelings, and sent presents or other marks of favour. The relationship between prince and nobility was that of members of the same social élite, whose common denominator was the court.[22] To be a member of the court in 1650 and to take part in tournaments one had to possess sixteen noble ancestors. This was also demanded of aspirants to the ruler's cabinet, a striking innovation in a territory such as Saxony where hitherto the bourgeoisie had played a dominant role in state administration. In the last decades of the century the nobility determined to exploit a situation favourable to themselves to establish their privileged position beyond dispute. In the meetings of their Diet (*Landtag*) in 1681–2 they demanded that the famous Princes School (*Fürstenschule*) at Meissen be reserved for scions of noble houses; furthermore, that they should have preference for officers' posts in the army, and that burghers might not buy landed estates from noble owners. They also required the newly ennobled to be excluded from *Landtag* membership. John George III, who was interested, as were many of his contemporary rulers, in winning the estates' agreement for the creation of a standing army, proved amenable: the subsequent struggle between the nobility and the burgher estate was resolved in the former's favour by a decree of August the Strong in 1700. The satisfaction expressed by a member of the nobility during the *Landtag* negotiations at what was happening was an eloquent testimony to a development, which was characteristic of most German territories in these years:

> Wornebenst denn dieses zu erwägen, wie einen hohen Regenten und Landesfürsten zu sonderbaren Splendor, Zierde und Hoheit gereiche, wenn er seine Lehen- und Rittergüter mit einem starken und tapfern Adel bewohnet weiss, welche zu Kriegs- und Friedenszeiten nicht allein ihr Gut und Blut freudigst aufopfern sondern auch bei Ausrichtungen, Solennitäten und Ritterspielen alle gehorsamste Dienste und Aufwartung erweisen könne.

> Wheretofore it should be recalled that it doth greatly redound to the splendour, the ornament and majesty of a mighty ruler and territorial prince, if he know that a strong and brave nobility occupy his fiefs and seignorial estates, for in times of peace and war they offer their goods and their blood most readily, and at the same time they are at hand to perform service and wait upon the prince on all occasions, solemn gatherings and tournaments.[23]

Chapter 3
The German nobility

An apt symbol of the diversity of her regional and social life, Germany's nobility in the early modern period is difficult to describe and classify without distortion or omission. With some simplification one can distinguish two main kinds of nobleman in 1648: the so-called *reichsunmittelbare* or imperial nobility, immediate vassals of the Emperor, and the territorial (*landsässig*) nobility, who were subject to a sovereign ruler.

I THE IMPERIAL NOBILITY

The immediate vassals were those secular and ecclesiastic princes, and the prelates, counts, barons and knights who owned land granted by the Emperor, and over whom the territorial sovereigns in which such land lay had no authority. Many of them were, however, also subject to other sovereigns in virtue of those of their lands which might adjoin but were not part of their imperial fiefs. This was particularly common in the areas around Würzburg, Fulda and the lands of the Counts of Henneberg in central Germany. New arrivals to the rank of imperial nobility were those men of comparatively humble origins, who had been granted *Reich* land in reward for service in the Thirty Years War – Wallenstein and his helpmate Aldringen from Luxemburg are cases in point. They succeeded to fiefs which had been declared forfeit to the crown because of their rightful owners' part in the Bohemian estates' revolt against the Emperor. This too was the origin of the Fürstenbergs, who were to be associated for many years in the eighteenth century with the principality of Münster as bishops or administrators, or of the Thurn and Taxis family, famous for their organization of the imperial post service.[1] Yet another group within the *Reich* nobility were the so-called *Personalisten,* such as the Windischgraetz family, prominent in Austrian military history, whose ancestor was raised to the rank of Imperial Count, although he held no *Reich* land. Most imperial fiefs lay in south Germany, and here imperial influence remained strong. Virtually all of Württemberg's native nobility had managed to have their lands made immediately subject to the Emperor by the end of the sixteenth century; they were therefore not eligible to sit in the local assembly of estates, which was thus unique in Germany in being composed solely of church prelates and commoners.

The imperial knights

Numerically the largest group within the imperial nobility were the knights. A natural bond existed between the Emperor and these members of the minor nobility; they looked to him and to the imperial privy council (*Reichshofrat*) to support them in their quarrels with the territorial princes; in their turn they could assist the Emperor in various ways. They could bring pressure to bear in the imperial circles (*Reichskreise*) in which they lived to support the Empire in time of war: the circles had been formed by the Emperor Maximilian I (1492–1519) to provide military contingents for the Empire's defence. Thus the Archbishop of Mainz, a member of the knightly family of Schönborn, proved an energetic ally in rallying the Frankish and Swabian circles during Louis XIV's invasion of Germany in 1679. The most important source of the influence of the knights, either as a body or as individuals, lay in the fact that they provided most of the candidates for the highest ecclesiastical offices in the land, the prince electors and prince bishops of the *Reich.* They had a traditional claim on seats in the cathedral chapters; generations of members of the same family asserted their right to a particular seat. The high imperial nobility, the counts and barons, are rarely found in these posts from the time of the Reformation onwards.[2] Some sovereign princes attempted to establish a 'secundogeniture' to the more important sees for their families: thus the Wittelsbachs of Bavaria always managed to install a younger member of the ducal or electoral house in the see of Cologne from 1538 to 1761.[3] The Habsburgs attempted to do the same for other sees, wishing particularly to gain control of Mainz, because the Archbishop of Mainz was the hereditary Arch-Chancellor of the Empire. But there were limits to the knights' devotion to the imperial cause; they vigorously opposed the appointment of Maria Theresa's youngest son Max Franz as Prince Bishop of Münster in the eighteenth century.

In the late sixteenth and early seventeenth centuries emperors had granted privileges to the knights, giving them 'quasi-sovereignity' in their often miniscule territories, which was confirmed at Westphalia in 1648.[4] Over the next century or more they gave evidence of a strong sense of corporate existence, which was nowhere more clearly illustrated than in the question of religion. The majority were Catholic or had converted because they lived in the ecclesiastical principalities and had greater opportunities for themselves and their children if they did so. Yet Protestant knights also had successful careers as administrators in a number of episcopal sees, for many had started to study law in the late sixteenth century to equip themselves for the service of a prince. This development was important for the survival of the knights as a class, since they did not have a great deal of landed wealth and large families were common among their ranks. Many knightly families had both a Catholic and a Protestant branch, in consequence of the tolerant practices observed in mixed marriages. The Tridentine Decrees which prohibited such marriages unless the non-Catholic partner pledged to bring up the children in the Catholic faith had been accepted by few German states. The customary practice among the knights was for the sons to be Catholic and the daughters Protestant, though in the late eighteenth century it became usual for the sons to follow the father's and the daughters the mother's faith.[5] Such tolerance sometimes manifested itself in quite eccentric institutions: the convent for the daughters of the nobility in Gebürg near Baireuth accepted an equal number of Catholic and Protestant nuns.[6] If, as occasionally happened over the years, the position in a cathedral chapter which was traditionally the perquisite of one family fell vacant and there was no Catholic available, a member of the Protestant branch usually was ready to convert.[7] In other words, the sense of loyalty to one's estate was greater in this period than one's confessional allegiance. If, however, disputes occurred between the confessions, appeal was made to the imperial privy council. Six seats were reserved for Protestant members, and on the whole the council acted promptly and impartially.

In order to preserve the family substance, it was customary for only one son to marry. Thus of the sixteen children of Friedrich Fürstenberg (died 1646), only the eldest married. Five of his brothers became, respectively, Prince Bishop of Münster and Paderborn, Dean of Salzburg, Prebendary of Mainz, of Paderborn, and of the Teutonic Knights of Mühlheim/Möhne; four sisters became canonesses.[8] Despite their frequent lack of wealth and landed property, the social status of these knightly families was highly regarded. An example of this was Friedrich Fürstenberg's descendant, Franz Friedrich, pioneer of reform in the territory of Münster, where he was the leading minister from 1762 to 1780, a friend of Nicolai, the Stolbergs and Princess Gallitzin. While still a young man on his 'Grand Tour' in 1753, he visited Vienna; here he was twice received by the Empress Maria Theresa.

Church dignitaries of noble birth generally only received the lower orders, and if the married brother should die, his sibling left church office, married and continued the line. For Protestant knights the opportunities were, however, considerably less, and in the Rhineland it was common for them to enter the service of Brandenburg in the seventeenth century – the Romberg and Syberg families, for example, served in the Prussian army for generations. Others went to the electorate of Cologne, both as officers and civil servants, and found their religion no barrier to their prospects. In central Germany some odd arrangements established themselves: The *Balleien* (commanderies) of the Teutonic Knights provided sinecures in Thuringia for Lutherans only, in Saxony for Catholics and Lutherans, in Hesse from the seventeenth century for all three confessions (i.e. Catholics, Lutherans and Calvinists). There were a number of religious foundations in northern Germany which had become Lutheran at the Reformation but where the inmates, the Teutonic Knights, still observed the vows of poverty, chastity and obedience. There were fourteen such houses in the Guelph principalities, with their own endowments left untouched by the local rulers, and the important monasteries of St Michael in Lüneburg and Loccum abbey. By 1700 the abbot of Loccum was permitted to marry and the *Loccum Hof* was built at Hanover to accommodate his spouse. When, in 1720, the then abbot wished to bring her to the monastery he was told by the elector's privy councillors: 'Er hätte den Loccumer Hof in Hannover, da könne er sich mit seiner Frau Gemahlin genügend verlustieren, aber in Loccum hätte sie nichts verloren' ['He had the *Loccum Hof* in Hanover; there he could lust at will with his lady wife, but in Loccum itself she had no place'].[9]

Some of the most prominent personalities of the time and some of the most able servants of the Habsburgs came from the ranks of the imperial knights: the Schönborns (already mentioned), the Dernbachs, the Stadions and the Metternich families. In the century 1650–1750 the

Schönborns produced two Archbishops of Mainz, two Bishops of Würzburg, and an imperial Vice-Chancellor, while the cathedral chapter at Mainz was populated by their brothers, cousins and connections. They were extremely well educated and cosmopolitan. Many of this traditionally Catholic family went to Leyden University, while their sisters were sent to the best convents in France. The Stadions, like the Schönborns, were raised into the high nobility by the Emperor to bind them more closely to his interest. Even such high church dignitaries as Archbishop Franz Lothar Schönborn, Archbishop of Mainz and occasional opponent of Leopold I, and the *Grosshofmeister* (Grand Master) Johann Philipp Stadion felt instinctively closer to Vienna than to Rome. When in 1727 the Pope introduced a new solemn mass for the feast of Gregory VII, these prelates protested vigorously to the Vatican; the quarrel between Gregory and the Emperor Henry IV in the eleventh century made such a celebration in their view grossly offensive to the Emperor. Whatever their personal differences with individual emperors might be, the imperial nobility felt a strong sense of commitment to the Empire and, increasingly, a desire to serve the *Casa d'Austria* as diplomats, civil servants and officers. Indeed a number of prelates had served as officers of the imperial forces in the Thirty Years War.[10] During the eighteenth century, and particularly during the centralization of government under Maria Theresa and her sons, opportunities were provided for the imperial nobility which they were well qualified to meet; their traditions of service to the ecclesiastical princes, and their knowledge of European countries through travel and family connections enabled some of their number to rise to the highest offices of the land.

2 THE TERRITORIAL NOBILITY

(*a*) *General character*

When we turn to the territorial nobility, the picture is rather different, although here too there was a considerable variety in wealth and standards of education between one region and another. In all German states the nobility formed the first estate in the land, and as such enjoyed certain rights and privileges. Yet already in the sixteenth century the growing power of the territorial princes affected their position adversely; at the same time their standard of living and of culture was often considerably inferior to that of the patricians and burghers of the major German towns. In the course of the following century things changed in their favour, and though they lost many of their political liberties, they gained important rights at local level as well as exclusive social privileges. Many noblemen acted as mercenary leaders during the great war and after 1648 found employment with the princes whom they had served. The political consequences of the war established their superiority over the bourgeois councillors who had gained ascendancy in territorial government during and after the Reformation. Nobles began in the seventeenth century to send their sons in greater numbers to university so that they might be equipped to take over positions in administration. In large areas of northern Germany the nobility won almost absolute authority over those who lived and worked on their estates. In the lands east of the Elbe the system of *Gutsherrschaft*, or manorial jurisdiction, conferred far-reaching powers on them; they exercised patrimonial justice, acted as magistrates, appointed candidates as ministers to the local churches, and supervised schools. Their sense of belonging to a privileged caste was reinforced by various prohibitions emanating from the territorial rulers: thus in early eighteenth century Prussia the members of the nobility were forbidden to intermarry with anyone below the rank of the upper middle classes – that is, officials or clergymen; if they did, such marriage would be null and void. They might not sell lands to commoners, nor enter burgher professions; to do so would entail forfeiting their noble rank. In the eighteenth century, pressure was brought to bear on them not to enter the service of other princes, and in Prussia Frederick William I forbade them to attend university outside his domains, thus cutting his subjects off from access to the universities traditionally favoured by Germans of Protestant faith: Leyden, Padua, Helmstedt and Heidelberg. Among the privileges designed to strengthen the nobility at the cost of other social groups was their relative immunity from taxation, though this varied very greatly according to region. Even their illegitimate children were accommodated, generally in the army, and usually had patents of nobility conferred on them (the children of ecclesiastical princes and their concubines, however, were of bourgeois rank).

The origins of the territorial nobility were fairly mixed. Thus 25 per cent of the nobility of electoral Saxony in the eighteenth century could trace their families back to the twelfth century, whereas many others had only been ennobled in recent times. The distinguished Tyrolese family, the Herbersteins, who produced a field marshal of the Empire in the early eighteenth century, had been tilling their own land in the fifteenth: 'Siegmund von Herberstein weiss anno 1530 noch dass es einmal sieben seines Namens gegeben habe, von denen nur einer Hosen trug, die anderen aber Bauernkittel' ['Siegmund von Herberstein still knows in the year 1530 that there once had been seven of his name, of which only one wore trousers, the rest the peasant's smock'].[11] The upheavals of the great war, the disappearance through plague and death in battle of many great families, the expulsion of others, and the many new creations by the Emperor for service or military success changed the character of the German and, more particularly, of the Austrian and Bohemian nobility. The older families naturally looked down on the newer ones, or on those who had risen from the ranks of the minor nobility to the peerage – such as Trauttmansdorff or Lobkowitz, contemptuously known for their acceptance of the confiscated Bohemian estates after 1620 as 'receivers of imperial tips'. However, up to about 1700 the different groups gradually intermarried, and spoke and thought as one. The differences between the nobility and the middle classes gradually became more marked, an expression of the hierarchical character of the contemporary court and of society generally. Rank and precedence became a veritable obsession, both in noble and burgher circles, and was much commented upon by visitors to Germany. Lady Wortley Montague, writing from Regensburg in 1716, said she believed it was their most absorbing passion.[12] The idea gained credence that the noble estate was necessarily superior to any other, and must be kept undefiled. Such views were propounded by the recently ennobled with much solemnity. The Silesian dramatist and syndic of the city of Breslau, von Lohenstein, whose father had been raised to the nobility, declared:

> Sintemal dieser [der Adel] doch allezeit von seinen Voreltern Tugenden, wie die aus Erzgebirgen entspringenden Adern etwas von ihren edlen Erzen mit sich führten. Wenn auch schon der Adel was Böses an sich nähme, liesse sich doch selbes von ihm viel leichter trennen, als den niedrigen Pöfel edel machen; wie es keine grosse Kunst wäre, Schlacken vom Golde scheiden, aber fast unmöglich, aus geringem Erze Gold machen.

> Since it [the nobility] possesses from ages past virtues inherited from its ancestors, just as the springs rising in the Ore Mountains carry with them traces of the noble metals found therein. Even if the nobility were to acquire evil characteristics, it would be far easier to purify it of these than it would be to refine the lower orders: just as it would be no great art to separate dross from gold, but practically impossible to win gold out of poor quality ore.

The nobility, he adds, should keep itself to itself: 'die Natur ist aufs äusserste bemüht, dass Nichts Ungleiches zusammenwachse. Eben diese soll die Klugheit, fürnehmlich in der Liebe beobachten' [Nature takes the greatest care that different things do not grow into one. Wisdom ordains the same, particularly in matters of love'].[13] Lohenstein belonged by birth to a class which not only considered itself equal to the nobility, but which already intermarried freely with it – namely, the patricians of the old free imperial cities. The title *'Junker'* (*'Jung Herr'* or 'young gentleman') was current as a form of address for Frankfurt and Lübeck patricians in the middle of the seventeenth century; in 1669 the Nuremberg patricians were acknowledged as nobles and in 1697 received the title *Edel*, meaning noble, the equivalent in English of 'Sir'. There was not a single aristocratic family in seventeenth century Bavaria without patrician ancestors. Contemporary portraiture of noblemen and patricians conveys the same sense of the high dignity and superiority of their class, which was not apparent a century earlier and of which the sitters seem almost excessively aware.[14]

The German nobility began to attend university in increasing numbers from the late sixteenth century onwards. Helmstedt University, founded in 1576 by the scholarly Duke Julius of Brunswick, proved particularly attractive to them, as can be seen from the lists of matriculated students. One of the most important appointments made in Helmstedt's early days was that of the distinguished humanist and doctor of law of Padua University, J. Caselius, who for almost a quarter of a century trained future state officials for a variety of north German states. The Guelph princes were very active in the field of education, and the general prosperity based on ground rents from large and well-run estates permitted many of their subjects to study. Such conditions never obtained in Brandenburg-Prussia, where apart from a few families who had enriched themselves by despoiling monasteries in the Reformation – the Arnims, Schulenburgs and Bredows – the nobility was relatively poor. In the eighteenth century only 3·7 per cent of the nobility of Kurmark – that is, those living near the capital – had attended university.[15] A substitute for university in many parts of Germany was the *Ritterakademie*, an institution first established in the sixteenth century and fairly widespread after 1648. The curriculum was more modern than in universities and grammar schools, teaching foreign languages and the natural sciences, as well as knightly skills, such as fencing, riding and dancing. It was as an extension of this topical view of noble education that the Pietist A. H. Francke opened his school for gentlemen in Halle in the 1690s, training them in both religion and in the practical tasks awaiting them, such as estate management. In Lutheran areas and among the Protestant nobility of Austria, the influence of the great Reformation humanist Melanchthon and his educational vision remained strong well into the seventeenth century. Surviving libraries from the castles of the rural nobility give evidence of cultivated minds and sophisticated tastes.[16]

The high nobility, or those who could afford it, favoured the Grand Tour for their sons, and this usually included a period spent at foreign universities. The young men were accompanied by a governor – the poet Gryphius acted in this capacity in Leyden for two Silesian noblemen – whose task was to see that his charges fulfilled their parents' instructions, which often included the keeping of a diary. Maria von Dönhoff quotes extensively from the diaries of of two such young men, connections of her family, in her book on East Prussia. Baron Friedrich von Eulenburg and Ahasverus Count Lehndorff left home in 1650 with their governor and a servant. Lehndorff was sixteen, his companion, Eulenburg, only thirteen; Eulenburg's father had laid down detailed instructions for their programme, which were apparently studiously observed. The purpose of the trip was to acquire 'knowledge and the virtues befitting their estate'. They were to be constantly aware of their duty to the honour of their estate; such matters as comfort or individual fortune were deemed to be of no account, to place store on them would be thought to be 'low class'. They must dress cleanly and simply, one summer and one winter 'habit' being sufficient. A weekly timetable proves that the tour was anything but a holiday: the boys were expected to be at their books by 6 a.m., studying until instruction began at 10 a.m. Mathematics, the study of fortifications and geography occupied the first hour, music the second. They had dinner at midday, and resumed class at 1 p.m. with poetry and stylistics, followed by a study period. Fencing or dancing at 4 p.m. provided relief after an arduous day. Three months before moving to a new country they were to study the language; 'auf den Stuben aber muss kein ander Wort als Latein geredet werden' ['in their rooms, however, no other word but Latin must be spoken']. In each country they were to study 'wie nemblich und von wem es regiert wird, worinnen dessen Einkünfte und Macht besthehen' ['how and by whom it is ruled, wherein do his revenues and power consist'], to see all the sights, 'insonderheit auf alle Thürme steigen, weil von denselben man den situm et justificationem loci am besten sehen kan' ['and above all to climb all towers, since from there one can best see the site and the reason for its location'].[17] This last was an eminently practical counsel. A young man who embarked on a military career might well find himself involved in an engagement in some of the many towns he had visited; military men covered enormous distances in the course of their careers, despite the primitive state of the roads. The fact that they were likely to serve a number of masters increased the likelihood of their fighting in many different countries. The Prussian officer Johann Georg von Arnim had, in the course of the Thirty Years War, served Sweden, Poland, Saxony and the Empire with equal profit; L. D. von Bönninghausen, a Westphalian knight, served Spain, the Catholic League, the Emperor, and finally the ruler of Hesse-Kassel, France's most important German ally, before returning to the imperial side once more.[18]

The route taken by the 'cavaliers' depended on their religion. Protestants visited the Netherlands, France and usually northern Italy; Catholics went to France, to Rome of course, and to the imperial court at Vienna. The overall effect was generally to make the travellers more tolerant in their religious views, by contrast with the sternly orthodox Lutheran country nobility, and very much more cultivated than the majority of the provincial barons and knights whose pleasures were food, drink and hunting, and whose daily life differed not a great deal from that of the peasants among whom they lived.

Towards the end of the seventeenth century the Grand Tour became less common for Germans, for a variety of reasons. The most important was the growing role played by the princely courts in the lives of the aristocracy. The practice of sending well born boys to court as pages became widespread; later they would enter the service of the prince as an official or officer. However, payment was irregular, prospects uncertain. Up to the end of the seventeenth century it was still customary for such men to move from one court to another in search of preferment – the career of the great political theorist Veit von Seckendorff is a case in point. In Prussia from the eighteenth century onwards the king put pressure on his nobles to remain in their native land, though his example was not generally followed in other German states. It was less the threats and prohibitions which prevailed on them to do so than something approaching a career structure. However restricting it was, and however ill paid in the early years, the service of the king had the great merit of relieving a nobleman of his most pressing problem: how to provide for his children.

(*b*) *The nobility in Austria*

The Austrian nobility was probably the most socially diverse in Germany. In Prussia and Saxony the ancestors of the old noble families had been colonizers of the eastern marches – Brandenburg and Meissen. In Austria the nobility went back to the royal servants of medieval times, to the great south German and Italian banking families of the late Middle Ages and to wealthy commoners who had served successive emperors from the time of Maximilian I and had been rewarded with land and title. The older houses liked to distinguish between themselves and the more recent creations, but in practice the differences were not great, since all were members of the provincial estates and eventually intermarried. Before the Thirty Years War the Austrian nobility was very powerful, largely because of the Emperor's dependence on their support against the constant menace of the Turk. Furthermore, the Austrian estates presented a united front to their sovereign, something which was not always true of estates in other regions of Germany. The reason for this was religious: the Austrian nobility and the towns were largely Protestant and they made their support of the Emperor dependent on his grant of religious privileges. He in turn made them pay dearly: even Maximilian II (1564–74), reputedly a Protestant, got almost two and three-quarter million florins in 1568 and 1571 from the estates of Upper and Lower Austria. Fifty years later the whole position of the Austrian estates and the Lutheran religion in that territory was in jeopardy. The reason was the rebellion of the Bohemian estates against Emperor Ferdinand II, who, as Archduke of Styria had already imposed the Counter-Reformation on his lands. In matters of religion Ferdinand was something of a reluctant fanatic. Naturally an agreeable, even easy-going man, his education, his strong sense of Habsburg mission, and the powerful influence of his spiritual advisers, urged him forward at crucial points in his reign. After the battle of the White Mountain in 1620, when the Bohemian Calvinists were routed by the imperial commander Tilly, and their cause lost as a result, Ferdinand began to suppress the Protestant faith in all the territories under his control. The Austrian nobility began to suffer the fate of the Bohemian, to face confiscation of their goods and threats to their persons if they did not convert. The result was emigration on a massive scale. From Styria alone 800 members of eighty-five different families left; from the small duchy of Carinthia 160 leading nobles left.[19] The consequences for Austria were momentous. Under the shattering effect of this blow the native nobility, apart from the Tyrol, which had remained Catholic, withdrew from public life. During the Thirty Years War only three of the thirty-seven imperial field marshals were native Austrians, and only nine of the seventy-five field marshals appointed between 1700 and 1740. The natural élite of Austrian society, the nobility, took little active part in administration or diplomacy over the next centuries. Its place was taken by members of the German, Spanish, Italian or French aristocracy, or commoners whose good fortune had been crowned with a patent of nobility by the Emperor. Only in one important sphere of public life were the native nobles still active as late as the beginning of the nineteenth century: the ecclesiastical hierarchy. Of forty-four bishops in eighteenth century Austria, all were members of the old nobility, only ten came from the *Reich,* all the rest were Austrians. However, one is struck by the predominance of Tyrolean names among them: twenty-one or possibly twenty-four came from that small province.[20] The heartlands of Austria, Lower and Upper Austria and Styria, lost their cultivated and enterprising élite in the Counter-Reformation and they were never able, in this period, to find an equivalent substitute.

(c) *The Prussian nobility*

The history of the nobility in Prussia is the best documented of any in Germany. Here the absolute rulers were more successful than elsewhere in freeing themselves from the restraints on their power provided by the traditional political liberties of the first estate. However, they did not alter the social status of the nobility, nor rob them of their important political functions in local government and the administration of the law. But no longer was the privileged status of the *Junker* in eighteenth century Prussia his by right of tradition: it derived rather from the important functions he was required by the sovereign to carry out in a rationally conceived, centrally organized state. This fundamental change in the character of the first estate was the work of three rulers, the first and third unusually gifted men, the second unusually energetic in his pursuit of a genial but grim vision of state: the Great Elector Frederick William (1640–88), his grandson King Frederick William I (1713–40), and his greatgrandson Frederick the Great (1740–86). From a position of relative political autonomy in the first half of the seventeenth century, able to exercise considerable influence over the ruler through their control of supplies and owning as a class far more territory than he, the Prussian nobility was gradually transformed into subjects of the sovereign, albeit uniquely privileged ones. It was in their character of royal servants that the privileged status of the Brandenburg-Prussian nobles now lay, in the functions allotted them by state in the army, and in civil service and local government. This found clear expression many years later in the *Allgemeines Preussisches Landrecht* (1794), in a frequently quoted phrase: 'Dem Adel als dem ersten Stand im Staate liegt nach seiner Bestimmung die Verteidigung des Staates sowie die Unterstützung der äusseren Würde und inneren Verfassung derselben hauptsächlich ob' ['The nobility as the first estate in the land is by its vocation charged with the defence of the realm as with the maintenance of its external dignity and its internal order'].[21] The most important change in the character of the Prussian nobility, and one which remained an integral feature of their lives until the present century, was the militarization of aristocratic values in consequence of Hohenzollern policies.

It is a moot point whether the Prussian nobility gained more than they lost in the process. By comparison with conditions for other social groups in Prussia, their lot was enviable, but the new role did not bring with it wealth or comfort. Even before the advent of absolutism, their economic position in most regions had been anything but strong. Apart from a few families, the members of the Prussian landed nobility were poor, their farming methods backward, their living conditions not those usually associated with the highest estate. Many were little more than peasants, living in thatched houses which did not differ greatly from the barns and sheds alongside, and were known mockingly as '*Krautjunker*'. Thus the dower house of a Frau von Barsdorf in 1697, who was the sister-in-law of the von Zieten family, consisted simply of a single room, with two closets opening off, in a former farmhouse.[22] The numbers of such nobles increased in the seventeenth century; their economic opportunities did not. Not only was Brandenburg one of the worst victims of the great war, but less than a decade after 1648 East Prussia was the victim of a disastrous invasion by the Tartars in 1656–7 which ravaged the populace and the countryside. They had neither the landed wealth of the high nobility in other parts of Germany, nor the chance open to the minor imperial nobility to place their sons in posts in the church: apart from the cathedral chapters of Brandenburg and Havelberg there was nothing of this kind in Prussia. Few were able to attend university; for the great majority the three Rs and religious instruction were their only acquaintance with education. A typical eighteenth century *Junker* was the former officer, Hans Gottfried von Klöden, who is recalled in the vivid memoirs of his grandson. The *Junker*'s education in the early decades of the eighteenth century consisted of: 'Lesen, Schreiben, Rechnen, Fechten, Jagen, Vogelstellen und Exerciren' ['reading, writing, arithmetic, fencing, hunting, trapping birds and drilling']. He knew 'seine Fuchtel zu führen und seinen Passionen standesmässig zu folgen, auch auf den sogenannten Ehrenpunkt mit grossem Eifer zu halten, kannte aber ausserhalb dieser Sphäre nichts als die Namen und Schicksale einer kleinen Reihe seiner Voreltern' ['how to wield a broadsword and to indulge his passions in a manner fitting to his estate, to keep his end up in the so called question of honour, but apart from this he only knew the names of a few of his ancestors and their destinies'].[23]

The gradual changeover from mercenary armies to a standing army, which was the work of the Great Elector, proved a godsend. Under his successor, the first king in Prussia, Frederick I (1688–1713), more and more nobles were drawn into the administration; Frederick William I, who often gave vent to hostile remarks about his nobility, in fact served their interest wholeheartedly. He restricted the savage recruiting system, and placed in the hands of colonels, majors and captains responsibility for recruiting and maintaining a fighting force based on a cantonal system. The men were usually recruited from their commanding officer's own tenants, and could be sent home for the greater part of the year to attend to the land.[24] He admonished them in a famous phrase that they must 'keinen Herrn kennen als Gott und den König von Preussen' ['acknowledge no master but God and the king of Prussia'], but he gave them employment: five out of every six of his councillors were noblemen.[25] More important, he stabilized agrarian prices and provided his land with a period of peace; the number of country mansions, gardens and parks laid out in his reign are ample evidence of the fact that the nobility enjoyed at this time their greatest economic prosperity of any time between 1600 and 1800. By contrast, Frederick II served the nobility much less well. The demands made on them by three major wars, the necessity for them to be absent for long periods from their estates while serving in the army or at court, the low salaries they received until, after nearly twenty years of service, they could be promoted to captaincy, led to their incurring a burden of debt which was carried on from one generation to the next. Nor could they easily marry before middle age, both for financial reasons and because the king disliked married officers. Prussian landowners were slow to create entails on their land: the younger sons were paid out sums raised by borrowing. The result was that by the end of the eighteenth century the Prussian nobility was burdened by debt; its whole future as a class was placed in jeopardy. Public opinion and informed critics in the years 1770–1806 were preoccupied with the whole question of the rights of hereditary nobility. Christoph Meiners, a popular philosopher and a widely read author, declared in the first volume of his *Göttingisches Historisches Magazin* (1787) that one could name 'unter den heutigen aufgeklärten Völkern Europens fast ebenso viele erklärte Feinde und Spötter des Adels als berühmte Schriftsteller' ['among the enlightened peoples of Europe today, one could name almost as many declared enemies and satirists of the nobility as one could writers'].[26] A member of the von Schlieffen house shocked and astonished his contemporaries when he wrote at the end of his *Nachricht von einigen Häusern der von Schlieffen* (*News of Some of the Houses of the von Schlieffens*) (1784) that 'Ahnenstolz unserer Väter, welcher verächtlich auf das mit diesem Narrengewand ungeschmückte Verdienst herabschaue ist des Lächerlichen würdig, womit die Vernunft ihn endlich brandmarkte' ['The ancestral pride of our fathers, which looks with contempt on merit which is not adorned with the fool's coat of noble pedigree, is merely ridiculous, and this has at last been branded as such by Reason'].[27] The most widely known (if not the best) novel of the time, *Sophiens Reise von Memel nach Sachsen* (1770–1) in five volumes by the Silesian pastor J. T. Hermes, devoted a lengthy chapter to the rights and wrongs of noble privilege, and unmasked the pretensions, the cruelty even, of such a system.[28]

Not only was the Prussian nobility impoverished, but its character had changed. By the beginning of the nineteenth century there were in the Kurmark only eighty-three families of the 259 resident there in 1540. One hundred and forty-two new families had come in over the centuries. However, one eighth of noble land was now held by commoners, and this was only the official figure; because of the prohibition on the sale of noble land, arrangements were usually made to conceal the fact of the sale; thus the real figures will have been considerably higher. The peasants were the first to suffer from the misfortunes of their landlords; a patriarchal relationship between landlord and tenant had existed under the old regime, but this was neither appreciated nor emulated by their bourgeois successors. By the end of the eighteenth century only a small proportion of Prussian nobles actually lived and worked on their land: in 1800 in the Kurmark it was 27 per cent, and a further 42 per cent came back after prolonged periods away from home in the royal service. Some 29 per cent lived in the town, either acting in official posts or living off some form of pension.[29] The case of Hans Gottfried von Klöden, erstwhile officer in the Bayreuth dragoons, chosen at random, illustrates the plight of an impoverished landed nobility. Returning home after almost a quarter of a century in the army, he married and had a son, but became increasingly frustrated by his failure to raise money to repair his house or farm. His son grew up half educated, and so embittered did the boy become at the prospects in front of him that he renounced his nobility, and enlisted as an NCO in the Prussian army, where a life of unspeakable wretchedness awaited him. Only in Silesia was a vigorous attempt made after 1763 to combat the kind of problems faced by Hans Gottfried and his kind. A system of mortgages with bi-annual repayments was introduced and had the effect of stimulating commercial and industrial enterprises on the land. The Silesian, as against the Brandenburg, nobility was not forbidden to engage in profit-making activities. At great cost to smallholders and cottagers, common lands were divided among the larger farmers and estate owners and the Silesian landlords prospered. In general, however, the overall picture of life in the first Prussian estate at the end of the eighteenth century excited concern rather than envy among contemporaries. For all its privileged status, the Prussian nobility had neither freedom from financial care, nor the leisure to enjoy it. Its dual function, to defend and represent the state and to create the basis of an existence befitting its position by cultivating hereditary lands, proved a burden too heavy to bear. It was Frederick II, in his successful pursuit of great power status for Prussia, who had laid this burden on the shoulders of his nobles. As the nineteenth century novelist, Theodor Fontane, astute observer and life-long critic of Prussia, speaking through his hero, Baron Stechlin, put it: 'Er war für sich und für das Land, oder, wie er zu sagen liebte, "Für den Staat". Aber dass wir als Stand und Kaste so recht etwas von ihm gehabt hätten, das ist eine Einbildung' ['He was devoted to himself and the land, or rather, as he liked to put it, "to the state". But to think that we as an estate and a caste really got anything out of him is fantasy'].[30]

(d) The Saxon nobility

The situation of the Saxon nobility was at first sight not much better. In 1787 32 per cent of noble land was held by commoners, 17 per cent under the sequestrator, and only 17 per cent was relatively free of debt.[31] Things were made worse by the fact that Saxony had been on the losing side in the Seven Years War; but here, by contrast with Prussia, if the nobility engaged in manufacture, it was not regarded as an offence against the honour of their estate. A number did in fact do so, encouraged by the success of a few dynamic men, recent recruits to the nobility, who played a leading role in the reform era in Saxony which began in the last year of the reign of Elector Frederick Charles, in 1762. Men whose families were to be among the most respected in the land in the nineteenth century, the booksellers, merchants and bankers, Thomas Fritsch (1700–75), Peter Hohenthal (1726–94) and the Austrian Wolfgang Riesch (1712–76), were all ennobled between 1717 and 1747. As new nobility they did not succeed in gaining entrance to the provincial estates or *Landstände*, but nonetheless they made a vital contribution in brains and wealth to their country. Such was the recognition afforded to their activities that a number were repeatedly offered posts in the Prussian, English and Russian services. Thomas Fritsch's son and grandson became ministers of state in neighbouring Saxe-Weimar; the Hohenthal girls were regarded as ornaments of the Prussian court in the nineteenth century, one of them, Ida, being for some years lady-in-waiting to Empress Augusta of Germany. Saxony's industrial pre-eminence in Germany before 1850 owed much to the enterprise of her new nobility. Not only did these new members found and finance projects, but they helped to encourage the founding of educational establishments specifically designed to foster new technical skills: the Freiberger Mining Academy (1765), the Mining Training

School (1775), the Drawing school at Meissen (1764). All these enterprises were aimed primarily at profiting the economic life of the state.

Business offered an outlet for the new nobility in Saxony in a way that was not typical of Germany as a whole until the second half of the nineteenth century. But the new men were not able to gain political or social recognition of their achievements in this field. The older nobility became sensitive to and intolerant of their ambitions. This was not peculiar to Saxony, but was characteristic of many other regions of Germany, especially in the north. For the attacks made by absolute monarchs on the autonomy of the old feudal estates had made the established nobility more jealous of its corporate existence. It closed its ranks to newcomers, guarded traditional rights and privileges and was even successful in certain areas, such as Mecklenburg, in extending them. The sovereign rulers, notably Maria Theresa and her sons in Austria, employed the new members of the nobility in their rapidly extending bureaucracy, granting them honours and titles, but they formed a highly respected 'second society' and had no social intercourse with the exclusive 'first society', the high or court nobility. 'Der Adelsbrief an sich' ['The patent of nobility itself], as Preradovich observes, 'ist zu keiner Zeit eine "Mitglieds-", sondern allenfalls eine "Eintrittskarte" gewesen' ['has never been a "membership card" but at best a "ticket of entry" '].[32] They intermarried with members of the banking and merchant families from which they themselves had emerged. In Prussia Frederick William I had initially disapproved of ennobled bureaucrats, but by the end of his reign was employing them widely, and in his territories there was in any case relatively little difference between the ranks of the nobility. Many families whose descendants are familiar names in nineteenth century Prussian history only came to the kingdom in his reign – for example, the Gerlachs, or the Stubenrauchs. Under Frederick II twice as many patents of nobility were granted as under his father; under his successor, Frederick William II (1786–97), there were over five times as many again.

The motive in Frederick William II's case – and he was not unique in this – was simply money. Of course, payment for titles was anything but new, it was an accepted part of imperial revenue. The conferring of the highest titles was reserved to the Emperor and the imperial court chancery at Vienna, but since the Middle Ages the office of count palatine (*Pfalzgraf*) had existed to confer honours and titles, to legitimize children, etc. Over 2000 counts palatine had been appointed between 1355 and 1806 – at least on record; there were probably many more.[33] The recipients paid well for the office, but could rely on it for a steady income. The office was granted either on a hereditary basis, and this was only given to smaller rulers, lest the power of the Habsburgs be diminished, or to individuals for their lifetime. Thus, the abbot of Kempten guaranteed a substantial debt of Emperor Maximilian II and was given the office of count palatine for himself and his successors for one hundred years. Honours granted in the early modern period by territorial rulers were not necessarily recognized outside that state, or only on payment of a sum of money. Even institutions could act in the capacity of count palatine, as did the law faculty of Innsbruck University in the person of its dean: a brisk trade in legitimizations was done in the eighteenth century at 13–30 florins a time, thus offering a valuable social service to the community.[34]

It was clear to many people by the end of the eighteenth century that there was a new mobility in society, and that individuals were prepared to pay a great deal of money for a patent of nobility, which they and others regarded as the outward confirmation of their success. The very increase in the numbers of the nobility made the whole basis of the nobles' claim to superior status questionable. The many contemporary treatises on the subject indicate how widespread was the feeling that change in the character and function of the German nobility was in the offing. For the cameralist Justi in 1756 nobility based on service was a good thing, but any nobleman who by his thirtieth birthday had not shown a particular talent for useful service should 'für seine Person des Adels für unwert erklären' ['be deemed unworthy of nobility for his person']. Half a century later in his *Metaphysik der Sitten,* Kant mockingly compared a hereditary nobility with the idea of a hereditary professor – 'ein Gedankending ohne alle Realität' ['a figment of the imagination, without any reality'].[35] The question of the ecclesiastic principalities preoccupied men's minds perhaps to an even greater degree, not primarily in an anticlerical or resentful spirit, but as part of an earnest and enlightened desire to improve society and political life. The response to the prize essay advertised by the Fulda prelate and president of the government, Baron Bibra, in his *Journal von und für Deutschland* in 1786, as to the causes of the poverty and impotence of the ecclesiastical states, was an overwhelming one. The most distinguished among many replies was the study by Frederick Carl von Moser (1787), judiciously criticizing the anachronistic character of these states. Public preoccupation with the whole question of the nobility, which received considerable stimulus from what was happening across the Rhine in the 1790s, was more an ethical inquiry than a political programme. When, therefore, Napoleon prompted the mediatization of all the ecclesiastic princes and a very great number of minor semi-sovereign nobles as well, when the *Reich* and the institutions of the *Reich* were abolished (1803–6), the reaction in Germany was far less violent than an outside observer would have supposed. A handful of radicals rejoiced at the passing of an anachronism, as they saw it, the individuals concerned faced the future with some trepidation, but the whole upheaval was minimized by comparison with the other political and military events which Napoleon's rule had precipitated in Europe. When the upheaval had passed, when Napoleon himself had been defeated and exiled, the members of the German nobility found that their resources were perhaps less than they had been, but that the ingrained habits of deference among those below them in rank helped them retain that privileged social status in fact which had so long been theirs in law.

Chapter 4
Town life in Germany

The Thirty Years War was long regarded by historians as directly responsible for a century and a half of economic decline or stagnation, particularly with regard to town life. If, today, regional and social historical studies have significantly modified our picture of Germany in the seventeenth and eighteenth centuries, it remains true to say that in general German towns decayed or failed to expand after the catastrophes of the early seventeenth century. Even major cities such as Frankfurt and Cologne did not expand beyond their medieval walls until the nineteenth century; Lübeck's population in 1800 was the same as it had been in the late fifteenth century, and Nuremberg's was not much more than half of what it had been then.[1] Germany's population had grown rapidly in the sixteenth century, despite epidemics and other crowd diseases which became common all over Europe from about 1560. Danzig, for example, had trebled its population between 1500 and 1640.[2] The war years reduced Germany's population by about 40 per cent in the countryside, 33 per cent in the towns. Before the war the population had recovered well from natural catastrophes: thus 790 people had died from plague in the north German town of Salzwedel in 1581; the number of weddings there declined in that year from the annual average of thirty to ten couples. Yet in 1582 ninety-four couples married and the number of births rose accordingly.[3] During and after the war this was no longer so in the urban areas. Although fertility was high, child mortality was alarmingly so; in Utzberg near Erfurt 91·74 per cent of children under five died in 1626–35, in Vieselbach/Weimar the percentage rose between 1628 and 1639 to 96·25 per cent.[4] The plague and crowd diseases such as typhus and smallpox were far greater killers than the marauding soldiers. The mortality figure was increased by the habit of peasants fleeing into the towns before the armies; if an epidemic broke out, the primitive sanitary arrangements facilitated its spread.

The social and political consequences of the war changed the character of town life in Germany and the conditions under which people lived. From being autonomous corporations, the towns in many parts of the country came under the authority of the princes. The well-to-do merchants then either moved away – in northern Germany, often to Amsterdam or Antwerp – or they sought service at court or with the estates. The craftsmen and shopkeepers worked either directly or indirectly for the court, but they were no longer responsible for the administration of their own town. In numerous towns throughout the land burghers were progressively excluded from political affairs, their competence confined to economic matters directly affecting them. Post-war conditions made it easy for certain rulers to subjugate towns in or near their borders, either by moving in troops to intimidate the town council, as happened in Brunswick in 1671, or by the prince setting up his official residence in a particular town and gradually eroding traditional privileges, as happened in Hanover in 1636, when Duke George of Calenberg-Göttingen moved there against the wishes of the townsfolk. The territorial rulers interfered with commercial life, erected toll barriers along roads and rivers which effectively frustrated Germany's economic development until the nineteenth century, and, in an effort to raise revenues, separated town and countryside by levying excise on goods coming in and out of the towns. Business initiative was stifled, enterprise constantly checked. To this was added the fact that Germany was cut off by the terms of the Treaties of Westphalia from direct access to the sea through her five great rivers: the mouths of the Rhine, Weser, Elbe, Oder and Vistula were all in foreign hands. Stettin (and Rostock) declined under Swedish rule, while Dutch control of the Rhine delta severely hampered internal trade along the river. Poor communications by road and water and a multiplicity of currencies kept regions apart from one another and fostered a parochial outlook which foreigners found characteristic of Germans in these years.

Yet, as always in German history, what is true as a general trend does not hold good everywhere; there was, in fact, considerable regional variation. Thus Danzig, despite the war, had the best year in its trading history in 1649. Andreas Stech's picture of seventeenth century Danzig burghers, painted in 1688, shows them walking outside their city, their rich apparel and stately gait indicating their wealth and status in society. The houses of some of Leipzig's successful merchants as portrayed in Peter Schenk's copper-plate engraving (1723) were more reminiscent of some great Mediterranean metropolis than of eighteenth century Saxony.[5] And throughout the whole period Hamburg's European importance contrasted with the fate of the majority of German towns in this period. As far back as 1597 Hamburg had a reputation for being 'the most flourishing Emporium of all Germany'. Not only was it virtually untouched by the war, its population growth unaffected by subsequent epidemics, but it continued to expand and to be able to defend its prosperity over the next centuries against all comers, except Napoleon. In Hamburg the burgher was master; no noble might reside within its territory. To be a citizen imposed a variety of duties – e.g. to bear arms and to contribute to the maintenance of various charitable organizations, hospitals, almshouses, orphanages, etc., which were all under the authority of the city government. But one enjoyed substantial privileges, too, and to be a citizen of Hamburg in the seventeenth century was probably, for Germans, the best guarantee of dying in one's bed. The town council of Hamburg had had a Dutch engineer fortify the city at the beginning of the century; in 1618 an army was engaged. Such foresight paid off. Hamburg was successful, as well as lucky, in contesting the Danish King's efforts to subjugate it. Accordingly, in the second half of the century, it attracted many enterprising merchants from other towns, such as Hameln and Brunswick, which had lost their autonomy to local rulers. A free imperial city, almost but not quite out of reach of the imperial authority, as the religious and civic strife of 1708–12 was to show, its citizens felt closer to Amsterdam, to its former Hanseatic trading partners in Lübeck, Danzig and Reval, than to inland towns. A certain arrogance characterized their feelings towards their fellow Germans, which increased as time went on. A typically patronizing attitude is expressed in the letters of a Hamburg merchant's wife accompanying her husband in 1790 on a business trip: 'Wie tot ist es aber gegen Hamburg!' ['How dead it all is compared with Hamburg!'], wrote Betty Schwalb in Brunswick. 'Ich glaub, man sieht hier in einen [sic] ganzen Tag nicht so viel Leute gehen als in Hamburg in einer Stunde' ['I do declare one sees less people here in a whole day than in Hamburg in an hour']. She dismissed the actors in the *Comödie* in Leipzig as 'elend' ['wretched'], adding kindly, 'aber wir Hamburger sind nun freilich ein bischen verwöhnt' ['But of course we Hamburgers are a little spoiled'].[6] Stateliness of dress and manners was typical of merchants in public life; 447 marks were paid by an eighteenth century Hamburg merchant for a 'suit of dragon green velvet'; French phrases adorned their speech – in the nineteenth century it was English. Yet there was a solidity and simplicity about the home life of even the richest merchants here. During working hours they spoke low German; relaxing at home they wore the dressing gown common to middle class German provincials everywhere. The patriarchal style of family life was not different from the rest of Germany; the children addressed their father as '*Sie*' and kissed his hand respectfully. Feastdays and birthdays, christenings, weddings and funerals were commemorated by members of the family in artless verse.

Hamburg's wealth was founded on its role as intermediary in the trade between Spain, Portugal and the Baltic, and later in trade with France and England. Its merchants imported and distributed colonial and other goods in Germany and played an important role in exporting the products of the Silesian linen industry; the fortunes of many families in the city were founded on this profitable trade. The city fathers showed wise foresight in welcoming the industrious religious refugees from Holland and Silesia, and the Sephardic Jews from Portugal. Their policy contrasted with the timidity of the council of seventeenth century Reval, whose refusal of domicile to foreign traders was a major factor in its decline.[7] In spite of their rigidity in matters of religious belief as orthodox Lutherans, despite their strong sense of tradition, the people of Hamburg were ready to use the talents of newcomers; one eighth of Hamburg's mayors from the time of the Reformation to the mid-nineteenth century were immigrants. The result was not only steadily growing prosperity but a sense of civic pride and patriotism among the population as a whole. Social distinctions did of course exist, evident when it came to marrying off one's daughter, but in essence it was true what J. K. D. Curio, himself an immigrant, said in 1803: 'Wir haben keinen Adel, keine Patricier, keine Sklaven, ja selbst nicht einmal Untertanen. Alle wirklichen Hamburger kennen und haben einen einzigen Stand, den Stand eines Bürgers. Bürger sind wir alle, nicht mehr und nicht weniger' ['We have no nobility, no patricians, no slaves, no, not even subjects. All true Hamburgers know and belong to but a single estate, namely the burgher estate. We are all burghers, no more, no less'].[8]

The nearest counterpart of Hamburg in the south was Nuremberg, the wealthiest city of early sixteenth century Germany. Its civic amenities and its orderly government had at that time few rivals among European cities. Streets were paved and cleaned regularly, baths and attendants were provided for the citizens at public expense, refuse disposal was, in theory at least, carefully controlled, while its own legal code, charitable organizations and defence systems all but guaranteed a good life for the virtuous among its population.[9] In the war Nuremberg had escaped the terrible fate of Magdeburg and other towns which lay in the path of advancing and retreating armies; although largely Protestant, it had paid the rapacious but discriminating Bavarian ruler, Maximilian, to protect it. Yet the war years affected it nonetheless. It was besieged by Wallenstein – who had been a student at its municipal University at Altdorf – and some 10,000 died of plague and disease. The old patrician families jealously guarded their dominant position in the government of the city even when, after the war, they were no longer active in commerce and finance. The prosperity enjoyed by Nuremberg until about 1685 and again between 1715 and 1765 was largely the achievement of newcomers, who resold colonial wares in south Germany, and finished and sold textiles from Saxony and Silesia. The mercantilist policies of Saxony and Prussia in the eighteenth century contributed to the city's decline, but the narrow minded and exclusive attitude of the ruling fathers was the principal cause of Nuremberg's failure to attract talent and enterprise.[10] The decline of Altdorf University, graphically described by Johann Miller of Ulm in his novel *Die Geschichte Gottfried Walters, eines Tischlers, und des Städtchens Erlenburg* (1786), was symptomatic of the decay of this once great city. Its population at the end of the eighteenth century was about 27 000, no more than half of what it had been 200 years earlier. By comparison with other inland European cities such as Milan, Lyons or Zürich, Nuremberg, Augsburg and the Swabian cities, once dominant in Europe, were in 1800 not much more than pleasant provincial backwaters. In 1796 the Nuremberg town council actually offered the city to the King of Prussia on condition he paid its debts. The offer was refused. Nuremberg was eventually absorbed by Bavaria in 1806.

The main trade routes in medieval central Europe had been the so-called Bernstein or amber route, running from the eastern Baltic through Silesia, Bohemia and Nuremberg to Italy, and the east–west Baltic route, dominated by Lübeck. The increase of sea traffic in the Mediterranean and Atlantic had changed this, as had the hegemony of the Scandinavian monarchs which had destroyed Lübeck's power. The beneficiaries of this were firstly Hamburg, and then Frankfurt and Leipzig. Frankfurt had long been important for its strategic position, and as the place where the Kings of the Romans were crowned. In the seventeenth century it became the chief money market of western Germany; a great deal of money was made by the inhabitants who hired houses and stalls to traders coming in to its fairs. By the early eighteenth century, however, Leipzig, an insignificant town before the Thirty Years War, had established its primacy over Frankfurt as the venue of the most important fairs in Germany. Leipzig was not, as Frankfurt was, a free imperial town, but its overlord, the Elector of Saxony, interfered relatively little in its affairs; when in 1670 he attempted to exclude Jews from the town, the merchants were able to persuade him to desist. The Jews from Russia, Poland and eastern Germany, whether merchants or small traders, were enormously important for Leipzig and it for them. Many a village in Pomerania, Posen and further east depended entirely on the Jewish pedlar for household goods, cloth and threads. When political factors interfered with direct trade, as happened, for example, to the Danzig merchants and their Russian partners in the second half of the eighteenth century, Leipzig offered an alternative solution. Thus Arthur Schopenhauer's grandfather, a leading Danzig merchant, instructed his Lyons suppliers to send their goods to him at Leipzig where he then sold them to the Russians.[11]

The consequent prosperity of the town was reflected in the civic amenities and the homes of its merchants. Leipzig had the distinction of being the only inland town in eighteenth century Germany where there were decent inns; the coffee houses were famous, and when the Frankfurt censorship became more rigorous in the 1690s, many booksellers removed to Leipzig, making it the centre of the German book trade. Indeed, for innumerable men of education in provincial towns and villages, Leipzig was their Mecca, and only if a local merchant visited Leipzig's book fairs could they have much hope of hearing about and getting new books. Very few German towns had bookshops until the second half of the eighteenth century. Leipzig started the vogue for public lending libraries and other towns followed suit. Its merchants founded the first professional pensionable orchestra at the *Gewandhaus.* Its university, a medieval foundation, remained one of the largest throughout this period, and attracted Protestant students from as far away as Transylvania and Lithuania.

These towns, as well as Danzig and the Silesian centres of the linen industry, such as Breslau or Hirschberg, were in fact the exception. The majority of German towns during the period 1648–1815 either came under the rule of a local prince or sank to the status of small country town. The territorial rulers hoped to use the towns within or near their borders to add to their wealth and hence augment their standing in the world. They crushed those traditional liberties which had been the source of enterprise and commerce, often, as the Great Elector did in Königsberg, with great ruthlessness. In some cases their intervention aided the town economically, in others their policies cut off a town from its former trading partners. The most significant effect of this on urban life, however, was not economic but social. The transformation of a town from an autonomous or virtually autonomous corporation, owing certain obligations to a prince, to being the seat or residence of a local ruler, brought with it a profound change in the urban middle classes.[12] This was so widespread and so far reaching in its consequences that it is worth looking at the process in detail in a particular instance, that of Munich.

In the late sixteenth century the Duke of Bavaria decided to take up his residence in the town; he and his successors withdrew or ignored time-honoured rights of the town council and citizens: the rights to trade in salt, to grant citizenship to whom it would, and to elect council members. Under Maximilian V a court official was imposed as head of municipal police, while towards the end of the war the town was finally forced to submit its annual accounts to the state for inspection. How could this come about? The process was only made possible through the attitudes of the patrician families who, as in Nuremberg, dominated the inner city council. In late medieval times they had begun to acquire property outside the city, to intermarry with the lower nobility whose ranks they aspired to join. In the sixteenth century they gradually withdrew from trade and commerce, living on the rents of their property and desiring to be held the social equal of the nobility so much less wealthy than they; many indeed were rewarded by a patent of nobility by the Duke. They were already remote from the preoccupations of their fellow burghers, when in the seventeenth century they began to take offices at court, while the Duke, now Elector of Bavaria, began in 1672 to reward his favourites by making them patricians of the city and therefore eligible for lucrative posts in the council. Just as the inner council was no longer composed of members of the indigenous ruling families, so the greater council ceased to represent those it governed. In the sixteenth century all craftsmen might belong to it; a century later it was recruited only from well-to-do merchants, vintners, and occasionally apothecaries and booksellers. The craftsmen lost caste and, along with the peasants and the lower ranks of urban society, were excluded from a say in their own affairs. The visitations of the wars in the late seventeenth and eighteenth century only served to increase the authority of the state in the lives of the Munich citizens. The apparatus of state bureaucracy was reflected in the number of buildings erected to house court and administrative officials, in the palaces of the nobles which rose round the residence of the elector; bourgeois Munich had given place to electoral Munich.[13] And yet Munich almost alone among south German towns grew in size, its prosperity owing much to the French subsidies which became a permanent feature of Bavarian policy. By 1800 it had a larger population than Hamburg and was the third largest city in Germany.

Vienna too owed its growth and its claims to be the largest city in central Europe to the decision of the Emperor Mathias in 1612 to make it, and not Prague, the imperial residence. Vienna had had no part in the great financial transactions of the sixteenth century which accompanied the rise of the Austrian Habsburgs. The Thirty Years War, the Counter-Reformation, and the subjugation of the estates by the Habsburgs, created a new class of nobility who were court officials and royal servants. To make room for their palaces, which are still an impressive feature of the city, the Viennese burghers were moved out of the town centre after the repulse of the Turks in 1683. The inhabitants of the city worked for the court; luxury industries and crafts developed as the principal product of native and immigrant labour. The lumbering bureaucracy with all the disadvantages of its Spanish prototype, absorbed more and more poorly paid but self-important officials into its machinery. Vienna's population was of mixed national origin even in the seventeenth century; the idea that military success would be rewarded by confiscated lands and a title had attracted Italians, Poles, Irishmen and others; after the war they were absorbed into Viennese society. The Spanish contingent dominated the inner councils of the Emperor until the eighteenth century, when Italians superseded them. The more successful business houses were nearly always German, usually from the imperial cities of the south. The fortunes of war and conquest in the eighteenth century brought Croats, Czechs, Poles, Greeks and more Jews into Vienna; the last two played a crucial role in making Vienna into the banking centre of south-east Europe, which it remained until our own century.

Closely related to the rulers and leading families of Austria and Bavaria, the prince bishops of the Empire played an important part in the restoration of urban life in the seventeenth and early eighteenth centuries, an achievement for which they have not received much credit from historians. The Archbishop of Salzburg gave the young architect Fischer von Erlach a free hand to build one magnificent church after another in his town, and to reanimate the building trade and dependent crafts. In Würzburg the bishop commissioned Baltasar Neumann to create his residence, and empowered him to vet all proposed buildings within the city; if these added to the elegance of the street, tax rebates were granted to the owner. Bamberg, notorious for the witch-burning zeal of its bishop in the 1620s, owed its revival after 1648 to the energy of his successor. The bishops of Passau, Eichstätt and Freising were active in their towns too. One can still see today in Eichstätt near Ingolstadt, which has changed very little since the eighteenth century, how completely the town was dominated by buildings erected by the bishop for his administration and pleasure.

Other lay rulers founded new towns to provide themselves with what they regarded as a fitting framework to display their power and authority, notably Mannheim, to which the Count Palatinate transferred his residence from Heidelberg in 1720, and Karlsruhe, which was famous for its magnificent layout, though sadly lacking in commercial amenities. 'One cannot even buy gloves here', a British traveller lamented as late as the 1830s. In 1716 Lady Mary Wortley Montagu commented acidly on the difference between such towns and the free imperial cities; here, all one saw was 'a sort of shabby finery, a number of dirty people of quality tawdered out; narrow nasty streets out of repair, wretchedly thin of inhabitants, and above half of the common sort asking for alms'.[14] Some of the north German princes built on old settlements or existing towns, as Hanover, Wolfenbüttel and Celle. Wolfenbüttel was in fact built by Duke Julius as a rival to Brunswick, whose council refused to allow him to reside there. It was financed by him and his successors through conscript labour from their lands and by forcing burghers under threat of 'military execution' to work or buy exemption. The burghers protested at the loss of civic amenities – six mills were demolished in the centre of Hanover during its rebuilding under Duke George of Calenberg-Göttingen – but compensation was hard to get and petitioning lengthy.[15] On the other hand the Guelph dukes and the Prussian electors offered substantial tax reductions to those who would improve or build houses in accordance with the town plans devised under the ruler's supervision. The princes took an informed interest in the whole process, since a knowledge of architecture was part of a gentleman's education. The smaller courts of central Germany should be mentioned here, for, despite their straitened means and large families, petty princes residing at towns such as Gotha, Weimar, Köthen, Meiningen or Dessau raised these to places of cultural importance quite out of proportion to their size and amenities. Musical and literary life flourished here – Prince Ludwig of Auhalt-Köthen, founder of the *Fruchtbringende Gesellschaft,* and the Guelph Duke of Celle, are but two examples – while their educational foundations, at Gotha under Duke Ernst, and the *Philanthropinum* at Dessau, did a great deal to stimulate the exchange of ideas in a period in Germany's history when political and economic difficulties discouraged movement of people.

Within the walls of German towns, however, life was constricting for most, and the facilities were primitive. People lived close together in dark houses which were tall and narrow because of the high ground rents. Thus the house which the Hamburg merchant Jobst Schramm bought in 1703 had cellars below, the business on the ground floor, a 'gallery' with living rooms opening out from it on the first floor, and above two storeys and attics for the family, dependent relatives, apprentices and tenants to sleep.[16] Electoral ordinances in Prussia demanded that people pave the ground in front of their house, but ordinances were not always obeyed. Leipzig was almost unique in Germany in that its centre was paved and lit. The muddy thoroughfares of German towns remained proverbial well into the nineteenth century. Water for washing was obtained at pumps, water for drinking from the water carts. Contemporary authors complained bitterly about sanitary arrangements. The barber Joh. Dietz in late seventeenth century Halle was proud to be the possessor of a privy; a satirist declared in 1782 that it was the rarest commodity in the city of Hamburg. The majority of town houses had buckets which were put outside at certain hours to be collected by the 'night women' and emptied into the nearest river, or even the gutter.[17] In many small towns pigs were more common than shops in the eighteenth century, though the Prussian government banned them, along with dung heaps, in 1660. The Prussian rulers were the most vigorous in their attempts to improve life in the towns. The 1660 ordinance laid down penalties for fouling the street, fines for the first offence, jail and pillory for subsequent offences; rubbish was to be collected on Saturday afternoons, wardens were to clean the streets. The Great Elector, who created the famous street, Unter den Linden, also ordained that anyone cutting down trees within the town would have his hand cut off. Draconian threats, coupled with constant legislation for the order of daily life, were typical of Hohenzollern rule. Frederick William I decreed in 1735 that twenty-eight dustcarts were to be acquired, painted with numbers and each assigned to specific districts in Berlin.[18] The proliferation of such orders throughout the period suggests that the population still found ways of obstructing bureaucratic attempts to reform their insanitary habits.

Just as there was a great deal of regional variety in economic life in Germany, so the style of life of merchants in different areas and under different regimes varied considerably. Cultivated, even sophisticated tastes could be found in a semi-rural environment, as for instance in eighteenth century Hirschberg in Silesia. In 1640 it had been a rural community, one century later it was exporting linen worth over one and a half million *taler* per annum. A few interrelated families dominated the industry, the Menzels, Buchs and Gottfrieds. They rebuilt the town in the prevailing baroque fashion, erecting a church with monumental burial chapels to record their standing and achievement for posterity. They had the long market square adorned with loggias, giving it a southern air, and erected fountains, hothouses, bathing huts and pools in the gardens they laid out outside the town. Here they sat in the summer with family and friends, here the linen was bleached. In their fine houses galleries, art and natural history collections told of unusually cultivated minds.[19] In the few truly commercial towns of Germany, artistic life was fostered by the merchants and financiers who cultivated poetry and music, such as the Hamburg notables who engaged Lessing in the 1770s to act as a dramatist to their theatre. A tobacco merchant in Leipzig, Zehmisch, founded the first theatre there in 1776, while in Frankfurt the Brentano family pursued their interest in all forms of art and acted as generous patrons.

Status, determined by differences of age, achievement and wealth, played just as important a role in the lives of the commercial classes as it did for the nobility; indeed, in the small towns it acted as a substitute for their lack of political function in the country as a whole. Inferiors, children and employees kissed the principal's hand; they would kneel to apologize for offences. Merchants, along with professional men, were people of rank in their towns (*Honoratioren*) and had to be treated as such. J. A. Stölzer, in his collection of biographies of merchants published in 1772–80, instances the case of a school performance of a play by Terence: in allotting the roles the schoolmaster had to have regard to the status of the boys' parents; one whose father merited respect could not play a humble role.[20] Marriages were usually arranged for business reasons, in fact a strong minded spinster could take affairs into her own hands. Stölzer reports one such vigorous lady of means negotiating with a bankrupt merchant, whom she married after paying his debts of 20 000 *gulden*; she then took over his property as security for future children.[21] Second marriages were usually agreed on by the partners themselves, often simply to provide for children of former marriages on both sides. Age differences were not generally considered. Practical questions were the more important when choosing a marriage partner, since family and business expenses were defrayed from the same purse. An extravagant wife could, and, as contemporary accounts so often inform us, often did, bankrupt an enterprise. A reckless business partner could also bring ruin to the family as well as the enterprise of his associate. Indeed, in the second half of the eighteenth century reports of bankruptcies in such circles abound; contemporary drama is full of reference to sudden loss of substance. In Prussia the fate of the victims was all too often the recruiting officer.

It was above all in German towns that the late eighteenth century economic decline was most apparent. Evidence of poverty and neglect was apparent in the decay of the building trade, in the fact that many houses destroyed by fire were not rebuilt.[22] Travellers commented more frequently on the depressing aspect of urban Germany, on the wretched state of her roads, the poor appointments and dirt of the inns. It was not, as Johanna Schopenhauer, always a perceptive observer of social change, recorded of her native Danzig, that wealthy families were lacking, but that commercial life had simply withered away:

> An alten reichen Familien, an einzelnen bedeutenden Handelshäusern, die mit grossen Mitteln und ausgebreitetem Kredit ihre merkantilischen Kenntnisse und Erfahrungen geltend zu machen verstanden, fehlte es zwar nicht, und diese verbreiteten allerdings noch eine Art von Scheinleben um sich her, durch welches dem oberflächlich darüber hinstreifenden Blicke das tief im Innern zehrende Verderben verschleiert wurde. Der Kleinbürger aber, der Ladenhändler, der Handwerker, alles was zum arbeitenden Mittelstande gehört, diesem eigentlichen Herzen grosser und kleinster Staaten, durch welches das Leben pulsierend sich weiter verbreitet, waren dem langsamen allmählichen Verarmen verfallen. Die Zahl unbewohnter, fest verschlossener Häuser mehrte sich überall, und nicht allein in kleinen abgelegenen Gässchen, auch in den sonst bewohntesten Hauptstrassen der Stadt.

> At first sight the presence of such families and of a few important commercial houses with wealth, connections and experience, gave a false impression of vitality to the business life of the city, concealing the canker of decay.... The small man, the shopkeeper and the artisan, all those belonging to the working middle class, the very heart of great and small states, the source of energy for the whole, had at last succumbed to penury. The number of locked up, uninhabited houses increased on all sides, not just in the small back streets, but in the once busiest thoroughfares of the town.[23]

Yet, when all this is said, it must also be remembered that citizenship conferred status, and that the status of a burgher was a privileged one, if only by contrast with the mass of the population. If it was in general an inherited state, the oath of loyalty to the council being renewed formally each generation, it could also be acquired by an outsider, after some period of residence and payment of a sum of money. This was common when a town's finances, whether because of decline in trade, war or plague, required further sources of revenue. The Treasury records of Lemgo in Lippe/Westphalia, for example, show that the sale of citizenship to newcomers and outsiders was a regular source of municipal income.[24] If a burgher moved away from his native town to another, he had to purchase citizenship in his new home, usually for cash, or by marriage, or a mixture of both. Even if the holder was no more than a humble artisan, with perhaps a couple of fields or a garden beyond the walls to supplement his earnings, he had importance in the community by reason of his burgher status and a theoretical right to a share in the administration of the whole. Citizens of free imperial towns, particularly in the south of Germany, still enjoyed in the seventeenth and eighteenth century a status not always in tune with economic reality. Thus Leutkirch in the Swabian Allgäu, whose population had suffered so grievously through war and plague in the 1630s and 1640s, formally retained the status and the civic institutions of far more famous and wealthy towns such as Augsburg or Ulm. For those urban inhabitants who were not citizens, the state seemed eminently desirable; to gain it, as in the case of Luther's father, appeared to the successful aspirant to be the crowning achievement of a career. Social barriers were very marked, even in the small communities, between those who were burghers and those who were not, and indeed between those families who traditionally dominated the council and those who did not. As Benecke has illustrated in the case of seventeenth century Lemgo, the ruling oligarchy was prepared to go to almost any lengths to defend inherited privilege, even to inciting the mob against so-called witches, and extending a reign of terror throughout the town. The property of victims was eventually shared out by the authors of the plot.[25]

Members of the 'oligarchic, self-appointed and self-perpetuating town councils'[26] set up by merchants and entrepreneurs in some of the more important towns in the fifteenth century onwards, and surviving into the eighteenth, were in fact, if not in name, a kind of patriciate, enjoying a status similar to that of the territorial nobility. Such families, quite in contrast with the mass of burghers, intermarried with each other outside their town and region, and, especially in the sixteenth and seventeenth centuries, sent their children away for their education; citizens of Nuremberg, for example, appear as students of the law schools of Bologna and Padua, merchants' sons from Hamburg and Danzig are met with by young noblemen on their travels in western Europe. But the leading citizens of most German towns in the period 1648–1806 were not members of a patriciate, but rather the town notables, the *Honoratiorenschicht*, comprising merchants, some officials and professional men, such as lawyers, and the artisans, working for a local market. Of these the last-named, the artisan craftsman, was numerically by far the most important, and in the late seventeenth and above all in the eighteenth century was virtually identifiable with the notion of burgher.

Even in the towns which were the seat of territorial princes, the craftsmen and their apprentices remained numerically the largest social group. Nowhere did the absolute princes abolish the guilds; in many south-west territories they actually reorganized or introduced them. However, the social status of the craftsmen had suffered a sharp decline in the sixteenth century, and their economic position worsened after the Thirty Years War. In his *Abbildung der gemein-nutzlichen Hauptstände* (*Portrait of the Chief Estates Serving the Common Weal*) (Regensburg, 1698), the author of a well-known illustrated book of costumes, Christian Weigel, warned his contemporaries against treating such useful members of society with disdain: 'Blickt niemand mit Verachtung an, Weil Gottes Hand leicht heben kan, den Niedrigen zu Ehren-Orden' ['Look with contempt on no man; for the hand of God can easily raise the lowly to an honourable estate'].[27] But it was clear that as a social group they had lost standing in society; the Frankfurt clothing ordinance of 1731, regulating what clothes different social groups might wear, placed the craftsmen in the fourth group alongside small shopkeepers, only one above the lowest rank in society, the day labourers and domestics.

Yet the craftsmen themselves retained a high regard for their own status and usefulness in the community. The guild system continued to exist far longer in Germany than in any other comparable European country. Their influence in German society from the sixteenth to the nineteenth century was a staunchly conservative one, affecting not only attitudes and social behaviour, but traditional methods of production and distribution, which they tried at all costs to preserve. The master craftsmen put obstacles in the way of competitors and opposed initiative in order to retain the privileges which still remained to them; they were successful in defending their right to exercise jurisdiction over their members throughout the seventeenth and eighteenth centuries, against both the Emperor and the princes. Their political powers had, however, been curtailed by the *Reich* Police Ordinance of 1530 and the *Reich* Guild Law of 1548. In theory their other powers were taken from them by the 1731 *Reich* Guild Law, but the princes who were required to enforce these measures rarely did so and the masters continued to impose fines on their members for misbehaviour or exclude them from the guilds if they felt it necessary. They continued too to determine prices and types of materials to be used by one trade and not another –

thus carpenters were allowed to use iron nails, cabinetmakers only wooden pegs. They could limit the amount produced; a swordmaker in Solingen might not make more than four swords per day; the bakers in Hamburg as late as 1811 took a master baker to court for using two ovens and thus producing too much bread; after many years they won their case.[28] In other ways the craftsmen defended their right to be regarded as persons of consequence. They continued in several towns to serve on the militia; to be a burgher of course implied the duty as well as the right to bear arms; in Hamburg this was part of the constitution of the city and not repealed until the 1860s. In the eighteenth century they managed to continue to be allowed to carry a dagger, less to protect themselves on the roads, which was not as necessary as it had been in the seventeenth century, than for its symbolic importance as the sign of a freeman. Although the authorities might contest the assumptions underlying such claims, their own social policies favoured the paternalist character and the conservative attitudes of the craftsmen.

If the attitudes of the master craftsmen remained similar all over Germany, there were considerable differences of income, often within the same community. In 1800 they constituted some 14–15 per cent of the population of Prussia but only a few paid income or property tax.[29] Yet Tieck's father, the ropemaker, owned house property, as did the father of Goethe's musical friend Zelter, the mason, who at times employed some 260 craftsmen. Keferstein, a paper miller of Halle in the mid eighteenth century, worked at his mill, and oversaw his men as his ancestors had done for five generations, and yet he could afford to entertain forty relatives to Sunday lunch after church every week.[30] Whatever their economic situation might be, the craftsmen regarded themselves as members of an 'honourable estate'. Thus the music master Müller, in Schiller's play *Kabale und Liebe*, awkward at expressing himself, fearful of the consequences, finds the courage to speak his mind to those high placed persons who have wronged him, because his 'honour' has been insulted.

This sense of status conferred by membership of a privileged group sustained its members in adversity even though those privileges were often more apparent than real. An example is the mother of the goldsmith Klöden, who has left us perhaps the most vivid account of artisan life in the late eighteenth century we possess.[31] This splendid woman, daughter of a surgeon and sister of goldsmiths, worked day and night to preserve the standing of the family by her handwork after her husband took to drink. She owed it to their social heritage. A trade generally secured one at least a minimal income, and above all one was beholden to no one. Thus the old Zelter ordered his son to learn the mason's trade and leave music to his leisure hours, reflecting in a fine rhetorical passage:

> Dass nur Handwerk gülden Boden habe; dass Handwerk über alles gehe, besonders über hohen Stand und herrschaftliche Abhängigkeit. Handwerk könne wohl sinken, niemals aber ertrinken; der Handwerker sei der wahre Bürger; das Gesetz, das ihn binde, beschütze ihn; die Mitte, wo er stehe, bewahre ihn; da er überall gebraucht werde, sei er frei; Ehre und Wert stehen im genausten Verhältnis; Schande und Erniedrigung seien ihm ganz fremd.

> A craft alone has a golden foundation; a craft is superior to all else, is above high estate and dependence on royal favour. A craft can decline but never perish; the master craftsman is the true burgher; the law which binds him, protects him too; his place is in the middle [of society], here he is secure; as he is needed everywhere, so is he free; honour and worth are in perfect correspondence; shame and humiliation are strangers to him.[32]

And although the trade was odious to the younger Zelter, although bricklaying damaged his hands, a serious matter to someone who was able to play three instruments at concert level, and whose services were much in demand in music-loving Berlin in the 1780s, he did what his father told him. He was a dutiful son, but he believed what he said to be true.

A craftsman's 'honour', expressed in the form of address given and expected by him, '*Ehrsam und Namhaft*', '*Ehrbar und Wohlgeacht*', in the use of the epithet 'honourable' in connection with the master and the craft, implied many things. It was based on a series of rights and duties in the community. It meant professional skill, a devout and moral character, and not least a sense of responsibility to the profession and its dependants. It imposed rigorous conventions, which were generally complied with, at least to the end of the eighteenth century. It implied a sense of responsibility to the community. Members of a guild must sit up with a sick comrade, and follow a dead one to his grave, ensuring, in the contemporary eighteenth century phase, that all was done to make him 'a fine corpse' ('eine schöne Leiche'). A man's family would expect to get some provision for themselves. This last aspect varied greatly from one guild or region to another; the miners were probably the best organized to care for dependants of the sick or accident victims. To be recognized and take his place in the community, a master craftsman must have a wife, yet he should not marry before he was qualified. He could not choose just anyone; his wife should come from the same social sphere as he. In fact, very many married the daughters or widows of the master whom they had served as apprentices. In eighteenth century Durlach in south Germany, for which detailed statistical evidence exists,[33] an average of 25 per cent of artisan marriages were with such widows, often women twenty or thirty years older; the reasons were invariably financial. Certain trades were not recognized as 'honourable' – such as streetsweepers or gravediggers – and an 'honourable' master might not ally himself with the daughter of such a man. Thus in 1725 the textile weavers of Neudamm put pressure to exclude a master because his wife's grandmother was a shepherd's daughter. A man who married someone whose reputation was in doubt, or even one whose wife, as in the case of the shoemaker in 1726, had a child some five weeks 'before her time' could be fined or even threatened with expulsion from the guild. Guild ordinances demanded of every master that he be 'von ehelichen Eltern aus einem rechten Ehebett erzeuget' ['conceived of legitimate parents in a proper marriage bed']. J. G. Hoffman observed in his *Zunftverfassung* (*Guild Statutes*) in 1803 with some truth that 'ein uneheliches Kind konnte zum Feldmarschall oder Minister aber nicht zum Schumacher – oder Schneidermeister reifen' ['an illegitimate child could rise to be a field marshal or a minister, but not a master shoemaker or tailor'].[34] There was, however, considerably more latitude in these matters in the south of Germany than in the north.

In the country towns, where most such people lived, the master's household was usually self-sufficient: 'Jeder hatte daneben seinen Acker und sein Gärtchen, wo er das, was er im Hauswesen brauchte, selber bebaute' ['Each had his plot and his little garden, where he himself cultivated what he needed in the household'], wrote Johann Miller somewhat idyllically in his novel of manners, *Die Geschichte Gottfried Walthers, eines Tischlers, und des Städtchens Erlenburg* (1786).[35] When Klöden's family moved from Berlin in 1795 to the small town of Märkisch-Friedland in Posen, they had the greatest difficulty in getting daily necessities. His mother did not know how to make bread, but there was none to buy; everyone made their own and they slaughtered their own animals and grew their vegetables. The brewing of beer, making of soap and candles, as well as making and mending of clothes, was all done at home, even in well-to-do homes, well into the nineteenth century. It must have added a heavy burden to the daily work of the mother of a family. Of course, the common practice of offering a home to younger sisters when one married, not to speak of parents and the occasional aunt, would have helped to alleviate this.

German towns remained little affected by the passing of time in the period of which we are speaking, despite the efforts of the authorities to tidy them up, retaining a rural character well into the modern era. In the late seventeenth century it was forbidden to keep pigs on the streets of Prussian towns; people put them in back yards instead. Erwin Mengers describes the practice of taking the cows out of the town to the fields by day in Brunswick; in the evening the herdsman brought them as far as the town gate and from there each cow found her own way home. This ws in 1869, in a town where an ironworks and foundry were already being erected.[36]

The patriarchal character of the German petty state after 1648, the complete dependence of the subject on the person of the ruler, was aptly reflected in the relationship between the master craftsman and his wife, children and apprentices. While portraits of kindly fathers exist in literature and memoirs, the more common type was the stern paterfamilias, himself often the product of a harsh struggle for survival. The care of the children and concern for the future seems invariably to have been the province of the mother, who both in literature and biography is almost always remembered by her children with affection. The influence of Pietism from the last years of the seventeenth century onwards was most widespread among middle class women, of the professional and artisan classes; one of its most far reaching effects was to encourage a more openly emotional relationship between mothers and children, and to provide them with a compelling interest in education as a source of self-improvement and social betterment. The head of the household regarded himself as *in loco parentis* towards his apprentices, and treated them to the same discipline to which his children were subjected. He was responsible for their attending church, and for their behaving well in public; he must pay fines if they were caught brawling with students, a common offence. In return, he could and did make demands on apprentices of fourteen or fifteen which made the majority recall their youth in later life with horror. An apprentice served five years with his master, three and a half if his parents could afford to pay debentures or the boy was well known in the community. His chief companions in these years in almost every trade were hunger and cold. The long hours, 5 or 6 a.m. in summer, an hour later in winter, until 7 or 8 p.m., were obviously taken for granted; few writers of memoirs dwell on them, for they were the norm for apprentice and master alike. But the cold and hunger remain vivid even in after years. Only a halfpenny roll for the whole morning; 'It really wasn't much', wrote Perthes, later Goethe's publisher, who had been a relatively privileged youngster when he began his apprenticeship in Leipzig in 1787. From 1 to 8 p.m. the apprentices got nothing; 'This is what I call hunger', but, Perthes added, it could have been so much worse.[37] And so it could. Johann Gotthilf Probst, who tried in his anonymous *Handwerksbarbarei oder die Geschichte meiner Lehrjahre* (*The Barbarity of Life or the Story of my Apprenticeship*) (1790) to publicize the brutalities to which apprentices were exposed, described what happened when he failed to clean his master's shoes to his satisfaction: 'Sobald als er mich sah, bewillkommte er mich mit vier Ohrfeigen, die mir an der einen Seite die Nadeln meiner Haarlocken tief ins Fleisch trieben. Ich erschrak und schrie laut über den unvermuteten Schmerz auf. Schreist du noch? Warte, ich will dich's lehren. Und nun etliche dreissig mit dem Peitschenstock' ['As soon as he saw me, he welcomed me with four boxes on the ear, driving a hairpin in my curls deep into my flesh. I screamed in terror at the unexpected pain. "You scream, do you, I'll teach you." And now it was a good thirty with the whip']. At that moment dinner is brought in: the boy has no appetite, but is forced to eat. Drunk with 'brandy and rage', the master compels him to swallow some food, beats him for disobedience until he falls unconscious to the ground. The extract ends with the wife shrieking that he is dead, and the neighbours listening to the performance at their windows.[38]

Most families lived so near the bread line that they could not afford to send food or money to sons away from home; this was known and accepted. The cold was perhaps worse. Snow fell on the young Klöden's bed in his master's attic, the washing hung over his head and dripped on him, for it took many weeks to dry in winter; he was not the only one to recall that for four months every year, one had to put up with festering chilblains. Perthes got frostbite from working in unheated warehouses.

The first few years as an apprentice were usually spent as a kind of dogsbody and general messenger, and often as the object of the master's or mistress's frustration at their own circumstances. How much worse if the fragile prosperity of the home was threatened by sudden indulgence in drink, as in the case of the wife of Perthes's master. Much of the literature of the last decades of the eighteenth century is concerned with current social and economic change and fears for the future; these perhaps affected the craftsman more than most. Before the 1780s most people regarded circumstances as immutable; one could only hope that things would not get worse, and that hard times would be short. The apprentices, like children, accepted their harsh environment. Occasionally lack of experience might prompt one to rebel against the indignity of his position; he rarely succeeded in improving things. If he lived away from home, he scarcely knew anyone to whom he could turn, and had few opportunities of making friends outside the house and workshop. As B. Riedel, a linen weaver's apprentice, remarked early in the nineteenth century: 'Handwerkergesellen stecken die ganze Woche im Futteral wie die Gesangbücher und gucken nur an Sonntagen heraus' ['Apprentices are stuck inside all week like hymnbooks in their cases and only peer out on Sundays'].[39] Although Klöden was apprenticed to his uncle, he worked for years as a household drudge, cooking the dinner as he operated the antiquated furnace, and being forced to go almost every evening to collect the querulous grandmother from her daughters' houses through unlit and muddy streets. Like many others, he contemplated running away, but the only possible employment was in the army, and being a Prussian NCO's son, he knew what that implied and decided to stick it out. Other apprentices were beaten by the masters, who could rationalize their brutality in the knowledge that God and society had placed them in authority over those whom they instructed in their trade.

Such conditions prompted many young men to wander far afield once they had finished their apprenticeship. In the late eighteenth century, there was a great vogue for geography and travellers' tales which, like the extraordinary popularity of Campe's *Robinson* and the fascination with air balloons, was part of a desire to escape from an oppressively narrow environment. Only the journeymen, students and soldiers could satisfy this impulse, and the former remained often years on the road, some even a lifetime. Many travelled astonishing distances; the seventeenth century barber and surgeon, Master Dietz of Halle, had taken part in more than one voyage to Greenland, and fought in Hungary against the Turks.[40] Life 'auf der Walze' [on the road] offered plenty of adventure; one could meet with one's own kind, but most shared the experience of the tanner Dewald of being robbed by such a new friend, usually at night in the hostel.[41] Most towns had a hostel specifically for the wandering craftsmen, where the newly arrived could also inform themselves of the type of work and master in the area. Here too they might learn that the craftsmen had decided to boycott ('Unredlichmachen') a particular master or even a whole trade, and be advised to move on. This was naturally frowned upon by the guilds, but it happened nonetheless, and had been customary for centuries. It afforded the craftsmen security through solidarity, and the *Reich* ordinance of 1731 which banned it proved to be unworkable. Thus the Breslau scissors masters curtailed some of the traditional and doubtless excessive holidays in 1744; the craftsmen left the city in protest, and the grinders, lest they make themselves 'dishonourable', refused to sharpen scissors. In 1747 the masters gave in and restored the original holidays.[42] In certain areas, masters were obliged to lend a craftsman a sum of money ('*Schenken*') when there was no work, so that they could subsist until the next town. In places where skilled workers were in short supply the richer masters secured the best for themselves by their gifts of money; in other regions *Schenken* was unknown and most turned at some stage to begging, or *Fechten*, as it was called. In lean years this practice became a nuisance and the beadle would be called out to make the unwanted artisan move on. No poor law or workhouse system as such existed in Germany, and each town or village regarded itself as responsible for its own resident poor only. When industrialization and bad times encouraged mobility, this rudimentary system broke down.

The journeyman was even more susceptible to changes in regional or national prosperity than the apprentice who at least had a roof over his head. For all of them a kind of grapevine existed throughout the *Reich* and beyond which advised individuals about conditions of work in a particular locality, and in the mid nineteenth century provided a useful warning to the politically minded as to which areas they should avoid. Another important source of general information was the *Volkskalendar*. This was a compendium of information about the profession, the weather and the stars. It even included such matters as advice on opportune dates for blood-letting, an activity which was taken seriously in these years and often occasioned a short holiday from work and celebration among one's family and acquaintances. In the second half of the eighteenth century, the *Volkskalendar* proved an important vehicle of enlightened ideas. Indeed, the Enlightenment in Germany had an astonishingly large following among the craftsmen, especially for its ideas on education. It was clear to many a humble artisan that education could provide the ladder to social status. Thus, Zelter's father, the son of a sapper, taught himself to write, gained admission to the mason's guild and rose to be the guild's leader in Berlin and a favourite of Frederick II. Klöden, who had had a primitive schooling and lived in abject poverty as an apprentice, taught himself French and Italian, geography and geometry, and became a well-known cartographer before finally being admitted to a degree course in Berlin and becoming head of the Graphological Institute in Berlin. Johann Ohm, a locksmith of Erlangen, son of an illiterate, painfully taught himself science and his sons became university professors in the nineteenth century. Knowledge and education meant more than mere social betterment: it represented a higher world to which one belonged by the fact of membership of a traditional craft, one which had known better days. Thus Paul Ernst's father, who mined silver ore for one and a half *taler* a week in the mid nineteenth century, spent six *taler* on Schiller's collected works which he and his descendants might read and treasure. Inventories of craftsmen's books, found in town halls all over Germany from the seventeenth and eighteenth centuries, provide evidence of the traditional importance of reading and the possession of books in the artisan home.[43]

The increasing interest in education in the eighteenth century under the influence first of Pietism and then of the Enlightenment had a profound long-term effect on the craftsman class. Once the economic situation began to change, as it did in the second half of the century, the better educated began to leave the workshop. Although the Napoleonic wars and subsequent depression slowed the pace of change, opportunity was there for those with initiative, and, what is surprising for us today, the humbly born could use chance encounters with the great to their own immediate advantage. Thus Klöden was allowed use of the royal library of the King of Prussia in Berlin for his studies, and J. C. Fischer of Schaffhausen, a metalworker on a visit to London, was admitted to hear Faraday lecture at the Royal Institute. Some of the best men were lost to the trade, but those who remained did not allow new ideas to affect their traditional way of life. As late as 1800 and beyond the centuries old ethos of the guilds still governed the training and outlook of the individual carpenter, tanner or mason, etc., and determined his social behaviour when he became a master. When in consequence of the reform movements of the early nineteenth century freedom of trade was introduced in certain parts of Germany, it aroused intense hostility. It was actually withdrawn in Kurhesse and the Palatinate, where the French had introduced it during the occupation, while Prussia, one of the first states to do so, modified it in the Trade Ordinance (*Gewerbeordnung*) of 1845. In the more traditionalist areas of Germany, in Austria, south Germany and Saxony it was not common until the 1860s. Even in those areas which were the first to experience the industrial revolution, habits of mind and methods of work continued to be influenced by the traditions of the guilds, as shown by August Bebel's memoirs of the 1850s and early 1860s, and were concerned primarily with protection for skilled workers such as they had enjoyed in the past. They were not concerned with 'freedom', an abstract concept which meant little to them, but with the 'restoration' of ancient rights. Class war, the triumph of the proletariat, they regarded with incomprehension or disdain. When a radical speaker addressed a number of artisans as 'proletariat' in 1848, the temper of the crowd grew violent, until he was persuaded to withdraw the term. In their own eyes such men were 'burghers' and their values and aspirations proved it, at least to themselves. As a class the artisans resisted industrialization as long as they could, not because they would suffer financially by going into the factories, but because to do so would rob them of their 'honour' as an 'estate', which was bound up with their identity as persons.

It is now clearly recognized by historians of early modern and nineteenth century Germany how important the traditions of regionalism and community were to its inhabitants; the variety yet overall compatibility of these were represented by the complex structure of the Holy Roman Empire, and they survived its demise by several decades. Industrial and political change in mid nineteenth century Germany paid little heed to particularist notions, regarding these as little more than obstacles in the way of the 'right' society and polity. It was because of the way in which personal identity of the individual was bound up with his regional or local loyalties, that the disruptive effects of the industrial revolution and the Bismarckian unification were socially so profound and sustained, in no stratum of society more than that of the small town artisans and tradesmen. These issues will be examined in greater detail in the second part of this book.[44]

Chapter 5
The educated classes

The most important influence on German education in the years between about 1530 and 1740 was the Reformation, and even during the late eighteenth century many schools and institutions continued to give priority to the teaching of religion over other subjects. Luther's own views on education were not very different from those men who had taught him; he did, however, provide a vigorous impulse towards spreading it over a much wider area in society. As regards the content and aims of teaching in schools and universities, the key figure and innovator was the spare and kindly Philipp Melanchthon, whom contemporaries so aptly called *Praeceptor Germaniae.* The development of Wittenberg University to being the leading school of Lutheran theology, the founding or refounding of the universities of Jena, Tübingen and Heidelberg, of Leipzig, Königsberg and Frankfurt, were all his work, or carried out with his advice and help. The principal author of the statutes of the University of Helmstedt, founded six years after his death by Duke Julius of Brunswick, was his pupil, David Chytraeus, who was also the reformer of Rostock University. Under two distinguished teachers, the lawyer J. Caselius and the divine J. Calixtus, Helmstedt produced some of the foremost lawyers and theologians of the following century. Melanchthon also drafted the Saxon school ordinance of 1528, which was to prove as fundamental to the future development of Protestant education as the Jesuit *Ratio atque institutio studiorum* of 1591 for Catholic lands. He also wrote a number of textbooks which were in use all over Germany for decades to come, on such different subjects as the classical languages, rhetoric, dialectics, ethics and psychology, physics and history. Moreover, his own personality helped, at least initially, to mould the kind of teacher employed: if a headmastership or a university chair fell vacant, whoever was responsible for filling the post turned instinctively to the learned professor at Wittenberg.[1] His friendship with individual scholars and princes bore fruit in the form of new institutions, such as the academy, later university, of Altdorf, founded by his friend and colleague Joachim Camerarius at the latter's native town of Nuremberg.

The Lutheran reformer laid particular stress on the need for an educated clergy. The new importance of the sermon in the Protestant rite, which was expected to provide religious teaching and uplift, as well as aesthetic experience through its scholarly allusions, modified the content of school and university teaching. The influence of the Renaissance, which was such a powerful factor in Melanchthon's own development, became apparent in the stress he laid on the teaching of the Classics, on Greek and Hebrew as well as Latin. However, before the end of the sixteenth century the humanist ideal, which Melanchthon had pursued all his life, had become confined to a small élite of scholars, linked across Europe by their common love of learning. In the universities where theology was preeminent over law, medicine and philosophy, the average graduate was a man trained in dogmatic Lutheran doctrine. He could dispute with eloquence in the old scholastic manner, and the rigorous defence of doctrinal purity, the defeat in debate of one's unorthodox rivals, seemed by 1600 to be the chief object of university training. Followers of Melanchthon, who sought to mediate between the different Protestant sects, could find themselves, as in the Palatinate in the 1570s, in prison for their pains. Caselius spoke bitterly of the persecutions he suffered at the hands of the divines even in enlightened Helmstedt.[2] *Rabies theologorum* became a cliché in these last decades of the sixteenth century, and, according to Friedrich Nicolai and other enlightened writers in the eighteenth century, was still malignant 200 years later.[3]

THE UNIVERSITIES

The decision to found or restore a university in the sixteenth century was nearly always part of religious reform, both in the Lutheran lands and in the Catholic territories, where the Jesuits established themselves in the universities of Dillingen, Graz and Würzburg. The new foundations of the seventeenth century, fourteen in all, were mainly designed to serve the needs of the native population. Among these were Salzburg (1622), Bamberg (1648) and Duisburg (1655). Duisburg was provided by the Great Elector for his Rhenish subjects, whom he thus hoped to stop attending the neighbouring establishment at Cologne, but it did not prosper, partly because it was poorly endowed. Other similar foundations closed again after a few years – Osnabrück lasted for a mere three years after its foundation in 1630, Cassel nineteen years from 1633. But size was no guide to success: some small universities played a significant role beyond the boundaries of their states; thus Rinteln, founded in 1618 by the Counts of Schaumburg-Lippe, had an important law school which was only obscured by Göttingen over a century later. Altdorf was probably the most important new foundation in the first half of the seventeenth century – it received its charter in 1622 – and in the second half Kiel (1665) and Halle (1694). Kiel, founded by Duke Christian of Schleswig, patron of the poets Oleander and Rist, had five professors of law on its staff, two of medicine and nine of philosophy, as against three of theology. Kiel thus marks a stage in the development of secular subjects at the cost of theology, which was to become the pattern over the next decades in most parts of the Empire. Halle, better endowed than Kiel, was destined to rise to preeminence among German seats of learning within a few years of its foundation. Some of the most able men of the time were associated with it, while the rationalist approach to knowledge of its teachers won it the support of the modern minded in the same way as it aroused veritable epidemics of *rabies theologorum.*

Many of the older establishments declined in size and repute in this century: Erfurt, belonging to the archbishopric of Mainz, suffered from being cut off geographically from the rest of Catholic Germany; Vienna, Cologne and Heidelberg became provincial places, though Cologne still had many students; Tübingen became almost exclusively Swabian. Indeed, it was a feature of the period 1648–1800 that the territorial rulers tried to prevent their subjects from studying 'abroad', i.e. at universities of other states, although few were wholly successful in their attempts. As early as 1564 the Elector of Brandenburg had tried to prohibit students leaving his duchy to study elsewhere; the Great Elector reiterated the prohibition in 1662, while his grandson King Frederick William I threatened dire penalties on those who disobeyed, including the threat to bar them from state service.

In two important respects the character of the German university changed in this period. The study of law began to replace theology as the most popular and lucrative subject of study; the poorer students, however, continued to study theology, since it was best endowed with scholarships, and promised the best hope of employment to those without connections or wealth. Wittenberg and Jena still remained important, attracting students from distant parts, from Silesia, Lithuania, Slovakia and Transylvania; they were, with Leipzig and Cologne, the only universities in the decades after 1650 with more than twenty professors. However, they gave the impression to many observers in the latter half of the century that they were out of touch with the preoccupations of the times, and the princes in particular became convinced that traditional university training was irrelevant to the needs of men in public life. Increasingly the court, the knightly colleges and the gentleman's Grand Tour came to replace university education for those sons of the upper classes who did not need to earn their living. For those that did, the law faculties provided the necessary qualifications for the service of the prince.

The demands of the territorial rulers on the better endowed and educated among their subjects brought about a further important change in the character of the German university in the second half of the seventeenth century. It ceased to be a privileged corporation with its elected head and professors and its own jurisdiction. It became a state institution, the leading members of which were appointed, promoted and dismissed by the state. The princes endowed scholarships for their subjects, but expected to get a return on their investment in the form of trained administrators. Already before the end of the century the professors and students had in some areas been subjected to visitations by commissions appointed by the ruler, who examined their teaching and investigated their private lives.[4] The tendency towards greater state control became general in the eighteenth century. Halle and Göttingen (1734) had their professors appointed by government ministers in Berlin and Hanover; in Göttingen's case it was expressly stated that this should be 'without consulting the faculties'.[5] The practice became common to require from the faculties a list of lectures given, and a register of student attendance, to be sent to the ministry at the end of the term or session. 'Useful servants of the state' were what the authorities looked to the university to produce, 'more precisely, servants of this territorial prince'.[6]

The orientalist J. D. Michaelis, professor at Göttingen (and father of the famed Caroline Schlegel), introduced his four volume work *Raisonnement über die protestantischen Universitäten Deutschlands* (1768–76) with a consideration of 'the advantages conferred on a state by a university'. According to him it was the lawyers of the Prussian University of Halle who first aroused a sense of patriotism among their fellow civil servants; what is taught by professors to their students permeates the whole of society within a single generation: 'Was von diesen Sachen auf der Universität gelehrt wird, das hören anfangs nur Studenten, aber nach und nach, etwa in einem Menschenalter, wird es der allgemeine Sinn des Volkes; der Bürger und Bauer glaubt dem Prediger, der Prediger glaubt im Staatsrecht was er von den Juristen seines Landes erzählen hört' ['What is taught of these matters in the universities is first heard by the students only; however, little by little, within about a generation, it is common knowledge among the populace; the burgher and the peasant believe the clergyman, the clergyman believes what he hears from the lawyers of his land about the law of the state'].[7] The last part of Michaelis's observation is an apt example of contemporary respect for the lawyer over the clergyman, a reversal of former social priorities. By the late eighteenth century the community of university scholars and teachers had become the servants of a particular prince and state. Social standing in the German territories derived now from the degree of recognition afforded one by the court. The professors gladly accepted such unacademic titles as court or privy councillors and continued to do so as long as the monarchical system remained.

The universities of the period 1648–1800 were small places: 300–400 students and fifteen to twenty professors constituted a good sized establishment. Thus of the four Prussian universities in 1716–17 Halle, unusually large, had 1202 students, Frankfurt an der Oder 190, Königsberg 400 and Duisburg 163.[8] Most professors lectured in their own homes, and the actual university buildings were generally a former monastery or even, as at Halle, a number of rooms in the former episcopal residence. Such apparent necessities as library facilities were minimal, if they existed at all. Halle had three rooms in the public weighhouse for the purpose in 1709; its annual library budget in 1768 was still only 100 *taler*. One of the great attractions of Göttingen was its fine library, where students could actually borrow books for home reading. The small size of the university had some practical advantages; in the seventeenth century many whole establishments could migrate in times of plague, as did the teachers and students of Heidelberg, Jena, Freiburg and Wittenberg on occasion.

The intimacy between pupils and teachers, who usually came from much the same social class, had a further advantage as far as the professors were concerned: the students often lodged in their homes and ate at their tables, thus supplementing their generally slender incomes. A further source of revenue for them, at least in the early years of the period, was the sale of wine and beer to their lodgers, the source apparently of much excess on the part of host and students; in some areas, it was said, the university teachers were not much more than innkeepers. There were no regular student fees in the seventeenth century; the professor was paid a small salary by the state, a professor of theology earning about 100–200 *gulden* a year in the early years of the century, a professor of philosophy about half that amount.[9] Private lessons were an important part of a teacher's income: G. F. Schuhmacher in eighteenth century Schleswig taught up to fifty hours per week. In addition university and teachers enjoyed perquisites in the form of housing, corn, wood and wine.

A student in the seventeenth century could expect to spend some 25 to 35 florins per annum, more than half of which was needed for food.[10] The teaching year was of course much longer than it is now, covering some eleven months of the year. The custom of offering a 'free table' to students in return for service was a common one: the two student library assistants in mid eighteenth century Halle got their dinner in return for their work.[11] Prices rose greatly for students between 1600 and 1800: in the 1770s Michaelis reckoned with as much as 300 *taler* per annum per student, though they themselves put it higher, 300–500 in Altdorf in 1795, in northern Germany anything between 200 and 1000 *taler*.[12] Students of means would spend far more than the top figure, since their dignity demanded that they be accompanied by servants. There was a great deal of difference between such smart young men and the ordinary student; they dressed extravagantly, comported themselves as cavaliers and were notorious for their duelling habits, particularly in Jena. Nicholaus Frangipani's contemporary etchings of the opening of Kiel University in 1665 show the student body apparelled in rich coats and knee breeches, their collars and cuffs adorned with fine lace, and splendidly plumed hats in their hands; full curling wigs covered their heads and shoulders. At the celebration banquet members of the academic body, similarly dressed, sat down to roast swan and wine with members of the ducal family and the estates of Schleswig.[13]

German students' taste for drink and brawling seems to have been remarkable, their chief opponents being the craftsman apprentices. That the students constituted a serious threat to the peace of the towns is clear from the records of most German universities. Indeed, every sort of licentiousness was reputedly common in institutions of learning. A satiric verse from the year 1617 declared:

Wer von Tübingen kommt ohne Weib,
Von Leipzig mit gesunden Leib,
Von Helmstädt ohne Wunden,
Von Jena ohne Schrunden,

Von Marburg ungefallen,
Hat nicht studiert an allen.

[He who comes from Tübingen without wife,
From Leipzig with a healthy body,
From Helmstedt without wounds,
From Jena without marks,
From Marburg without a fall,
Has not studied there at all.][14]

Wallenstein was sent down from Altdorf for being involved in four major incidents in the space of a few months, during one of which a certain Corporal Fuchs was killed. The annals of Altdorf report that the future generalissimo had 'bey des Fuchsen Ableib das seinige gethan' ['done his bit in the matter of Fuchs's decease'].[15] Things hardly improved in the eighteenth century. In his generally reliable novel of manners, *Gottfried Walther* (1786), Johann Miller describes how the son of the town clerk of Erlenburg, a most respectable young man, was transformed by his period at university in Erlangen. As a student he sported: 'beschmutzte Reuthosen und grosse Stiefel mit Spornen, eine Reutjacke, einen fürchterlich grossen tief ins Gesicht gedruckten Hut mit einer schwarzen Feder drauf, und seine Haare hingen unordentlich um den Kopf herum und ins Gesicht. Mit einem kräftigen Fluch' ['dirty riding breeches and great boots with spurs, a riding jacket, a frightful big hat, pulled low over his face, with a black plume in it, his hair hanging untidily about his head and into his face. With a mighty oath' he told of the 'Fressereyen, Saufereyen, Zwisten, Schlägereyen, Ansonsten und dergleichen edlen Lustbarkeiten' ['guzzling and boozing, fights and brawls, other and suchlike noble pleasures'] of the students, who carried daggers at their sides and whips over their shoulders.[16] Laukhard refers in his memoirs, written about a decade later, to the extremely high rate of syphilis among university students.[17] The poorer students, almost invariably those studying theology, lived a different kind of life. Many were lodged in supervised houses, where they were forced to submit to examinations to test their academic progress. This idea was copied by many universities. The Jesuits in Dillingen exercised a stern discipline over their students, though at the other Bavarian university of Ingolstadt, where the future Emperor Ferdinand II and his cousin, Duke, later Elector Maximilian of Bavaria, had studied, the young men liked 'eine zimbliche libertatem' ['a fair liberty'], according to a report in 1602.

It was at Halle that a sustained effort was made to provide a new type of education, which many felt necessary in the climate of the time.

Those responsible for the organization of the new establishment aimed to produce devout yet practical men, who were at the same time equipped intellectually to serve society and the state. It was here that efforts were successful to set aside the notion that dogmatic theology was the sum of academic learning. The Pietist A. H. Francke was one of the moving spirits behind this, and it was as a refugee from the persecution of rabid orthodox Lutherans in Leipzig that he came to Halle in 1690. The university was founded by the last Elector and first King of Prussia in 1694, for those Lutheran subjects of his realm whom his father had prohibited from going abroad to study. The first rector was to have been the famous political theorist and servant of princes, Veit Ludwig von Seckendorff, but he died in 1692, and Francke seemed the obvious choice as successor. Two years later the university opened its doors in a ceremony of pomp and splendour which Elector Frederick loved, but it only got its own buildings in 1834.

Besides Francke, the lawyer and philosopher Christian Thomasius (1665–1728) had been recruited. If Francke represented the powerful force of religious fervour which people in late seventeenth century Germany sought as a kind of emotional reaction to the aridity of the Lutheran authorities' position, Thomasius stood for the ideas which superseded both, the rationalist philosophy of the early Enlightenment and the revived interest in the natural sciences. A contemporary saying expressed their different positions: 'Hallam tendis? Aut pietista aut atheista reversurus!' ['You go to Halle? You will come back a Pietist or an atheist!][18] Thomasius was the sort of lecturer who enjoyed irritating his colleagues by playing to the student gallery: he lectured, not in the traditional sober robes, but in modish dress, 'hung with gold' we are told, and a dagger at his side. Much more enterprising, he lectured from the very first in German. Even before he came to Halle from Leipzig, he had published a monthly review in German – the *Monatschriften* (1688–). Through his lectures and work he helped to create in the German public mind an association between modern ideas and the use of one's native tongue, in a similar manner to his other great contemporary Leibniz, or the dramatist, political novelist and diplomat, D. C. von Lohenstein of Breslau. Both Thomasius and Francke, for all the profound personal differences between them – Francke had dismissed his colleague's wife from his congregation for being too richly dressed – were at one in their efforts to free education from the domination of religious dogmatism. In this they were initially successful. Students believed that Halle had something special to offer and came in numbers that were unusually large for the time. Within thirty years of its foundation, 14 148 students had matriculated; by 1742

Halle with 1500 students was the largest German university.[19] Christian Wolff (1679–1754) joined Halle in 1706 to teach philosophy, mathematics and much else besides. Until his expulsion by Frederick William I, he encouraged his hearers to rely on their reason rather than the authority of church or professor, to pursue truth rather than to memorize uncritically a mass of traditional learning. The King of Prussia expelled him as a dangerous influence on young and pious minds; by doing so, he helped spread Wolff's ideas. When he returned after seventeen years in Marburg his philosophy was everywhere triumphant. The sermons of numerous clergymen, the works of the most influential writers – such as Gottsched – and the lectures of academics were informed by Wolffian rationalism.

Although the Saxon universities of Wittenberg and Jena declined in the face of such competition, the oldest Saxon foundation, Leipzig, augmented its reputation, changing its character considerably in the process. In the sixteenth and seventeenth centuries it had attracted students from north and north-east Europe on religious grounds; now it became the fashionable university, 'Little Paris', renowned for its dandies even before Goethe arrived there in the 1770s. The university certainly benefited from the commercial life of the city, and especially from Leipzig's challenge to Frankfurt as the centre of the German book trade. It was Göttingen, however, founded by George II of England, Elector of Hanover, for his German subjects, which first established the international reputation of German universities, providing also an opportunity for Germans to become acquainted with English thought and culture. From the first the new establishment was exceptionally well endowed: it had 16 000 *taler* per annum, twice as much as Halle. Its revenue came in large part from the former monasteries, which the Guelph rulers had administered since the time of the Reformation as a separate fund.[20] It was expensive to study there, and attracted an unusually high proportion of noble students from Hanover, from the south and west, including many members of the imperial nobility. They came to study history, political science and law, and in particular to hear the renowned exponent of imperial constitutional law, heraldry and genealogy, J. Pütter (1725–1807). By 1788, eleven princes, 148 counts and 14 828 'other persons' had studied there.[21]

Yet Halle and Göttingen, although so successful in attracting renowned teachers and large numbers of serious students, represented the exception rather than the rule in the history of universities in Germany at this time. They achieved fame partly because of their role in equipping future servants of the state – this was especially true of Halle, at least to 1740 – and because they rejected the claim so long upheld that theology and its ancillary subjects should dominate the curriculum of school and university. But the vast majority of German students, who came from fairly modest families, sons of clergymen and officials, continued to be taught in the traditional manner at the other universities and colleges, to accept the doctrinaire approach of the ecclesiastical authorities. This was also true of the Catholic regions. In the Jesuit schools and universities which supplied the educational needs of the upper and middle classes, and in certain areas such as the Rhineland also provided primary school teaching for the poor, allegiance to the authority of the church was rigorously stressed. It was not until the suppression of the Order in 1773 that the state was forced to take responsibility for the education of its citizens in Austria, Bavaria and the Rhineland.

THE 'RITTERAKADEMIEN' OR KNIGHTLY ACADEMIES

Many gentlemen's sons, whose fathers desired that they should be accomplished men, never went to university at all, or spent at most one or two terms there as part of the Grand Tour. The lack of suitable facilities for those destined to rule was a matter which preoccupied philosophers and educationalists in the seventeenth century. Seckendorff made the point in a memorandum which he submitted to the Elector Palatine in 1660.[22] Balthasar Schupp (1610–61), a Hamburg preacher well known for his pioneering ideas on education and who had visited many courts on his travels, protested at the practice of giving young princes pedants for their masters, and allowing them to become 'magistri ... und Land und Leute mit der Metaphysik regieren' ['schoolmasters ... to rule land and people with metaphysics']. He subscribed to the view, held by many members of the well-to-do bourgeoisie as well as the aristocracy that 'wenn auch grosse Herren nicht studieren haben, so hat ihnen doch die Natur gemeiniglich etwas Sonderliches mitgeteilt und die Natur tut mehr als die Kunst' ['even if great lords have not been to university, Nature has generally endowed them with special gifts, and Nature is more effective than Art'.][23] Prompted by these current views and by their own desire to raise the tone and reputation of German court life, which was not high, a number of princes founded *Ritterakademien* to teach courtly address, modern languages and knightly exercises, in addition to traditional subjects. The Tübingen *Collegium illustre*, founded as far back as 1589, served as a prototype; another early foundation was the *Collegium Mauritianum*, founded by that most accomplished of princes, Landgrave Maurice of Hesse-Kassel, in 1599, which did not, however, survive the great war. The decades after the war saw a host of such colleges: St Michaelis in Lüneburg (1655), Wolfenbüttel (1687), maintained by prince and estates jointly, then in the new century Brandenburg (1704) and Berlin (1705), which became a cadet school under Frederick William I in 1717. In Vienna the estates of Lower Austria opened their school in 1682; over half a century later Maria Theresa founded the 'Austrian Eton', the *Theresianum* (1746) for the nobility of the Empire, which was much favoured by the Hungarians.

The essential difference between these academies and the old grammar schools and universities lay in the curriculum. The best academies stressed the greater importance of modern languages, 'modern' political science rather than theology and philosophy; a good deal of time was set aside for riding, fencing and dancing. In practice most cost a lot and had little to show for it, their main purpose being to attract well-born young men to the court and help to defray expenses by having court employees act as tutors. Some idea of what was envisaged can be gleaned from the description sent out by the Wolfenbüttel Academy to potential applicants. It was held out as a particular advantage that 'die Akademisten *permission* haben den fürstlichen Hof zu frequentieren, dass sie dann *ordinarie* gewisse Tage in der Woche bei Hofe kommen und denen ausgestellten *divertissementen*, Bällen und dergleichen mit beiwohnen und von der vorfallenden *honesten conversation* mit profitiren können' ['students of the Academy have permission to frequent the court, so that in the normal course of events they come to court on certain days, and can avail themselves of the opportunity to assist at the appointed *divertissements*, balls and such like, and profit from the *honnête* conversations of these occasions'].[24]

At Hildburghausen (Saxony), opened in 1714, the young men were promised the use of the prince's Spanish, English and Turkish horses and lessons from his master of horse. The language in which the advertisements for the academies are couched shows that the later seventeenth century German courts were at pains to appear thoroughly French in style and manners. At the Hildburghausen Academy the students might learn knightly exercises from the prince's own masters: 'Im Fechten und Tanzen haben S. Hochfürstl. Durchl. nach der eignen Experienz in dergleichen *exercitis* solche *maîtres* choisirt, deren *capacité* und *dexterité* in *informatione* jeder gute Kenner wird approbiren müssen' ['For fencing and dancing His Royal Highness, rich as he is in experience in such matters, has appointed *maîtres* whose *capacité* and *dexterité* in teaching will win the approval of every connoisseur'].[25] The Brunswick *Collegium Carolinum* (1748) and the Württemberg *Karlsschule* (1778) were the products of a different concept; they were designed primarily to produce useful material for the service of the prince, and the discipline, as Schiller bitterly recalled, was that of a barracks rather than a school for gentlemen's sons.

THE EDUCATED MIDDLE CLASSES UNDER THE ABSOLUTE STATE

The overall effect of the *Ritterakademien* was to exacerbate a development which was to have profound consequences in the following centuries – namely, the separation of the nobility and the upper bourgeoisie from the rest of society. With the decline of humanism and, after the great war, of the German towns, the German bourgeoisie had no longer an autonomous culture, and they had little opportunity to develop their talents in their own sphere. In the second half of the seventeenth century, they began to be drawn into the ambience of the court, where they played a crucial part in helping to establish absolute government. 'Eines der wichtigsten Mittel zur Konsolidierung des Absolutismus ist die Einbeziehung von Adel und Bürgertum in den Staat, die für sie das Aufgehen ihrer ständischen Selbstsständigkeit bedeutet' ['One of the most effective methods of consolidating absolutism is to involve the nobility and the bourgeoisie in the state; this means their relinquishing their former character as separate estates'] A. Hirsch.[26] For the German of bourgeois origins the ideal ceased to be a devout man of learning, versed in the classics as well as in theology, and possessed of a professional qualification, and became instead the '*galant homme*' of the Spaniard Gracián's famous *El Politicón* (1653). Gracián's work was very widely read in Germany in a French translation at the end of the century, and it provided the model for ambitious individuals as well as for numerous novel heroes from Christian Weise's books to J. M. von Loen's much-read *Der redliche Mann am Hof* (1747).[27]

Weise's career and writings illustrate the change taking place among men of his type and background. Born in the Lusatian town of Zittau, he went to university, and entered the service of Duke August of Sachsen-Weissenfels at the Halle court; he then became professor of politics, rhetoric and poetry at the Weissenfels grammar school (*Gymnasium*), where boys of good family were prepared for official careers. He eventually became rector (headmaster) of the Zittau grammar school, marrying the daughter of one of the town's leading families. He made his pupils familiar with the new ideas he had absorbed earlier in his career and won considerable acclaim for his writings on these matters, and for his novels. These are interesting in the present context for the way they depict the burgher associating with noblemen and imitating their style. Weise wrote several manuals on skills likely to be useful to a man embarking on a career in the service of the prince, and from their numerous reprintings these seem to have enjoyed great success. Entitled variously *Der politische Redner* (*The Political Orator*), *Der kluge Hofmeister* (*The Wise Tutor*), *Chr. Weises curiose Gedanken von deutschen Briefen* (*Chr. Weise's Curious Thoughts on German Letters*) and *Der politische Academicus* (*The Politically-Minded Academic*) and published between 1675 and 1705, they projected a new type of educated commoner, who disdained learned pedantry and sought out the specialist in order to inform himself on a variety of useful subjects. These might include mining, optics, currency, law, and geography, so that one day such a person might 'dem Fürsten und dem Vaterland mit klugen Consiliis ... zustatten kommen' ['oblige the prince and the fatherland ... with wise counsels'].[28] The Lutheran theologian Theodor Grossgebauer commented ironically on the new development; instead of religion, men were concerned with

> viel höheren und nötigeren Sachen ... nämlich wie der Staat zu befestigen, Tribute zu steigern, Steuern zu legen, Cantzleyen zu bestellen, Hofhaltung zu ordnen, die Hoheit mehr zu beobachten, Vestungen und Schlösser zu bauen, Reuter zu werben. Dazu gehören kluge Etatsräte, listige Finanzräte, verständige Kuristen, versuchte Hofmänner, weltkluge Doktoren, künstliche Baumeister, geübte Kriegsobersten.
>
> much higher and more urgent matters ... namely how to secure the state, increase tribute, impose taxes, appoint to chanceries, order the conduct of the court, have more regard to sovereignty, to building fortresses and castles, engaging cavalry.... For these ends one requires clever councillors, dexterous financiers, wise clerks, tried courtiers, cosmopolitan doctors, gifted architects, experienced army colonels.[29]

Besides practical knowledge, a modern young man of ambition must acquire the appearance and the conversation of a man of parts: 'weltmännisch soll nicht nur das Auftreten, sondern auch das Urteil sein' ['cosmopolitan, not solely in his manners, but also in his judgement'].[30] The late seventeenth century produced many treatises on the subject of modern education and opportunities, their rationalist, almost calculating tone in sharp contrast with the religious resignation of the war generation. Thus Chr. Georg von Bessel advises an ambitious young man in his *Politischer Glücksschmied* (1681) to equip himself to serve both God and the Fatherland: 'muss man sich müglichen Fleisses bemühen ... bey Fürsten und Herren bekandt zu werden, und sich in dero Gnaden zu setzen, wodurch man sich den Weg zu einem Dienst bahnet' ['one must try as hard as one can to become known among princes and lords, and to win their favour: this is the avenue to a post in their service']. For, as he astutely remarks in an observation which could well be applied to the whole of German society over the next century, 'es wird ein ehrlicher obgleich geschickter, aber ausser Herren Bedienung lebender Mann nicht viel geachtet' ['a man who is not in service to the highborn will not enjoy much regard, however honest and able he may be'].[31] In the writings of contemporaries the Christian virtues of hard work are frequently seen both as a command of God and, equally, as a sensible way of getting on in the world. Thus Chr. Thomasius entitled his guide to students: '*Chr. Thomasius eröffnet Der Studierenden Jugend einen Vorschlag, Wie er einen jungen Menschen, der sich ernstlich fürgesetzt, Gott und der Welt dermalens in vita civilii rechtschaffen zu dienen, und als ein honett und* galant homme *zu leben, binnen dreyen Jahre in der Philosophie ... zu informieren gesonnen sey*' (*Chr. Thomasius Unfolds a Plan for Young Academics: how he proposes to instruct in a matter of three years in philosophy a young man, who has set himself in all earnestness the task of one day serving God and the world in a righteous manner and of living as an honest and* galant homme) (Halle, 1689). He followed this with another treatise whose title is a nice illustration of that happy blend of self-interest and altruism which was so characteristic of the early Enlightenment in Germany: *Kurtzer Entwurff der politischen Klugheit sich selbst und anderen in allen menschlichen Gesellschaften wohl zurathen zu einer bescheidenen Conduite zu gelangen* (*A Short Sketch on the Political Wisdom of Assisting Oneself and Others in Human Society and Achieving a Modest Provision*) (*1710*).

Political adroitness was to be at a premium in the struggle for preferment in the German courts of the next decades. One type of person who lost status in consequence was the man of learning, the humanist scholar who was often a theologian as well, striving to inform himself over a field so wide that people in the seventeenth century had spoken of such men as possessing 'universal knowledge'. To be sure, a few individuals still managed to combine the address of a *galant homme* with great erudition, and to enjoy access to the circles of the great. One such was Leibniz, who served the genial Johann Philipp Schönborn, Archbishop and Elector of Mainz, became the confidant of Queen Sophie Charlotte of Prussia and was sought out by the Emperor Leopold himself. But the old international community of scholars which had existed at the beginning of the century had largely disappeared in Leibniz's time. In 1600 or a few decades later such a scholar automatically had belonged to such a community; he could write to, visit and recommend his friends to colleagues whom he had never seen, and expect to enjoy their hospitality as he himself was ready to confer it on them. To be the possessor of the title of doctor in those days was to be entitled to the social status ordinarily reserved to the nobility; one was by right a member of the *nobilitas literaria*, a concept recognized and embodied in the police ordinances of the time.[32] Learned doctors must be given the highest place at table in bourgeois gatherings, they could not be submitted to corporal punishment nor torture, and in law their voice must carry more weight than that of an ordinary commoner. If a tradesman disturbed a scholar, he could be forced to move elsewhere. Such men naturally regarded themselves as a class distinct from the rest of society; most in fact were well born or had been fortunate to secure the patronage necessary to allow them to acquire their prodigious learning. They entertained truly vast correspondences on matters of mutual interest with their colleagues. The humanist Puteanus, for instance, left 16 000 letters among his effects on his death in 1646. They were not specialists, but men both profound and versatile: the great Silesian dramatist and poet Andreas Gryphius held the responsible post of secretary to the town of Glogau; he was capable of lecturing in astronomy and metaphysics, and on occasion he conducted a dissection of Egyptian mummies at a meeting of learned men in the city of Breslau. As so many of his kind, he had studied at several universities, in Leyden, Italy and Strasburg. Gryphius, Hofmannswaldau and Lohenstein, fellow writers and Silesians, combined prodigious learning with a demanding public position. Hofmannswaldau was the longest serving councillor of the city of Breslau, Lohenstein chief syndic of the same city, a post which carried in 1670 a starting salary of 800 *taler*.[33] The three most famous Silesian writers served important municipalities. A century earlier men such as they had been the chief councillors of princes. Until the early seventeenth century

> alle entscheidenden Stellungen des sich bildenden Staatswesens wurden von Juristen und Theologen besetzt; und diese stammten zumeist aus dem Patriziat bzw. Ratsmannenfamilien der Territorien, gelegentlich auch aus dem mittleren Bürger- und Bauerntum. Die Kanzler, Räte und Amtleute der Fürsten waren noch allein entscheidend im Lande; sie erwarben zumeist auch ausgedehnten Grundbesitz, erhielten vom Fürsten Lehen und Rittergüter.

> all important posts in the state and administration were filled by lawyers and theologians; most of these came from the patriciate – that is, the families of town councillors of the territories, and sometimes from the middle-ranking burghers and peasantry. The chancellors, councillors and officials of the princes had a decisive

> voice in the land; they generally acquired considerable landed property and received from the prince fiefs and seignorial estates.[34]

Such people, like the Brunswick chancellors Reinharter, König and Fischer-Piscator, kept their bourgeois names. After the great war, however, and especially in Austria, the bourgeois state officials aspired to join the ranks of the new court nobility. Increasingly, they saw the executive posts being reserved for men of noble birth, while they had to be satisfied with administrative tasks. However, the bourgeois secretary could still wield considerable influence; Schiller's *Kabale und Liebe* provides a later example, or, as a Hanoverian aristocrat put it in the nineteenth century: 'mein Vater [war] Minister des Inneren; er war es unter dem ersten Sekretär Schulze' ['My father (was) Minister of the Interior; he held the post under First Secretary Schulze'].[35]

What was different about the later decades of the seventeenth century onwards as regards the bourgeois councillors was that the special characteristic of generations of German burghers from late medieval times on, a high standard of academic achievement, was no longer valued for its own sake, nor regarded as essential equipment for public service. This change was bound to affect the standard of learning generally and also its status in society. Furthermore, the German courts, although increasingly the focal point of local life, were small places, with vast ambitions but straitened means; they could only absorb a limited amount of talent. Of the many aspirants to public preference only a minority could be satisfied; the rest had to be content with the numerous but very poorly paid subordinate posts in the administration of the absolutist territorial state. The absolutist system restricted the movement of men and goods and therefore of ideas in Germany. The ideas and discoveries of alert minds in France, Holland and England reached the inhabitants of German states with a certain time lag. In the eighteenth century, therefore, Germans became more provincial than they had been in former times, and, what is more, they felt so themselves. It was difficult for a studious man not to feel isolated from his kind and to indulge his solitude in the pursuit of eccentric ideas and hobbies. No longer was the scholar someone to be treated with extreme respect, but rather as something of an oddity – as the heroes of middle class novels from the time of Hermes and Nicolai until the nineteenth century were to show.

THE SCHOOLS

Reading the biographies of famous Germans in this period, such as that of J. J. Winckelmann, or the translator of Homer and writer, Heinrich Voss, who set out on their eminent careers equipped only with what the local school could provide, one can only marvel at their subsequent achievements and at their endurance. For, with some exceptions, the average German school was pitifully inadequate. It had become a widespread practice from the late seventeenth century onwards for those who could afford it to employ tutors for their children instead of sending them to school. They did so because they found state and municipal schools unsatisfactory, but their action only exacerbated the problem. Nor did the absolute rulers do much for education before the later decades of the eighteenth century, and then – as in Frederick II's case in Prussia – their efforts were often misguided. Not only was the teacher in the German (primary) school and in the Latin (secondary) school badly paid, but the low status of his work meant that his post was often filled by men without training or inclination for the job. Candidates for orders were widely employed as teachers while they waited for a position in a parish. As a contemporary observed, 'Der Theologe [sah] das Schulamt wie ein Fegefeuer an, ... welches die Regierung dann mit einer guten Pfarre vergütigte' ['The theologian (regarded) schoolteaching as purgatory ... which the government compensated for by the grant of a fine parish'].[36] Some waited for life, their only hope of promotion being that of *Konrektor* or *Rektor*, deputy or headmaster. As the century progressed, and the prices of basic commodities trebled or quadrupled while salaries stagnated, there was a serious shortage of teachers. Retired officials were recruited and, in Prussia, invalid or elderly NCOs were directed to the schools. J. D. E. Preuss, author of the pioneering but hagiographic study of Frederick II, was forced to admit that his primary school policy was 'ein trauriger Schlag für die Landesschulen' ['a sad blow for the schools of the land'], adding perceptively that the real source of the problem, at least in rural areas, was the lack of rich farmers.[37] In other parts of Germany, especially in the last decades of this century, craftsmen who failed to make a living often turned to teaching in the local school.

The physical hardship of struggling to maintain a family on a teacher's salary warped many a man, and remained vivid in the memories of their children: Jean Paul, for example, suffered bitterly from the violence of his father, third teacher in the impoverished Fichtelgebirge region. The salary of an experienced teacher compared unfavourably with the earnings of a minor official or small craftsman. Thus the headmaster of the Latin school at Witzhausen-Hesse (*c.* 1650 inhabitants) received in 1747 from various sources, including salary, school fees and money for wood, $94\frac{1}{3}$ *taler* per annum plus living accommodation. The deputy earned 64, and the master of the German school 59 *taler* and a corn allowance of 4–5 cwt. There was a girls' school, too, and the master here got a mere 18 *taler*, but free accommodation and 11–12 cwt of corn.[38] If parents were slow to produce the fees (*Schulgeld*), the teacher had to go from house to house to collect it; contemporaries record that they made them feel like beggars asking for alms. Another source of income, and one which was equally humiliating, was conducting the school choir at weddings and funerals, the latter in all weathers, out of doors. The straitened circumstances of teachers and indeed of subaltern officials generally is best appreciated with reference to the price of food. In Leipzig, wheat, rye and lentils rose in price in the period 1657–1800 by between 400 and 500 per cent, meat by 300 per cent. Some princes raised the salaries of their employees, but most remained the same. Details from Augsburg, Frankfurt and Würzburg tell the same story. It became virtually impossible to live without some other source of income, which was frequently an illegal one.[39] Recent work in this area suggests that corruption was more widespread than was hitherto thought.[40] Klöden recalled his father, a Prussian excise official, taking bribes to overlook illicit distilleries.

The teacher's external appearance reflected his lack of means. Though Klöden's first teacher in Berlin had a black coat and powdered wig for public occasions, in school he always appeared in a flowered calico dressing-gown and slippers, the virtual uniform for men of his profession from the eighteenth to the mid nineteenth century. Kaplan Meerkatz in the provincial town of Märkisch-Friedland wore a very old 'Pudelmütze' (bobble-hat), a flannel jacket and 'alten abgeriebenen Manchesterhosen von unbestimmbarer Farbe, herabhängenden Strümpfe und Schlorren an den Füssen' ['worn serge trousers of indeterminate colour, stockings hanging down and slippers'].[41] So meagre was the salary of the teacher Rektor Pax in Preussisch-Friedland in the 1790s that he could not afford a housekeeper and took to drink to save the bother of getting breakfast. The vital concession offered him by the better-off citizens of a *Freitisch*, or free dinner in their houses, was withdrawn in consequence, and he eventually perished from want on the high road. 'Man glaubt nicht, wie viele edle Kräfte im Lehrstand untergehen in Folge der jämmerlichen Umstände, in welchen man sie vergehen lässt' ['People have no conception of how many fine talents in the teaching profession are condemned to perish as a result of the wretched circumstances in which they are allowed to rot'], commented his humane and perceptive pupil.[42]

In their standard of living and outlook teachers belonged to what would be called the '*Kleinbürgertum*', the lower level of the bourgeoisie. Yet outside the big towns they undoubtedly belonged to the 'notables' (*Honoratioren*) of their community. The poorly dressed and fed schoolmaster had his place as of right in this 'élite' because of his profession. When a travelling theatre came or a concert was held, he had his place in the front rows. What Paul Ernst noted of his native village in the Harz, where traditional manners lasted long into the nineteenth century, was true of most small communities in eighteenth century Germany too: those who were not actually dependants of another man provided a homogeneous group of senior citizens. There was no '*Grossbürgertum*' now, as in earlier centuries, and so the headmaster, his deputy, the doctor, postmaster, master craftsmen and officials were the notables. In Paul Ernst's native Elbingerode, the only man of consequence, the *Amtsrichter,* or county court judge, had no one of his own rank, and was constrained to associate with the rest of the local 'élite'.[43]

The earliest form of schooling for children in the eighteenth century were the so-called ABC, *Klipp-* or *Winkelschulen,* usually patronized by the children of the poor. They were generally presided over by some crone, not much more than a babyminder seeking a living, as Tieck, Hamann or Klöden recall. Parents who had the leisure taught their children the rudiments of reading from the Bible or a simple grammar book. The age at which children first went to school seems to have varied from one region to another. Schooling was to be obligatory for all from 'dem 5ten, längst dem 6ten Jahr' ['the fifth at the latest the sixth year'], according to the authorities in Eisenach in 1705; seven years later a report declared that only 50 per cent were complying.[44] Penalties threatened parents who failed to send their children to school from their fifth to their fourteenth year in a Saxon ordinance of 1769, but a renewed ordinance issued in 1773 showed these to have been ineffective. In rural areas children were often kept at home to help on the land; where poor schools did exist many were 'zu stolz ihre Kinder in solche zu schicken, weil sie sie für nachteilig für ihre Ehre [hielten]' ['too proud to send their children to such schools, because they (thought) they would detract from their honour'].[45] It was not until the nineteenth century that schooling became everywhere obligatory and the methods to enforce it effective. Even then many children did not attend if there was work for them in the area. Some states had a better record in education than others; the old Lutheran lands of Saxony and Württemberg had long shown an enlightened interest in primary schools as well as in higher education. Saxony had attracted many reformers to its schools, and had introduced some of the methods propounded by the great Bohemian educationalist Jan Comenius. In the Rhineland the Jesuits had begun to introduce primary schooling for all classes in the mid seventeenth century. But it was all very piecemeal and it was not until the late eighteenth century that one can discern a concerted effort to provide good schooling for all citizens. Even so, it is clear from the numerous late eighteenth and early nineteenth century memoirs that schools left many a gap to be filled by private study or perhaps a tutor. It is clear that the Enlightenment provided great stimulus to people to improve themselves, and the reader of memoirs will come across astonishing instances of endurance and success in apparently hopeless circumstances by those desirous of bettering themselves through education. However, these necessarily belong to the minority. The educational standard of the majority probably lay somewhere between the opinion of the Bochum judge who declared in 1763 that 'unter 100 erwachsenen Leuten kaum derselben erfindlich [seien], die im Lesen und Schreiben tüchtig' ['among 100 adults there are hardly any who can read and write properly'], and the reputation of the Solingen smiths, of whom it was said 'kaum sechs unter 100 waren des Lesens und Schreibens unkundig, viele schrieben sehr schön und waren im Rechnen sehr gewandt' ['scarcely 6 per cent were not able to write; some wrote a very fine hand and were very good at arithmetic'].[46]

For the children themselves entering school the process of education was not likely to be a pleasant one, not so much because of the general dreariness of the material to be learnt or the form in which it was presented, but because of the methods generally thought necessary to impress it upon their minds. 'Die ersten Werkzeuge zur Erziehung in den Händen der Eltern, der öffentlichen und der Privatlehrer waren die der körperlichen Züchtigung, die man an den Wänden aufgehangen oder vor die Fenster wie ein Zeichen hingestellt sah, dem nur die Überschrift fehlte: hier erziehet man' ['The first tools of education in the hands of parents, state and private school teachers were those to administer corporal punishment; one could see them hanging on the wall or in the window, a kind of trademark, with only the motto lacking: "Here we educate"'], wrote the merchant and educational reformer of Hamburg, J. G. Büsch, of his childhood.[47] The object of schooling for small children was to make them sit still and behave themselves, and for the older children to learn by rote the rudiments of religious doctrine, reading, writing and addition, which their parents and grandparents had done before them. The authority of the teacher was maintained by punishment which must seem barbarous to people today, but which was in fact a feature of many schools in other parts of

Europe until comparatively recent times. F. X. Bronner, who spent many years as a monk, recalled his first village school in Hochstädt in south Germany:

> Da bekam einer mit der Ochsensehne einen mörderischen Spaniol auf die gespannten Beinkleider; dort wickelte der Lehrer einem anderen dem Mantel um den Kopf, damit er nicht schreyen könnte, und führte ihn in das sogenannte Speckkämmerlein, wo ihn entweder mit der Ruthe oder gar mit der Ochsensehne das nackte Sitzfleisch fürchterlich durchgegärbt ward. Wenn so ein Bube wieder heraus-kam, wälzte et sich gewöhnlich vor Schmerzen auf dem Boden.
>
> On one side someone was getting a murderous thrashing on the seat of his trousers with the strap, on the other the teacher was winding a coat round the head of another, to stop him screaming and led him then into the so-called bacon larder, where his naked posterior was frightfully tanned with the rod or even the strap. When such a lad emerged again, he usually rolled about the floor in agony.[48]

Such murderous ill usage, so frequently dwelt on in memoirs, was possible because many parents treated their children likewise. Klöden wrote of his maternal grandfather, a surgeon in mid eighteenth century Berlin: 'alle seine Kinder wurden bei der geringsten Kleinigkeit unbarmherzig gezüchtigt, wobei er mit mannigfachen Strafinstru-menten abwechselte und den Grundsatz aussprach: Kinder können nie genug Strafe bekommen! Dies war in jener Zeit nichts Ungewöhnliches' ['all his children were beaten mercilessly for the least transgression, and he would vary the instrument of punishment, as he voiced the principle: children can never be punished too much! This view was a common one at that time'].[49] Punishments in school of this nature were also in part the consequence of the teacher's own low status and lack of training, which allowed him to work off his frustrations on obstinate or stupid children.

The content of teaching was generally very meagre. 'Vier Stunden vor- und drei Stunden nachmittags gab unser Vater uns Unterricht, welcher darin bestand, dass er uns bloss auswendig lernen liess, Sprüche, Katechismus, lateinische Wörter und Langens Grammatik' ['Our father gave us four hours of instruction in the morning and three in the afternoon, which consisted merely in his making us learn by heart sayings, the catechism, Latin words and Lange's Grammar'].[50] The methods of Jean Paul's father did not differ very much from those recorded elsewhere. In Märkisch-Friedland Klöden and his companions learnt portions of the Bible by heart each day; by frequent application of the rod they developed a facility for finding quotations at great speed which they never lost. The Bible was the children's reading book; every lesson in the five hour day had direct reference to religion, he recalled, except tables and sums. Nothing was explained, everything learnt by heart. Comenius's *Orbis pictus*, the first school book with pictures and for many decades the only one, was greatly loved by those fortunate enough to get hold of it. In Klöden's remarkable memoirs one gets the impression of a gifted child starved of visual stimulus and virtually without books. If one lived in the provinces and was poor, there was very little chance that books would come one's way. He read such few as he had time after time, and to the end of his life never forgot the sense of wonder he experienced when, as a boy of ten or so, he was given Campe's *Robinson*. The idea that the grown-ups in this story were as eager to explain things to the children as they were seen to learn struck him as extraordinary. Nobody ever did at school, and at home people had neither the time nor the ability.[51]

Against this depressing picture of educational conditions in seventeenth and eighteenth century Germany, the old grammar schools afford a certain relief. They were in general founded and maintained by the municipalities, the territorial princes and the Jesuits; despite many vicissitudes in the course of their history, they continued in this period to provide a sound education. Here the ideas of the great educational reformers, the energetic and intolerant Ratke or Ratichius, the Moravian bishop Comenius, or Superintendent Kromayer of Weimar, had lasting influence; they tried to get away from the old methods of learning by rote, and by means of carefully devised textbooks to help the pupils to understand what they had learnt. Although the ideal of the Strasburg reformer Johannes Sturm, *sapiens et pietas eloquens,* still remained the ultimate aim of the majority of such schools, the use and study of the German language made progress in the seventeenth century, much stimulated by the great baroque writers. In the Jesuit schools, however, it was forbidden to speak German in class, and sixth formers might not even use it among themselves. The grammar schools attracted pupils from far off; some were boarding schools, for the rest provision would be made for pupils from outside the town to lodge with a relative or friend, either for money or in return for some service on the part of the boy. Among the best of the municipal grammar schools were the Elisabeth and the Magdalene in Breslau, Aegidianus at Nuremberg, St Anna at Augsburg, Regensburg's *Gymnasium poeticum,* and the Jesuit *Tricoronatum* at Cologne, where the great pastoral theologian and poet Friedrich von Spee was educated and many members of the Fürstenberg family, who served as statesmen and prelates in north-west Germany. In many towns, such as those mentioned above, the presence of Jesuit colleges since the Counter-Reformation nurtured a keen academic rivalry between schools. One should not allow the biased views of nineteenth century writers to suggest that there was inevitably hostility between the teachers and pupils of the municipal or state and Jesuit schools; much evidence suggests that the contrary was true (see Chapter VI, pp. 104ff). The two Lutheran schools in Breslau started to put on their dramas in alternate years in imitation of the Jesuits, who had taken over the old university premises as their new college in 1638 and produced plays acted by the pupils. Gryphius and Lohenstein had each made their debut as dramatists at their school, the Magdalene Gymnasium, Gryphius writing his first Latin drama for performance when he was sixteen, and Lohenstein taking part in a public 'declamation' at the age of eleven. Their school had a large library which 'wenig Bibliotheken Teutschlands dörffte weichen' ['need cede pride of place to few other libraries in Germany'], as a contemporary put it;[52] here, too, the philosopher Christian Wolff was educated.

The most renowned grammar schools maintained by territorial princes were to be found in central Germany, where Ratke had advised the able Duchess Dorothea Maria of Anhalt-Köthen, mother of Duke Ernest of Gotha, and where Comenius's writings inspired the reforms of less well-known figures. Duke Ernest's grammar school at Gotha was perhaps the most reputable of such schools in the seventeenth century; the Duke was shrewd enough to secure the services as headmaster of Andreas Reyher in 1641. Reyher, a practical, immensely hard working and dedicated teacher, was faced with the seemingly impossible task of making good the devastations of the war, appointing teachers prepared to work for years on small or non-existent salaries – 'ein Vorgeschmack der Höllenstrafen' ['a pre-taste of Hell-fire'], Reyher called these first years at Gotha.[53] He made discerning appointments, introduced a kind of prefect system, wrote some forty textbooks on the three Rs, foreign languages and philosophy. His approach is characterized by an opening sentence in a section of the much-printed *Schulmethodus* of which he was the main author: 'Die Arithmetica sol solcher gestalt getrieben werden, das man nicht von den *Praeceptis*, sondern von der *Praxi ipsa* anfahe' ['Arithmetic should be taught primarily from the point of view of practical use rather than from principles'].[54] This was to be the approach which characterized the best school reformers of the eighteenth century in German-speaking lands. He also introduced the idea of a scholarship class for the best pupils, and of certificates for those who wished to go on to university; this anticipated the introduction of the *Abitur* or leaving examination in Saxony in 1718 (Prussia 1778). Gotha's fame began to draw pupils from as far away as Westphalia, Swabia and Silesia – including Gryphius's son; by the 1660s pupils were coming from Poland and Hungary. Duke Ernest's connections with the German community in Moscow led to Reyher's textbooks being used there. Other distinguished schools were Pforta, Meissen and Grimme in Saxony, and Joachimstal in Brandenburg. The standard of teaching in these schools varied considerably from one period to another; the person of the teacher was more influential than in later, more standardized times. Thus Wieland owed his discovery of the great authors of the Enlightenment, of Bayle, Voltaire and Wolff, to masters in his Pietist boarding school at Klosterberge near Magdeburg, where his father, a Swabian parson, had sent him to ensure a sound religious education. Kügelgen's portrait of his hugely eccentric and marvellously stimulating preceptor, Pastor Roller at Dresden, is but one of a vast number of portraits of able teachers drawn in memoirs.[55]

Many eighteenth century rulers, clergymen and teachers were concerned to provide a type of education more suitable to the practical requirements of trades and crafts. Francke's pupil was Julius Hecker, who had also been a teacher at his *Pädagogium* in Halle, and who founded the Berlin *Realschule* in 1747; by 1762 he had 1095 pupils, including 300 scholarship boys. Hecker also founded a teachers' training college attached to his school to train primary school teachers. Many projects of this kind were discussed and some attempted in the last decades of the eighteenth century, the most illustrious being the *Philanthropinum*, founded by the genial J. Basedow (1723–90) in 1774 under the aegis of Prince Leopold of Anhalt at Dessau. It aroused a great deal of excitement among contemporaries, and Basedow knew how to appeal for public support in fine rhetorical passages: 'Der Schulstaub liegt seit Jahrhunderten!' ['The dust of school lies centuries old!'], he cried: 'O wie mancher gehorsame Knabe und sittsame Jüngling wiederholt in täglich verwünschten Schulstunden die durch Striemen eingeblauten Worte eines Gesandten Gottes oder eines Weisen unter den Menschen, und leider um sie nie zu verstehen, oder doch nie zu verehren' ['O how many an obedient and virtuous youth must repeat in daily accursed lessons the words he has beaten into him by an emissary of God or sage among men, and he will never, alas, understand them or learn to honour them'].[56] Basedow's rhetoric was, alas, not matched by his organizational powers. The *Philanthropinum* was much less successful than its authors had hoped. However, the cumulative efforts of this and other short-lived foundations, as well as the writings of Rousseau and the Swiss educationalist Pestalozzi (1746–1827) and others, proved vital. At the beginning of the nineteenth century the German states, notably Prussia under Wilhelm von Humboldt, submitted their educational systems to a thorough reform, which at last established the teacher as a professional man in his own right, and as such worthy of respect in society at large.

Chapter 6
Religious life and the clergy in Germany

I THE PROTESTANT CHURCHES

Religious life in seventeenth century Germany was coloured by the war and the natural catastrophes associated with it, the effect of which was to make God, mortality and the hereafter of much more constant and immediate concern that they were to later generations. The more we learn of the uncertainty of life at all social levels at that time, the better we understand why this should have been so. Though 1648 brought an end to the war, it did not bring peace: in the campaigns against Sweden, France and the Turks during subsequent decades, Germany remained the battleground. The plague recurred at frequent intervals throughout the century, claiming among its victims many great men, including the distinguished authority on poetics, Martin Opitz, and the Jesuit poet, Friedrich von Spee. The French historian, J. Neveux, has pointed out its importance in determining both the movements and the religious or political allegiance of distinguished men in this epoch.[1] It is no cliché to say that death was ever present in men's minds; as Gryphius wrote in one of his many powerful passages on the subject:

> Was itzund Atem holt, muss mit der Luft entfliehen,
> Was nach uns kommen wird, wird uns ins Grab nachziehn.
> Was sag ich? Wir vergehn wie Rauch von starken Winden.

Those who now draw breath must vanish in the wind,
Those who are born after us, will draw us to them in the grave,
What say I? We disappear as smoke in a storm.[2]

The case of the Prussian divine A. Calovius who buried five wives and all his thirteen children is by no means isolated. The biographies of contemporaries are a constant witness to the transience of life.

And yet, when one studies the accounts of religious life in these years, one hears far more of theological conflict than of spiritual experience. Political affairs and personal life histories seem to be dominated by questions of doctrinal allegiance. The main area of conflict was Saxony, which, as Luther's homeland, claimed to act as arbiter of religious matters in Protestant Germany. Whether one belonged to the pro-Saxon orthodox party, or to that of its opponents, determined many a young man's future career, friendship, marriage and political allegiance. It was the Saxon orthodox Lutherans' persecution of the followers of Melanchthon in the late sixteenth century, the so-called crypto-Calvinists, that drove many of them to sympathize with and eventually to support the Calvinist interest in the Empire. A typical example is that of Ludwig Camerarius of Nuremberg, whose grandfather had been a colleague and friend of Melanchthon. He entered the government service of the Count Palatine, followed the young Frederick V to Bohemia and acted as his chancellor during his brief reign as King of Bohemia. He continued to identify himself with the Calvinist cause after the débacle of 1620, and ended his career in the Hague, as ambassador of the King of Sweden. Camerarius thus combined in his person experience of the main centres of Calvinism in the Empire: the free imperial cities with their long traditions of prosperity and independence in political and religious matters, the wealthy lands of the Palatinate and Bohemia, and finally the refuge of the Reformed Church in Europe in the seventeenth century, the Netherlands.

The defeat and humiliation of the Calvinist cause in the Palatinate and Bohemia during the Thirty Years War meant that Protestantism was now confined, outside the cities, to north and central Germany. However, there were considerable distinctions between the different areas and many of the smaller states favoured neither Lutheranism nor Calvinism. The fact that the inhabitants of a region felt its historical character and traditions threatened by a powerful neighbour in this acquisitive age tended to draw them together in some distinctive form of worship. Thus Silesia, threatened by the Austrian Counter-Reformation in Bohemia and Moravia, turned increasingly away from orthodox Lutheranism, which seemed close to the Catholic position, towards sectarianism, with forms of worship akin to those of Calvinism. Educated Protestant Silesians had no university of their own, and they went in considerable numbers to Leyden, in the steps of Opitz and Gryphius, where many of them actually became Calvinists. Similarly in Lusatia, threatened by Saxony on the one hand, and Austria on the other, the cobbler and mystic, Jakob Boehme, attracted adherents to his highly individual form of Christian belief from the craftsmen as well as the patricians of his once prosperous home town, Görlitz. To many contemporaries he came to symbolize resistance to any sort of theological or political orthodoxy. The deeply felt piety of Boehme's circle, the intensity of religious experience shared by men of different social origins, had a parallel at the end of the century in Pietism. Some of the small independent states, such as Reuss or Wittgenstein-Berleburg, or those areas such as Halle or Magdeburg which had been taken over by a larger power, in both cases Prussia, became centres for Pietist conventicles. It was as if their sense of local community found expression in the more intimate form of worship characteristic of all Protestant sects, in which, unlike Lutheranism or Catholicism, the humbly born were equal to the well-to-do, even in the sight of man.

The Treaties of Westphalia did not significantly alter the religious boundaries of Germany established at the peace of Augsburg in 1555. What the war had done was to prevent the encroachment of the Austrian Counter-Reformation into the lands of central Germany, while on the other hand, the death of Gustavus Adolphus of Sweden probably destroyed the possibility of a unified Lutheran power in the north. The main Catholic territories were now Austria, Bavaria, the ecclesiastical principalities of the Rhineland – Mainz, Cologne and Trier – whose territories often stretched far into the surrounding countryside, a number of important bishoprics in the south, centre and north-west – Würzburg, Constance, Bamberg and Münster, for example, as well as Baden, and numerous petty states and enclaves, mainly in the south and north-west. The principal Lutheran territories were the Saxon duchies, the Guelph duchies, Mecklenburg, Hesse-Darmstadt and Württemberg, where Lutheranism was restored after a period of Catholic rule. The peace treaties in 1648 recognized the Calvinists as one of the three official religions of the Empire, but Calvinism had lost much ground, being confined largely to the Palatinate and the lower Rhine, to Hesse-Kassel, parts of Silesia and a number of towns. However, since 1613 the ruling house of Brandenburg, the Hohenzollerns, had been Calvinist, as was the Silesian branch of the Piasten dukes. Also in Silesia the princely Leszczynski family welcomed Calvinist families to their small but culturally distinguished court. Here at Lissa (Leszno) a number of men were educated who later functioned as Calvinist court preachers to the Hohenzollerns in Prussia.

The extinction of a ruling house could bring about a change in the sovereign's religion, but should not affect that of his new subjects unless they freely converted to the same faith. Thus, when Elector Sigismund of Brandenburg became a Calvinist in 1613, he gave a pledge to continue to protect his Lutheran subjects: the strongly entrenched Lutheran estates saw that he carried out his promise. When in 1697 Elector Augustus of Saxony became a Catholic, his lands remained virtually untouched by his decision, except in the stimulus it gave to baroque architecture in his capital, Dresden. In the Palatinate the inhabitants suffered persecution after the Elector became a Catholic in 1685, but this was dictated by French domestic policy, not religious hatred. Throughout the period 1648–1806, religious freedom was guaranteed to every member of the Holy Roman Empire if he belonged to one of the 'drei im Reich rezipierten Religionen' ['three accepted religions of the *Reich*']. However, a sharp distinction was made between liberty of conscience, which was meant here, and freedom of public worship, which was much more circumscribed. The right to public worship was regarded as a sovereign right of the territorial ruler, and the rights of religious minorities in any state depended on whether they could establish the fact that in the year 1624 they had enjoyed an *exercitium religionis.* They could only be expelled if they had not at that date enjoyed freedom of worship. Those professing a religion other than the recognized ones, i.e. the Jews, had no claim to the right of public worship or liberty of conscience. The territorial system, particularly in Protestant areas, largely determined the character and influence of the churches. The secular ruler here claimed that the right to appoint church officials was vested in him; he appointed general superintendents and the supreme ecclesiastical council in his dominions. In the eighteenth century the Protestant churches became increasingly subordinate to the secular power. The freedom of worship enjoyed by them was justified in the eyes of the state because of their usefulness as an instrument of social control. The churches – both Catholic and Protestant – were expected to teach the faithful obedience and submission to authority at all times, and this they did throughout the period.

In the seventeenth and even in the eighteenth century the German clergy, notably the orthodox Lutherans, wrangled acrimoniously in Saxony, Magdeburg, Hamburg and Königsberg, but on the whole religious fanaticism was verbal rather than violent. Confessional quarrels submitted to the Emperor and the *Reichshofrat* were frequent in this period, but they were almost always concerned more with sovereign rights than strictly religious matters. Despite the atrocities of the Thirty Years War, there was probably less religious persecution in the Empire (apart from Austria) than in those countries such as England, France and Spain which regarded themselves as much more civilized. This is one of the more positive aspects of Germany's past which we are prone to overlook, even if the degree of religious tolerance was, according to our modern understanding, rather relative. The variety of religious opinions and beliefs to be found within the compass of Germany made in the long run for a degree of mutal acceptance, particularly after the experience of the war, which had spared few regions. Many aristocratic families had Catholic and Protestant branches, who met and intermarried. It was in Germany, too, that the first concerted efforts were made to bring about a union of churches, the most celebrated being that made in the 1690s by the philosopher Leibniz, the Catholic bishop Spinola from Gelderland and the Calvinist court preacher at Berlin, Jablonski, whose grandfather had been the illustrious Bohemian educationalist, Jan Comenius.

The exception to this tolerance was Austria, which emerged from apparent defeat in 1648 to a new era of hegemony in Europe. In making the point, it is important, however, to distinguish between the Austrian ruler in his capacity as territorial sovereign and as Emperor. As Emperor he saw to it that committees appointed to deal with religious disputes in the Privy Council were composed of members of both confessions involved; as territorial ruler he sought to impose a unified religion and culture on his disparate domains. In this he was prompted and abetted by the Spanish party at court in Vienna, the Jesuit order in the field of education and a number of mendicant orders preaching to the populace. Foreign political considerations could increase or modify the severity of the authorities towards their Protestant subjects. Thus during the Spanish Succession War the revolt of Prince Rákóczy in Hungary won concessions for the Protestants, though these were lost soon after, in 1711. The essence of Austrian intolerance was political rather than religious: the Austrian nobility was largely Protestant, as were the towns in the mid seventeenth century: it was to break the power of the estates that the Habsburgs gradually withdrew the religious rights they had once enjoyed. Harassment increased inexorably, given new stimulus under Leopold I (1657–1705) by his Spanish consort. Protestants might now no longer hold services in their homes, employ Protestant tutors or servants. The case of the poetess Catharina von Greiffenberg (1633–94) illustrates the insidiousness of the persecution: she spent her youth and fortune trying to obtain the release of her husband and the restoration of his property after he had been cast into prison on a trumped-up charge; an acquisitive Catholic neighbour desired to seize his estates and was able to use the religious issue to veil his motives. Like other Austrian Protestants, Catharina was forced to journey as far as Nuremberg if she wished to attend service and receive communion. As the years passed, even these journeys became fraught with difficulty and she, and many others, decided to settle permanently in that city.[3]

The Austrian authorities did not spare expense or imagination in their efforts to impose uniformity of religion on their lands: they erected the architectural glories of the baroque parish and monastery churches; they had a forgotten holy man, St John Nepomuk, canonized in 1729 and his statue erected on bridges throughout the land, in an attempt to make people forget the 'other John', the martyred Jan Hus of Bohemia.[4] If few Austrian noble families chose to remain Protestant by the eighteenth century, the same is not true of the peasantry. Right down to the end of the century peasants in many remote areas led a double life, attending mass on Sunday in the village church and holding Lutheran services secretly in their homes.[5] This was often known to the priest, who, however, was dependent on their goodwill for his slender income. A Cistercian monk, Baltasar Kleinschroth, fleeing in 1683 from the Turks in Lower Austria, barely escaped death at the hands of angry Protestant peasants who told him that the persecution of their co-religionists in Hungary had been the cause of the Turkish invasion.[6] Efforts to eradicate Lutheranism continued down to the reign of Joseph II (1765–90). The most notorious solution was found by Archbishop Firmian of Salzburg who expelled some 21 000 subjects in 1731, as Goethe commemorated in his epic *Herrmann und Dorothea* in 1797. The Empress Maria Theresa rightly felt that this was economically too costly. Her policy favoured migration: Protestants were settled in the sparsely populated but fruitful lands of Transylvania in the years 1752–60. More genial and, from a religious point of view more effective, was the decision taken by herself and her sons to provide better pastoral care for remote congregations and encourage greater participation by the laity in church. The liturgical reforms of Joseph II and Leopold II are remarkable in their time for their attempt to bridge the gap between clergy and laity in a way not realized until the Second Vatican Council.[7]

The efforts of the Saxon authorities to provide a similar confessional unity to the Lutheran church were less ruthless than in Austria, but also by the nature of things, less effective. True, the universities of Wittenberg, Jena and Leipzig attracted students from as far away as the eastern Baltic and southern Hungary, and the theologians here were frequently referred to in matters of doctrinal orthodoxy. But the universities tended to train candidates to dispute in Latin rather than to preach in German, and so make the clergyman remote from the common people. The war had certainly encouraged scepticism about such matters among many who might have echoed Grimmelshausen's hero Simplicissimus when he said to the parson:

> Welchem soll ich glauben? Vermeint der Herr wohl, es sei so ein geringes, wenn ich einem Teil, den die zwei anderen einer falschen Lehre bezichtigen, meines Lebens Seligkeit anvertraue? ... Zu welchem Teil soll ich mich dann tun, wenn je eins das andere ausschreit, es sei kein gutes Haar an ihm. Sollte mir wohl jemand raten hineinzuplumpen, wie eine Fliege in einen heissen Brei? Ich will lieber ganz von der Strass bleiben als nur irre laufen.
>
> Whom then should I believe? Does the gentleman think it is such a trifling matter for me to entrust my hopes of heavenly bliss to one party, whom the other two accuse of false doctrine? ... Which side should I support when each berates the other, saying there is not a word of truth in him? Shall we counsel a man to plop in, like a fly into hot porridge? I'd prefer to stay away from the road, than to wander round in circles, hopelessly lost.[8]

There was a growing tendency in the seventeenth century for pious men to look outside the churches for spiritual solace and direction. Long before the emergence of Pietism in the 1680s, radical religious and social thinkers were being widely read. Johann Arndt's devotional work, *Paradiesgärtlein,* was published in 1612 and reissued constantly during the next decades; Johann Valentin Andreae's *Christianopolis* (1617) offered a Christian Utopian view of society which was much discussed, as was Christian Hoburg's *Vaterlandes Praeservatif* (1677). Here the author urged his countrymen to emulate the Dutch, to set aside the traditional barriers of religious and social prejudice in order to bring peace and happiness to the land. The critics of orthodox Lutheranism were convinced that the Reformation had lost its idealism, that it had, above all, become too closely identified with the vested interests of princes and estates. The fact that appointments to parishes lay in the hands of the local landowner or municipal council made this in a sense inevitable. The Lutheran church had become as hierarchical as ever the old church had been. In many churches theatre-like 'boxes' were constructed to accommodate the nobility; as the clergyman handed out communion he addressed the common people in the familiar, the nobility in the polite form; in the 1670s the Saxon knights requested the right to baptize their children at home, as 'it was not thought fitting that a highborn child should be baptized with the same water as the children of the common people'.[9]

Critics of the Lutheran church came from very different social backgrounds; one was that most perspicacious of seventeenth century German princes, Duke Ernest of Gotha, who lived on in popular memory as the 'father of the *Volkschule*' and a solicitous ruler of his people. He regarded the Thirty Years War as a visitation by God on His wayward children, and he determined by organization, visitation and discerning appointments, such as that of the political theorist Veit Ludwig von Seckendorff and of the Pietist Francke's father, to make his little state exemplary in the practice of the faith. More humble souls, such as Paul Gerhardt, Christian Scriver, author of the popular *Seelenschatz* or *Treasury of Souls* (1675–92), and Joachim Bethkius tried to inspire devotion by composing prayers, hymns and manuals. Bethkius was the author of *Excidium Germaniae,* written during the war but only published in 1666; the full title was *Full and True Account of the Reasons why at the Time of the Old Testament the Jews and at the Time of the New Testament Germany became a Tenfold Sodom, and how God Allowed it to Perish Through the Sword, Through War, Famine and Plague as Visitations of His Anger.*[10] Unlike the Catholic church of the Counter-Reformation, with its shrewd and subtle understanding of the popular mind, the authorities of the Lutheran church failed to appreciate the unease of many of its members, or, indeed, to cater for the spiritual needs of the lower orders. The craftsman class, the domestic servants and the peasantry responded with alacrity to the reforming impulse of the various sects and movements, particularly to Pietism and Count von Zinzendorf's Brethren in the eighteenth century.

Pietism is so fundamentally important for an understanding of German history in this period that it is hard to understand why many modern historians have chosen to ignore it. Its most fertile sphere of influence was Prussia, where its principal institutions were built, and where the rulers, after initial reluctance, gave generous patronage. Pietism had a profound effect on the ethos of the Prussian army and bureaucracy. Stressing usefulness to the community and subordination of the individual to the good of the whole, Pietist leaders inspired a tradition of service which lasted in secularized form down to the dissolution of the Prussian monarchy centuries later. The founders of the movement were Philipp Spener (1635–1705), and August Herman Francke (1663–1727). Spener spent most of his life in Frankfurt, Dresden and Berlin, from where he exercised an immense personal influence over the faithful in remote parts of the country. He even arranged marriages among his adherents; a well-known union was that of the clergyman Petersen and his highborn wife, who spent long years of matrimony in unusually energetic service of the Lord, writing, exhorting, visiting, addressing and generally organizing the faithful. But it was Francke, practical, zealous and inventive, who was really responsible for the spread and institutionalization of Pietism, a man who aroused bitter hostility, as much for his success as for a certain disguised ruthlessness in pursuit of his magnificent vision. He put into effect a vast series of projects for financing his charitable organizations, for the Pietists believed in the primacy of good works as an expression of true faith. He instituted a vigorous trade in publishing and a wine importing business with both the Prussian army and the Duke of Marlborough as his customers, for although the believers themselves abhorred intoxicating liquors, they knew that the Hungarian wines were a profitable trade; he founded a research centre for medicine and a laboratory to make and dispense patent medicines; this last was the most lucrative of all his ventures, and was launched by means of a thoroughly modern advertising campaign.

Francke was more than a religious reformer. He was a social radical who believed that by education one could change society fundamentally. His educational principles were the cornerstone of his practical religious activity. These were rooted in Christian belief, and he was convinced that prejudice based in ignorance could be eradicated by sound pedagogical methods. In this, as in much else besides, he was close to the thinkers of the early Enlightenment. His most famous foundation, the orphanage or *Waisenhaus* at Halle, was genial in concept and fell only a little short in practice. Like the Utopia of some baroque visionary, it bristled with inventiveness and catered for innumerable spiritual and physical needs. His system of central heating in the dormitories, which also operated the bakery, aroused the disapproval of contemporaries: orphans should not, they alleged, be treated softly. But, Francke pointed out, this device and the 'motion' and fresh air which he favoured for the inmates, benefited their general health. What could be wrong with that? He soon catered not just for orphans but for the sons of merchants and noblemen. Each boy was to be allocated to a class according to his natural gifts; as in the ideal comprehensive school, he would go to different classes for different subjects; courses were both academic and practical. Francke even included the daughters as well as the sons of the nobility in his project to train the landed gentry in household and estate management. Of course in practice the divisions of society were not so easily set aside, even by so persuasive and inspired a person. Yet he certainly facilitated the social advance of many boys of humble origins whom he prepared for the service of the state. The curriculum was designed to train administrators, soldiers and diplomats as well as Christians, and the Prussian state, particularly under Frederick William I, made ample use of the talent available at the *Waisenhaus* and the Potsdam Military Orphanage which the king set up with Francke's help in 1724.

The influence of Pietism in Prussia and in Germany was socially very diverse. Since 'conversion' (*Erweckung*) was almost invariably the result of personal contact, the presence of a charismatic individual in a conventicle or group of worshippers, be he nobleman, artisan or scholar, acted as a focal point for a whole region. The movement encouraged self-analysis through diary and letters, hence its importance in literary history in Germany. Most leading Pietists conducted a truly vast correspondence with like-thinking men, or with weaker brethren in need of encouragement. They recommended acquaintances to each other, looked after distant relatives and friends, as their Lutheran, Catholic and Calvinist contemporaries did for each other.[11] But the letter writing of the Pietists was on a much greater scale: they established a network of friendship and refuge for those who suffered harassment in staunchly orthodox areas, such as Saxony or Mecklenburg. Their social egalitarianism, their abolition of the distinction between clergy and laity, which Luther had failed to achieve, ran counter to the feudal world in which people still lived in the late seventeenth and early eighteenth centuries. The Pietist's strong sense of equality of all before God was a genuine impulse, shared by those princes and noblemen who joined the movement – the Reuss princes, Henry XXIII and Henry XXIV, Counts Ernest of Wernigerode and Casimir of Wittgenstein-Berleburg. Often the ingrained habits of deference were too much for lowborn Pietists. The eighteenth century Prussian chronicler, Büsching, recalls the story of the preacher whom Henry XXIV Reuss invited to his table; the poor man was:

> so ängstlich blöde ... dass er an der gräflichen Tafel weder essen noch trinken konnte. Der Herr Graf ermunterte ihn zwar, wider die Hofgewohnheit, zum Essen und Trinken und verlangte, dass er sich einbilden sollte, er sei zu Hause bei den Seinigen ... aber es war nichts auszurichten. Er liess vor Angst sehr oft die Serviette fallen, wagte es nicht, nah genug an den Tisch zu rücken, und das Zittern der Hände verstattete nicht, den Löffel, eine Gabel und ein Glas an den Mund zu bringen. Er stand also so hungrig und leer wieder auf, als er sich niedergesetzt hatte.

so stupid with nervousness ... that he could neither eat nor drink at

> the Count's table. The Count encouraged him, contrary to court custom, to eat and drink, saying that he should imagine himself at home with his family ... but to no avail. From sheer nerves, he let the serviette fall several times, did not dare to sit close enough to the table, while his trembling fingers prevented him from bringing spoon, fork or glass to his lips. So he stood up as hungry and empty as he had sat down.[12]

It was this apparently blatant disregard for social differences which aroused the passions of the movement's opponents. Its appeal to the lower orders explains the vehemence with which its adherents were attacked, as for instance in Hamburg, where the Pietist pastor Horbius barely escaped from the city with his life. The patrician senate of that city, many of whose members were allied in marriage with orthodox pastors' families, believed that the sentiments of the Pietists stimulated the *Rat* or town council, representing the craftsmen, to revolt against their own authority. Bloody conflict broke out in the first decade of the eighteenth century between the two sides, and a fragile peace was established only after the Emperor himself had intervened through his representative.[13] Indeed, had the Great Elector and his son Frederick I not protected the Pietists in the early years, they might have succumbed to their enemies, the most vociferous of whom were the Lutheran estates at Halle. It was the grudging enthusiasm of that astute monarch, Frederick William I, that established Pietism in Prussia, if not as the national religion, at least as a powerful reforming influence. It is an instance of Francke's realism and determination that, despite his religious objections to war, he should have accepted the inevitable role of the army in the Prussian state, even to producing at the *Waisenhaus* press a devotional manual for soldiers, the *Soldatenbüchlein* (1715), which aimed to inspire a more Christian way of life among the Prussian forces. This move was unexpectedly successful, partly because Francke had many sympathizers in the officer corps and at court. When the King introduced the canton system for recruitment, abolishing the worst excesses of the pressgangs, he also appointed military chaplains who 'all must have studied in Halle' according to his wish. Theirs was a daunting task. As a contemporary put it, 'for a military chaplain it was not a case of "I send you among wolves", but "I send you among devils".'[14] However, the new institution did have a civilizing effect. Büsching, a well-informed commentator, could attribute the devotion to duty and the achievements of the Prussian army in the early years of Frederick II's reign not least to the religious spirit of generals, officers and common soldiers. In the later years of that reign, however, King Frederick's indifference to religion and the growth in the number of foreign mercenaries eroded much of the former influence of Pietism among the troops.

Frederick II's religious indifference was not the main cause for the decline of Pietism in Prussia or elsewhere. By the middle of the century it had become institutionalized and its followers intolerant. In her popular satirical comedy *Die Pietisterey im Fischbeinrock* (*Pietism in a Whalebone Coat*) (1737), Frau Gottsched mocked at the foolish antics of devotees, Frau Glaubeleichtin (Mrs Believeanything), Frau Seufzerin (Mrs Sigh) and Frau Zankenheimin (Mrs Quarrelhome), who are completely under the spell of the rapacious and hypocritical preacher Herr Scheinfromm (Mr Seempious). Contemporaries found it very funny. However, what at that time seemed to many simply foolish excess was in part the result of a widespread decline in religious belief and practice, which was particularly apparent in Protestant regions in Germany. The rationalism and religious scepticism which was characteristic of the age of the Enlightenment later provoked in its turn a resurgence of religious feeling but also of charitable activities associated with Pietism. This occurred in the last years of the eighteenth and the beginning of the nineteenth century and therefore will be dealt with in a later chapter.

The Protestant clergy

What kind of a person was the clergyman in Germany between the Thirty Years War and the French Revolution? What were his functions in the community, his social status? In both these respects there was a considerable difference between Protestant and Catholic lands. Before the Reformation a sharp division had existed in the educational level and the status of city as opposed to country clergymen. Bishop Wedego of Havelberg had asserted in 1471 that it sufficed for a young man to be ordained priest if he knew the Creed, the Lord's Prayer and enough Latin to read the Mass; he should also 'know about' the sacraments. While the often ignorant and sometimes boorish country clergy at that time could not satisfy the spiritual needs of their flocks, the clergy of the cathedral towns were often too worldly to do so. One of the achievements of the Reformation in Germany was to create a class of educated, even scholarly pastors and to eradicate, at least for a time, the divisions within their body. Because the Protestant clergymen were no longer celibate, they passed on their cultivated tastes and their libraries to their descendants. They generally sought their wives from among their own kind – for economic necessity made it a common practice for widows of clergymen to marry their deceased husband's curate; traditional modes of behaviour were therefore established and the clergy felt themselves a distinct and unique element in society. In the leading areas of the Reformation, Saxony, Württemberg and Nuremberg, educational establishments were set up to perpetuate the work of training enlightened men – the universities of Marburg (1527), Königsberg (1544) and Jena (1548–55), the renowned Tübinger *Stift* (1536) and the *Fürstenschulen* created in their wake, are all part of the institutionalization of the Reformation which had important social consequences. In Württemberg alone out of some 2700 clergymen in the sixteenth century, 1779 are known to have studied at university, 1678 of them at Tübingen.[15] Church visitations were another important innovation in the same direction. The early superintendents found much to do; they set about reforming, instructing, dismissing hangers on, and putting the new pastors' livings on sound economic foundations. They instructed the clergy and left them with 'reading lists' to be studied before the next visit. They introduced them to Luther's catechism to teach the faithful. This drive was imitated by the reforming Council of Trent (1545–63) in the Catholic church and by the Jesuits and the Capuchins, of whom Peter Canisius and Martin of Cochem are perhaps the best known as catechists. As a result of such endeavours, the Lutheran clergy soon enjoyed a high social standing, although their origins could be humble. Melanchthon had been the son of an arms maker, Spalatin of a tanner and Osiander of a smith. In wealthy towns such as Hamburg and Königsberg the city preachers continued to enjoy the highest esteem until well into the eighteenth century, allying themselves in marriage with the patrician families. In Prussia, where social distinctions at the top of the scale were perhaps less pronounced than elsewhere, it was by no means unknown for noblemen to marry clergymen's daughters. When, for example, the nineteenth century Prussian Minister of War, Albrecht von Roon, married into a *Pastorenfamilie*, there was no hint of condescension on his part. Among the so-called Baltic barons further east, the acceptability of such marriages was long established and continued to be so down to our time, the pastors being regarded as part of the 'upper class'.[16] In Prussia the court preachers might even be ennobled. An interesting and fairly typical case is that of Benjamin Ursinus. The preachers to the Hohenzollern court belonged to the Reformed church since the conversion of the Elector to Calvinism in 1613. Ursinus's father, a Silesian, had found refuge from Counter-Reformation persecution at the court of the Leszczynski family at Lissa, one of the few remaining havens in Catholic eastern Europe. The family later moved to St Peter's church in Danzig, and Benjamin became a preacher at Cologne, and later at Berlin, where he married a Dutch girl. He took part with Dr Jablonski in the attempt to form a union between the Lutheran and Reformed churches, and was ennobled in 1705 as Ursinus von Bär. Through his son's marriage he became connected with such distinguished families as the Kleists, Bonins, Puttkamers and Stojenthins. He enjoyed the princely salary of 1950 *taler*, which he won by a shrewd mixture of unction and hard bargaining. His style of address to the king suggests that, whatever society thought of him, in his own eyes he was a man of consequence: 'Obwohl die Schrift (I. Tim. 5: 17 und 18) denen, die lang am Wort gearbeitet, doppelte Ehre und Salarium zuerkennet, verlange ich doch nichts zur äusseren Pracht oder Üppigkeit und Überfluss, sondern nur eine genügliche Substanz' ['Although Holy Writ (1 Tim. 5: 17, 18) would grant double honours and salary to those who have toiled long to preach the Word, I ask nothing for external glory, luxury or excess, but only a modest provision'].[17]

By comparison with other clerics, this was a lot of money, 50 per cent more than any other incumbent enjoyed before the nineteenth century. Cathedral preachers commanded at most 600 *taler* at that time, while parish clergy earned between 150 and 300 *taler*, depending on their parishes, though they had their incomes supplemented by gifts and perquisites. The payment of parish clergy up to the nineteenth century was based on the income from a benefice, which might include a farm as well as a garden, on tithes and on the surplus fees or payments made for baptizing, marrying or burying parishioners, which were often in kind. With the encroachment of the secular authorities on church land in the seventeenth century, the value of benefices declined all over Germany, and while clergymen after the Reformation had been fairly well off economically, this was not so in general by the eighteenth century. Tithes were abolished in the nineteenth century, either as part of early nineteenth century reform movements, or in 1848, and the state gradually took over the payment of the clergy in money instead of in kind shortly after. In many parts of Germany prior to this a candidate for a post, whether a parish or as a court or town preacher, would probably only be successful if he promised to support the widow and children of his predecessor.[18]

But Ursinus's financial and social standing and that of other Calvinist court preachers whose sons followed them in their office, Cochius, Ancillon or Jablonski, did not lie in the fact that they were important churchmen, but that they were personal ministers of the monarch, instruments of his policy. In this respect the Calvinist Prussian court preachers are a unique class. The leading churchmen in Lutheran areas, and the superintendents and chief superintendents in Saxony or

Württemberg, enjoyed considerable authority within their own sphere, but in the seventeenth century they lost the special position which they had enjoyed as counsellor, guide and friend of princes. Indeed, noblemen now rarely sent their younger sons into the church. Clergymen, as contemporaries noted, were everywhere less highly esteemed than previously. 'Vornehmer, reicher Leute Kinder sind nunmehr zu hoch zu Theologie und Kirchendienst' ['The children of the quality and the rich are too high now for theology and the service of the Lord'], noted the theologian Theodor Grossgebauer in his *Wächterstimmen aus dem verstöhrten Zion* (*Voices of the Watchmen From the Ruins of Zion*) (1661). Instead they chose the service of a prince, the army or the law. In the eighteenth century the inclination to regard the clergy as a socially inferior class was even more pronounced, although individuals still commanded respect for their learning. Theology was the best endowed faculty at university and from a practical point of view it provided gifted young men without means an opportunity to escape from a narrow environment. But because so many sought this solution, the number of candidates for the ministry was far too great for the places available. The majority were condemned to the social humiliation of spending a lifetime as tutor to noble families or miserably paid teacher in some provincial school. Portraits abound in literature – notably during the *Sturm und Drang* period (Lenz, *Der Hofmeister*) – and in memoirs: Johanna Schopenhauer, the philosopher's mother, recorded a wonderfully feeling portrait of her own clumsy but able pedagogue.[19]

Regrettably little is known about daily life among the parish clergy before the nineteenth century: much work remains to be done here. In the few important cities which survived the decline of town life in early modern Germany the chief dignitaries of the Lutheran church enjoyed great authority and social prestige, not least in their capacity as inspectors of schools. In eighteenth century Danzig 'das damals sehr gefürchtete Oberhaupt der Geistlichkeit' ['the greatly feared head of the clergy'], Dr Heller, ruled his clergymen with the sternest of hands. Should a young cleric dare to be seen wearing furs in the icy winter, 'Die Hoffnung, jemals eine Pfarre zu erhalten, war für ihn immer verloren, denn Doktor Heller achtete ein solches Vergehen der ärgsten Ketzerei gleich. Nicht nur die Kandidaten, auch die schon angestellten Prediger, und sogar ihre Frauen, durften an Theater, Konzert und ähnliche Vergnügungen gar nicht denken' ['The hope of ever getting a parish was lost for ever, for Dr Heller regarded such a *faux pas* in terms of dire heresy. Not only the young candidates for the ministry, but those who were already established, and their wives, dare not even consider going to theatres, concerts and such entertainments'].[20] Such posts were, however, few in number by the middle of the eighteenth century. Most clergymen were appointed by the prince or the local landowner, not, as in Catholic areas, by the bishop. Much of their time was spent in their capacity as the arm of the secular power. As Seckendorff declared in his *Teutscher Fürstenstaat* (1656): 'Die Hohe weltliche Obrigkeiten, welche niemanden denn den höchsten Gott über sich haben ... auch in geistlichen und Kirchensachen ... das Regiment zu führen haben, lernen wir aus dem Wort Gottes, welches diesfalls keine Ausnahme machet, sondern alles der Obrigkeit untergibt; ['The sovereign rulers, with no one over them but God, have authority in spiritual and ecclesiastical matters also. ... This we learn from God's own Word, which brooks no exception but consigns everything and everybody to the charge of the (secular) authority'].[21] The pastor was expected to appoint the village *Vogt* or bailiff, to supervise tax returns, conduct a census if necessary, be responsible for the school and even organize such menial tasks as repairs and cleaning in the village and maintenance of the public ways. Herder, himself a clergyman, commented bitterly on the low standing of his kind: 'A minister is only entitled to exist now under state control and by the authority of the prince, as a moral teacher, a farmer, a list-maker, a secret agent of the police.'[22] The underlying causes of this were the decline in religious belief generally and the reputation for doctrinal wrangling among clergymen – in the late eighteenth century the celebrated quarrel between Pastor Goeze of Hamburg and Lessing confirmed many intelligent people in their prejudice against churchmen. The memoirs of Magister Laukhard, published in the 1790s, gave a vivid account of quarrels and scandals at parish level, and of victimization of rivals, which gained wide credence.[23] Young men in the *Sturm und Drang* period in the 1770s and 1780s were critical of the clergy's subordination to the secular power and of their failure to protest at the tyranny of individual princes. The general educational standard of parish clergy was, outside Swabia, less high than in former times. The decline of the universities, especially of Leipzig, Jena and Giessen, as well as the general laxness of examiners, allowed candidates for orders to leave university without the intellectual training to carry on the hallowed traditions of scholarship of the Lutheran church.

But in the long run, and speaking in the broadest terms, the most important factor in the social evolution of the Protestant clergy in eighteenth century Germany is that, in contrast with the Catholics, they did not retain their spiritual authority over their flocks. The Catholic parish priest might be ignorant, he might be worldly or simply inadequate, but he was appointed by his ecclesiastical superiors primarily to care for the spiritual needs of the people. Of course, in Catholic territories he filled a secular role as well, but this was secondary to his spiritual capacity, and the faithful retained a respect for him. The relationship of the Protestant clergy to their secular superiors and the rationalistic approach to religion of many pastors in the mid and late eighteenth century set them apart from the preoccupations of ordinary people, as is illustrated by the Mecklenburg lady who enjoyed talking with the local pastor on all sorts of subjects but always avoided religion: 'Dat versteit he nich' ['He doesn't understand that'], she said.[24] On the other hand, the cultural achievement of the Protestant clergy in Germany as a social group was second to none. They were responsible for pioneering new methods of husbandry in their gardens and farms, they nurtured and developed the splendid musical traditions of the sixteenth and seventeenth century, both in their churches and in their homes. The *Pfarrhaus* was often a little island of culture in remote areas of Germany, and it was also the nursery of some of Germany's finest thinkers and writers: from Gryphius in the seventeenth to Lessing, Herder, Wieland, Claudius and Lenz, Schelling and the Schlegels in the eighteenth, and Burckhardt and Nietzsche in the nineteenth century.

2 THE CATHOLIC CHURCH

It is still today more difficult to write an informed account of the Catholic church and Catholic life in Germany than it is of the Protestant churches. To some extent Catholic life in this period is a casualty of the 'Prussian view of history', which trained successive generations of scholars to neglect regional history in favour of national history, and which helped to establish the assumption that the Catholic areas, being less open to modern thought than the Protestant, were therefore less 'relevant' to German history. An older and more valid prejudice against the methods employed by Counter-Reformation princes to reconvert their subjects to Catholicism, especially in Austria, made a black and white picture of the Catholic church broadly acceptable. German historians in the nineteenth and early twentieth centuries were often prepared to overlook the fact that the policies of persecution of those of different faith, which they condemned as typically Catholic in Austria and Bohemia under Emperor Ferdinand II or Leopold or Archbishop Firmian of Salzburg, were enacted with at least equal fervour in the same periods by James I of England, Cromwell or Queen Anne. It would, of course, be pointless to try to justify Ferdinand II by citing the case of Cromwell: what is necessary is to try and go beyond the stereotyped portrait of the Counter-Reformation in Germany and of religious life in subsequent years to understand the character of Catholic life as it appeared to contemporaries.

So much remains to be done in this field that it will not be possible to give more than an approximation. The history of the different religious orders, which played so vital a role in the Counter-Reformation and which helped to sustain religious life in wide areas throughout the rest of the life of the Holy Roman Empire, has been studied in detail, but not in recent decades. Many of these studies tend to be occasionally uncritical, at times positively hagiographic. There is plenty of material available; the annual reports to Rome made by each head of Jesuit houses, for example, are as yet unprinted. They promise valuable insight into the most neglected field of all, day-to-day pastoral life, as well as primary education in the seventeenth century. Fr. Oorschot's reference to the diaconess movement in the Rhineland in his life of the Jesuit poet, Friedrich von Spee, whose collected works he is editing, or E. Gatz's work on the later period, *Kirche und Krankenpflege im 19. Jht.* (1971), give some indication how modern research at local level might substantially modify our picture of how Catholic life and institutions impinged on society in general.

Catholic life 1648–1806

In the century before 1648 the Catholic church had experienced far-reaching reforms in response to the shock and challenge of the Lutheran Reformation. Although the political aspect was much in evidence throughout, there is no doubt but that the spiritual regeneration of Catholic life was profound and lasting. The impulse towards reform, both in those few lands which had remained faithful to the old church, and those which were to be won back in the course of the Counter-Reformation, as this movement was called, had come from outside. A leading German authority in the field, E. W. Zeeden, has expressed the view that the role of St Ignatius Loyola, founder of the Jesuits, was as important in this movement as Luther or Calvin had been for the Reformation.[25] The Jesuits came into Germany, principally the Rhineland, Bavaria and the Austrian territories, from the Netherlands and Spain.[26] They received much encouragement from the Habsburg princes, the most zealous of whom usually had Jesuit confessors. Other new orders, the Capuchins, Piarists, Servites and Barnabites, worked alongside the Jesuits, often caring for the spiritual and material life of the less fortunate social groups. Their efforts were supported by the papal nuncios, but not in general by the

Catholic hierarchy. There were of course striking exceptions, one such being Bishop von Galen of Münster, not for the last time in the history of that distinguished family. Bishop J. B. von Galen was a redoubtable prince on any reckoning. He succeeded as Bishop of Münster the Wittelsbach son of Duke William V of Bavaria, who had held the sees of Münster, Liège and Paderborn, as well as being archbishop of Cologne. He was selected by a chapter weary of Bavarian domination and pluralism, and fought vigorously against clerical ignorance and the lack of discipline among religious orders, as well as caring for neglected or deserted parishes. He managed to combine his role as spiritual leader of his flock with his activities as diplomat and captain of an army. His army was renowned for its artillery and he used it with some success against the expansionist Netherlands. His military successes were nullified by Imperial and Bavarian diplomacy, but his spiritual reforms in the diocese of Münster were long lasting, and helped to establish Münster as a stronghold of Catholic life for many years to come.

Those who desired the reform of the Catholic church after the Reformation faced a formidable task. This was not only because of the advance of Protestantism, but also because territorial rulers and the feudal upper classes in the Catholic regions had long been accustomed to regarding the cathedral deaneries and other prebendaries as the material basis of their own privileged existence. Highborn prelates were simply not prepared to accept the decrees of the Council of Trent (1545–63), which provided both the guidelines and the most powerful impetus to the spiritual renewal of the Church.[27] The ignorance of the clergy, which the Jesuit apostle, St Peter Canisius, described so forcefully in his letters, was a serious obstacle to improvement at parish level. The leading figures of the Counter-Reformation therefore imitated the Protestant reformers' concern for education; however, it took them at least a century to build up seminaries and schools. It was significant for the future of the Catholic clergy and intelligentsia that the majority of these seminaries for the training of priests and the Catholic boarding schools were situated in small towns or in the country, where opportunity for contact with educated minds and men of different allegiances was negligible. It was difficult to foster the rise of a Catholic educated class comparable with that of the Protestant, whether Lutheran or reformed, on account of the celibate character of the clergy. The majority of priests, and in Bavaria and the Tyrol even of abbots and priors, were men of humble origin. Such education as they acquired, excellent though it might be, was not passed on to the next generation. The strong cultural influence of the Protestant

Pfarrhaus or vicarage, which was such a crucially important factor in the rise of the middle classes of central and northern Germany, had no equivalent in Catholic areas. Clerical celibacy increased the respect of the parishioners for the priest or member of a religious order who cared for their spiritual needs, but it isolated him too. An individual priest who was a man of learning, who took an informed interest, say, in archaeology or local history, would find fellow enthusiasts to converse or correspond with, but he could not make his presbytery a cultural force in the community at large. The hierarchy was in a different position, especially the bishops and abbots of the Rhine and Main valleys. They were cultured and travelled men, for they were aristocrats, connected by birth with the best families of the state or neighbouring countries. Catholic culture in these years was an aristocratic culture. The residences built by the prince bishops, the mansions erected by their nephews and relatives who held a sinecure in the cathedral, and the great monasteries such as Melk or Göttweig on the Danube or St Blaise in the Black Forest, housed treasures of art and witnessed musical performances which betokened a sophistication of taste among the inmates, equal to that of the most cultivated secular princes of their age.

As elsewhere in Europe, the education of the Catholic upper classes lay predominantly in the hands of the Jesuits. Their strength in the different regions lay in contacts made with convinced local Catholic families: such families became patrons of the order and sent their sons to their schools. The Jesuits in their turn welcomed local boys, including the less well off, as potential candidates for admission to the order. They thus became acceptable to the local Catholic population.[28] The *Leopoldinum* at Breslau, the *Tricoronatum* at Cologne, and the Jesuit college at Dillingen which eventually included a boarding school and university, had many distinguished pupils in the course of their history, and they were just three among many such foundations. In contrast with the somewhat haphazard if often excellent Protestant schools, where so much depended on individual teachers and on the local environment, Jesuit education was highly organized and standardized. It was inspired by a profound belief in the importance of the task: *puerilis institutio est renovatio mundi,* and was based on the 1591 programme known as the *Ratio atque institutio studiorum.* Single minded in their desire to mould the whole person of the pupil, the Jesuits were sufficiently flexible to adapt themselves to the particular local requirements. As one commentator put it: 'La société a rarement réalisé tout ce qu'elle a vu, elle s'est contentée de faire ce qu'elle a pu' ['The society has not often realized all that it envisaged but has contented itself with achieving what has lain within its power'].[29] The Jesuits set themselves to win control of the faculty of arts as well as theology in the universities where the order was taught, despite the occasional opposition of the local bishop and the steadfast hostility of the cathedral chapters in towns such as Würzburg, Bamberg or Fulda. Apart from their very great importance in the development of Catholic education, these universities gradually became centres for the spread of the Counter-Reformation through the efforts of the Society of Jesus. Thus Dillingen and Ingolstadt became the focal points of the Counter-Reformation in Swabia and Bavaria, Würzburg and Bamberg for Franconia, and Fulda for the hostile Lutheran lands of Saxony and Hesse.[30]

Besides acting as university lecturers, prefects and masters of study for adjacent Jesuit boarding schools, the members of the order also pursued missionary activities in the surrounding countryside. They preached in the village churches as well as the university chapels, they took on the care of the sick and of prisoners, following the example of St Peter Canisius at Ingolstadt in the sixteenth century. Friedrich von Spee, who died a victim to the plague at an early age in 1631, combined the offices of university teacher and confessor to soldiers stricken by the plague and to the 'witches'. Bitter attacks were made by members of the university of Ingolstadt on the Jesuits for turning the students' prison into an infirmary; these critics failed to appreciate the force of the Jesuit ideal of piety combined with practical religion.[31]

The Jesuits are often charged, by their co-religionists as well as others, with being excessively preoccupied with the souls of the great and wealthy. It is certainly true that the order has always known how to win itself friends in high places, and has in its turn been attractive to the powerful and educated classes, who admire the intelligence and cosmopolitan culture of its members. It should be said, however, that in the Rhineland and possibly in other parts of Germany also, they undertook pioneering work in the instruction of the poorer classes and can be regarded as being among the first in the field of primary education in this area.[32] Another aspect of their activity, which had a long-lasting effect on the spiritual and on the social life of the church as a whole, was the special stress they laid on the rite of first communion from about 1680 onwards.[39] The Marian congregations which were founded for laymen about the same time, and which attracted the membership of many students, helped to spread their own zeal over a wide social and geographical area (all the victorious commanders over the Turks at Vienna in 1683 were members).[34] Such practices gave the church a new sense of solidarity which embraced the powerful and educated as well as the humbler souls: village churches, which now were rebuilt in the baroque manner in the late seventeenth and early eighteenth century or which had, as it were, a mantle of baroque art thrown over them, were not different in style nor in message but only in size from the great monastery and pilgrimage churches which became the centre of Catholic worship in this age.[35]

Nineteenth century German historians of the so-called liberal Protestant school liked to picture German Catholics as being in thrall to Rome. Curiously enough, although the Holy Roman Empire was by tradition and by nature a Catholic institution, and all its executive offices were held by Catholics, even after 1648, the relationship between the German hierarchy and Rome was not at all cordial. The *Reich* constitution as enshrined in the Treaties of Westphalia ensured a greater mutual tolerance between the confessions than could possibly be acceptable to the Counter-Reformation papacy. Of course, the attitude of a Catholic to other Christian churches depended on where he lived and worked. A Catholic bishop or abbot attending the *Reichstag* sessions at Regensburg, meeting his Lutheran colleagues at a reception given at the house of the counts of Thurn and Taxis on the other side of the town from the assembly hall, would regard Protestants in quite another manner than would a cleric at Rome, who might never set eyes on a Lutheran or a Calvinist in the flesh. The German ecclesiastical princes knew that the *Reich* could only function if a modicum of tolerance was observed. They also knew the benefits which the Holy Roman Empire conferred on them, and were pledged in their own interest to support it. It became the practice in the seventeenth century for the confessions to vote separately at *Reichstag* sessions on most major issues. This was known as *Itio in partes,* a pairing off of the *Corpus Evangelicorum* and the *Corpus Catholicorum.* The division into Catholic and Evangelical parties was something which now had to be taken for granted: accommodation by both sides was necessary in order to preserve what almost all the Imperial estates desired during this period, or at least up to the late eighteenth century – the preservation of the *status quo.* To German ecclesiastics this state of affairs may not have been ideal, but it was workable; the Counter-Reformation papacy could hardly be expected to view things in the same light. Many practices common in the German Catholic church must have seemed distinctly irregular to Rome: the existence of mixed congregations and chapters in parts of north Germany, the alternation between Catholic and Lutheran bishops in the see of Osnabrück, and the accommodation between both sides over the question of mixed marriages. To the many south European clerics and noblemen who thronged to the court of Vienna in the seventeenth and early eighteenth century, German

Catholics must have seemed as good (or as bad) as Protestants.

Just as the rivalries between orthodox Lutheranism and Pietism were more acrimonious than the Protestants' feeling towards the old church, so too the mutual distrust between the pro-papal party and the German clergy as a whole was often more considerable than their hostility towards non-Catholics. The hierarchy in Germany actually ignored vital aspects of the Tridentine Decrees, such as those on episcopal elections. It was not until 1803 that the old oligarchic practice of members of a cathedral chapter choosing one of their number as bishop was ended, and replaced by a more constitutional – and canonical – form of election. The bishops' hostility to the Holy See and the Council of Trent increased when the Pope began to appoint nuncios to aid the cause of reform in Germany. Many of these were astute diplomats, able and willing to command the ear of the secular princes. They soon made their presence doubly unwelcome to the hierarchy by attempting to win powers of dispensation, etc., which normally lay with the bishops. One of the most effective of the nuncios was the Italian, S. A. Tamara, papal nuncio at Cologne from 1687 to 1690. The issue was still a topical one when the ruler of Bavaria, Charles Theodore, re-established a nunciatur in Munich in 1785 to improve pastoral care and to limit the power of the bishops.

The progress of the movement known as the Enlightenment in Catholic lands has attracted much less attention from scholars than that in other parts of Germany. In some general works one even gets the impression that, apart from the reforms undertaken by the Austrian rulers (*Josephinism*) and the movement to create a national church associated with the name of the auxiliary bishop of Trier, Febronius, it was not of great moment. This is not the case. Politically, the Enlightenment contributed directly to the ending of privilege, and to the secularization of the ecclesiastical territories in 1803, which in turn precipitated the end of the Holy Roman Empire in 1806. This aspect is fairly well known and accepted. What is much less generally appreciated is the spiritual effect of the new thinking, both of the reforms of Maria Theresa and Joseph II, her son, and the reaction to them, and of the new emphasis on pastoral care instead of ecclesiastical privilege which characterized the reform. This approach is especially marked in the case of the most distinguished enlightened reformers in the church, such as Febronius, whose real name was Nicholas of Hontheim, or Bishop Sailer of Landshut and Bishop Ignatius Sattler of Ingolstadt, both former Jesuits. Their support for reform in the late eighteenth century had a good deal to do with the fact that the titular bishops commonly employed auxiliary bishops and theologians to do their work for them.

These men were generally of burgher origin, and they were university graduates. They had little or no social contact with the aristocratic members of the hierarchy, who even in the latter half of the eighteenth century were not always ordained priests. It was Rome's tolerance of what must have seemed rank abuses to the open-minded and zealous spiritual reformers that gave a distinctly anti-papal character to the Enlightenment in Catholic Germany. It also encouraged tendencies towards a national church which had been mooted in German Catholic circles as far back as the conciliar era and during the Reformation. Many entertained a warm regard for their Protestant acquaintances – this was the period of deep spiritual friendships between members of different confessions – one thinks, for example, of the influence of Matthias Claudius on Princess Galitzin and the convert Count Stolberg, or of the circle around Franz von Fürstenberg in the diocese of Münster in the last decades of the eighteenth century. Catholic enlightened thinkers such as Hontheim, who published his famous work, *De statu ecclesiae,* in 1763, were even prepared to consider waiving the celibacy rule in order to facilitate reunion between the confessions. Although the hierarchy was attracted to the idea of a national church for political reasons (i.e. that it would lessen the influence of the papacy, particularly the power of the papal nuncios) they disapproved of the rest of the reformers' ideas. They tried to exploit Hontheim's work for their own political advantage, but failed in general to appreciate the spiritual power behind them. The bishops accused Hontheim's colleague, auxiliary Bishop Heimes of Mainz, of vengefulness, when he suggested curtailing noble rights to appointments of bishops and abbots. Heimes, similar to many men of enlightened views, was practical as well as logical. He declared that if Catholic princes and noblemen wanted posts for their unmarried sons and daughters, they ought not to be dependent on ecclesiastical benefices and places in convents for them. It ought to be possible to provide for them in another way, without, as it were, spiritual strings. The current arrangement of putting unsuited men and women of noble birth into influential positions in the church was a grave source of scandal.

Catholic enlightened thinkers rejected the idea that because practices were hallowed by centuries, this was sufficient justification for perpetuating abuse. Had the hierarchy as a body shared the desire of their subordinates for spiritual reform, the ecclesiastical territories might have found greater support among the Catholic population during the Napoleonic era. As it was, a new type of prelate succeeded to office in the nineteenth century. Usually of burgher or peasant origin (especially in Austria and Bavaria), he did not have the cosmopolitan manners and wide culture of his predecessors, but he was first and foremost a churchman, which they had not been.[36]

In no territory did the Enlightenment have such a profound effect on religious life as in Austria. The two brothers, Joseph II and his successor Leopold II, were the principal authors of ecclesiastical reform in this state. Joseph became the object of the most bitter attack for his alleged destruction of religious life, especially because of his dissolution of monasteries. His motives were thoroughly utilitarian. He was unable to appreciate the importance of contemplative orders in the life of the church, and dissolved these and many other types of religious houses as being useless to the community. Only those monks and nuns who cared for the sick, the poor and the aged or who taught in schools were permitted to continue as such. Many of the rest were directed into parish work, and it was here that the positive aspects of his drastic measures may be found. Joseph created several hundred new parishes in the course of his reign. In Lower Austria and Styria alone they numbered 416, for he believed that no one should be more than an hour's walk from his parish church. The Emperor was prompted in this by his desire to have trained local officials: parish priests now began to execute the administrative tasks of the state which their Protestant counterparts had long been doing in Saxony or in Prussia. The Council of Trent had tried to persuade parish priests to keep registers, but not always successfully. Joseph succeeded by making the surplice fees into payment for these duties. Recent research by Reinhardt and others has shown how the Enlightenment fostered liturgical reform, and was responsible for the truly modern idea of lay participation in the mass and other services: one of the fruits of this was the great German mass, *Hier liegt vor Deiner Majestät*, by Michael Haydn, brother of Joseph.[37] However, the populace in Austria, unlike the clergy and the officials, took violent exception to their Emperor's well-meant efforts. They were incensed at seeing their processions curtailed, their pilgrimages frowned upon, at being told to abandon 'irrational devotions', such as saying their rosary at mass. In some rural areas resistance was resolute and protracted. In consequence Austrian (and Bavarian) Catholicism tended to be of two kinds – either the rational and somewhat sceptical religion of the educated classes, or the frankly emotional but nonetheless often deeply convinced belief of the masses. This division was modified during the last years of the period by the movement associated with the Redemptorist Clemens Maria Hofbauer in Vienna, who had started life as a baker's boy. As a priest he created a new concept of pastoral care in parish life and aroused a keen response among the laity. The resurgence of spiritual life which he prompted – and which was also in part a reaction to Josephinism – attracted a number of leading German Romantics to Vienna, among them the convert Friedrich Schlegel, and Zacharias Werner, whose flamboyant sermons became a feature of Viennese life. The influence of this was far reaching but belongs more properly to the nineteenth century and will be discussed fully later.

The picture drawn here of Catholic life in the century and a half after the great war is fragmentary and in certain points perhaps hypothetical; it is possible that at some future date I will be forced to alter it radically in the light of new work. It is also possible that the rather unsatisfactory nature of what is presented here will tempt scholars to undertake work in this neglected field, and one for which a great deal of material lies ready to be discovered and evaluated.

Chapter 7
Army life

The conduct of war in sixteenth century Germany lay in the hands of mercenaries. This remained the case long after the Thirty Years War, despite a change in contemporary ideas on the function and character of the army in the state. At the turn of the sixteenth century, many rulers had tried to reanimate the old medieval idea of the military levy (*Landesaufgebot*), believing this to be more economic and more reliable than a mercenary army. Maximilian, Duke and later Elector of Bavaria, had personally supervised the training of local militia between 1595 and 1615 to defend his territory. The thirtieth, tenth, fifth or third man of those fit to fight were picked and equipped to be trained each Sunday in the use of arms.[1] Special rewards were given to those skilled in shooting, and the granting of citizenship was made dependent on the applicant possessing such skills. In 1609 Duke Henry Julius of Brunswick had demanded that all his subjects be ready to serve in the army if necessary; the rulers of Hesse and the Palatinate followed his example; in Brandenburg 16 000 men were called up, in Saxony 15 000. But the communes sent their least able men, 'unbrauchbare Gecken' ['useless jackanapes'], as one Saxon inspection report put it.[2] The war proved the inadequacy of such troops, the Bavarians in particular making a very poor showing in defence of the land against the Swedes. The German and foreign princes gradually had ever greater recourse to hired soldiers. The mercenaries' power developed in the course of the war, since they alone were capable of prolonging the fighting, and it was in their interest that it should go on. A typical mercenary leader not only had absolute charge of the troops he recruited, he was also responsible for the administrative side of fighting. The colonel of a regiment was out to make money, an entrepreneur, who might win a title as well. The most obvious though not entirely typical case of entrepreneurial success is Wallenstein, but there were many different kinds of leaders. There was Bernard of Weimar, member of a ruling house, the imperial general Tilly, aggrieved to climb no higher in the social ladder than a count of the Holy Roman Empire while his colleague and rival Wallenstein became a duke and, in contemporary terms, a millionaire to boot,[3] and Derfflinger, the Austrian craftsman's son who became a count of the Holy Roman Empire and commander of the Prussian army. Gerhard Oestreich aptly terms these men 'military merchants', and their captains at their side as 'petty entrepreneurs'.[4] Ethical concepts such as loyalty or honour, or indeed patriotism, had no place in their ranks. The mercenary leader made a contractual agreement, known as a capitulation, with the territorial prince whom he served for so many years, or perhaps only months. It was a business arrangement, nothing more. Derfflinger once refused to execute a command of the Great Elector who employed him: it was not, he argued, in the capitulation. At the end of the stipulated time, or earlier if the contract had been broken by either side, he renewed it or went elsewhere, not infrequently to the other side. Nor were his men bound to the colonel mercenary leader by loyalty, although the strong personality which such individuals generally possessed created a sense of attachment beyond that which men usually feel for those who provide them with their livelihood. They probably followed him at the end of a term of service as being the most likely source of income for their future.

The social composition of German armies changed considerably between the sixteenth and eighteenth centuries. Under the *Landsknechte* of Renaissance times, soldiering had been a profession; the men had felt themselves part of a kind of corporation, much as craftsmen or peasants were, even if their way of life made them rough, or indeed even barbarous creatures. However, the mercenary soldier of the great war was usually the dregs of society, or, as happened in the last decade and a half, the war brutalized those noblemen and peasants who had drifted into the armies after being made homeless by pillaging and burning. 'Es haftete am Soldatenleben das ganze Jahrhundert lang der Makel des Entgleisten oder Untauglichen zu bürgerlicher Beschäftigung und Ehrbarkeit'. ['The whole century long the soldier's life had the reputation of that of one who had gone off the rails, who was not fit for the life or work of an honest citizen'].[5] The soldier's life was most insecure; regiments which had been together for years could be disbanded overnight, if the military entrepreneur went bankrupt, or if he decided to retire after making his fortune. It is not surprising that the mercenaries tried to make the most of the opportunities offered to enrich themselves. In the early years of the war plundering was usually punishable by death, as it was also in the Swedish army while Gustavus Adolphus was alive. In the last years discipline collapsed and punishment was rarely enforced. The most brutal were usually the camp followers who had no regular income; they and the soldiers commonly plundered the bodies of the dead on the battlefield and murdered the wounded for their possessions. The latter would possibly have died anyway, for there was virtually no provision for care of the wounded and sick. Even in the eighteenth century the military profession was regarded outside Prussia as a kind of a haven for social misfits. In 1769 the Elector of Bavaria decreed that the following be sent in to the army: 'Vaganten und Müssiggänger überhaupt, sonderbar aber die Dienst- und Herrnlos Bursche, herumgehende Schreiber, Studenten und Jäger, item sowohl inn- als ausländische Handwerksbursch, welche ohne Legitimation, oder vor der Zeit aus dem Dienst trettende Ehehalten, und nicht minder auch andere liederlich, ungehorsam und incorrigible Leut' ['Vagrants and layabouts, but especially the lads without service or master, wandering scribes, students and huntsmen, similarly all native and foreign apprentice boys who are without papers or who have left their service before time, and also all good-for-nothing, disobedient and incorrigible persons'].[6]

Mercenary leaders were usually noblemen, who could stake the limited capital, men and provisions to be had from their lands in the hope of increasing the stake many times over. Such were, besides Wallenstein, Piccolomini and Montecuccoli, familiar to readers of Schiller's *Wallenstein*, who became princes of the Holy Roman Empire, and Aldringen, Gallas and Werth, who became counts. Although a number were born commoners and rose to the highest ranks, such as Derfflinger, Mercy and Sparr, this became rare as the century progressed. Then and later the highest posts were reserved for members of the ruling houses and their social circle, the high nobility. A striking number of great European generals came from these ranks: Princes Maurice and Henry of Orange, the Great Elector, Charles of Lorraine, and in the following century the inimitable Eugene of Savoy, Leopold of Anhalt-Dessau, independent-minded soldier servant of the Kings of Prussia till he died, still active, aged eighty, in 1747, and Max

Emmanuel of Bavaria. Such leaders, wrote G. A. Böckler, author of *Schola militaris moderna, Neue Kriegs-Schule* (1665), the leading military manual of the time, were distinguished for their 'Kriegserfahrenheit, Witz und Geschicklichkeit, dazu ein heroisches Gemüt und ein unverzagtes Herz' ['military experience, quick wits and flexibility, courage and endurance'].[7] Certainly the strategy and tactics of the baroque age, with the slowness of movement and the rigidity of the canons of military thinking, offered a tremendous opportunity to the individual commander to display his genius: Gustavus Adolphus, the Great Elector, and Prince Eugene gained legendary renown, as did Wallenstein (though he did not share their popularity), for their active intervention and personal leadership on the field of battle.

Bitter experience in the great war brought home to German princes the high cost of the mercenaries. The Treaties of Westphalia acknowledged the military sovereignty of the prince in his own land, and encouraged the notion of a standing army. Just before the war a new concept of citizen defence, as expounded in late sixteenth century Holland by the prominent jurist Justus Lipsius, had begun to be discussed in some German states by those who had travelled in Holland or who had served under Prince Maurice of Orange or his cousin William Ludwig of Nassau. As military leaders they exemplified the idea of an officer responsible for the welfare of his men, who repay him with devotion and loyalty.[8] The war brought these ideas to nought, but something of the new thinking reappeared in the armies of the rulers of Brandenburg. The Great Elector was much influenced by the country of his first wife, Louise of Orange. It was the Hohenzollerns who revolutionized the legal and social position of the army officer and many states attempted to follow suit. The relationship between ruler and officer was no longer a contractual one: the prince was bound to defend the state and the subjects committed to his care and they in turn must obey the commands he gives in their own and his interest. 'Dem Fürsten standen Untertanen gegenüber, keine Vertragspartner, auch im militärischen Bereich' ['The prince had subjects, not contractual partners, in the military sphere as well'].[9]

The commander of a standing army was usually a member of a ruling house, often of the territorial princely family itself; he was generally chief of a regiment by his twentieth year, a general five years later. The ordinary officer rose very slowly. He was forced to exist as a lieutenant on meagre pay, until, twenty years or so after his entry, he became a captain and could pay his debts. However, his promotion was virtually automatic after that time if his health held and he did his job with reasonable competence. The actual term officer came into use about

1600 for all those who held some military office, including the NCOs. The gradual distinction between the latter and those holding a commission emerged in the course of the century, but it was not until 1713 that the articles of war for 'NCOs and soldiers' appeared in Brandenburg-Prussia, which did not apply to subaltern and senior officers. The sharp distinction which was already existent in practice was graphically described in 1669 in Grimmelshausen's satiric vision of the army as a tree: the NCOs and common soldiers were represented by the lower branches, above whom towered the main part of the tree on which officers from ensign upwards were perched. The trunk which separated them was '[mit] seltsamer Seife der Missgunst geschmieret, also dass kein Kerl, er sei denn von Adel, weder durch Mannheit, Geschicklichkeit noch Wissenschaft hinaufsteigen konnte, Gott geb wie er auch klettern/könnte, denn er war glätter poliert als eine marmorne Säule oder Stählerner Spiegel' ['smeared with the strange soap of ill will, so that no fellow, unless of noble birth, could climb higher, neither by virtue of his bravery, his ability or his knowledge, however God gave him to climb, because it was polished more smoothly than a marble pillar or a steel mirror'].[10] External marks distinguished the two elements from 1707 onwards in Prussia, when the then Crown Prince, Frederick William, demanded that all officers wear sash and gorget. Uniform was introduced during his reign, among other reasons to encourage home textile manufacture.

But the nobility for whom officers' posts were almost exclusively reserved had shown themselves loath to profit from the opportunity. Many of the estates fought a bitter struggle between the Treaties of Westphalia and the end of the century against accepting a standing army which must increase the personal power of the ruler. In some areas the estates managed to keep control of supplies and therefore determine the size of the army; in Prussia they were foiled by the dexterous policies of the Great Elector. His grandson, King Frederick William I, turned the honour of being an officer into a singular burden. The order issued in the form of a circular in 1717 gave the sovereign the right to grant or withhold permission for an officer to marry. In fact Prussian officers were discouraged from marrying long into the nineteenth century; their salaries were very low until they reached middle life and few had the alternative means to enable them to marry: the illustrious Helmut von Moltke was almost fifty before he could afford to do so. Usually a Prussian nobleman or *Junker* served twenty to twenty-five years, then retired to his estate to farm and to marry. However, in the course of Frederick William's reign, the Prussian nobility began to realize the advantages of an army career. They were a poor nobility, with some few exceptions; the army offered them not only the favour of the sovereign and a secure post, it also made them members of a caste within which there was real equality. All officers up to and including the rank of colonel wore the same uniform; so did the king. Frederick William was not personally fond of aristocrats, nor they of him, but in Otto Büsch's words, he had a sharper eye for social realities than his more famous son, and was well aware that they were the only suitable estate on which to base the military system which he planned for Prussia.[11] His was a down-to-earth assessment of the situation; Frederick II on the other hand credited the nobility with exclusive intellectual and moral qualities and based the Prussian tradition of the superiority of the military over the civilian element on this assumption.

In the rest of Germany things were different. In Austria and Bavaria the native nobility showed little inclination to serve, unless as an outlet for 'verlorene Söhne' ['lost sons'] or 'missratene Sprossen' ['wayward offspring'].[12] They preferred to seek a career in the state or court offices, and leave the army to members of the *Reich* nobility, or to foreigners, among whom Prince Eugene of Savoy is the most famous example. Frenchmen and Italians were so common in the Bavarian army that the Elector Max Emmanuel complained at the beginning of the War of the Spanish Succession that he had scarcely a dozen members of his own nobility there. The senior posts in the Austrian and Bavarian armies were the preserve of the high nobility: of 157 field marshals in the eighteenth century Austrian army, thirty-two were members of ruling dynasties and seventy-six came from the imperial nobility – i.e. German, not Austrian – and only thirty-five came from the minor aristocracy.[13] There is a great deal we do not know about the social composition of the armies of the German states, apart from those of Prussia, Austria, Bavaria and Mainz, where conditions were somewhat similar to Bavaria. Modern military historians warn against assuming that Prussia was typical for the rest of the *Reich.* True, certain features of the Prussian cantonal organization were imitated. The Bavarians tried to copy it, to raise the abysmally low educational level of their troops, and to abolish the sale of commissions. A cadet corps was founded in 1756 and a high standard of education achieved here, but in general the Bavarian rulers lacked the necessary energy to implement their reforming projects, and continued to use the army to accommodate antisocial elements. The appointment to the command of Charles Theodore's energetic *aide-de-camp,* the shrewd and incisive American, Benjamin Thompson, later Count Rumford, came in 1789. Although he was full of constructive ideas, such as putting his men to civic duties – he had the English Garden in Munich created by them from a marsh – his appointment came too late for him to make the necessary changes before the French wars exposed the gross inefficiency of the troops, and he resigned.

What was the soldier's life like in this period in Germany? Here, too, we have much detailed information about Prussia, particularly from the eighteenth century, which is not valid in detail for the rest of the country. The Prussian rulers set out to organize Prussian society for the purpose of producing an efficient army. 'Die preussiche Armee war Anlass, Mittel und Basis zugleich für die Errichtung, Ausbildung und Aufrechterhaltung dieses sozialen Systems' ['The Prussian army was the occasion, the means, and at the same time basis of the formation, development and maintenance of this social system'],[14] wrote Büsch on the opening page of his brilliant study. The main burden fell on the countryside, on the peasant most heavily of all. During this century the percentage of those under arms rose from 4 per cent to almost 17 per cent of those fit for service, and the military budget rose to two thirds of total expenditure, thus exceeding the revenue collected from the provinces. The nobility paid feudal cavalry dues (*Pferdegeld*) and the burghers provided the excise. In Prussia the town was rigorously separated from the countryside; the peasant had to pay excise on his wares coming into the market and on what he bought there and he also provided war contributions, transport in time of war, and fodder for the horses. Frederick William dissolved the old militias, declaring it to be the will of God for young men to serve their prince with their possessions and their blood. In the early years of his reign the recruiting officer was the most feared man in the kingdom: suicide, mutilation and selling one's possessions to buy oneself off were widely recorded. Similar acts of self-inflicted mutilation occurred in the late eighteenth century among those desperate to get out of the army, yet prohibited from doing so. Soldiers, poor ignorant creatures, were even known to kill a child so as to escape their life of torment by execution – to their simple minds this was a lesser crime than murdering an adult, for the innocent child would go straight to heaven. The recruiting officers attacked students, despite university laws protecting them – many such instances at Halle were given great publicity by the Pietists there – and they blackmailed or tricked unfortunates into enlisting, as Uli Bräker, author of *Der arme Mann in Toggenburg,* was tricked. The following letter speaks for itself; it was written by a young man called Nicholaus Schmidt who had fled to Hamburg to escape the recruiting officers in 1720, and whom his father had begged to return:

Geehrter Herr Vater. Bei meiner heutigen Zuhausekunft finde von demselben vor mir unterschiedliche Briefe, welche ich hiermit in aller Kürze beantworten will und dienet, dass der Herr Vater das Porto woll ersparen, imgleichen das Papier zu was Notwendiges gebrauchen mögen. Wozu dienet, dass er mir das Soldaten-Leben anpräsentieret, er wiss es ja, dass ich die Zeit meines Lebens keine Lust dazu gehabt, viel weniger werde jetzo die Lust dazu bekommen, ich habe bis daher allen Respekt vor dem Vater gehabt, auch mich allzeit gegen demselben so aufgeführet als ich zu tun schuldig gewesen, nunmehre aber, da er mir ein solches anmuten und zu ein solches Leben animieren will, ist der Gehorsam und die Liebe gegen denselben hiermit aufgehoben, sie mögen mit Euch machen, was sie wollen, wenn sie Euch auch das Leben nehmen, ja gar in vier Stücke zerteilen, so komme ich nicht.

Honoured Father: On my return home today find before me several letters from yourself, which I will answer in all brevity, which will serve to save you postage; thus your paper may find a better use. What is the point of your praising to me the soldier's life, you know that all my life I have had no desire for it, and now far less will develop such a desire. I have always had respect for my father, as is my duty, and always behaved towards you as I ought, but now that you want to persuade me to do this, and lead such a life, the [obligation to] love and obey you is set aside; they can do to you what they will, even if they take your life, nay, quarter you, I shall not come.[15]

It was only the imminent decay of the peasant estate that made Frederick William decide on an alternative. In 1733 he introduced the cantonal system, whereby the captain of a company, who was usually the local landlord, recruited his own tenants, who were allowed to return after training to work on the land. Most served an initial one to two years and then spent two months of each year with the army.[16] There was widespread contempt in Europe for the slavish treatment of the Prussian officer, which became legendary, although in individual cases religious feeling mitigated the officers' treatment of the men. Schwerin, Schmettau, Zieten and Belling were officers of this type, who came under the influence of Pietism in their early careers. The system, however, encouraged officers to exploit their authority and to trade on the material advantages offered to the captain or colonel. Apart from what they could make from equipping and provisioning the troops – and it was by no means rare for jackets and waistcoats to be made too tight so that they could sell the extra cloth for profit – they might win awards, sinecures and tax exemptions for success in battle. In the bad years after the Seven Years War (1756–63), contemporaries contrasted the luxury enjoyed by the upper ranks of the Prussian officers with the wretchedness of the junior officers. A captain would earn about 92 *taler* a month, plus 15 for fodder, 22 for repair allowance, 19 for gun allowance, 7 for medicines for the horses, and 36 for recruitment expenses; other perquisites brought the annual income in the late eighteenth century up to over 2200 *taler* a year; a major got over 2700, a colonel over 5000, in a dragoon regiment as much as 6500. This was very much more than they got under Frederick William, and the salaries were paid in gold; a common soldier got about 2 *taler* a month.[17] After 1806 salaries were put on a fixed scale, which brought those of senior officers down by almost a half.

In the second half of the eighteenth century the Prussian army relied increasingly on mercenaries, who were often pressganged in their own homeland by Prussian recruiting officers. In 1776 only 90 000 out of a total of 187 000 were natives.[18] Discipline and punishment, always overemphasized in Prussia, became draconian, as desertion grew more frequent. The poet Ludwig Tieck recalls the case of his friend Daschieri, who was seized by such a gang in Strasburg, made to serve seven years, and then pressed for a further seven. After fourteen years, when he tried to get released his officer started an incident which ended in Daschieri's being condemned to beating by broadsword and he died from the injuries received. One of the most graphic accounts of life seen from below occurs in the memoirs of the NCO's son, Klöden. Running the gauntlet, and beatings with sticks and broadswords were not only common in the Berlin garrison where he spent his early life, but they offered entertainment to a spectacle-loving public, much as did the reviews and parades. The married quarters for an NCO consisted of two rooms, which his wife and their children shared with '*Schlafburschen*', young recruits given into his charge in case they deserted. One of these, a Pole, was an example of the state of near bestiality to which people were reduced in these conditions. He would get drunk, lie about unconscious for several hours, taking his frequent punishments with a philosophic 'Juckt mir wieder mein Puckel, so sehr muss schröpfen lassen' ['If my back itches, I must be cupped (bled)'].[19] Klöden's father was given unpaid furlough for four months on one occasion. For the peasants who went back to their farms this was a relief; for the Klödens living in the garrison, it meant hunger, perhaps starvation, had not the neighbours been kind. Klöden senior was never promoted, for he was too poor to equip himself with the smart uniform which would have appealed to the regimental commander. He ended his life, as so many Prussian soldiers did, in a poorly paid post as an excise official and then as a guard at the gates of a small provincial town.

Even petty German princelings regarded it as imperative to their honour to keep an army: Karl August of Weimar had thirty-six officers, whom he drilled with due solemnity at four o'clock in the morning, and whom Goethe termed somewhat contemptuously in his diary, 'militärische Makaronis' ['military macaronis (Wops)'].[20] Others maintained troops as a rich source of revenue. The decision to sell troops to the British to fight the Americans, which caused such an outcry in Germany in the 1770s, helped to found the fortunes of the landgrave of Hesse-Kassel, which, shrewdly invested on the advice of Nathan Rothschild, made the ruler of this small territory into the richest of German princes. Bavaria, too, though a state of some importance, depended for much of its revenue on subsidies paid by France to maintain an army. In Austria, although it had heavy military commitments during this period against Turkey, France and later Prussia, and extended the so-called 'military frontier' all along the south and south-east of its possessions through colonization, the army did not play the dominant role in society and in the state which it held in Prussia.[21] The nobility did not favour the cadet schools set up by Maria Theresa; indeed the middle classes began to play an ever more important part in the Austrian officer corps, and as their members were promoted they joined the new nobility from the higher bureaucracy.

In the eighteenth century German armies the common soldiers as a whole were mainly recruited from the peasantry, from the second and third sons who could not inherit, and from the cotters and hirelings. To a growing number of commentators in the last decades of the century who were concerned with agrarian matters, this practice exercised a malignant influence on the economy and therefore on the whole of society. For the soldiers were kept in the army for long periods, from upwards of twenty years, even when there were no hostilities. 'A prince who does this sort of thing', averred one such critic, Friedrich Carl von Moser, in 1787, 'loses (through such a policy) his best peasants and finally retains cripples whom he cannot feed himself (and) who either are a burden to others, or to his disgrace must beg their way through the world.'[22] Although some rulers sought to kill two birds with one stone, as it were, and employed criminals and beggars as common soldiers, the drain on the rural labour force continued; at a time of rising population and increasing demand for food, this was, as many agrarian reformers pointed out, foolhardy and dangerous. In general German rulers were moved by ill considered notions of prestige to maintain forces which they and their states could ill afford, and the numerical ratio of soldiery to civilian population was much higher in Germany than in other European states.[23]

Chapter 8
The peasantry

'The peasants', wrote Oswald Spengler in *The Decline of the West,* 'are without history.' Written or pictorial records of life as experienced by German peasants are undoubtedly far less extensive than those of court or town life. However, anyone acquainted with the local and folk art museums, or with the '*Bauernstuben*' or peasant parlours in the farms of the Black Forest, Bavaria or Saxony, would hardly agree with so summary a judgement. The historian of rural life in the years between the end of the great war and the end of the Holy Roman Empire is faced with what Wilhelm Abel, the leading authority on the subject, has called a 'chaotic variety' of tenures, conditions of life and social relationships. It is difficult to generalize about the degree of freedom, prosperity and contentment (or lack of it) in rural areas of the Empire at a given period. For one thing we still know too little of local life,[1] for another a variety of legal systems still existed after 1648, though attempts were made, as in the 1655 Decree of the Supreme Court of the Empire, establishing serfdom as an estate, to legislate for social relationships over the whole area. The peasant, whether freeman or serf, was a tenant and paid rent; he did not own his land. The few exceptions, known as *Eximirte,* enjoyed a status in early modern Germany equivalent to that of territorial nobles, burghers and officials.[2] The village provided the environment in which most people lived. Peasants were members of a corporate body; they managed communal resources and looked after the communal life, supervising paths and ditches, allocating grazing rights and seeing that public order and morals were in a satisfactory state. A village court dealt with minor offences or acted in an advisory capacity to the seigneur's court. The community was initially responsible for drawing lots for conscripts. In the seventeenth century the authority of the village declined, the power of the seigneur grew greater and the financial burdens more onerous. Yet the village community still retained a good deal of importance for its inhabitants.

Equality was never a feature of the peasant world. The better-off peasants had long recognized the need, in their own interest, to limit the right to participation in decisions. In Lower Saxony only certain houses carried the right of their owners to vote, while in Austria it was limited to householders with a certain minimum amount of land. Smallholders, hired hands, lodgers and servants, and usually women too, were excluded. In the canton of Zurich only householders had the right to use the common lands. In other regions use was permitted by custom, though not by law, to the cotters and labourers; when in the late eighteenth century pressure was put on the village by governments and lords to divide the common lands in the interest of greater productivity and profitability, these people were excluded. They had no legal title and, deprived of the means of pasturing a goat or cow, or of collecting firewood from the communal forests, they drifted to join the agrarian proletariat, which became Germany's chief social problem at the turn of the century. The superior status implied in the possession of a vote was confirmed by marriage practice. The large farmers intermarried among themselves; they also generally managed to keep the office of village headman or *Schultheiss* in their families for generations. However, in the years after 1648, and in certain regions earlier, the elective or hereditary office of headman came to be controlled by the lord. Once the local lord appointed a man to this office, he was no longer regarded by the villagers as wholly one of them. He was unpopular in bad times and was blamed for their shortcomings by the lord. Grievances erupted in violence against his person; the abbot of Selau in Bohemia, for example, found himself driven to impose heavy fines on the villagers who beat up their headman.[3] The perquisites of the office, usually in the form of tax remission, still attracted villagers to the post, but in the eighteenth century Rhenish provinces of Prussia, the officials of the ruler began to oust the headman and assume the task of maintaining public order. In other regions this development did not occur: in the central cantons of Switzerland, in Swabia, Tyrol and parts of the Black Forest and north-west Germany, the village or the farmers of substance remained in charge of their affairs, although they had to pay dues and services to an overlord.

Within the individual farming household, life was patriarchal: the relationship of the family and dependants, and of the household and farm servants to the master of the house was one of respectful submission.[4] To those living under such a system, as to the peasants themselves in their subjection to the sovereign or seigneur, it was the natural order of things. The head of the household was not only entrusted by God with the care of their life and their work, but also with their religious observance and moral conduct. He delegated some of this authority to his wife, who oversaw the work carried out by the female servants, in which she shared. Life in a peasant household was not very different, except in scale, from that of a rural nobleman's house, as described by Wolf Helmhard von Hohberg, a seventeenth century landowner from Lower Austria. In loving detail and with ample illustration, Hohberg describes in his *Georgica curiosa* (1682) how and when the various tasks of the year are to be done on farm and in house, and how the household resembled a *res publica* in miniature.[5] Hohberg's work is part of a body of writings on the subject of farming written in this period, and suitably known as '*Hausvaterliteratur*'; these treatises advise the heads of household in practical terms how to organize their work and exercise their authority. The servants enjoyed each a special status according to their age and task, which was duly acknowledged in their wage, and where they ate their meals.[6] Until the eighteenth century, the indoor servants ate with the family and addressed the children as '*du*'; in many regions the outdoor servants and wage labourers also shared a common table with the rest of the household. The Enlightenment and economic pressures were responsible for the gradual erosion of the old patriarchal way of life in rural households. In an effort to protect the underprivileged from exploitation, enlightened reformers helped to create an awareness of class barriers between servants and master; with their stress on legal title as against customary right, a characteristic of that age, they undermined the sense of corporate solidarity which, though open to abuse, had generally been a positive feature of the farming household.

An East Frisian, recalling his childhood days in the early nineteenth century, remembered the effect on local society when the larger farmers began to give the hired hands their meal separately and to educate their children apart. Formerly the sons of big farmers and of day labourers had gone to school, worked in the fields, and enjoyed themselves together on Sundays and festive days; now, all this changed, and mutual hostility crept into their relationship.[7]

The wide variety of systems of tenure and of natural resources in the German countryside, the 'chaotic variety' of which Abel speaks, meant that, while many peasants laboured under burdensome obligations and minimal return for their labour, others prospered. Thus, while the farmers in some parts of the Bergisch-Land, north-west of Cologne, had solid oak furniture in their parlours, and gold and silver jewellery to wear on festive days in the seventeenth century, a few kilometres away there is no trace of such wealth.[8] In general one can say that, where the farm was passed on intact to the next generation, the peasants retained their substance. In the early seventeenth century there was much wealth on the land: wardrobes and chests, household articles and implements as well as fine peasant parlours, survive from Swabia, the Black Forest, southern Bavaria, Thuringia, Hesse and Lower Saxony.[9] Later in the seventeenth and in the eighteenth century peasants who left their farms in western Germany, for religious and other reasons, to settle in distant Prussia or south-east Europe, brought considerable assets with them. An estimated 300 000 settlers brought some 2 million *taler*, 6000 horses, 8000 cattle, 20 000 sheep and 3000 pigs.[10] When farmers were in a position to engage in an alternative trade, such as seafaring in northern Germany, they could become rich men. The accounts of a Dithmarschen (Holstein) farmer, named Jeff Tygesen of Emmerleff, have survived for the years 1743–1800; they show how a farmer of substance could make money letting off his arable land and from supplying with food the shippers of draft animals on their way to Holland. Tygesen received colonial products from them in return, including luxuries such as silk handkerchiefs and a 'blue doublet'.[11] In Schleswig-Holstein the carrier trade was a lucrative source of income; one farmer was able to give his three daughters a dowry of 14 000 *taler* in 1729 on the profits. The Greenland whale trade was another important source of livelihood; along the North Sea coast subsidiary manufacturing of whale products prospered for a time.[12] Abel concludes a recent survey of German agrarian life at this time with a warning against seeing it in too dark colours.[13] Where opportunities arose to better themselves economically, the peasants were able to profit from them. However, they were the last in the line and were the group that bore the heaviest burden of taxation. They could hope for less return on their labour than almost any other estate.

The bulk of the rural population was not of course the farmers with large and medium sized holdings, but tenant farmers in central, south and west Germany owing dues to a number of lords, and, in the east, the serfs who were bound to the soil. The peasants were not only the chief source of revenue for the prince until the nineteenth century, they were also the main producing class. Yet it was not until the end of the eighteenth century that political thinkers and public officials began to appreciate how unproductive the agrarian system was, particularly the labour services owed by the peasant. A sixteenth century chronicler, Thomas Kantzow, described in his *Pomerania* the state of the local peasants: 'Die haben an den Höfen kein Erben, und müssen der Herrschaft so viel dienen, als sie immer von ihnen haben wollen und können oft über solchen Dienst ihr Eigenwerk nicht tun und müssen derohalben verarmen und entlaufen'. ['They have no inheritance from the farms, must serve the lord as much as he will, and can therefore often not do their own work and so must become impoverished and run away'].[14] The same could have been written about the Lower Austrian, Bohemian and Silesian peasants a century and a half later. J. G. von Justi, from central Germany, who made a name for himself as a leading cameralist at the Vienna court, declared in 1761 that labour dues were simply not profitable:

> Der Bauer, der diese Arbeit mit Unwillen und Verdruss verrichtet, arbeitet dabei so wenig wie möglich.... Das ist auch eine der hauptsächlichen Ursachen, warum die Ernte auf solchen Gütern in Ansehung ihrer Grösse und Proportionen allemal viel schlechter ausfällt, als auf kleinen Gütern, die aufmerksame Wirte aber keine Frondienste haben.

> The peasant who does this work with ill will and resentment works as little as possible. ... This then is one of the main reasons why the harvest on such estates, considering their size and proportions, always turns out so much worse than on small estates, where careful farmers have no labour obligations.[15]

The services took the form of tilling the fields, providing the lord with horses for transport and beaters for the hunting season – perhaps the most bitterly resented task – and carrying messages and letters. Nor did the peasantry get much benefit from what they themselves produced: the bulk of German exports, particularly from the east, was agricultural produce: over 100 000 tons of corn was shipped annually through the port of Danzig in the first half of the seventeenth century. The cattle trade was very important in central Europe; Vienna, Brieg and Breslau in Silesia, Posen and the insignificant little town Büttstadt, north of Weimar, were the main centres; in the latter as many as 16 000 head of cattle might assemble for a single fair. Yet the money received from agricultural produce did not go to buy the kind of technical means of improvement of husbandry then being applied in western Europe: it was spent on luxury goods, jewellery and porcelain, glassware and textiles for rich men's houses and rich men's wives.

The peasants were inevitably the worst sufferers during the Thirty Years War, and, for many years after the peace, at the hands of marauding soldiers. Yet, as has been said already, some areas suffered little or not at all. The north-west was scarcely involved at all in the last, most brutal period of fighting; Austria and Switzerland escaped entirely. The Swiss made so much money out of supplying food and other materials to the belligerents that contemporaries told of whole villages where the old houses were pulled down to make room for new and imposing ones. Even in war-torn regions, some districts were spared the butchering and looting of peasants and their families which Grimmelshausen describes in *Simplicissimus Teutsch.* Thus in Franconia around Nuremberg, the Upper Palatinate and the Bavarian forest, rural officials elaborated an extensive news service, to warn villagers of approaching troops. On receipt of the news, provisions would be hastily collected with money to buy off the soldiers as soon as they arrived. The sight of these was usually sufficient to prevent excess, but it was essential to have the cash and food ready beforehand. The same was done in the county of Lippe, where the Swedes fought with imperial troops along the banks of the Weser river.[16] Horror tales are all too numerous. The chronicle of the Odenwald parson Minck, covering the years 1633–48, tells of complete disregard for the peasantry on both sides, and describes in lurid detail the fate of country folk at the soldiers' hands.[17] Some rulers had sought to anticipate events by training local defence forces from among the peasantry, but it was not particularly successful. The Hesse militia proved as helpless against the Imperial general Tilly as did the Bavarian peasants defending their homes against the Swedes in 1632. Elector Maximilian of Bavaria, who knew the value of money better than most, had to confess that what he had spent on their training had not been worth it.

The most important overall effect of the war for the peasant was that he became increasingly bound to the soil he tilled. The ravages of the fighting, the weakness of state power in eastern Germany and the adjoining lands in the mid seventeenth century, gave added impetus to the tendency already at work in the previous century to increase the rights of the nobles at the expense of the peasantry. The population growth in sixteenth century Germany had made land more valuable. Many lords had taken deserted peasant land back into cultivation and, when the opportunity presented itself, had added it to their own. The relative annual increase in the size of some 412 noble estates in Brandenburg was greater between 1480 and 1624 than at any time from the fourteenth to the nineteenth century.[18] After the war territorial sovereigns were so anxious to restore their lands that they lent support to a host of ordinances designed to give the lords greater power over their peasants. These powers were in any case more considerable among the landowners in eastern Germany, whether they were the descendants of the original settlers, or colonizers of noble and peasant origin, than was the case in the west. Labour was so scarce after 1648 that the lords were quick to exploit the legal position to bind the peasants to the land; here, in contrast with western Germany, the lord's right over the peasant was derived from possession of the land – '*Gutsherrschaft*' – and it was owed to him alone. Such a manorial domain was a kind of state within a state; the scarcity of villages in the lands east of the Elbe made it easier for the landowner and his officials to take over the running of peasant affairs in their area. Peasants began to be counted like domestic animals, as part of the estate. 'Untertanen können bei Kauf und Verkauf, Pacht und Verpachtung nicht anders als nach den Präständis Geld, Vieh oder Dienst nach Propertien in Betracht kommen' ['In the buying and selling of land, hiring and renting, the subjects can only be considered proportionally in terms of money, stock or service'], stated one writer on the subject in the eighteenth century.[19] However, ordinances and treatises do not necessarily give an accurate picture of the country as a whole. The obligations exacted from the peasants varied very considerably from one area or one period to another. Thus in East Prussia in the early seventeenth century, where there were several families owing labour service, the average demand worked out at one child per family being sent for a year's service. On the other hand, it was required that every peasant family with two sons or two daughters send one of them to serve the lord. They were paid a wage which was not increased between 1653 and 1832, when such services were finally abolished in the area.[20] In general the larger and more densely populated an estate was, the lighter the obligation. The peasants on crown land usually fared better than those working for a noble estate owner. The sovereigns, especially in the eighteenth century, showed growing concern for the material welfare of those under authority, a sense of obligation which was prompted by the desire to increase the yield of goods and taxes for the crown. The big landowners thought primarily – as a general rule – in terms of production and profit, especially those in north-east Germany who were involved in the corn export trade. One landlord who stands out among his kind for his energetic efforts on behalf of his peasants was Eberhard von Rochow. The peasants in his native Brandenburg were, he declared, as 'Tiere unter Tieren' ['beasts among beasts'], instead, as they should be, the sinews of the state.[21] The peasants on holdings too small to provide tax revenue were the worst off: they were required to render the heaviest services. In eighteenth century Silesia their labour was also employed in the commercial enterprises and manufacturies which the landed magnates were beginning to develop. One of the worst features of the system in the west of Germany was the multiplicity of overlords. While the urban taxpayer had only one lord, most peasants owed some obligation to as many as four – his political overlord (*Landesherr*), the lord who exercised personal authority over him (*Gerichtsherr* and *Leibherr*), the lord to whom he paid tithes (*Zehntherr*) – often the most onerous of all – and finally the one who actually owned the land he worked (*Grundherr*). The difference between the lands east of the Elbe was that labour services or *Fronen* were performed for private individuals, whereas in the west they were for the state or community (maintaining the roads, or, as in the case of the Electorate of Mainz, for example, the banks of the Rhine).[22]

In eighteenth century Prussia it was the peasants who bore the chief burden of the military establishment, and it was a heavy one. The population policies of successive Prussian rulers were designed to increase the numbers of the peasantry, since they provided both recruits and revenue to equip and maintain the army. 'Der Bauernstand [ist] für den Staat sehr wichtig; er bildet seine Grundlage und trägt seine Last; er hat die Arbeit und andere den Ruhm' ['The peasantry is very important for the state; the peasantry is its foundation and bears the burdens; it does the work and the rest have the glory'], wrote Frederick II in his *Political Testament* in 1768.[23] His father, the 'soldier king', had begun the military organization of the country on succeeding to power in 1713. The peasantry was to provide the main source of manpower. The excesses of the recruiting officers, however, caused whole villages to emigrate, especially from the western provinces of the kingdom,[24] which moved the king to forbid forcible recruitment in 1721. Yet he contradicted himself in two patents of the following years, declaring that 'derjenigen Untertanen und Landeskinder Vermögen, so aus Furcht vor der Werbung ausgetreten, ... konfisziert ... sein soll' ['the property of those subjects and children of the land, who flee for fear of being pressed into service, will be confiscated'].[25] The 1733 ordinances divided his realm into cantons, giving local landlords as captains the power to recruit, usually their own tenants, and to allow these to work on the farm when not actually training. If this was in fact but a legalization of forcible recruitment, it did have the advantage for the peasant of letting him know what he could expect.

The war contribution paid by the Prussian peasant usually represented by far the largest part of his income. A cotter in Magdeburg in 1740 paid 4 *taler* annually, the same amount as his small house and garden cost him in rent; a farmer in Further Pomerania paid 18 *taler* from an annual income of only 22.[26] The peasant also paid cavalry money in lieu of fodder when the horses were stabled in the garrisons; he had to supply forage where demanded at less than market prices; perhaps the most exacting part of this obligation was the long journey to the garrison with the forage, which was arduous and time consuming. In addition, he paid excise on what he bought or sold in the market town, and might have to support a son or relative during his army service, for the pay the recruits received barely covered the cost of food. Otto Büsch summarizes his meticulous account of the peasant in eighteenth century Prussia thus: 'Das Militärsystem des alten Preussens war, soweit es das bäuerliche Leben berührte, keineswegs nur die Organisation zur Rekrutierung und Versorgung der Armee. Dieses System erfasste vielmehr den ganzen Menschen als soziales Individuum in allen seinen Lebensbereichen' ['The military system of old Prussia, in so far as it touched on peasant life, was not merely the organization for recruiting and provisioning the army. This system encompassed the whole person as a social individual in all spheres of his existence'].[27] The peasant in the western provinces of Prussia fared better; in East Frisia, for example, they were free men, something that was incomprehensible to the landlords of the east; these peasants usually managed to commute military service for money payments. In the east the peasant, absolute subject of his lord, became, through the cantonal system of recruitment, subject to the authority of the regiment of which his master was captain or colonel. Where he lived, how long he served, even his marrying, depended on what the regiment decreed; permission cost money, and his superiors put illegal pressures on him to squeeze even more out of him. The punishments meted out on the parade ground were imitated by the lord at home, teaching him that blind obedience was his only choice.

In western Germany the territorial rulers intervened to check the power of the landlords. In Lower Saxony their policies helped to preserve the old farms more or less intact into the present century. The tenant farmers were forced under threat of military service to take back into cultivation lands devastated in the great war. Although taxes were heavy, they succeeded in restoring the former prosperity of this area in little more than a generation after 1648. Other regions were less fortunate and less well governed. The price collapse after the war, the shortage of labour and stock, protracted the agrarian depression until the end of the century. The Palatinate, most blessed by nature, suffered terrible devastation in the wars of Louis XIV, barely a generation after the end of the Thirty Years War. The 'Palatines' became refugees in many lands, emigrating to America, to south-east Europe, even to Ireland, where they gave their name to a celebrated song, *The Palatine's Daughter,* who, as befits a daughter of this talented and industrious people, is a wealthy and desirable match for an ambitious young man. The peasants fared worse under alien landlords, such as the soldier adventurers who bought up devastated or abandoned lands to make their fortunes. Bavarian peasants therefore could count themselves lucky that the church and not strangers bought up much of the land of the impoverished nobility in their state.

However, if the Bavarian peasant probably had a less harsh life than many of his fellows in other regions, his political rights were less than those of peasants in most other south German territories. Here at that time it was not uncommon for the peasants to have some representation in the provincial assemblies and to have a voice in granting supplies. The south of Germany contained many miniscule territories – Sausenberg and Rötteln between Basel and Freiburg are examples of two of them which have been studied in depth[28] – where constitutional rights and privileges were not clearly defined and where sudden demands might be made on the ruler for arms against the Turkish or other invaders. Such a situation gave the peasants bargaining power. Together with the ruler and in consultation with the guilds, they decided important matters such as currency values, and prohibition on the sale of corn and cattle outside the state. Peasants were also represented in the local diets in Alsace, the Black Forest, Voralberg, Tyrol and Salzburg. It was in the Tyrol that their powers were most effective; here they succeeded in establishing their right to be represented as a separate estate alongside clergy and nobility. In some of the larger territories the expense of sending representatives to the assembly, and maintaining them while it was in session, proved too onerous. The tangible benefits did not seem to make it worthwhile. By the late seventeenth century peasant representation had disappeared from many states, such as the Margravate of Baden. In the smaller territories the peasantry showed evidence of long memories and the native cunning associated with their kind in resisting authority. One such case concerned the monastery of Kempten in Swabia. On the basis of an agreement (Memmingen Treaty of 1526), made between the then abbot and the peasantry, they successfully contested increased dues imposed on them in the seventeenth century. In the next century they managed to have their labour services commuted to money payment, and a ban on export of produce lifted; they even initiated what today would be called a social programme, which included a savings bank for their members, farming credits and a poor relief, with 10 per cent of the local chamber's budget at its disposal.

In general it can be said that the south German peasants, particularly in Swabia and the Tyrol, had a sense of corporate solidarity which proved politically and economically effective. The decline of the towns in the seventeenth century contrasted with the relative prosperity of a number of rural districts in the region. In north Germany peasant representation was uncommon, though it was known in East Frisia; and it was also found in some of the imperial counties of central Germany, such as Sayn, Waldeck and Reuss.

One important feature of peasant life in the period 1648–1806 was the frequency with which peasants resorted to violence to express specific or general grievances. Although in the north of the country sporadic disturbances did occur, peasant uprisings on a large scale were confined to the south, especially common in those areas where the Peasants War had broken out, and despite the legendary brutality with which it had been suppressed. Peasant rebellion, it could be said, was endemic in Austria, prompted by religious as well as economic grievances, for many peasants continued to oppose the Counter-Reformation policies of the Habsburgs after their own native and Protestant nobility had been forced to emigrate or to comply, and a new non-native nobility had been established. This was the case in Bohemia and in parts of the Austrian archduchy itself. The most violent and prolonged outbreak had been in Upper Austria in 1626; it was in fact a full-scale war. Led by the legendary Stephen Fadinger, who inspired the rousing 770-line *Fadingerlied,* it won considerable support from the local nobility and the towns, as well as the peasants themselves. In the end the revolt found the fate destined for almost all such events: execution, mutilation and exile of the rebels and their supporters. Unrest remained endemic, however, lasting in some districts of both Upper and Lower Austria into the nineteenth century.[29]

The peasants rebelled too in Switzerland and Bavaria, especially in districts where once the peasants had enjoyed local representation, or whose neighbours in adjoining regions were thus represented. The peasants in northern Switzerland, who were subject to the local towns, strove to acquire the status of the free peasants of the central cantons. Rebellious peasants in Austria, south Germany and Silesia were moved to revolt by a combination of religious and social grievances; in these traditionally Catholic areas, many showed unexpected loyalty to Lutheranism and even to Anabaptism. Economically speaking, the seventeenth century was a bitter time for the rural inhabitants of these regions. Invariably the peasantry rebelled, not against the ruler, the *Landesherr,* but against their lord. Again and again they sent representatives to

Vienna, to seek the protection of the Emperor (or his consort or his mother), believing that here they would find justice. Not until the time of Maria Theresa and Joseph II was their tenacity rewarded; the Empress cared deeply for their well-being and, similar in this to the Prussian kings in the eighteenth century, improved their lot on the crown lands, though without success in the case of that owned by noble landowners. The Austrian nobility was very largely absentee in this period, demanding ever greater dues from their tenants to pay for city palaces and expensive habits. When they came to visit their estates, it was generally to hunt, a pastime which wreaked devastation on the fields and meadows. This was a most bitterly resented grievance of peasants in widely different regions of Germany: even the Elector August of Saxony, a sovereign well disposed towards his subjects, demanded that the peasants remove all fences and hedges so as not to impede the chase; he even considered the idea of removing the entire peasantry of one area near the Bohemian border in order to improve the hunting terrain. In Germany, as in other European countries, the penalties for poaching were brutal; in the sixteenth century the death penalty was introduced for it, when mutilation had proved an insufficient deterrent.

Strikes, go-slows and court cases were employed by the peasants in defence of their rights; in the village of Reudnitz, near Greiz in central Germany, they took their local lord to court fifteen times between 1648 and 1789. Such instances were not isolated. Peasant protest rarely led to a sustained improvement in their lot. One exception is the case of the Bavarian rising against the occupying forces of Austrian troops in 1705; here the peasants were successful in resisting conscription. Yet despite a long history of failure they proved, if only to themselves, that they felt and acted as a corporate estate. In the long run their persistence probably prevented further deterioration in their condition; certainly in the eighteenth century it brought home to political thinkers and to the rulers that wholesale reform was needed, and eventually emancipation was mooted.

A new political awareness was at work among the peasantry of territories west of the Elbe in the last decades of the century, fed by the popular *Bauernzeitung*, or farmers' journal; although it was written by the type of urban dwellers responsible for the moral weeklies, the journal showed an insight into the peasant mind. It appeared in the main in central Germany, and was unknown in the Catholic south or Prussia, apart from Silesia. However, in most regions of the country the popular almanacks and calendars, which are a feature of the age of the Enlightenment, began to include political and agrarian features and information. The growing vogue for scenes from rural life in contemporary literature was not lost on members of the peasant estate; one farmer delivered a load of wood as a gift to the poet and professor Gellert, in appreciation of what he had written on rural life. Many leading literary figures in mid and late eighteenth century Germany showed an interest in the environment and sympathy for the peasant's lot – Albrecht von Haller who wrote *Die Alpen* in 1729, Salomon Gessner, author of *Die Idyllen* (1756), extolled the simple virtues of the countryman, and by implication contrasted his virtue with the vice or dissipation of courtiers and others; the poets Bürger and Zachariae championed his case against princely huntsmen. The image of the peasantry underwent a striking change in this period. The ideal peasant of modern times, a true '*Socrate rustique*' in Rousseau's sense, was discovered for contemporaries in the person of the Swiss Jakob Cujer, known as Kleinjogg. The Zurich burgher H. C. Hirzel described him in his widely read *Die Wirtschaft eines philosophischen Bauern* (*The Farm of a Philosophic Peasant*) (1761), Margrave Karl Friedrich of Baden sought him out and the Duke Ludwig of Würtemberg publicly embraced him as his moral superior. Goethe himself visited him and spoke enthusiastically of him. Kleinjogg, sound peasant that he was, seems to have taken it all in his stride.[30]

The peasant of the seventeenth and early eighteenth century had been, as in previous times, a stock figure of comedy, the butt of crude satire, ignorant and boorish, cunning by instinct but easily outwitted by the astute. Whether this image corresponded in any way to the facts is difficult to say; we have very little direct evidence of how peasants thought and felt at that time. From the middle of the eighteenth century onwards we have an increasing number of memoirs and accounts of rural life, of which one of the most memorable is that of the Swiss Ulrich Bräker, author of *Der arme Mann in Toggenburg* (*The Poor Man in Toggenburg*) (1789). Bräker was indeed a poor peasant, so poor in fact that he felt recruitment into the army to be preferable to life in his village. His service with the Prussians taught him his mistake, but it was years before he managed to escape home; his natural realism prevented him idealizing by contrast the life to which he returned. Among other features of his tale is the stark report on rural poverty, which affected both producers of food and village craftsmen. At the time in which he wrote, many regions of Germany were experiencing a prolonged agrarian depression, which culminated in the famine years of 1771–2. Agricultural techniques had not improved sufficiently to provide food for the increased population. Even for those farmers who could affort to employ labour, the budget for household expenses was often extremely straitened. The peasants of the village of Petze in Brunswick, who farmed on average some 80 acres of land and owned thirteen to fourteen head of livestock, went to court in 1774 to dispute their high tax and other burdens. It was shown that some 20 per cent of their produce was sold and the proceedings used almost wholly to supplement their taxes and dues; these already claimed 40 per cent of their total turnover; 45 per cent in wages, seed and feed stuffs; the remainder had to cover the expenses of the household, including materials for spinning and weaving. Illness and other emergencies could not be budgeted for; at the end of each year they were in deficit and could only keep going, they said, because their farms 'von alters her in gutem stande sind, also vorerst zusetzen können; ['had, since times of old, been well maintained and they could still live off the capital'].[31]

Although farmers are traditionally reluctant to admit to any degree of prosperity, it seems that even men of substance were justifiably anxious about the future. The numbers of independent and semi-independent farmers declined inexorably during the eighteenth century, and the population increase concentrated itself among the lower strata of rural society. This process can be illustrated in the case of electoral Saxony: in 1550 the number of peasant holdings large enough to support a family was 50 per cent of the total; by 1750 this had fallen to 25 per cent and in 1843 was only 14 per cent; in the same years the cotters and landless peasants increased from 18 to 38 and 52 per cent respectively.[32] The cotters were not necessarily poor men; in seventeenth century Mecklenburg they owned cattle and sheep, sometimes even horses. They too shared in the sea trade on the mouth of the Oder, and might rise in the world. Kellenbenz quotes the case of one Christian Brennmöhl, son of a serf who became a shipper; in 1699 he was first mate of a ship, two years later a burgher of the city of Stettin.[33] Customary rights allowed these people to graze their animals on the common lands and many had other trades as well, most commonly weaving, or they hired themselves out as hands. When labour was at a premium, as after the great war, they might secure favourable conditions, but when the population put pressure on scarce resources and rational methods of cultivation became fashionable, the farmers made common cause with the lords to divide the common lands, often greatly underused. Those with no legal title lost, as has been observed, an essential source of their livelihood. It was this new 'rural proletariat', as a later generation termed them, which provided the new manufacturing enterprises with a substantial part of their labour force. In some regions, such as Baden or Swabia, such pressures encouraged the lower strata of peasant society to engage in crafts more than they had done previously. At all events the long-term effects of the agrarian depression in the eighteenth century was to introduce a greater social mobility into rural life, which in some way anticipated the industrial revolution of the following age.

However, in this, as in so many areas of peasant life, it is difficult to generalize. Kellenbenz points out in the article already quoted that scholars' preoccupation with the manorial system had tended to make them ignore the variety of life and of sources of income in this social sphere. Future research may modify our view of peasant life in Germany, but it is unlikely to alter the impression that frequent need and at times great hardship was the lot of the majority of German peasants in the years between the end of the Thirty Years War and that of the Holy Roman Empire in 1806.

Chapter 9
The fringes of society

Society in Germany in the years 1648–1806 was still organized on a corporative basis; its members derived their legal status from the corporation to which they belonged: nobility, clergy, merchants and craftsmen's guilds, university, and peasantry. The rights and duties of these were generally accepted by the absolute princes, as is evident from the large body of legislation dealing with social distinctions and privileges. Seckendorff listed among the duties of the prince in his *Teutscher Fürstenstaat* (1656) that he 'preserve proper distinction between social classes in respect to conduct, clothing and general consumption'.[1] Such divisions were marked by external appearance and habits. The medieval clothing ordinances, laying down what fabrics different social groups might wear, continued to appear well into the eighteenth century. Thus in 1604 the Elector of Brandenburg forbade all unmarried girls of the first rank to wear velvet or satin, while men and women alike in the third rank might not appear in silk. Silk dresses, bodices and camisoles worn by servant girls and 'common women' would be publicly taken off them, the choleric Frederick William I of Prussia decreed in 1731. The value of presents and the numbers attending feasts on the occasion of births, christenings, weddings, etc., were carefully prescribed according to the different classes. Yet all of these ranks within society were accorded privileges deemed necessary for their proper functioning within the social structure.

There were, however, several other groups of people who did not fit into the traditional social groups, who had no corporate existence and therefore no legal status. Yet they existed in Germany, growing in numbers, harassed and persecuted, sometimes expelled from one territory or even from the *Reich,* but invariably returning to preoccupy the authorities and the population. These were the Jews, the gypsies, pedlars and beggars, the victims of wars and natural catastrophes who were too numerous to find care in their places of origin; lastly there were those cast out from society on the charge of being in league with the powers of darkness: witches and sorcerers.

1 THE JEWS

At the end of the Thirty Years War there were relatively few Jews in Germany. In medieval times they had been under the protection of the Emperor, who, for economic reasons, frequently defended them against the violent hostility of the populace. The presence of a group of people outside society, so obviously alien in dress, manners and above all belief from everyone else, who prospered even in times of distress, provoked sporadic outbursts of hatred throughout the late medieval and early modern periods. Usually such episodes were fomented by religious or popular leaders, by Christian merchants jealous of their prosperity or by peasants who had borrowed money at the high rates allowed to the Jews, and got into debt. Luther certainly helped to make such attitudes respectable by his vitriolic pamphlet *Concerning the Jews and Their Lies.* No general *Reich* laws existed governing the rights of Jews in Germany. From late medieval times the territorial princes issued their own *Schutzbriefe* or patents of protection for Jews in their lands. The terms of these varied from one area to the next; they generally permitted residence for a limited number of years on payment of an annual sum but could be withdrawn without notice. The Jews did not enjoy civil rights and were dependent on the prince for their personal safety. Thus when the Elector Joachim II of Brandenburg died in 1571, the Jews he had protected were arrested in large numbers, and their property plundered; his successor expelled the remainder. No Jew was permitted to settle in Brandenburg for the next 100 years. After 1648 many rulers recalled Jews to their territories; Jewish international contacts put them in a position to help to restore trade and above all supply credit to the princes in lands devastated by the war. By the end of the century the numbers of Jews in Germany had grown rapidly, both the *Schutzjuden,* resident Jews under the prince's protection, and numerous unlicensed Jews who had simply come into the country hoping for the best.

Society's need of Jewish talent and connections was such that they generally managed to stay, as long as they were in a position to pay for the privilege.

The Jews living in Germany during the seventeenth and eighteenth centuries were almost all Ashkenazi, who had come originally from Poland and Russia. An exception was the colony of Sephardic Jews, originally from Portugal, who settled in Hamburg and Altona in the seventeenth century, through its international trading connections,[2] and helped to found the unique prosperity of Hamburg. Although sporadic attacks were made on Jewish persons and property, the history of the Jews in Germany in the late seventeenth and eighteenth centuries was more peaceful than in previous centuries. Contacts existed between Jewish and Christian traders, between the heads of Jewish communities and the state authorities, and between the Jewish peasants and their Christian overlords in those regions, such as Hesse, where they were allowed to live on the land. They were excluded from the professions and the guilds, but were allowed to act as moneylenders and to practise a number of trades, such as tailoring and metalworking; they could also deal in second-hand goods. The German Jews were organized, not on a national or territorial basis, but in autonomous communities. They elected leaders who were then responsible for worship, for education, and for the payment of taxes to sustain the community, and to buy tolerance from the state.[3] Although it would have been in their own interest for the Jews to organize themselves in one body, in fact the Jewish communities clung jealously to their local autonomy as an expression of their separate identity. Considerable differences existed between communities, both in regard to religious observance and to the community's relationship with its Christian environment. In the long run, this local exclusiveness delayed integration of the Jews into society and state. Most of the religious leaders realized and welcomed this fact, at least up to the time of the Enlightenment. In those areas where contacts existed between the Jews and their Christian neighbours, such as in Berlin in the time of Frederick II, integration seemed relatively easy; in eastern regions of Prussia and Austria, in Posen, Silesia, Bohemia, Moravia and Cracow, many Jews retained the external features of their separate identity until the twentieth century: they lived in the ghetto, and wore the distinctive Jewish dress, beards and sidecurls.

Yet even established communities were constantly at the mercy of a sovereign's whim. Thus in 1670 Leopold I acceded to the demands of his Catholic Empress and expelled some 4000 Jews from Vienna. Most found refuge in Bohemia and Moravia, but a number were received by the Great Elector in Brandenburg-Prussia, where they were to play an important economic role in years to come. Leopold I had no sooner got rid of his Jews than he found himself unable to do without them. They were after all one of the few groups in the state who paid their taxes regularly. He therefore had recourse in 1673 to a practice which numerous princes all over Germany employed in the seventeenth and eighteenth centuries: he appointed one Samuel Oppenheimer as his *Hoffaktor* or Court Jew. In return for extensive privileges, Oppenheimer arranged credit facilities for the Emperor, and was soon responsible for purveying every conceivable type of goods and services to the court. He and his successor Samson Wertheimer were typical of the Court Jew of the absolutist period. They brought off the most extraordinary feats of supply, despite difficulties of transport, currency changes, lack of regular markets and the tariff demands of the petty princes. Despite all this, they supplied building material for the royal castles, fodder for the animals, payment and uniforms for the army and the court officials, ships for the Danube fleet, jewels, wine and even preserves for the imperial household.[4] Oppenheimer's death in 1703 caused a major financial crisis, since virtually all sources of revenue were mortgaged to him. But the state refused to pay, and Oppenheimer's daughter-in-law declared after her expulsion in 1723 that the family had lent the state some 100 million *gulden.* Time and time again we hear of princes refusing to repay the capital lent by Jewish financiers; however, the interest rate generally sufficed to found their fortunes. Descriptions of the houses of this new class of privileged Jew show that most knew how to conserve what they had gained and to protect themselves against exploitation. Samson Wertheimer, Openheimer's successor, was more careful. He died in 1724 leaving nearly 2 million *gulden*; his descendants were the aristocracy of the Viennese Jews. Maria Theresa disliked the Jews intensely, but her husband, Francis Stephen, with his customary shrewdness in financial matters, appointed the son of a former clerk in Wertheimer's office, Adam Arnstein, as his *Hoffaktor.* Arnstein died leaving his son Nathan a fortune and a house full of tapestries, Chinese silks, Japanese vases and Dresden statuettes. Here Mozart performed in 1784 to Nathan and Fanny Arnstein's guests, whose names indicate the new social milieu of the privileged Jews: princes and princesses Auersperg, Starhemberg, Montecuccoli, Liechtenstein, Kaunitz and Schwarzenberg were among their number.

Not all Court Jews ended their careers in such surroundings. The horrific fate of Oppenheimer's relation Jud Süss of Württemberg in 1738 was not unique. In the eighteenth century, however, most princes came to recognize that the services of these men were too useful to allow them to be exploited beyond measure. They founded the wealth of individual sovereign houses (Hanover, Hesse), and in other states, such as Prussia, the importance of the Court Jews in the history of Germany is very great indeed.

> They were the first who rose in the princes' favour from the position of traders to that of economic policy makers, and their economic and social rise was closely linked with the development of the German states from medieval-patrimonial state structures into modern state and economic structures. They were the Jews with whose assistance the princes destroyed the powers of the estates and the feudal order, founded the mercantilistic state economy and built the centralized unitary state.[5]

For the history of the Jewish community in Germany the Court Jews are of interest as being the first to pursue their careers and achieve positions of importance in the state while remaining faithful to the religious observance of their fathers. They were in fact the forerunners of emancipation.

For the vast majority of the Jews living in Germany in the seventeenth and eighteenth centuries, the mansions of an Oppenheimer and the contacts of an Arnstein were as remote as the palace of the Emperor himself. Most Jews earned their living as small traders or pedlars, living usually in the pocket territories of the *Reich,* for many of the larger states, such as Württemberg or Bavaria, refused to allow them to settle in their hereditary lands. In a time of poor communications the Jewish pedlars provided an important service and contacts with the outside world, as they appeared at regular intervals with their materials, laces, ribbons and small household utensils. They carried their cooking pots with them to observe the ritual laws, and generally only returned home once a year at Passover. In times of epidemics these Jews were in great danger. They were regarded as carriers of the plague, refused admittance to towns and often set on by the populace. In the poor regions of the east, there existed a fluctuating horde of Jewish beggars (*Pletten*) who would come into the towns and villages to celebrate the feast of Atonement. Full of bugs and dirt, they were unwelcome guests in the houses of local Jews, who, however, were forced by religious custom to invite them to their table.

The partitions of Poland brought a large Jewish population under the Prussian crown, particularly in West Prussia and Posen, where they often comprised up to half the population of a town. And yet, as contemporaries record, here there was little ill will between Christian and Jewish communities, apart from an occasional act of rowdyism. The son of a local excise official, K. F. Klöden, writing of Märkisch-Friedland in the 1790s, recalls the keen interest provided by the Jewish festivals in the impoverished lives of himself and his companions. The Christian children were invited to the performance of Esther during the Purim, and enjoyed it immensely. Jewish weddings, with the music making which accompanied them, were another thing they looked forward to. Some of the brighter children, such as Klöden himself, were allowed to attend lessons given by the Rabbi or his pupils.[6]

If one was destined by fate to live the difficult life of a Jew in Germany in this period, it was no doubt best to live in Prussia. In 1670 the Great Elector noticed the prosperity of Halberstadt, which he had recently acquired, and rightly attributed it to the Jewish community there. Accordingly he invited fifty of the Jewish families expelled by Leopold to settle in Brandenburg, and granted them privileges such as Viennese Jews did not enjoy until over a century later; they could acquire houses and worship in public. He did not regret his decision. The Court Jews under his successor, King Frederick I, Schulhoff, Liebman and Koppel Riess, stimulated trade and commerce and won considerable religious concessions, though they paid for them dearly in other ways. His grandson, Frederick William I, was savage in his language, but more fair minded in his treatment of the Jewish minority. When he invited one of the most distinguished Jews of his time, the west German merchant Moses Levi Gumperz, to be his *Hoffaktor,* he allowed him the unique privilege of carrying a dagger and of travelling freely in his dominions. Both Frederick William I and his son Frederick II went further than their fellow sovereigns; they passed general regulations governing the rights and duties of the Jews. If Mirabeau was justified in calling Frederick II's General Privilege of 1750 a '*loi digne d'un cannibale*' because it did not go far enough, one is forced to apply a relative standard in judging these matters. At that time neither the state authorities nor individuals thought to question their right to treat Jews differently from other human beings. It was something of a shock to traditional habits of thought when the Prussian official Chr. Wm. von Dohm wrote in his epoch-making work *On the Civic Improvement of the Jews* (1781), 'the Jew is more a human being than he is a Jew'. This was news indeed to most. It was in keeping with such prejudice that the German Jews owed the impulse to relief from their disabilities, not to humanitarian principles, but to the view that thus they could be more useful to the state.

A further impulse to reform came from cordial relations which grew up in Frederick II's time between a number of privileged Jews and their

Christian neighbours. Under Frederick such men as Veitel Ephraim, Daniel Itzig and others began to play a vital part in political and economic affairs. In fact it is not too much to say that they helped Frederick avoid defeat in the Seven Years War through veritable miracles of supplying troops and equipment, and by helping to restore the devastated economy thereafter. They did not achieve this without arousing prejudice. Post-war inflation was blamed on the Jews, especially as the King had granted Veitel Ephraim the right to mint all coins for the realm in 1762. A coin was minted by his critics showing Frederick stroking Ephraim's face with the caption, 'This is my beloved son in whom I am well pleased'. A satiric verse scoffed at the new coinage: 'Von aussen schön, von innen schlimm. Aussen Friedrich, innen Ephraim!' ['Outside lovely, inside nasty. Outside Frederick, inside Ephraim!'].[7]

But it was largely due to Veitel Ephraim's efforts, and those of his associates, that the trade and commerce of Prussia was placed on a sound financial basis and the foundations of a modern economy were laid. Seventeenth century Court Jews were rewarded with honorific titles and valuable gifts. The '*Juifs de Frédéric le Grand*', as they came to be known, preferred concessions which could lead to more permanent fortunes. In the last years of Frederick's reign and under his successor Frederick William II, the Berlin bankers and merchants merged with the cultured upper classes of the capital. It was an extraordinary time for Germany, but perhaps more extraordinary still for the history of the Jews. Despite the fact of the French revolutionary wars there seemed more time than ever for things of the spirit, for philosophy, poetry and music, and in their pursuit Jews played a leading role. The salons of Henriette Herz, later of Rahel Levin, provided the meeting place for poets, musicians, scholars and the nobility. Marriages with sons of wealthy Jews in other parts helped to spread ideas and culture. Thus when Fanny Itzig, Daniel's daughter, married Nathan Arnstein of Vienna, her salon was open to visitors from all parts and new ideas in Berlin were widely discussed here. When Frederick II's former court music director, J. F. Reichardt, came on a visit to Vienna in 1808, he was delighted to hear of Fanny's daughter, who had married into the Dutch Jewish family of Pereiras, playing the piano quartet in F minor by Prince Louis Ferdinand of Prussia. Reichardt's letters from Vienna, written after that happy visit, did much to eradicate the poor impression of Viennese customs and manners which the somewhat humourless Nicolai had established in northern Germany after his travels fifteen years earlier.

The active role played by Jews in Berlin life in the 1780s and 1790s naturally promoted interest in the question of Jewish civic disabilities, particularly since they themselves were changing. Itzig and Ephraim had won permission to establish a Jewish school in Berlin in 1762 to improve general education. A group of younger Jews, David Friedländer from Königsberg, his brother-in-law Isaak David Itzig, and Moses Mendelssohn's friend Naphtali Wessely, founded a more ambitious one in 1776 which soon grew rapidly. Friedländer and his brother-in-law also founded a Hebrew periodical on the lines of Biester's *Berlinische Monatsschrift,* which was to provide a link between the liberal minded Jews all over Prussia and Germany. While the generation of Daniel Itzig and Adam Arnstein, who died in the 1780s, remained strict observers of Jewish ritual, their children believed that orthodox observances were the chief cause of the disdain in which their people were held; these stressed their separateness and encouraged people to ill use them. It is remarkable that four out of Moses Mendelssohn's five surviving children became Christians, as did most of Daniel Itzig's large family. Many submitted to baptism, not, as in the nineteenth century, for opportunistic reasons, but because they had come to share the rational belief of one of their champions, Lessing, that all religions were fundamentally one. Certainly the climate of opinion in Berlin in these years was sympathetic to the Jews, and there are many literary works from the mid and late eighteenth century which argue the case for greater tolerance: the dramas, Lessing's *Die Juden,* Nesselrode's *Der adelige Tagelöhner,* Bischoff's *Judenfeind,* and the novels, Hermes's highly popular *Sophiens Reise von Memel nach Sachsen* or Jung Stilling's *Theodor der Schwärmer.*

Meanwhile Joseph II's Patent of Tolerance (1782) for all the Jews in his realms had caused great excitement all over Germany. It was widely hailed as a splendid example of things to come, but in fact it failed to provide the freedom of public worship for which Austrian Jews long hoped. Jews in Austria were now entitled to bear arms for their country; a patriotic Jew executed two engravings showing his co-religionists drilling in their uniforms, while lampoons mocked at their lack of dexterity. In other parts of Germany Jews had to wait until the nineteenth century for further measures. Across the Rhine the French revolutionary assembly brought full and immediate emancipation to the French Jews in 1791, and when the French invaded Germany the same rights were automatically extended to those living under their rule. This was a fundamentally different approach from that of the German authorities. The German governments and educated opinion generally inclined to the view that a gradual process of educating the populace and the Jews themselves for full emancipation was the best method. Dohm's book, mentioned earlier, is a typical example of this mentality. Indeed, his views are not only typical of Prussian attitudes towards the Jews but of a more general view of the role of the state in Germany in the late eighteenth and the nineteenth centuries. A passage from the beginning of *The Civic Improvement of the Jews* is therefore perhaps worth quoting at length:

> It is the great and noble business of government so to attenuate the exclusive principles of all those various societies that the common link which embraces them all is not impaired; that each of these divisions shall stimulate only emulation and activity rather than dislike and distance; and that all of them are resolved in the great harmony of the state. Let the government allow each of those special groupings to indulge in its pride, even in innocuous prejudices; but let it also strive to instill yet more love in each of the members, and it will have achieved its great task when the nobleman, the peasant, the scholar, the artisan, the Christian and the Jew is, beyond and above all that, a *citizen*.[8]

This is the view of the state as the guardian of civic society which found expression in the Prussian Code of State Law (*Allgemeines Landrecht*) (1794) and the Prussian liberal reform (1806–19). Although disabilities were reimposed on the Jews after 1815 in Prussia as elsewhere in Germany, it was in Prussia that assimilation was most rapid and that the Jews made the most diverse contribution to public life.

2 THE POOR

(*a*) *Vagrants*

Vagrancy had had a long history in Germany even before the seventeenth century; as early as 1400 it was organized as a regular and profitable business. A considerable gypsy population was present in Germany by the early sixteenth century, as well as a host of beggars, unemployed soldiers and strolling players. The *Liber vagatorum*, published in Augsburg in 1509, contains a full and illustrated account of their types, their manners, customs and language, *Rotwelsch.* Martin Luther wrote a preface to the nineteenth edition in 1528; here he urged the state and municipal authorities to distinguish between the destitute, whom they had a duty to care for, and the felons. Discharged soldiers constituted a serious menace to public safety throughout the sixteenth and seventeenth centuries, both on the highways and in the villages. The habit of leaving the bodies of hanged and broken robbers to rot on gallows and wheel beside the roadside did little to deter them; theirs could be a lucrative life in an age, especially between 1570 and 1650, when an honest living was hard to come by. The *Reichstag* had deliberated the problem of vagrants and the *Reich* Police Ordinance of 1548 contained punitive measures to be used against them. However, there was no machinery to enforce these, and the territorial princes began to legislate themselves. In Nordhausen the Elector of Brandenburg conferred with neighbouring princes and in 1572 instituted controls on the movements of strangers within his lands: they must make themselves known to the local authorities, and innkeepers were required to give particulars of travellers staying under their roof. Brandenburg suffered severely in the war, and by 1648 the whole area was infested by brigands. One of the achievements of the Prussian military system under the Great Elector was that it cleared the roads by the end of the century of marauding soldiers, either by hanging or recruiting them.

The problem of vagrancy was more difficult. Absolute princes in Germany were the more opposed to mendicancy because it was unproductive, and it discouraged the destitute from finding work. Between 1670 and 1684 the Elector of Brandenburg issued four edicts for the control of beggars, vagrants and gypsies, instructing the rural *gendarmes* to evict them from the Mark. In 1689 a new policy assigned such people to houses of correction, notably to Spandau, where they were employed to spin wool for the Prussian wool industry. The practice was one which the Prussian ruler had observed in Holland, and was imitated by other German states. Soon the poor and destitute were sent to join them. King Frederick I of Prussia (1688–1713) tried to combat the unsolved problem during his reign by imposing heavy penalties on city magistrates and rural authorities who tolerated foreign beggars.[9] In Würzburg Bishop Frederick Charles von Schönborn (1729–46) appointed border guards and watchmen at town gates to keep beggars out; if necessary armed force was to be used.[10] But the very frequency of such ordinances suggests that the law was not being enforced. Beggary certainly increased in the eighteenth century. Indeed, the term used in Austrian legislation to describe such persons, *Schubpersonen,* 'push-people', indicates the attitude of authority in face of so intractable a problem.[11] The populace was slow to cooperate with the authorities. In some areas, such as along the eastern borders of Germany, gypsies threatened the local population with arson if they reported their thefts. In general, however, people seemed to feel some sympathy towards beggars; their tolerance was perhaps prompted in part by a sort of passive resistance to increasing coercive bureaucracy. Grimmelshausen's hero Simplicissimus confesses to liking 'dissolute, idle beggars, vagrants and idle vagabonds'. In literature up to about

1730 the beggar is often represented as an amusing, often likeable figure, the Jew on the other hand, virtually never.

(*b*) *Poor relief*

The large number of beggars in towns and villages in early modern Germany was to a great extent the result of the state's failure to solve the problem of its poor. In medieval times it had been thought right and necessary for salvation to give to the poor. Municipalities, well-to-do men and landlords founded institutions to care for the poor and aged in their area. Nothing approaching a national or territorial poor relief system existed. The Protestant reformers in the sixteenth century rejected the kind of alms-giving practised in medieval times and condemned begging as dishonourable. Instead they instituted collections for the poor during divine service and hoped to administer some form of poor relief from a fund provided by confiscated church wealth. This was also needed to pay the salaries of the clergy, and funds soon proved inadequate. Accordingly an imperial edict issued in 1530 imposed a duty on towns and villages to cater for their resident poor; territorial princes issued similar ordinances in their lands. Catholic rulers were more lenient, perhaps more realistic, about the poor; begging certainly took some of the onus off the state, and it continued to be allowed, if more controlled than in former times. Thus the duke of Bavaria issued a series of ordinances from the end of the sixteenth century onwards; these permitted victims from fire, former prisoners of the Turks and (in 1655) the veterans of the Bavarian and the Imperial armies, to beg. However, in an attempt to prevent pauperization the Bavarian state imposed limitations on marriage among the poor and on subdivision of land; draconian penalties were also laid down against foreign beggars coming into Bavaria. However, the various charitable foundations continued to function, in the ecclesiastical states in particular, and the Catholic areas in general could not but attract vagrants from other parts. Society, one could say, by regarding those without property as outsiders, actually encouraged the poor to take to the roads. The *Reich* Ordinance of 1731 specifically rejected the old custom of regarding certain activities – peddling, bird fancying, etc. – as 'dishonourable'. But people continued to regard them thus, and the guilds continued to prohibit marriage between their members and descendants of such people.

The authorities proscribed and threatened, they reissued limitations on marriage and residence to those under a certain income, but they did not do much to alleviate the problem. Where were the funds to do so? Real poverty increased alarmingly in the eighteenth century; many found it impossible to feed their families, i.e. at a time when prices increased rapidly over wages; others, a very great number, if we are to believe contemporary reports, were simply work-shy, especially in the Catholic regions. The beginnings of manufacturing helped to deal with the problem. The Nuremberg Foundlings Home, Francke's Pietist foundations and the Potsdam Military Orphanage had consigned the poor to work. Indeed Francke's predecessor in the Pietist movement, Philipp Spener, had declared as early as 1674 in a sermon on jails and workhouses: 'For one thing, there is more good to be expected from such institutions than if we were to build more churches.'[12] Contemporary opinion regarded the late eighteenth century manufacturing and 'putting out' enterprises as aiding, not exploiting the poor. The social composition of early factory workers gives some indication of the extent of the problem. It included disbanded soldiers and their families, unemployed craftsmen, bankrupt traders and burghers as well as vagrants and felons. Not only was trade uncertain in these decades after the Seven Years War (1756–63), but calamity was always close at hand, remedy elusive. From the biographies of contemporaries, especially those in the middle and lower ranks of society, we see how the death of a father could in so many cases bring a family close to penury, even though he had been a member of a guild who tried to look after dependants. How much worse for them if he had not. Even the widows of eminent men could be indigent – Bach's wife, for example, finished her days on a slender pension from the city of Leipzig. The death of a mother, remarriage of the father and the survival of several children could put an intolerable strain on a household. Death from diseases contracted through undernourishment was common at the lower levels of society, affecting adults and children alike. Orphan children were a serious problem too. Among persons belonging to the middle groups of society, merchants, craftsmen and professional people, the larger family unit as it then existed usually gave a home to bereft minors. A man on marriage in such circles might expect to give a home to his bride's sisters and her mother if necessary. Among lower income groups the family might not be in a position to do so. The hosts of destitute children begging in the streets of Prussian towns prompted Francke to found his famous orphanage, King Frederick William I to apply his legendary energy to creating a military orphanage, the Königsberg court preacher Dr Mel to emulate their example in his home town of Hersfeld. However, arrangements by family, friends and the state to cater for those in need began to show signs of strain towards the end of the eighteenth century. The increase in population was mainly at the lower end of society, and this made demands on a system which was in any case little more than a series of *ad hoc* measures.

By 1800, although not yet known by that name, wide areas in Germany were affected by the problem of pauperism on a major scale.

3 WITCHES

In seventeenth century Germany, and in some parts of the country well into the second half of the eighteenth, a far more horrible fate than hunger and neglect awaited some members of the community, especially those from among 'the lowly and the elderly, the feeble- and simple-minded ugly country folk':[13] they were accused of witchcraft, tried, tortured and generally burnt at the stake.

Germany thus shared in a phenomenon that was characteristic of early modern European history, but showed certain chronological and regional variations. Witch hunting occurred in southern France and Switzerland in the fourteenth century, but although it came to Germany a century later, first to the Rhineland and then into southern and central parts of Germany, there are relatively few known trials in the late fifteenth and early sixteenth centuries. One of the most notorious exponents of witch hunting was a German Dominican, J. Springer, whose *Malleus Maleficarum* or *Hammer of Witches* (1485) was to be much quoted in defence of the practice in later years. Yet it was not reprinted once in the years 1520–66 – that is, between the early years of the Reformation and the onset of the first major trials. The period in which witch hunting became a veritable mania in certain regions of Germany, that is between the 1560s and a little over a century later, lies mainly outside the time covered by this study. However, the incidence of trials and execution of witches lasted longer in Germany than in western Europe: the last execution in England took place in 1685, the last known trial in 1717, whereas in Kempten in Swabia, a woman was executed for witchcraft as late as 1775.[14]

There are other features of witch hunting in Germany which puzzle the historian. The Peasants War of 1525 and the worst phases of the Thirty Years War, notably the years after 1630, saw relatively little persecution, and, in the case of the latter years, a time of severe plague and famine, there was a sharp decline in the practice by contrast with the previous thirty years. Moreover, during the witch panics of the century mid 1560s to 1660s, Jews were relatively little molested. It is not true to say that witches and Jews were interchangeable scapegoats, at hand to bear the brunt of the fears and frustrations of an ignorant and superstitious populace. The incident of the so-called Hall Witches Bath provides a somewhat bizarre illustration of this. The colonel of a Bavarian regiment, occupying the free Imperial town of Schwäbisch Hall near Stuttgart during the Thirty Years War, decided to counteract rumours of witchcraft among the wives of his soldiers by conducting a trial by immersion in water. He offered the substantial reward of 12 *taler* to any unsuspected person who would submit himself voluntarily to the test, it being held that an innocent person would float. A Jew named Löb was the only volunteer and, after floating three times, collected his reward. That he should have felt sufficiently confident to do so at such a time is remarkable. It is recorded that the wives of both officers and men were less fortunate or less adept. Several were now forced to submit to the test, sank, were found guilty and executed.[15]

In his erudite study of witch hunting in south-west Germany, the American historian Erik Midelfort has introduced to the German field the insights of an anthropological approach to the subject, without, however, wholly accepting their relevance for early modern German social history. Here, as so often since the 1950s, critical and sensitive American scholars, in most cases the products of schools founded by emigrés from Hitler's Germany, have provided a bridge between modern historians in the United States and western Europe, with their readiness to learn from other disciplines, and the more traditionalist German approach. Midelfort puts forward some interesting views on the possible origins and causes of decline of witch hunting in the south-west. The area covered is that of present-day Baden and Württemberg, at that time an area of great territorial complexity and mixed religion. He notes that up to 1600 there was considerable diversity of opinion on witchcraft among the theologians of all three confessions. This appears to have derived from two distinct traditions with regard to the power and influence of the witch. The one saw evil and natural disaster as part of Divine Providence and refused to accept that the witch could possess the powers over other human beings generally attributed to her; the other condemned witchcraft as heresy, and stressed the witch's pact with the devil and her power for evil in the community: this approach made it a duty for the authorities to hunt out and punish with the greatest severity those guilty of spiritual as well as secular crimes. Before the beginning of the seventeenth century no one confession could be linked with either tradition. After about 1600, with the growing dynamism of the Counter-Reformation and perhaps an even greater readiness than before to perceive the forces of darkness arraigned against the hosts of light, the milder observance towards witches became rare among Catholics, though it still appealed to many Lutherans. Not only were the numbers of Catholic trials more numerous in the areas examined, but the number of those executed per trial was considerably higher. However, the pattern of witch hunting is peculiarly complex and general statements are often misleading: the last and some of the bloodiest large-scale trials in Württemberg in the 1660s all took place in Lutheran territories.

An important factor in the witch panics of early modern Germany was a change in the legal system. In 1532 the *Codex Carolina* had permitted the use of torture in the trials of witches; at the same time it was demanded that sufficient evidence exist before the accused be brought to trial and certain limitations on its use were prescribed. Among the many gruesome features of the witch panics was the readiness of the many authorities to dispense with these safeguards in later years. Part of the trouble was the confused wording of the *Carolina*. Individual territorial rulers accordingly introduced new codes for their lands with more specific and harsher procedures – Württemberg in 1552, electoral Saxony in 1572, the Palatinate and Baden in the following decade. Moreover, whereas early German law had been private law, in which the plaintiff exposed himself to severe penalties if the case was not proven, in the second half of the sixteenth century the state began to take over the role of accuser; it became common for judge, prosecutor and torturer to be the same person or panel of persons. If we recall that the torturer (and the executioner) was paid per victim, the dangers to which the accused might be exposed are manifest.[16] Moreover, it was common in the seventeenth century to regard witchcraft as so heinous a crime that the accused were permitted no legal aid, and even kept in special prisons of unimaginable horror. The use of torture to extract confessions and force the witch to name her associates was based on the idea that only under severe pain would the victim be momentarily released from the thrall of the devil and speak the truth; the very success of the ghastly efforts only confirmed its veracity to men haunted by a sense of evil all about them, an awareness fed by plague, famine, natural catastrophe and war, or, more frequently, by the dread of these things in the immediate future. Their fears might be fed by the sermons of their local pastors or by the reading of popular works on demonology (*Teufelsbücher*) which became a veritable spate in the late sixteenth century. The detailed confessions of accused witches confirmed people in their certainty of demonic possession and horrid acts against God and society. (But, as Erik Midelfort points out with reference to the seventeenth century witch panic in the Swabian town of Ellwangen, it would be quite easy to reconstruct the witches' confessions from the questionnaires of their accusers.) Few contemporaries were prepared, as was Johann Weyer, physician to the Calvinist Duke of Jülich-Cleves, to declare quite simply that women (and men and children also) were prepared to confess and to suffer the ultimate penalty of death at the stake in preference to being thrust back to daily torture and hideous dungeons (in *De Praestigis Daemonis*, 1563).

In other parts of Germany a number of seventeenth century ecclesiastical princes were most savage in their pursuit of witches, notably in Trier, Bamberg and Würzburg. If the witch panics of the south-west were largely a response to mass mood, there was a very strong political element in these trials, particularly in the case of the prince bishops of Würzburg and Bamberg. In the latter case the bishop virtually eradicated the upper class of the town, husbands and wives alike; between 1626 and 1630 nearly 200 persons were burnt, including the mayor, several clergymen, lawyers and doctors. It was as a result of what he had witnessed as a student at Trier, and was to see later in Würzburg where he acted as chaplain to accused and condemned witches, which prompted the Jesuit poet Fr. von Spee to write in 1631 his *Cautio criminalis*, attacking the whole concept of witch hunting. He declared that he had never been convinced that a single one had been guilty of the crimes accused, and in an appendix which dexterously and audaciously compared the sufferings of the 'witches' with those of Nero's victims, Spee called for the support of the Emperor and the German people. Spee's arguments were legal, not theological, and though not immediately effective in counteracting the terror, the fact that the *Cautio* was reprinted sixteen times in the following hundred years seems proof of its eventual influence, especially among judges and magistrates. The powerful Archbishop Elector of Mainz, Lothar Philip von Schönborn, who spoke with great admiration of Spee to Leibniz in later years, was moved by his arguments to prohibit the practice in his lands in 1647, some twelve years after Spee's death. The decline in the mass witch panics was brought about, in Professor Midelfort's view, not by rational persuasion or humanitarian considerations, but by satiation. When the bishop of Bamberg found himself and his chancellor accused of witchcraft in 1630, he suddenly called the trials to cease forthwith, and even instituted regular memorial services for the innocent victims.

If at the beginning of a spate of witch hunting and in the early stages of large trials, the accused were almost invariably of the type described above, the ugly old crone of legend, very soon prominent citizens and their wives were drawn into the vortex. Victims were invariably tortured to make them name their associates, and if innkeepers and midwives figured largely as victims, this is not surprising, since animosity was likely to be directed at well-known, notorious and rich citizens; the number of prominent citizens involved had a good deal to do with the fact that such people were creditors of those who named or accused them. In the mass trials of the seventeenth century men and children fell victim in ever increasing numbers to the witch mania. Children accused themselves of gross crimes, and in some trials the number of child victims exceeded that of adults.[17] The bishop of Würzburg even had his own young nephew burnt. As it became impossible to identify the witches, no one was safe. Thus a loss of confidence in the judicial procedures caused the decline in witch panics in the second half of the Thirty Years War, though they erupted sporadically in the following decades. The smaller witch trials, for which an anthropological explanation would seem appropriate, continued to serve as a kind of social mechanism to channel local fears and frustration against the eccentric members of the community: the victims of these small trials continued to be the stereotype witch, the elderly or feeble-minded women, living alone. Since the social structure was geared to the patriarchal family, widows or spinsters whose parents had died – that is, those living without the control of husband or guardian – were automatically regarded by society with suspicion.

In accounting for the onset and spread of witchcraft in Germany and in Europe generally in the early modern period, scholars nowadays incline to the view that changes in the marriage patterns at this time meant that both men and women married later and that there were greater numbers of dependent women in existence than society could cope with.[18] At the present stage of historical research it is not possible to establish this conclusively. The ultimate decline of witch hunting in the eighteenth century came when the courts were able to find persons guilty of specific crimes – murder, arson, fraud or superstitious practices, rather than of witchcraft, with all the accompanying traditional notions of heresy, devilish pacts, carnal intercourse with demons, witches' sabbaths, etc. At local level, particularly in rural areas, the eccentric and the ugly, or even the very beautiful continued to be the object of suspicion and often to be physically molested as witches, but without, in general, serious consequences.[19]

Part II: 1806–1914

Introduction to Part II

The year 1806 is a milestone in the history of Germany. In the summer of that year the Holy Roman Empire ceased to exist; in the autumn, on the battlefield at Jena, the army and social order of Prussia suffered an annihilating defeat at the hands of the same agent who had brought the Empire to an end: Napoleon. One year later a young privy councillor and Prussian official, von Altenstein, analysed the causes of defeat and commented: 'There was no nation in the state, not even provinces in the proper sense of the term; there were just separate estates in the various provinces, each with its own special interests, with no common ground between them.'[1] Altenstein was overstating the case, but in his observation he put his finger on the central problem of Prussian and German society at the beginning of the nineteenth century and one which foreign visitors continued to comment on for many years. For although in the winter of the same year, 1807, the Romantic philosopher Fichte held the first of his famous *Addresses to the German Nation,* in fact at the time the German nation was still not much more than the postulate of a fairly narrow segment of society, namely the early German liberals.

However, for a decade after the demise of the 1000-year-old Empire, men of liberal views found themselves in a position to exercise influence on public opinion and even on the policies of governments. Many, indeed most, were of bourgeois origin, academics of the type of Fichte, or Thaer, doctor and pioneer of artificial fertilizers in agriculture, or businessmen, merchants and publishers, such as Perthes, established in Hamburg, or Buchholtz of Berlin, whose interests took them to or linked them with many parts of Germany. Others, provincial clergymen and other professional men, whose experiences as tutors in noble houses had made them fiery critics of absolutism in youth and sympathetic to liberal ideas in middle age, corresponded with like-thinking diplomats and state officials, who, as in the case of Baron Stein or Wilhelm von Humboldt, had come in contact with English political philosophers or with the writings of Adam Smith while at the Hanoverian University of Göttingen.[2] Most liberals in early nineteenth century Germany had been strongly influenced by the German Enlightenment. They had developed their ideas in the clubs and reading societies and in the debates conducted in the learned journals which had been so numerous in the last decades of eighteenth-century Germany. Despite an initially widespread and enthusiastic response to the French Revolution among German intellectuals, few were radical. Their debates and discussions, conducted between members of very different social backgrounds, especially in the unusually fluid society of Berlin in the 1790s and early 1800s, were speculative and rational in tone, rather than programmatic. Many intellectuals and public figures believed that the opportunity – or the vacuum – brought about through the events of 1806 would enable them to reform society and the state on a liberal basis.

The humble origin of many of the most energetic and articulate spokesmen of liberalism made social reform a central preoccupation. Furthermore, while the passing of the Empire had made so many of the traditional feudal privileges seem not only obsolete but without any justification in social function, it was apparent that some could even be a burden to those whom they were intended to distinguish. Thus members of the Prussian nobility were prohibited by their caste from selling their estates to commoners or 'demeaning' themselves by pursuing commerce. In fact, as East German historians have demonstrated in detail, a considerable proportion of such land was indeed owned by commoners by 1806, though not officially in their names.[3]

Moreover, despite much adverse comment at the time, the traditional marks of feudal society, the distinctive dress and forms of address peculiar to the various estates, were rapidly disappearing by the end of the eighteenth century, and it seemed reasonable to acknowledge this in legislation. Thus the titles '*Herr*' and '*Madame*', formerly the prerogative of the upper classes, were already common in *Kleinbürger* circles in the early nineteenth century, although in some parts of Germany until 1848 the patronizing '*Er*' was used to subordinates, even minor officials and teachers, instead of the polite *'Sie'*, and *Demoiselle* instead of *Fräulein* (that factory workers and domestics until 1918, common soldiers in Bavaria until 1868, were addressed by the familiar *'Du'* was less the natural survival of feudal custom, than a wish to prolong paternalist authority in the home and places of work).[4]

The reform programmes introduced into several German states in the wake of Napoleonic conquest, most notably Prussia, were motivated in a general way by a belief in the need to replace a caste society by a more efficient and liberal state. More immediately they were a response to the needs of the moment – namely, fiscal considerations, and the necessity of finding the war contributions which were the price of defeat or domination by the French. From the latter point of view the reforms, particularly in Prussia, were successful to the point of making Prussia financially the most solvent of all German states in the first half of the century. The economic liberalism of the reform programme was sedulously adhered to by successive Prussian administrations until mid century, and prepared for the prodigious expansion of the economy in that state after 1850. The measures granting powers of self-government to the municipalities, initially resisted for financial reasons, contributed in the second half of the century to the rapid growth of towns and cities; their administrators remained staunch advocates of economic liberalism long after other groups had become disillusioned with the accompanying political risks and social cost.[5] The massive task of agrarian reform proceeded at a different pace in different parts of the country; in some parts, notably Austria, reforms were not implemented until the time of the revolution of 1848, in Mecklenburg later still. In Prussia the agrarian programme and the measures raising restrictions on trade brought about a massive transfer of property at the lower end of society. The resultant social mobility and the prodigious expansion of population which accompanied it – a 60 per cent increase in Prussia alone between 1815 and 1848 – were vital contributory factors to the economic and social crises of the Restoration period.

The social context of the 1848 revolution is now firmly established. Historians continue to corroborate in detail the scale of local grievances which contributed to the outbreak.[6] The political frustrations of the Metternich regime made the constitutionalists the natural leaders of the revolution. (Although their grievances were most acutely felt in Prussia, where the King had failed to implement his promise – made on five occasions – to grant a constitution and where the reform movement had failed to dislodge the privileged élite, the existence of constitutions, as in the south German states, was no guarantee of individual freedom.) It was, however, the intensity of social distress and the feeling that the authorities had abandoned their traditional role of protector in time of need which provided the revolution with the necessary mass support. Agrarian discontent, especially in the heavily populated south and south-west, was much more acute than governments realized, and it provided the motor force for the outbreak of revolt in the early months of 1848, in places even before the actual occurrence of the February revolution in Paris. Across the broad spectrum of the middle classes, support for the revolution came from the distressed craftsmen and small traders for whom material want brought not only physical suffering but a sense of loss of status in the community, from the educated without or with few prospects, and from middle and lower ranking state employees dissatisfied with conditions and with official policies.

However, the revolutionary assemblies and new liberal ministries failed to deal with social problems. This was a vital contributory factor to the failure of the revolution as a whole. The apparent neglect of their concerns by the newly constituted authorities and the solidarity experienced in the strikes, the congresses and associations of working men, and in the violent clashes with the military in the autumn of 1848 and spring of 1849, all helped to forge a sense of working class consciousness, something which had not been there before. Moreover, the experiences of 1848–9 persuaded the broad mass of the lower middle classes and economically deprived groups in towns and the countryside, particularly the small tradesmen, to forsake their liberal allegiance and support the conservative forces of the Counter-Revolution. This phenomenon was a most important long-term consequence of the 1848 revolution. It was exacerbated by the growth, from the 1860s onwards, of the most important new social group to emerge in the nineteenth century – namely, the urban wage labourers – and of its organization, the social democratic movement. Already by the 1850s those groups who had been political liberals in the pre-March days, besides the lower middle class, the academics and minor officials, also such groups as rural innkeepers, no longer held liberal views.[7] With their leaders emigrated to Britain or the United States, and themselves disillusioned with the notion of progressive social change, they looked to the traditional establishment to remedy what they saw as their vital needs – namely, economic and social protection, rather than political enfranchisement. Partly as a result of earlier policies, but mainly by a matter of fortunate timing, governments, particularly in Prussia, were given credit for the sudden upsurge in the economy which followed the revolution, and was sustained, with brief intermissions, for nearly a generation. The commitment of the middle ranks of society in Germany to a conservative government and social order in the second half of the nineteenth century was naturally strengthened by the unification of Germany under Prussia, after three successful wars in 1864, 1866 and 1870–1. At the same time it was continually reinforced by the distrust felt by large sections of the community for Manchester-type liberalism on the one hand, and by a fear of organized labour on the other.

Even the new plutocracy, which was the product of the industrial revolution, assimilated itself, as did most other groups within the upper bourgeoisie, to the values and attitudes of the traditional ruling classes, rather than acting as a leaven upon them. Contacts, whether social or professional, between the upper middle classes and the nobility remained fairly tenuous even in the decades immediately preceding the 1914 war, because of the official policy of the preferment of the wellborn in the prestigious posts in the army, the diplomatic career and the civil service. Prestigious educational establishments, such as existed in one form or another in Western countries, where the élite of both strata could meet, did not exist in Germany (rather did education in the form of grammar school (*Gymnasium*) act as a well-nigh insurmountable barrier between upper bourgeoisie and *Kleinbürger*). To be sure, many marriages did take place between scions of noble German houses and wealthy bourgeois during the Second Empire (1871–1918); patents of nobility were granted (at a price) in increasing numbers and with the reluctant acquiescence of the old Emperor William I. This was designed to furbish the coffers of conservatism and to assure the continued loyalty of the well-to-do and the educated to the established order. But the scale of both was insufficient to bring about any integration of the two classes. On the other hand, as recent research indicates, a high degree of integration was achieved between the bureaucrats and the professional middle classes in late nineteenth century Germany and their sense of cohesion *vis-à-vis* other economically dependent groups was fostered.[8]

Overall, and especially by comparison with France or Britain, Germany did not discard that hierarchical and stratified character in the nineteenth century which earlier foreign visitors, such as Madame de Staël and Fanny Trollope, had considered to be a salient feature of her society. Contemporaries had noted that one of the effects of the failure of the 'bourgeois' revolution of 1848 had been to encourage a tendency for social groups to think in terms of their own kind and their own preoccupations, rather than of society as a whole, or of such notions as bourgeois culture and progress (provincial society in West Germany today still retains much of this character).

The fact that the dual revolution experienced by Germany in the nineteenth century, industrialization and unification, did not alter the traditional character of its society is a central problem of recent German history. The rapidity of change – economic, demographic, and political – the failure of the 1848 revolution to alter the basic social structure or effect a transfer of power from the pre-industrial élite, created what is known as 'the general crisis of modernization' in pre-First-World-War Germany. This was in effect a refusal to modernize, a refusal to entertain as possible, or indeed as inevitable, that German society might evolve along the lines of that in Western constitutional states: it was exemplified in a particularly crass manner in attitudes of the rest of the community towards the urban wage labourers as forming inevitably a 'dangerous' or 'hostile' force in their contemporary world.

Perhaps only in death could it be said that the development of society in nineteenth century Germany had approximated to the pattern in other parts of Europe: in the last years of the Holy Roman Empire it was still customary for members of the nobility to bury their dead within the church or cloister, while the 'populace' found their graves outside in the churchyard. By contrast, the growth of the cities and of the population in nineteenth century Germany produced the type of large purpose-built cemetery where the only distinguishing feature between one social group and another was the degree of ostentation of the gravestone, no longer determined by membership of a particular estate but merely by differences in wealth and social pretension.

Section 1
The authorities

Chapter 10
The courts and the nobility

An informed observer visiting Germany in the year 1806 would not have given much on the chances of the hereditary nobility surviving in its present form. It was not only the revolutionary changes under Napoleon's administration that threatened privileged position, but the consensus of opinion in ministries and educated circles seemed unfavourably disposed towards the aristocracy in general. The ease with which the ecclesiastical states had disappeared from the map between 1803 and 1806, and the so-called mediatized princes, former sovereign rulers of petty states, had been absorbed by the member states of the Confederation of the Rhine, seemed to point to a new order of society in which the nobility would play a much diminished role. Yet when the time came to reorder the map of Germany at Vienna in 1815, in the aftermath of Napoleon's defeat, it was the wishes of the sovereigns rather than national feeling that determined the form of government. The rulers of the new German Confederation (1815–67) clearly considered the privileges of the nobility as a guarantee of their own position. Although the nobility lost certain legal privileges, particularly in connection with the land reforms of the first decades of the century, many of its political privileges survived until the revolution of 1848; socially its preeminence was unchallenged before the fall of the monarchy in 1918.

The most anomalous position in the complex history of the German nobility in the nineteenth century was that of the mediatized princes (*Standesherrn*). They were concentrated in Swabia, Franconia and the Wetterau in north-west Germany. Their loyalties were diverse, often determined by the accident of which state army members of the house had happened to serve in. Many, especially the Catholics who were in the majority, felt a strong bond with Austria; after 1806 they transferred the loyalty they had felt for the Holy Roman Empire to the Habsburgs and many, such as the Windischgrätz of military fame, settled in Vienna. When, in the mid nineteenth century, a guardian was sought for the young orphan heir of the Thurn and Taxis family, the Emperor Francis Joseph himself was not thought too elevated to be asked and he agreed to act. Württemberg earned their particular hostility and the title of 'purgatory of the mediatized princes', for its king refused to acknowledge their claimed equality of rank with himself as ruling prince and insisted on compulsory attendance at court under threat of confiscation of a quarter of their income.[1] The question of rank was a favourite and often exclusive preoccupation of these princes, still an issue in 1872 when Baroness von Spitzemberg, a Swabian noblewoman, so acute in registering the 'feel' of the time, confided resignedly to her diary: 'ich kam an des Kronprinzen Tisch zu sitzen, mit lauter Standesherren, so dass ich mich sehr mässig unterhielt' ['I was placed at the Crown Prince's table, with nothing but mediatized princes, so had a rather dull time'].[2] Although it was not a fact always appreciated by them, Prussia treated the mediatized princes most generously. Many found posts in government service there. Count Solms-Lamberg performed a useful task of conciliation after 1815 as *Oberpräsident* of the Rhineland, whose inhabitants were unwilling to be part of the Prussian kingdom; Otto von Stolberg-Wernigerode played a similar role in Hanover after 1866, while members of the various branches of the Hohenlohe family served as diplomats, military attachés and *aides-de-camp* to the Kings of Prussia.

The mediatized princes provided much talent at national level and in the administration of the states they chose to serve. Furthermore they were a vivid link with Germany's earlier particularist traditions. The bond between the nobility as a whole and that other great conservative institution, the church, was strong throughout the century, in Protestant as well as Catholic regions, and perhaps in no group more than the Catholic mediatized princes. It was, after all, one thing to have been a prelate in some wealthy monastery of the feudal *Reich* church, and quite another after 1815 as bishop or abbot to be forced to defer to some niggling minister of the interior in one of the German federal states. The effect of mediatization therefore was to make them more conscious of their loyalty to the church, though not necessarily pro-papal. In Austria mediatized princes continued to be appointed to the highest ecclesiastical posts – Cardinal Archbishops of Prague and Olmütz, where they ruled as feudal lords, uninfluenced by the ferment of social thought agitating some of their German colleagues. Not only sons of princely families but young Catholic noblemen in general tended to be sent to boarding school, especially to the Jesuit houses in Feldkirch, Innsbruck and Kalkburg, making contacts here which would serve them well in later life. The earliest Catholic political groups formed in 1848, and the Centre Party in its early years, were led by members of the nobility, among them the Lothringian mediatized family of Arenberg. Members of two other such families, the Löwensteins and Prince Alois Liechtenstein, played an energetic part in the Catholic associations of the late nineteenth century, their conferences an important source of inspiration for Leo XIII's famous social encyclical, *Rerum Novarum.*[3]

The history of the mediatized princely nobility is a fascinating but extremely diverse one, and has been told in painstaking detail by Heinz Gollwitzer. The history of the rest of the south German nobility has been much less studied, and information must often be gleaned from memoirs and correspondences. On the other hand, very many monographs have been devoted to the north German aristocracy in the nineteenth century, particularly from the East Elbian provinces. In general, common to them all in the years after 1815 was an entrenched position of privilege, though their legal position and economic stability might vary considerably. Thus in Hanover they owned but 6 per cent of the land, yet had legal privileges unequalled by the nobility of any other state of the Confederation; in Mecklenburg the nobles had experienced none of the intervention by the ruler in rural affairs characteristic of Prussia, and had built themselves up vast estates through expropriation of the peasantry; their peasants were serfs of the kind found in Russia. In Saxony and in Prussia the nobility lost certain legal rights during the land reforms, but still dominated rural life, especially in the east, and they continued to find preference over commoners in the army and government. Silesia was one of the few provinces in which a really wealthy landed aristocracy was found, who invested in trade and industry, behaved as great magnates in their sumptuous castles and consorted with their peers from France and Russia, Italy and Bohemia at the foreign resorts which their fellow countrymen, the Prussian *Junkers,* could not afford.

In general the German nobility, despite the privileges its members retained, especially in the first half of the century, survived in their position of preeminence only in so far as they were economically successful. This could mean many things: it could mean transforming their estates, as did many East Elbian *Junkers,* into capitalist enterprises, it could mean placing one's children in secure, if not well paid, posts in the army or state service, it could mean securing the hand in marriage (this was most common at the end of the century) of a wealthy Jewess or member of an industrial or banking family. But, as a class, survive they did, and although commoners were ever more successful in aspiring to the kind of posts noblemen considered acceptable, they retained a percentage of the most prestigious posts quite out of proportion with their numbers.

Under the Second Empire the nobility effectively dominated most institutions of state, the army and the upper chambers of state legislatures, and in Prussia the lower house; they filled virtually all prestigious posts and many of the rest in the diplomatic service and they had a 'strategic position within the apparatus of administration' at local and national level, as well as considerable influence in appointments to senior posts in government and bureaucracy.[4] Although the actual percentage of noble officers declined from 65 per cent in 1865 to 30 per cent in 1913, a closer look at the positions they held shows developments in a somewhat different light. Thus in 1913, 80 per cent of cavalry officers were noblemen, as were 48 per cent of infantry and 41 per cent of the field artillery, but in the traditionally less respected technical regiments of sappers they numbered only 4 per cent. Sixty-two per cent of all Prussian regiments had more than 58 per cent of noble officers, and the officer corps of sixteen regiments were exclusively noble; in 1908 – though this figure is not representative of the average – the Guards regiments had only four bourgeois officers. Moreover, 83 per cent of all *Oberpräsidenten,* chief administrative official of a province, 50 per cent of the *Regierungspräsidenten* or president of government boards and district president or sheriff were noblemen, as well as 40 per cent of all *Reich* ministers.[5] 'Noble' included the many new creations which were a feature of the 1870s, part of the policy supported by Bismarck, despite the patrician reluctance of his Emperor, to win support from the old bourgeoisie and the new plutocracy for the conservative monarchical state. Contrary to this trend to buttress the privileged position of the first estate, even in the so-called bourgeois age, was the practice in the churches, both Protestant and Catholic. High offices in the German churches were less frequently held by noblemen than had been the case in former years, though many of the wealthiest and most prestigious prelates (Cardinal Archbishop of Prague) or the most forceful (Archbishop Ketteler of Mainz or Chief Superintendent Friedrich von

Bodelschwingh) came from their ranks.

A patent of nobility in Germany and Austria was, in the words of N. von Preradovich,[6] a ticket of entry, not a membership card; it often took several decades before a newly ennobled family began to intermarry with the old nobility and to be accepted by them. In nineteenth century Austria the two did not merge socially; however, the service nobility won positions of power and influence both in the army and the administration, including even the diplomatic corps. They met little opposition from the exclusive established families, who wished neither to recruit new blood in the manner of the British or Prussian nobility, nor to play a prominent role in the political life of their country.[7] The senior diplomatic posts were traditionally the preserve of the highest families, but all the foreign ministers between 1818 and 1871 came – apart from two Lothringian aristocrats in 1848 and 1864–6 – from the German nobility; after 1871 they were generally Hungarians. The strength of the Prussian nobility on the other hand was their ability to attract and absorb new blood. On court occasions the demonstrable superiority of the older families over the new was made apparent in the ceremonial order; where it mattered, in the army and the administration, in the foreign service apart from the key posts and in parliament, a common ideal of service to the state and intermarriage greatly facilitated the integration of the two classes of nobility. A patent had to be earned in Prussia, but this achievement was respected. The father of General Gneisenau, who distinguished himself in the wars against Napoleon, had been a buildings inspector in Oppeln, Silesia; yet the Gneisenaus were able to intermarry with such distinguished families as the Plessens, Bonins and Kottwitzes. The Rauchs, connected by marriage with the Moltkes, Levetzows, Brühls and Bismarcks, and who provided Prussia with seven generals and a minister of war in the nineteenth century, were greatgrandchildren of a teacher in the village of Peterskirchen.[8] The Prussian nobility, old and new, dominated the conservative parties under the Second Empire, both in the *Reichstag* and the Prussian Diet; the Rhenish and south German, on the other hand, being Catholic, were to be found in the ranks of the Centre Party, where in 1881 they reached their highest proportion ever – some 26 per cent of the members. In Bavaria the pattern was different again; here the public service was dominated by members of the bourgeoisie or the newly ennobled, but they did not intermarry with the native nobility. The latter, as in Austria, took very little interest in public affairs; nobles active in the state administration or the army were almost invariably from Franconia or Swabia.[9]

The pioneering land reform programme, introduced by Baron von Stein into Prussia in 1807 and imitated in various forms in most German states thereafter, was motivated by a desire, firstly, to improve agricultural production and, secondly, to instil a concept of citizenship into all ranks of Prussian society, which the corporative privileges of the nobility had formerly denied them. The impetus for such thoroughgoing reforms was the fruit of over a generation of discussion and criticism, reflected in journals, newspapers and pamphlets in which the whole idea of a hereditary privileged nobility was questioned.[10] Hardenberg, Stein's colleague and successor in the Prussian ministry, and himself a nobleman, declared programmatically in 1807: 'Jede Stelle im Staat, ohne Ausnahme, sei nicht dieser oder jener Kaste, sondern dem Verdienst und der Geschicklichkeit und Fähigkeit aus allen Ständen offen' ['All posts in the state are open, not just to this caste or that, but without exception to merit, ability and talent'].[11] However, circumstances changed between the time of the initiation of the programme in the aftermath of Prussia's defeat at Jena, which had been seen above all as a failure of the hitherto dominant nobility, and the years of peace after 1815. The vested interests of ruling princes in preserving a hereditary nobility close to the throne, as well as the German and particularly the Prussian nobility's strong sense of self-interest, proved effective in preserving their position. Moreover, the final effect of the agrarian legislation enabled most to strengthen the economic basis of their power, although individual families succumbed in crisis periods of German agriculture during the next decades.

In south Germany a feudal form (*Grundherrschaft*) of landownership was usual and the nobility lived from rents rather than, as in East Elbia, farming the land themselves. Service and feudal dues were commuted to money payments in the course of the land reform, which, however, extended over a period of almost half a century and was not completed until after the revolution of 1848. As a result many noble families, not least several mediatized princely houses, having spent the monies received in compensation, found themselves deprived of their regular income, and were forced to seek employment in bourgeois occupations. Others, more enterprising, exploited the resources on their estates; thus Ernest of Hohenzollern-Langenburg, married to Queen Victoria's stepsister Feodora, and their son Hermann, cut down their forests and sold the timber to industry and the railway companies; after that inauspicious beginning – the Langenburgs, who had existed on an income of £600 when they married in 1828, were literally saved from penury by an annuity from the young Victoria – they completely restored the family fortunes. Many of the Bavarian landowners showed equal initiative and invested manorial dues or quit rents in industrial enterprise on their lands.[12]

It was in Prussia that the most vigorous efforts were made by the nobility to survive as a social class in the face of change. The overall effect of the agrarian reforms had in fact been to strengthen the economic position of those *Junkers* (and bourgeois owners of seignorial estates) who managed to survive the general depression of agriculture between 1806 and 1825, and particularly the crisis years of the early 1820s. The amount of land held by the owners of *Rittergüter* increased substantially in the half century following the Stein-Hardenberg legislation; most important of all, they transformed themselves from something the equivalent of self-sufficient gentlemen farmers into capitalist entrepreneurs. Undoubtedly the presence of bourgeois landowners in their midst contributed notably to a new attitude towards farming. These had bought up bankrupt estates at the turn of the century, or when prices plummeted in the early 1820s, and many of them tried out the new rationalist methods such as those propounded by Albrecht von Thaer in his *Grundzüge der rationalen landwirtschaft* (*Principles of Rational Farming*) (Berlin 1809). The East Elbian landowners learned to profit from a favourable economic situation, with easy access to overseas markets for their grain exports up to the middle of the century, and a growing demand on the home market. During the half century from 1825 to the mid 1870s it was not aristocratic privilege but efficient farming which determined the continued possession of land by noblemen. However, in the *latifundia* of the eastern provinces – that is, estates of 5000 hectares or more – bourgeois or newly ennobled landowners were few. In the early 1880s there were but ten of these among a total of 159.[13] The surplus population of rural labourers in eastern Germany, which was one of the consequences of the agrarian reform, coupled with the very great increase in fertility among this class, and the fact that German industry was not in a position before the late 1860s to absorb their numbers, provided the landowners with an apparently limitless supply of cheap labour.[14] Several decades of economic prosperity, plus the fact of their privileged status in the local community and in society at large, made the East Elbian landowners regard their position less as a privilege than a right, and to make them psychologically unprepared for the political assaults on their status in the 1848 revolution and the liberal era of the 1860s; it made them determined to resist the disagreeable economic facts of life, when the long years of agrarian prosperity came to a sudden end in the 1870s.

Despite the emancipation of the peasantry, the legal changes and economic upheaval in their midst, the political and social position of the

Prussian landed nobility was still largely unchanged in the middle of the century. The revolution of 1848 brought them the loss of their patrimonial jurisdiction; in 1861 their tax concessions on land were abolished, while in 1872 the new district code (*Kreisordnung*) took from them their police powers in the village and their absolute majority in the district assemblies or executive council (*Kreistage*). Bitter scenes marked the passage of the bill in the Prussian provincial diet, as those affected fought to preserve their traditional role, under threat of mass creation of peers. In the event the changes proved more apparent than real: their political position had been entrenched by the virtual transformation of the upper house of the Prussian diet into a hereditary house of lords; the tax reforms of 1861 were to be virtually nullified by the financial policy of Miquel, minister of finance in the 1890s. The district code of 1872 really only changed the source of noble authority, at least in the eastern provinces. Nearly all the *Landräte* or sheriffs continued to be landowners, though their claim to the position might be no longer inherited privilege but the approval of the central government.[15]

However, in the mid 1870s the free trade which had brought German agriculture such prosperity in the previous decades suddenly threatened the whole economic future of the grain and fodder producing landowners It was not merely that the cheapness of production made American and to a lesser extent Russian grain a serious threat to their grain, with its high production costs, but that the price war among American railroad companies and the ever lower tariffs of transatlantic shipping made the future blacker still; in 1893 the transatlantic freight rates would drop to one fifth of what they had been in 1874.[16] Russia, meanwhile, through the port of Odessa was building up a profitable trade with central and southern Europe, threatening traditional Prussian markets as well as the increasingly significant home market. It was then that Prussian landowners began, with what Ralf Dahrendorf has aptly termed the 'remarkable inventiveness' of the Prussian élite, to agitate for tariff protection.[17] As founders of the new German Conservative Party (1876), they were able to bring political pressure to bear in the *Reichstag* and elsewhere. It was fortunate for them that Bismarck's animus against the German liberals at this time harmonized with his own private interests as a large landowner. Protective tariffs were introduced into the *Reichstag* and became law in 1879. Between 1879 and 1887 the corn tariff was increased fivefold.[18] As Bismarck put it, 'Wer die Klinke der Gesetzgebung in der Hand hat, wird sie auch gebrauchen' ['Whoever holds the handle of legislation, will use it'].[19] Moreover, special low freight rates on the railways benefited the East Elbian landowners; a complex, not to say devious, arrangement of export credits for their agricultural products kept the Prussian estate owners in business – at a cost to the consumer. This privileged élite were confident that the deeds of their ancestors and their own function in the state as food producers – as well as army officers administrators – entitled them to special treatment. Their awareness of the economic fragility of their position – the price of grain on the German markets sank alarmingly in the 1880s[20] – and their dependence on a political system, rigged as it was in Prussia, Saxony and Mecklenburg by an anachronistic three-class franchise, made them hysterical in defence of their rights and in condemnation of the aspirations of rural social groups.

The remarkable success of the Prussian *Junkers* in buttressing their economic position in a time of crisis owed much, as has been said, to the newly ennobled or bourgeois estate owners in their midst. Partly in order to win acceptance from the established élite, partly because they clearly recognized the consequences for themselves, these new men showed themselves bitterly hostile to liberalization in society and the state. In the character of von Gundermann in *Der Stechlin*, Fontane created a typical example of these successful and aggressive parvenus. It was in fact three bourgeois owners of *latifundia* in the east, Major Riedmann, the banker Ferdinand Hansemann (both recently ennobled), and the economist and civil servant Kennemann who refused a title, who founded the pressure group closely associated with East Elbian landowners, the *Verein zur Förderung des Deutschtums im Osten* (The Association to Promote Teutonism in the East). One of the most successful pieces of propaganda in support of noble privileges was the 'agrarian myth', the notion that rural life and the paternalist relationships on the land were more 'wholesome', that they were productive of values important to the community at large and an effective counterweight to the 'evils' of city life.[21] Peasant literature of mid century, the family journals with their serials from the several hundred *Bauernromane* or novels of rural life, written in the second half of the century,[22] all played their part in disseminating this view among the reading public of Germany. On public occasions the East Elbian landowners harped on this theme, succeeding in convincing many people of quite different regional and social backgrounds that traditional social patterns in the east were a pledge of German strength in a threatened border region. Yet the very people who so effectively presented themselves as standard bearers of German patriotic and cultural values were responsible at the turn of the century for bringing large numbers of seasonal Slav workers from Russia and the

Austro-Hungarian monarchy as a cheap labour force. Similarly, they showed the greatest alacrity in exploiting the well-endowed Commission for the Resettlement of German Colonists in the East, which forcibly purchased Polish estates in order to increase the German population in areas such as Posen and West Prussia. Bankrupt or just enterprising Prussian landowners used the Commission, which paid high prices, to get rid of estates at far more than their market value: in fact, while Polish landowners were paid some 30 000 000 *reichmarks* in all, Germans received over 220 000 000 *reichmarks*.[23]

Criticism of the thus privileged landed nobility was less widespread than the situation warranted, largely because the educated and propertied classes in the rest of Germany feared the implications of change. The most persistent and incisive critics, apart from individual journalists, the Social Democrats, particularly the *Reichstag* deputies, were prevented from reaching a wider audience by the very fact of their party allegiance.

The political clichés in which most Germans thought dismissed socialist or left liberal criticism as self-interested and partisan – a situation which Heinrich Mann portrayed so tellingly in his novel of pre-1914 Germany, *Der Untertan* (serialized 1911–12 in the satirical journal *Simplicissimus*). Yet, leaving aside the iniquities of a privileged class system, since this was in fact accepted by all but the social democrats and a few others, the preferential treatment of the landed nobility and their fellow agrarians by the state was open to criticism on purely economic grounds. Their vaunted claims to special status on account of their contribution to food production were not justified; progress in agriculture in the Second Empire was almost wholly the achievement of small farmers, who specialized in cattle and dairy and garden produce, and whose costs were increased by the tariff on fodder. The kind of food produced in the East Elbian estates at a high cost to the taxpayer – rye and potatoes – was suitable for times of mass pauperization, as in the 1840s, but was no longer acceptable as their exclusive diet to a population of rising incomes. Not only were diet habits changing, but consumption was rising, and countries which were taking German industrial products also wished to place their agricultural products on the German market – at a price advantageous both to exporter and consumer. Between 1873–7 and 1903–13, the mere fact that food imports – meat, dairy produce and fruit – into Germany increased fourfold in value[24] was a telling refutation of the agrarian interest's claim. The strength of that interest was demonstrated from 1893 onwards, when the Agrarian League was founded, led by the East Elbian landowners, attracting the support of many peasants also. The best organized of all the pressure groups characteristic of political life in the last years of the monarchy, it won important concessions, often at a high cost to other social groups.[25]

The focal point of the social life of the aristocracy was the court. The protocol which governed it appeared to the nobility as a public demonstration of its own social preeminence. There was of course a great deal of variety between one court and another, ranging from the exclusive Austrian court to the village-like atmosphere of the small central German courts such as the theatre Mecca, Saxe-Meiningen, or Weimar, which still preserved a certain cultural nimbus generations after Goethe's death. Dexterous marriage policies and excessive generosity in granting patents of nobility made the Coburg court remarkably well connected but irritating to brother monarchies. Queen Victoria was a regular visitor, for this was the Prince Consort's home, though its scurrying court photographer and numerous provincial-looking holders of court office made it seem something out of a comic opera. By contrast, at least before 1871, Dresden, seat of the Saxon court, was far more lively and culturally distinguished than Berlin, where the Crown Princess of Prussia, daughter of Queen Victoria, was shocked at the ill appointments and musty smell of the palace where she was destined to live. From 1871 this changed. As Berlin grew into its new role of imperial capital, the Prussian court, without essentially modifying its traditions, attracted the cream of native and resident foreign society. During the season court society assembled, the members of the Hohenzollern family at the head, followed by holders of the most preeminent court offices, the mediatized princes, Prussian princely houses, generals, *aides-de-camp* and officers of the Cavalry Guards, army and civilian chiefs and finally officers of the other guard regiments and landed nobility. The mediatized princes were often reluctant to attend since they regarded themselves as equal in rank with the ruling monarch and disliked being placed after court officials. Court occasions were organized with military precision and attention to detail: 'Mit preussischer Korrektheit verteilte man die Gäste, je nach Kategorie, in verschiedene Säle: die Excellenzdamen, die übrigen verheirateten Frauen, die vorgestellten und die noch vorzustellenden Mädchen' ['With Prussian correctness, the guests were divided according to category and allotted the various rooms: the wives of their Excellencies, the other married women, the girls who had already been presented and those who had not'],[26] wrote Marie von Bunsen in her memoirs, which, perhaps because she was three-quarters English, are full of the kind of details contemporaries take for granted and fail to record. Throughout the Empire the superiority of military over civilian office-holder was amply demonstrated at the Prussian court, where the Kaiser and even the chancellor invariably appeared in uniform. In Vienna on the other hand, except on gala occasions, uniforms were not welcomed. A young lieutenant of noble birth was eligible to appear at the Berlin court; a bourgeois civil servant would have to be well advanced in his career before this should happen. The notion of the court as a meeting place of the 'family', with the monarch as the 'father' and members of the nobility as his beloved children, still lingered on despite the growing numbers of 'new' peoples now for policy reasons admitted to exclusive gatherings. By contrast, in Munich bourgeois academics and ministers of state supplied the main element at court, and mixed with such members of the nobility as appeared. In Berlin William I's Spartan upbringing and soldierly traditions made the court social round lacking in glamour and at times an unpleasant and onerous duty. However, he was popular with the ladies for his kindly manner, and his somewhat eccentric and intelligent consort, Empress Augusta, was able to attract a variety of talent to her circle. His thrift increased with age, and the young and socially ambitious grew restive in the 1880s at the court's unimaginative style. By contrast, his grandson William II put all his considerable histrionic talents into the pageantry of court life, and if he upset the sensitivities of many, he was more ready than any of his fellow monarchs to receive at court distinguished subjects not traditionally eligible. Around 1900 there were actually some fifty-six classes of those eligible to appear: a source of some considerable disquiet to the hereditary nobility.[27] The scions of noble houses were expected to divert themselves under one roof with 'frischem Beamtenadel, geadelten oder ungeadelten Plutokraten, getauften oder ungetauften Kleiderjuden, ja, bisweilen selbst mit gekämmten oder ungekämmten Gelehrten' ['recently ennobled civil servants, rich men with or without a patent of nobility, baptized or unbaptized Jews from the ragtrade, indeed on occasions even with intellectuals, both long-haired and shorn'].[28] Besides the actual court occasions, members of the established nobility and of prestigious regiments enjoyed the hospitality of those houses whose exclusiveness ensured that an invitation to a social function there was a membership ticket to the 'best society'.

Social obligations of this kind were very expensive and many entitled to appear at court never did so. However, the season did provide the opportunity of marrying one's daughters well and finding rich brides for one's sons, and also afforded occasion to have oneself or one's relations considered for posts in the army, diplomatic or government service. For those who had to watch their resources, it might still prove a good investment. To the nobility living in the provinces or whose personal circumstances made attendance impossible, news of the royal family and court doings were the very breath of life, especially for the ladies: 'Nachrichten vom Hofe wurden tagelang besprochen. ... Starb ein Mitglied einer regierenden Familie, so wurde die an dem Berliner Hofe verordneten Trauerzeiten wie auf vielen Schlössern, so auch in Kaminietz auf Tag und Stunde eingehalten' ['Court news was discussed at length. ... If a member of a ruling family died, the official mourning period, as laid down at the Berlin court, was observed in many castles, as at Kaminietz, to the day and hour'],[29] wrote Count Strachwitz, whose mother had been a friend of the Crown Princess Vicky in her early married life at Berlin. When the sovereign died the ladies of the castle went round in long black garments, black crepe veils on their heads. 1888, as Baroness Spitzemberg observed, was a disastrous year for fashionable tailors; the court literally never came out of mourning, and both summer and winter trade was lost (William I died in March, his son Frederick in June). The most important function of court life for the participants, as well as those who relived memories in their provincial world, was that it brought them into direct contact with the monarch in his capacity as head of society and the state, thus giving them a sense of involvement in the state far above and beyond their profession or political function. For the members of the nobility, knowledge of their preeminence at court reassured them of their continued role as the country's élite.[30]

One of the most characteristic features of everyday social life in aristocratic circles was the mobility membership afforded. 'Family' included not only distant cousins but their connections by marriage, running in some cases into a hundred or more, and scattered throughout the country. A young nobleman studying away from home or visiting a strange city would present himself at the home of such a 'connection' in the confident expectation of hospitality. Thus Count Hertling, later Bavarian prime minister and one of the last *Reich* chancellors, was on a modest provenance as a young man, for he had lost his father early; visiting Cologne at the age of seventeen he was able to present himself at the house of A. von Reichsperger, one of the leading members of the Catholic nobility in the Rhineland, who looked after him throughout his stay; as a student in Munich it was self-evident that he should be a regular guest at weekends at the house of a distant connection by marriage.[31] Members of the high nobility found equally easy entrée into society when they were abroad – though not in Austria. Thus while sojourning in Paris, Prince Chlodwig von Hohenlohe, from a somewhat impoverished mediatized family, and in no way equipped to reciprocate hospitality, expected to be invited to dine and be present at parties every night of the week: he was not disappointed. While in Berlin as a young civil servant he dined every week with the king himself, with whom of course he regarded himself as equal in rank.[32] In Vienna the high nobility were not merely exclusive, they were also generally uncurious of strangers, as Fanny Trollope, the mother of the author, and before her Madame de Staël, had observed. The Prussian military attaché in Vienna, Prince Kraft von Hohenlohe-Ingelfingen, in 1854–5 received few invitations in the months following his arrival. However, a dearth of dancers owing to the mobilization of the Austrian army during the Crimean War provided him with an entrée. 'Also habe ich mich eigentlich in die Wiener Gesellschaft weniger eingeführt als eingetanzt' ['And so I danced myself rather than introduced myself into the society of Vienna'].[33]

In other residences and in the fashionable spas where the best people were to be found, in Karlsbad and Marienbad, in Teplitz and Baden-Baden, there was plenty of opportunity to meet one's own kind, and to be invited to Silesian castles to hunt or to shoot on Pomeranian estates, or indeed to join Pietist landowners, such as the Kleist-Cummerows and the Thadden-Trieglaffs, for prayerful and emotional weekend parties in their country mansions. Such arrangements greatly facilitated marriage within one's circle, though Prussian history is full of incidences of intermarriage with 'suitably disposed' or simply just wealthy commoners. Among the older, more exclusive families, especially in the centre and south, and in Silesia, equality of rank rather than size of income was generally what was looked for. So many noblemen, from the mediatized princes downwards, had modest incomes that the lack of worldly goods was not the problem it might have seemed. Within the same family very considerable differences of income could exist, since all children inherited their father's title, but usually only one the family estates. Thus Count Strachwitz, brother of the ballad writer and associate of Fontane in the literary group *Der Tunnel*, lived modestly as a civil servant in Gleiwitz, Silesia. In 1884 his elder brother Rudolf died, and the Count felt it his duty to take over the castle and estate of Kaminietz in Upper Silesia and 'represent' the family. Here life was thoroughly feudal: even the servants sat at three different tables, according to their rank in the household. Open house was customary: 'Immer wieder ergingen Einladungen zu grösseren und kleineren Essen, zu Jagden, Scheiben schiessen und Whistpartien. Getafelt wurde meistens um 5 Uhr abends. Auch in denen Jahren, also in den 80ern, war es Sitte, dass die Damen am Abend Toilette machten und mit langen Schleppen einherrauschten' ['Invitations were continually going out to banquets and smaller dinner parties, to hunting parties, target shooting and whist evenings. One dined usually at about 5. And in those years, that is, the 1880s, it was customary for the ladies to appear in "haute toilette", with long trains rustling after them'].[34] The Silesian magnates, many of whom, unlike their Prussian neighbours, did not disdain connections with industry and exploited mineral deposits on their lands, had a name for a lavish, even ostentatious life style. Many bourgeois industrialists from Berlin and the Rhineland invested in land in Silesia during the Second Empire, and cultivated the aristocratic pastimes and excellent culinary tastes of their new neighbours.

Literary and artistic tastes were in general the province of south German and Austrian aristocrats, though it was rather as patrons of the arts and artists than as practising writers and musicians. Marie von Ebner-Eschenbach, widely known for her novels and stories of Austrian rural life, warned a correspondent: 'Beim künstlerischen und wissenschaftlichen Beruf wird Dii der Adel hinderlich sein, denn ein einstirniges und fast unbesiegbares Vorurteil begrüsst seine Mitglieder auf den geistigen Gebieten, welche den meisten von ihnen fremd geblieben sind' ['In the profession of a scholar and artist, your nobility will be a hindrance to you, because its members have a narrow and virtually ineradicable prejudice on the subject of intellectual pursuits, which are an unknown terrain for most of them'].[35] Literary work was rather more suspect than cultivation of musical or artistic talent, which could be admired in the family: there was something not quite in keeping with aristocratic exclusiveness in wanting to publish writing for all to read. Such attitudes were expressed most forcibly in the case of highborn women, very many of whom, as their memoirs and correspondences show, tried to give meaning to their often uneventful lives through creative writing. Many became well-known authors – such as Bettina von Arnim (born von Brentano), Countess Hahn-Hahn, somewhat of a man-eater for all her one-eyed ugliness, and the indefatigable Bertha von Suttner,[36] a pioneer of pacifism, to name but a few. The descendants of the von Brentanos of Frankfurt had many talents and great taste in artistic matters, and many connections throughout Germany; in Munich the Bavarian royal family was particularly eager – over-eager perhaps – to make Munich a genuine artistic capital, and attracted many noble families, generally from outside the state. In northern Germany on the other hand, particularly in Prussia, there may have been a larger proportion of aristocratic poets than elsewhere, but the general cultural level of the landed nobility of Prussia, Mecklenburg or Hanover was not high. Kurt von Stutterheim, born and brought up in Coburg (and later a connection by marriage of Anthony Eden), was overwhelmed by the philistinism of Prussian *Junker* students at their favourite (non-Prussian) university of Heidelberg at the end of the nineteenth century. He joined the prestigious and socially exclusive Saxo-Borussia fraternity there on account of his north German ancestry – his father was a former Hanoverian officer and his mother a Baltic noblewoman. His fellow members regarded him with the amused tolerance which they considered adequate to the south German aristocracy, but he felt utterly out of place among students whose only interest was fencing and drinking. It was not as if they did it in a spirit of youthful exuberance: the corps activities were rigorously laid down, occupying most of their time, and providing them with that unthinking and all-absorbing discipline to which they were accustomed at home, school and in the army.

> Während sich die Söhne des gebildeten Bürgertums bemühten, ihre Geisteskräfte zu schulen und ihr Wissen zu erweitern, hielt der Adel sich von Künsten und Wissenschaften fern, ja, es galt kaum als passend, sich dafür zu interessieren ... Mensuren, Kneipen, Witze, Jagdgeschichten und die nicht endenwollenden Feststellungen von Verwandtschaften bildeten das Hauptgesprächsthema.

> While the sons of the educated bourgeoisie were engaged in disciplining their minds and extending their knowledge, the nobility kept away from the arts and sciences; indeed it was thought not quite the thing to show any interest in such matters ... fencing duels, drinking, jokes, hunting tales, and the unending discoveries of kinship between individuals were the main themes of conversation.[37]

It was above all the association of the arts with the 'bourgeoisie' which made them socially unacceptable to these young Prussian noblemen. In marked and somewhat idiosyncratic contrast was the traditional respect exhibited by the Baltic nobility for the educated. Professors, pastors and creative artists were known as '*literati*', and had long been considered acceptable marriage partners; thus Helene Marie Zoege von Manteuffel, of an old and distinguished Baltic family, was able to persuade her father to let her marry a painter, Gerhard Kügelgen (their son was Wilhelm von Kügelgen, author of one of the best-loved memoirs of the nineteenth century, *Erinnerungen eines alten Mannes*).[38] A member of one of the highest noble families from the Baltic declared on one occasion during the Second Empire that he would never take his hat off to the wealthiest banker in the land, but would not hesitate to do it to a learned professor.

In general, however, membership of the nobility, particularly of the old families, brought with it segregation from the rest of society, especially from the urban middle and lower classes. In private or cadet school, in the army and university and the social round, contact with those of inferior rank was rare. It was the lack of such common experience in early life, coupled with the increasing sense of threat from hostile social classes or financially more robust social groups, which encouraged aristocratic exclusiveness in the last decades of the monarchy. This was much more pronounced in the north than in the south, where human contact was easier. Here too the absence of an established landed nobility, characteristic of the lands east of the Elbe, made social barriers more fluid, though they were not denied. The members of the nobility married their own kind, though by no means always their own confession, but they had considerable contact with the notables of the local townships and academic and artistic worlds.

The German bourgeoisie under the Empire has been much criticized by historians for accepting its own inferiority of birth and failing to overcome this natural disadvantage by identifying itself with the backward-looking conservatism of a social élite, which in an age of industrial and technological advance no longer had time on its side. This is undoubtedly true, but in order to judge the behaviour of its members more fairly, one should recall the situation of the individual aspirant to professional and social preeminence at the time. The social exclusiveness of the German nobility was not what caused ambitious members of the bourgeoisie to emulate them. As with the nobility in Latin countries, this was a traditional feature and could have been accepted and ignored by the rest of society. It was the fact of having to compete professionally with a nobility which in Germany was forced to earn its living and which, for reasons of government policy, was almost inevitably preferred for promotion to senior posts. Lacking a commercial burgher class outside the Hanseatic cities and the old trading towns of Bavaria and Swabia, and therefore lacking too that pride and self-respect which only tradition can confer, talented and wealthy members of the German bourgeoisie felt they had no alternative.

The German nobility had been shattered and weakened during the Napoleonic wars[39] but it was not abolished, as some of its members had feared. The determination of princes and statesmen in the aftermath of Napoleon's fall to restore not just individual rulers to their thrones but to encourage paternalism in society at large, made them regard the nobility as a vital element of reconstruction. They too, as all other classes of society, were to be made directly subordinate to the state, in a way that had not existed under the old Empire, but they were paid for their allegiance by important social, political and fiscal privileges.

The vigorous discussion about the function of an aristocracy, which had been a feature of the late eighteenth century, died away in the Metternich era, but after the experience of 1848, many leaders of the nobility felt it necessary to encourage plebeian apologists to put their case to the educated public. Hermann Wagener, Fr. Julius Stahl, Victor Aimé Huber presented the aristocracy as the natural protectors of the lower classes, particularly the oppressed craftsmen and rural workers who were represented as the victims of unfeeling progress. Many of the East Elbian landowners and their apologists used religious arguments to appeal to their public. To Fontane, a conservative by nature and inclination, the self-interest, not to say hypocrisy, was all too evident. In 1852, when he was English correspondent of the Prussian conservative *Kreuz-Zeitung,* he had an interview with the editor. The sofa was adorned with a cushion on which was embroidered an iron cross; above there hung a picture of Christ on the cross. The conversation, he reported later, 'das anfänglich wie zwischen dem eisernen Kreuz und dem Christus mit der Dornenkrone hin- und herpendelte, belebte sich erst als die Geldfrage zur Verhandlung kam' ['which, to begin with, moved backwards and forwards between the Iron Cross (i.e. conservative politics) and Christ with the crown of thorns (i.e. religion) really only got going when the financial question was mentioned'].[40] Hypocrisy is no more attractive for being unconscious, though it would not be correct to suggest that the conservative landowners of East Elbia used their religion to cloak their ambitions. Their sentiments were indeed genuine, though their religious duties did not conflict with their worldly ambitions. Von Thadden-Trieglaff, one of the spokesmen of aristocratic privilege and a leading Pomeranian Pietist, would no doubt have been grievously offended to have been accused of such a fault, when he observed with reference to enclosure of peasant land in his area in the 1830s: 'Ich bin bekanntlich ein Konservativer, weil geschrieben steht, wer da hat, dem wird gegeben, und als echter Preusse verstehe ich den Wahlspruch unseres Hauses "Suum cuique" nicht bloss als, behalte, was du hast, sondern nimm, was du kannst, aber wohlverstanden, was du mit gutem Gewissen bekommen kannst' ['I am, as is well known, a conservative, because it is written, to him who has will be given, and as a good Prussian I understand the device of our house, "To each his own", to mean not just keep what you have but take what you can get – meaning, of course, what you can get with a good conscience'].[41]

'Adelssauce mit einem Bibelspruch als Champignon – aber ranzig' ['Noble sauce with a Bible saying as the mushrooms – but it is rancid'], commented Fontane of such attitudes.[42] In addition to the support the nobility received, especially in northern Germany, from the state authorities, their image in society was enhanced by the Romantic writers; these were the proponents of a so-called 'organic' society, composed of social groups distinguished by their function in the community and separated by 'natural'' barriers; set against this harmonious creation was the 'artificial' class society, the product of revolutionary violence and social envy.[43] In the 1880s the pioneering sociologist Ferdinand Tönnies in a widely read systematic study contrasted the traditional '*Gemeinschaft*', the characteristic form of society in Germany, with '*Gesellschaft*' or class society, the brainchild of the rationalist West. The natural leaders of the 'community' were the traditional nobility.

Germans on the whole accepted authority easily once they could identify it with a person or a family. In Prussia in particular, the fact that the nobility were resident landowners, who frequently worked alongside their tenants, goes far to explain the acceptance of conditions of life and work which would have seemed intolerable in other countries in the nineteenth century. Undoubtedly it suited interested parties to romanticize the relationship between estate owner and peasant, but paternalist relationships were not at all uncommon on the land in the middle and latter years of the nineteenth century, until seasonal workers began to be used as cheap labour. Elard von Oldenburg-Januschau's somewhat self-congratulatory memories of his life as a landowner are therefore not untypical:

> Das Geheimnis zur Lösung der Leutefrage auf dem Land habe ich immer darin gesehen, den Arbeitern ein gerechter Vorgesetzter zu sein ... Freilich war ich niemals nachsichtig, sondern hielt darauf, dass im Betrieb Gehorsam der oberste Grundsatz blieb. Auf diese Weise bildete sich im Laufe der Jahrzehnte auf allen meinen Gütern zwischen meinen Leuten und mir ein Vertrauensverhältnis, dessen Formen manchen nicht aus dem Osten stammenden Deutschen vielleicht eigenartig erscheinen mögen.
>
> I have always seen the key to the solution of our relationship with the landworkers to lie in being a just employer and master. ... Of course, I was never soft, but saw to it that obedience was the first principle. ... And so over the years a relationship of trust grew up between me and my people on all my estates, whose form would perhaps have struck Germans who were not from the East as an odd one.[44]

The notion of army discipline between landowner and peasants goes back to the eighteenth century Prussian tradition of having the landowner act as a company captain to his own tenants.[45] Even bourgeois writers in the Second Empire liked to cite the case of that incorrigible aristocrat Fr. August von der Marwitz as an example of the virtues of paternalism. As a young officer in the guards, Marwitz, who was later confined to the fortress of Spandau for his outspoken opposition to the Prussian emancipation of the peasantry, used to ride home for the weekend to oversee his estate at Friedersdorf and to check that all was well in school and church in 'his' village.

In conclusion it can be said that the German nobility proved remarkably successful in the nineteenth century in retaining access to sources of wealth and influence. Individual members of the class, it is true, suffered severe curtailment of income, and the life style of many differed little from that of the less wealthy members of the upper middle class. Industrially and commercially Germany on the eve of the First World War was one of the most advanced countries in the world; politically and socially its development had been arrested in the nineteenth century, an age associated elsewhere in western Europe with liberal values, material progress and emancipation of the bourgeoisie. Nowhere was this fact more evident than in the survival of a privileged nobility, whose members, however, were animated by a sense of grievance at the increasing loss of their rights, which past achievement justified in their eyes. Just how far the special status of the German nobility in social and political life was derived from the past was expressed – quite without conscious irony – in the entry under *Adel* in the fourth edition of the semi-official *Staatslexikon* (1911), where it was stated that the (lower) nobility 'besteht in der Gegenwart weniger in Vorrechten als in einer auf ehrenvollen historischen Erinnerungen bestehenden erblichen Titulaturauszeichnung von gesellschaftlicher Bedeutung, welche der Staat anerkennt, verleiht und gegen Missbrauch schützt' ['nowadays less a matter of privileges than a distinguishing hereditary title, which rests on the memories of an honourable historical past, and which the state recognizes, grants and protects against misuse'].[46]

Chapter 11
The churches and religious life in the nineteenth century

The recent interest shown by German historians in social history has brought much new or forgotten material to the attention of scholars and the public. An ever increasing number of publications seek to inform us about social life in earlier times; the nineteenth century is particularly well represented in these endeavours. A number of collections of documents have appeared, the most oustanding of which is probably G. A. Ritter and J. Kocka's recent *Dte. Sozialgeschichte 1870–1914* (1974). A feature common to all these works, however, is their neglect or indeed omission of any reference to church and religious life. None of the 301 sections in this last book refers to the clergy or the churches as part of the German social scene. This strikes one as rather odd, especially since modern social historians affect to be particularly concerned to depict the life of the anonymous masses, and devote much space, as is proper, to conditions of life and work among the lower classes. Yet it was in the lives of such classes that the churches played a major role, perhaps social more than spiritual, but a role nonetheless. No one will pretend that religion was not a declining force in nineteenth century Germany, but those with pretensions to depict the past 'wie as eigentlich gewesen ist' ['as it really was'] can scarcely deny that religion was still a considerable force in people's lives or that public attitudes and behaviour were profoundly influenced by it, if often only by way of reaction. The neglect of nineteenth century German religious life by mid twentieth century historians, partly because many mid twentieth century historians are not interested in religion, has naturally affected the state of primary sources. As for the earlier period, much remains to be done both at national and local level, and the standard works of a generation ago are still a major source of information. However, the third edition of *Die Religion in Geschichte und Gegenwart* (six vols, Tübingen, 1957–62), although by its nature not exhaustive, is an invaluable compendium with useful bibliographical references.

1 GERMAN PROTESTANTISM

The religious outlook of the German Protestant at the beginning of the nineteenth century was generally formed by one of two influences: Pietism and rationalism. Pietists in the late eighteenth century were widely known as '*die Stillen im Lande*', quiet people, both for their lack of ostentation in behaviour and religious observance, and for their political quietism. They were not dispersed evenly through the *Reich*, but maintained their association with certain areas – Saxony, the eastern provinces of Prussia, and Württemberg, where the movement had a genuine popular base. The religious colony of Herrenhut in Saxony, where Zinzendorf had founded the Moravian brethren, was one of the most important institutions to spring from the Pietist impulse, and it continued to exert a strong but subtle influence on religious attitudes among the upper classes until the beginning of the nineteenth century. The religious indifference of Frederick II had caused the Pietists to lose their foothold in the state-controlled universities and schools in Prussia; their most serious loss was Halle which thereafter became the stronghold of theological rationalism. However, the boarding school at Herrenhut, and less well-known but similar institutions at Bunzlau, Niesky, Barby, etc., provided many prominent Germans, among them Novalis and Schleiermacher, with their early education; such men helped mould the religious ideas of a whole generation of influential Germans.

As a formative influence on religious belief and practice, Pietism was intense rather than diverse. Much more typical of the attitude of the 'average German Protestant' in the early nineteenth century was the rationalism taught in the theological faculties of the universities and preached from the pulpits of town and village churches all over the north and centre of Germany. In contrast with France, Spain or Italy, the Enlightenment in Germany had been dominated by religious-minded men, who were primarily interested in ridding the churches of intolerance and excessive preoccupation with theological controversy. Matters of faith and doctrine seemed to both enlightened clergymen and laymen alike of considerably less importance than the moral and pedagogical role of religion. From about 1775 onwards, at least in Lutheran areas of Germany, the concept of the church became secularized; people began to regard its prime function as serving society.[1] Such a rationalistic approach to the church and religion generally was reinforced in Prussia by the state tradition of requiring clergymen to perform utilitarian tasks in the community, to act, in fact, as one commentator put it, as '*Polizeibeamte im Talar*', police officials in vestments. It was indeed ironic that Halle, once upon a time under Francke a kind of Rome for the Pietists, should have become the place where generations of rationalist clergymen were educated. The theology professors at Halle during the century from about 1740 and 1840 proved to be able teachers, many with forceful personalities; they left their imprint on the religious thought and practice of individual parish clergymen and their flocks for three or even four generations.[2] It was ironic too that the Pietists' own stress on the importance of the individual's relationship to God without the mediation of priest or church helped to prepare for the acceptance of the Enlightenment, or *Aufklärung* in Germany, especially since they were to be the bitterest critics of the secularist implications of the later Enlightenment.[3]

Theological rationalism appealed above all to the educated classes in Germany, who were not generally interested in social and political questions. It seemed commonsensical and 'modern' to them to reject miracles and superstitious practices, to regard theological dogmatism as irrelevant to contemporary life and injurious to one's advance in personal virtue and wisdom. Such attitudes were obviously more likely to appeal to Protestants, both Lutheran and Reformed, who lacked the clearly defined authority of the Catholic church; however, many German Catholics did indeed share these views and rejected the traditional role of religion in society. During the period 1775–1840 the popular conversation lexicons and encyclopedias reflected changing views in bourgeois German society about the function of the church in the modern world. These widely read compendiums of useful knowledge were usually compiled by associations of scholars; the best known were Meyer's or Brockhaus and they were bought and consulted by the kind of people who would today feel it necessary to have a Chambers or Pears encyclopedia in their sitting room bookcases. But in Germany, in contrast with England, learning, or at least the air of scholarship, carried much social prestige; the opinions and definitions of these works were quoted with a flourish and listened to deferentially by those less well informed. On the question of the church's role in society there was considerable agreement among the leading works of this kind. Thus the seventh edition of the *Allgemeine deutsche Real-Encyklopedia für die gelehrten Stände* (*General German Encyclopaedia for the Educated Classes*) defined it in 1827 as 'Vereinigung der Menschen zu irgendeinem gemeinsamen Zwecke' ['Union of human beings for some common purpose'], comparable with bourgeois society or with marriage, while the *Neuestes Conversationslexikon für alle Stände* (*Latest Conversational Lexicon for all Classes*) (1835) declared it an 'Institut für religiös-moralische Zwecke' ['Institution for religions and moral questions'].[4] Such views were widely current among the educated classes of north and central Germany by the early decades of the new century. The protests of orthodox clergymen against the critical attitudes towards authority fostered by theological rationalism were not very effective; one of the reasons for this was that intellectual stature tended to be the prerogative of the *Aufklärer* and their supporters. Pockets of orthodox resistance remained, just as certain areas where Pietism predominated, but the majority of Lutheran clergymen tended towards tolerance or even scepticism in matters of faith and doctrine and preached to the flocks accordingly.

However, the French revolutionary wars and Napoleon suddenly impinged on Germany and, as in so many spheres of German life, acted as a kind of watershed. The resistance to Napoleon, especially in Prussia, engendered a patriotic enthusiasm which was akin to religious feeling. A keen sense of foreboding, of being gripped in a historic conflict between the forces of godlessness and destruction on the one hand, and traditional values on the other hand, awakened in many Germans the desire for a restoration of the churches as a bulwark of society and state; this feeling was particularly powerful among the ruling classes; many influential men and women found a new strength and optimism in communal worship and genuine religious conversion. Individual clergymen played a crucial role in attracting people back to the churches; thus in the Wuppertal Fr. Krummacher's sermons were described by a government official sent to investigate his following as 'einzig in ihrer Art und hinreissend' ['quite unique and overwhelming']. Goethe's comment was more laconic: he called Krummacher 'narcotic'.[5] Clergymen all over the country had been quick to denounce the French Revolution as the work of Satan, to condemn revolutionaries as his agents, for their attempts to usurp God's power and divine plan by holding out hopes of a paradise on earth (the same argument would be repeated much later in the century by clergymen and the establishment in condemnation of the Social Democrats). A certain pastor from

Frankfurt am Main, by the name of Mencken, later influential in the neo-Pietist revival, compared Napoleon's monarchy with the kingdom of Daniel. The Prussian government began to appreciate the potential usefulness of such attitudes in resisting Napoleon, and encouraged clergymen to galvanize support for the national struggle. Not only did they enlist voluntarily as chaplains and soldiers in the wars of 1813–14, but Nicolovius, head of the Department of Cults, issued a 'call to the clergy of the Prussian state' (1813), urging them to use their influence on their congregations. Schleiermacher, a genial preacher, exhorted Germans to heed the call to arms; he preached to those departing for the front and their relatives. His eloquence and deep sincerity won for him a reputation of 'the second Luther', which in the vicissitudes he encountered under a timorous and reactionary era after 1819 he never again lost.

After the war prominent clergymen who had heeded the government's call for support were rewarded by promotion and decorations, which often brought with them handsome salaries and emoluments. The court preacher, Eylert, sycophantic biographer of Frederick William III, was appointed bishop in 1818. General Superintendent Borowski, who liked to address clergymen during the war as 'soldiers of the king' – he did not mean King of Heaven – rose to be chief court preacher and archbishop, and in 1829 was ennobled. Schleiermacher was certainly the most talented and versatile of Prussian clergymen at the time; he had played a prominent role as a colleague of Wilhelm von Humboldt in the educational reforms during the Stein-Hardenberg reform era, but as a liberal critic of the religious and social system in Prussia he was now regarded as a grave embarrassment. Indeed, but for his very considerable popularity, he might well have shared the fate of his colleague in the faculty of theology at Berlin, De Wette, who was dismissed in 1819.

It was over the question of liturgical and church reform that Schleiermacher became a bitter critic of Frederick William. Personally very devout, the monarch was deeply interested in ecclesiastical matters and resolved to strengthen the cause of religion by bringing about a union of the two Protestant churches in his realms, the Lutheran and the Reformed confessions; it had greatly pained him that he, as a member of the Reformed church like his ancestors, had not been able to take the sacrament with his Queen Louise, who was a Lutheran. His decision to create a new 'Evangelical Christian' church on the 300th anniversary of the Reformation was acceptable to the theology professors and to the Reformed congregations in Berlin. However, the way in which the king determined to impose his new liturgy and centralized structure, the so-called *Agende,* aroused the opposition of his critics. The new church was closely bound to the state, with the executive power lying in centrally appointed consistories instead of the old local synods; the King reformed the offices of superintendents, appointed evangelical bishops with the rank of provincial governors (*Oberpräsidenten*) and an archbishop with the rank of privy councillor. It was clear that the government looked on the clergy as instruments of state authority. Schleiermacher and those who felt as he did recognized the dangers of royal policy for the spiritual authority of the church, but most clergymen submitted without a struggle. It would have been easier for those who disagreed with the general authoritarian policies of the state after the end of the reform era in 1819 to have challenged them on this matter, had they not been conditioned by their earlier history as officials of a state church, and had the king and his cabinet advisers been less sincere in their own religious belief and practice. For personal piety was a striking feature of upper class society in Prussia in the years of the wars of liberation and thereafter; very many high officials and officers experienced a religious 'awakening'. In almost every case this experience had been the result of personal contact with one or other circles of like-minded believers. The social composition of these intimate groups of worshippers varied considerably, and included both artisans and peasants, but the most influential spirits were a number of East Elbian noblemen, landowners or crown officials, such as Kottwitz, Thadden-Trieglaff, Senfft-Pilsach and the four Gerlach brothers, Ernst, Ludwig, Leopold and Otto.[6]

A revived interest in religion as a conservative social force was characteristic of the ruling classes of several countries in the wake of the Napoleonic wars, notably France and Austria. However, in no other country did the religious revival so completely win the approval of the monarch or the church and become such an important element in government policy. In consequence, the social composition of the Prussian Protestant clergy underwent a remarkable change. Since the late seventeenth century the church had been a poor man's profession (apart from the Reformed court preachers, of course) and had attracted few highborn recruits. From about 1815 onwards, however, we find a striking incidence of landowners', officers' and officials' sons entering the ministry. The government showed itself eager to encourage this trend and provided scholarships for the less well off noblemen, as well as for the sons of teachers and artisans who evinced the 'right attitudes'. The candidates had to be personally pious – the term neo-Pietism came into general vogue at this time; they were expected to be hostile to social and political change and to theological rationalism which was sincerely believed to nurture revolutionary tendencies. Many key men in the Prussian bureaucracy and among the king's advisers had been exposed to Pietist influence in their youth. They had come to believe that conservative social policies could best be implemented at local level by the appointment of truly religious – that is, Pietist – clergymen. One of the most influential men in the government was Nicolovius; in his youth a candidate for orders, he had decided that he could do God's work more effectively as a government official and had entered the state service. When, in 1810, the administrative and personnel policies of the state church in Prussia were merged, he was the obvious choice as head of the Department of Cults in the Ministry of the Interior. Among his friends was Baron von Kottwitz who frequently suggested the names of suitable candidates for appointments to church office. Nicolovius lent a ready ear to the suggestion that a seminary be set up in Wittenberg in 1817 to prepare candidates (the famous university here had been closed down in 1815 after Prussia acquired this portion of Saxony at the Congress of Vienna). The man put in charge of the new foundation was one Heubner, a former lecturer in theology, whose motto in life was, as he put it: 'Seid untertan aller menschlichen Ordnung um des Herrn Willen' ['Be ye subject to all human authority for the sake of God's will'].[7] Heubner's case illustrates how the association of humbly born clergymen with the nobility in their common zeal for combating rationalism could overcome the traditional class barriers of Prussian society. These were to be numerous such cases in the decades to come. Orphaned at a tender age, Heubner's religious fervour and meekness commended themselves to Baron Kottwitz, who introduced him to his own Pietist circle. Heubner soon fulfilled the hopes placed in him at the Wittenberg seminary. Known as the 'Holy Three', Kottwitz, Nicolovius and Heubner devoted themselves to training a new clerical élite who would disseminate neo-Pietist religious views in universities, schools and parishes. The government gave scholarships to candidates and provided them with posts on ordination. At a time of critical shortage of opportunities for graduates, this policy was a form of favouritism; the young men concerned repaid their debt by zealously defending the established order and combating the *Zeitgeist*, or, as Nicolovius put it in a letter to Heubner, 'den Drachensaat des Rationalismus' ['the dragon seed of rationalism'].[8] For the next three or even four decades it was made abundantly clear that the authorities favoured neo-Pietism as an important means of inspiring religious fervour and therefore, they argued, political docility among the people. From the 1820s onwards, the government's highly selective distribution of posts and honours demonstrated that there were limited but attractive possibilities for a successful career if one possessed, besides talent, the 'right' creed and political leanings.

The close association between the 'awakened' aristocrats from the eastern provinces of Prussia and deferential clergymen brought about further sociological change in the clergy: intermarriage with the nobility. The Lutheran and the Reformed clergy in Prussia and Germany had been a homogeneous social group; they had married their own kind, and the sons had frequently followed their father's profession. This now changed. There were many such cases of intermarriage. Superintendent August Kahnis, a tailor's son, Tholuck, son of an impoverished goldsmith from Breslau who became an influential professor of theology, August Hahn, superintendent of Königsberg, son of a poor village teacher – all these married noblewomen.[9] Many such marriages came about because of the nature of neo-Pietist worship, which was centred on the home. Eminent Pietists, such as Baron Kottwitz and the immensely energetic Gerlach brothers, welcomed fellow worshippers to their homes in Berlin; Pomeranian landowners, who took such a prominent part in the movement – von Thadden-Trieglaff, Kleist-Retzow and others – held the religious equivalent of weekend parties on their estates. As many as thirty or forty clergymen and layfolk attended. The communal prayer meetings were scenes of great emotional intensity. It is hardly surprising that the daughters and sisters of the hosts were ready to admire and fall in love with eloquent clergymen, nor that their guardians' objections to what might be considered a *mésalliance* were swept aside by their belief in the importance of these men's careers for the cause. Most such marriages were very successful: Mathilde von Gemmingen-Steinegg, to quote but one case, married Tholuck in 1838 and proved of stern stuff in supporting her unstable but pugnacious husband through his quarrelsome career.

The general standard of living and the social status of the clergy benefited from the keen interest shown in religious affairs by the dynasty and government. As part of the administrative reorganization of the church after 1815 standardized procedures were introduced to train the parish clergy: a prescribed period of study leading to an examination was followed by ordination, which was rather in the nature of an appendage to theological studies than its culmination. All appointments to livings were made by the central ministry in Berlin. This was greatly resented by the landowners accustomed to select their own clergymen, and became a source of animosity between provincial Pietists and the bureaucrats in the following decades. The recently Prussianized Rhenish Calvinists were equally angry at this, used as they were to a presbyterian form of church government. In course of time a compromise was worked out in the form of nominations made by local representatives to the minister who then selected a candidate. Promotions, transfers and dismissals all lay in the provision of the ministry, although the clergy were paid by the congregations – apart from the provincial superintendents, theology professors and chaplains. The faithful were naturally reluctant to increase the number of churches and posts which they were obliged to maintain, and in consequence the numbers of Evangelical clergymen failed to keep pace with the rapid rise in the population. In 1847 there were some 5783 such clergymen in Prussia as against 5714 in 1822; the population, however, had increased from 10 million to over 16 million between 1800 and 1850.[10] Eventually this brought about a downward trend in the numbers studying for the ministry. At Halle, the most important university, theology students fell from 1500 in the 1820s and 1600 in the 1830s to 700 in the late 1840s. That so many embarked on so uncertain a career can be explained by the economic security enjoyed even by the lowest paid clergy, once an appointment was secured. This situation compared favourably with other government posts, such as subaltern officials and teachers. The ambitious and self-confident were bound to be attracted to a career where the holders of the highest offices, the court and cathedral preachers, the theology professors and superintendents, consistory councillors and chaplains, commanded impressive salaries. G. F. A. Strauss, professor of theology at Berlin from 1822 and court preacher, earned 1500 *taler* from each post. As professors Schleiermacher, Tholuck, Hengstenberg and Otto von Gerlach earned 2000 *taler*. Bishop Sack had 1000 *taler* as bishop, 1600 as chief court preacher and 300 as chief consistorial councillor.[11] This was a great deal of money on any count, particularly in frugal Prussia. In addition, clergymen at all levels received payment in kind – rent, wood and grain allowances. The government showed its benevolence in other ways: Tholuck, whose nervous disposition suffered from his own pugnacity, was given the agreeable post of chaplain to the Prussian ministry in Rome, which seems to have been used as a general rest cure; Hengstenberg could enjoy a restorative trip to the fashionable and invigorating Marienbad spa at the state expense whenever he so desired.

By 1830 leading Evangelical clergymen in Prussia identified themselves readily with the conservative political and social system, and acted with forcefulness, even aggression, to implement official policy in matters of religion. They denounced liberal theological views and intrigued against their exponents. De Wette was dismissed from one of the chairs of theology at Berlin in 1828 and Hengstenberg appointed in his place; even Schleiermacher had cause to fear for his future. The rationalist theologians who had educated generations of clergymen at Halle and Königsberg and at Frankfurt a.d. Oder before it was transferred to the new foundation at Breslau, became the objects of bitter criticism in public and intrigue in private. Not only these men were attacked, but others who on grounds of tradition or for other reasons opposed the King's Agenda. In Silesia the Lutherans resisted vigorously; General Superintendent Kahnis actually had recourse to the military to enforce official rulings, earning himself the title of Commissar Kahnis. Rather than submit, numbers of clergy and their flocks emigrated to the New World to practise their faith unmolested; contemporaries reported the sound of their fervent voices singing outside the royal palace at Berlin as the boats taking them and their possessions moved down the Spree.

There is no doubt that the religious policies of the king, government policy in appointments to ecclesiastical office, and the publicist talents of a few vigorous churchmen, greatly increased the political role of the state church in Prussia. Although the majority of parish clergymen, apart from the eastern provinces, continued to preach a mildly rationalist view of religion to their congregations, most were ready to conform in public to the official line. To those wishing to get on in their careers this was imperative. However, with the quickening of interest in political issues, characteristic of educated circles in the 1830s and early 1840s, came the first organized protests and some prominent casualties of the system. Some of the most talented young men of their time, who, because of limited means had entered schools of theology almost as a matter of course, began to dispute the social and political views of their church; Bruno Bauer, later known for his materialist philosophical views, and Gottfried Kinkel, revolutionary tribune of 1848, were two such men. They and their associates among the so-called Young Hegelians had been deeply influenced by D. F. Strauss. In 1835 Strauss had published the most controversial work of the Restoration, *Das Leben Jesu*, in which, with all the learned apparatus so deeply respected by the educated German public, he disputed the historical authenticity of the Gospels. That there was no place in the Prussian state church for men who questioned the established order in such terms was clear enough: even in a more tolerant system the Young Hegelians would scarcely have remained within the Christian fold, though they might have asked other questions: they might have become historians or lawyers, and they almost certainly would have entered politics.

Of greater significance for the history of the Protestant religion in Prussia and the neighbouring states was the defeat of the popular liberal movement within the Lutheran church known as the Friends of Light. This was an association of liberal minded, mainly urban Protestants, which was founded in Saxony and spread rapidly eastwards from Halle and Magdeburg to Berlin, Breslau and Königsberg, and westwards to Brunswick and Bremen. In a sense the Friends of Light movement was a substitute for the lack of political opposition, but there was a genuine religious element in it as well; its most colourful personality, Pastor Uhlich, earned himself the title of the Saxon O'Connell, no small tribute in the 1840s to his rhetorical talents. In his Magdeburg parish he organized discussions on matters of general and religious interest, at which he also gave public addresses. These proved so successful that within a short time he began to look further afield and hit upon the genial notion of using the newly opened railway stations as meeting places. At Köthen in Anhalt, an important railway junction, a large restaurant had been built providing facilities for travellers; here Uhlich and his associates soon found themselves addressing crowds of several hundreds. It would not be right, as some have done, to see in the Friends of Light merely a political movement expressing itself in church language. The rank and file provincial clergy in Prussia were seriously concerned in the 1840s at the position that government policies had placed them in; their own liberty of conscience seemed to be imperilled. Other governments had followed the Prussian church policies and many of their clergymen were becoming restive. When Frederick William IV ascended the Prussian throne in 1840 he appointed Eichhorn as Minister of Cults, a zealous bureaucrat who had openly stated that in the question of religion the government was not neutral but 'biased, totally biased'.[12] Ludwig von Gerlach, his influence now greatly enhanced since his friend, the former crown prince, had succeeded to the throne, spoke of the 'liebender Aggressions- und Erholungstrieb' ['loving aggressive and reforming principle'][13] of the Pietist faction. With the acrimonious Hengstenberg at their head, the Pietists inveighed against the 'masses' of the Friends of Light. However, the Prussian authorities were well aware that the kind of people who were coming to listen to Uhlich from the Prussian provinces, from Silesia and the Rhine, and further afield from Schleswig-Holstein, Franconia and south-west Germany, were respectable, educated people, farmers, merchants and even officials. In 1844 Uhlich's radical associate, Wislicenus, a clergyman of Hungarian descent, challenged the government's right to impose the Agenda on the clergy against their will. For this he was suspended from his parish. The movement's leaders now began to travel widely. Wislicenus spoke to several thousand people at Köthen and 6000 greeted Uhlich at Breslau. The Prussian conservatives were particularly enraged by the participation at a meeting in Berlin of, as Hengstenberg put it, 'women, wives of *literati*, dressmakers and embroiderers'; it was outrageous that a pastor should welcome the 'shameful spectacle of women entering the public scene'.[14] In 1847 Uhlich too was suspended and, despite 20 000 signatures collected on a petition for his reinstatement, the king refused. There followed a wave of dismissals of parish clergymen who had supported him, and with that the movement collapsed. It had been a significant interlude, and in many ways anticipated the political groupings and the dilemmas experienced by the liberals in the 1848 revolution.

From the point of view of church politics the most significant development in mid century was the way in which the neo-Pietist faction had succeeded in identifying the state church in Prussia with a reactionary social and political system. God was invoked, not for the last time in Prussian history, to justify the use of arms in supporting the establishment. The revolutionaries of 1848 were firmly identified in the minds of the ruling classes with the godless. On November 9, 1848, as General Wrangel moved his forces to crush the Berlin revolution, the king wrote to his friend Gossler: 'Heute ist der grosse Wurf geschehn. Die Kugel rollt unter Gott Fürsehung. Ich habe das Werk im Namen unseres göttlichen Herrn und Heilandes begonnen. Er weiss, dass ich nicht lüge' ['Today the die has been cast. The ball rolls under the guidance of Divine Providence. I have begun the task in the name of Our Lord and Saviour. He knows that I do not lie'].[15] Success only confirmed the righteousness of their cause in the eyes of the king and his advisers. But a sense of guilt haunted the monarch for having 'allowed' the revolution to happen; he devised the idea of a day of prayer and penance in November 1849, *Buss- und Bettag,* which has remained an official church fixture to this day. In an attempt to bring the churches of the German states together he had inaugurated an annual conference, the *Kirchentag,* which first met at Wittenberg in September 1848; he mooted the idea of a German unified Protestant church to stem the 'flood' of revolutionary agitation. However, the example of what this had brought with it in Prussia repelled church leaders, particularly the Bavarian Lutheran leader, Harless. The 'Sündenfall der Revolution' ['fall of man in the Revolution'] remained a favourite theme of sermons long after the generation which had experienced it had passed away. Not only in Prussia but also in Mecklenburg, Hanover and Electoral Hesse and in the relatively enlightened Saxony and Baden, church leaders supported the efforts of governments to restrict or even withdraw constitutions granted 'under duress' during the revolution 1848–9. In the second half of the century the assumption became widespread that the church was a bulwark (or fortress, dyke, dam, according to the preference of the speaker) against the threat offered to the 'natural harmony' of society and state by revolution, communism, socialism, or even, after about 1880, liberalism. An important factor in disseminating these views were the *Kirchentage* of the post-revolutionary years which met again in Wittenberg in 1849, in Stuttgart in 1850 and in Elberfeld, Bremen, Berlin and Frankfurt in subsequent years.[16]

The political aspects of Protestantism in Prussia have been treated at some length because of their effect on religious life and belief. Educated middle class Germans had long been less devout than the ruling classes; now a deep and lasting antagonism was aroused in such circles against the established church by the religious and educational policies of Frederick William IV and his advisers. 'Was hat Goethe mit Luther zu tun?' ['What has Goethe to do with Luther?'] asked Julius Stahl, author of *Rechts- und Staatslehre auf der Grundlage christlicher Weltanschauung* (*Jurisprudence and Political Science based on Christian Principles*) and official philosopher of Prussian conservatism, as in accordance with royal notions of restoring society to its prerevolutionary innocence, the classical writers were banned from Prussian primary schools in the 1850s. Some efforts were made both inside and outside Prussia to organize liberal-minded people within the Evangelical church to challenge official attitudes in this and other matters. They were not successful; in Protestant and in Catholic circles the current of religious opinion was running too strongly in favour of traditional forms of state and social organization. Inevitably, then, the church and its ministers seemed but another pillar of the ruling élite, alongside the army and the bureaucracy, which failed to attract the men of liberal conviction and individual enterprise which had invigorated its ranks earlier in the century.

The clergy invoked God's aid in the wars of 1864–71, and success was attributed to God's pleasure at the superior virtue of His Germans. Prussia had become great, it was declared after 1871, and Germany unified, by 'throne, bayonet and catechism'. The new *Reich* was widely referred to by the establishment as a manifestation of the 'Protestant spirit', and church leaders tried to regain popular support by associating religion with the burgeoning national spirit. Protestants outside Prussia, especially the Pietists, had come to support the cause of national unity because they believed that their social programme of aid to the needy would be much easier to implement in a national rather than a particularist framework. By subscribing to the false analogy between the religious revivalism of the years after 1813–14 and the wars of liberation, they looked to a similar religious fervour among the German people, stimulated by the successful outcome of the wars of unification. On every occasion of patriotic celebration in the years after 1871, to which the authorities and the populace were much addicted, church dignitaries graced the platforms as inevitably as representatives of the Prussian–German army provided military music and parades. When in 1881 in response to a wave of aggressive national feeling stimulated by the historian von Treitschke at Berlin university, the *Bund deutscher Studenten* was formed, students of theology took a prominent part in the organization. A deeply pious religious leader, Friedrich von Bodelschwingh, one of the most respected figures of his generation, did not see anything incongruous in instituting an annual *Sedan-Feier* commemorating the Prussian victory over the French on 2 September 1870, designed to renew the religious life of the people. The patriotic form of the occasion must attract a wide response, while the form of the festival, a religious service followed by children planting an 'oak of peace' and all the hallowed accompaniments of the traditional German excursion, food and drink in the open air, singing and decorous merriment, would, he believed, engender sentiments of gratitude to a benevolent deity. The Sedan festivals continued to be organized for over twenty years, but the religious hopes placed in them were not destined to be realized.[17]

But while devout Protestants were usually Prussian or German nationalists, it did not follow that the reverse was true. True, the nobility continued to be faithful to their church – up to the end of the Weimar Republic the parish boundaries of the Evangelical church in the eastern provinces coincided with those of the party districts of the Conservative (later German National) Party; educated circles tended to subscribe to a mildly Protestant ethic, on which Hegel had had a more formative influence than Luther. In the Second Empire men of property and education found in an increasingly aggressive nationalism an adequate substitute for the religion of their childhood. They liked their wives to be devout, however, and regarded religion as a most necessary custodian of the social order with which they now – in the 1880s and 1890s – liked to identify themselves. In a typically humorous formulation, Fontane's successful concert singer of humble origins, Maria Trippelli (*Effi Briest*), neatly summarized contemporary attitudes among such classes:

> Ihr Vater sei freilich ein Rationalist gewesen, fast schon ein Freigeist. ... sie ihrerseits sei aber ganz entgegengesetzter Ansicht, trotzdem sie persönlich des grossen Vorzugs geniesse, gar nichts zu glauben. Aber sie sei sich in ihrem entschiedenen Nichtsglauben doch auch jeden

Augenblick bewusst, dass das ein Spezialluxus sei, den man sich nur als Privatperson gestatten könne. Staatlich höre der Spass auf, und wenn ihr das Kultusministerium oder gar ein Konsistorialregiment unterstünde, so würde sie mit unnachsichtiger Strenge vorgehen.

Her father had been a rationalist, to be sure, almost a free thinker.... For herself she was of the opposite persuasion, despite having the great personal advantage of not believing in any religion. But she was constantly aware in her firm unbelief that this was a special luxury to be enjoyed only as a private individual. From the point of view of state, however, there was to be no nonsense, and if she had charge of the Ministry of Cults or even a consistory, she would be severe and unrelenting to a degree.[18]

The most serious casualty – from a religious point of view – of the developments in the Evangelical church over the previous decades were the urban masses. By the time the German Empire was founded, migration on a vast scale was taking place from the countryside to the towns, especially of northern Germany. Rural workers had always gone to church, since those who ordered their lives expected it of them; once living in the cities, there was no pressure on them to do so, and for those in employment there was very little spare time at their disposal, even on Sundays. An Evangelical pastor who worked in disguise as a factory worker for some months in 1890 in order to experience life as it was lived by the urban working class, recorded that almost all adult males were constrained to work in some other job on Sundays, just to make ends meet.[19] The parson, whether in rural areas or in a city parish, was for such people the agent of established authority, the dispenser of orthodox spiritual comfort and perhaps of charity, accompanied by admonitions to practise self-denial and gratitude; he was not someone who spoke their language or came from a similar social background. The sermon, not the communion service, was the focal point of church worship; the rhetorical style favoured by the parsons and their educated listeners was standard in poor parishes as well; this could have little meaning or solace for those who were oppressed with bad housing, low wages, uncertain employment prospects and malnutrition. Nor could the German Protestant churches offer the kind of escape or imaginative stimulus in the shape of popular devotions, colourful pictures and statues which the Catholic church offered the lower classes. In a crude cartoon in 1890 the Berlin satirical paper, *Kladderadatsch,* showed the energetic city preacher, Adolf Stöcker, who tried to win back the masses to Christianity, as a missionary in an Africa which was divided between the two Christian confessions: there were no candidates among the natives for Stöcker's tracts lying in a neat pile on his table, while over in the Catholic side cannibalistic natives were rushing enthusiastically to secure a rosary or holy picture – to be devoured at leisure.[20]

The type of nonconformist congregation which played such a vital social as well as spiritual role in the lives of the British working class had no equivalent in Germany; the Pietists might have been expected, from their early history, to have remedied the deficiency, but they were now too closely identified with the establishment. When Adolf Stöcker, a controversial exponent of social commitment on the part of the Evangelical church, visited the textile manufacturing town of Barmen in the Wuppertal in 1880, he declared angrily that the local clergy 'nicht unter das Volk gestiegen seien. Wer kein Mitleid mit der materiellen Not der Arbeiter hat, sei kein echter Christ' ['did not come among the people. He who feels no pity for the material need of the workers is not a proper Christian'].[21] There were indeed a number of free church congregations and sects in Germany, but these were to be found rather among the artisans and domestic workers, notably the weavers; they were in the main individualistic, mutually intolerant and, in some cases, not a little self-satisfied.

It would be wholly wrong to give the impression that the Protestant churches in nineteenth century Germany overlooked the existence of poverty and distress among the lower classes. Many devout clergymen and members of the laity dedicated their lives to the problem, notably Wichern of Hamburg, the Rhinelander Fr. Bodelschwingh (whose father as a Prussian minister had introduced the first factory act into Prussia in 1839), and Adolf Stöcker of Berlin.[22] Wichern, a man of humble origin, founded the institution known as the *Rauhes Haus* in 1844, a hostel for neglected or orphan boys, who were trained in a trade or craft. This was unusual for the time, and psychologically penetrating; orphanages usually trained their inmates only for menial tasks, as though their unfortunate condition did not entitle them to become useful and respected members of society. The idea spread rapidly through most German states in the 1850s. Wichern, a tireless organizer and splendid persuader of the rich and powerful in the interests of his charges, extended his activities to found the Inner Mission. This was a project which aroused considerable publicity throughout the whole of the second half of the century, and was intended to rekindle religious fervour among all classes in the giving and receiving of charity. Charity was the key concept and, at the same time, the chief obstacle to the success of the Inner Mission. Because of their training as servants of the state as well as of the church, because of the church's static view of society which she shared with the establishment, in which the prosperous had an obligation to succour the less fortunate and the latter had an equal obligation to bear their preordained lot in humility, grateful for charity received, the clergy could not appreciate that it was social reform, not bounty, that was needed, that the church must rethink its social role before it could hope to appeal successfully to the victims of dynamic industrial change. To the conservative establishment in the Second Empire reform was close to revolution, and revolution like modern society generally an aberration.[23] Members of the ruling classes and their satellites liked to blame drunkenness and immorality for the conditions in city slums; they did not appreciate, to take one example, the influence of bad housing on family life and the crying need to check the activities of the property speculator in a city such as Berlin.

Wichern and Stöcker joined the philanthropic reformer, Victor Aimé Huber, in calling for workers' settlements; some paternalist employers, such as Stumm-Halberg, built them, but submitted the inmates to close surveillance and practically forced them to go to church on Sundays. Both Wichern and Stöcker were men of humble origin whose activities and talents had introduced them to the highest in the land – Stöcker became court preacher in 1874. They could not envisage pursuing schemes of social welfare against the wishes of the ruling classes. Stöcker's attempt to found a Christian Social Party was a fiasco; the masses to whom he tried to appeal saw in him simply an appendage of the establishment; their class consciousness aroused by the Social Democratic movement found its intellectual expression in scientific materialism; Stöcker's religious arguments seemed merely out of date. However, he gradually attracted support from the lower middle classes of the self-employed, shopkeepers, small traders, minor officials and employees, for whom his emotive association of the so-called enemies of religion and orderly society, socialists, liberals and Jews, was a persuasive one. He became a controversial if not popular figure among the antisemites in Berlin in the 1890s. As a religious leader his career ended in failure; Kaiser William II, who had associated himself with the Inner Mission as a young man, dropped his former favourite in a typical gesture: in a telegram he declared: 'Christlich-sozial ist Unsinn. Die Herren Pastoren sollen sich um die Seelen ihrer Gemeinden kümmern, die Nächstenliebe pflegen, aber die Politik aus dem Spiel lassen, dieweil es sie gar nichts angeht' ['Christian-Social is nonsense. The pastors should concern themselves with the souls of their parishioners, cultivate Christian charity but forget about politics, because it has nothing to do with them'].[24] Perhaps more serious – again from a strictly religious point of view – than this programmatic statement from the head of the Evangelical church in Prussia was the fact that the *Oberkirchenrat,* a leading church dignitary, who had warmly recommended the Christian-Social policies to parish clergy in the past, now persuaded the General Synod to confirm the Kaiser's line. The philosopher, William Dilthey, a representative spokesman of educated but sceptical Protestant opinion, commented: 'Der Oberkirchenrat tut in seiner grauenhaften Unsicherheit und Sklavennatur das Seine, wie der Grossinquisitor in Don Carlos' ['the Chief Consistorial Councillor, with his ghastly lack of confidence and a slavish nature, does his bit, like the Grand Inquisitor in *Don Carlos*'].

The Lutheran and Reformed churches in the non-Prussian states retained their independence under the Empire – with the exception of those areas such as Baden, Nassau and the Bavarian Palatinate who had joined the Evangelical church in 1817, but they were inevitably affected by the developments of religious life in Prussia, which occupied some three fifths of *Reich* territory. It would not be wide of the mark to suggest that the position which the German Protestant church occupied in the last years of the Wilhelmine Empire was one that did not deeply concern the majority of its members. It was one of the acknowledged 'pillars of state' and clergymen enjoyed considerable social prestige and respect, though they provided by 1900 a decreasing proportion of the élite of German society.[25] On important national occasions the church service was an accepted item on the programme, although church attendance had declined considerably over the previous decades. To its critics both inside and outside the church its basis seemed ever more exclusively that of a particular social class or even merely of a party – the conservative agrarian interest.

2 THE CATHOLIC CHURCH

The problems facing the Catholic church in nineteenth century Germany bore an immediate resemblance to those experienced by the Protestants. However, the political situation in which the Catholic church found itself was a radically different one. At the beginning of the century, with the fall of the Holy Roman Empire, the church lost the basis on which her temporal power rested. Fears were expressed in Catholic circles as to whether the church as an institution would survive at all in Germany. However, the political difficulties brought about sociological changes in church leadership which had positive effects in the spiritual sphere. Members of the Catholic hierarchy in the nineteenth century came increasingly from the middle and lower ranks of society, in marked contrast to former times. This undoubtedly helped the lower classes to identify with their pastors in a way that was not typical of Lutheran areas.

Political confrontation between the state and the Catholic church in Prussia during the 1830s and 1870s aroused a keen sense of loyalty among the faithful from every class of society. The Catholic political interest group formed during the 1848 revolution at Frankfurt emerged as the Catholic Centre Party in 1871; from 1871 to 1933 the Centre provided talented men with a highly motivated career in parliament and public life which was bound up with their religious faith. In one other important respect the Catholic church proved itself resilient in an age of unbelief, namely in its attitude to the social question. Although the church was naturally committed to a hierarchical and even authoritarian form of society, Catholics in Germany did not have the same vested interests in a static social structure as did the Lutheran clergy and laity, at least in Prussia. The Catholic landowners in Silesia and the south-west apart, Catholics were less privileged members of the community and did not have the same urgency as did many of their fellow Christians to defend the old order against the onslaught of social change. Thus when faced with the human problems created by industrialization, the Catholic clergy and laity recognized the need to be involved in social problems; indeed, many proved themselves unexpectedly pragmatic. Individual Catholics played a little-publicized part in succouring the distressed and in pioneering institutions to care for categories of the needy. Many church leaders came to accept what their counterparts in the Evangelical church found difficult to accept – namely, that charity was not enough, and that reform of social conditions was mandatory. Outstanding social vision was characteristic of only a very few, however; much more typical was the pragmatic approach expressed in the reluctant decision on the part of the Catholic authorities to authorize the founding of a Christian Trade Union movement in the 1890s in order to counter the appeal of Social Democracy for Catholic workers.

However, the impact that such social awareness might have had in the direction of liberalizing the German Catholic church was prevented by external causes from taking place. The intransigent rejection of modern ideas by Pope Pius IX (1846–78), culminating in his unfortunate decision to publish the *Syllabus of Errors* (1864), was followed in Prussia by the *Kulturkampf*, a violent confrontation between state and church. This episode drew Catholics all over Germany together, but their militancy was increased at the cost of liberal elements in their midst. This was an extremely significant, and in some ways fateful, development for the church. Of course the *Kulturkampf* was not Bismarck's brainchild nor even exclusive to Prussia. It was a tactical device employed by the Chancellor with strictly domestic political aims in mind. However, the favourable response from the non-Catholic middle classes, many of whom were still technically members of the Evangelical church, was characteristic of similar clashes between governments and the Catholic church in other European countries, notably France and Austria. To such people Catholicism was a symbol of reaction in a progressive world, and the church an institution which held its members in thrall to an intolerant and scientifically indefensible doctrine. Many Germans believed that the international connections of the church, and the power of the Jesuit order in high places, represented a kind of world conspiracy, which could be invoked against national power – much as people decades later were prepared to give credence to the notion of a Jewish world conspiracy based on financial connections.

Yet there were many Catholics for whom the Syllabus represented not only a major tactical mistake on the part of the Papacy, but a menacing claim; there were others who, like the able and popular Munich theologian, Ignaz Döllinger, were prepared to secede from the church over the proclamation of the dogma of papal infallibility in matters of faith and morals in 1871. The anti-papalism characteristic of the Catholic upper classes in Germany was prompted both by a long established dislike of the Vatican and a tradition of mutual regard and tolerance for their Lutheran cousins and friends.[26] But in consequence of the *Kulturkampf* there was little place left in the German Catholic church from the 1870s onwards for the liberal, the tolerant or even the critical voices. The subsequent purging of liberal critical elements in the Catholic leadership, both in the clergy as well as the Centre Party and the Catholic *Vereine* or associations which had such a profound influence on Catholic life in the decades before 1914, fostered a ghetto mentality among German Catholics, which seriously prejudiced the church's development up to and beyond the two world wars. The German Catholics' sense of solidarity forged in these years not only changed their relationship to the Vatican, making it more friendly than perhaps for centuries, it also altered their attitude to the conservative society in which they lived. The tactful rapprochement between state and church which the new Pope, Leo XIII (1878–91), made possible, further modified their relationship, and by the late 1880s Bismarck could regard the Centre Party as a possible ally in domestic policy, since each shared a dislike of liberalism, socialism and modern materialism. Moreover, the question raised by Bismarck during the *Kulturkampf* as to whether Catholics could in fact be loyal to the German Empire and to

Rome was one which the up and coming Catholic middle classes could not afford to have repeated. New careers, new opportunities were being opened to them; they had to seem as good Germans as the rest. A marked sense of national inferiority was characteristic among the Catholics after the founding of the Second Empire, which could easily be represented as the triumph of Protestant (or liberal) *Kleindeutschland* over the Catholic south or *Grossdeutschland* which had included Austria. Catholics tried to overcome their sense of inferiority by ceasing to question the authoritarian nature of that state. The popular democratic tradition of the Catholic south and west, which had been a factor of some potential in Germany's evolution in the first half of the century, had virtually disappeared.[27]

Thus in the last years of the monarchy German Catholics, like German Protestants, were closely associated with one political party and were generally conservative in their attitude to the modern world. However, in most other ways the two churches had developed differently in the century which had elapsed since the fall of Napoleon. The Centre Party was socially the most comprehensive in the country, and if it was the interest party of members of one faith, it was also the only political party in the country which was not the economic interest group of a particular social class. Moreover, both clergy and laity had come to accept the primacy of social over political questions for the church; in consequence of this the body of the Catholic working class had not lost its sense of involvement in the life of the church. In order to maintain the authority of an institution, people must be able to identify themselves in some way with the persons who represent it. This was possible for Catholics because of the presence of a number of dedicated and able men and women who devoted themselves to the pastoral care of those affected by social upheaval, and, in a more general way, because of the mixed social background of the hierarchy and clergy in the nineteenth and twentieth centuries.

German Catholicism had, as already remarked, suffered a body blow at the hands of Napoleon, who undermined its political influence in the *Reich.* In 1803 the ecclesiastical states were secularized, the lands and their inhabitants divided among secular princes, many of whom were Protestant; three years later the ancient edifice of the Holy Roman Empire followed the ecclesiastical states into the obscurity of history. With its demise Catholic influence in central Europe was inevitably vastly diminished. The *Reich* church was not, as Alexander Dru put it in his brilliant essay on the church in nineteenth century Germany, 'violently overturned, but legally buried'.[28] The same 'legality' accompanied the redistribution of population and territory during and after the Napoleonic wars. Only three territorial rulers survived: the Archbishop of Mainz, now however virtually landless, the Grand Master of the Teutonic Order, and the Master of the Knights of St John. In 1815, at the end of the Congress of Vienna, there was no Catholic German state; even Bavaria was partly Lutheran, through its acquisition of Franconia and Bayreuth-Ansbach; the Catholic Rhineland had been given to Prussia, while the many Catholic principalities and abbeys in and near its territory had gone to Württemberg. In subsequent years the Vatican negotiated a series of agreements with some of the secular rulers to secure the position of the Catholic church in their lands. A concordat was signed with Bavaria in 1817; in other areas papal bulls regulated the administrative liberties of the church, as for example the bull *De salute animarum* with Prussia (1821).

These external changes took place against the background of a much needed religious revival within the Christian fold. Late in the eighteenth century a number of devout and thoughtful men and women, both Lutheran and Catholic, and of very different social origins, had found themselves drawn together by common concern at the state of spiritual life in Germany and at the assaults being made on the churches as institutions both in France and in their own country. Educated Catholics were not unaware of the state of superstition and ignorance which passed for religion in many parts of Germany and of the general cultural inferiority of Catholics *vis-à-vis* the Lutherans. Eulogius Schneider, one of the most outspoken advocates of the Enlightenment within the church, had asked bitterly in 1789: 'Are we differently made from our Protestant brothers? Do we breathe a Boethian air while they live under an Attic sky?'[29] Princess Galitzin, an aristocratic Catholic of considerable influence, described her own humiliating experience of Catholic education in her memoirs. After leaving her convent school in Silesia, where the girls were made to pay deference to the innumerable statues of saints, as though they were practisers of polytheism, she came to Berlin and was invited with her parents to court. During a walk in the park grounds with the royal entourage she made a profound curtsy to what she believed were two marble statues of the Virgin Mary and St John Nepomuk and provoked the wildest merriment among the assembled courtiers: it was a naked Venus with her lover Apollo.[30] When her own children were growing up, the princess came to Münster to have them properly educated and joined the influential circle there. Its focal point was Bishop Franz Fürstenberg, with his friends Overbeck and Count Stolberg; they studied and discussed religious questions and maintained lively contacts through correspondence with friends in other places. One of the most important influences in their circle was the poet and Lutheran pastor Matthias Claudius, who had translated the great Fénélon and introduced his Catholic friends to this genial influence, who had rediscovered the baroque poet Angelus Silesius and through him opened up access to a half-forgotten but powerful mystical tradition within the church; at great spiritual loss to themselves the Jesuits in Germany had long been prohibited from reading the German mystics, since to the authorities these had smacked of Protestantism.

Other influential figures in the Catholic reform movement at the turn of the century included Bishop Dalberg at Aschaffenburg and Wessenberg who began to use German in celebrating the liturgy, and the greatest of all, J. M. Sailer (1751–1832), a former Jesuit whose personal piety and theological writings made a formidable contribution to the revival of pastoral theology in Germany. It was typical of the ferment of these years that reforms were proposed and even briefly implemented – such as the use of the vernacular – which were to become accepted practice in the universal church only a century and a half later. The most constructive aspect of the reform was the practical concern of clergy and laymen for religious education, which they rightly saw as crucial for the future of Catholic life. Here Sailer was unsurpassed. He has been compared by many historians to Fénélon himself, a man of deep spirituality, practical and warmhearted, admired and even loved by all who came in contact with him, by people as diverse as the bookseller Perthes, Claudius, the lawyer Savigny, and the ebullient Bettina von Brentano. Sailer's rejection of traditional scholasticism in favour of a revived pastoral theology, flexible in its interpretation as befitted a changing world, made him suspect to his own superiors. This prevented his appointment as Archbishop, but by a fortunate paradox this very fact recommended him to the secular authorities under Montgelas in Bavaria as a suitable candidate for the chair of moral and pastoral theology at Landshut university. Moreover, his influence in this position proved far more diverse, and in the case of individual students such as Franz von Baader, the social thinker and philosopher, Diepenbrock, later Cardinal Archbishop of Breslau, and Clemens Brentano, more intense than could possibly have been the case had he been appointed bishop.

Sailer was one of those people whom the church has produced throughout its history, whose simplicity and goodness has disarmed critics – though more effectively those outside the fold – and yet whose intellectual qualities were formidable enough to engage their serious consideration.[31] He had a genius for friendship, had wide contacts with other Christian circles and was in fact the first German Catholic to obtain a general hearing.[32] His deepest concern was with the primacy of pastoral care in an irreligious age, and it was for this reason that he developed his renowned *Vermittlungstheologie,* or theology of mediation, which was to bear fruit many years later in the modern ecumenical movement. In his own time the most lasting effect of his concern was found at parish level, where others, such as Clemens Maria Hofbauer, baker's boy turned Redemptorist preacher in Vienna, sharing his concern, tried to implement his ideas.

The interest of a number of leading German Romantic writers and thinkers in the Catholic revival was of enormous potential for the church.[33] They included Friedrich Schlegel, Joseph Görres, whose exceptional journalistic talents were placed at the service of religion, and Clemens Brentano. Unfortunately that potential was not fully realized, partly because personal and financial circumstances forced them to enter the service of Restoration regimes for whom the Catholic revival was merely a useful buttress of legitimacy and a reactionary society. Schlegel entered the stultifying service of Metternich and Gentz at Vienna; here his attempts to foster understanding between Catholics and Lutherans through his periodical *Concordia* made him suspect to his hosts, as did his friendship with Hofbauer; Görres meanwhile found a platform for his ideas and a wide audience in the Munich of Ludwig I (1825–48). Here the Catholic revival was made official and submitted to the kind of hothouse treatment which inevitably favoured the conservative, even feudal, influences within the church. Such patronage, effectively submitted, smothered the probing and original, but profoundly spiritual, reexamination of the role of religion and the church in the modern world, to which members of the Romantic movement had given a vital impulse. An illustration of that spirituality is to be found in the poetry of Eichendorff, a Silesian nobleman who spent most of his working life in the Prussian civil service and wrote in his leisure hours, especially in his use of symbolic landscapes and nature images to explore spiritual states.

The primacy of Munich in German Catholicism remained unassailed until the abdication of Ludwig I in 1848, the death of Görres and the dispersal of the group of well-connected Catholics associated with the institution known as the Round Table. Although Heine's satiric barbs at their self-satisfaction, not to say intellectual and religious intolerance, were often apt, in one vital aspect they differed from their co-religionists in France – namely, in their appreciation of the primacy of social problems for the church. Unlike French Catholic leaders such as de Maistre, Bonald and Lamennais, who concentrated their concern on the relations between state and church, these Germans were not trying to secure a political position for the Catholic church in Germany. A number of thinking Catholics were convinced – and here the impulse from Romanticism remained influential below the surface – that the greatest dangers to religion would come, not from the hostility of a secularized state, but from the secularization of culture and the indifference of the masses. Though most Catholics were conservative by inclination and favoured a corporative organization of society, they had less interest in defending the inviolability of the *status quo* than their counterparts in the Evangelical church. Franz Baader, professor of philosophy at Munich and an original social thinker, had been the first to discern the nature of the social change taking place as a result of economic factors, and probably the first to use the term '*proletair*' in the modern sense of propertyless class.[34] A number of Catholics, prominent and obscure, intellectuals and working men, showed sensitivity to the needs of the working class many decades before the state did anything to remedy their distress. The theologian Pilgram saw clearly that mere charity could no longer suffice to relieve need on the scale it was experienced in the 1840s; Buss, a professor of theology at Freiburg University, proposed the introduction of factory acts in 1837, while Adolf Kolping, a journeyman apprentice, founded the *Gesellenverein* or journeymen's association in his native Elberfeld, the first in a nationwide network of hostels for working men. Through the various religious orders Catholics had, as it were, an accumulated knowledge of conditions of poverty and distress. Most people had an aunt or uncle, a cousin of their mother or grandmother, in a convent or monastery; a very large number of such orders existed in Germany, and the variety and scope of their charitable tasks has only recently been more fully investigated, although not yet acknowledged by social historians.[35]

Perhaps the most important practical aspect of Baader's social ideas lay in the formative influence he exercised on a Westphalian aristocrat who rose to be primate of the church in Germany, a man who later confessed that on taking holy orders the greatest sacrifice he was called upon to make was having to give up his gun: Archbishop Ketteler of Mainz (1810–78). A man of 'few but clear ideas' (Dru), no stereotyped Roman prelate but rather an officer among his clergy, Ketteler eventually acquired great moral authority in Germany. When still a relatively young man, he was called upon to preach the Lenten sermons in the Frankfurt cathedral in 1848 and chose as his theme 'The great social questions of the time'. Here was a man with the will and ability to lead, and the flexibility of one active in practical affairs. In the 1840s and 1850s he saw the social question in terms of the artisan class, but by the following decade, influenced by Lassalle, he began to concern himself with the industrial proletariat. Despite his aristocratic background and natural preference for a hierarchical society, he, like Lassalle, advocated universal suffrage in order to give the workers influence on their conditions of life. His book *Die Arbeiterfrage und das Christentum* (*The Worker Question and Christianity*) (1864) inspired many Catholics from a variety of social backgrounds to involve themselves in these problems and thus to fulfil the missionary duty imposed on them as Christians in the modern world.[36]

The sense of commitment to their faith was meanwhile being reinforced by current political events. In 1837 there occurred the so-called Cologne Incident, a clash between the Rhenish hierarchy and the Prussian, mainly, though not exclusively, over the question of mixed marriages. This was a topical issue, since the Prussian officials coming to work in the Rhenish provinces married Catholic girls, and the Prussian authorities, not surprisingly, objected to the church's insistence on the children of such unions being brought up as Catholics. Archbishop Droste-Vischering of Cologne, who formulated the church's stand, found himself arrested and confined to fortress detention without trial; his colleague in Posen, Archbishop Dunin, suffered the same fate. The reaction among the people of the Rhineland showed that the secular authorities had unwittingly challenged deep local loyalties, of which Catholicism was but one; they were bitterly incensed at the arbitrary nature of such an act, at the confrontation, as they saw it, between police state methods and their own popular traditions. In a letter to the Prussian diplomat Varnhagen, Heine compared his fellow Rhinelanders to the Belgians, in whose recent successful struggle for independence the Catholic organizations had played a prominent part: 'was diese den Holländern gegenüber sind, das sind meine Landsleute gegenüber den Preussen' ['their role with regard to the Dutch is like that of my fellow countrymen with regard to the Prussians'].[37] The Cologne Incident was eventually patched up and after his accession Frederick William IV tried to conciliate his Rhenish subjects by organizing a fund to complete Cologne cathedral, to which non-Catholics made substantial contributions. It was important in showing the strength of the popular element in Catholic regions, where political instincts were often genuinely democratic.

However, this was another area of Catholic life where potential was not destined to be realized. The most intransigent critics of the Rhenish Catholics were Prussian liberals, such as the writer Karl Gutzkow, and it was the liberals to whom Bismarck looked and found support during the *Kulturkampf* in the 1870s; the association in the minds of religious leaders between liberalism and anticlericalism gradually isolated and eventually suppressed the liberal and democratic traditions within the Catholic church in Germany. The importance of the *Kulturkampf* in the history of religious life in nineteenth and twentieth century Germany lies less in the successful way in which the church was able to galvanize the energies of its members against the secular and often arbitrary power of the state, but in the manner it reinforced the conservative and acquiescent elements at the cost of a liberal, critical spirit. This development cannot be attributed merely to the Prussian government policies towards the Centre Party and the Catholic church. The Syllabus of Errors and the proclamation of papal infallibility in 1871 caused a deep split within the church. The publication of the Syllabus, just two years before the expulsion of Catholic Austria from the German Confederation and the foundation of Prussian hegemony, attached a reactionary label on all things Catholic. The dogma of papal infallibility seemed to liberal Catholics to establish the authoritarian nature of the Roman church for all times. Lord Acton, by instinct an opponent of the dogma, feared for his life in Rome as a result. Chlodwig Hohenlohe believed to the end of his long life that his brother, the Cardinal, had been expedited from this world by the Jesuits, when he, a doughty critic, died in Rome at the time of the Vatican Council.

The *Kulturkampf* was only possible in the hysterical atmosphere engendered by these developments; non-Catholics lent a ready ear to the notion of an international Catholic conspiracy directed against the young Empire, while Bismarck successfully aroused a crusading Protestant spirit as well as appealing to the liberals when he condemned the 'reichsfeindlich' [hostile to the state] character of the Catholic Centre Party, founded in 1871. By 1876 all Prussian bishops were either imprisoned or exiled for their resistance to the May laws of 1873 and the subsequent legislation limiting clerical power; 1800 parish priests were in similar straits. Expressions of solidarity from all parts of the country forged a new sense of identity but also of political power among the Catholics. When the authorities in Münster decided to auction the effects of the recalcitrant bishop of Münster, the local populace bought them back and carted them to the prison where he was held. Prussian officials working here were boycotted and deliveries of milk, bread, etc., to their households ceased. However, when the diplomatic Leo XIII succeeded Pius IX in 1878, he found that the very resistance of German Catholics to the inroads of the state had bred a new intolerance among them; German church leaders were unwilling to cooperate with his policy of conciliation. This was especially the case with the head of the Centre Party, the diminutive but redoubtable

Windhorst, of whom Bismarck once said that God had given him to love and to hate, his wife to love and Windhorst to hate. Eventually, however, a compromise was reached between the opposing parties, but in subsequent decades the leaders of the Centre Party who had received their political education in these years evinced the ghetto spirit typical of a once persecuted minority. Church leaders too tended to confine Catholics within their own world, to shield them from loss of faith by maintaining their ignorance of the modern world. The education of German Catholics lagged seriously behind that of their fellow countrymen. The Bavarian prime minister and later *Reich* Chancellor, Count Hertling, made a powerful attack on the complacency of his co-religionists, when in 1896 he spoke of the grave moral irresponsibility of those in charge of Catholic education.[38] However, he aroused little positive response. The prosperity of the times, the dominant position of the Centre Party within Catholic areas, and the powerful indirect influence on political life, activated against change and encouraged, in Dru's apt phrase, 'the impassive conservatism of the ghetto'.[39] Individual Catholics critical of the accepted image of the church might win a local following – Carl Sonnenschein in Berlin is the most outstanding example in the early 1900s and during the Weimar Republic[40] – but vested interests denied them the opportunity of genuine reform.

One further effect of the German unification under Prussia and of the *Kulturkampf* deserves elaboration, because it conditioned the instinctive reaction of German Catholics to an authoritarian state up to and including the time of the Third Reich. This was their sense of national inferiority *vis-à-vis* the Protestant majority. Many Catholics had favoured the Austrian side in the 1866 war, and were extremely apprehensive at the prospect of the exclusion of Catholic Austria from Germany. 'The world stinks', commented one prominent Catholic politician in 1866, Hermann von Mallinckrodt. Most German Catholics believed in 1871 that the Empire must seriously disadvantage them. They found it difficult to identify with the exuberant nationalism of the new state, with the constant references on public occasions to the 'Prussian Protestant spirit', to the commemoration and the statues of German heroes, soldiers, statesmen and artists, few or none of them Catholic. They were made aware that they had contributed little to the culture of nineteenth century Germany, to its philosophy or its history, to literature or music. The generation which grew to maturity at the turn of the century had not been influenced by the victory of Prussia over Austria; they felt real loyalty to the Empire and hoped that the opportunities offered them by the increasing power and prosperity of their nation would advance them in their careers. Yet in all sorts of ways they felt at a disadvantage when they came to compete with non-Catholics for appointment in the civil service or universities.[41] A Catholic publicist collected statistics on the so-called parity question in 1899 and concluded, not without justice, 'dass mit der Bedeutung der öffentlichen (nicht bloss staatlichen) Stellungen die Verwendung von Katholiken abnimmt, um in den höchsten Stellungen fast ganz zu verschwinden' ['that with the increase in importance of public – not just state – office, the proportion of Catholics declines, to disappear almost entirely in the higher posts'].[42]

Essentially the relations were based on fear – on the part of Lutherans and liberals, fear of the international power of the Catholic church and, in domestic matters, that the solidarity of the Catholic party would give them preponderant influence, and among Catholics a sense of real discrimination against them by their own government and fellow citizens. Constantly reminded of their status as a political minority and conscious of their cultural backwardness, they began to feel something of second class citizens, and in times of national crises, as in the twentieth century, to try and win trust and confidence by stressing their character as 'staatserhaltende Kräfte' ['pillars of the state'] – in the current phrase, conservative, authoritarian, nationalist. This was evident in the years before the outbreak of the First World War, when the Centre gave its support to the parties of the Right, and more particularly in the response of the party to Hitler in 1933. The founding of the Christian Trade Union movement against the determined opposition of Catholic entrepreneurs, academics and a wide section of the middle class, seemed to prove the underlying strength of the social involvement of the Catholic church. The new movement supported the workers' right to strike, but it led to the embittered 'trade union conflict' within the ranks of the hierarchy. The body of Catholic opinion was in fact thoroughly suspicious of such developments, fearing the taint of socialism in the eyes of the authorities and of society in general. Here too the ghetto mentality, the lack of self-assurance towards the rest of the nation, is evident.

The Weimar Republic offered the Centre Party its greatest opportunities and its leaders readily rose to the challenge. Its most able politicians in these years came from the ranks of the trade union movement and the professional classes; but the influence of men from these social groups received a sharp setback in the last years of the Republic, when, under Brüning's chancellorship, the leadership passed back to the traditional right wing circles in the person of Mgr Kaas. It was the group of upper class Catholics associated with Kaas who made the fateful decision that the interests of religion and the liberty of conscience would best be preserved by ready acceptance of the absolute authority of the state in political matters. In this, the gravest crisis which the German Catholic church as an institution was called upon to face in its modern history, its leaders, with some notable exceptions, showed an alarming lack of assurance which was in great part the product of the church's chequered history in the nineteenth century.

Chapter 12

The German army

The history of the German army in the nineteenth century is very largely, though not exclusively, that of the Prussian army. The special relationship between the monarchy and the army which had characterized the Prussian state under the early Hohenzollern kings did not disappear with the advent of the new century. If anything, despite the reforms associated with the liberal era, 1807–19, the privileged position of the officer corps was actually enhanced. Nor was the aristocratic character of the officer corps and noble predominance in the highest posts effectively changed before the end of the monarchy in 1918. True, the catastrophe inflicted by Napoleon caused some rethinking of the system on which the Prussian army and society had been based. The King himself drafted the terms of reference in 1807 for a commission for the reorganization of the army. On the question of the social composition of the officer corps he asked (Point 5): 'Should not some change be made as regards the admission of bourgeois, and more of them be admitted?'[1] However, as in many other aspects of the Prussian reform, the principle was accepted by the authorities, only to be diluted or ignored in practice in subsequent decades. The Prussian nobility distinguished itself in the wars of liberation, regaining self-confidence and the trust of the king which they had lost at the battle of Jena. In the years of reaction after 1819 it became difficult for members of the middle classes to enter the officer corps in Prussia, or, once in, to win a fair share of the scarce promotions available. Throughout the next fifty years the *Junkers* fought a rearguard action to secure their dominance of the armed services, firmly convinced that they had a monopoly of those virtues which the profession of a soldier demanded. In the cavalry they were most successful, but a prejudiced observer in the 1850s (Major von Schweinitz) declared that the infantry now admitted 'the sons of postmen, tax inspectors, ticket collectors, superannuated students, post office clerks, etc.', while the artillery was 'the God-sent dumping ground for everyone who could not get into any other branch of the Service'.[2] While the percentage of non-aristocrats among infantry officers grew in the second half of the century, the artillery, as a result of vigorous efforts on the part of the Inspector-General of Artillery, von Hahn, became a highly regarded and thoroughly 'smart' branch up to the time of the First World War.

The unique personal relationship between the Hohenzollerns and their officers was a powerful force in maintaining an aristocratic tone in the Prussian army as a whole. Even the youngest lieutenant was '*hoffähig*' and William I at least knew all his officers personally. To Prussian monarchs the *Junkers* were their own kind, with the same habits and attitudes as themselves. Frederick William IV liked to drop in for afternoon chocolate without ceremony at Schloss Tegel, the home of Wilhelm Humboldt near Berlin;[3] in letters to his wife in the 1840s Roon recorded the easy atmosphere and congenial relations with members of the royal family at court.[4] In Prussia at that time both royalty and nobility were unostentatious, even austere, in their private lives; indeed one of the charges made against bourgeois officers in the mid nineteenth century was that they got into debt irresponsibly. Aristocrats, on the other hand, were used to doing without things.

The *Junker*'s son intended for an army career would be sent at an early age to one of Prussia's eight cadet schools (in Bavaria as in Saxony there was but one such school, reflecting perhaps the importance of the army in the state relative to Prussia). The cadet schools and the officer corps were not unlike the English public school system, both for the austerity and discipline prevailing there, at least in the early nineteenth century, but also for the sense of loyalty they fostered and the professional and social advantages conferred in later life. They provided free or assisted schooling for the sons of officers or poor noblemen, and although only a minority of officers attended them, the personality and style of these institutions exercised a formative influence on the entire military élite to 1918.[5] Albrecht von Roon, later Minister of War under William I, and a typical representative of the Old Prussian army officer, was sent at an early age to the cadet school at Kulm and later at Berlin.

He was an orphan and knew virtually no other home than this, but for his companions too home and family were often remote. They saw them only for short holidays during a period of years. School, on the other hand, and the officer corps afterwards offered a life that was both absorbing and the source of rich and intimate friendships. The King, a frequent visitor to the cadet schools, was a kind of father figure to the boys and on close terms with many of his officers. The most vivid memoirs of army life were written by the successful and intelligent, men such as Roon, Moltke, and Kraft von Hohenlohe-Ingelfingen, and their attitudes are naturally very positive; but even allowing for that, the reader cannot but be struck by the keen sense they all felt of belonging to a large and homogeneous family. As the Chief of General Staff, Count Waldersee, put it in another context many years later (1890): 'Die Armee ist eine Korporation wie eine Familie, deren intime Fragen nicht vor die Öffentlichkeit gehören' ['The army is a corporation like a family, whose most intimate concerns are not for the public eye'].[6] Typical of Prussian officers, he automatically identified the officer corps of which he was speaking, with the army as such. For a young officer in the long peace time years between Napoleon's defeat and the wars of the 1860s, there was plenty of free time. Individual officers would attend their clubs in Berlin, the casino in provincial garrisons, or they might pursue a variety of interests. Intellectual interests seemed to have played a much more prominent part in the early decades of the century, when the Romantic movement still influenced the upper classes, than in the later years, when the current tone in many casinos was aggressively anti-intellectual. Moltke attended a course of lectures on Goethe and another on English at Berlin University when he was a young officer at the War Academy. Between one third and one half of the audience were officers like himself. Money was for most of them a major worry; promotion was extremely slow. In nineteenth century Germany one was promoted to captain after fifteen years, and to a major after a further ten on average, but in Moltke's young days it was slower still.[7] He took on the arduous task of translating Gibbon's *Decline and Fall* in order to meet expenses on being transferred to the General Staff; the 500 marks he was promised worked out at the equivalent of the cost of two horses and their equipment. Roon was more fortunate; as well as being an instructor in the War Academy he was examiner and military tutor to the royal princes. He found himself in the enviable position of being able to marry in his early thirties; Moltke was forced, mainly on financial grounds, to wait over ten years longer.

Officers' wives inevitably took second place, even outside working hours. An officer was expected to spend his leisure hours with his regimental companions. William von Humboldt's granddaughter, the young and pretty Lella von Bülow, was only married a few weeks to her adored Leopold von Loen before she was writing in her diary 'Um mit gutem Gewissen seinem Vergnügen zu leben, liess er seiner Frau Gemahlin Plinsen mit Apfelmus aus dem Kasino holen – die Portion war gut, aber nicht für eine hungrige Seele berechnet' ['In order to devote himself with a good conscience to his pleasures, he had his lady wife sent apple pancakes from the casino; it was a good helping but not for a hungry soul']. This was no ordinary quarrel of newly weds, but something that most wives came to expect. When Leopold did come home, he generally brought his friends too, whose healthy appetites were a disaster for the meagre housekeeping allowance.[8]

Towards the end of the century, and particularly under William II, ostentation, luxury even, became characteristic of officers' lives. The older men spoke scornfully of such tendencies, blaming them on the bourgeoisie in their ranks, but the real reason was the immense increase in national wealth which had benefited the nobility as well as other propertied classes. After long years of peace the officers of the Second Empire spent their lives between manoeuvres, often an important social occasion at which the ladies appeared in colourful fashions to be presented to the monarch, and the somewhat effete and intellectually barren atmosphere of the casino.

Although nominally a conscript force, the Prussian army until William's time was not in fact a large one. The *Wehrgesetz* (Defence Law) of 1814 laid down the peacetime strength as 40 000 and this remained in force until 1858 despite the increase in Prussia's population between 1820 and 1858 from 11 million to 18 million. The main reason for this state of affairs was the realistic parsimony of Prussian officials, who saw clearly that a conscript army was more than a poor country could afford, particularly since defence spending in any case claimed over half the state budget. Thus although nominally everyone did two years military service, apart from the one year volunteer force, a sizeable portion of the populace was never called up. In 1852 it was calculated that, out of 62 000 eligible for service, 28 000 escaped entirely.[9] After initial training many of the recruits were sent home on unpaid leave and only recalled for the autumn manoeuvres. Those who had completed their service were liable to be called up in time of war to the Reserve; here too the old adage was valid: to him who hath, etc. 'The notorious situation resulted, when the army was mobilized in 1859, that some 150 000 reservists, most of them married men, were recalled to the colours, leaving their families as a burden on the rates, while 100 000 young men were left undisturbed' (Michael Howard).[10] The officials of the War Ministry were well aware of the absurdity of a military system which depended on the older age groups, pointing out that if the fathers should fall, the families of reservists must be reduced 'to the proletariat in the worst sense of the word'.[11]

This was an important factor in the army reforms of 1859 associated with Roon, but which William himself had planned since 1852. Besides his belief in the need for reform on military and social grounds, William clearly saw that control of the army in nineteenth century Prussia, as in seventeenth century England, conferred sovereignty. He therefore pursued his goals with a dogged determination unequalled by any of his advisers, and was prepared to risk a head-on confrontation with parliament, the Prussian *Landtag,* and even abdication, rather than compromise.

William succeeded his brother as King in 1861. For him the simplicity of a soldier's life was something that helped to make it morally superior to any other, one which he hoped would act as a model for Prussian society at large. As a man who had made his career in the Service – he had been an active soldier until he was fifty-one, in 1848 – he came to power, determined to increase the efficiency of the army. His military advisers included personal friends, notably Roon and Manteuffel, and with their aid he was also determined to retain the traditional bonds between the sovereign and a mainly aristocratic officer corps. He chose to ignore the liberal temper of the state over which he had assumed power, recalling only his unavailing attempts in the previous thirty years to have the length of service for conscripts extended from two to three years. He was convinced that the 1848 revolution would never have occurred had the 'right attitudes' been implanted in the recruits by three years at the colours.

It was less the massive increase in the army – almost double – than the extension of the two year service and the amalgamation of the territorials with the line that aroused the opposition of the liberals in Prussia. The bourgeois character of the territorial officers and the popular myth about the role it was alleged to have played in Napoleon's defeat made its preservation as a separate identity important for members of the propertied and educated classes from Berlin and the provinces at that time, for whom the professional army was a symbol of reaction. Militarily speaking, the King and Roon were correct in their estimation of the territorial army and bourgeois opinion was misinformed. The military party's provocative stand incensed public opinion and created wide support for parliament in the early 1860s. William and his advisers had – could have – no appreciation of the position of the liberal reformers in the *Landtag* – had not Roon described their fellows in 1848 as 'die Mittelklasse nämlich, d.h. die Konstitutionellen par excellence, die Liberalen in Glacéhandschuhen, die zahme Schar der liberalen Geheimräte und Professoren usw., die ganze gemütliche Gesellschaft' ['the middle class – that is, the constitutionalists *par excellence,* liberals in kid gloves, that tame crowd of privy councillors, and professors of liberal notions, the whole bunch of them'], and the citizen militia in the same year in these terms: 'die Canaille hat jetzt Gewehre' ['now the *canaille* bears arms'].[12] The obduracy of the military party was founded on unquestioning selfrighteousness; Bismarck's genial bullying of the *Landtag* and the extraordinarily fortunate timing of the successful wars against Denmark (1864) and Austria (1866) brought them victory in the Constitutional Conflict, although some face-saving manoeuvres for parliament were devised by the prime minister. He had presented the conflict in terms of foreign and national policy, whereas in fact it had been about budgetary control of parliament and the determination of the King and Prussian conservatives to preserve the position of the army as the 'absolutist kernel'[13] of the state. By accepting a peacetime army of 1 per cent of the population and agreeing to reviewing the position every seven years, the Prussian parliament had surrendered its annual budget right. In the whole affair Bismarck had shown himself a better friend to the army than its own chiefs, who had been prepared – as they were to be in the 1890s – to unleash a *coup d'état* in defence of their position. Bismarck's policy, his brilliant exploitation of Prussian victories, made the army acceptable to the nation in a way observers in the early 1860s could never have believed possible.

The army's politically privileged status was now assured. The victory over France and the founding of the Second Empire in 1871 confirmed the army's claim to be regarded as the founder of Germany's new status in the world. This naturally strengthened the bond between the monarchy and the officer corps. A clear connection was established, both among the military and in the nation as a whole, between the brilliant performance of Prussian arms and the special relationship between the King and his officers. Innovation and experiments devised by individual officers had been put into practice with gratifying results, simply because military matters aroused keen interest and support in the highest circles in the land. One can appreciate the importance of this by contrast with a country such as France. Here army officers were also drawn from traditional officer families, many of which had a long and distinguished history of service to the state; however, the military families were regarded with a certain disdain in influential French circles, for their relative poverty and lack of political influence. Napoleon III showed an intelligent interest in the technical side of military reform – among other things the *chassepot,* which had been developed from the highly effective Prussian needlegun – but he did not have William's power to override opposition. In Prussia, and after 1871 in most of Germany, army leaders retained a certain independence of the political administration. There were limits beyond which even Bismarck could not assume to go as far as the military were concerned. William's own obstinacy in defending the special status of the services was dictated by his view of that relationship. He saw it in feudal terms of mutual obligation, protection and service. He gave the Chief of General Staff the right of direct access to the ruler without the presence of his *Reich* Chancellor. Neither he nor the Chief of the Military Cabinet was answerable to parliament in any way. The only minister of the crown to whom parliament could make representations was the Prussian Minister of War (an Imperial Minister of War did not exist). By cabinet orders of March and May 1883 all matters of personnel, recruitment and promotion were taken away from the Minister of War who was merely in charge of administrative matters.[14] The concept of the military as a privileged section of society was given added substance from the very first day of William II's reign. On 5 June 1888, the day of his father's death and his own accession, he issued commands to the armed forces; three days were allowed to elapse before he found time to address his people. In subsequent years he paraded his view of the special relationship by holding regular meetings with the service chiefs three times a week at specified hours; the imperial chancellor had no such statutory arrangements for audience with the Kaiser.[15]

The social prestige of the officer corps in Prussian-dominated German society was everywhere evident from 1871 onwards. At the solemn act of proclamation of the Kaiser in Versailles in 1871 no civilian was present in his entourage apart from the chancellor, Bismarck, in the uniform of a Prussian general.[16] In subsequent decades the new plutocracy and the well-to-do professional classes began to try and get their sons into the army, a career which they would not have contemplated a generation earlier. In doing this they had no plans for reforming the erstwhile symbol of reaction from within; rather they were concerned with assuring their own upward social mobility. It was inevitable that the bourgeois element in the army must now grow rapidly. The very scale of the army reforms of the 1860s which had brought an almost 100 per cent increase in officer corps and ranks had dictated this. William I might declare solemnly in 1870: 'It is a grave offence against the army, which made him what he is, for any regimental commander to help undermine the well-deserved reputation for officers as a class by accepting officer-cadets who are "unsuitable".'[17] By this he meant those not belonging to traditional military families. Moltke, much less passionate in his convictions than many of his associates, denied that the nobility were preferred in the service, but agreed in conversation that middle class candidates were frequently rejected 'teils weil es unbrauchbare junge Leute sind, die sich zum Militärdienst melden, weil sie in einer anderen Karriere nicht fortkommen können, teils weil sie die Gesinnung nicht mitbringen, die man in der Armee bewahren muss' ['partly because they are useless young people who come forward for military service because they have got nowhere in any other career, partly because they have not got the right attitudes, such as must be preserved in the army'].[18] However, by the 1880s demand was already outrunning supply. 'Suitable' candidates were clearly no longer there. In 1865 65 per cent of all Prussian officers were noblemen; by 1913 the percentage was only 30 per cent. Even in the higher ranks, still predominantly aristocratic, the trend was towards *embourgeoisement*: 86 per cent of generals and colonels had been noblemen in 1865, in 1913 52 per cent. Even the élite of the army, the General Staff, had an equal number of noble and bourgeois officers by 1913.[19] As Germany's population continued to grow, more and more officers were required. When William II came to the throne he announced as policy what had been grudgingly practised as – it was hoped – a temporary expediency. In future, he declared in an order of the day, 29 March 1890, nobility of temperament was to rank alongside nobility of birth as qualifying a man for membership of the officer corps. Men would be welcome from 'honourable bourgeois families with a love of King and Fatherland, warm feelings for the army and Christian culture'.[20] The officer corps grew enormously between the mid nineteenth century and the eve of the 1914 war; when William I came to the throne, he knew his 3000–4000 officers personally; by 1893 there were 22 500 army officers in Germany and 70 000 NCOs in an army just over half a million; twenty years later, the numbers were 29 000 with appropriate increases in the other ranks.[21]

However, the increasing proportion of non-noble officers did not alter the aristocratic dominance of the corps. The wealthy and influential nobles thronged to join the cavalry or guards regiments, or those attached to the court of a German sovereign. The opposition parties in the *Reichstag* constantly drew attention to the fact that an overwhelming proportion of 'good' regiments were still the preserve of an exclusive social group. Such protests were quite ineffectual for, in Berlin at least, if not in Vienna or Munich, as the acute Marie von

Bunsen observed, it was much more important to be a member of a smart regiment if one wanted to move in high society, than to own a good pedigree or a favourable bank balance. 'The Foot Guards were in the ascendant at our house, and those of our set, more especially our favourite second regiment of the Foot Guards. The Alexander Guard regiment passed muster, the Kaiser Franz, the Fusiliers of the Guard and the Artillery of the Guard were rather lower down the scale. We were not aware of the existence of the Engineers and Sappers of the Guard.'[22] But even in the officer corps as a whole, attitudes of mind associated with a bygone age gradually became normal for bourgeois and aristocrat alike. The practice of selecting officers – apart from the cadet corps – lay with the regimental or battalion commanders, who made sure of getting the right kind of man. They corresponded with the applicants' fathers about the allowances they would give their sons and inquired into the social background of their families. A candidate might pass his military examinations with ease, but he would not be promoted to officer in a regiment until he had passed the more formidable test of acceptance by his future comrades, who first invited him to the casino to discover his 'attitudes' on essential subjects. In an article published in the *Militärwochenblatt* (1899) an anonymous contributor described the relevant attitudes with some pathos:

> Der bürgerliche sowie sowohl wie der adlige Offizier vertrete das gleiche Prinzip, die aristokratische Weltanschauung gegen die demokratische. ... Die dem Urgendanken des Offizierstandes entstandenen Gesinnungen sind: dynastischer Sinn, unbedingte Treue gegen die Person des Monarchen, erhöhter Patriotismus, Erhaltung des Bestehenden, Verteidigung der seinem Schutz anvertrauten Rechte seines Königs und Bekämpfung vaterlandsloser, königsfeindlicher Gesinnung.
>
> Both the bourgeois and the aristocratic officer stand for the same principle, the aristocratic outlook, as against the democratic. ... The attitudes rooted in the very depths of the officer's estate are: devotion to the dynasty, absolute loyalty to the person of the monarch, high patriotism, preservation of the *status quo,* defence of the rights of his king, who has entrusted himself to him, and hostility towards anti-patriotic, anti-monarchic attitudes.[23]

If individual bourgeois officers adopted the mentality of an exclusive caste in order to be accepted themselves by the élite of the nation, so did the bourgeoisie as a whole come to accept military values and the military tone particularly associated with Prussia. Prussian and German society underwent a process of militarization which forcibly struck those who came to visit the Empire from abroad. Everywhere uniforms were to be seen, not only those of professional soldiers, but state and municipal officials also. They stressed the idea of the omnipresence of the state, regulating the lives of the citizens, guarding their interests; they added life and colour to the scene – thus the cabdrivers in Berlin in the 1870s wore red braided jackets with black patent top hats – in the 1890s these were replaced by white patent leather. Even the holders of the highest civil office in the land, the *Reich* chancellor, generally wore uniform. Bismarck favoured that of the cuirassiers with which he had once served; even Bethmann-Hollweg (1909–16) made his first appearance in the *Reichstag* in a major's uniform and his name was mentioned in the promotion lists of 1914 as '*general à la suite*'. A uniform was deemed intrinsically superior to the best cut suit, and carried authority without reference to the wearer, as the famous incident of the captain from Köpenick was to prove. In civilian dress, according to the character of Schlettow in Carl Zuckmayer's play of the same name, one felt like 'half a portion, with the mustard left out'.[24] An incident experienced by my father as a student visiting Berlin in 1913 aptly illustrates the militarization of German society which foreigners found so strange. He had come to Berlin to meet and bring the greetings of Irish colleagues to Kuno Meyer, the renowned professor of Gaelic, at the Humboldt university. Walking together along the Kurfürstendamm, they were approached by a young officer with a crimson stripe on his trousers, denoting membership of the General Staff. Meyer stepped down on to the roadway as he passed; my father, protected by his ignorance of the language and the customs of the country, walked on. He was less astonished, when he had understood what was going on, by the anger of the officer upbraiding him than the anxiety of the professor to explain to the young blood that my father was a foreigner and knew no better.

A vivid external sign of the militarization of German society in the Second Empire was the proliferation of nationalist political organizations. Some grew out of veterans' associations after the wars of unification. In Prussia the *Preussischer Landeskriegerverband* whose function was initially social rather than political, had some 27 000 members in 1873. By 1890 it had 400 000, ten years later 1 million. The character of the association had obviously changed in the intervening years, and, as with the many other conservative associations, had become a political pressure group. Count Westphal, president of the *Landeskriegerverband,* was also on the committee of the national organization, the *Deutscher Kriegerbund*; in 1886 he had announced the intention of the movement's leaders to turn the local branches into

'Kampfstätten gegen die Sozial-demokratie' ['centres of hostility towards Social Democracy'].[25] William II agreed to become patron of the Prussian association. Here, as well as in the various nationalist groups which first appeared on the scene in the 1890s and early 1900s, the Pan-German League, the Navy League, the *Reich* League Against Social Democracy, the Defence League, etc., retired and active officers of both the regular army and the reserve played a prominent role. The honorary presidency of the local branch was frequently taken by a senior officer from the garrison, the anniversary of the founding of the *Reich,* or Sedan Day, would be suitably celebrated with an address from some prominent military man. The numerical expansion of these organizations – the *Reichsverband* had 2 800 000 members in 1912! – aptly reflects the aggressive nationalism of the pre-war years and anticipated the *Kampfbünde* or para-military organizations during the Weimar Republic, which prepared the way for fascism.

The importance of extra-parliamentary control of the army in the German Empire lay principally in the fact that it questioned the whole validity of Germany as a constitutional state. As the former Hanoverian chief minister, Rudolf von Bennigsen, put it: 'Die Kriegsverfassung, die Heereseinrichtung bilden ... bis zu einem hohen Mass das Knochengerüst der Verfassung eines jeden Staates, dass, wenn es nicht gelingt ... die Heeresverfassung und die Wehrverfassung einzufügen, in die konstitutionelle Verfassung überhaupt, die Konstitution in einem solchen Lande überhaupt noch keine Wahrheit geworden ist' ['The defence constitution and the army organization are to a very large extent the backbone of the constitution of any state, and so, if these are not successfully absorbed into the constitution, it is not really possible to speak of that state as a constitutional one'].[25a] What the leader of the National Liberal Party in the *Reichstag* could say of the situation in the 1870s was still valid some forty years later at the time of the outbreak of war. Military expenditure was after all by far the greatest item in the budget of the *Reich*: in the North German Federation (1867–71) it had accounted for 95 per cent of the whole; in Germany in 1913 75 per cent of the greatly increased *Reich* estimates went on defence. The numbers of men under arms increased steadily throughout the Second Empire, though the actual number of officers and men at any time was something less than those on paper:

1880	45·1 million	434 000
1890	49·2 million	509 000
1900	56·1 million	629 000
1913	67·0 million	864 000

Thus thirty years brought an increase of almost 100 per cent, the cost of maintaining the whole military apparatus rose by 360 per cent.[25b] Yet the Crown and the military authorities could see nothing incongruous or offensive in denying parliament's right to a voice in the apportioning of expenditure; indeed, the very notion that civilians could claim any right beyond that of voting supplies for the army seemed to their spokesmen nothing short of treasonable.

The most effective means of what was in fact a 'Prussianization' of German society in the Second Empire was the institution known as the Lieutenant of the Reserve.[26] Those with the required educational qualifications, whose parents could afford it, served only one year (instead of the statutory three up to 1893 and two thereafter) as unpaid volunteers. If a man proved himself, he became an NCO after nine months and shortly before leaving was promoted to Officer of the Reserve; in subsequent years he was liable to be called up to take part in military exercises. To be a Lieutenant of the Reserve carried considerable social cachet in the drawing rooms of the Second Empire; it was also of considerable help to a man in his professional career. In the years before the war the Reserve officers were looked to for support by the authorities in their efforts to unite conservative opinion in the country. They were, after all, a sizeable element in the population, numbering 120 000 in 1914. Before 1900 politics had been something that an officer, whether professional or Reserve, did not sully his hands with. However, with the new century a growing sense of threat haunted the upper classes in Germany, articulated as a fear of foreign 'conspiracies', or of social revolution from below. Basically this fear had its roots in the refusal to accept the fact of a changing world, to admit that the privileged élite of a former age was not really competent to deal with the immense political and social problems of a mighty industrial economy such as Germany had now become. The German authorities and the upper classes tried to deal with the problem by galvanizing 'loyal elements' of the population into giving political support to the *status quo.* The change in attitude is well expressed in a widely read essay on the Reserve officer, the eleventh edition of which appeared in 1911:

> Was nun die Politik betrifft, so waren längere Zeit merkwürdige Anschauungen über das Verhalten des Offiziers vorhanden. Man glaubte eine Zeitlang, durch vornehme Zurückhaltung fülle man seinen Platz auch als Reserve-Offizier am besten in der Politik aus. Diese Ansicht beruhte auf Unterschätzung des Gegners, der mit grosser Rührigkeit, ohne ängstlich in der Wahl seiner Mittel zu sein,

den Kampf führte. Die Erfolge der staatsfeindlichen Parteien ermahnen zum tatkräftigen Kampf!

As for politics, some odd views used to be current with regard to the officer's attitude: a discreet distance used to be thought the most correct line for a reserve officer to take. Such ideas were based on an underestimation of the enemy, who took up the struggle with great energy and without heed as to the type of weapons he used. The success of the party hostile to the state warns us that we too must be prepared for action.[27]

Should, however, an officer so far forget himself as to give support to a left liberal party or to the Social Democrats (in 1912 the largest party in the state), he would be summoned before a court of honour and stripped of his office.[28]

If the Reserve officers were responsible for spreading a military code of behaviour and conservative political attitudes among the bourgeoisie, the non-commissioned officer was the chief instrument of educating the ranks in what the great Moltke fondly described as 'the school of the nation'. Popular myth attributed to them – and to primary school teachers, many of whom were former NCOs – a vital role in training the troops for the victorious wars of unification; in the Second Empire they were 'Respektspersonen der Staatsgewalt auf der untersten Ebene' ['the lowest ranking people worthy of respect in their official capacity']. The social bridge between them and the ranks was fluid, but between themselves and the officer corps stood a virtually insuperable barrier. Their social origin was peasant and rural labouring class or small tradesmen, and their term of service was initially for twelve years. The talented and ambitious generally left at the end of the statutory time, because of lack of prospects in the forces, and many rose to be middle ranking officials. Caprivi tried to secure their loyalty by the reward of a 1000 *Reichmark* bonus, raised to 1500 in 1914,[29] which was nicknamed the 'Schiess- und Gesinnungsprämie' ['prize for shooting and having the right attitudes'] by socialist critics. The economic position of NCOs improved very greatly after 1890, partly because of a general rise in the standard of living, partly also because the government was forced to compete with industry, which could offer a variety of alternative careers to these people. Various status symbols and privileges were conferred on them according to the Royal Ordinance of 1909 in a further effort to increase recruitment – their own private dining rooms ('NCOs' casinos'), dispensation from carrying baggage, late night leave, etc.; this policy proved successful and the number of NCOs in the Prussian army – that is, about 75 per cent of the whole – rose from 8434 in 1909 to 9536 in 1913. They also had by this time a prescriptive right to special consideration for posts in the imperial and municipal service after leaving the army. They formed in the manner of the time their own special mutual protection society to increase their chances of employment, the *Bund deutscher Militäranwärter*, and aroused much hostility on that account among civilians applying for such jobs. However, there were some 16 000 former NCOs waiting for vacancies in the state and municipal service in 1914, a time of general prosperity, so it would appear that they were not particularly successful.

One of the reasons for this was undoubtedly their low educational attainments. The official line was that too much book learning was no advantage in such a post – quite the reverse in fact. In 1890 the Inspector of NCO training establishments declared that their knowledge was getting too extensive: the implication was that ignorance was somehow a pledge of loyalty and absolute obedience. This undoubtedly had the disadvantage that they relied on a parade ground bark to discipline recruits, a method effective enough on raw country lads, but the object of much satiric comment in the popular journals, such as *Kladderadatsch*, and, from 1896 onwards, the south German *Simplicissimus.*[30] Education was a much discussed topic in German army circles throughout the nineteenth century. The Prussian authorities were opposed to raising the educational standard for entry to the officer corps on the grounds that this might exclude the very type of old noble families they most wished to attract. Character, not general education, was, they said, what was required in a leader of men. 'Die Ausbildung entsprach jener Überzeugung' ['The training was in line with such convictions'], as a modern German military historian drily remarks.[31] A school certificate, *Primarreife,* roughly corresponding to a pass at O-Level, was deemed sufficient for a Prussian officer. In Bavaria, on the other hand, all officers had to have their *Abitur* since the time of Prankh's army reform in 1868; this meant they had attained the standard necessary to enter university. It is worth noting that when the Bavarian military reformers wished to raise the status of the officer in public estimation, they should place such stress on a high level of general education. German naval officers were also distinguished by their educational attainments; on the eve of the First World War 90 per cent had their *Abitur* and looked upon their army counterparts with a certain disdain. It was characteristic of the members of the Military Cabinet in the Second Empire, which had the ear of the monarch, that they should oppose the demand for school leaving as a basic requirement for officers. The Prussian War Academy, which had been an example to other European countries in the middle of the century, placed ever more emphasis on purely technical matters. The War Academy had in fact been taken away in the 1870s from the Inspector of Military Education and given to the General Staff. Even the redoubtable Moltke could declare in his guidelines for that institution in 1888 that 'seiner ganzen Anlage nach auf einer gründlichen Berufsbildung hinzielen, darf sich nicht in das weite Gebiet allgemeiner wissenschaftlicher Studien verlieren' ['The whole structure of army training is geared to professional competence and cannot afford to lose itself in the broad spheres of general education studies'].[32] Such attitudes contrasted with the ideas which led to the foundation of the Imperial Defence College in Great Britain and in France of the Centre des Hautes Etudes Militaires.

In south Germany and in Saxony, which had retained certain regalian rights in the 1871 constitution, things were initially somewhat different.[33] The 'unmistakable conformity in general civilization and social structure' of south Germany[34] showed itself in the greater elasticity of the social requirements for admission to the officer corps. The standing of Bavarian officers had not been especially high before mid century; royal favour rather than individual merit had been the key to promotion. Maximilian II (1848–64) proved far less arbitrary in this, as in many other respects, than his father Ludwig I, while under the rule of his son, Ludwig II, an important military reform was implemented by the Bavarian Defence Minister von Prankh. The new defence law of 1868 was closely modelled on Prussia, making a three-year military service obligatory and successfully establishing the military alongside the court and state officials as constituting the social élite of Bavaria.[35] However, despite the influence of Prussian military ideas on the organization and professional training of Bavarian soldiers from now on, the Bavarian army remained distinct in two important respects. The first was the higher educational standard demanded of its officers in the Prankh reform – as a general rule the *Abitur* – and also the bourgeois character of the officer corps, which prevented it from becoming a separate caste within society.[36] Indeed, the militarization of society in north Germany was regarded with considerable scepticism in the south, particularly in Bavaria, where both officers corps and populace were confident that the special position accorded to the Bavarian contingent within the German army as a whole would protect her relative independence. The efforts of the Prussian military authorities under William II to curtail the Bavarian monarch's sovereignty in this respect aroused considerable bitterness in Bavaria, and what was regarded as cynical contempt for their special position by Prussia during the First World War was an important cause of the deep hostility of Bavarians in general towards Prussia during the revolution of 1918–19 and throughout the Weimar Republic.

About life at the bottom, as it were, in the ranks of the Prussian and German army, a wide variety of opinions existed. The authorities were hypersensitive to the danger of 'infection' from socialist propaganda and laid special emphasis on the need to eradicate 'revolutionary' proclivities among the lower classes and left-wing intellectuals during military service. Certain drill sergeants were famed for the way they treated the one-year volunteers, whom as educated men they suspected of liberalism or worse. However, experience of life in the ranks whether during military service or as a regular soldier was usually less disagreeable than socialist critics liked to make out. Indeed, for many a small townsman or peasant, his army years were the great experience of his uneventful life; meetings with former comrades in later life were important social occasions and the whole affair often commemorated by appropriate pictures or souvenirs adorning the walls of living room or workshop. Discipline was certainly stern, and in individual cases brutal. The Kaiser announced his intention in a command on 17 September 1892 to show the greatest sternness to those who ill treated their men, but it is clear that many cases did occur and went unpunished. The memoirs of known socialists, such as Franz Rehbein, or the letters of academic volunteers, such as those of Max Weber,[37] speak eloquently of humiliations and physical violence. Social democrat recruits were sent, as a matter of policy, to isolated garrisons; socialist reading material was prohibited, as was attendance at public meetings; however, as these were frequently held in inns, the publicans concerned protested with some vigour and eventually, through the *Reichstag*, with success. However, the comradeship and experience of life offered by the army caused others, even social democrats, to change their mind about 'the school of the nation'. The material conditions gradually improved. Feeding of the troops grew better, the military authorities not disdaining to seek advice on modern methods of cooking. In the late nineteenth century the army abandoned the former system of allowing the soldier so much per day to feed himself and instead introduced meals in common. Payment also contrasted favourably with that of any other comparable conscript army in the world, being (for 1912) two and a half time as high as in Austria, nearly four times as high as in Italy and eight times as high as in Russia.[38]

'Besonders die militärische Welt überschlägt sich' ['The military world in particular is getting beyond itself'], wrote Fontane in 1887, 'er ist der verwöhnte Sohn im Hause, weil er am besten reiten und tanzen kann, sich unter Zustimmung der Eltern alles erlauben darf' ['It is the spoiled child of the family, just because the military are the best riders and dancers, and the parents let them do anything they want'].[39] Only a decade and a half later the primacy of the army in the public mind was threatened by the rise of the navy. For the wealthy citizens of the Second Empire the latter had considerable advantages. It was a symbol of the world power status of their nation, and it was an institution with which the bourgeoisie could readily identify itself in a way not possible with the army. The army officers remained an exclusive caste, which new men might successfully aspire to join: the naval officers were, on the other hand, almost all of middle class origin, a very high percentage coming from academic families.[40] Furthermore, the public support needed, if the navy was to expand, was stage-managed by that master of modern propaganda, Admiral Tirpitz. The Kaiser, the *Reichstag* and the public gave the navy the fullest support in the early years of the twentieth century, and the army languished in its shadow. Then came growing fears of encirclement by rival European powers. The army began to win back the esteem of the nation and primacy in financial policy too, as the 1912–13 army estimates clearly show. In 1912 the Defence League (*Wehrverein*) was founded, yet another of those nationalist organizations in which Wilhelmine society sought its identity. Together they helped to condition the populace for war in 1914, and, perhaps equally significantly, to accept the dominant role in the political and economic life of the country which the military thereafter assumed.

Section 2

'Bildung und Besitz': Education and property

Chapter 13
The bourgeoisie

Social historians, and many others too, experience serious terminological problems in discussing the historical evolution of the middle classes. Social historians of Germany writing in English have their difficulties compounded because of the absence of an equivalent English word for the German *Bürger/Bürgertum,* a term closely linked with traditional ways, and whose historical meaning was of a person who was a citizen of his place of residence. Nineteenth century Germans tended to distinguish between *Bürgertum* and *Bourgeoisie,* the latter being a product of the industrial revolution. Fontane, writing in the last decades of the century, uses this distinction consistently in his novels and letters to express feelings of dislike by members of the older and economically weaker social groups towards the new rich. A further difficulty exists in the absence of a neutral equivalent for the term *Kleinbürger,* which, up to the end of the nineteenth century, meant someone whose economic circumstances put him at the lower end of the middle rank of society, but who in his own mind was an established element in the solid citizenry of the state. 'Petty bourgeois' or 'lower middle class', which is acceptable nowadays as a translation of the term, fails to do it justice in earlier centuries, since it does not convey the notion of self-regard so important to the *Kleinbürger,* a vital source of social stability to the state. Even though a man's subjective self-esteem might not correspond to his actual social or economic position, it made him and his kind content with their circumstances. The same was largely true of the German middle classes as a whole. It was only when the individual and the group became aware of the disparity between fact and image, which occurred in the years before the revolution of 1848, and from the late nineteenth century onwards, particularly during the Weimar Republic, that the stability of German society was dangerously undermined.

In this section, which examines the propertied and educated middle classes, the term bourgeoisie is used both in the sense of the German *Bürgertum* and, more particularly for the period after 1850, also of the *Bourgeoisie.*

The nineteenth century was generally regarded by those living at the time in western Europe as the age of the middle classes. In Germany this was true to a much more limited extent. The very sequence of the phrase *Bildungs- und Besitzbürgertum* indicated that Germans associated middle class status primarily with education, and only secondarily with property, for until after 1850 the German middle classes were relatively poor. However in nineteenth century Germany the bourgeoisie did not win political power and influence from the feudal class, as was the case among her western neighbours. What a recent writer on France in this period, Th. Zeldin, could say about the French bourgeois could not be applied to the German, that 'he developed his own moral and economic doctrine and formed an original class with spiritual unity. At the same time he became an object of attack, satire and animosity, far more concentrated than ever before.'[1]

It is true that the so-called *Biedermeier* or pre-March period, 1815–48, was characteristically bourgeois in its life style: the cult of beauty in simple things, frugality in daily life, the cult of the domestic virtues, were the hallmark of middle class life and were cultivated by other social groups, including royalty, in conscious imitation of bourgeois standards. Early photographs of the Saxon court show the King and his relations playing skittles, the Queen and her ladies occupied with handwork. The King of Prussia appeared promptly each night at the theatre at 6 p.m., to retire at 9 p.m. to supper and early bed. His children, later Frederick William IV and his brother William, recalled their father's forbidding them to comment on the unusual plenty at a dinner given to Tsar Alexander I in 1807; many years later, when William was German Emperor, he still observed the frugal habits acquired in youth: after lunch he would solemnly mark on the bottle the level of wine drunk at the meal, before having it put on the sideboard.

For a time in the years before the 1848 revolution, especially in the

Rhineland, East Prussia and parts of Saxony and southern Germany, and during the 1850s in central Germany and parts of Prussia, a liberal middle class consciousness seemed much in evidence. It was reflected in literature, in the works of novelists such as Karl Immermann, Karl Gutzkow, Gustav Freytag and Friedrich Spielhagen, and in the widely read journals of the time. In general, however, the concept of 'noble' and 'bourgeois' as a pair of opposites is not very meaningful for Germany in the years between the Congress of Vienna and the First World War. The dividing line, if it must be drawn, ran rather between those who formed part of the 'authorities' and those who did not. The 'authorities' included officials and their assistants in very humble positions; there was some truth in Fontane's allegation that the boy who fetched the newspaper for the minister enjoyed more 'status' than those responsible for editing and producing it (letter to Fr. Stephany, 9 December 1883). Certainly the nobility had political and social privileges in the nineteenth century which set them apart from the bourgeoisie, but the latter had a sense of involvement in the process of government and administration, either through membership of the state service, or the academic professions, which were in effect an extension of the bureaucracy.

At various times during the nineteenth century pressure was applied on governments by members of the bourgeoisie and their friends and associates from the aristocracy: their aim was to gain a meaningful voice in public affairs, but in general, and particularly in contrast with western and southern Europe, the middle classes in Germany showed reluctance to engage in politics. The development of German society after 1866, and more particularly after the founding of the Empire in 1871, showed clearly that the authoritarian state and its privileged upper classes were largely acceptable to the middle ranks of society, not least because they themselves had a direct or a vicarious share in the status associated with authority in Germany. Outside a few trading towns, the origins of the bourgeoisie were official, not commercial. As has been said, Germany remained a fairly poor country until the second half of the nineteenth century. Economic considerations in most German states made ambitious and educated men put a premium on security of employment rather than on individual liberty. Some independent-minded spirits protested; but they were dependent on the system and they knew it. Thus E. Th. A. Hoffmann, the Romantic poet, turned the full blast of his satiric powers on the official world, or escaped from the pettiness of such a life into the realms of fantasy; however, after a number of years as a musical odd job man, he was glad to avail himself of the opportunity of returning to a post in the Prussian bureaucracy in 1816, which political circumstances had forced him to quit eight years previously. He even became a member of the judicial commission set up in connection with the notorious Carlsbad Decrees (1819), to examine those suspected of anti-state activities.[2] The excess of educated men, which Lenore O'Boyle has shown to have been a European phenomenon of the early and mid nineteenth century, increased the economic pressures on those without a fortune; thus minor officials and clergymen of humble birth and few contacts learned to value security over initiative, and to practise the virtues of deference and frugality.[3] German attitudes to the creative artist in the nineteenth century are revealing in this connection. A bourgeois profession, which most writers were forced to seek for economic reasons, gave them credibility in the eyes of their readers. Conversely, society seemed to distrust an artist who attempted to live by his pen. Such attitudes remained in force well into the twentieth century, though an exception was made in favour of those who wrote on certain approved subjects, notably national themes.

Intermarriage was by no means rare between members of the nobility and bourgeois from an official or clerical background. The Prussian code of 1794, in attempting to classify the various types of burgher, had referred to 'exempt, high bourgeoisie and rich citizens'. It was from such circles that most of the new nobles of the late eighteenth century had been created: the Saxon Hohenthals, Goethe, or the father of Karl Rotteck, the south German liberal historian. It was men with knowledge of other territories and life styles, whom affairs of state or their own business interests had brought to different parts of the country, who began to identify themselves at the turn of the century with the administrative reforming ideas of the Enlightenment and with new views about the state's role in society. The fact that many of those charged with the tasks of government in the early nineteenth century were of middle class origin especially, but not only, in Prussia, did much to foster a sense of bourgeois self-confidence in such circles. But their self-awareness was not of themselves as a new middle class force, but rather as an enlightened and educated section of the government class, opposed equally to archaic feudal privilege and to narrow burgher attitudes.

In the many small towns spread across the map of Germany, particularly numerous in central and south Germany, a different and specifically burgher sense of social cohesion existed, which the power of the state and economic pressures tended to undermine in the years after 1815. The political awareness of the inhabitants was centred on preserving things as they were, even to the point of looking to the ruler to defend them against his own bureaucrats. They did not conceive of, much less aspire to, political power for themselves. The fact that many of the bureaucrats were of 'bourgeois' origin was no consolation to the small-town notables: quite the reverse in fact. In the case of an aristocrat they might feel confidence in his respect for traditional ways; with a 'jumped-up bourgeois' they could not.[4]

The continued survival of regional loyalties, the lack of a capital before 1871 to provide a goal for the ambitious, and a national centre of government, social and commercial life, inhibited in Germany the development of the kind of middle class consciousness which we associate with Britain and France in this period. In the larger territories of northern Germany, notably Prussia and Saxony, where well before 1850 industrialization was under way, a kind of bourgeois self-awareness did emerge in the pre-March period, though we would do well to remember Ludwig Beutin's wise words, written over thirty years ago, that 'it was all on a much more modest scale'.[5] Equally relevant is his shrewd observation that the political awareness of the German middle classes between 1815 and 1871 was based, not on present achievement, but on past memory – namely, the wars of liberation against Napoleon. The social groups which gave meaning to the term bourgeois, the civil servants, the Rhenish, Saxon and Berlin merchants, the university teachers and the publicists, were primarily concerned with rationalizing administration and promoting the commercial development of the country in the interests of the whole. The academics, the writers and the journalists saw it as their function to make their fellow countrymen 'politically aware'. By this they did not mean that they saw their class as potential heirs to noble privilege, but rather as the leaven of a somewhat idealistically conceived community, of a nation which would be a kind of extended family, in which each member would try to promote the good of the whole.

The term 'liberal bourgeoisie' is frequently used with reference to the pre-March years, and rightly so, though it does in fact include many individuals with '*von*' in front of their name, who were fellow students, colleagues and lifelong friends of the middle class liberals. It was such men who revitalized the Prussian state in the years after Jena, who laid the foundations for the economic liberalism characteristic of Prussia in the years 1815–79. It was very largely bourgeois officials in the Prussian ministries who provided the expertise and the impetus for the reforms which overcame the most divisive element in German life: poor communications. A sense of the rapid increase in the pace of life now began to impress itself on contemporaries. As the Prussian official Th. von Hippel put it to Chancellor Hardenberg in 1817, 'Everyone wants to go at a canter nowadays, no one is prepared to proceed at a dignified pace'. The number of people travelling by mailcoach increased tenfold between 1821 and 1837.[6] When in 1834 the famous Customs Union was set up, establishing under Prussian aegis a free trade zone over a large part of Germany, enthusiasm was greatest in middle class circles. The blend of idealism and sentimentality with which the popular poet Fallersleben, professor of German at Breslau, greeted the Union was thoroughly representative of the response in academic and professional circles (and provides an instance of their tolerance of bad poetry in a good cause). In a collection of poems characteristically entitled *Unpolitische Lieder* (*Unpolitical Songs*) (1842), he apostrophized the various items which now passed freely across state frontiers within the Confederation, from cows and radishes to dolls and scissors:

> Denn ihr habt ein Band gewunden
> Um das liebe Vaterland,
> Und die Herzen hat verbunden
> Mehr als unser Bund dies Band.

> For you have woven a bond of union around our dear Fatherland and it is our hearts more than our union – i.e. the German Confederation – that this bond has bound together.[7]

The institution of the railways in 1835 was greeted with the most ardent enthusiasm, more particularly since it was almost entirely the work of middle class entrepreneurs – in Germany, though not in Austria. Between 1845 and 1849 private investment in the railways reached one quarter of the total annual budget for Prussia.[8] The great economist, Friedrich List, was able to attract a sizeable readership to his propaganda journal, the *Iron Journal* (1835–7), and his *Customs Union Paper* (1843–6), designed to win support for the economic union of Germany. Two thousand people travelled daily on the line between Berlin and Potsdam only a few years after it had been opened, reported the diplomat Varnhagen in the early 1840s. The enthusiasm was undoubtedly fostered by the enormous profits made by investors in the early stages of the railway programme.

The pioneers of the industrial revolution in the Rhineland, men such as Harkort and Camphausen, Hansemann, Beckerath and Mevissen, who were also directly or indirectly involved in building railways, became household names in many parts of the Confederation as examples of a new bourgeois spirit. This was achieved principally through the columns of the *Rheinische Zeitung,* edited for a time by Marx, and by the more moderate but influential *Kölnische Zeitung,* in which the speeches of these and other delegates to the United Diet at Berlin in 1847 were published. The United Diet itself provided a powerful impetus to a sense of political sympathy between these men and their opposite numbers from the towns of East Prussia, Danzig, Königsberg and Elbing, from Prussian Saxony and Silesia; it also gave them an awareness of themselves as a progressive and largely bourgeois stratum of society.

In southern Germany in the pre-March years society was more old-fashioned, and the economic dislocation caused by pauperism was, or seemed to be, less severe. Yet in spite of the hierarchical character of local society, the temper of the south was more liberal than that of the north. Many of the states had constitutions, granted in the aftermath of Napoleon, and they had assemblies which met and worked. The bourgeoisie was more sedentary here, but liberal by tradition, not by conversion, as it were. The families of academics at Tübingen or Freiburg, government officials in Karlsruhe or Darmstadt, Munich or Stuttgart, and the wholesale merchants in Bavarian and Swabian towns, were more like the Swiss liberals in Gottfried Keller's stories, proud of local traditions, and suspicious, especially from about the 1840s onwards, of the 'great' cities of Berlin, Vienna, or even, in some cases, Munich.[9]

The participation of the liberal bourgeoisie in the revolution of 1848 from both parts of the country was motivated by social and economic anxiety, brought to a head by the ever-increasing problems of the economy, as well as by their desire for a greater share in the public life of their country. The failure of the revolution administered a severe blow to the self-confidence of the middle classes, though the full effect of this was not immediately apparent. The course of the revolution divided them politically, a development exacerbated by the events of subsequent decades. These divisions were to prove particularly significant for the lower strata of the middle classes, the so-called *Kleinbürger*, who felt threatened by the phenomenon of organized labour on the one hand, while at the same time they found their claims to regard themselves as part of the 'middle rank of society' unacceptable to a growing section of the bourgeoisie. The take-off into sustained growth which coincided with the years immediately after the revolution, exacerbated divisions within the broad spectrum of the middle classes, by greatly increasing differences of wealth. Meanwhile employment prospects for the academic professions did not improve significantly in the 1850s and 1860s; this put pressure on members of a status conscious group within the bourgeoisie to accept the *status quo* of an authoritarian state and a privileged élite. For a large proportion of the middle classes the national movement became a kind of sublimation of their former political ambitions: the educated certainly believed themselves to be the prophets of that sense of national identity which had so long proved elusive to Germans, and which 1848 had so signally failed to translate into fact. Their appetite for, and their endurance in the cause of national commemoration was impressive – as was proved in one singular instance: a dozen lengthy plays on themes of German history by the patriotic dramatist Fr. von Raumer were played to capacity audiences for a whole fortnight.

In the second half of the nineteenth century, the German middle classes showed themselves content with a vicarious share in the triumphs of successful governments. In anecdote and ballad – especially popular in the years between 1840 and 1870 – in historical novel and drama, in anniversary speeches and apt quotation from those held to be the classical exponents of German-ness, as well as in the collections for national monuments to commemorate past heroes and events, the bourgeoisie seemed to find an extension of themselves, a heady sense of participation in national events. It was not the least of Bismarck's extraordinary political skills that he was able to divert the enthusiasm and energy of the middle classes for the national cause into channels which did not threaten the authoritarian state and society which he believed was best for Germany.[10]

From about the mid 1860s, during the so-called *Gründerzeit* or Promoters' Boom, when the first wave of industrialization had already transformed the economy, and wealth was concentrated in certain areas, something approaching an upper middle class on the French model emerged. The villas built in Berlin by wealthy bankers and entrepreneurs in the better class suburbs, or by successful businessmen in north-west Germany, the Saarland and Saxony, were not so different from those of prosperous Parisians or Belgians, nor did they differ significantly in their life style and cultural values from the plutocracy in the rest of Europe. The members of the German entrepreneurial class were aware of how much they had contributed to the economy and to generating the wealth which had benefited much of society. Members of the academic professions, who enjoyed status if not general wealth, were proud of what they regarded as their contribution to 'the cultural supremacy of Germany'. Such sentiments did not lead to a search for a specifically bourgeois political or social programme. Constitutional reforms in the 1860s and 1870s brought many of the typical features of a bourgeois era, universal suffrage for the *Reichstag*, a free press (though there were limits), industrial enterprise on a large scale, liberalization of commerce and transport; these, however, were for the most part the gift of the state. As historians have frequently emphasized, the last decades of the nineteenth century in Germany did not see the nobility becoming bourgeois, but the bourgeoisie being 'feudalized'.

The so-called Great Depression of 1873–95 played a crucial role in making the German middle classes conscious of their sense of solidarity with the nobility against a real or imagined threat to the social order by the working classes. The immediate effect of the slump of 1873 was to create a climate of pessimism and anxiety, which was more severe and more enduring in its psychological effects than its actual economic significance warranted. It affected heavy industry first and most profoundly: in the six years between 1873 and 1879 the consumption of steel in Germany fell by 50 per cent; miners' wages were halved. The crisis caused two distinct pressure groups to emerge within the ranks of the industrialists, whose aspirations and fears determined their political alignment in subsequent decades. While the representatives of heavy industry began to put pressure on the government to introduce protective tariffs, those in the export-orientated consumer and light industries formed a separate group to oppose them. The recurrence of a further, if less violent, slump in 1882–6, after initial recovery between 1879 and 1882, administered another sharp shock to German society, but particularly to the upper classes. Of the twenty years of Bismarck's chancellorship, only four were years of prosperity. If we remember this, it is perhaps more easy to appreciate the climate of anxiety characteristic of this time in Germany for all the great achievements of the recent past. To this was added the problem of a rapidly rising population, which increased by a staggering 10·4 million in the Depression years alone: this naturally created a growing demand for additional work places at a time of recession or stagnation. The very length of the Great Depression and the sense of uncertainty it engendered throughout society helps to account for the unusual convergence of apparently conflicting economic interests, in the form of the mainly bourgeois captains of heavy industry and the east German grain producers. Both sides hoped to benefit, at the cost of other groups in society, from Bismarck's tariff policy of 1879 onwards. In the words of the conservative economist Gustav Schmoller: 'Under Bismarck's patronage the alliance was formed by industrial capitalists and large estate owners, which dominated Germany from the late 1870s onwards.'[11] Its dominance in fact lasted well into the twentieth century. In their short-sighted clamour for protection – short-sighted economically, quite apart from the political consequences – in the train of the East Elbian feudal landowners, these German captains of industry demonstrated what was meant in practice by the 'feudalization of the bourgeoisie' in imperial Germany.[12]

Apart from the relatively brief but highly significant clash in the 1860s between the liberal Prussian *Landtag* and the monarchy over the army, the Prussian bourgeoisie did not challenge the role of the nobility or the army in society, and under the Empire the rest of Germany gradually accommodated its attitudes to those of the dominant state. Rather did the sons and grandsons of successful members of the bourgeoisie enter typically aristocratic professions, buying estates in Silesia or Pomerania to become agrarian capitalists, or entering the officer corps. Parliament did not play the kind of role in the political consciousness or social ambitions of up-and-coming Germans, as it did in Anglo-Saxon countries. Indeed in the last years of the century men of property and education began to be apprehensive of constitutional reforms and to rationalize their feelings by deriding politics as something ignoble. They were frightened that the logical outcome of universal suffrage must be for the socialists to gain a majority – by 1890 they had the highest number of votes (though not of seats) in the *Reich* parliament, despite the restrictive legislation against them. For fear of similar developments in Prussia and Saxony, the state, with massive support from the upper and middle classes, firmly opposed altering the antiquated and unjust three-class franchise in those states. Fear of socialism, which men of substance all over the country equated with revolution, drew the nobility and the bourgeoisie closer together, their illiberal temper reflecting something of the Iron Chancellor's own misanthropy and pessimism for the future. Fear of the proletariat had helped to create a sense of solidarity between the bourgeoisie and the state in the aftermath of the 1848 revolution; by the late 1870s they feared, not so much mob rule, as the dominance of organized labour. Their concern was not simply to preserve property and wealth. Equally important to them was the complex system of rank and status in society, which seemed to the majority a wholly adequate substitute for political power.

Chapter 14
The bureaucrats

Of those social groups which helped to form the concept of a German bourgeoisie in the early nineteenth century, namely, the academics, merchants and state officials, it was the last who had the strongest sense of group consciousness. They regarded themselves, especially in Prussia in the early decades of the century, as being the most progressive element of the educated classes, and during and after the Prussian reform era (1806–19) enjoyed high social prestige. Humboldt remarked in 1819 'that, because of the loss of prestige by the nobility, only the state official commands respect; accordingly everyone is trying to enter this class'.[1] Although in most German states the cabinet and the army remained the preserve of the nobility, the bourgeois officials dominated the administration in the years after Napoleon's fall and wielded considerable power. The prestige of state service owed much in the decades between 1815 and 1840 to the lead taken by a number of gifted and enlightened administrators during the Prussian reform era; it was much enhanced by their administrative and economic measures, which not only inspired imitators in other German states, but above all gave a sense of common material interests to German burghers everywhere, the most significant of which was the Customs Union (1834).

The Prussian bureaucracy originated in the seventeenth century and was greatly expanded under Frederick William I and his son; under

Frederick William II a reputation for favouritism and corruption crept in, and it was part of the effort to raise national morale after the defeat at Jena that his successor, Frederick William III, agreed in October 1807 that henceforth the service should be open to competition on merit. From this date forward the civil service began to attract progressive elements among the educated classes in and outside Prussia, the majority of whom were of bourgeois origin.

'Kein Staat hat sich liberaler bei der Wahl seiner Beamten bewiesen, kein Beamtenstand ist gebildeter, unabhängiger als der preussische' ['No state has shown itself more liberal in the choice of its officials, and no class of officials is more cultivated and independent than the Prussian'], declared a pro-Prussian writer in the highly respected *Augsburger Allgemeine Zeitung* in 1832, 'everywhere the dynamic elements in the state belong almost without exception to the burgher estate'.[2] But already by the mid 1830s the position was beginning to be reversed in favour of the nobility. Both in the central and the provincial bureaucracy the highest positions (provincial president, governor, etc.) were increasingly the preserve of the old landed families, while the elective position of the *Landrat,* the chief administrative officer of rural Prussia, was being secured by the country nobility for one of their number. Ten years after the optimistic declarations of the *Augsburger,* the critical *Rheinische Zeitung* published a table of comparative figures showing the predominance of the nobility at all levels in the army and the bureaucracy, apart from the judges; of 306 *Landräte,* 234 were noble.[3] Frederick William IV was by nature suspicious of the bureaucracy as impinging on the royal prerogative; he was particularly ill disposed towards the educated and liberal bourgeoisie in important administrative positions, an attitude which changed to open hostility after the role played by many of them in the 1848 revolution. The 1850s were a difficult time for the officials, particularly those of burgher origin, but although Bismarck increased rather than reduced the political pressures on the service when he came to power in 1862, he provided far greater opportunity for employment of middle class officials than had ever existed before. However, the tendency to reserve the more senior posts for the nobility was not reversed under the Empire: quite the contrary in fact. The extraordinary powers of self-preservation characteristic of the Prussian nobility in the nineteenth century were demonstrated here, as also in their increasing predominance in the Prussian lower house (*Landtag*). The ministers of state sound like a catalogue of old noble names – Bodelschwingh and Puttkamer, Posadowsky and Eulenburg with the occasional newer name, such as von Boetticher, demonstrating that the assiduous and successful bourgeois could at least hope for promotion once he had cleared the hurdle into the ranks of the new nobility.

In the decades before the 1848 revolution, however, the Prussian state service seemed the most desirable goal for a young bourgeois of ambition and with some private means seeking a career. Here above all was the opportunity for a man, who was not of landed stock nor of the patrician merchant class from the Hanseatic towns, to make his mark in public life. The Prussian bureaucracy, always more effective under its weaker monarchs, had been more constructive under Frederick William II and III than under the capricious Frederick II. The prospect was an exciting one in spite of Prussia's reputation for pettifogging discipline. Moreover such a young man knew, as the dramatist and novelist Immermann when he was appointed judge to the High Court at Düsseldorf, that once he had secured a permanent post in the civil service, he had an easy entrée to the best society in the place of his appointment. It might not always be as agreeable and cultivated in the eastern provinces of Prussia as in the Rhineland, but one enjoyed the gratification of considerable social prestige.[4] The apprenticeship served by the aspirant was not easy; it grew progressively more arduous and the future more uncertain in the 1840s as the numbers of applicants increased, while the number of posts remained static. Until the 1840s, when a university degree and two stiff competitive examinations became compulsory, a young man accepted into the state service learned his job from his superiors, starting at the most menial tasks of copying and running messages, and eventually winning promotion, as in the army, on age rather than merit. A feature of his apprenticeship was that he was expected to accompany his superiors to the *Bierkeller* or *Weinkeller* of an evening, to hear them discuss work and interests. For the first few years he had no security, and probably no pay either. The majority of officials therefore came from families who could afford to keep a son for several years after he left grammar school, very frequently from a family where the father was himself an official. As the service was socially fairly cohesive, particularly within the branches, such as central administration and judiciary, the young man was also invited to his boss's home to enjoy the frugal but aesthetically pleasurable hospitality of a Biedermeier home. Memoirs of officials from these years, 1815–48, give evidence of a widespread interest in music making, reading, reciting and writing verses. These arrangements had of course the added advantage of giving one's daughters the opportunity to meet possible suitors. Even in a town as small as Berlin was at that time – about 300 000 – the middle class bureaucrat's social life was thoroughly segregated. Even the cafés he frequented were different from those noblemen went to, or army officers or merchants, though in the 1840s he began to make contact with businessmen and academics drawn by a common interest in liberal ideas. Wives and daughters were equally segregated: 'the wives of public officials had no contact with the ladies from the diplomatic corps. Nor did they have regular connections with the wives of financiers', Delbrück, who joined the service in the 1830s, recalled in his memoirs.[5] In provincial towns the barriers between the different middle class groups were less; Heinrich Simon, a young lawyer from Breslau, who was to play a prominent role in the revolution, describes in his (unpublished) diaries the local club, where dances were held in winter for all the families of the town's 'notables', and where one could go to read papers and journals and have a quiet smoke and chat.*

The difference between salaries at the top and the bottom of the scale was quite extraordinarily large. In 1800 the president of the chamber of war and the domains got 3000 *taler* per year, a clerk 50 *taler*.[6] Indeed, the lowest paid officials were among the regular recipients of poor relief in Berlin in 1800.[7] A post official who entered the service at nineteen in 1840, spent the first four years on trial, receiving no more than free lodging and about 60 *taler* per annum. He then received tenure and a salary of 300–350 *taler*, which rose to 500 after twenty years' service. Marriage for such a man brought, in the words of a contemporary, 'the most severe restrictions'; children could bring the family near the poverty line. W. H. Riehl, author of a widely read study of contemporary society, *Die bürgerliche Gesellschaft* (1851), published in 1850 an essay in the *Deutsche Vierteljahresschrift* in which he spoke of the Prussian subaltern officials, school masters, junior lecturers, candidates for the ministry, journalists and artists as no more and no less than 'educated proletariat'. The situation was exacerbated all over Germany especially in the 1830s and 1840s by the fact that Germany, like France and England, suffered from an excess of educated men without sufficient private means to support them. In Germany the prestige of a university training was particularly high, and although in Prussia the authorities actually appealed to parents not to send their sons into university lest it arouse false hopes of a future career in the state service, they not only continued to do so but they also continued to apply for posts in the administration and judiciary. In 1840 some 2500 unpaid lawyers were employed in the judiciary alone, whose qualifications entitled them to a permanent position.[8] Inadequate pension arrangements meant that elderly officials did not retire until very advanced in years, while the cautious authorities feared to overextend the limited national budget by

* I would like to thank the librarian of the John Rylands University Library (Manchester) for permission to use these diaries.

expanding the bureaucracy. Furthermore, salaries, which had been reviewed in 1825, remained the same until the 1850s, although in mid century the cost of food, clothing and heating soared.

The prestige enjoyed by the service could not compensate for the hard fact of being unable to make ends meet. Long engagements made brides tearful and prospective parents-in-law restive: some got married and lived off their brides' dowries, but this was, of course, risky. The uncertainty about material prospects, apart of course from political reasons, helps to explain the involvement of so many young civil servants in the 1848 revolution in Prussia. Even for the successful 2 per cent who actually received a higher paid post, the cost was high and the rewards not necessarily commensurate. An Oldenburg district governor described the process as he experienced it, also about this time, in the years before the March revolution; he considered his own case to be fairly typical of those fortunate enough to secure a senior post. From the age of fourteen he spent four to five years at grammar school, and then three to four years at university, costing his parents some 2667 *taler*. Parental support was needed for a further five years or so, while he was in a junior position, but even at thirty he was not yet in a position to marry. His salary of 2000 *taler* as governor would seem princely to struggling subaltern officials, but in fact, as many found, official entertaining, an integral part of the job, cost such a man more than what he received from the state.[9] Indeed, the need for a private income was a feature of the Prussian state service at higher levels; Gabriele von Bülow, Humboldt's daughter, whose husband was appointed Prussian minister to London, found the cost to their private fortune alarming. Much later in the century, two chancellors, Bismarck and Hohenlohe, discovered that their salaries scarcely defrayed half of their outgoings; admittedly, Bismarck was extravagant, and he had many unpublished sources of income, but the fact remains that the Prussian state did not materially reward its servants according to their qualifications and their deserts. Yet what was the alternative? The opportunities for employment outside the state service were limited in the first half of the nineteenth century. Most of those who went to university, apart from the theologians, studied law, and what they were taught there fitted them far better for the bureaucracy than for the world of business or the free professions. Even after the take-off of Germany's industrial revolution into sustained growth in the 1850s, it was some time before graduates began to seek employment in commerce and industry.

In spite of the differences in salary at the two ends of the profession, and in spite of the singular material difficulties facing junior members, the Prussian bureaucracy up to the 1840s was a socially cohesive if paternalistic organization. In 1843, in an effort to limit the number applying for senior posts, the authorities made a university degree a condition of entry; this did not solve the problem of numbers – the period of waiting for tenure, which in the 1820s had been about two years, now stretched to ten or even twelve years. But the measure did drive a wedge between the higher and the subaltern officials, which had not really existed before, and which was to be further increased in the second half of the century when numbers at last began to rise. But the service had changed in another more serious way: the bureaucracy as an institution both in Prussia and in other areas such as Bavaria had somehow lost the confidence of ordinary citizens. People were ever less concerned in these difficult years of rising costs and widespread pauperization with national issues, with the idea of overall material progress through the wise administration of a distant government. What they wanted was something done about the day-to-day problems of their region, their particular social and economic group. Rather unfairly, people identified the bureaucracy with the state, and many a master craftsman fallen on hard times, many an impoverished landowner, directed his resentment at the 'faceless men' who had failed to prevent the present crisis. The younger officials in particular felt isolated in society, and resentful at the government for allowing this to happen. In Prussia the members of the bureaucracy felt that the new king, Frederick William IV, did not like them – as indeed he did not, resenting in his turn the power they had wielded over affairs during his father's reign. The younger officials, men such as Viktor von Unruhe and Heinrich Simon, who were to play a prominent role in the revolution, felt particularly incensed when the king introduced a system of personal files on officials, which were to include such matters as debts – impossible to avoid during the long apprenticeship – and also their political opinions. Pressure was put on officials who showed an interest in liberal matters – in 1845 Simon, who had pioneered protests against the 1844 regulations allowing the government to transfer judges even against their will, was forced to resign. When the revolution broke out in 1848 many officials took part, some few actually mounting the barricades, others officering the burgher militia or getting themselves elected to the Frankfurt parliament or the assemblies at Berlin or Vienna.

The involvement in the revolution of so many officials – 'his servants', as he saw it – had a traumatic effect on the king. It was not however until the 1850s that his government tightened its control over them and reintroduced the notorious personal files. The younger men were naturally the chief target of surveillance, though in the paternalist system a good word from his superior would usually satisfy the king about a junior official. The long-term effect of this attitude was to make all but the most resolute or the financially independent desist from all independent political activity or interest as harmful to their careers. Timidity and conformity gradually became characteristic of the Prussian bureaucrat where ten or twenty years ago he had seen himself as a progressive element in society, and, even if of bourgeois origin, a member of the social élite of his state. The Prussian liberal historian, Gustav Droysen, spoke in sorrow as well as in anger of the 'complete dependence of this once proud and independent Prussian bureaucracy'.[10] Things were far worse for the individual official in other German states, such as Hanover, where the King, who liked to refer to bureaucrats as 'royal servants', refused promotion and holidays, or arbitrarily transferred those who did not please him. In Baden, even in the 1860s, the majority of officials were legally bondsmen of their Grand Duke, a state of affairs which could not but influence their independence of mind, even if they served a master known for his liberal views. What made the new developments in the Prussian bureaucracy seem so lamentable, however, was the sense of contrast with the earlier traditions of progressive administration, a contrast which was accentuated by the decline in the numbers of able bourgeois in important posts. During the Constitutional Conflict of the 1860s, some of the old spirit of independence seemed to revive; twenty officials challenged Bismarck and were disciplined by him. In fact, his critics were the same officials who had been young hotheads in 1848: they had no successors among the younger members. Bismarck used various methods to bring pressure to bear on civil servants; he disliked the idea of officials standing as members of the Prussian lower house, largely because of what had happened in the Constitutional Conflict. In 1848–67 38 per cent of the members of the Prussian *Landtag* had been officials (in 1855 it was as high as 50 per cent), in the period 1863–1912 the average was only 24 per cent.[11] The Prussian government showed a certain subtlety in rewarding those who gave up political activity with position in the service. A striking case is that of Benedikt Waldeck, whose famous trial in 1849 for his part in the revolution ended in a fiasco for the government after the state witness perjured himself; Waldeck resigned as a deputy but was allowed to retain his post as a judge. Rudolf Gneist commented sardonically on the judicial officials, once the most radical critics of reactionary government which Prussia was now experiencing under Bismarck: 'with fixed salaries, with set promotion to higher positions, with the immovability and untransferability of judicial personnel, they think they have everything necessary to maintain the independence of the judiciary.'[12] The criticism was not unjust.

The Second Empire saw the steady growth both in the number of German civil servants and of their status in society. In 1849 Prussia had just under 7500 higher civil servants; by 1907 they were two and a half times that number, though in the *Reich* as a whole the increase was less.[13] The middle ranking officials grew steadily in numbers, from 40 000 in 1849 (in Prussia) to over a quarter of a million in 1907.[14] Moreover, the increasing obligations assumed by the state and the municipalities provided opportunities for those with professional and technical qualifications: one need only call to mind the prodigious expansion in the last years of the century of services such as street lighting and paving, direct water and gas supply to firms and dwelling houses, and sewage works. The extension of the *Reich* postal system and the gradual takeover by the state of the railways in Prussia provided further state employment: the length of railway line owned by the Prussian state in 1878 was less than 5000 km; by 1890 it was 25 000, in 1910 it was 37 000.[15] Although minimal by modern standards, some idea of the rate of increase of the state's involvement can be measured by the budget increase: the *Reich* Ministry of the Interior spent 8 000 000 *Reichmarks* in 1890; by 1910 the figure was 108 000 000 *Reichmarks.*[16]

Many began to question the type of education required by the state of its officials, but there was no radical change before the advent of Weimar. Admittedly, in 1879, in response to public pressure, the four-year period of compulsory training at the law courts was reduced to two, with two further years in the provincial administration, but lawyers still continued to dominate the service; one quarter of the entrants to the higher civil service in the 1890s were doctors of jurisprudence. 'The civil servants who administered the most dynamic society in Europe were thus trained lawyers with little or no practical experience.'[17] Even in the technical departments there were few who were not trained in this way. Professor Post, a chemist from Göttingen, was called to the ministry of trade in 1891 by the progressive Freiherr von Berlepsch, but such deviation was most unpopular, as Chancellor Hohenlohe found when he tried to get a Bavarian university professor to the secretariat of the Prussian ministry of state. 'Whoever has not been a Prussian *Landrat,* Prussian *Regierungsrat,* for the required number of years, cannot enter this sanctuary. . . . If the *Reich* Chancellor and even his Majesty fail in the attempt to appoint an able and decent man to the Prussian bureaucracy, then I must concede defeat and record with dismay that the bureaucracy is more powerful than the Kaiser and the Chancellor.'[18]

Perhaps the most marked contrast between the Prussian bureaucrat at the beginning and at the end of the nineteenth century was the energy and general progressiveness of the former by contrast with the extreme conservatism of the latter. Bismarck was largely though not wholly responsible for this. He not only worked assiduously to stultify independence of mind among his subordinates, but he prevented the younger element, if they valued their careers, from criticizing and thus modifying the natural conservatism of their elders. After he was gone, the service, still rightly famed for its honesty and relatively high degree of administrative efficiency, failed to attract men of originality or dynamism, or prevented them from developing these qualities if they did possess them. The determination on the part of the authorities to keep out 'the wrong type' formalized what Max Weber called 'unofficial patronage' – in other words, family, personal influence, fraternity membership and reserve officer commission were what mattered. Thus in 1910, 75 per cent of leading Prussian officials were sons of officials, army officers or landowners.[19]

Although the service was nominally open to all, in fact discrimination was widely practised against the 'wrong type', which included, besides Jews and those with left-wing views, one third of the total population of the *Reich*, namely the Catholics. Julius Bachem, a Catholic publicist, investigated the so-called parity question or proportionate appointment of members of the different confessions to public office, and discovered that out of a total of ninety chancellors, state secretaries and ministers holding office between 1888 and 1914, only eight were Catholic. It is certainly true that the Catholics were less well educated than the Protestants, but it was obviously not merely a matter of education. The best educated, the Jews, found it virtually impossible to gain admission to the civil service unless they were baptized, and even then it was not easy – even for a Rothschild. As Alexander von Hohenlohe put it in his memoirs: 'If father or grandfather had been baptized ... and the son if possible had managed to give lustre to the faded glory of some noble family with his inheritance by marrying one of the daughters of the house, then people were prepared to overlook the matter of race, if it was not all too apparent in a man's face.'[20] A further means of exclusion was the continued predominance of the nobility in the higher administrative posts: 62 per cent of the *Landräte* and the *Oberpräsidenten* in 1891 were of noble birth, 73 per cent of the *Regierungsprisidenten* and 83 per cent of the police directors appointed between 1888 and 1891. Indeed, in the century before 1914 which had seen such remarkable changes in German society, the number of noblemen in district and provincial governments declined by less than 10 per cent.[21] Although the ministries of justice, finance and public works were staffed predominantly by men of middle class origin, the Ministry of the Interior, which controlled the provincial administration, was aristocratic and conservative. There was only one bourgeois Minister of the Interior in the whole history of the Second Empire, Ludwig Herrfurth, dismissed, it was said, only three years after appointment in 1891, because he had given too many posts in the provincial service to non-nobles.[22]

The state official in Wilhelmine Germany, even of bourgeois origin, was not likely to criticize a system which ensured him, along with the army officer, high social prestige, and which might well reward him, if successful, with a coveted decoration and even a title. William I, with some reluctance, acceded to Bismarck's policy of ensuring the loyalty of various social groups by the judicious reward of patents of nobility. Most officials, no less than successful businessmen, tried to ape their betters in dress and behaviour, so that Delbrück's reaction on receiving this honour was much commented on in Berlin: he simply wrote in by hand on his printed visiting cards the predicate '*von*'. Baroness Spitzemberg, for one, found it most refreshing that someone at least was prepared to be true to type, traditionally cheeseparing and pettifogging perhaps, but honest, efficient and unimpressed by ostentation and new Prussian fashion. However, the Delbrück type was already a thing of the past. In the years before the First World War the reservoir of trained and experienced officials diminished, while those who possessed the acceptable political and social qualifications were for that very reason unfitted to deal with the complexity and variety of problems which the Second Empire faced. 'It is appalling', wrote Alexander Hohenlohe in 1899 in connection with a vacant ministerial post, 'how few suitable people there are.'[23]

Chapter 15
Education and élites

THE ACADEMICS

Education, not wealth, was the main factor in social stratification in nineteenth and twentieth century Germany outside the nobility. The educated formed an élite in society, which did not replace or even equal the traditional ruling élite, but enjoyed a high social regard and certain important political privileges. They did not aspire to positions of political influence, nor, the majority of them bourgeois in origin, did they seek political emancipation for their class in the semi-feudal environment in which they lived. They did not do so for three main reasons: their social background and traditions, the powerful influence of German idealism on their concept of state and society, and, lastly, the content and emphasis of higher education in Germany.[1] Moreover, the educated provided the most significant source of talent for the bureaucracy in states of very different social complexion. This was true of Prussia, where the hereditary nobility still retained control over the leading positions at court, in the ministries and the army; in Bavaria, on the other hand, the native nobility showed virtually no interest in administrative posts, and public office was almost entirely in the hands of the educated bourgeoisie. It was possible for the educated to attain the status of an élite in the era following absolutism, where, in general, state government rather than the ruler held the reins of power, because institutions of learning were themselves state institutions, and their senior staff were state officials. The concept of official or civil servant in Germany did not – and perhaps still does not – have the association sometimes given it in west and south European countries of personal unfreedom and narrow intellectual horizons. It was associated rather with status and privilege on the one hand because of the high regard in which the state was held, on the other on account of the economic security state service conferred. Even today a teacher leaving the profession is obliged to solemnly renounce his 'rights as a civil servant' (*Beamtenrechte*), a ceremony which must bring home the sense of surrender of personal status.

How did one become a member of what had become known from mid century as the '*Bildungsbürgertum*', the cultivated and educated citizenry? One of the most surprising features of the educational scene in early nineteenth century Europe is the continued supremacy of classical over scientific or technical education. In Germany it was widely believed by those responsible for the far-reaching educational reforms associated with the name of Wilhelm von Humboldt in the second decade of the century, that a classical training was the best preparation for future responsibility. Men believed this, not simply because a study of the classics developed intellectual powers, but because they were convinced of the moral influence of classical antiquity on personal culture. Moreover, the special role which the study of Greek civilization had played in creating a new national awareness among cultivated Germans in the late eighteenth century enhanced the classics in the eyes of all patriotic citizens. Humboldt had hoped that the Prussian liberal reforms would be broadly democratic, developing the abilities of pupils independently of their class and property, and patriotic, in that they would create a nation of German citizens. Yet it was already clear that the recipients of a classical education must by the very nature of things be but few in number. The economic situation of Prussia and all German states in the early nineteenth century was such that education had to be limited to a minority. Who should compose that minority was very largely determined in the Restoration era by the state authorities. The activities of radical students in the years immediately after the Congress of Vienna contributed to the growing unease felt by governments about the role of the university and all higher education in future. Heads of government came under pressure from Metternich, Austria's chancellor, who saw all too vividly the implications of liberal and national ideas for the multinational state he governed and for the loosely organized German Confederation. In 1819 the Carlsbad Decrees imposed severe restrictions on students and university teachers in the classroom, and censored the content of what was taught there. The state was in a position to exclude those politically unacceptable through its extensive influence over appointments to schools, universities, the bureaucracy and (Lutheran) church livings. The excess of educated men over the number of posts available in this era put even greater pressure on individuals to conform politically. Heinrich Laube, the young German writer who later became director of the Vienna Burgtheater, recalled the feelings of university students in the late 1820s: 'Everyone looked to the state for his advancement. The world was enclosed in a fence called office, minor office.'[2]

Of all aspects of Humboldt's educational reform, the notion of the superiority of a classical education survived the longest, its effect being, contrary to Humboldt's hopes, to limit the numbers enjoying higher education and to segregate these off from the rest of society both in fact and their own self-esteem. Fichte, Romantic philosopher and first rector of the new Berlin university, lost few words on the subject: the educated were in his view part of a higher stratum.[3] The system became to a large extent self-perpetuating, in that state officials who had been the recipients of a classical education supervised the university and supported the appointments to school and university posts of men of a similar background to themselves, who in turn educated future bureaucrats.[4] It was this intimate association which made the idea of challenging the state's right to order higher education irrelevant. The products of the system enjoyed status and security, or if, as in the 1840s, in Prussia and Saxony, too many teachers were trained, they found employment in other German states. Attempts to cater for more modern subjects in the curriculum, or to alter the emphasis from classical philology to modern languages and mathematics, were successfully resisted by university professors and teachers. Thus in Bavaria efforts to set up two distinct types of school, one classical and traditional for scholars, the other for '*Realien*', subjects suitable for the more practical professions, were thwarted by the minister of education for that state, by origin a Saxon.

As the century progressed, it became increasingly more difficult to get to university at all without a classical grammar school (*Gymnasium*) education. One entered the grammar school at the tender age of six and remained there for the following thirteen years (longer, should one be forced by idleness or illness to repeat a class). 'Parents and teachers were forced to make essentially permanent educational plans for five year olds. ... Inevitably a "cultured family background" often became the actual measure of the capacity for culture.'[5] The cost of grammar school education increased significantly in the second half of the century, effectively excluding the children of less well-off parents, despite the nominal equality of opportunity existing. Statistics available from the last decades of the century show clearly the extent to which higher education (university and grammar school leading to *Abitur*) was the preserve of the upper classes, particularly the bourgeoisie. The percentage of academics of lower middle class origin – that is, minor officials, primary school teachers, artisans and small tradesmen – was fairly constant at about 20 per cent;* the percentage of working class was absolutely minimal, even after 1918; up to the end of the Second World War there was but a very slight increase in the numbers of students of working class background, though the early 1930s also saw a decrease in the number of upper class students.[6] The one exception to the general trend was the student of Catholic theology, for Catholic priests came from a much wider social background than any other students.[7] In general, the prevailing system militated against Catholic students of all faculties until after 1945; the same is true, to an even more marked degree, of women.

The social function of education in the Second Empire caused ambitious industrialists to submit their children to the narrow and rigid curriculum of the classical grammar school, rather than to provide for them the kind of education their future careers would seem to demand. Countless memoirs of famous men recall that the education they received had little to do with cultivation of the mind, with literature, history and culture such as Humboldt and the German idealists had understood antiquity to communicate, but saw Greek and Latin grammar as an end in itself. However, the fact remained that, with six years attendance in the upper forms of a *Gymnasium,* a man was entitled to volunteer for the one year military service without pay, in place of the obligatory three (from 1893 two) year service which was the lot of the rest of society. He could enter a Prussian forestry department or building institution, postal service or provincial bureaucracy at a certain level. Above all, the holder of the *Abitur* or school-leaving certificate, and even more so of a university degree, knew he had the means of entering the upper class.

The relationship between teachers in grammar schools and higher education and the state was based to a considerable degree on mutual advantage. This became more evident as the century progressed. There were undoubtedly certain areas of conflict, notably in the Restoration era; Prussian officials used their powers to impose appointments to university in 322 cases against the will of the faculties concerned.[8] In

* This remained a feature of the German educational scene long into the twentieth century.

the much publicized incident of the Göttingen Seven in 1837, distinguished professors of law, history and literature – including the Grimm brothers, Dahlmann, and Gervinus, author of the first history of German literature – challenged the right of the new Elector of Hanover, the Duke of Cumberland, to abrogate the Basic Law of the state; they were dismissed. Their action aroused very wide interest and approval all over Germany; it also helped to establish university teachers in the vanguard of the national movement. The academics' participation in the Frankfurt Assembly earned it the name of the professors' parliament. It was a professor of literature – Hoffmann von Fallersleben, at Breslau University – who composed the most lasting of German national anthems, *Deutschland, Deutschland über alles,* to the tune of Haydn's *Kaiserhymne* in 1841. He was dismissed by the authorities for his political views in 1842. Individual teachers and scholars were victimized for their liberal and national views. The cases of Jahn, the gymnast, and E. M. Arndt, the bard of early German nationalism, who were dismissed in the aftermath of the Carlsbad Decrees, are well known; but even the most tolerant of regimes – and of colleagues – would not have found them easy. A more flagrant case of victimization was the liberal and clear-sighted Adolf Diesterweg, a disciple of Pestalozzi and head of a teachers' training college in Prussia, who lost his post in the 1840s for his enlightened views.[9]

In general, however, the status and growing opportunities for advancement in their careers, as the economy expanded after 1850 and the state began to invest in education, reconciled leading members of the teaching profession with the political quietism expected of them. In the universities the career structure committed the young scholar to the post of unpaid lecturer (*Privatdozent*), dependent wholly on such student fees which an unknown teacher could attract, until such time as he could by his publications secure himself a professorship. The degree of privation suffered by the individual academic is well illustrated by the case of the orientalist Paul Bötticher, known as Lagarde, whose extraordinary gifts as a scholar had to wait decades for recognition.[10] The position of *Privatdozent* constituted membership of what one mid nineteenth century commentator called the academic proletariat.[11] However, once the academic teacher had received a chair, and could marry and establish himself, he enjoyed the fruits of patience and industry and was unlikely to challenge the system which counted him as a member of the élite. If one looks at individual cases in the nineteenth century, many achieved their professorships at an age which seems early to us, particularly the so-called extraordinary – that is, roughly the equivalent of associate-professorships; Ranke, who had been a school teacher in the provinces, was thirty, Treitschke twenty-seven, Burckhardt twenty-nine, Liebig only twenty-three.

Teachers in the secondary and tertiary sectors were only a small percentage of the whole profession. The vast majority taught in a wide variety of primary schools. Their status and salary improved considerably over the century, and in Prussia after 1866 they enjoyed public approval. It was claimed and later widely accepted that the battle of Königgrätz, when Prussia defeated Austria and excluded her from Germany, was won by the discipline and devotion to duty instilled in the classrooms of the nation by the primary school teachers. German primary school education has perhaps enjoyed an undeservedly high reputation, perhaps by way of contrast with the state of things in mid nineteenth century Britain. The myth that the battle of Königgrätz had been won in the primary schools of Prussia enjoyed wide popularity over the next fifty years or more, sometimes being attributed to Bismarck. Actually it goes back to an essay, published in 1866 by a Leipzig geography professor, Oskar Peschel, entitled *Wert der Mathematik für die Kriegführung* (*The Value of Mathematics for the Conduct of War*). The reality was often far different from the image. The association, inherited from seventeenth and eighteenth century practice, between schoolmastering and menial tasks such as drawing water, chopping wood for church and school, kept men of genuine pedagogic talent and interest out of teaching, unless forced into it by circumstances. The low regard expressed by the village for their teacher Oswald, himself the son of their former schoolmaster, in Zschokke's *Das Goldmacherdorf* (1817), expressed their low social standing at that time. Well into the nineteenth century the Prussian state regarded primary schools as a useful repository for invalid or elderly soldiers and unsuitable minor officials. Something approaching a sense of professional solidarity emerged in the first half of the century, when economic security preoccupied men's minds. The fact that elementary teachers were not citizens of the village or town in which they taught – the Hanseatic towns, as in so many other respects, were here an exception – made their existence especially precarious.[12] As part of the Prussian educational reforms, a network of teachers' training colleges were set up from 1817 onwards. Although they were appointed by the ministry, the individual directors largely determined the character of the institution; the strictest subordination was demanded of the candidates, in all aspects of their life and studies.[13]

An exception to the authoritarian mould of most directors was Adolf Diesterweg, already mentioned, who headed the Berlin college from 1832, and who in 1848 founded the *Allgemeiner Deutscher Lehrerverein*

(Germam Teachers Union), one of the first professional interest bodies in Germany. A radical in his opposition to the repressive education policies of the state in the 1840s, he was forced to resign in 1847 and pensioned off in 1850. His subsequent career was unusual for a teacher; he entered the Prussian *Landtag* in 1850 as a member of the opposition and remained so until his death in 1860. In Prussia the status of the elementary teacher was probably better than in most states, although they were unsuccessful in their efforts to get themselves raised to the status of official. In Bavaria they succeeded in this, but the decision was rescinded in 1841 – indeed in parts of the state they were so poor that many took employment as navvies in the holidays. In Baden they were not allowed cover from the state fund for state officials, on the grounds that they lacked 'the requisite degree of education'; to put them on a par with state officials would be 'highly offensive' (*Beschimpfung*) to the latter.[14]

The years immediately following the revolution saw a severe reaction directed against teachers in Prussia. Training colleges, on the express wish of the King, were to be transferred to rural areas in order to keep future educators of German children free from the contaminating influence of liberal cities. The notorious *Stiehlsche Regulative* of 1854, issued by the Minister of Cults and Education, banned German literary classics from the curriculum of primary schools. It was not merely the curriculum that was affected by a narrow pedantry and timorousness, but the way in which subjects were taught. Fontane recorded a conversation with an acquaintance in the 1850s, whose youngest son surprised and delighted his disillusioned parent with the news that they were going to study natural history. A few weeks later the boy started coming home late: he had to sit behind to learn his natural history. The father discovered that natural history consisted solely in learning by heart the 160 bones of the human body. For the last fifty years, Fontane recorded in his diary in 1861, the ministry officials in charge of education, with one exception, 'had and have no children'.[15] A further serious factor in the unsatisfactory state of primary education was that, although the state began to invest more and more in higher education in the second half of the century, it devoted few funds here. Raabe's portrait of the tubercular schoolmaster who contracted the disease because of conditions in the schoolroom, in his novel *Der Hungerpastor* (1864), was an eloquent attack on abuse. His views were confirmed by accounts of rural schools in the memoirs of philanthropic landowners or their wives; the system still obtaining, in practice if no longer in theory, that the landowner in the manorial east was responsible for the local school, was obviously open to abuse.[16]

Despite their inferior status and often difficult economic position by comparison with grammar school teachers, the elementary school teachers regarded themselves in the second half of the century as a cut above their fellow members of the lower middle class. They could justify their attitudes by reference to their greater 'moral earnestness', and the sacrifices they were prepared to make for their children's education. William II, who was genuinely interested in educational matters, called a *Reich* conference of teachers in 1890. Although he did not raise the prestige of these teachers by raising the entrance requirements to their profession, he fulfilled their social ambitions in a psychologically satisfying manner: from 1900 they could share the privilege of absolving their military service as one-year volunteers and hence be promoted to officers of the Reserve.[17] In fact not many could afford to take advantage of this privilege, but it enhanced their social status considerably, not least in their own eyes. In the war, very many elementary school teachers served as officers.

Teachers at all levels and university students were strong supporters of monarchy and Empire in the years before 1914. The Berlin teachers retained their somewhat radical traditions, but for the rest, discipline and loyalty to 'throne and altar' were accepted and highly regarded virtues: for elementary schools, the close association between school and church, which also determined the kind of candidate likely to be appointed, precluded the kind of anti-clerical and critical attitudes associated with the French teaching profession in the nineteenth century. Teachers in Germany gave enthusiastic support to the various national anniversaries and organizations of the Empire. Many members of the Pan-German League, founded in 1893, were members of the teaching profession; large numbers had fought in the wars of unification in their youth and looked back on those days as their finest hour. Teachers, as also officials and tradesmen, were hostile to parliamentary democracy; they regarded the state as the guarantor of the conservative, national values, indeed many of them found in aggressive nationalism, or in Bismarck's social imperialism, an adequate political creed.[18] In the years immediately preceding the outbreak of the 1914 war, it became increasingly clear to the educated and the propertied classes that the dynamics of a modern industrial economy and the introduction of genuine parliamentary democracy must threaten the *status quo*. A sense of social unease, made more acute by the rigidity of social stratification in Wilhelmine Germany, fostered illiberal attitudes. Teachers in higher education shared with other members of society with an academic training the belief that they belonged to an élite, the *Bildungsbürgertum*: elementary teachers excluded by their educational achievements from forming part, identified themselves with the values and standards of the class, and hoped that their children would one day be members. They justified their defence of their position, as élites have done before and since, by representing themselves as guardians of ethical values, the cultivation of mind and spirit, the disdain of material values, which they attributed to their opponents, the socialists, the new rich Jews, or, in the years of colonial and naval rivalry, the British. The astonishing popularity of the nationalist historian Treitschke in the 1870s and 1880s, so puzzling to the outsider, can be understood if it is realized how he reassured the members of academic professions that their image of themselves and their social position was fully justified and ought to be preserved. Thus he pandered to their self-regard when he said of universal suffrage: 'Our idealism has always been our strongest national asset; thus it is absolutely un-German to let stupidity and ignorance have the decisive voice.'[19] As Fritz Stern put it in a now famous essay, underlying the unpolitical attitudes of this highly respected class was the cultured person's fear of the rapidly growing proletariat and his suspicion that culture and democracy, if not incompatible, were certainly opposed to each other. Without surrendering his unpolitical pretensions, the cultured German could, for the sake of his culture, support every conservative measure and oppose every radical move.[20]

By the time of the founding of the Empire, the university teachers were part of the establishment. Few attempted to question the foundations of the authoritarian state or criticize its representatives. Among those who did were Theodor Mommsen, the great historian of ancient Rome, who had a celebrated controversy with Treitschke over the Jewish question in 1879–80, and the Lutheran theologian Ewald, who was actually committed to prison in his seventies in 1871 for stating that Frederick II and Bismarck had fought unprovoked wars against Austria. The vast majority were, in Karl Kupisch's felicitous phrase, official and pensionable representatives of the German mind.[21]

2 ARTISTS AND WRITERS

Yet the representatives of the German intelligentsia who were not part of the academic world, the creative writers, critics and journalists, had a considerably less secure place within the ranks of the bourgeoisie. Certainly the national appetite for the printed word grew prodigiously in the nineteenth century; the number of books and journals, and their circulation, increased yearly. From the 1850s onwards the interest in national affairs, in political economy and modern science, kept pace.

Publishers satisfied demand and stimulated the public appetite still further. The economic situation of the writer, which had been precarious in the first half of the century, became so favourable for those able to cater for taste and fashion that – to take but one example – when Bertha von Suttner, a friend of Alfred Nobel, found herself and her husband without means of support in the early 1870s, they began to write essays, stories and travel pieces, and very soon earned enough to satisfy their needs. However, when one considers the now famous writers of nineteenth century Germany, one feature of their economic position strikes one: the vast majority wrote only in their spare time and spent their days in some 'respectable' position. Initially the main reason for this had been lack of alternative. In the Restoration era, as has already been said, writers were glad of the security offered them in state employment. Eichendorff, for instance, might fret under the sterile yoke of Prussian bureaucracy, in his post as legal official, and it undoubtedly influenced the imagery of his work by way of reaction, while Grillparzer was equally unhappy in a government post in Austria, but neither could hope to live on their writings. Immermann was a district judge, Mörike a parson, Keller a municipal official, Fontane a restless state employee for many years, and for a few weeks a reluctant state official (*Beamter*). In some cases the discipline and sense of service to the community imposed by their professions helped writers in their work – the case of Keller is an illustration of this, and also Goethe. In most other cases the reverse was true. For at bottom nineteenth century German society and the authorities mistrusted the creative artist and misunderstood the nature of artistic freedom. The attacks on Gutzkow and the Young Germans, the dislike and fear of the Young Hegelians, the support given to repressive measures against their work, were motivated by the feeling that to earn one's living solely by one's pen was socially irresponsible and dangerous. It was as if one's bourgeois existence, seen in terms of a solid profession, provided a guarantee to the public of the general reliability of what one wrote. In the latter half of the century a number of talented writers attained fame and even fortune through their novels – Freytag, Dahn and Spielhagen were the most successful of these. They and von Scheffel, author of stories and epics on themes from the medieval German Empire, and von Wildenbruch, the Hohenzollern 'house dramatist', were successful because they wrote on approved patriotic subjects, answering a need felt by very different social groups to orientate themselves in the new unified Germany.[22]

Writers whose reputation is established without dispute were, on the whole, not appreciated in their time and felt keenly what they regarded as the anomalous position of the artist in nineteenth century German society. Many tried desperately to secure a bourgeois position, none perhaps more than Hebbel, whose lowly origin and protracted struggle to establish himself nurtured a morbid sense of social inferiority. Similar to Klaus Groth, a fellow Holsteiner, his first step on the social ladder was to enter the service of a local church warden, where for eight years, from his fourteenth to twenty-second year he was employed as errand boy, coachman and clerk. In between he had long hours of free time and permission to use his master's library: years later he wrote to the philosopher Arnold Ruge that the reading done at this period of his life had provided him with ideas on which he drew all his life. At the age of twenty-two he prepared to take the next step upwards and become a student at Heidelberg, then at Munich University. Forced by lack of funds to walk back home to Hamburg, his rucksack on his back, he was careful not to have it on his person when he arrived in the city: 'Someone might meet me, who knew me and would notice', he wrote in all earnestness, just as years before he had angrily protested to his Hamburg patroness for giving him food to take home from her house; to expect him to carry things of this kind was 'an indelicacy, which must mark me as a beggar before the whole neighbourhood'.[23] One of the most characteristic features of bourgeois existence in nineteenth century Europe was that one delegated menial tasks: a gentleman or an aspirant to that rank did not carry parcels.

In the correspondences of German writers – in the absence of a capital city and cultivated society, letter writing provided an important source of intellectual stimulus – we find constant reference to the material problems of existence, but also to other problems besetting the artist, the vagaries and oppressions of the censorship in the first half of the century, and in the second half of the century a sense of public belittlement of his function. 'The position of the writer is a miserable one', wrote Fontane in 1891, '... Those who trade in literature and the politics of the day grow rich; those who make them, hunger or barely get by.' What can one do about our 'Cinderella existence', he asked in the course of this sketch on the social position of the German writer, published at his request anonymously in 1891. His own ironic solution showed how shrewdly he appreciated his position and that of the intellectual generally in the Second Empire: 'There is but one way: state approval, official label. ... The power of public approval, always considerable in our country, is increasing steadily. The belief that only exams, certificates, official approval, office, titles, orders, in short everything which smacks of state, can confer worth and value: this belief dominates people's minds more than ever before.'[24] There were many writers who conformed to the accepted image of the artist as a kind of laureate of bourgeois taste and chauvinistic doctrine. These – Spielhagen the novelist is a case in point – made a great deal of money from their works and were greatly respected; and almost all are forgotten today. Fontane himself was in fact one of the few to reject official label, a decision which cost him social disapproval and a protracted estrangement from his wife, Emilie.

By the late nineteenth century the state authorities and the majority of the educated classes in Germany – the cultured part of the nation, as they liked to style themselves – felt a mutual need of each other in the crisis situation of their times. Whether this sense of crisis was justified or not on objective grounds is not easy to decide. Change in national status and economic development so rapid that it deserved the epithet revolutionary, unprecedented social and regional mobility without accompanying change in the image and values of the society affected, all these things had nurtured in the élites of hereditary nobility, army, bureaucracy and academics a sense of fear, which Bismarck's own misanthropy, a product of the near megalomania of his late years, had sedulously fostered. A polarization in German society became even more apparent in the years before 1914 between the supporters and the beneficiaries of the authoritarian state and the organized masses, the former united in Dahrendorf's telling phrase, a 'cartel of fear', the latter, restive, frustrated, uneasily aware of their existence on the fringes of state and society. There was no room in Germany for the critical intellectual to question the assumptions on which the much vaunted national unity and greatness were based. Fontane, no social reformer, but a sensitive and perceptive critic, recognized this when he ironically attributed to the two most impressive characters of his last novel, *Der Stechlin,* the old Prussian landowner Dubslav, and the pastor Lorenz, social democratic views. If you are not with us, you are against us: to criticize the establishment in Wilhelmine Germany was, as Heinrich Mann illustrated to the point of caricature in his *Little Superman,* to stamp oneself as an outsider. The rewards of loyalty, on the other hand, were economic security and an uplifting sense of one's duty done, which were reflected in the regard of one's equals and the deference and respect of one's inferiors.

Chapter 16
The industrial entrepreneurs

In the last few years a great deal of work has appeared in Germany dealing with the early history of industrialization in that country. Historians have studied the growth of the leading industries and the social groups most affected by the process – craftsmen and migrant workers, businessmen and factory hands. There is agreement among these scholars that the traditional date marking the beginning of the first wave of industrialization, 1849–50, is too late, and that industrialization in the Rhineland and Westphalia was already under way in the 1840s, and in Berlin almost a decade earlier: the 1850s marked a tremendous acceleration of expansion rather than its initiation.

During these years, the industrial entrepreneurs contributed more than any other social group to revolutionizing the German economy, thereby indirectly affecting its political development profoundly. As a social group, aware of their achievements and responsibilities, they were new. However, individual entrepreneurs had played a role in Germany's history since the seventeenth century. They had acted as licensees of a prince, exploiting a monopoly in tobacco, tea or coffee, or they had been employed directly by the ruler to develop mining and metal industries, textiles or porcelain, in the traditional centres of manufacture in Germany, the Rhine and Ruhr valleys, Saxony and Silesia, Berlin or the Tyrol. These men had been of diverse social origin, noblemen or ennobled burghers, craftsmen or merchants; some had been the victims of religious persecution, such as the Counts of Donnersmarck, the Lutheran branch of which came to Silesia from Austria in the years of the Counter-Reformation; one of their descendants, Count Guido von Henckel-Donnersmarck, made a prince in 1901, pioneered the Silesian railway network on monies borrowed from Parisian bankers in the 1850s. The textile industry of eighteenth century Wuppertal was in the hands of Protestants – largely Calvinist refugees from Spanish Brabant and from Jülich-Kleve – who had settled there in the seventeenth century; immigrants from Bohemia settled in Saxon manufacturing centres; in Berlin and in many other places there were French Huguenots and Jews with patents of protection who earned their living in commerce, in banking and manufacture.

In the eighteenth century there was a sudden upsurge of industrial activity in certain areas of Germany. Thus between 1730 and 1786 the manufacture of knives in Solingen doubled in tonnage, while the number of master weavers employed in the Wupper valley increased from 300 in 1730 to between 1000 and 1100 in 1780.[1] The population of Krefeld, engaged primarily in silk manufacture, increased by 500 per cent in the eighteenth century. In the late eighteenth century a strong sense of family pride became characteristic of the more successful commercial houses whose members helped to finance enterprises. Cologne banking families, Hanseatic merchants and the owners of textile and metal work concerns began to invest their wealth in fine houses, to show a degree of ostentation in their dress and habits which had not been seen in earlier years. The Napoleonic wars brought bankruptcy to many old established firms, but they also offered opportunities to men of talent but little capital. These were of diverse social origins, a number being, curiously enough, clergymen's sons, who would join a firm as apprentices and work their way up to partnership or ownership through marriage. The early entrepreneur usually had a commercial training; although an interest in technical problems was almost always characteristic of the most successful, it was knowledge of markets that was above all demanded of him. He prided himself on his commercial skills; even in the 1860s the founder of the Dortmund Union and one of the biggest industrialists of his day, Friedrich Grillo, and the steel magnate, Alfred Krupp, spoke of themselves as members of the 'commercial estate' (*Kaufmannsstand*).[2]

The entrepreneurs were not a class, but a type. However, contrary to generally accepted views, the German entrepreneur in the age of the industrial revolution was rarely a self-made man, one who had come up in the world socially by dint of skill, business acumen and good luck. There was of course some considerable degree of social mobility in the industrial and business world; upward social mobility generally spanned two generations, but the majority of leading names came from families already engaged in commerce or manufacture. After the early years of the nineteenth century only a relatively small number were craftsmen or craftsmen's sons, although some of the most famous pioneers of industrial processes or captains of industry, including August Borsig and Carl Zeiss, came from this social group; a few were sons of professional men, of clergymen, teachers or officials; Werner Siemens was the son of a tenant farmer; the biggest manufacturer of furnishing fabrics in Berlin, Lehmann, was the son of a horse dealer; none at all came from the lowest ranks of society, the rural wage labourers or the urban lower classes. Between 1800 and 1870 54 per cent of all German businessmen followed their father's profession, though they might be more prosperous than he had been; during 1871–1914 the percentage was 54 per cent, and in 1923 64 per cent.[3] For the same periods only 31, 30 and 10 per cent respectively came from the middle ranks of society, none from the lower. In Berlin for the years 1855–70 as many as 78 per cent of the leading bankers, industrialists and merchants came from business families; only 10 per cent were the sons of craftsmen, traders and shopkeepers, 12 per cent of professional men.[4] The social origin of the successful businessman naturally varied according to the industrial enterprise with which he was associated. Thus the textile industry, which was the earliest to be mechanized, attracted men with a commercial rather than a technical background, while in the metal and engineering industries it was the reverse. The last named required skilled operators; most of the leading personalities spent a decade or more as foremen before setting up on their own. Financiers and merchants helped to pioneer the railway building programme, the 'eigentliche Motor des industriellen Aufschwungs in Rheinland-Westfalen' ['the real force behind industrial expansion in Rhineland-Westphalia'],[5] as of Berlin too, and to develop the insurance business in mid century. Some came from well-established houses, as the Beers and Mendelssohns in Berlin, others, Camphausen and Mevissen in western Germany, or Samuel Bleichröder, whose son was Bismarck's banker, came from provincial towns where they had been engaged in commerce.

Upward social mobility was not, therefore, an essential feature of the nineteenth century industrial entrepreneur in Germany, partly because of the more rigid social barriers in German society, by contrast with the USA or Britain, or even France at the same period, partly also because of the absence of an established commercial middle class in Germany as a whole. The revival of craftsmen guilds in mid century for political reasons put another obstacle in the way of expansion among the craftsman class. In Prussia the Trades Ordinance of 1849 made it difficult for those who wished to transform their workshops into modern industrial concerns. Where intergenerational mobility did occur, it usually took, as has already been said, two generations. In very many of such cases the newly made wealth was either dissipated by the third generation, or the enterprise sold or wound up. The grandsons or granddaughters of the founder of a firm began in the latter half of the century to depart from the tradition of intermarrying with their own kind: from the time of the founding of the Empire onwards, many chose their partners among the landed class, if they were successful, or themselves invested in land.

A feature of the German entrepreneur in the years before 1871 was the fact that he was often different in religion and way of life from the community in which he lived and worked. Thus in the Wuppertal and the Ruhr, most merchants and factory owners in the early years of industrialization were Protestants, generally members of Reformed communities, in a predominantly Catholic area; the same was true of the Lutheran merchants of Aachen and Cologne and the Jewish bankers, the Oppenheims, also of Cologne. In Berlin something of the order of 50 per cent of the businessmen were Jewish, but unlike the Westphalian Calvinists, who had lived for several generations in the same place, they were mostly recent immigrants. They came from a variety of regions: from the provincial small towns of the Mark Brandenburg, from Saxony and Silesia, from West and East Prussia or Posen. Indeed some 60 per cent of all Berlin businessmen in the mid nineteenth century were immigrants, but they became absorbed without friction into the resident community, which was also Protestant or Jewish in more or less equal proportion to the newcomers,[6] and because initially they had little contact with social groups other than their own.

The evolution of the German businessman in the nineteenth century is best illustrated by a number of individual cases. One of the earliest types was the craftsman who travelled, first as a journeyman and later as a master craftsman, visiting contacts abroad, and whose natural curiosity about technical inventions and innovations in production methods made him want to inform himself, in order to try them out at home. J. C. Fischer (1773–1854) of Schaffhausen was on any reckoning a remarkable individual, yet, outwardly at least, his case is not untypical of the craftsman exploiting the opportunities of his age. He was born into a well-established craftsman family, and trained by his father, a coppersmith. When the time came for him to seek experience as a journeyman in 1792, he set off with a two-volume work on the principles of mathematics and his father's suit for Sundays; he went first to Frankfurt am Main, then to Chemnitz in Saxony, to Potsdam and on to Copenhagen, where his great-uncle was in charge of the royal art cabinet. This uncle introduced him to interesting and useful contacts; Fischer then did what so many of the great German entrepreneurs were to regard as a necessary and desirable part of their training: he went to England. It must seem surprising to learn of his mixing with distinguished society at lectures which he attended at the Royal Institute, but Fischer was an unusually resourceful man; he watched experiments on gunpowder and shrapnel at the Arsenal in Woolwich; both then and later he was at pains to learn as much of new processes as his hosts would permit. Shortly after his return home from this first visit to England, in 1802, he took over his father's firm and began to expand the labour force and introduce new machinery. He discovered crucible steel independently of the English, who had kept the process secret, and published his discovery in 1804; he became one of Switzerland's most eminent industrial personalities, but in his life style and relationship to his workers he remained a traditional master craftsman, referring to himself simply as 'a coppersmith and bell caster by trade, as well as manufacturer of cast steel and files'.[7]

Heinrich Kunz, also of Switzerland, born in 1793, was the son of a country putter-out who also did some farming. Heinrich was sent as a commercial apprentice to work in a textile mill in Alsace; he wrote letters home to his father in which he gave detailed costing of machinery and advised him to introduce such machines into his own business. On his return in 1811, he helped to expand the works, and rose to be one of the leading textile manufacturers of the continent, known later as the 'spinning king'.[8] Not all would-be entrepreneurs had such cooperative fathers. The sons of another Swiss manufacturer, Sulzer, attempted to get their father to borrow money and build a new foundry. His reply was characteristic of the older generation: 'Never, but never, on borrowed money. Neither grandfather nor I ever did that. A man of honour only undertakes what he can do with his own powers.'[9] Another case of the craftsman who became an industrial pioneer was the carpenter's son August Borsig, born in Breslau, who came to Berlin as a mechanic and entered Egell's metal works where so many of his kind served their time: Carl Hoppe, a clergyman's son from Naumburg; Wöhlert who worked twenty-five years for Egells and for Borsig before opening his own firm in 1842; and Schwarzkopff, the armaments manufacturer. Borsig had worked at Egell's from 1823 to 1837, rising to be a foreman, and in 1837 set up on his own with fifty workers. In his case and in many similar ones, progress was unbelievably rapid. Within a few years Borsig had made the firm's first steam engine, five years later the 100th was put into service, and in 1854, shortly before his untimely death, the 500th was handed over to the transport authorities: Borsig now employed over 1000 men; Carl Hoppe also employed some 1000 only ten years after founding his firm. However, history books rarely mention the many entrepreneurs who failed to make the grade, often because they invested in textile machinery in the 1840s when this branch of industry was no longer expanding, or because of the shortage of capital which in the late 1840s was so serious for the smaller firms and those just setting up. A decade or so later, in the early 1860s, it was no longer possible for the Borsig-Wöhlert type, men with skill and experience but without much capital, to set up on their own and become successful entrepreneurs; the cost of enterprise and the size of concerns was by now too great.

Another type of entrepreneur was the inventive genius who set up in partnership with a craftsman. The outstanding example of this is Werner Siemens from Hanover and his associate Halske, a mechanic from Hamburg, who together created the German electrical engineering industry and in time were to pioneer the international firm with branches all over the world, employing by 1913 almost a quarter of a million men: truly 'an empire on which the sun did not set'. Siemens, the son of a tenant farmer and eldest of eight brothers, had gone into the Prussian army as a youth since it offered the only means of getting the training he wanted. Typical of the resilience of the man, he enjoyed it all immensely. His inventiveness was extraordinary: he seemed capable of a stroke of genius when he most needed it. An important invention was produced to save him from relegation to provincial garrison service as punishment for taking part in a public demonstration; he determined to make himself useful to the army authorities so that they would want to keep him in Berlin; he succeeded. In partnership with Halske whom he joined in 1847, he designed an underwater cable resistant to corrosion, and won the contract for laying telephone cables across the Atlantic. With his brother Karl as his partner he laid the telegraph system in western Russia; in conditions of quite extraordinary difficulty and under pressure from the Tsar, they connected Odessa and finally Sebastopol by telegraph with the capital during the Crimean War just in time to learn of the fortress's fall.[10] Other famous partnerships included such legendary names as the Berlin physicist Abbe and the craftsman Carl Zeiss, who together revolutionized the manufacture of optical instruments; between the engineer Rudolf Diesel and the businessman, Heinrich Buz, and towards the end of the century between Daimler and

Karl Benz, son of an engine driver.

To contemporaries the most impressive figures among the new class of entrepreneurs were the bankers, whose close links with industry are characteristic of the German industrial scene from the first. Many of the great names of mid century were Jewish, especially in Berlin; the best known perhaps is the Mendelssohn family; Abraham had moved from Hamburg at the beginning of the century to Berlin, where his wife's family, the Itzigs, had been established as bankers since the days of Frederick II – Daniel Itzig, his father-in-law, was one of 'les Juifs de Frédéric le Grand'; in mid century the firm was headed by a nephew, Paul Mendelssohn-Bartholdy. Less well known than his eminent composer brother, Meyerbeer, was William Beer, another banker, whose Berlin salon in the 1840s was distinguished for its company and lack of ostentation from one who was, as contemporaries agreed, in a position to be so.[11] Bismarck's banker and the founder of his immense fortune in land, Gerson Bleichröder, was the son of a perfume manufacturer from a provincial town in the Mark of Brandenburg, Samuel, who had worked for some time as an agent of Rothschilds.

Many early German industrialists founded banks to finance their enterprises. David Hansemann, originally a Rhenish wool merchant, who won the contract for the Cologne-Aachen railway from his rival, L. Camphausen, because the Cologne banking house of Oppenheim gave him their support, founded the influential Disconto-Gesellschaft which lasted till modern times. Like his business rival Hansemann, Camphausen was to become a member of the United Diet and a well-known parliamentarian and in 1848 a minister. Camphausen had begun his career as an oil and corn merchant in Cologne, and like Hansemann went into banking, with his brother as partner. The leading industrialists spread themselves into a variety of enterprises. Hansemann was a founder member of the Aachen fire insurance company in 1815; Mevissen, a fellow Rhinelander, though almost a generation younger and the dominant figure in the economic life of the provinces in the 1850s, was founder and director of the Schaaffhausen Bankverein, the largest credit institute of Rhineland-Westphalia, president of the Rheinish railway company and a founder member of two other banks, one insurance company, three mining companies and several factories. The brothers Oppenheim, besides being directors of their own bank in Cologne, held similar positions in three mining companies and they sat on the boards of no less than thirty-one enterprises.

The close links which existed between the numerically few big businessmen in the middle years of the century were often cemented by marriage. A number of the Jewish bankers in Berlin had been baptized –

as had for example the Mendelssohns – but they still continued to marry their own kind; the same faithfulness to their own social milieu is typical of the largely Protestant families of Rhineland-Westphalia. David Hansemann declared he would not marry until he could afford to marry someone of his own class and background. In two generations there were six marriages between the vom Rath and Böninger families; such people when they spoke of 'society' used the term 'among ourselves'.[12] An exception was made – as it traditionally was in Hamburg too – in favour of clergymen's children, who were thought suitable marriage partners. In the eighteenth century the manufacturers and merchants had tended to marry within the community of the local church; it was a sign of the times, of the new interest in expansion when the van der Leyens, an old Mennonite family of Krefeld, married one of their children to a son of the Cologne banking house of Herstatt (which went into liquidation only a week prior to the time of writing). The marriage habits of the middle ranking businessmen in mid nineteenth century Germany were similar or, as in the case of the Berlin textile merchants for whom we have records, even more exclusive: scarcely a single one married someone not the daughter of a businessman.[13] The group as a whole had perhaps a greater sense of social cohesion than the leading industrialists, though these had more contact with the ruling classes; it is clear, at least for those in Berlin about 1850, that, while they might not aspire to the sons of officials and the military as possible bridegrooms for their daughters, they were no longer prepared to see them marry into craftsmen's families; they mixed socially with their own kind and with academics, clergymen, teachers and doctors.[14]

They had their own clubs in Berlin, the *Verein der Freimüthigen* and the *Verein der Freunde* with several hundred members. In the 1860s such people began to hold 'evenings' and invite academics and artists to their houses, in particular actors, for both men and women in their circle were devotees of the theatre. A vivid portrait of this society is contained in the memoirs of the actress Helene von Racowitza, daughter of a Prussian official, for whom Lassalle lost his life in a duel.[15] Richard A. Meyer, writing of the period 1860–75, recalls the *Verein Berliner Künstler* (Association of Berlin Artists) as one of the focal points of social life for the well-to-do bourgeoisie: 'Their winter balls were the most elegant public entertainments after the subscription balls in the opera house, which are still flourishing and patronized by the old Kaiser.'[16] The officials, Meyer goes on to say, were not prominent in such circles, although politically at that time they sympathized with the business and academic circles. In fact the relations between the business community and the officials in Prussia were not particularly cordial in the decades before 1871, although much of the original impetus and encouragement for industrialization in the early nineteenth century had indeed come from enlightened Prussian bureaucrats, such as Beuth, Vincke, Maassen and others. In the middle years of the century the two groups did not have a great deal of contact at work, nor did they have much occasion to meet socially; in the Rhineland the Prussian officials were long regarded with dislike, which erupted into active hostility when a senior official in 1854 revealed the extent of the bribery by industrialists to exempt their sons from military service;[17] in consequence, 150 young persons were sent to fortress arrest. The image of the official as someone who was not his own master was strong in their minds: 'Dependence on the favour of the great was the element in which I could not exist', wrote the Rhinelander, Peter Conze, in the 1840s.[18] Carl Hoppe, owner of a leading Berlin engineering works, refused an administrative post in the royal mines in Silesia; he preferred, he said, to be independent.

The life style of the early entrepreneurs was in some respects similar to that of established commercial families in the old German trading towns such as the Hansa cities or Frankfurt. It was patriarchal in character, simple, even frugal in everyday life, although if occasion demanded it, hospitality would be munificent. In the textile manufacturing towns of north-west Germany a number of manufacturing families had been established in the same place for many years. Their families formed a group of town notables which dominated not only the business life of the community, but also the social and the church life. Thus in Barmen in the Wupper valley names such as Wichelhaus, Engels, Schuchard and von Eynern, manufacturers of yarn, recur throughout the late eighteenth and early nineteenth centuries in positions of responsibility; they were active both in municipal affairs and in the church; the latter was also the centre of social life for themselves and their womenfolk. Although only a minority were Calvinist, the Lutheran majority was much influenced by the Calvinist ethos, and indeed it was often difficult for an outsider to distinguish between the two. Most were deeply religious men, dedicated in their work to the service of the Lord. They believed that their prosperity was a sacred charge given them to administer for the public good; Schuchard, for example, promoted legislation against considerable opposition in the 1830s to limit the employment of child labour in the mines and factories. During the mass starvation of 1816, many merchants and manufacturers in this area contributed to a fund to distribute corn to the needy. The reward of their virtuous endeavour was to be sought, as one J. W. Fischer, a leading organizer of the fund, put it, in 'the silent recognition by the best among the burghers, but, above all, a pure, quiet conscience, and the glorious certainty of having protected Barmen in the hour of need from hunger and want'.[19] When the scope for their abilities widened, they began to look beyond the narrow confines of their factory and their church. In the 1820s they were sending delegates to the provincial Diet, and from the 1830s they were representing their town in the Chambers of Commerce. The Pietist revival of the 1820s and 1830s found numerous adherents in Westphalia and the Lower Rhine and among Protestant business circles in Cologne and Aachen. As the Bonn theologian Karl I. Nitsch put it in 1838: 'All is church and trade, mission and railways, bible and steam engine'.[20]

The combination was proving commercially sound, for by this time a number of textile manufacturers could afford to build themselves spacious houses outside the towns where they worked. The Mennonite Beckeraths of Krefeld dwelt in Cracau castle, though inside the frugal way of life was maintained. Pictures might adorn the walls, but the walls themselves were covered in a simple lime wash, and most members of the family sat on benches, not chairs, in the great hall to a simple supper which might consist merely of herrings and eggs, or porridge. The children were strictly brought up; they must not speak unless spoken to; they must learn early to understand the value of hard work and money. The boys worked in the factory or the office from an early age, the girls, even of well-to-do families, did their own washing and mending. Until about mid century the church provided recreation, if it may be termed this, for women, while the men began to frequent their clubs. 'These people lead a frightful life', wrote Engels, admittedly not an impartial observer, of his own kind in Barmen in the 1840s, 'and they are so content with it: the whole day long they bury themselves in figures in their offices, with a fury, with an interest that is scarcely credible; in the evening at the appointed hour all go into company where they play cards, talk politics and smoke, and at the stroke of nine they all go home.'[21] By mid century the strong religious convictions of this group had been modified, and although the leading businessmen were still patriarchal towards their dependants, both family and labour force, a new group of entrepreneurs had emerged, many of whom were former craftsmen or 'middle men' between the factory owner and the domestic weaver, and who, in their new position, thought simply in terms of profit and loss, and felt no personal sense of responsibility towards worker or community. The two groups continued in existence side by side in the community, each having their separate clubs, which now from about the middle of the century catered for the womenfolk too, with balls and concerts in the winter, and where members of other social groups, the military, officials and members of the professions might also come.

The prodigious expansion of industrial activity and of population after mid century inevitably changed the character of these communities – in the period between 1850 and 1875, for example, the town of Essen grew from 9000 to 55 000 inhabitants, an increase of 620 per cent. In subsequent decades many businessmen began to invest in land and houses and many descendants of the prominent families began to move to other more attractive towns, such as Wiesbaden or Godesberg, to live on investments. Others adopted a style of life which they thought fitting to men of their wealth, but which was a far cry from the traditions of their parents and grandparents. Thus the grandchildren of the tobacco and sugar merchant, William Carstanjen of Duisburg, might not enter the drawing room without their kid gloves on. The readiness to abandon the thrifty and self-contained life hallowed by tradition was more common among the younger generation of Rhenish and Berlin industrialists than it was in the older commercial communities. They began to covet social recognition in the form of titles and decorations from the Prussian government. To the latter such behaviour was typical of the parvenu; the *Bremen Handelsblatt* commented caustically in 1869: 'The Hansa cities have made an exception in this process of catching and taming the savage: there are no commercial and privy commercial councillors in their ranks ... and it is hoped that they will remain an exception at a time when a supposed honour from Berlin turns a rich and philanthropic Hamburg merchant into a kind of Young German Peabody.'[22]

Perhaps such commentators did not really understand the position in which the average German industrialist found himself. By French or British standards the industrialists were a powerful class; yet they knew they did not possess the status or the political influence which their wealth and their achievements in the economic life of the country might be thought to entitle them. Of the two, social status meant more to them; they shared in general the feeling of contemporaries that government was a matter for those trained for the job, the officials, though they welcomed the opportunity through membership of the provincial and national diets to protect their interests. Laurenz Hannibal Fischer, in his book *Der teutsche Adel* (1852), put his finger on it when he wrote 'Ambitious men of the prosperous bourgeoisie, thoroughly aware of their wealth, have no time for the principles of equality of the former classes (Communists and Democrats), but they take great exception to the fact that the princes and the bureaucracy do not accord them a position of honour in the social hierarchy which their wealth would seem to indicate'.[23] The award of the title of *Kommerzienrat* or indeed something higher seemed to the recipient the recognition by the authorities and by society of his just deserts. It was more than a mere label, it meant that one was shown deference in public by one's social inferiors, while the use of the title at all times drew the attention of those who didn't know one to the fact that a person of consequence was around; and of course one's wife enjoyed the satisfaction of prompter service in shops, as well as a certain eminence within her own circle. The Prussian government, in one of its rarer moments of psychological insight, used moral blackmail in the form of the award of titles and decorations to detach businessmen from their natural allegiance to the liberal cause during the Constitutional Conflict of the 1860s. They were particularly successful among the Rhenish industrialists who had once been so hostile to anything Prussian, and among the Berlin businessmen recently arrived from the provinces. Another incident connected with the Bonn University jubilee celebrations in 1867 illustrates the sense of social inferiority among such people. The Governor of the Rhine province, Adolf von Pommer-Esche, had the leading industrialists approached for contributions, but got little response; of the fourteen towns in his area, only one, Krefeld, replied. A personal approach was then tried, either by visit or personal letter; this tactic was immensely successful; contributions flowed in, accompanied by apologies for lateness.

Contact between businessmen and the ruling classes, the higher officials and the military, began to increase during the 1860s, when investment seemed to offer all and sundry the means of getting rich quick. Shareholders in the big enterprises included members of the landed aristocracy and senior bureaucrats, who were sometimes invited to sit on the board. The successful entrepreneur found himself lionized in Berlin in these years; wherever Friedrich Grillo went 'he found a swarm of admirers: noblemen, bankers and merchants surrounded him, to learn from him and be allowed by him to participate in his projects'.[24] The legendary 'Iron King', Strousberg, who made a fleeting but enormous fortune from dealing in railway shares, attracted a host of noble customers, many of whom lost their money in the process. Business morality reached a low ebb in the 1850s, but got worse still in the years just before the stock exchange collapse in 1873; the lawyer Edward Lasker's revelations, in the *Reichstag* in 1873, of the scandalous deception of the public, named leading bankers and their noble business friends and government officials among those responsible. A vivid literary portrait of the corruption and deception is contained in Friedrich Spielhagen's *Sturmflut* (1876). But there was positive collaboration too between these different social groups. The leading businessmen took an active interest in communal action to alleviate distress and sat on committees with members of the government and their representatives to discuss measures. Those working to help the victims of the great Hamburg fire of 1842 were moved by other considerations. They wanted to be regarded by the ruling classes as responsible and trustworthy citizens. They sat on committees and provided funds for relief. Their wives were invited to take part in the ladies' committees such as the *Ladies Committee to Succour Need Among Small Manufacturers and Artisans*; meetings followed in cafés, clubs and drawing rooms. After the founding of the Empire contacts between leading businessmen and the ruling classes grew much more intimate. Many began now to invest in land, to buy estates for their sons, who might then in time sell their father's firm and either live on investments or work their lands according to modern capitalist methods. The cases of two Westphalian industrialist families illustrate the trend: Friedrich Wichelhaus from Barmen (born 1801) married to Juliane de Weerth, had six children; both daughters married businessmen, but only one son went into the family firm; two other brothers became estate owners in Upper Silesia, one of them being ennobled at the age of forty-four in 1875; the fourth became a professor in Berlin. Of the five children of William von Eynern, also from Barmen, married to Emilie de Weerth, one daughter married her cousin Wichelhaus, an estate owner; one of her brothers also bought an estate in Upper Silesia, while the three remaining brothers lived off investments, one in Bonn, one in Kiel and the last, a cavalry officer, in Berlin.[25] The fact that the last mentioned should become a cavalry officer is very revealing. The Prussian army had stood for all those things the west German industrialist of a generation ago had most disliked. Now more and more successful businessmen were sending their sons into the Reserve, for social as well as business reasons, and a number into the regular army.

What in fact was happening during the early decades of the Empire was that the wealthy plutocracy – if one may describe them as such – was beginning to imitate the habits and if possible acquire the manners of the old ruling classes. For years the industrialists had disdained academic training for their sons, regarding it as poor substitute for the skills acquired in their own firms or those of their associates; now many began to send their sons to university, where they joined the prestigious fraternities. Julius Leverkus, son of the pharmaceutical manufacturer

Carl Leverkus, joined the Pfälzer at Bonn, 'the princes' university'; L. R. Peill joined the Teutonia and later the Frisia. During the early years of industrialization the German businessman was, with the exception of those from Silesia, almost invariably of bourgeois origin; he had little contact with or sympathy for the nobility. Practical and hardworking as they were, the bankers and captains of industry had scant respect for a way of life which in their eyes was unproductive in terms of goods or material progress. In the Rhineland and Westphalia there was a strong prejudice against the ruling classes generally in the years before the revolution of 1848. The revolution and its consequences helped to modify their attitudes. Their earlier sense of sympathy, if not of solidarity, with the craftsmen who worked for them underwent a change; the anger and frustration of the latter class with an economic situation which was endangering their livelihood, classing them with the 'proletariat', was focused in many instances on the factory owners whom a decade earlier they had been calling 'our factory masters'. These, in their turn, began to be aware of the 'working class' with interests and ambitions which might clash with their own. The terms '*Arbeitgeber*' [employer] and '*Arbeitnehmer*' [employee] were first used in 1848; the employers, who prior to 1848 had specified the task of their employees – deskworker, mechanic, silk master, etc., in subsequent years, lumped them all together as '*Arbeiter*' [worker].[26] Although the conservative elements in Prussian society and government were bitterly opposed to the industrialists and championed the craftsmen in the decade and a half after 1848, a number of officials – and not least Bismarck himself – understood the importance of winning their support. Not many entrepreneurs were ennobled before the founding of the Empire, apart from a number of Berlin bankers. Thereafter, and especially after the breakdown of the alliance with the liberals in 1878–9, Bismarck persuaded the Emperor to bind the leading entrepreneurs to the conservative cause by judicious award of patents of nobility. With the emergence of a united social democratic movement under its most able leaders Bebel and Liebknecht at Gotha in 1875, many industrialists were all too ready to agree with the establishment in regarding organized labour as a threat to state and society. Not all industrialists felt this way, but most appeared to do so. Even those who had nothing to do with workers – the academics, for instance – indulged themselves in an irrational fear of their power. Contemporary newspapers and journals satirized such attitudes – *Simplicissimus* in 1897 pictured the proletariat (*Der Pöbel*) as a gang of workers held in check by the army, the crowd (*Die Menge*), clerks, farmers, respectable citizens of limited means gently controlled by a policeman, and the people (*Das Volk*) walking along in procession, bemedalled, top-hatted and elderly – but they did not alter them.[27]

As for the workers themselves, only a minority were active members of the Social Democrat party or of the trade unions before the 1890s. Most were politically apathetic, interested only in making enough to meet their needs. Few thought about 'getting at' the master; if they didn't like their jobs, they moved on; labour mobility was very high indeed in some areas up to the end of the century and beyond. Many industrialists gave considerable thought to the welfare of their workers in the late nineteenth century, for a variety of reasons. Some, as the gas industrialist Oechelhäuser of Dessau, were characterized by progressive thinking, others, such as Stumm-Halberg, owner of vast interests in the Saar, or the mine owner Emil Kirchdorf, by hopes of nullifying the appeal of Social Democracy. Stumm-Halberg built houses and places of recreation for his workers, as did Werner Siemens and many others. Such men saw the labour force as part of their property, their fiefs, for so they had come to regard the fruit of their industry. Werner Siemens referred to the various concerns he owned as 'industrial dukedoms'; the term 'industrial baron' became commonly used of the great industrialists. Given such attitudes, it is not surprising that industrialists tried to influence the political views of their men. Karl Fischer, in his evocative memoirs of a nineteenth century factory hand, recalls how he was summoned to vote for the boss's candidate Miquel, later Prussian Finance Minister, when the latter was mayor of Osnabrück in the early 1870s. He and his fellow workers were instructed to appear in their best clothes and go together to the polling booth.[28] In 'Saarabia', as Stumm-Halberg's concerns were popularly termed, things were even more rigorous. Anyone reading a Social Democrat paper was dismissed, and informers were installed in the workers' settlements to report on any expressed political interest. The entrepreneurs of the Second Empire tried to cultivate loyalty on the part of their workers to themselves, using such devices as torchlight processions on the employer's birthday or a jubilee of the firm, followed by free beer for all. In the older or more settled industrial areas, such as the Zurich Oberland, where the textile manufacturers employed the same families for two or even three generations, a real bond existed between employer and employee, loyalty and devotion on the one hand and a truly paternal care in good and bad times on the other.[29] A number of liberals, politicians, academics and industrialists had earlier founded the *Verein für Sozialpolitik* in 1872 to try and foster progressive social policies. The *Verein* published some seminal works on the subject in the following years, but the introduction of the Socialist Law in 1878, which seriously compromised the liberals who had supported it and isolated socially and politically those who opposed it, made their work increasingly difficult. Bismarck and the conservative interest were particularly astute in the 1880s in identifying 'national' attitudes with conformity to the prevalent reactionary policies, and those who tried to show an interest in progressive labour relations could easily find themselves dubbed socialists or Marxists. Even the most able among the liberally inclined thus found themselves in a dilemma impossible to solve: this includes Walther Rathenau, industrialist, statesman and writer, who was later assassinated when Foreign Minister of the Weimar Republic, as well as Gustav Stresemann, a successor to Rathenau in this post, and one of the most able political figures in Germany from the early 1900s to his death in 1929.

The rise of the industrialist in Austria was somewhat different from Germany. The qualities of enterprise, inventiveness and business acumen were not highly regarded by the authorities in Austria: 1242 bankers, merchants and industrialists were ennobled in Austria between 1701 and 1918; in contrast 8596 officers and officials were ennobled.[30] In the eighteenth and nineteenth century the state encouraged many higher officials to engage in manufacture, but the negative effects of state intervention were felt in the many regulations, privileges, etc., which hampered the development of a healthy spirit of competition in that country. The role of immigrants in Austria's industrialization, in the view of Herbert Matis, a leading authority on the subject, can scarcely be exaggerated: in textiles it was the Dutch, then the Italians, French and Swiss; in the metal industries, and later in the railway programme, Englishmen. Although the Jews played a crucial role in the reorganizing of commerce and the credit system in nineteenth century Austria, they rarely went into manufacturing. On the other hand the Bohemian nobility, using their tenants as a labour force, launched into a diverse variety of enterprises in this period, above all manufacturing industries connected with agriculture. Some of these magnates showed all the initiative (and even some of the dubious business morality) associated with the 'new' bourgeois entrepreneurs: Count Hugo Salm personally smuggled out of England plans for a mechanized wool spinning machine, while the origin of Skoda works was as an enterprise on the Waldstein estate.[31] Even members of the royal family engaged in such ventures: the Cardinal of Olmütz, Archduke Rudolf, built a technically very advanced foundry, while the idiosyncratic Archduke Johann, later Regent during the Frankfurt Parliament, prided himself on having worked as a wheelwright. In the years after the 1873 stock exchange crash, many members of the nobility withdrew from capitalist enterprise, for numbers of them had lost heavily in speculation. In the last decades of the century Austria continued to attract foreigners to her industries, in increasing numbers Germans, especially from the Rhineland. However, increasing state intervention and bureaucratization hampered industrial enterprise to a far greater degree than in Germany, and the hope aroused by the promising beginnings of industrialization in the Austrian Empire in the early nineteenth century were not fulfilled.

In the years of Germany's second industrial revolution, from about 1890 to 1914, industry and business expanded so prodigiously that the role of the individual entrepreneur became less important. A few major names still stand out, such as Krupp and Kirchdorf, Rathenau and Thyssen, Stumm, and Ballin of the Hamburg shipping company, but in general the trend was towards the formation of powerful industrial cartels and syndicates which put pressure on parliament and government agencies in pursuit of their particular wants. The cartels, a characteristic feature of the German industrial scene in the last years of the century, placed unheard-of power in the hands of relatively few men who were not necessarily owners of firms but included a new phenomenon, the managing director. The cartels and syndicates formed in the 1870s and 1880s had been a response to the stock exchange crash of 1873, defensive in character and short lived. Those of the 1890s were concerned above all with power, political as well as economic. The different branches of industry might and did have conflicting interests, but the growing hysteria about the future power of social democracy, which businessmen as well as the ruling classes in general identified with revolution, helped to bridge their differences. The socialists, despite the pressures against them, despite the unfair distribution of electoral districts which favoured their opponents, increased their share of the vote progressively at every *Reichstag* election (apart from 1907) and in 1912 emerged as the largest single party. The propertied classes in Germany had painted a lurid picture of social democratic ideals in practice; they therefore showed themselves ready to support provocative measures against the urban working class in the fond belief that this must destroy the movement. The industrialists' interest groups were only too ready to help. In 1899 the *Zentralverband deutscher Industrieller*, representing heavy industry, contributed 12 000 *Reichmarks* to the *Reich* Ministry of the Interior (at its request!) to spread propaganda in support of a bill currently before parliament. This bill, entitled 'for the protection of those willing to work', proposed prison for strikers.[32] However, revelation of the deal in parliament prevented its passage. The cartels exercised the economic functions characteristic of cartels in England and the United States, but their political influence was at least as significant. They sought to extend their influence over public opinion by giving their support to those groups, which are a further typical feature of this period, the mass political associations such as the Pan German League, the Navy League, the *Reich* League against Social Democracy, etc., in the not incorrect belief that public opinion was a powerful factor in determining government policy. The individual membership of these movements and associations ran into several hundred thousands in the years before the Great War, the corporate membership twice that figure.[33] The aggressive nationalism and imperialism which they preached formed a common bond between the very disparate elements of German society in the years preceding 1914, at least of the majority of the property owning classes.[34]

The German industrialist on the eve of the Great War was a very different sort of person from the entrepreneur of the early and mid nineteenth century. The latter had generally been the son of a merchant or businessman, or perhaps an artisan whose commercial or technical ability coupled with initiative helped to found or to expand a firm, and to become prosperous and locally respected. Despite his wealth, the life style of the early entrepreneur remained essentially that of his father or grandfather, while his interests outside his work rarely went beyond those of local community or church. In the late 1830s and 1840s a number began to engage in politics, in the interest of a greater liberalization of the commercial code, setting their hopes on Prussia because of her lead in tariff reform and the setting up of the Customs Union (1834). Some, especially the Rhenish and Westphalian businessmen, took an active part in the new order ushered in by the 1848 revolution, but with the failure of the revolution and the prodigious expansion of industrial and commercial life in the years immediately following, more and more devoted themselves exclusively to economic matters and left the political future in the hands of bureaucrats and ministers. However, the industrialists, especially those members of the newly formed party of the National Liberals, collaborated successfully with Bismarck between 1867 and 1874 to liberalize and unify commercial legislation of the German *Reich*. The stock exchange crash of 1873, provoked by reckless speculation and followed by a long period of comparative stagnation until the early 1890s, altered the temper of society in Germany. Liberalism became equated in the public mind with ruthless exploitation, a widespread pessimism succeeded the optimistic atmosphere of the *Gründerzeit* (Promoters' Boom) of the 1860s and early 1870s. In 1879 Germany changed over to protective tariffs – a political move by Bismarck but one which, despite the fears of the more progressive industrialists, proved remarkably successful for the majority of interests, for heavy industry as well as agriculture. The German business community began to take on the conservative values characteristic of the ruling classes, to intermarry with the landed aristocracy and to seek acceptance at court. With some notable exceptions they acquiesced in the Anti-Socialist law, and publicly expressed their belief in the need for authority in the state and at work. Despite their wealth they did not see themselves as an independent and potentially powerful plutocracy, but sought social recognition by conforming to the patterns of behaviour of the military and bureaucratic establishment of Prussia-Germany. Fontane's *Kommerzienrat* (Commercial Councillor) Treibel in *Frau Jenny Treibel* (1892), or the figure of Gundermann, the ennobled industrialist in his last novel, *Der Stechlin*, offer a satiric but also subtle psychological interpretation of this process. As members of parliament in the conservative interest, as presidents or members of the committee of the various nationalist pressure groups supporting the national interest, German captains of industry were rewarded with the business contracts and the social eminence they desired. The values normally associated with western European society in the nineteenth century, the trend towards greater equality of opportunity, and even of wealth and property, was therefore not characteristic of Germany in the period of her industrial revolution. Fearful of social unrest which might destroy the prosperity of the country, fearful too in the last years before 1914 that other nations, envious of Germany's achievements, would try to rob her of them, the industrialist, like the military, the bureaucrat and indeed the average German burgher, was ready to subscribe to the opinion expressed by Max Weber in his inaugural lecture given at Freiburg in 1895: 'Not peace and human happiness is our heritage to our descendants on their way, but rather the preservation and refinement of our national way of life – the social unification of our nation, which modern economic developments have shattered.'[35]

Chapter 17
The Jews

The Jews in early modern Germany had seemed a social group permanently outside the order of society, possessing, in the view of their Christian neighbours, immutable and unacceptable characteristics. Yet by the end of the eighteenth century the influence of the Enlightenment had at last modified the image of the Jew and his role in society. A change in the environment and the legal status of Jews would inevitably, it was declared, modify their national character and habits. In a number of the larger states the idea of the social usefulness of the Jew was mooted,[1] and it was in line with such thinking that Joseph II of Austria introduced his Patent of Toleration in 1782. Under the Patent Jews became eligible for military service, and this, far from being considered a wearisome obligation, was regarded by them as a mark of privileged status. In 1846 the Jews of Posen were actually to petition the government to make them liable for conscription. It was events in France, however, which awakened German Jews to the possibilities of full emancipation in their own country. On 28 September 1791 the National Assembly emancipated all Jews of France despite opposition from several quarters; they now shared the rights and duties of other French citizens. The importance of the step was clearly realized by contemporaries: as Isaak Berr of Nancy jubilantly proclaimed: 'We are now recognized not just as human beings, not just as citizens, but as Frenchmen.'[2]

This pioneering act by a European state – France was the first country apart from the USA to emancipate the Jews – aroused the keenest hopes of similar developments across the Rhine among the far more numerous German Jews.[3] However, the French initiative was to prove disadvantageous for them: the association between revolutionary France and Jewish emancipation confirmed the traditional and instinctive dislike of German élites for the whole concept of Jews as citizens of Germany, which they liked to consider as contrary to the natural order of things. Furthermore, the variety of German states and of existing statutes and measures concerning the Jews within their borders made national agreement on emancipation difficult. Some areas of Germany such as Posen or Pomerania had a very high Jewish population; others, such as Bavaria and Württemberg before 1806, had scarcely any at all. In some regions the Jews were established, prosperous and respectable (as in Berlin and Frankfurt), in others they lived close to destitution. The readiness of the authorities or of leading citizens to alter the present status of the Jews bore no relation to the size of the Jewish community in their midst or to the percentage of Jews in the population as a whole. Anti-Jewish feeling in the early nineteenth century and political antisemitism from the 1870s onwards was often greatest where the Jews were few in number. But the complexity of their status and the sporadic eruption of anti-Jewish feeling convinced the authorities that full and immediate emancipation on the French model was out of the question. The solution proposed in Prussia and elsewhere was very much in the spirit of German state paternalism: the Jews and the public were not yet ready for full emancipation; both must be gradually prepared for it.

The actual process of civic and legal emancipation in Germany spans three quarters of the century; in the early years, privileges were extended from individuals to groups, then to a whole territory; subsequently, in response to local demonstration or individual pettiness or malice, they were amended or withdrawn until full emancipation was granted in the 1860s. Thus in 1812 the Prussian Edict of Toleration, the work of Wilhelm von Humboldt, offered the Jews living in the older states of the kingdom almost full rights. However, it was not extended to include those Prussian lands in the east, notably Posen and West Prussia, which were restored to Prussia in 1815, where the Jewish population, numbering as much as 50 per cent in the provincial towns of the region, had virtually no legal rights at all. Extraordinary anomalies were allowed to survive in consequence of this 'gradual' approach: thus in the county of Wittgenstein, acquired by Prussia from

Hesse in 1816, the 1573 law declaring 'heathens, gypsies and Jews' as outlaws was still in force in 1842.[4] In the period of reaction following the Congress of Vienna, many Prussian government officials advocated severe curtailment of Jewish rights, despite the fact that Prussian Jews had enthusiastically enlisted to fight Napoleon. The line of argument of the Minister of Justice, von Kircheisen, was not untypical: 'other reasons aside, a display of courage on a particular occasion does not disprove the general assumption that Jews are less moral [than Christians]'.[5]

At the Congress of Vienna the failure of Austria and Prussia to win uniform legislation, the energetic but ineffective protests by the Jewish representatives from the communities of Frankfurt, Hamburg, Bremen and Lübeck at the loss of rights they had enjoyed under Napoleon, and the redistribution of territories with Jewish populations, kept the Jewish question before the public eye. States such as Bavaria and Württemberg, where in the days of the Holy Roman Empire the Jews had not been permitted to reside, now gained substantial Jewish populations: in Bavaria it was as many as 50 000. Article 16 of the Federal Act of the Congress of Vienna (1815) contained a vague pledge that the constituent states would legislate in favour of the Jews, but it proved of little value. Baden granted some rights to their Jews in 1807–9, Bavaria in 1813; only in the tiny states of Anhalt-Bernburg and Anhalt-Köthen in central Germany was emancipation virtually unqualified;[6] Württemberg did nothing until 1828, Saxony and Hanover until 1838 and 1842; Austria, with the largest Jewish population of any German state, delayed until 1848. The multiplicity of legal measures, petitions by the Jews to improve their lot, efforts by state and municipal authorities to restrict extant rights, in order, it was said, to protect craftsmen and peasants from the menace of Jewish competition: all these factors kept the inferior status of Jewish subjects before people's minds. They also gave the Jew a sense of isolation in the community and helped to create a 'Jewish problem'.

The period between the Congress of Vienna and the revolution of 1848 saw a widespread if sporadic revival of attacks on Jewish property and persons in many parts of Germany. These were atrributed to religious motives, by the authorities and the ringleaders, but they were mainly a reaction to economic and social distress. In Germany and in Central Europe generally there had long been a correspondence between economic difficulties and natural disasters and the Jews. As a later slogan had it: When the share prices fall, antisemitism rises up. The revolution in the German economy in the nineteenth century did not alter this; if anything it exacerbated the tendency for the economically and socially frustrated to avenge themselves on the eternal scapegoat. In the primitive rural economy of early modern Germany and Austria, the Jew as pedlar and moneylender, as innkeeper and horse, cattle and grain dealer, had played a crucial role and was to continue to do so in the eastern provinces up to the beginning of the twentieth century. He was an easily identifiable victim of popular resentment in bad times, an unhappy situation which the authorities did little to counteract. Indeed the representatives of government were often, in their private capacity as landowners, in debt to the Jews and indifferent, to say the least, at the sight of their illtreatment. The easing of restraints on trade and movement in mid nineteenth century Germany encouraged the Jews to move to the cities, where they soon dominated certain branches of the economy, notably banking and ready-made clothing. The demand for cheap labour in the textile industry brought the rural labourers, men and women alike, to work in the towns and cities: in the brief slump periods between 1850 and 1873, accusations of Jewish exploitation of German labour were occasionally heard. It was, however, the large numbers of Jews involved in stock exchange dealings which unleashed the most serious and sustained wave of antisemitism in the country's history – that which followed the crash of 1873. A number of Jews had been prominent in shady dealings, notably the 'Railways King' Strousberg who made an enormous fortune out of real and fictitious railway shares. It was very much in the interest of the establishment to deflect attention from the high proportion of their members, notably Prussian *Junker* families, who had sought to climb on to the bandwagon of Strousberg's genius for moneymaking by making the Jews as such into a scapegoat. Many small investors, who formerly had stuck to government bonds and 'safe' securities, had been tempted by the vast profits being made during the *Gründerzeit* in railway bonds and the construction industry. They had saved not only to provide for their old age but in order to finance their children's social rise, by means of a grammar school and university education. It was the small investor of this type who was the main victim in 1873, and it is psychologically understandable that they were all too ready to blame others for their own foolishness and greed. A number of Jews did indeed make away to the USA and elsewhere with the savings of investors; their photographs under the heading 'Wanted' adorned the advertisement pillars on the streets of German towns and the columns of newspapers for many months, thus imprinting a visual image of the 'exploiter' on the minds of the gullible.

The long period of stagnation following the crash lasted until the early 1890s. It coincided exactly with the rise of modern political antisemitism in Germany and Austria, with the appearance of such destructive and influential tracts and books as Wm Marr's *Der Sieg des Judentums über das Germanentum* (1873, 12th impression 1879), Lagarde's *Deutsche Schriften* (1878–81), Eugen Dühring's *Die Judenfrage als Racen- Sitten- und Culturfrage* (1881) and Pater (later Professor) August Röhling's forgery *Der Talmudjude* (1881).[7] An Antisemitic Party was founded in Germany in the 1880s, and won some sixteen seats in the 1893 *Reichstag* elections; one year earlier the Conservative Party had officially adopted antisemitism as part of its programme (Tivoli Programme). In 1893 the conservative agrarian pressure group, the *Bund der Landwirte* and the petty bourgeois shop assistants organization, *Handlungsgehilfenverband* excluded Jews from membership; student athletic groups and fraternities had been doing this since the early 1880s.

However, the sudden upsurge of the economy in the mid 1890s, which lasted to the outbreak of war, made antisemitic programmes and policies seem less relevant to national life, and became largely the preserve of eccentrics. The socialist leader A. Bebel, perspicacious in most of his judgements, could confidently assert in 1906 that 'It is a consoling thought that it [antisemitism] has no prospect of ever exercising a decisive influence on political and social life in Germany.'[8]

The important difference between the antisemitism of the late nineteenth century and that of earlier times was that the former was based not on religious difference, but on race. Furthermore, it gained adherents in circles which a generation earlier had been predominantly, even passionately, liberal: among academics and the educated bourgeoisie in general. The Crown Prince of Prussia, noted for his liberal views, could declare in 1881 that antisemitism was 'the disgrace of the century', but his words did not arouse a positive response; they were no longer intellectually acceptable. However, the early prophets of antisemitism, Marr and Dühring in Germany, and Georg von Schönerer in Austria, attained notoriety as key figures only in our own century in the light of the holocaust of the Third *Reich.* They were not widely recognized as such at the time. Dühring was undoubtedly prominent for some years as an academic economist, but he lost his teaching post in 1877 for vicious and malignant attacks on the university; symbolically, perhaps, he went prematurely blind. There is a certain parallel between him and Schõnerer, whose brief and violent political career ended prematurely, a victim of his own incipient paranoia.[9] Far more influential at the time, or so it seemed, and the source of deep disquiet in Jewish circles, were the attitudes of public personages, such as Wagner, and the changing attitudes of the popular press. In 1874–5 one Otto Glagau published a series of articles in the immensely popular family journal, *Die Gartenlaube,* which had been known in the 1850s and 1860s for its liberal views, castigating the influence of emancipated Judaism on German life.[10] The *Frankfurter Zeitung*, one of the country's most important newspapers and which was Jewish owned, took issue with recent developments in an article headed 'Zur Judenfrage' (4 November 1880): 'Etwas' ['Something'], wrote the editor perspicaciously, 'muss gestürmt werden; nach dem äusseren Düppel* wurde das innere Düppel gestürmt, nach dem Franzosenkriege der Vatikan, nach diesem der Sozialismus und jetzt, wo kein anderer Krieg in Sicht ist, und man doch nicht die Brutalität im Leibe behalten kann, muss der Jude herhalten' ['has to be stormed; after the external Düppel, it was the turn of the internal Düppel, after the war against the French it was the Vatican, after that Socialism, and now, since there is no other war in sight and one cannot be expected to keep one's brutality to oneself, the Jew must remedy the deficiency'].[11] And yet there was something so inconsequential, not to say irrational, about antisemitism at that time, that, hurtful and distressing though it was to German Jews, most could satisfy themselves that it was an aberration, part of the process of accommodation to the new Germany, which time would doubtlessly take care of. Thus Bismarck would in 1880 defend the role of the Jews in finance to his Minister of the Interior, Puttkamer, yet was prepared to castigate 'das besitzlose Judentum in Presse und Parlament' ['the propertyless Jewry in the press and parliament'].[12]

Wagner applied the full force of his vituperative talents and malice to the Jews, prominent among them Meyerbeer, to whom he owed so much, trumpeting in a letter to Ludwig II of Bavaria in 1881: 'I hold the Jewish race to be the born enemy of humanity and of all that is noble; it is certain that the Germans in particular will perish through them, and I perhaps am the last German able to testify against Judaism, which holds all beneath its claw.'[13] And yet many of the finest interpreters of Wagner's music, both in his own lifetime and later, were Jews, as were many of the maestro's favourite performers. Wagner showed a sustained preference for them, so much so that Hans von Bülow, his conductor, would lament ironically to a colleague: 'O why were my father and yours not circumcised?'[14] Joseph Rubinstein, the Jewish pianist, was perhaps an extreme case: desolated at Wagner's death, he committed suicide on his grave. But there were many others:

* This referred to the famous storming of the Düppel redoubt by the Prussians in the war against Denmark (1864).

Karl Tausig, the pianist, Angelo Neumann, the tenor, to whom Wagner pledged the world rights of *Parsifal* outside Bayreuth, and, most singular of all, Hermann Levi, whom Wagner, with a calculated balance between affection and maliciousness, called his 'alter ego'.[15] Nor was the admiration of the known antisemite Wagner confined to interpreters of his music: many of the greatest enthusiasts were to be found among the Jewish middle class, who regarded themselves as completely assimilated and felt peculiarly drawn to this most 'German' of composers.

The dilemma, indeed the tragedy of the liberal Jews in Germany was this: the hunger for education characteristic of the ghetto Jews of the eighteenth century had been directed into rabbinical studies. In the nineteenth century geographical and social mobility brought thousands for the first time into contact with German schools and culture. Many abandoned their traditional religion, some from an idealistic belief in the equal value of all religions and a desire to further mutual tolerance, others as part of an intellectual rejection of what they saw as outmoded rituals, a third group from expediency, others still from a combination of motives. Classical humanism in its German form or positivist belief in science and human progress provided adequate substitutes for very many of the new Jewish bourgeoisie in Germany, and a passkey, or so they believed, for complete assimilation. The children and grandchildren of the first generation of assimilated Jews did not accept the label often given them in the second half of the century, 'German of Jewish faith': they felt only German. What Ignaz Maybaum wrote of the renowned rabbi Franz Rosenzweig, who spent his youth in Cassel/Hesse in the 1890s, '[He] grew up like many sons of Jewish families in Germany before the First World War – parental love, the best education, a cultured home in which Goethe and Beethoven played the chief part and Judaism not at all',[16] could have been said about a whole class of educated German Jews. The term 'Jew' might be used by hostile individuals and groups in the Second Empire as a synonym for features of contemporary society which they rejected or disapproved of: capitalism, socialism or that vague but emotive concept, 'modernity'. To the individual Jew the realization that his fellow citizens regarded him as different from themselves came often as a bitter and sustained shock. Walter Rathenau, son of the founder of the electrical company AEG, Emil Rathenau, and himself an industrialist, economist, intellectual and practical man of the world all at once, experienced this most acutely. In his person Rathenau began to comprehend the tragedy of the German Jew, whose image of himself was the product of his environment and which experience constantly reinforced. 'There comes a moment in the life of every young Jew', he wrote, 'which he remembers all his life: when he fully realizes for the first time that he has come into the world as a second-class citizen, and that no virtue and no merit can free him from this situation.'[17]

Wilhelmine Germany's rejection of its Jewish citizens as not quite equal was tacit rather than overt. Otto Klemperer recalls his experience at what was undoubtedly an enlightened Hamburg school: although consistently top in his class, he was always put second in the annual reports; it would, it was assumed, be derogatory to the 'German' boys if they were shown to be less able. Memoirs of Jews written long before Hitler recall numerous instances of physical violence as well as occasional abuse at school, and that it generally went unpunished. Gustav Mayer (born in 1871), the historian of the Social Democratic movement and the son of a prosperous tradesman in Prenzlau/Brandenburg, records how on one occasion when he was an undersized fifteen-year-old, a schoolboy four years his senior and several inches taller stuffed his mouth with pork fat to the delectation of his whole class. They could see nothing dishonourable in the disparity of age and size. Mayer's reaction to the petty persecution – and this seems to have been a common one – was to try and emulate his Gentile neighbours, to excel against them in the things they admired, such as physical force and duelling. 'I tried to accommodate my ways as far as I could to theirs, and did not pay any heed to whether the way of life I thus forced on myself might appeal to me or be acceptable to my parents'.[18] His experiences of antisemitism at the university were wide ranging, he became aware that an unbaptized Jew could not aspire to that hallowed status of Wilhelmine Germany, Officer of the Reserve, and that it was difficult to become a higher civil servant. Yet he was not really disturbed by it all: 'I found antisemitism simply a bore', and discrimination in public life seemed merely 'a survival of past ages', which the progress of civilization would soon cast on to the scrap heap.[19]

The burden of hindsight has made the historians of German Judaism hypersensitive to manifestations of antisemitism in previous centuries. However, it is probably true that antisemitism in the last decades of nineteenth century Germany had a more destructive influence on its instigators then on its victims. The response of many Jews to the phenomenon was, at least initially, to increase their efforts to assimilate: Theodor Herzl was one of many Jewish students who took an enthusiastic part in a duelling fraternity at Vienna, and, although forced to leave in 1881 in response to a wave of anti-Jewish feeling in the university student organizations, he always cherished a high regard for the practice and actually proposed introducing it in the new state of Israel. Many Jews accepted the premises of antisemitism and condemned the practice of forming cliques to protect each other, and advance their career and business interests, as provocative and counterproductive. Others, of whom Karl Kraus is an extreme example, actually adopted antisemitic arguments to break the Jewish monopoly in certain branches of the press and in finance.[20] Yet another response was that of the Jews who had remained faithful to their religion but in a substantially liberalized form: Hermann Cohen, Herzl's distinguished opponent over the question of Zionism and professor of philosophy in Marburg University, believed, as did a number of Jews in northern Germany in the early years of the Second Empire, that Judaism was in essence identical with Protestant Christianity. Consulted by a Catholic colleague as to whether he should attend a Lutheran celebration in the university, he replied: 'If I shouldn't be there, who should?'[21] Cohen subsequently modified his views but his response is indicative of the optimistic belief in harmony and tolerance characteristic of most educated Jews in the latter part of the nineteenth century. A number of others, however, and men of the keenest intellects, rejected both their traditional religion and the very premises of bourgeois society in which they now lived: these included Karl Marx and the anarchist Moses Hess, as well as many of the intellectual leaders of German Social Democracy – Edward Bernstein, Paul Singer, etc.[22] Towards the end of the century, the vision of the state of Israel, inspired by Theodor Herzl, and brought into the realms of practicality by the support of Baron Hirsch, seemed to offer to many Jews a permanent solution to the problems of assimilation and antisemitism. However, it was a vision which had a far stronger appeal to the poor and unemancipated Jews of eastern Europe than to the average German Jew, either at that time or later. Although Herzl proposed to offer them 'German theatre and German opera' and 'Viennese coffee houses' in their new home,[23] they were, or felt themselves to be, far too rooted in German culture to want to seek a new identity elsewhere.

It is possible, as Freud later averred,[24] that prejudice and petty discrimination against Jews in Germany and elsewhere acted as a stimulus on them to excel in very many fields. Certainly the German Jews made a contribution to the scientific and cultural life of their country in the nineteenth and early twentieth century, and to its industrial prosperity, which was out of all proportion to their numbers. However, to write an account of the social history of German Jews in the nineteenth century merely from the point of view of antisemitism and their response to it, would be to give a false picture. The fact that this is often done, by non-Jewish as well as by Jewish writers, is understandable: hindsight in this case is too terrible not to persuade one of its constant relevance; it would be even more fallacious to suggest that it did not continually react on the attitudes of German Jews throughout the period discussed here, 1800–1914, and influenced their choice of career and their prospects. But to look back at their history in this period simply from the vantage point of the second half of the twentieth century could easily allow one to fail to appreciate the very great variety of forms of Jewish life in Germany, and would give a stereotyped view of the individual Jew and his response to his social environment.

In the beginning of the period the type of employment, social status and financial circumstances of German Jews varied considerably, according to the area in which they lived and the privileges their people had been able to win. Thus in southern Germany, in the provinces of Hesse and the Rhineland which were acquired by Prussia in 1815, there was a sizeable Jewish population in the villages. These people spoke a German dialect with some Hebrew words, and continued for many years to use Hebrew in their accounts and correspondence. The rural communities were often well integrated, and their menfolk acted as cattle dealers, pedlars and in general as the link between the countryside and the local town. Berthold Auerbach (1812–82), a literary lion of Berlin drawing rooms in the years when Spielhagen and Freytag were at the zenith of their fame, was the son of such a pedlar, and wrote his immensely popular *Tales of the Black Forest* (1843–54), reminiscences of life on the road. In the vast landscape of east Germany, where towns were few and the traditional land tenure had made villages the exception rather than the rule, the Jewish pedlar and dealer was more essential as a supplier of goods and services. Jewish jokes from eastern Europe still recall the kind of role played by them in the primitive rural economy.[25] Their numbers were particularly high in Pomerania, West Prussia and Posen, former Polish territories where their ancestors had settled in the early modern period after expulsion from the Holy Roman Empire. In some townships they numbered as much as 50 per cent of the population, as they were not allowed to reside on the land. It was from here and from the adjoining areas such as East Prussia and Silesia that the main body of immigrant Jews in mid and late nineteenth-century Berlin came. The Jews living in the villages of south and west Germany also declined in number from the 1860s onwards: 70 per cent of Jews living in rural areas of Bavaria left for the towns, or, further still, for the New World between 1870 and 1900.[26] There were new opportunities offered by the growing markets in the era of industrialization. Typical of the transition from rural life and traditional trades was the case of the Mayer couple, who in the early nineteenth century were regular stallholders in the country markets of Pomerania selling manufactured goods; they eventually founded in 1828 a store in Prenzlau which became a household word in north Germany: owners of famous drapery firms in Berlin which dominated the German market before the First World War had trained as apprentices in Ascher Mayer's of Prenzlau.[27]

Even as early as the middle of the century only half of Prussia's Jews were active in the traditional role of money lending and small trades. A respected minority were wholesalers, factory owners, bankers and members of the free professions. By 1900 it was estimated that Jews occupied some 25 per cent of the seats on boards of industrial and financial enterprises, and 14 per cent of the director's posts.[28] They were over-represented in these social groups in Germany as a whole because they were excluded in fact if not in theory from a number of more prestigious careers, such as the diplomatic service, the higher civil service and the officer corps. Even the teaching profession offered only limited access: the Christian confessional character of German schools made entry difficult even for baptized Jews, at least in the lower school, and both in grammar schools and the university a tacit *numerus clausus* operated on appointments of Jewish academics. In the liberal wing of politics, in the press and publishing, Jews gradually won an important, even a key, position, just as those student fraternities and clubs which did not exclude Jews as members tended to be dominated by them.[29]

If we turn to the biographies of individual Jews, we find a wide range of life styles and individual achievement. Perhaps the most talked-of Jew in cultured circles in the first thirty years of the nineteenth century was one who had never been to university or academy, had no career, and who was not even good looking: Rahel Levin (1771–1833), daughter of a Berlin merchant, whose Jewishness was an important part of the fascination she exercised on contemporaries. Extremely well educated alongside her brothers, as was usual for Jewish girls of good family, her conversation and her personality enthralled the most discriminating connoisseurs of feminine qualities, including Goethe, while Heine congratulated himself at his superb good luck in gaining access to her salon. She corresponded with many of the most eminent of her contemporaries, with wealthy and able men many years her junior, and when she eventually married the Prussian diplomat and man of letters, Varnhagen von Ense, some nine years younger than herself, even her women friends felt that it was he, not she, who had made a good match. Apart from her extraordinary personal fascination which she still exercises through her letters and diaries a century and a half after her death, she is interesting as a representative of that remarkable period in German, or more particularly Berlin, history, when conventional social barriers and racial prejudice seemed to be set aside by cultured men and women, when a love of music could bring together Prussian officers – including a scion of the Hohenzollerns, Prince Louis Ferdinand – and a mason, Carl Zelter, and when Jewish houses were the centre of musical and literary life. In this brief period from the 1790s to the end of the wars of liberation, people could show a remarkable awareness of feelings and loyalties very different from their own, yet treat them with tact and delicacy. The Prussian king, King Frederick William III, no natural friend of the Jews, gave an outstanding instance of this: when awarding Amalia Beer, mother of the composer Meyerbeer, with the Order of Queen Louise for her services in charitable work, he suggested that a medal be substituted for the usual cross, which a Jewess would not wish to wear. It was entirely because of her own personal magnetism that Rahel's home continued to be a meeting place for Jew and Gentile, and for members of different social classes after the return of reaction in the 1820s, and that it remained so till her death in 1833. Some years before she died, members of the same social group, of the same profession, were already tending to confine their social intercourse to their own kind, and their intellectual and personal horizons were becoming more narrow.[30] The general retrenchment by government and local authorities on the question of emancipation was already beginning again to affect the individual Jew seeking to promote his career. The case of the lawyer Eduard Gans, to take but one such instance, was something of a *cause célèbre* in the early 1820s: in 1822 he was appointed to the chair of law at Berlin university only to have his appointment quashed on grounds of religion.[31] Gans decided to submit to baptism and was immediately instated. It was in connection with him that Heine made his celebrated remark about baptism as being the 'entry ticket to European culture'. Yet Heine too, for all his sarcasm, and despite a real if tortuous devotion to Judaism, was to follow his example. So too did the writer and journalist Ludwig Börne, one of the most acid and perceptive commentators on German political life in the Restoration period, who had had to abandon his career as a policeman in 1815, when a Jew was decreed unsuitable for posts in the state service.[32]

That baptism was not essential to success was illustrated by the careers of two very different men: Giacomo Meyerbeer (1791–1865) from Berlin, and Gabriel Riesser (1806–63) from Hamburg. Meyerbeer's father was for many years a member of the council of elders of the Berlin Jews and played a prominent part in the agitation for emancipation in the years before the 1812 Edict; his mother was a descendant of Jost Liebmann, Court Jew to the Great Elector. When he was a young man Meyerbeer promised his mother that he would never be baptized and he kept his word.[33] However, throughout his career he was excessively sensitive to the social and professional disadvantages of his position. His generation was very aware of frustrated hopes and pettifogging discrimination. His family and many of his co-religionists had enthusiastically supported the campaign against Napoleon; his own brother William had joined up as a volunteer and looked forward to a career as a regular officer in the Prussian army. However, as soon as peace was made, Jews learned that they were to be excluded from the officer corps: they could only become non-commissioned officers. William resigned from the army, and became a wealthy and successful banker, married to one of Berlin's beauties, Dorothea Schlesinger. Meyerbeer always interpreted success or failure of his musical works in terms of his Jewishness, and even at the pinnacle of a truly remarkable career was unable to convince himself that he would not have been an even greater success, had he not been born a Jew. Yet only three years after the first performance of his opera *Robert the Devil* (1829) it was on the repertoire of seventy-seven different theatres; by 1901 his *Huguenots* was performed for the thousandth time in Paris: even Wagner never knew such success.[34] Meyerbeer's achievements as a great composer for the theatre, who satisfied the public's voracious appetite for spectacle, were rewarded by his enjoying an *entrée* into the best society in Europe, whether at Paris, Monte Carlo or Rome. Yet he never lost this basic insecurity, and despite a happy marriage remained a lonely man, subject to intense depressions, which the editor of his letters and diaries attributes to his early experience as a Jew in a hostile environment.[35]

Gabriel Riesser, almost a generation younger than Meyerbeer, knew nothing of the high expectations and dashed hopes of German Jews during the wars of liberation and the Congress of Vienna. However, as a child in Lübeck he had experienced the outbreak of violent anti-Jewish feeling, part of the Hep-Hep (*Hierusalem est perdita*) movement of 1819. His entry into the university teaching staff at Heidelberg was prevented and later his career as a lawyer in Hamburg was checked on the grounds of his Jewishness. An ambitious and realistic man, he did not seek solace, as did the Rhenish Jews Karl Marx and Moses Hess, in challenging the ethical and political foundations of contemporary society, but instead sought to make his a test case and force a change in the law. He refused to be baptized and agitated for a review of the position of public service with regard to the Jews. He founded a controversial publication, with a provocative title, *Der Jude*, in which he not only attacked the constraints on his co-religionists, but also the hypocritical conversions. He took a prominent part in the Frankfurt Parliament, was one of the delegation which offered the imperial crown to the King of Prussia in April 1849. That he eventually succeeded in his efforts on behalf of the Jews and in 1861 became the first Jewish judge in Germany was not only the result of his transparent honesty and the logic of his arguments, but also of the era in which he lived: the temper of the educated classes was progressive in the 1850s and 1860s, though their rulers were not, and a significant body of opinion supported the view that the emancipation and assimilation of German Jews was now but a matter of time. Even Treitschke could be moved to describe Riesser, in conscious contrast with Heine and Börne, as 'a German in the best sense of the world'.

The contrast in the attitude towards the Jews between these years and the so-called Great Depression of the late nineteenth century can be gauged when one considers the career of perhaps the most successful and influential of German Jews in the Second Empire, the banker Gerson Bleichröder (1811–82). Bleichröder's father was one of the many enterprising Jews who came from the provincial towns of Brandenburg to Berlin, in his case from Strousberg, where he had owned a perfumery business.[36] He acted as agent for the Rothschilds and founded a bank, which his son took over in due course. A unique partnership with the founder of the German Empire, Bismarck, brought him unprecedented influence as well as wealth, and he repaid the chancellor by promoting him to be – unknown to the general public – one of the largest landowners and richest men in Germany.[37] Whereas the older generation of bankers, Abraham Mendelssohn from Hamburg, father of Felix the composer, or Meyerbeer's brother William, entertained discreetly if lavishly in their Berlin homes, Bleichröder's *soirées* were famed for their ostentation and panache, and were thoroughly in keeping with the spirit of the *Gründerzeit*. The crash of 1873 had little effect on Bleichröder's fortune and position, though it did greatly encourage envy and resentment on the part of the less successful. One of the most disagreeable features of the social scene at that time, as the acute Marie von Bunsen recorded in her memoirs, was that the German aristocracy, old and new, thronged to the Bleichröder parties, yet could hardly wait until they were on the stairs to criticize everything they had received, and the next morning to apologize for having been seen at the house of a Jew.[38]

All those discussed here – and they are representative, despite their very individual talents, of many thousands of German Jews in this period – belonged by circumstance and achievement to the middle and upper classes of society. In spite of disabilities in the early decades of the century, and discrimination throughout, they were able to acquire the education and also the houses and landed property which befitted their social position. Yet they were only a minority of the half million Jews living in Germany at this time: much more numerous were the poor Jews, small traders and craftsmen living in the eastern provinces, or those who came in the second half of the century to the cities but failed to rise in the world. Their lives are of necessity much less well documented than the famous and prosperous, and, where records do exist, they are concerned mainly with physical conditions of life. The biography of a Jewish teacher from Posen, Moritz Jaffe, born in 1795, which survives in the memoir of his son,[39] is therefore of particular interest for what it has to tell us of the lives of this section of the populace, and also for showing how the process of emancipation affected the fortunes of an individual Jew. Jaffe lived in one of the poorest areas of Prussia and existed throughout his career on or below the poverty line. The Jews of Posen comprised some 6 per cent of the population of the province, but between 30 and 50 per cent in the towns. They were almost all small traders or poor scholars. A Jewish upper class was virtually non-existent here, and a state ban on freedom of movement until 1847 kept all but the most enterprising from leaving home. In religious observance and social customs these Jews were extremely conservative; before the middle of the nineteenth century they knew little of the enlightened ideas which had so profoundly influenced their co-religionists in Berlin or Vienna. If any individual Jew in Posen made a name for himself, it was due to his own efforts or to the rare inspiration of an able teacher. For most, life was a struggle to keep alive and to sustain the communal religious life: there was little time or energy for self-improvement. Jaffe was one of the first teachers to be employed in accordance with the new Prussian regulations of 1824, which made schooling compulsory for Jewish children. He was obliged by the state authorities to submit to a three-day examination at the Bromberg teachers' training college in 1828 to prove that he was fit to teach primary school pupils. Although he failed to pass a number of subjects (including geometry and singing), the lack of qualified Jewish teachers decided the examiners to employ him after all. For the next thirty-five years he taught in various schools of the province, often forced to seek another post after one or two years, because the Jewish communities were often too poor to employ a regular (and pensionable) teacher. His annual salary at the small town of Budzin in 1846 was 110 *taler* a year plus allowances for rent and heating. The contract with the magistrate and school authorities required him to teach the full number of hours laid down by law and, in addition, 'morality' for two hours on a Saturday afternoon. He was also responsible for seeing that his pupils attended the synagogue regularly and behaved themselves when they got there. It throws an odd light on contemporary practices when we learn of a condition of his appointment: 'during teaching hours Herr Jaffe must be fully and properly dressed and must not engage in any other task in the schoolroom, nor eat there or indulge in other improprieties'.[40]

The demands made on Moritz Jaffe and the meagre reward for his services had little to do with the fact that he was a Jew. Primary school teachers were among the worst paid in society: in mid century Germany an elementary school teacher was paid 120–200 *taler,* while a *gendarme,* a sergeant and a prison guard earned between 200 and 225 *taler* a year. But the insecurity of Jaffe's existence was largely the result of social and economic changes in early nineteenth century Germany which had profound consequences for the Jews. He belonged to the generation of poorer Jews just emerging from the ghetto, yet not able to integrate into their Christian, or rather secular, environment. He owed his original appointment to the lack of trained applicants. By the 1840s, the first graduates of the Jewish teachers training college (founded in Berlin in 1840) forced him and his kind out of their posts in the larger towns to seek whatever employment they could find. The Prussian Edicts of 1847 and 1850 giving greater liberties to the Jews had a further adverse effect on Jaffe's career. The Posen Jews were now granted freedom of movement and they immediately began to move to the cities, especially Breslau and Berlin. The opportunities of employment were thus diminished. The Jewish population of Posen declined by almost 50 per cent in the second half of the nineteenth century, though the number of inhabitants as a whole rose by just under a third. Cholera decimated the school children in Wirsitz where Jaffe was teaching in 1855; the Jewish school was closed and he was retired. Furthermore, it was becoming common practice in certain areas for Jewish parents, concerned about their children's material future, to take them away from Jewish schools and send them to the Christian schools where general subjects were usually better taught. Jaffe on his retirement was dependent on his pension of 36 *taler* a year until a Jewish teacher's charitable organization provided a tiny supplement of 50 *taler*. But the insecurity of his career and the poverty of his existence were largely limited to Jaffe's generation. His own son Marcus, born in 1832, was able to get his diploma in the state teachers' training college in Thorn, and on the basis of this to obtain a permanent teaching post in Deutsche-Krone in West Prussia. When Marcus Jaffe retired in 1899 the local paper described the ceremony at length and mentioned the names of the mayor, the district school inspector and the rector as among those present. But by that date the Jews were commonly assumed to have been successfully integrated into German society.

The story of the German Jews in the years between the end of the Empire and the First World War is on the whole one of remarkable achievement. From being a barely tolerated minority of which a few, a very few, aspired successfully to share the life of the upper classes, they had penetrated all ranks of society. In the late nineteenth century Jews appeared at public functions and court balls; a few, notably Emil and Walther Rathenau, father and son, and particularly Albert Ballin, the head of the Hamburg-Amerika shipping line, and an unbaptized Jew, were on good, even intimate terms with the Kaiser himself. They were represented in, and in some cases dominated, the most important branches of German industrial society. Their sons and especially their daughters were sought after as marriage partners by members of the élite of society. The upward social mobility of some Jewish families was as rapid as it was remarkable, occurring in a European rather than merely a German context. Thus of Heine's family, one brother, Gustav, became a Catholic and an officer in the Austrian cavalry; he had a knighthood conferred on him in 1867, a baronetcy three years later, and he owned several estates. Marriage linked him with several members of the Austro-Hungarian nobility and he died a millionaire. A further brother, Maximilian, studied medicine and entered the Russian service, and was also ennobled, while their sister, who married a Hamburg banker, saw her son made a baron and her two daughters marry Italian princes.[41] Heine's father had been in the textile trade, on a modest scale. Of Meyerbeer's three daughters, two married noblemen (one became the mother of the poet Leopold Andrian, last director of the imperial court theatre), while the son of the third was made a member of the hereditary German nobility. The motive behind such marriages and granting of titles was blatant: money was needed to save the estates of many an impoverished aristocrat. The authorities, despite their ingrained prejudice against the Jews, gave their blessing to an institution which offered to salvage the traditional ruling class, particularly in Prussia. Most wealthy Jews accepted with alacrity, and it was distinctly unusual when Moritz Warburg, senior partner of M. M. Warburg & Co. of Hamburg, refused to become a member of the hereditary nobility in the 1880s, commenting, with a telling mixture of Jewish wit and

Hanseatic self-assurance: 'But I preferred to keep my kosher three millions for myself.'[42]

The social success of individual Jews was perhaps less noteworthy than the scale of their contribution to German cultural and political life. They made outstanding contributions to higher learning in a variety of fields, both as scholars and as teachers. In the decades before 1914 (and for twenty-five further years) their most signal achievements lay perhaps in fundamental science and medicine, among other branches notably neurology, psychiatry and pediatrics, and psychoanalysis.[43] As patrons of the arts and publishers they played an important role in the cultural life of their country; for members of the artistic community, and for scholars, Jewish drawing rooms in the larger cities were important meeting places; in the Viennese home of Josephine von Wertheimstein, a descendant of the Habsburg Court Jew Wertheimer, the Jewish salon of the late eighteenth century experienced a splendid revival. Most people, however, chose to disregard such things: they were much more conscious of the particular role of German Jews in parliament and the press; it was this which conditioned the attitude of the authorities and the average burgher to them in the years before the Great War. It was almost inevitable that their parliamentary allegiance should be mostly to the liberal parties, or to the socialists. Well-to-do Jews did not, in general, subscribe to the process characteristic of the German bourgeoisie under the Empire, the so-called feudalization of the middle class. Emancipation had been the fruit of liberal political policies, and even when from the 1880s these had begun to be regarded with some suspicion in Germany, the Jews retained their belief in the necessity and the inevitability of liberalization of society and state in the future. Even more than their support of the progressive parties, Jewish domination of the liberal press, particularly the activities of individual journalists, such as Maximilian Harden of *Die Zukunft,* aroused strongly voiced resentment against the Jews in pre-war Germany and Austria. The satirist Harden, as his former admirer, the Viennese Jewish journalist Karl Kraus, acidly observed on many occasions, was responsible for provoking widespread antisemitic feeling by his calculated and often venomous attacks on cherished establishment values and personalities. Germany, unlike Austria, had no native satiric tradition; people did not understand political satire and they did not like it. To criticize the establishment and what passed as bourgeois values even in a constructive manner was thought reprehensible; how much worse to make jokes about something as serious as the new German nation. The activities of the politically articulate Jews in both Germany and Austria thus confirmed the authorities and the citizens generally in their inherited dislike of minorities in general and the Jews in particular. Thus in the last years of the monarchy it was the unthinking and widespread acceptance of a stereotype image of the Jew, which, more than anything else, kept him as a separate and easily recognizable element in that society in which he lived and of which he felt himself an integral part.

Chapter 18
Artisans and small traders

The first half of the nineteenth century brought profound changes to the artisans and small traders as a group. These changes were by no means uniform, nor did they occur in all branches or all regions at the same period. In consequence it was some time before the economic and social reality of their situation was reflected in their status in the community and in the regard their members enjoyed in the public mind. Despite a general if sporadic liberalization of the trading laws, which had an adverse effect on the economic situation of the majority of these people, their social attitudes and habits of mind continued to be very similar to those of the more fortunate sections of the middle class. Up to the 1840s it was still possible to speak of a common culture linking such different groups as the artisans and the teachers, state officials in small communities and rural clergymen. For many artisans, the desire for education and culture brought them into contact with what could be termed the academic classes. Literature and music, enjoyed in their own homes or in the small circles, which are typical of the Biedermeier era, offered them reassurance as to their continued membership of the burgher class, despite the pauperization of many of their members. The possession of books and musical instruments was more than a status symbol; they answered a genuine need, and belonged to the tradition of artisan culture.[1] Ludwig Tieck illustrated this point in his story, *Der junge Tischlermeister* (1836), which is an interesting document, both for what it has to say about artisan attitudes (Tieck of course was the son of an artisan) and for the way the terms referring to status and social aspirations recur in writings by and about artisans down to the time of the Weimar Republic.[2] Leonhard, the young cabinetmaker, and his wife set great store on the ritual quality of their lives, on modest but aesthetically pleasing household appointments; their relationship with the apprentices is thoroughly paternalistic. At one point Leonhard tries to explain to a well-born friend why he chose to be a craftsman. His words are sententious, but they assume the speaker to be part of the cultivated middle class: 'I have always felt elevated by man's instinct to want things that are in daily use to be both functional and beautiful: thus a rich man or an educated man will want nothing in his home which has not been transformed into something higher by the addition of ornament.'[3]

Contemporary painters, of whose work there are many examples in south German museums, recorded the likeness of local artisans, dressed in their Sunday best and accompanied by their families. There is nothing in the dress of these people to distinguish them from members of more prestigious occupations in the middle class.[4] A fundamental feature of the whole burgher estate was described by K. A. M. Schlegel, brother of the Romantic writers, in 1817: it was, he averred, having or being able to earn enough to meet basic necessities, plus a little more – in short it meant a state of moderate prosperity.[5]

He was quite correct. The basis of social cohesion within the burgher class was indeed at least a modest provision. The economic crises of the Restoration era (1815–48) were selective in their targets, but the collective effect was to destroy that social cohesion. Contemporaries' awareness of what was happening can be remarked in the increasing use of a special term to describe those members of the burgher class who were the victims rather than the beneficiaries of economic and social change – namely, *Mittelstand.* The term was not new; it had been used occasionally in the seventeenth century and in the following one had come to be applied to those who were neither noble or '*Volk*'. By the time of the 1848 revolution the emotive nature of the word *Mittelstand* was already in evidence: this was to remain its characteristic as late as the Third *Reich.* Both Marx and Bismarck used it in the same sense in the late 1840s, the former in the Communist Manifesto: 'Those who up to now were members of the middle estate, the small industrialists, merchants and rentiers, the artisans and farmers, are sinking into the proletariat'[6]; Bismarck, speaking in the Second Chamber of the Diet, declared that artisans were the very 'heart' of the *Mittelstand,* 'so necessary for the life of the state that the sacrifices demanded [for its protection] shall not be considered too high.'[7]

Marx's interest in the artisan class was a scientific one, but Bismarck's views were much more representative of contemporary attitudes, especially of those in authority. The concern he expressed was based on the assumption that property was the source of political morality, of 'good citizenship', binding men together in spite of their many differences. People appreciated the connection between the political and social situations, particularly having become aware in the 1830s and 1840s of the declining number of those who could acquire or afford to maintain property.[8] The ever-increasing numbers of skilled artisans who failed to establish themselves as masters in these years, the pauperization of tradesmen of all kinds in the 1840s, were eloquent witness to the widespread decay of the property-owning class. The years before the outbreak of the revolution saw many petitions to state governments and town councils, as well as a host of treatises and tracts from the pens of politicians and officials, philanthropists and academics, on the causes, the state and the grave social and political consequences of the decline of craftsmen and traders.[9] The extent to which anxiety about their future led them to offer support to the revolution, at least in the early stages, is beginning to be documented for other parts of Germany besides Prussia.[10]

The artisans took an active part in the revolution, but, although there were a number of radical figures among them, the majority supported it in the belief that the liberal reform programme offered the best chance of a solution to their many problems. The years prior to the outbreak had witnessed a growth in political awareness among those not normally noted for their political interests. R. M. Bigler, in his recent work on the Prussian Protestant church in the Restoration era, has shown with what lively interest artisans and their womenfolk attended mass meetings of liberal preachers. Such occasions offered the opportunity to exchange views, ostensibly on religious matters, in which many artisans were deeply interested, but also to articulate hopes and fears about the present situation. The journeymen, who travelled across Europe in these years, provided links between members of their trades in different parts of the country, and acted as sources of information in provincial Germany about what was going on in the big world.

The serious economic situation of many artisans was a major cause of revolution, but an important psychological cause was their growing sense of division within their own ranks. Many were conscious that their burgher status was under attack; others felt a sense of solidarity with the working man and hoped that a new liberal government would lend its support to improving and safeguarding his livelihood. As the former theology student, the revolutionary leader Gottfried Kinkel, put it: 'Half the artisans belong to the bourgeoisie ... the other half sends its children to the poor house and lives a mean and miserable life on its daily earnings.'[11] For the journeymen, the facts that the masters were putting obstacles in the way of entry to their ranks, and that masters' daughters were now reluctant to become engaged to journeymen, brought home to them the seriousness of their position. In his topical *Die drei gerechten Kammacher* (published 1856), Gottfried Keller described in grotesquely humorous terms the pursuit of the 'mistress' by three penniless journeymen. From the first, journeymen took a prominent part in revolutionary activity in 1848: of some 230 people killed in the street fighting in Berlin in March, 40 per cent were journeymen.[12] The following months saw dedicated and energetic men from their ranks working, often with bourgeois intellectuals, to improve the lot of their fellows. Their activities usually took the form of instituting working men's associations (generally for educational and not political purposes), sending petitions to the assemblies, and organizing congresses and strikes. One of the best known of the artisan leaders was Stephan Born, who came from Lissa in Posen and was the son of a Jewish broker called Buttermilch. Although his family had once been reasonably prosperous, they had fallen on hard times, and Born had been apprenticed to the printing trade. Typical of his kind, he was determined to improve himself, and attended lectures at Berlin University during his lunch hour. He went to Paris as a journeyman in 1846, where he met Engels, and departed on a proselytizing tour to Lyons and Switzerland on behalf of the Communist League. He then went to meet Marx at Brussels and worked there with him. Despite his sympathy for Marx's ideas, his own practical nature, and the humane and moralistic tradition of the German artisan caused him to distance himself from him. His practical ability was in evidence when he organized a successful printing workers' strike in April 1848 in Berlin; he was also active in helping to set up working men's associations in different parts of the country. He came to share the belief of most German artisans involved in 1848 that self-help in the form of organization, and government aid, not violence and radical solutions, offered the best hope for the working man.

Initially most artisans – masters and journeymen alike – had faith in parliament and constitutions to achieve their aims for them, and they hoped to formulate these aims for submission to the Frankfurt Parliament at the artisans' congresses of the summer of 1848. However, the course of events demonstrated that their confidence was misplaced. Moreover, the summer months brought home to the journeymen that their interests were not the same as those of the masters. The Journeymen's Congress in Frankfurt and the All German Workers Congress at Berlin aimed at nationwide organizations of workers: this was an implicit rejection of the guild system which the masters, attending the Artisans Congress at Frankfurt, wanted to see restored. The masters meanwhile were growing anxious lest the journeymen and the non-guild workers become too powerful. In fact the split between the two groups was the chief cause of the failure of the working men's movement in 1848 and the disappearance of their associations in 1849. Yet despite their failure, the organizational efforts of German artisans in 1848–9 anticipated the future form of labour organization in Germany, while the congresses of individual trades, such as the cigar makers (who incidentally held the first nationwide strike in German history in 1848) or the printers and tailors, represent the beginning of modern trade unionism in that country.[13]

The discussion about the fate of the artisans as a class continued on well into the twentieth century; the interest of the *Verein für Sozialpolitik,* and the survey undertaken by the economist Schmoller in the 1890s, gave an important stimulus to it. In the second half of the nineteenth century the term *Bürgertum* could no longer be applied in any meaningful way to all sections of the 'middle classes', but only to the upper strata. It was then that the artisan began to be represented in the speeches of conservative politicians and many popular writers as a type of ideal burgher, whom the impersonal machine of economic progress was crushing inexorably. The way of life of the artisan and his culture was invested with moral values by those who did not belong to his social stratum, and it became fashionable to contrast these values with the materialism and the disharmony of present society. The nostalgia for that happy state, that golden age, when the artisan was master in his house, was exploited by writers and publishers. Novels and tales of medieval and early modern guildsmen, and of small town life, enjoyed very considerable popularity. The picture of artisan life, as found in the *Deutsche Lebensbilder* of Fanny Lewald, or in Scheffel's work, to mention but two popular writers, in the paintings of Spitteler and Schwind, or the serials in family magazines, could not have withstood the test of confrontation with reality, but this was either unknown or disregarded, by artist and public.[14] A different form of nostalgia for past and more 'wholesome' times was the vogue for artisans' memoirs in the late nineteenth century, and again after the defeat of Germany in 1918. Former artisans, most of them elderly men when they wrote, and enjoying often very different positions than their social origins might seem to have destined them for, recorded their memories of a bygone age. Amateur and professional historians delved into second-hand book shops and into archives to discover and edit forgotten or unknown earlier works of this kind. While many authors recalled the deprivations they had suffered, most shared the sentiments of Karl Scheffler, the art critic, who spoke of the artisan's life in terms reminiscent of Zelter's father: 'In the exercise of a craft, all contradictions are overcome. The craftsman's work requires thought and skill, it is the least one-sided of all professions. The man who practises his craft has a sense of perspective, he is not tempted to extremes of one kind or another; his is the work of the golden mean, equally removed from wealth or poverty, from arrogance or faint-heartedness.' Such sentiments – and they were common ones – tell us more about the attitudes of Germans living at the end of the nineteenth century than they do of the artisan in the industrial age. For to an increasing number of Germans, disorientated by the speed of change, the artisan was a symbol of belonging, to a community, to a regional world. The artisan's life, Scheffler went on, is one 'which engenders a sense of home, in a way no other way of life does'. The ideal type of burgher, unlike his counterpart in Wilhelmine Germany, was alleged to have an unquestioned sense of identity, of '*Heimat*'.[15]

Behind the mid century concern about their future and the later nostalgia about their 'golden' past, lay certain economic facts. In what ways had industrialization affected their lives?

Long before the beginning of the nineteenth century, it was clear that the corporative organizations of artisans had lost most of their legal and economic powers to the state. However, the guilds and the associations of apprentices still exercised an important social function in caring for their members and giving them a sense of corporate solidarity. Yet by no means all branches of trade were organized in guilds, nor were all members of any one trade or craft under the authority of the guild; thus in Vienna in 1734 only one third of the local masters were members.[16] Moreover the word 'guild' in English is used to render a variety of institutions with different meanings and different local applications. The strict rules and prohibitions, such as the ban on rural crafts, were no longer effective in many places by the late eighteenth century, though where business was bad, the masters operated a closed shop and many competent journeymen had little hope of establishing themselves. As the authorities on the subject of artisan life remind us, it is hazardous to make general statements about the period before reliable statistics are available. However, an overall trend seems clear: the restrictive character of guild organization in Germany on the eve of the nineteenth century was much more in evidence than its function to promote the general welfare of the artisan class. Instead of the customary three to six years 'wandering' prior to setting up a permanent business, we learn of journeymen moving about for half a lifetime. It has been said that the main effect of the guild system for a substantial percentage of the artisans, was that it depressed them legally, economically and socially.[17]

The state had already begun to intervene in the relationship of the guild masters and the apprentices before 1800, ostensibly to succour the victims of oppression. In fact such efforts were part of a larger programme designed to bring the whole of society under the authority of the state, and also to increase revenue. The liberalization of trade, introduced by several state governments in the first half of the nineteenth century, was part of the same approach. The guild system, the manorial system and serfdom, were part of the inherited social structure. The introduction of freedom of trade (*Gewerbefreiheit*), as of peasant emancipation, was bound to bring about major social change. It was the source of much bitter petitioning of governments in the 1840s and it occupied a large part of the debates during the Artisans Congress in Frankfurt in 1848. But neither the legislation nor the expected social consequences happened overnight. Nowhere is the regional diversity of Germany more apparent than in this area: different time scales operated in different districts, and even within the branches of one trade. Thus in the early 1850s over 1000 men were employed in the Borsig works at Berlin, many of them former artisans from the metal workers guild; at the same time master craftsmen in the small towns of Württemberg were shaking their heads and discussing well-tried methods of getting rid of '*Bönhasen*' (ground rabbits) and '*Pfuscher*' (botchers), names given to those artisans who pursue their calling without being guild members.[18] In south German states the master craftsman, whatever his income, was a person of consequence in his community, entitled, as he and his fellow citizens believed, to respect and economic protection, on the grounds that his class provided order and stability in society. In north Germany, where industrialization occurred much earlier, in the textile towns of Westphalia, in Berlin, or along the new railway lines, there were numerous artisans employed, who had been unable to meet competition from machinery, or who had been unwilling to submit to the traditional discipline of a trade, which seemed to offer neither financial reward, status or freedom.[19]

The introduction of freedom of trade had no immediate or sweeping effect for two main reasons: the first was that it was introduced piecemeal, withdrawn or modified within a few years, because of the opposition it had aroused, or because the consequences proved harmful to those it was designed to aid. In Austria, Saxony and south Germany, it did not come until the 1860s, although the restrictions operating were being widely ignored in practice. Prussia introduced it in 1810, as part of the liberal reform. Yet even here there were many anomalies: it was brought into East Prussia in 1806, and to Lithuania in 1808; the Edict of 2 November 1810 applied to the whole country, but it was not extended to cover those provinces reconquered or acquired in 1813–15. In most of the Rhineland complete freedom of trade had existed since the French occupation in the 1790s, in Westphalia from 1808–10 onwards; in 1815 this was no longer to apply. Oldenburg, Hanover and Hesse, also formerly under French rule, lost in 1815–16 the freedom of trade they had enjoyed. A number of state governments, such as the Bavarian, merely forbade masters to exclude qualified craftsmen, but did not abolish the examination conducted by the masters which was a condition of entry. It was thus easy to exclude potential business rivals by failing the candidates. Police permission in areas where freedom was legal was often withheld from would-be settlers to protect the local craftsmen. Wolfram Fischer, a leading authority in this field, summarizes the complex picture: 'Characteristic of the legal position of the German artisan in the first half of the nineteenth century is a constant to-ing and fro-ing between abolition and reintroduction of the guilds, of weakening and strengthening their privileges.'[20] The second reason for the lack of impact of liberal legislation was that it was frequently simply an acknowledgement of current practice. In Saxony as late as 1861 artisans were forbidden to set up in rural areas. Yet evidence proves that between 1849 and 1861 more artisans were actually working in rural areas than in the towns.[21]

The craftmen's centuries-old monopoly of trade, in theory if not always in practice, made them blame the liberal measures for economic hardship. In fact the removal of restrictions on trading in the first half of the nineteenth century was more effect than cause of economic dislocation. The rapid rise of the population, which in Prussia alone had increased by 50 per cent between 1816 and 1843, had not been accompanied by an increase in food resources. The artisan population had increased most of all, masters in Prussia by 80 per cent, artisans by 120 per cent in the same period.[22] Certain trades were hopelessly oversubscribed and demand was falling. This was particularly acute in the textile trades, where machinery was first introduced and English competition was keenest. In general the increase in artisan population occurred before industrialization had got going, often as a result of an influx into their ranks of workers from domestic manufacture, who belonged to the lower orders of society. It was these people who were to be effectively absorbed into industry in large numbers in the second half of the century. In the 1830s and 1840s, however, there was as yet too little need for their services. Writers on the 'social question' and the authors of petitions and protests from the ranks of impoverished artisans condemned the machines as the villain of the piece, as the cause of destitution in so many regions of Germany. Many philanthropists and state officials, such as the Swabian lawyer Robert von Mohl, accepted mass production as something economically advantageous, but considered the social consequences a disaster for 'the workers themselves, and for the prosperity and security of the whole of bourgeois society'.[23]

Other writers during the 'Hungry Forties' tried to bring home to readers the scale of human suffering among artisans by comparing their situation with the horrors in Ireland. The fear of revolution as a consequence of such social dislocation was uppermost in commentators' minds, before it actually occurred; when it did break out, it is not surprising that so many of the master craftsmen believed a return to the old restrictive system would eradicate both social and economic ills.

The situation of the artisans as a whole was much more differentiated than they or contemporary observers could appreciate. The harrowing accounts of the plight of some trades and regions, such as the moving account of conditions in Silesia by Wilhelm Wolff, *Das Elend und der Aufruhr in Schlesien* (1845), were by no means fanciful. Less widespread in effect, but equally worrying for the future, were the conditions of the stocking weavers in Franconia, and the tailors and shoemakers in many areas, who had hitherto enjoyed a steady local demand, and were now being threatened by machine-produced goods from at home and outside. Machinery was already beginning to erode local autarky in many regions by mid century; even apart from their lower price, machine-made goods had the attraction of novelty. Competition in the local market was made possible by the rapid development of transport in the 1840s and 1850s. This was all the more striking by contrast with the proverbially bad state of German road and river communications a few decades earlier. The years after the Napoleonic wars had seen gradual, then sudden improvement. A series of river acts abolished the heavy dues levied on the Rhine, Elbe and Weser, which facilitated the movement of goods. The Prussian government began a road-building programme, which reached a total of 12 888 km in 1837 and 28 000 km in 1862, while the railway network, begun in 1835, reached 18 600 km by 1870.[24] Moreover, the Customs Union of 1834 reduced the toll payable on highways, promoting the movement of goods and of people. Manufactured goods began to be sold in areas where people had always bought from the local tradesman only. In the 1850s the Berlin-based ready-made clothing began to expand into a highly organized and lucrative business. It employed large numbers of women and former domestic workers and took work from tailors all over the country. Alternative employment in the form of piece work was poorly paid and was felt to be humiliating by the artisans. Paul Ernst recalls in his vivid memoirs how a cabinetmaker in his native Elbingerode, obliged to work for the local factory and produce what he regarded as inferior goods, hanged himself in his own workshop for 'betraying his craft'.[25]

But there were many trades where skilled men were in demand, such as the metal industry, and in the second half of the century the food industry; later still, when the mass market was well established, a demand arose for what was known as *Kunsthandwerk* (arts and crafts). The increased national income in the late nineteenth century created a demand for specially commissioned articles by skilled craftsmen, especially in the leather and fashion trades. In the middle of the century a number of artisans rose to be foremen, some even entrepreneurs. Masters with enterprise expanded their workshops to provide the kind of repair work which industry did not provide, or, as in the electrical industry later on, artisans were employed to install and service the products of industry. The number of artisans employed in factories grew steadily in the period of take-off in the 1850s and 1860s. In Prussia in 1846 they numbered 4 per cent of the total employed, in 1867 it was as many as 10 per cent.[26] However, those who had neither the skills nor the character to adapt themselves, especially those from rural regions, drifted from one menial task to another, content to have a roof over their head, but unable to do more than earn enough to keep body and soul together.

The handcraft trade, then, was not destroyed by industrialization, but learned after initial losses and setbacks, to exist alongside it. The artisans often suffered the greatest deprivation in regions where there was little industry, such as Silesia in mid century. In Saxony, by contrast, the state with the largest artisan population and the one where industrialization was most rapid, they accommodated themselves to the changed economic situation, finding alternative employment if their particular skill was no longer in demand because of mass-produced goods, or developing new skills. Moreover, as German households changed to being consumer organizations, buying the goods they had once produced, artisans found a demand for their services in the home, a development reflected in the contemporary meaning of the term *Handwerker*.[27]

In the early phase of industrialization, artisans had associated factory workers with deprived or asocial elements, regarding the need to earn a living there as personally and collectively degrading; by the late 1850s and early 1860s, skilled artisans in industry were beginning to see themselves as an élite. By the 1870s the majority were identifying themselves with the other wage labourers, and were to provide some of the most able leaders of the socialist movement. August Bebel was by trade a turner, and had pursued his training as a journeyman apprentice in many parts of Germany in the 1850s,[28] Friedrich Ebert, secretary of the party in the early 1900s and later President of the Weimar Republic, had been a saddler. The artisan tradition of self-help and self-improvement survived and found a new outlet in the labour movement. Moreover, the experiences gained as journeymen in their young days, gave the leaders of the movement knowledge and insight into conditions in other parts of the country, and horizons beyond their own locality and class.[29]

Wilhelm Wernet, one of the leading historians of the artisan movement in Germany, suggests that there are three stages in its history from the late eighteenth century to the present time: 1780–1840 was, in his view, a time of stagnation, 1840–1900 one of change and gradual accommodation, and the third stage, 1900 to the present, one of evolution, despite setbacks and crises.[30] During the second period the artisans believed they were doomed. Between 1861 and 1895 the population of Germany rose by 38 per cent, the masters by 30 per cent. Whole groups of artisans dwindled or disappeared – dyers, bleachers, spinners and weavers foremost among them. One-man concerns declined in the period 1882–95 by 13·5 per cent, in 1897–1907 by 19·6 per cent, while firms with more than fifty employees rose by 89·2 per cent in the first, 61·8 per cent in the second period.[31] However, by 1900 it was becoming clear that the trend towards ever-larger industrial concerns was not an absolute one, and that there was indeed a continuing need for the small craftsman too. The discovery of the electric motor in the 1890s played a vital role in helping artisans to adapt to the new conditions: they now could use a large variety of tools. Schmoller, who in the late nineteenth century had prophesied the disappearance of the craftsman, was forced to modify his views later. The sociologist Th. Geiger could state in 1932, despite the current sense of victimization among such people, that 'No one, unless he wants to make himself ridiculous, speaks any more about the disappearance of craftsmen and small traders.'[32]

The German artisan had been forced in the nineteenth century to share the 'cake' with a new class of industrial workers and others. By the end of the century the 'cake' had vastly increased in size, and it was clear to pragmatic observers, such as the Prussian statisticians Viebahn and Engel, that there was a share for both industry and craft. Yet a strong sense of loss of status remained with the artisans and those of a similar background and life style, the shopkeepers and small traders. They felt close to another somewhat disgruntled section of society, the subaltern officials and the clerical workers in industry, who were anxious about their status and whose pay and prospects were often less good than those of people whom they looked on as their social inferiors. Both groups resented the pressures on them to accommodate to an industrial society, with which they had little sympathy. The psychological support given them in the Empire by the state authorities, because of their conservatism, only nurtured their sense of being hard done by the modern world, which an objective comparison between their standard of living in 1900 and that of their kind a century earlier would scarcely have justified. Political developments under the Second Empire had an important bearing on the outlook of these groups, now known as the 'old' (artisans and traders) and the 'new' *Mittelstand* (white collar workers at subaltern levels). They felt they could not succeed in joining the 'bourgeoisie' but they felt threatened by the growth and particularly the organization of the labouring classes, with their energetic and charismatic leaders. The authors of the so-called *Sammlungspolitik* in the last years of the century, the Prussian Finance Minister Miquel and his associates, appealed to them for support in their attempt to broaden the basis of conservatism. The imperial 'cartel of fear', as the conservative alliance of big business and agrarian capitalism was called, needed the numerical strength which the *Mittelstand* could supply. Their spokesmen were prepared to offer a price in return for support – the protectionist crafts law of 1897 was one such price.

Such appeals were the more successful since the small traders had neither political party nor spokesmen of their own. In the first half of the century they had been genuinely open to liberal and national ideas, although probably unaware of the implications of these for their own position. In many ways 1848 had been a watershed for them. Many enterprising artisans and traders had emigrated to the United States; others left their traditional way of life for industry in the following years; those who remained, especially if they were not prosperous, felt a sense of group solidarity as victims of social change. In fact – and this was to be a salient characteristic of these groups up to the 1930s – their sense of victimization was not wholly justified. It was understandable that they should feel this way, since in the artisan tradition the weak were entitled to expect protection, and the strong were restricted. This was now no longer accepted, and those whose living standards had declined, and particularly those affected by the crash of 1873, blamed their lack of credit facilities on others. Because they had no party or leader of their own, they were susceptible to radical agitators who could 'identify' their 'enemies' for them. One such figure was Adolf Stöcker, who initially set himself the task of converting the urban wage labourers from socialism to Christianity. Unsuccessful here, he discovered that he could draw heady support from shopkeepers and artisans on a platform of antisemitism. Contemporaries recorded the impact of Stöcker's speech in 1876, of the chanting chorus from the audience in answer to his repeated questions, who was responsible for present ills, and the answer came back each time: 'the Jews!'[33] Stöcker was a man with unconscious demagogic powers, and techniques which Goebbels would use with even greater instinctive skill a half a century later. For his audiences, in the brief decade and half of his notoriety, it was less his programme – if he had one at all – than his charismatic presence and well-timed attacks on the Jews. Stöcker's ability to make the resentful members of the *Mittelstand* see socialism as part of the general Jewish takeover of the economy was possible because of their inherited dislike of the Jewish pedlar or shopkeeper who, back in their former homes in villages and country towns, had 'undercut' the 'burgher' tradesman. In the decades after 1873 the Jew became for the tradesman, as for the bourgeois intellectual and the rural landowner, a symbol of modernity and change, of that progress which recent events had made seem illusory.

The sense of being hard done by stayed with the majority of small tradesmen from the 1870s to the Third Reich. However, from the 1890s to the time of the war, the appeals for support from the conservative parties and pressure groups gave them a sense of belonging to what was known as the '*staatserhaltende Kräfte*', the pillars of state and society. They began to give their support to organizations of social imperial policy such as the Navy League or the Pan-German League; a number emulated the economic interest groups of other classes by setting up organizations such as the Shop Assistants Association. Common to all of them was a belief that their loyalty to the authoritarian order entitled them to special treatment, at least to the right to a status distinct from and above the labouring classes, and therefore to the means to retain it.

Section 3
Rural life and its problems

Chapter 19
The peasantry and rural labourers

One of the most important changes in the social structure of Germany around the turn of the eighteenth to nineteenth century affected the peasantry. This change was preceded and conditioned by a large number of works on the subject of 'economy', as the cultivation of land was then called, and on the present needs of rural inhabitants. They were mainly of two kinds: learned tracts, pamphlets and articles, or works of poetry and fiction. They were aimed at the educated reading public, were thoroughly didactic in tone and intention, and dealt with such diverse matters as controversial farming methods, legal tenure and the rural social structure. The body of opinion expressed in these writings helped to create a new climate of opinion favourable to the peasant, and to channel energies into an impressive agrarian reform programme.[1]

The second half of the eighteenth century had been a time of rising agricultural prices. Favourable opportunities for farmers existed in many regions of Germany, as for example in Schleswig-Holstein, where the peasants were emancipated as early as 1780 under enlightened conditions, favourable both to landlord and tenant. In general, however, the condition of the peasant was not an enviable one. To the majority of those who bothered to think about him at that time, he was a brutish creature, by his very nature destined to remain so. The picture of the witless tiller of the soil, animated by low cunning, but an easy dupe of his social superiors, persisted long into the age of reason. It was logical, therefore, that one of the abuses most resented by the peasants, the indiscriminate damage wreaked on agricultural land by the hunting gentry, was deemed hardly worthy of comment by them, since it was mere peasant land. Rousseau was one of the first to try and show that the peasant was not constitutionally ignorant and base, but that he was the product of conditions in which he was condemned to live. The peasant, he wrote in *Emile* (1761), lived like an automaton, ceaselessly occupied with repetitive tasks; he was therefore governed by custom and obedience, not by reason. Gradually the interest in educational reform characteristic of the German Enlightenment began to benefit the peasant. This process was stimulated by a much more positive image of rural life, depicted in the works of a number of Swiss and German poets, already mentioned in an earlier chapter. The peasant began to feature in the numerous discussions of social evils by enlightened publicists or those who merely wished to seem so. The very simplicity of his life made him a useful weapon in the arsenal of those who criticized vice and extravagance at princely courts and other high places. Schubart, owner of the best-known model farm in Germany and a controversial pamphleteer, wrote angrily in 1783: 'These people, however, are looked upon as if they had different bodies, different souls, different blood than those to whom a prince (also a mortal human being like others) has given rank and title.'[2]

Others, such as the generous-minded reforming landowner von Rochow, believed that education must help the peasant to learn good methods of husbandry and so contribute to solving the problems of rural overpopulation and meeting the needs of the state at large. Extraordinarily diverse in its influence, inspiring imitators far beyond its author's native Switzerland, was Pestalozzi's novel *Lienhard und Gertrud*, published in the same year as Rousseau's *Emile*, 1761. It was didactic and simplistic, peopled with archvillains and weak sinners; its heroes were a strong and loving wife, a reformed husband and a kindly paternal landlord, and it satisfied its readers with a happy and moral ending. *Lienhard und Gertrud* succeeded in persuading an admiring public that very many of the ills of village life were only due to ignorance. The bonds of drunkenness and ignorance have held Lienhard in thrall for many years and endangered his family; his valiant wife appeals to the landlord, who is astonished to hear of the blackmail and threats perpetrated in his name; with his support, Lienhard and Gertrud work to educate themselves and their neighbours in a moral life of thrift and hard work, and eventually bring prosperity to the village. Pestalozzi had many imitators over the next half century. They wrote for a growing rural reading public as well as the educated. Specific abuses were made the subject of novels and stories, as for example in the works of the altruistic Heinrich Zschokke, an unusually prolific writer, who settled in Switzerland after an active political life in Germany. His short novel *Die Branntweinpest* (1836) drew attention to the evils of rural alcoholism, and came as a shock to readers quite unaware of the widespread misery and physical suffering caused by the disease. By Zschokke's time, the village tale had already established itself as an independent literary genre. The social compass of its readership showed how far the image of the peasant had progressed since the middle of the eighteenth century. However low the literary level of such stories might have been, they enjoyed a remarkable vogue and did much to establish in the public mind the notion of the peasant as a citizen in his own right, with duties and privileges equal to the rest of society.

Such a concept was central to those state officials in many parts of Germany, but most notably in Prussia, who brought dedication and an extensive knowledge of the subject to their work of reforming agricultural tenure and social relationships on the land. The formative influences on their views included Rousseau, Pestalozzi and Adam Smith. Many were animated by a bias against the privileged nobility, especially in their relationship to their peasants. The reformers felt that such privileges were unjustified by any present function the nobility might claim to perform in the state. The forthright advocacy of peasant proprietorship of the soil, which we find in the works of eighteenth century Germans, such as Justus Möser of Osnabrück, or those of the Swabian Fr Carl von Moser or the Saxon Schubart, seemed to many a viable alternative to the inherited rural social structure. Admittedly these men wrote about areas in which agricultural conditions were reasonably good, and the peasantry did not labour under the onerous burdens typical of other regions, such as East Prussia, many of the crown lands of Austria and parts of south-east Germany. However, the cause was taken up in the late eighteenth century by officials concerned with the emancipation of servile peasants in just these areas, as well as in Baden and Schleswig-Holstein, and was given a warm welcome by advocates of economic and fiscal reform. Such a man was the influential cameralist, J. G. von Justi, who had been employed by the Saxon and Austrian courts, who had taught at Göttingen, Hamburg and Berlin, and who believed peasant proprietorship would increase production and state revenue. The enlightened philosopher and statesman, Josef von Sonnenfels, confidant of the Empress Maria Theresa, had gone so far as to advocate breaking up the great estates into small holdings to support increased population. By the end of the century educated people were keenly interested in agriculture; some idea of their concern with the practical side of the problem can be gauged from the sheer volume of works on the many aspects of agriculture and rural life: Benedikt Weber, professor at Breslau, published in 1809 a *Handbuch der ökonomischen Literatur*, a bibliography of such works; it contained some 6000 titles, 231 of them practical manuals on husbandry.[3] The years preceding the Prussian agrarian reform measures of the Stein-Hardenberg era were characterized by an intense preoccupation with agrarian matters. The tempestuous and prolific professor of philosophy, history and 'statistics' at Göttingen, August Ludwig Schlözer, editor of the eighteen volume *Staatsanzeigen* (1783–93), scarcely allowed a single issue to appear without some reference to the question. 'Eventually a dissertation on turnip culture almost had to end with a peroration on the evils of the agrarian social structure.'[4]

However, efforts on the part of individual rulers in the eighteenth century, such as Frederick II, to come to grips with the deep-seated problem of agriculture, had failed because of the rigidity of the social structure and the vested interests of the landowning nobility in keeping it so. In the early years of the new century it became clear to a number of educated and energetic state officials, who were not themselves landowners as their predecessors had been, that it was insufficient merely to advocate improved techniques of farming; they must introduce major legal and social reforms, one of which was peasant emancipation. It was at Göttingen that many of the key personalities concerned in the Prussian reform had developed their future policies. Göttingen University, so incisive yet so diverse in its influence on German public life, had also among its professors Pütter and Sartorius, who in the 1780s introduced some of their ablest pupils to the works of Adam Smith. These pupils included Albrecht von Thaer, author of the pioneering manual of modern farming, *Handbuch der rationalen Landwirtschaft* (Berlin 1809), and founder of a model farm, Baron Stein and his successor at the ministry, von Hardenberg. Stein's own copy of the *Wealth of Nations*, which has survived, is underlined at the passage where the author asserts: 'It appears, accordingly, from the experiences of all ages and nations, I believe, that the work done by free men comes cheaper in the end than that performed by slaves.'[5]

Smith's views on the importance of personal freedom and the identity between enlightened self-interest and the common good made sense to these practical and energetic men. Stein himself had occasion to travel through Mecklenburg, where the conditions of the peasantry on the great estates was one of extreme servility; his observations brought home to him with considerable force the brutishness of life and the low standard of production under traditional conditions. Under the impact of Napoleon's defeat of Prussia, Stein, as chief minister of the King of Prussia, believed he had the opportunity to help the subjects of the kingdom help themselves and at the same time restore national morale and wealth: the liberation of the peasantry was to be a central feature of this programme. To many of his associates in the Prussian liberal reform era, between 1806 and 1813 in particular, to the soldiers Gneisenau and Clausewitz, to Luden, the son of a Hanoverian peasant and influential professor of history at Jena, as well as to Stein's personal friend E. M. Arndt, the bard of young German nationalism, grandson of a serf from Swedish Pomerania, the peasant appeared to be source of national regeneration. He was not only the prime producer of the national wealth, but the moral backbone of the nation. He represented a special sort of citizen, simple and loyal, close to the soil, an embodiment of those ancient customs and traditions which made up the national identity of the '*Volk*', who would supply the main body of the armies to liberate Germany from the French. Thus gradually under the impact of patriotic stirrings which preceded the wars of liberation against Napoleon, 1813–15, the peasant had attributed to him a special status among patriots. On a more practical level, the state officials concerned with the details of the agrarian reform programme in these years regarded the emancipation of the peasants from their feudal state as a means of bringing the mass of the populace into a direct relationship to the state without the intervention of privileged intermediaries.

Peasant emancipation is the term used to describe a whole series of land reform measures beginning in the late eighteenth century and culminating in the October Edict of 1807, announced a few days after the Peace of Tilsit. Legislation was concerned with two distinct questions: the personal legal status of the peasant in Prussia and his tenure. The personal freedom was decreed for all peasants whose holdings were above a certain size and who owned draught animals, both those on crown lands, who had been the object of special consideration under previous regimes, and those on noble estates, who had not. At the same time the peasant was freed from the obligation of personal services and dues arising from that servile status; in return he paid quit rents or surrendered a portion of his land to the landlord, one third if he had hereditary tenure, one half if he had not. The exclusion of those peasants from the legislation, whose holdings were below a certain size, was based on the belief that they could not achieve the degree of self-sufficiency necessary to survive. The obligation to surrender part of peasant land and other measures in favour of the nobility which were incorporated in later edicts, were designed to make the 'package' acceptable to the nobility, who, at least in most of Prussia, proved to be the real beneficiaries of the reform. In other parts of Germany, governments imitated Stein's example in liberating the peasantry from their servile status; in south Germany similar measures were incorporated in the constitutions issued by state rulers after 1815.[6] Mecklenburg, on the other hand, was characterized after 1815 by mass emigration of rural wage labourers: the exploitation of their weakness, and the foreclosure of their lands by the landowners proceeded even to the point of overriding the decrees of the grand duke contained in the reform ordinance of 1820.[7]

The agrarian reforms of the early nineteenth century in Germany have been called one of the 'most incisive and far-reaching events of modern [German] history'.[8] In contrast with the French, German peasants were not animated by hatred of the feudal system; with few exceptions their grievances were about individual cases of oppression or excessive labour and money dues. Only in Schleswig-Holstein had the peasantry come in contact with the ideas of the Enlightenment, and felt actively involved in reform measures; here the landowners preferred to grant hereditary tenancies or sell land, rather than to form large estates. In consequence the peasantry emerged strengthened. In the rest of Germany the peasants were generally not more than reluctant witnesses of changes designed by officials and intellectuals in their interest. Economic and fiscal considerations apart, the reformers aimed to absorb the rural population into a new liberal and rational social order, which was their ultimate goal. In the process a complex series of personal relationships was overthrown, and in its place was put the legal and political equality of all before the law. Yet, as an early sociologist observed in a much quoted phrase, 'for the peasant custom takes precedence over the law'; changes in the law of inheritance did not, as a rule, cause a break with inherited ways of doing things.[9] Besides, the old habits of deference to the lord, whose authority remained virtually unassailed in the village, survived in many regions until after the First World War. Although the establishment of peasant proprietorship ended the lord's obligation to protect his peasants in hard times, in some areas, such as East Prussia, the old paternalist relationship was too deeply ingrained for it to disappear. That is to say, it survived in districts where estates remained in the same family for several generations. This was, however, becoming even rarer: lands changed hands several times within a couple of decades. In 1885 only 25 per cent of East Elbian landed estates had been in the same family for more than fifty years.[10] In practice, what the landowners and the authorities liked to refer to as 'paternalism' often meant the economic dependence and social subordination of the peasant to the local landowner. As late as 1910 in more than 15 000 administrative districts the landowner was still virtually the only employer, with a decisive voice in appointing parson and teacher.[11] Among its many insights into the inevitable process of social change, Fontane's last novel *Der Stechlin* conveys with great sublety the illusion on which such authority was based, and how the emergence of political awareness of rural inhabitants – although as yet they are merely manipulated by the political parties – must eventually destroy it. A further aspect of this dependence was that the personality and energy (or lack of it) of the individual landlord determined the physical aspect of a whole district.

In general, therefore, the goal of early nineteenth century Prussian officials to create a more socially equitable and economically resilient system on the land was foiled by circumstances. In the aftermath of the Napoleonic wars, the landowners had been able to amend legislation in their favour, as a severe agrarian crisis compounded the confusion and in some cases misery of the newly emancipated peasants. Cattle disease, a series of bad harvests, lack of credit, inability to cope with the quit rents and payments due, prompted many peasants to surrender their land. In East and West Prussia, in contrast with the south and west of Germany, it was not felt degrading for a peasant to sell his land; over a million hectares passed to large estate owners in the next decades in consequence; between 1816 and 1859 2·8 per cent of peasant farms, about 10 000 in number, disappeared.[12] Many got no more than a fraction of the true value, because of the collapse of the market in the 1820s. The peasants were not, however, the only victims; many noble landed proprietors were so heavily in debt by this time that they were forced to sell up. By 1824 about half the landowners in East Frisia were bankrupt, while in East Prussia hundreds of noble estates remained on the market unsold at a fraction of their 1800 value (1825 represented the nadir; from that point on the value of land began to increase steadily, and continued to do so, until the renewed crisis of the 1870s; by 1875 the price of land was three times what it had been fifty years earlier).[13] The peasant vendors either settled in the village, living for a time on the proceeds, or obtained employment as rural labourers on the estates. One of the fears haunting the proprietors at the time of peasant emancipation had been labour shortage. This was a further reason why peasants who did not own draught animals, or whose holdings were below a certain size, had been excluded from the reform measures. They too contributed to the pool of available labour, indeed were forced to do so, because in the division of the common lands which preceded or accompanied the reform, they had been excluded too. Unable to feed an animal to supply milk and butter, and without a source of firewood, they were dependent on the chance to earn a wage. Throughout the Restoration era, the problem on the land was not shortage but excess of labour, in fact a rural proletariat, which the economy could not yet absorb. Prior to emancipation, the peasant without land had at least hereditary tenure and therefore some security. The landless peasant, like the unemployed artisan without the niche in society which security conferred, was a new and disturbing phenomenon for political and social thinkers after 1820.[14] The problem was just as pressing in the south-west, because of density of population since the eighteenth century and the practice of dividing holdings between all the heirs. In the years between the Congress of Vienna and the mid 1850s, emigration was a favoured solution for the younger and more vigorous elements. Here, as in the eastern provinces of Prussia, the problem of the sheer numbers of landless peasants was made worse by the widespread tendency of these social groups to marry young and have large families. In eighteenth century Prussia the landless peasants, and in parts of central Germany the younger sons of peasant families who had no hope of inheriting, usually went into the army – 'to the Prussians', as the phrase had it.[15] After twenty or thirty years they were either dead or they came back to live as lodgers, elderly bachelors doing odd jobs about the house and farm. Now, in the aftermath of the land reform, and with the introduction of conscription, these men were absent for only two or three years. On their return they either managed to get a small plot of land, where they could grow potatoes and other crops to feed their families, or worked for low wages on the estate, many becoming a growing burden on the community. In bad times the temptation for the rural poor to move to the towns in search of work was countered by a variety of acts regulating the employment of servants and farm labourers; according to these wages would be withheld until the period of contract was up; prosecution threatened those who left the land without their employer's permission. As a contemporary pertinently asked: 'Is this any different in practice than bondage?'[16] In a sense such people were not much better off than the old servile peasants of the pre-reform era. Personal unfreedom among rural labourers was not limited to the great estates of the east but was also characteristic of other areas, such as the large farmlands of Bavaria.

In general there was a good deal of truth in the adage, much repeated in the Restoration era, that the reform 'made gentlemen of the peasants and turned us (cottagers, lodgers, etc.) into beggars.'[17] Franz Schnabel describes what happened as a mass proletarianization such as Germany had not known prior to the inflation after the First World War.[18] While the problem of the 1820s was low agricultural prices, that of the 1840s was scarcity of food, mass starvation on the land and in the towns. The new rural proletariat had, as in Ireland, become too dependent for its food on the potato, had been encouraged to marry because of the cheapness of this commodity and the possibility of feeding a family on a small plot of land. The population explosion of this period – the population of East Elbia between Berlin and Warsaw, which was to be a major source of industrial labour in the late nineteenth century, rose by 100 per cent between 1815 and 1870[19] – was bound to be a major problem, though it was not in fact the fundamental cause of the social misery characteristic of mid century. As Peter Reichsperger, one of the leaders of the new Catholic faction in 1848, was to put it: 'The sickness for Germany lies not in the excess of population, not in the machine system nor in the superfluity of industrial factories in general; rather it lies precisely in the lack of those machines which ought to create work and employment for our workers instead of the English.'[20]

On the other hand, those peasants – and those noble and bourgeois estate owners – who were able to weather the crisis years between 1816 and 1825 reaped signal advantages; the land reform established them as a vigorous class of farmers. Farming methods improved, the extent of land under cultivation increased, and more rational methods were employed. The writers of village tales, such as Heinrich Zschokke, helped to spread propaganda in favour of the new ideas. In his popular *Das Goldmacherdorf* (1817), he has the enlightened school teacher, Oswald, measure and map the holdings of the whole village, and have the results displayed in the local tavern. When the more ambitious peasants realize the amount of time they waste travelling from one strip of land to another, they listen to his plans for concerted exchange and consolidation. In real life the difficulties were considerably greater than Oswald admitted to, but it is certainly true that by the 1830s unified holdings began to predominate. In some areas, such as Saxony, the old three-field system was deliberately retained and sheep fed on the fallow, but, in general, crop rotation was well established by mid century; from 1840 the application of science to new industrial products, such as artificial fertilizer, brought benefits to the wealthier farmers, under the aegis of the great chemist Justus von Liebig. Though Liebig came from Giessen, he spent most of his working life at the University of Munich where the signal distinction accorded him by the King of Bavaria and the respect of his colleagues helped to publicize his discoveries. Farming districts around the growing towns were especially quick to try out the new ideas – the Rhine and Ruhr in particular. In such areas farmers' wives developed individual enterprise in building up a trade in dairy products with town-dwellers. Farming all over the country gradually became geared to a money economy as the decades passed, until towards the latter years of the century dowries and the old people (*Altenteil*) began to be paid in money rather than in kind.

Writers of peasant literature, which by the 1830s had established itself both among the discriminating reading public in the towns and the literate rural labouring class, reflected current liberal progressive beliefs in the importance and the viability of a strong peasantry. However, it was characteristic of such writers as Immermann or Gotthelf, as of the advocates of peasant proprietorship in the eighteenth century, such as Justus Möser, that they were familiar with rural conditions only in regions of strong peasant traditions. Their works and those of their contemporaries even before the 1848 revolution are imbued with a sense of threat to the way of life about which they write; after the revolution this fear is expressed by an open hostility to urban life and idealization of conservative values which the peasant is alleged to embody. The Swiss Jeremias Gotthelf (1797–1854), whose main works appeared in the 1840s, anticipated the kind of arguments used by German conservatives in the second half of the century, though his portrait of rural life has nothing of their pallid sentimentality. His magnificent epics, the greatest of them *Geld und Geist* (1843), deserve to be ranked alongside the major works of European realistic writing. He contrasts the serenity and security of the hard-working peasant, a 'nobleman', his wife and 'little queen' in their small world, with the rootless and vicious townees, many of them former peasants, who failed to attend to their duties and were forced to sell up and drift from the land. Feckless surrender of the land which had been in the family for generations, in return for cash and the consequent proletarianization of families were common social phenomena to Gotthelf's contemporaries and to the much larger readership of Karl Immermann's *Der Oberhof*, a novel of peasant life in Westphalia, where its author was a district court judge. However, where Gotthelf with his strong moral and didactic sense makes failure appear the result of idleness and vice rather than economic forces, Immermann's peasants both in the *Oberhof* and in the references to the subject in his earlier novel *Die Epigonen* (1836), are seen to be threatened by pressures beyond their control. Two aspects of Immermann's work attracted a sustained interest in his work for many decades to come. The first was his realistic portraiture of peasant life. A gentleman from a neighbouring court comes to the farming community in search of a rural idyll, and is gradually forced to accept the toughness and ruthlessness, alongside the more positive qualities of its representatives. The second had an even longer, but more chequered history: the peasantry is seen as the incarnation of the nation, through its 'healthy blood' the source of national regeneration. It is not surprising that Immermann was acclaimed as their spiritual ancestor by the prolific manufacturers of 'blood and soil' epics in the 1920s and the Third *Reich*. Immermann's portrayal was that of a townsman, who, keen observer though he might be, was primarily interested in the moral problems created by economic and social change. As a portrait of rural life 'as it really was' (Ranke) and as literature, *Der Oberhof* does not measure up to Gotthelf's novels nor to the work of that other splendid portraitist of the problems and the quirks of contemporary peasant life, Fritz Reuter. Reuter wrote in Platt, the dialect of the north German plain, and in his most renowned work, the novel *Min Stromtid*, he created unforgettable characters, while at the same time focusing the attention of the public on pressing problems of the peasantry, as for example the lack of credit facilities; in the portrait of Moses and David, he drew attention to the all-too-common fate of the unsuccessful peasant – falling into the hands of usurers.

The peasant novel enjoyed a continuous vogue in Germany up to and after the First World War, though after the era of Gotthelf, Reuter and Immermann, it attracted only minor talents. The simple moral tale of rural life remained popular with country-dwellers, while the many admirers of such works among the propertied classes read them as a form of escapist literature. The exaggerated fear of the proletariat engendered by pauperism, revolution and rapid industrialization made them idealize traditional rural life as they understood it.[21] The 'true peasant' – the peasant novel was not interested in the pressing problems of the rural proletariat and usually ignored their existence – was presented as a link between past and present, embodying and keeping alive values of authority, order and 'German' culture, which social upheaval and economic progress were attempting to destroy. Property was in fact the key issue here: the representation of the true peasant as a man of property seemed a pledge of stability. To destroy such a class must, it was believed, 'open the floodgates' (or one of many such images current in the language of the propertied classes) to revolution.[22]

Although observers of the social scene had been oppressed by the increasing urbanization of life and its consequences for over half a century, it was not until after 1871 that Germany's predominantly rural character began to change. It was not only that 64 per cent of Germans in 1871 still lived in communities of less than 2000, or that well over half her population still earned their living in agriculture; the actual physical appearance of the country had so far been very little altered by industrialization before the large-scale internal migration from the late 1860s onwards, and the rapid expansion of the railway network and road transport from about the same time. There had in fact been some considerable movement of population occasioned by the peasant emancipation, the crises of the 1820s and 1840s and the failure of 1848; some 2 000 000 Germans left the land between 1820 and 1860, many to go to America.[23] However, the sustained rise in population had made this loss less significant or apparent. From the 1860s onwards, however, the growth of industry and the state's propensity to assume responsibility for a variety of services, hitherto in the hands of individuals or local authorities, created opportunities for all social groups. The increase in literacy and the proliferation of family journals made town life the object of growing curiosity to country-dwellers on a scale hitherto unknown. In the 1870s came a major slump in agriculture; bankruptcy among farmers was widespread, compounded by the fact that liberal commercial policies in the previous years had abolished the limits on bank and private lending rates. Small, inefficient or simply unfortunate farmers fell into the hands of usurers, often their own more provident and unscrupulous neighbours. Forced to sell up, many chose the call of the city rather than face the loss of caste in their village. A graphic account of the inexorable path to bankruptcy and its social consequences, typical among small farmers in many parts of Germany and Austria in the late nineteenth century, is to be found in the memoirs of Karl Renner, later Chancellor of Austria. He came from southern Moravia, a region of wine growing and mixed farmland. He was the youngest of a family of eighteen children, born in 1872, and grew up in circumstances that became ever more straitened as he grew to adolescence. In contrast with the straitened conditions of his childhood in the 1870s and 1880s, his eldest brother had been set up in farming in the good years of the mid 1850s, and had extended his holdings of draught animals, which he hired out to contractors in railway, road and bridge building. He had married young and his large family grew up to provide cheap labour on the farm; he was already a rich man when Karl was a child. His own father, on the other hand, with sickly sons and many daughters, forced to hire labour, experienced a succession of bad harvests in the 1870s, made unsuccessful investments and borrowed at high interest rates. Meanwhile the cotters and squatters in the village, used to working for their richer neighbours, found that the introduction of machinery had made their services unneeded. The differences in income within the village became ever more noticeable, and this underlined the differences in 'honour'. 'The expropriation of the small vineyard proprietors by the big ones, who were also traders, by means of usurous loans and subsequent bankruptcy substituted for the old and honourable difference in rank the rivalry of two different classes'. The very order in which people sat in church reflected the changing social structure of the village. Only the wealthy farmers retained their pews, for which they paid, the rest sat at the back, among them those who once had been holders, or they ceased to come at all. Karl's siblings, like so many such villagers, left the land for the big city, as porters, concierges, factory workers, or, as in his own case, that of an extraordinarily resourceful and persevering youth, to put himself through university and then to join the Austrian Socialist Party.[24]

It is of course quite impossible to generalize for the whole of German agriculture in any one period, although one can appreciate how important historical traditions were for the character of agrarian conditions and social relationships in any given area. Thus even as late as the Second Empire in south-west Germany, where peasants continued to divide up their lands among their heirs, a peasant proprietor was not so different in status or living standards from the rural wage labourer in the same village. Part of the reason for this was that here the common lands had been preserved, to be let as allotments by the village or given to individuals to cultivate; in the second half of the century this stimulated cultivation of garden produce to sell in the town. In the big farms of Bavaria, Swabia and Switzerland the head man and head maid (*Grossknecht* and *Grossmagd*), although servants in name, ate their meals with the family, were treated with deference by the other servants and farm hands and enjoyed considerable status in the village. In Bavaria and the Alpine regions primogeniture had ensured a sound agricultural structure, and here a sturdy medium and large peasantry existed as a class. Apart from regions near growing urban centres, the way of life in the countryside changed very slowly in the last decades of the nineteenth century. Nor did German agriculture tend towards greater concentration, as was the case in the industrial sector. Despite the continued existence of the large landed estates in East Elbia, in Germany as a whole the percentage of small and medium sized farms – that is, those between 2 and 20 hectares – actually increased in the period 1882–1907 as against those of 20 hectares and over.[25] The lack of credit facilities, the bane of small farmers' lives, the fear of the usurer, had begun to be remedied by a number of new institutions. The first of these were the rural savings banks and credit organizations, the work of the philanthropist Raiffeisen, still known today as Raiffeisen banks. He opened the first of these in 1860 and had many imitators in the next decades. The institution of fire and weather insurances and the establishment of rural cooperatives were also important innovations; there were as many as 3271 cooperatives for dairy produce by 1909.[26] In general it was the medium and larger farmers who took advantage of the opportunities offered; it was they who took the farming journals to learn new methods and who sent their sons to agricultural colleges. From about the mid 1890s onwards, German farming, which for economic or other reasons had lagged behind Britain and France, became increasingly mechanized; artificial fertilizers were used more and more widely to raise production, while selective breeding improved the quality and weight of livestock. Over the period 1870–1914 the value of agricultural production doubled,[27] though the number of people employed in agriculture rose very little. Relative to the rest of the population, which was still rising rapidly, the agrarian sector was in fact already beginning the inexorable decline which in our own time (1967) was to reduce the percentage to a mere 10 per cent of the whole population (Federal Republic only).[28] In 1882 42·2 per cent of all employed worked in agriculture and forestry, 33·8 per cent in industry and crafts, 8·5 per cent in transport and commerce. On the eve of the war, the first two groups were almost equal, by 1925 it was 30·5 per cent as against 41·5 per cent, with 28 per cent in the tertiary sector.[29]

The full social implications behind these figures – industrialization, internal migration and flight from the land, the transformation of Germany from a food exporting to a food importing country – were not immediately apparent to those most concerned. As was the case with so many other social strata, it was not until the last years of the war and the Weimar Republic that the effects became manifest. The psychological impact was profound nonetheless, even before the war, and showed itself in demands for greater protection from state and society, on the part of farmers all over the country, in the constant self-preoccupation which was a feature of their class. Very relevant in this context is Lothar Gall's observation in a recent article that the greater part of the rural *Mittelstand*, as well as the artisans and small traders, had abandoned their support of liberalism well before the 1870s.[30] The landowners and farmers on the one hand, and the authorities on the other, saw agricultural problems principally in political terms. They considered that their production of basic foodstuffs was an all-important factor giving Germany a freedom in her military policies which she would not otherwise have had. They considered that their function in the community and their conservative and monarchical sympathies entitled them to special treatment. The first instance of this special treatment took the form of protective tariffs on grain, imposed in 1879 and extended in subsequent years. These benefited the large landowners, however, rather than the peasant proprietor, while the cost was borne by the rest of society, falling heaviest on the urban poor. In the 1890s the East Elbian landowners' use of cheap labour from Austria-Hungary and Russia, often imported illegally with the connivance of the police, had a very serious effect on the living standards of rural wage labourers in that region. Immigrant labour was satisfied with minimal pay and gradually forced the local labourer to move away from the land in search of employment. Indeed it would be no exaggeration to say that the prodigious expansion of industry in Berlin, central and western Germany from the mid 1890s to the eve of the war, was founded on the influx of labour from the eastern provinces.

In defence of their self-interest East Elbian landowners formed in 1893 the so-called *Bund der Landwirte*, the Farmers' League. Although only 1 per cent of its members were great estate owners from the east, it was they who effectively dominated the organization. Their extraordinarily adept propaganda, their success in projecting an image of 'farmers in distress', and finally the lack of effective rival associations in other parts of Germany made opinion accept their projected image, as a kind of 'Green Front' or representative organ of the whole agrarian interest in Germany. There had been a number of farmers' organizations prior to this in Westphalia, Bavaria and south-west Germany; local farmers had either founded these or supplanted the original noble founders. However, they were not numerically strong enough and they certainly lacked the demagogic appeal and propaganda apparatus which the 1893 foundation so rapidly developed. Although many of the mainly Catholic farming organizations of the west and south disliked the Prussian character of the Farmers' League, its growing power was too useful to resist it effectively, especially in the years before the war. The polarization of German political life, so characteristic of the pre-war years, between town and country, the tendency to see change in personal status or economic power in terms of 'conspiracy', the antipathy of conservative landowners or conservative Catholic farming circles to 'progress', all helped to rally the farming interest, very diverse as it might be in itself, behind the state, and to make them regard the supporters of liberalism and democracy as 'the enemy'.

The rural labourers who left the land did not, in general, bring to their new homes hostility to the principal authors of their altered circumstances; it is true that a number did indeed find their way to the socialists, often, in the way described by Franz Rehbein, author of the graphic *Memoiren eines Landarbeiters*, through their experiences in the army.[31]

Those who remained on the land were not, until the war changed them, politically aware, but tended to accept the views of those in authority. Schmoller collected evidence in a survey, undertaken as early as 1882, that these people and the small peasants of the eastern provinces, had identified themselves with the prejudices of the landowners against certain groups and trends in contemporary Germany. He found instances in Pomerania, Mecklenburg and Posen of deliberate incitement to hostility against the Jews, and a readiness to lay the blame on them for economic and social ills. In other parts of Germany a kind of passive antisemitism existed, based partly on inherited suspicion against the Jews as outsiders, and partly (and this is particularly the case in the Catholic farming regions of the south, Silesia and Westphalia) on conservative Christian prejudices. An important step in the identification of the interests of the rural classes with the national community through their self-appointed spokesmen was taken at a meeting between representatives of the Farmers' League and the Pan-German League, which took place at the Berlin headquarters of the former one year before the outbreak of war. On 6 July 1913 a spokesman for the Farmers' League made a report which was a programmatic statement for the coming years. He declared:

> Democracy's fight against agriculture threatened the very roots of the German nation. But the democratic onslaught had become so strong that it could no longer be warded off only by a defence of agriculture's economic interests; the national threat of this onslaught must be emphasized more than ever. In consequence the Farmers' League must occupy itself more than before with national questions and set itself national goals, and as the League (the Pan-German) was not yet quite at home in this sphere, closer contacts with us are particularly welcome.[32]

Underlying this and other similar statements by interested persons or bodies is the claim to the superior moral and national values of rural life, and the obligation of the rest of society to maintain it in its present form, without reference to economic realities or the cost to other groups in that society. The constellation of agrarian pressure groups and aggressive nationalists was to be a significant factor in the aftermath of the war and the Weimar Republic, and the sense of betrayal which they felt by the state, from whom they had learnt to expect privileged treatment, was an important element in attracting the rural vote to the right wing parties, especially the NSDAP.

Section 4
Lower orders: manual workers

Chapter 20
The industrial labour force

During the early years of industrialization in Germany – that is, from about the late eighteenth to the middle of the following century – the social origins of the labour force were very diverse. In the main the workers, both male and female, came from domestic craft and manufacture, or from the artisan class. We would be wrong to see in these people a faceless mass of human misery, exploited by the 'masters': there were in fact considerable differences in social status, skill, traditions and conditions of work between one industry and one factory or another, and even within the same factory. In the beginning of the period the highest and lowest paid type predominated; as the nineteenth century advanced, numbers of low paid workers familiarized themselves with processes and developed others which enabled them to rise into the middle rank of workers.

The prevailing image of the early period of industrialization in Germany as elsewhere has been formed by our knowledge of the textile industry, initially the largest employer and the one where skills were least and conditions worst. Here the proportion of women and children was very high; they could do the same jobs as men in many instances, and could be paid half or even one third of the man's wage. When English competition forced manufacturers to lower their prices, the argument for taking on ill-paid labour was a cogent one. Textile manufacture had been first developed by a number of Germany's absolute rulers as occupation in female houses of correction – hence the association between prison and spinning houses. Frederick William I of Prussia and Maria Theresa, to name but two such rulers, had encouraged projects in order both to give gainful employment to the growing numbers of poor and destitute in their kingdoms, and as a kind of reformatory for the idle and feckless, in the hope of making useful citizens out of them. In the late eighteenth century middle class bankrupts, soldiers' wives unable to live on their husbands' meagre pay, and single or deserted women, had come to seek work. Many lived on the factory premises, in primitive and unhealthy conditions. The women's section of the Schwechat cotton factory (just outside Vienna) in 1810 was described by an observer thus: straw mattresses with a sheet and pillow lay so close together on the floor that one could barely move between them, yet over each bed, if one might call it that, another was suspended; the proximity of so many sleepers made an unbearable stench by night.[1] There was also an infirmary for women – a very high proportion of industrial workers suffered from chronic ailments and disease caused by working conditions right to the end of the nineteenth century. This had five beds and opened on to the factory hall so that the inmates were forced to breathe in the dust inevitably associated with an early cotton factory. Despite such conditions, work was so hard to find that men brawled with women who 'robbed them of their livelihood' by taking up work in factories; in 1770 and again in 1802 the clashes in Austria were so violent that the police were brought in and the offenders sentenced to hard labour.[2] Yet even within the textile industry there were considerable differences in the type of worker employed. It was mainly in the mechanical spinning of cotton that women and children predominated; as spinning techniques were developed, there was less work that children were able to do. In weaving it was the less skilled who went into the factories, since the fine work continued to be done by hand until more sophisticated machines were developed in the second half of the nineteenth century. The tobacco industry also paid very low wages and depended mainly on female and child labour in the early nineteenth century, as did, somewhat later, the food industry. Here too it is necessary to qualify general statements: the tobacco industry also had some of the best paid and highly organized sections of the work force, as became evident in their activities during the 1848 revolution.

In the mining of coal and ore, the social composition of the work force was very different. In marked contrast with nineteenth century England[3] the German miners represented the traditional élite of workers. Mining was endowed with privileges possessed by few workers; in the *ancien regime* they had enjoyed freedom from feudal dues and taxes, and even sometimes military service. Their hours, wages and employment were regulated by the state and their dependants were compensated in case of accident. The miners' organizations, the so-called *Knappschaften,* had their own bands, festivals and parades, and regarded these as expressing their superior social status. However, their behaviour was subject to numerous controls; they were required, as for example by the terms of employment in the Saar-Nassau region, to show their superiors 'deference, obedience and respect' and to greet them dutifully.[4] Miners were solid, respectful and thoroughly conservative. They took no part in the revolutionary disorders of 1848; some actually opposed reform. In the 1850s, however, the legal distinctions covering the status of the miners were abolished in Prussia. Mines all over the country were taken over then and in the following years by entrepreneurs for capitalist exploitation. The miners were so used to being protected by the state that they continued to look to authority for help; thus they sent delegates to seek a personal audience with the Kaiser for aid during the 1889 Ruhr strike. Catholic miners responded to the interest taken in their conditions by the Catholic church, so much so that the 1872 strike was known as the 'Jesuits' strike'. Despite considerable efforts in defence of miners' rights, socialist leaders made few converts among miners before 1890. Thereafter, however, they were successful, especially in the Ruhr area, and from about 1895 onwards more and more miners embraced socialist views, until by the turn of the century the socialist miners became the most powerful of all mining organizations in Germany. The social origins of the Ruhr miners were different from those of central Germany, the Saar and Silesia in that no guild tradition existed here. Labour was mainly recruited from the rural areas. Some came from the surrounding regions, others from as far away as eastern Germany. They included former farm hands and day labourers, or even peasants from places where no domestic crafts existed to help them to eke out a living in bad times. It was among the rural workers recently come to work in industry that the symptoms of disorientation and uprootedness were greatest; the contrast between the poverty stricken but familiar village from which they had come and the anonymity of the town, and the proximity of one's colleagues and neighbours was for many an overwhelming and frightening experience.

The machine tool industry, which was already flourishing in some parts of Germany before mid century, was different again. Right to the end of the nineteenth century its workers came from the craftsmen class, the factories were like workshops on a larger scale.[5] These were among the élite of industrial workers in the nineteenth century, well paid and very conscious of their status as skilled operators. This was especially marked among those working in areas such as Saxony, the Rhineland, Alsace and Switzerland, where there was a demand for textile machinery. In other words, there was a marked difference both in social prestige and in outlook between those who came from the manufacturing industries which demanded special skills and the mass of unskilled labourers of diverse social origins. Operatives working in those branches of industry which had originated with a privilege granted by a local ruler or which were a state monopoly, such as glass, porcelain and armaments, and where trade secrets were carefully guarded, enjoyed special privileges. Not only did they regard themselves as persons of consequence, but their wages were often very much higher than those in many bourgeois occupations. The individual workers were also rewarded at different rates according to the degree of skill required of them; recently discovered material in the Prussian and Saxon archives illustrates this. Thus a man who could copy scenes from Watteau on to porcelain earned in the mid eighteenth century some 377 *taler* a year, whereas one painting a battle scene got 333 and a landscape painter 191; the man who fired the china in the same enterprise received between 84 and 156 *taler*;[6] fifty years later the lowest paid official in Prussia earned not more than 100 *taler* a year, while the artisan's earnings, if he were lucky, were perhaps on average 150. Specialist workers enjoyed not only higher wages but privileges such as exemptions from military service and from taxes. Although these privileges were lost in the nineteenth century, the traditional hierarchy within such enterprises was preserved for many decades to come.

The early period of industrialization in Germany was not characterized, as has often been alleged, both at the time and later, by a general lowering of wages and mass proletarianization of the workers, though of course this did occur to some extent. Different functions carried different incomes and social status, the latter still determined by pre-industrial traditions which continued operative well into the nineteenth century. The social status of the worker could also be influenced until about the 1850s by his legal status deriving from earlier centuries. Thus in Prussia there were miners of the first and second class, and in addition there were day labourers. They were paid on different scales, according to the original agreement made by the state government who owned the mines; some had insurance rights but no freedom of movement, others the latter but not the former.[7] In other branches of industry, such as paper manufacture, guild workers considered themselves better than their colleagues who were not, and might even refuse to work in the same workshop. The different function of workers was the most important factor in determining social status in factory and workshop.[8] Subjective factors were also important in distinguishing one group of workers from another: local and linguistic differences are a case in point. The native worker who was a citizen of the town he lived in thought himself far above the immigrant who was not. The immigrants remained close together, especially if they came from a distance: East Prussians brought their brides to join them from home. Even at the end of the century, this tendency remained: between 1885 and 1915 some 160 000 East Prussians settled in the Ruhr town of Gelsenkirchen.[8a] The existence of different types of bread or roll in Barmen, such as the 'Waldecker', the 'Kasseler' etc., shows how long the loyalty to one's place of origin could last, even in the apparently anonymous life of a textile worker.[9] There were very marked differences in outlook and social mobility between the town worker and the rural immigrant. The former usually spared himself at work and often devoted what little free time he had to improving himself by reading or study; the latter, used to hard work and long hours, did not spare himself and used his free time for sleep.

In industry and manufacture, as in most occupations in early nineteenth century Germany, the pay scales varied enormously between the top and the bottom; some groups of skilled workers got as much as eight or twelve times that of the lowest paid child, and four or five times that of the lowest paid male worker. In a Baden factory in 1848 the foreman's wage was eleven times that of the lowest paid worker, while out of a work force of 128 in 1844 Krupp paid his skilled men 25 *groschen* a day, the least skilled 6 *groschen.* In bad times the average wage actually rose, suggesting that the skilled workers were kept on, at the expense of the unskilled.[10] The tendency over the century as a whole was for the wages to level out. However, such differences as did remain, as well as differing function, status, social origins and subjective factors, helped to delay the emergence of a sense of class consciousness among workers until well into the second half of the century.[11] This was further delayed by the patriarchal relationship between workers and employers in the early factories; the masters demanded and usually got the loyalty of their employees, whom (as in Barmen during the famine years of 1816–17) they cared for in times of distress. A worker, and particularly one who had skill, felt a sense of obligation and sometimes of commitment to the 'master', but with fellow workers in other factories he had little contact.

Hours and conditions of work varied from place to place. After the Napoleonic wars a flood of unskilled labour, including demobbed soldiers, led the Austrian authorities to limit the hours of work in order to accommodate more persons. English competition, now that the continental blockade had been lifted, and the fall in demand because of the high food prices and shortages, had serious, even disastrous effects on manufacture and handcraft in many parts of Germany. Many were ready to endure grim conditions in the factories in order to earn a wage. It was not until the middle of the century that the state began to intervene to limit the hours worked on grounds of humanity, although in 1829 the Prussian government had taken tentative steps to do so merely because the physical calibre of such workers was not up to army requirements when they presented themselves for military service. In the late 1830s and 1840s industry and manufacture, long regarded by governments as an important source of prosperity, revenue and employment, began to be blamed for the relentless growth of pauperism. 'Industry', abruptly declared the Prussian Minister of Finance, Thile, to some Wuppertal merchants in 1846 'is a canker of the land'.[12] Prussia had introduced restrictions on child labour in 1839, forbidding the employment of children under nine, and limiting to ten the hours those aged ten to fourteen might work; Bavaria and Baden followed suit, as did Bremen (for the cigar factories only). Austria laid down maximum hours for all workers under seventeen. In practice these regulations were not adhered to; parents often depended on the earnings of their children, especially in these bad times, and it was not until the 1860s that an efficient factory inspectorate was created.

The average hours worked in the mid nineteenth century, in many cases without time off for meals, were as much as fifteen and sixteen per day. At that time the founder of the Erbreichsdorfer cotton factory in Austria agreed with his son that sixteen hours was 'normal', a verdict confirmed by Dr Knolz of the Vienna medical school when he investigated conditions in the spinning works of Lower Austria in 1843.[13] Work began at four or five in the morning, continuing until eight or nine at night. The primitive nature of the early machinery made the actual work so much more burdensome: 'Who can possibly wield an eleven pound hammer for eleven hours a day?' complained a metal foil worker of an eighteenth-century factory at Neuhausen in Austria.[14] Perhaps even more wearing was the lack of ventilation and in certain branches of industry the dust and fibres; legislation to provide for adequate ventilation was not enforced until the end of the century when absence of workers through illness decreased significantly. The average number of absent female workers in unventilated premises in 1886 was 55·7 per cent, in one actually 91·2 per cent. The proportion fell to 44·4 per cent in a reasonably ventilated works.[15] By the 1870s eleven hours' work per day was about average for industrial workers, not including rest periods, though in times of high demand this could be extended and many worked even on Saturday afternoons. The efforts of the trade unions in the last years of the century gradually bore fruit, and the ten-hour day was the norm in most industrial enterprises by 1905.[16] On the eve of the First World War a ten-hour day was general; some firms only worked an eight- or nine-hour day. When speaking about hours of work, we must remember that the concept of annual holidays was unknown, and that the many feast days enjoyed by the worker in medieval and early modern times had almost wholly disappeared, except in some Catholic regions. The artisans claimed their traditional day off, 'blue Monday', even after entering factory work, but they were not successful. However, the frequent crises in industry and manufacture resulted in men being laid off, and an average of three months' enforced idleness or at least unemployment seems to have been common.[17]

As for payment, it was only in 1849 that in Prussia the iniquitous truck system was abolished. The authorities were not indifferent to the pitifully low wages paid in some areas, as was shown by their generally lenient treatment of all but the ringleaders of the two Wuppertal strikes in 1855 and 1857, in both of which some thousand dyers apprentices were involved; in the second strike they were successful in getting increased wages. The Prussian Finance Minister von der Heydt visited Elberfeld in 1855 and observed, '4 *taler* a month does not seem much'. In general, however, the state preserved its paternalist attitude towards the entrepreneur and refrained from intervening in 'family affairs', the relations between employer and employees.

It is difficult to discuss minimum wages with reference to our own time; standards and expectations were so very different. A working man's household in about 1850 with the average manual labourer's wage of 100–150 *taler* would have only about one fifth of the income of a comfortable bourgeois family, but would be regarded as having a standard far above that of the poor. There is a further difficulty in estimating the real value of his wage; we do not know how much a worker paid his employer for food and lodging at the factory, or for a house, since especially in the early decades of the century the masters built houses for their employees, and this remained the policy of individual firms, Siemens, Krupp and Stumm. This was partly done to attract workers, partly for political reasons; the authorities and the propertied classes feared nothing so much as a Paris-type commune incident and tried to encourage industry in rural areas where the workers could not become 'disaffected'. Some actually enclosed working premises and living accommodation with a high wall, and permission had to be asked to leave the settlement, even on Sundays. In the latter half of the century this practice became rare, and the masters themselves preferred to move away from their place of work and establish themselves among respectable bourgeois society in a 'better' part of the town (Fontane makes a discreet reference to such pretensions in the opening chapters of his satire on the industrial bourgeoisie, *Frau Jenny Treibel*, 1892).

In some regions, as in the early factories around Vienna, it was customary for whole families of workers, such as the Croats from nearby Burgundland, to come with provisions for a week to the factories, and return home to replenish supplies at the weekend.[18] Those who, like the Croats, had their own source of food were obviously likely to fare best. Conflicting evidence exists on the diet and health of factory and domestic workers throughout the century; much depended on the region and on the period of time to which reports, analyses and memoirs refer. In many working men's households an ox or pig was slaughtered and preserved annually well into the century; many made their own butter, which suggests they kept a cow or goat. Opinions differ widely among historians as to how widespread the possession of a garden allotment was among industrial workers as a whole. In trying to generalize one can only say that the rapid growth of cities, especially after 1871, made this less common, and that where workers did not have such an alternative source of food, their vulnerability to distress in bad years was so much greater. Even after the beginning of the first wave of the industrial revolution in Germany, 1850–73, expansion was not steady, but rather alternated with checks, and even recessions, of which 1857–8 was the most serious. In the 1850s and early 1860s Prussian government inspectors and county commissioners examined the conditions of the labouring classes, and were appalled by what they found. The mill hands in his area, reported the Aachen factory inspector, lived almost exclusively on a diet of bread and so-called coffee water, varying this occasionally with potatoes and oil.[19] The county commissioners for Silesia, where the weavers' revolt had taken place a decade previously, produced harrowing tales of near starvation among both the weavers and the factory workers in the province. It is clear from these reports that for many workers physical survival was a major problem, even at a time when industry was in a position to absorb more and more labour.

Factory workers enjoyed higher wages in the years up to 1848 than domestic workers and craft apprentices, though their social status was generally regarded as lower. They also enjoyed greater material security at a time when mechanization seemed to threaten craftsmen and domestic workers. It is therefore not surprising that the first working men's associations attracted chiefly artisans in a precarious economic position, particularly the craft apprentices unable to gain a master's title because their trade was oversubscribed and the demand for their goods was less. From about 1848 a gradual change began to come about in the relationship of different categories of workers to each other, which was expressed in the changing meaning of certain words, as for example '*Arbeiter*'. '*Arbeiter*' had hitherto been looked upon by the artisan as an unskilled labourer, while a skilled worker even in the factory was referred to by his particular trade – cooper, tanner, saddler, etc. An observer in Frankfurt noted the change when he wrote in 1848: 'If in bygone times someone had denied the title of "apprentice" to a young artisan and called him a "worker" he'd have given him a dubbing.'[20] One couldn't just 'be' a craft apprentice, you had to 'become' one by diligence and skill. However, factory owners in Berlin in 1848–9 began to use the term '*Arbeiter*' of the employees regardless of their function, and gradually this came to be accepted by more and more of those concerned.[21] On the other hand, the term 'proletariat', which began to be current in the 1830s and 1840s with reference to the growing numbers of paupers, was long regarded by working men as a term of abuse: an enthusiastic journalist, one Zacharias, addressing a group of workers in 1848 as 'proletariat' was forced by the angry meeting to retract. Marx, inspired by developments in France, made few converts among the fourth estate in his own country when he used the term in his famous opening words to the Communist Manifesto. The most politically minded among working men in mid century were the wandering artisans, who came into contact with radical groups in France, Switzerland and Germany, concerned to improve the conditions of the lower classes, and to organize a working class movement. However, in contrast with their colleagues in France, Belgium or even England, German artisans were more interested in national or religious questions than in labour movements. Communist literature was scarcely known to them, though some of the writings of contemporary anarchists appealed to the Utopian streak which many of them had. However, some sense of what later generations would call working class consciousness was aroused in a number of journeymen, who came across the workers' associations founded by exiled intellectuals in Paris, London, Brussels and Zurich. Their sentiments and aspirations about national unity and international brotherhood are recorded, if not immortalized, in the radical artisans' lyrics which they sung on the road or in the inns.[22] At home in Germany a number of these workers' associations were set up in the 1840s, but were stamped out in the court actions of those years and in the aftermath of the 1848 revolution. Their place was taken in part by educational associations which proved so popular in the late 1850s and early 1860s that as many as fifty-four could be represented at the first conference held in Frankfurt in 1863. One reason for the resurgence of a working class movement in the 1860s was the decline of pauperism; as the demand for labour grew and wages began to rise, working men became more ambitious and more aware of their status in society.[23] Their loyalties were initially regional rather than national, and the majority aimed to improve themselves socially and intellectually rather than politically. In fact not a little of working men's opposition to Lassalle, founder of the first workers' political party, the *Allgemeiner Deutscher Arbeiterverband* (1863), derived from the fact that he was trying to separate them from the bourgeoisie whom they aspired to join.[24] Lassalle's supporters numbered only a few thousand in his brief career as a worker's leader which ended in his death in a duel in 1864. However, he did create the basis of a class party at national level, and the remnants of his movement eventually merged, at Gotha in 1875, with the *Sozialdemokratische Arbeiterpartei* founded in 1869 by the Saxon Bebel and the Hessian Liebknecht. This was a reorganized version of their earlier creation, which they called the *Verband deutscher Arbeitervereine* (1863), to establish a connection with the workers' organizations of the revolutionary years.

The strong national and democratic element which had been characteristic of the earlier associations was also a feature of the political movements of the 1860s. Craft apprentices still formed the backbone of the membership, especially those employed in the small industrial concerns of rural Saxony and southern Germany. Where members were recruited from among factory hands, the movement was much weaker. This is equally true of the Lassalleans as of the followers of Bebel and Liebknecht.

The leaders of the social democratic movement were predominantly petty bourgeois in origin. To name but a few: August Bebel (1840–1913) was a wood turner, who became a relatively successful businessman on a small scale; Edward Bernstein (1850–1932) was the son of a plumber who later became a railway engineer; he himself worked for ten years as a bank clerk; Johann Dietz (1843–1927) was a printer who went into publishing. But there were also many who had been to university and came from well-connected families, notably William Liebknecht who was descended from a long line of Hesse officials and could even count Martin Luther among his ancestors, Georg von Vollmar, whose father had been a government minister, and

Karl Kautsky (1854–1938) who came from a wealthy Viennese Jewish family. In the first decades it was necessary that they should have a source of livelihood; even in the early twentieth century the long hours worked in factories made it difficult to combine factory work with the duties of a party functionary: those who came from such a background generally found employment elsewhere. Journalism was one of the few jobs that could offer them an income, but even this was always precarious because of police powers to search and confiscate issues of socialist publications; after the passing of the Antisocialist Law journalists, publishers and printers suffered. Even much later, after 1890, there was an element of risk involved for socialists. However, the challenge of the situation made people inventive: the so-called 'Red Postmaster', Julius Motteler, organized the printing and smuggling into Germany of the paper *Der Sozialdemokrat* from Zurich, and, after the police seized large numbers in 1884, was able to arrange for secret printing to be done in Germany. Thus many who would have been out of employment were kept involved in the movement, while well-to-do sympathizers showed great generosity in giving financial support to those in real need. Because of the political and financial insecurity of their position, many socialist functionaries in the years of the Antisocialist Law 1878–90 were younger men, without family responsibility. After that date the party was able to employ paid officials, as was the trade union movement. With the new security and gradual growth of the SPD to a mass party, the type of functionary changed, though his social origins might be similar to those of his predecessors. In the years of persecution, a radical temperament was required, but from the 1890s onwards the socialist official developed the conservative, even bureaucratic mentality towards his job and his organization, which became generally characteristic of socialists for many decades to come.

Both Bebel and Liebknecht had been democrats before they became revolutionaries; Marx had little influence on the German working class movement in the 1860s (and on few writers before the end of that decade) for he, like Engels, was impatient of national matters. It was not until the early 1870s, nurtured by their bitter hatred of Prussia and their disappointment at the form of German unification, that Bebel and Liebknecht came to share Marx's views. Kautsky was later to write that it was the needlegun and Moltke's genius which had decided the issue against the German revolution and the unification of all Germany in favour of Bismarck and unification under Prussia. He might have added that Marx and Engels were also the victors of 1866 and 1871, since their ideas would never have come to be accepted in the 1870s and 1880s as the official socialist party doctrine had Germany been united with Austria under a democratic constitution.[25] The strong support which Bebel and Liebknecht's party had won in Saxony and in southern Germany came from Prussia's sternest critics, democrats rather than socialists. Bebel was elected to the *Reichstag* of the North German Confederation on its formation in 1867; he immediately registered his protest against a federation which proclaims 'not German unity but its splitting up, a federation which will turn Germany into a great barracks'.[26] When the Prussian authorities decided to continue to wage war on France even after the capture of Napoleon III, Bebel and Liebknecht, who was also a member of parliament, opposed the voting of war credits in the *Reichstag*. For this they were arrested on a charge of high treason in December 1870. The stand taken by these leaders had profound long-term consequences for relations between the working classes and the rest of German society in the next decades. Although they had in fact misjudged the mood of those whom they represented and their party lost much support in the winter of 1870–1, the affair of the Paris Commune intervened to make good the loss. The Commune was established on the very day of the twenty-fifth anniversary of the outbreak of the 1848 revolution in Germany. The subsequent fate of its supporters inspired working men in Germany, as in many other countries, to see in it a symbol of the international solidarity of the masses against the vested interests of inherited privilege, capitalism and the churches. Until May Day became the traditional labour festival, in the 1890s, politically conscious working men in Germany chose 18 March as their special celebration, rather than the anniversary closest to the hearts of most citizens of the Second Empire: 2 September, or Sedan Day, when Napoleon's defeat was commemorated. Just to give expression to their feelings on the subject, many socialists paraded on 2 September in memory of the fallen Communards, their comrades, to the outrage of the other classes. It was not as if the socialists had consciously made their choice in favour of international solidarity of the working man against the state in which they lived, but rather that they were drawn by a long tradition of opposition to rally to the defence of whichever was under attack. Until the threat of war became imminent in 1914 – when the socialists voted overwhelmingly for war credits – it was clear to them that their class was in greater need of their support than the Prussian-led Empire. The effect of all this on the rest of German society was traumatic. To the property owning, God- and Kaiser-fearing classes in Germany, the Commune was the very incarnation of anarchy and social evil.[27] The attitude of the socialists was incomprehensible, unless, as they increasingly supposed, these men were intent on destroying the whole laboriously erected edifice of the glorious German Empire. As the years passed and the Social Democratic Party (as it was now called) became not only the best organized labour party in the world, but also captured an ever-increasing percentage of the popular vote, the attitude of the German establishment became little short of hysterical. Baroness Spitzemberg noted in her diary that the bourgeoisie would not allow their children out of doors on May Day.[28] Kaiser William II referred publicly to the socialist members of parliament in abusive terms; in 1895 the chancellor Hohenlohe commented on their boycott of the Sedan celebrations as an act 'hostile to culture and to the nation by those who know no Fatherland'. In the idiom of the time, invective could go no further.

The psychological effect of this on the urban working classes, about one-third of whom were members of the socialist party or of the trade union movement by the end of the century, was naturally considerable. Not only were they regarded with suspicion by the rest of society, but the attitude of their leaders made it difficult for them to know where they stood with regard to their nation and to identify themselves with the society in which they lived and worked. Yet the attitude of the state and society did much to increase the appeal of socialism to the working classes, and to encourage the militancy of its leaders. The efforts of the authorities to strangle the movement betrayed rather their own nervousness than its threat to the state. The editors of socialist papers were harassed by the authorities; two or three were constantly in jail. The innumerable court cases involving labour leaders and journalists often brought to light corrupt practices on the part of the state, suborning of witnesses, use of informers, police spies, etc. In 1878 Bismarck decided to ban all extra parliamentary activity of the SPD. Bismarck's antisocialist legislation of 1878 caused severe hardship to members of socialist organizations and journalists, many of whom lost their livelihood; by June 1879 some 127 periodicals and 278 other publications had been suppressed. During the period of the Antisocialist Law, the police hounded real and supposed offenders, yet their action, which seemed to imply a dual standard, one for working men, another for the propertied classes, helped to keep alive a sense of commitment to the movement and caused its rapid expansion after the repeal of the law in 1890.

The German socialist movement exercised a strong attraction for those who flocked into the towns and cities during the great internal migration of the second half of the nineteenth century. Most felt isolated and friendless in their new environment. Unlike British workmen they had no church with which they and their wives could identify themselves, no local nonconformist minister from a similar environment or social group to whom they could turn for material succour or friendly advice. The Evangelical church ministers were too closely identified in their minds with the powers that be for them to seek their aid; in any case the association in clergymen's minds between industrial workers and socialism made most of them unsuited for such a role. A number of Lutherans did try to organize movements to wean the people from socialism, but they were not a success. In Catholic areas, by contrast, where local priests had long been aware of the social problem, socialism made few converts. Lily Braun, a prominent though highborn socialist, described an incident in her memoirs which helps to explain in very few words the appeal of socialism to the urban working class and the loyalty which they showed to their party. She visited a poor shoemaker living with his daughter Martha; both had been unable to find work. Then Martha came across the socialists. 'The old man stroked his daughter's cheek with a wrinkled hand: and so she saved my life! We were no longer alone. Now we had something to live for.'[29] In fact both the Social Democrat Party and the trade union movement had a vital social role to play in their members' lives: they provided them with the opportunity to 'belong'. The socialist movement also gave them the chance to educate themselves – the educational organizations of socialism brought working men into contact with many able and highly motivated intellectuals, who lectured, led discussion groups and edited socialist publications. In addition there were a variety of associations for leisure pursuits, singing, bands, allotments, youth and sport clubs, which were organized at local level.[30] The worker who joined the party, and who was intelligent and loyal, had every chance of becoming a person of consequence in his locality. After 1890, when the party had several hundred paid and thousands of voluntary workers, he might achieve personal success at regional or national level. There were precinct groups, which were integrated into the branch organizations of the regions; these in turn were subject to the national organization, and all of these had their presidents, secretaries and treasurers, offering scope for a man of ambition and dedication at several levels. The German trade unions were both labour associations and friendly societies. As was the case with the British trade unions in the decades before the war, they spent more money on sickness and disability benefits than on strikes.[31]

A strong sense of social cohesion among industrial workers, whatever their origins, emerged in the 1880s in response to the attitude of state and society towards their class.[32] One factor which contributed to this was the tendency of urban workers of very different backgrounds to live in the same area of the city; another was the greater mobility of labour in the late nineteenth century. In former times artisans had been mobile, even radical in youth, but once established as masters had taken on the manners and outlook of the petty bourgeoisie. From the 1870s onwards workers moved easily from one part of the country, often living from hand to mouth for years, as many workers' memoirs, such as those of the onetime baker's apprentice, the railway and factory labourer Karl Fischer, illustrate.[33] From the worker's point of view it emphasized the rootlessness of his existence in the nation to which he was supposed to belong, and prejudiced him in favour of socialism – the party, as the establishment and the bourgeoisie constantly reiterated, of those without a fatherland. A further factor, which emphasized the worker's separate status in the community and increased the attraction of working class associations, was the two years' obligatory military service. The experience of military service could be a traumatic one for working men, particularly for those who had connections with or showed interest in labour organizations.[34] Drill sergeants submitted known socialists to all kinds of humiliation and seemed to regard urban workers as potential socialists, *ergo* traitors, and determined to show them forcibly the error of their ways.

After the ending of the Antisocialist Law in 1890 the growth of the labour movement was impressive, not least to the members themselves. Trade union membership increased from 135 353 in 1889 to 320 213 in late 1890,[35] rising to some 2·5 million in 1910 out of a work force of some 17·8 million (this included the Christian and liberal trade unions, at about 20 per cent of the total). The trade union leaders concentrated their efforts on improving the economic and environmental condition of the workers, with some success in the years before 1914. Meanwhile the SPD grew in size and influence: electoral support rose from 1·5 million in 1890 to 4·5 million some twenty years later. In 1912 it was the largest parliamentary party in Germany; in March 1914 it had 1 085 905 members.[36] It drew its support from those members of the urban working class who grew politically aware as their earnings and conditions improved in the great industrial expansion from the mid 1890s to the eve of the war, and whose political consciousness was sharpened as the brief but recurrent depressions of March 1900 to March 1902, July 1907 to December 1908, and April 1913 made them sensible of their vulnerable economic situation. Socialism also attracted support from those who felt alienated by the dominant culture of '*Bildung und Besitz*', but despite the intellectual and moral stature of its intellectuals, the Social Democratic Party remained an urban working man's movement.[37] In the years between 1890 and 1914 a gradual rapprochement took place between the authorities and socialists in the south German states. The extension of the franchise increased working class representation in the federal assemblies (*Landtage*), but also (perhaps more important) in local administration.[38] However, the dominant position of states which resolutely opposed the extension of working class influence in public life, namely Prussia and Saxony with their unreformed franchise, determined the overall attitude of Wilhelmine society to labour organizations. Yet despite the Marxist doctrine of the party programme and the rhetoric of their leaders, the behaviour of its adherents gave little substance to upper class fears that a German revolution was imminent. If the establishment chose to interpret strikes, such as the 1905 or 1912 miners' strikes in the Ruhr, in that light, it was for political reasons, an attempt to unite public opinion on their side, not from genuine conviction. Despite their alienation from state and society, the urban working class had little thought of direct confrontation. Undoubtedly, too, Bismarck's social welfare scheme of the 1880s, although it had failed to undermine working men's support for their party, made them less hostile to society. And if the socialist leaders as a reaction to an unfriendly environment had provided through its organization for leisure as well as work, a kind of subculture for the urban working classes, and thus isolated them from the community, it also made them more content to live their lives peaceably within that subculture.[39]

As late as 1914 party membership remained overwhelmingly skilled working class, though the share of the factory proletariat among party votes was increasing rapidly. But the bureaucratic and politically passive attitude of party functionaries, for all their radical ideology, was attracting a good deal of criticism from party supporters in the years before the war. At the same time, despite the impressiveness of working class organization in Germany, both as to size and structure, many urban workers and almost the whole of the rural working class were without contact with it, and until the experience of the war, the majority were virtually without political awareness. Sporadic efforts were made to win support for socialism among the rural labour force; individual leaders attempted to incorporate agrarian policies in the party programme in 1895 but were roundly defeated by party members in some 223 special meetings between July and October.[40] Political passivity was equally characteristic of workers in the public service also, though there were outstanding exceptions. The trade union movement was very unevenly represented in different branches of industry. The majority of German unions in the pre-war period were craft unions, which fulfilled an economic and social function, but did not give a political lead to their members.[41] In many areas, such as iron and steel producing concerns, unions had no foothold, and the employers successively maintained their role as 'masters' up to the war. Karl Kautsky in the 1890s declared: 'the trade union movement does not organize the worker as worker, as a member of his class, quite the reverse, the individual worker is organized in his character as printer, carpenter, compositor. The trade union movement as such is not merely not a class movement, it is the opposite: in place of solidarity with one's fellow workers, it confers a sense of solidarity with one's professional colleagues.'[42] Kautsky's observation was oversimplified, but there was a good deal of truth in the idea of the German urban worker in the pre-war years as a kind of Jekyll and Hyde, a radical socialist in his theoretical allegiance, and at the same time a man taking an old-fashioned professional pride in his craft. However, in the large modern industries, with relative mobility between different branches and little of the tension between skilled and semi-skilled workers such as was characteristic of the older type of craft unions, this was not so. Here, as in the railways and in the metal industry, militancy was strong on the eve of the war. The metal workers' union (DMV) was the most powerful and efficient union in Germany at that time and dissatisfied with party and union leadership. Its administrative offices in the cities and larger towns were gradually winning influence in the party associations; during the later years of the war, its members would identify themselves with the left wing critics within the socialist movement and be active in the industrial and political unrest which precipitated the revolution.

The political allegiance of German workers is probably the best documented chapter of their history in the later nineteenth century, though here too modern scholars are making us aware that there was far less integration between different groups of workers on the eve of the war than had once been supposed. About many matters of working people's lives, matters which affected everyone, such as the impact of industrialization on their relationships and habits, and on family life, much less is known. However, work is in progress and some has already appeared. One such field which has attracted the attention of scholars, especially in the United States, is the alleged 'destruction of morality and family life' which contemporaries, especially the propertied classes, alleged had taken place as a result of the industrial revolution. It is, however, open to question whether industrialization did have such an effect, and whether, if a change in social mores really took place, this was its principal cause. It is not easy to discover how those concerned, the workers themselves, both men and women, experienced life in the towns and cities as different from that which they or their parents had known in the village and farm. A body of workers' autobiographies exists, covering the years when the flight from the land took place, from the late 1860s onwards. These have been discovered and much discussed by social historians recently, although those with an interest in central European life have been acquainted with many of them for years. What these writers have to say about family life and sexual relations is not very explicit, but is sufficient in conjunction with other evidence to suggest that the differences between the age which preceded industrialization and that of the industrial revolution itself was not as great as was commonly supposed. Of course the restraints such as the village community could exercise on its members no longer existed for the factory workers or those in the textile industry who did piecework at home or the workshop. The proximity of male and female workers in the factory and the almost total lack of facilities for the latter until the end of the century, the appalling overcrowding in the poorer quarters of the cities where by 1900 the majority of Germany's population lived, all were bound to have an effect on the habits and outlook of those concerned. A number of workers' autobiographies speak of the sense of shock and confusion at things witnessed or experienced, such as factory girls submitting to the foreman in the hope of better wages.

One of the most generally cited, if oversimplified, indications of greater promiscuity among the lower classes is illegitimacy. Social historians have pointed out that illegitimacy was in general higher in the towns and cities than in rural areas. Statistics have been quoted to prove this. In Munich between 1879 and 1888 an average of 30 per cent of all live births were illegitimate, compared with 16 per cent in the rural area of Oberbayern in which Munich is situated.[43] For all of Germany in the year 1900 the ratio of children born to unmarried women was 9·14 in towns above 2000 inhabitants, 6·16 in small towns and rural areas.[44] Yet what figures cannot tell us – rather obviously – is when conception took place. Many births registered in the towns might well have been to recent arrivals there. The natural thing, as countless examples in recent times have shown, is for a country girl, who becomes pregnant and whose boyfriend cannot or will not marry her, to seek the anonymity of the city. Many of the prostitutes in late nineteenth-century Germany were such country girls who had drifted into their trade because it was the easiest way to support themselves and possibly a child in the city where no one knew them. What is not proved is that industrialization was a cause of the rise in illegitimate births. In some instances, such as in Rhineland-Westphalia, a highly industrialized area, the figures of illegitimate births are considerably lower than the national average: in the years 1896–1900 they were just 4 per cent, though the high proportion of men in the population may account for this. In fact long before the industrial revolution in Germany, society had witnessed an extraordinary increase in illegitimate births. This was not confined to Germany but was a European phenomenon, which dates from about the middle of the eighteenth century.[45] A number of social historians have therefore concluded that it was not industrialization as such that altered the relationship between the individual and his family and encouraged greater promiscuity among the working classes, but rather a process of what they have termed 'modernization', which was initially brought about by worsening economic conditions and a new view of the individual. From about 1750 onwards there occurred a sharp and sustained rise in the cost of living without an accompanying rise in real wages; falling demand made it difficult for young artisans to establish themselves as masters to be in a position to marry; enclosure and the well-intentioned agrarian policies of governments, designed to increase agricultural produce, had the effect of increasing the number of landless rural workers without prospects. Meanwhile the traditional prohibitions, enforced by state and municipality on marriage for the lower orders not in a position to support a family, gradually ceased to be effective. At the same time, particularly towards the end of the eighteenth century, novels and tracts make increasing reference to a new spirit of insubordination among the lower orders, a taste for the dress and habits of their betters, which prohibitions of various kinds seemed unable to discourage. The penalties which used to act as an effective deterrent on premarital intercourse, illegitimacy and adultery for the majority were no longer invoked; a Bavarian ordinance of 1808 stated specifically that 'fornication penalties' were now abolished. These and other factors apparently overruled the economic and social constraints in the lower ranks of society and account for the astonishing rise in the illegitimacy rates in Germany. From something in the order of between 1 and 3 per cent in Bavaria, Leipzig and Frankfurt, for example, at the beginning of the eighteenth century, these rose to almost 20 per cent in the Napoleonic era, to reach almost 24 per cent of total births in the 1850s and 1860s. Though the ratio of illegitimate to legitimate births declined from about the 1880s in Germany as a whole, the actual number remained fairly constant.

An indication of changing moral standards among the urban working classes in the Second Empire is the practice of limiting births. On the basis of several hundred interviews conducted by the German sociologist Max Marcuse in 1917, and evidence supplied by the workers' autobiographies, it seems clear that knowledge of these was fairly widespread before 1914. For, unlike the illegitimate birth rates, legitimate births declined in periods of economic crisis and rose again when things got better. It seems that it was the better paid workers, many of whom had advanced or socialist views, who consciously sought to limit their families in order to improve their own lives and to provide a better future for their children. As a thirty-seven-year-old Berlin factory foreman put it bluntly to Marcuse 'a person owes it to his future to limit births. . . . We workers are no longer as stupid as before when we supplied children for the rich and the state – factory and cannon fodder – that doesn't go any more.'[46] Similar if less blatantly class conscious views were expressed by others.

Does this point to a 'demoralization of the lower classes' in consequence of changing economic conditions? The changing attitudes of the working classes were rather part of a process of individual emancipation which began long before the industrial revolution and urbanization but which became more articulate during that time. The religious and social sanctions, which had guided their lives in former times, gradually lost their power to influence them. After 1871, working men and women who lived in the overcrowded poor quarters of towns and cities of Germany had ever less physical contact with churches and ministers, or with the kind of paternal authority which their parents and grandparents had deferred to, either in the form of the local landowner in rural areas, the notables of the small towns or the early nineteenth-century type of factory or workshop owner whom they called 'master'. They lived in a society which seemed hostile or at least indifferent to them as a class, which was ever ready to identify the workers with socialism, and which saw in official Marxist views on marriage and free love concrete evidence of lower class promiscuity, subversion of the moral and political order. The more sophisticated workers might articulate their attitudes with reference to class conflict or rejection of 'bourgeois' morality, for the majority changes in attitude and behaviour were the expression of secularized, more rationalized values, by which they hoped to exercise control over their private lives.

Chapter 21
Domestic servants

Up to the end of the eighteenth century, and in some parts of Germany for much longer, domestic servants were reckoned as part of the household. Their status was similar to the children of their master, although their authority within the house naturally depended on personality and length of service. It was usual for the indoor servants to eat with their masters, at least in the smaller households and in the country, to use the familiar '*du*' to the children and to have their masters address them in the same way. The mistress of the house, whether she were the wife of a merchant, a country landowner or a modest burgher, had always been used to work with her maids in the kitchen, linen room, etc., as numerous manuals on household and estate management of the seventeenth and eighteenth century illustrate.[1] Even in the nineteenth century, both in bourgeois and country aristocratic households, the housewife took a much more active part in the work of the household than would have been the case at the same social level in England or France. However, the general tendency towards greater self-consciousness among what is vaguely termed the middle classes, which included the well-to-do farmers as well as the urban bourgeoisie, under the influence of the Enlightenment, had the effect of changing the relationship between mistress and maids, between master and servants, from a familiar one to that of employer and employee. The history of the domestic servant in nineteenth and early twentieth century Germany, as in many other countries, is that of an inferior social class, something that was not necessarily true of their position in preceding centuries.

The German household – speaking generally – remained both a producer and consumer organization well into the industrial age. Slaughtering and sausage making, making butter and preserves, as well as spinning, weaving, and a variety of forms of needlework, formed part of the routine of most households, except at the very top and bottom of the social scale. In better-off houses a large number of domestics would be employed, and outside help brought in to do specific tasks, such as washing and ironing, but also tailoring and hairdressing, as is still the case in many Spanish households today. In the eighteenth century the guilds expressed their dislike at the practice of craftsmen being employed in noble or bourgeois houses in this way; popular novels depicted the simple craftsman acquiring the habits of easy living or a debilitating taste for luxury while working in the homes of the well-to-do. The guild masters disliked being unable to control workmanship and payment of their colleagues when they were employed in this way, but those concerned usually earned higher wages and had a greater degree of financial security in hard times. The marked increase in indoor servants at the end of the eighteenth century suggests that more and more people were prepared to accept the loss of liberty in return for such security. The eighteenth-century servant might indeed be a person of many talents. The enlightened professor Carl Friedrich Bahrdt told of his *Hausmeister* (male housekeeper) who was an excellent cook and judge of wine, and also a carpenter, potter and turner.[2] Sachse, author of *Der deutsche Gil Blas* (1768) has one of his 'gentleman's gentlemen' observe: 'A perfect servant should possess every accomplishment, he should be able to serve, shave, dress hair, drive, make music, declaim, speak French, be a tailor, a gardener and ideally be able to read aloud.'[3] This is of course a typical example of the master–servant profile, according to which all masters exploit their servants, while according to the masters their servants are idle rogues; yet it is also a valid social observation of the time in which it was made. Seventeenth- and eighteenth-century servants filled a variety of roles. In the small German courts, such as those of the Saxon dukes and the central German states, the members of the court orchestra duplicated as huntsmen, cooks and lackeys: it was, after all, a matter of finance and of the resources available. In the underdeveloped economy people acted as servants to the ruling classes who in other circumstances would have filled a variety of posts. Intelligent men among them were sometimes able to take advantage of the opportunities offered of improving themselves socially. Graf Brühl, chief minister of Saxony in the mid eighteenth century, placed a number of his personal servants in official posts. Almost all of Goethe's servants, whom he trained to copy his manuscripts and be generally useful to him, found employment in the Weimar state service later – though this is perhaps a special case. The social origin of personal servants, both male and female, in the pre-industrial age was often what we might call bourgeois. Girls of good family might spend some time in an aristocratic or patrician household to prepare themselves for household management on marriage. Not only girls of good family; craftsmen's daughters, whose services at home could be or had to be dispensed with on financial grounds, were glad to find employment in domestic service. The personal situation of indoor servants could vary considerably: an intelligent servant in the house of a tolerant and educated master might be able to improve himself both intellectually and socially. One of the most interesting aspects of Professor Engelsing's stimulating studies on the neglected field of domestic servants in the eighteenth and nineteenth centuries is the scope offered them by the use of their master's library, and the readiness of some employers to permit them to use it freely.[4] Thus Hebbel was employed as errand boy, coachman and clerk to the church warden at Wesselburen for some eight years; when not actually working – and such servants had a long day but frequent periods when they were not required to do anything – Hebbel read in his master's library; years later he wrote to Arnold Ruge that the reading done in this period of his life provided him with all the ideas on which he was to draw for the rest of his life.[5] Klaus Groth, the dialect poet and later professor at Kiel and Bonn universities, who came from a background as humble as that of Hebbel, held a similar post in Holstein.

However, for all the advantages their position might hold for them – and this depended of course on many factors – such people were isolated in society. Senior servants, or those in direct contact with their employers, if only as valet or clerk, felt themselves immeasurably superior to those who earned their living in more menial posts. Yet even if the former came from 'respectable' families, their legal position was that of someone who was unfree. Tutors and governesses came in for some sympathy in the works of *Sturm und Drang* writers in the 1770s and 1780s, and in the novels of half a century later, but this did not alter the humiliations they were so often forced to endure. The limited opportunities for employment among the educated who had no private means meant that such posts remained in demand well into the nineteenth century, especially for girls. Despite their background and training, they remained servants in the eyes of their employers, and were frequently reminded of their status. The case of Hebbel is particularly interesting in this connection. Once he had managed by study and writing to become a member of the bourgeoisie, he was constantly at pains to be seen to do nothing that might make people recall his former status: although experiencing real physical want, he was outraged when a well-meaning patroness tried to make him presents of food to take home. Should he carry – or rather be seen to carry – such things home he would immediately advertise his inferior social status. If a patroness lent him a journal or paper to read, he had some maid bring it back to her. His morbid sensitivity had much of the egoist, but his reaction is also worth commenting upon as an instance of the change that had taken place in the social image of the domestic servant. In the eighteenth century the kind of upward social mobility from washerwoman's son to respected writer which Hebbel had achieved was rare; however, the status of domestic servant was at that time less socially degrading than it came to seem to the self-conscious bourgeois in the mid nineteenth century, for whom '*Bildung und Besitz*', education and property, in some way represented personal merit.

The status of household servants and their social origins changed in the decades before the advent of the industrial revolution, because the whole concept of what constituted the family unit had changed. In medieval and early modern Europe there existed the 'whole house' (*ganzes Haus*) economy made familiar to modern historians by Otto Brunner.[6] The dependent relatives and the servants formed part of a kind of extended family, working, taking their meals and saying their prayers together, and all were under the authority of the master, who was responsible for their moral and physical welfare. Under the influence of the ideas of the Enlightenment, as well as for other, largely economic reasons, the better-off began to resent the proximity and familiarity of their own children and the servants. In the large farms of the north-west and in the towns all over Germany it began to be customary for the servants to take their meals separately from the family, for the lady of the house to work apart from her maids.[7] Even more significant, servants began to be assigned to specific functions, and the place of work of the master to be separated from his place of residence. The servants who had once worked in the house, acted as messenger or clerk in the warehouse, the shop or workshop, or even been employed in garden and estate when occasion demanded, the body of dependants known in former times as '*Gesinde*', was now, at the turn of the eighteenth to nineteenth century, divided into domestics, employees, manual workers, each with their particular place of work and living quarters. Many of these no longer lodged in the house or on the premises, but found themselves somewhere to live in the area; they no longer formed part of the 'household' and could not look to their employer for moral and physical support as in earlier times. Contemporaries were well aware of what was happening and discussed it passionately. In what was perhaps the best known book of etiquette, Baron Adolphe von Knigge's *Uber den Ümgang mit Menschen,* which went into six editions in the first ten years after its appearance in 1788, the author condemned the changes roundly: 'Our sophisticated way of life has robbed one of the first and sweetest relationships, that between the father of the house and its inmates, of all its dignity. The rights and joys of the father of the house have fairly disappeared. The servants are no longer seen as part of the family but as hirelings.'[8]

Not all agreed with this view; in novels, sermons and tracts ignominy was heaped on those servants who were getting 'above themselves'; many, it was said, were no longer faithful to their master, dressed ostentatiously, tried to imitate the social habits of their betters, and were idle and insolent. It was true that although unfree and forced to be at the behest of their employers for long hours, many domestics were well rewarded by comparison with craftsmen and small farmers in the lean years of the later eighteenth century. In Hamburg at this time a lady's maid would receive about 96 *taler* a year and her keep, plus presents at Christmas and from visitors. A married labourer with a family to support would be hard put to earn as much, and certainly there was many a craftsman's wife who was far worse off than she. The number of servants went on increasing in the more well-to-do German towns, despite protests on both sides about the calibre of master and servant, until the Napoleonic wars disrupted trade, destroyed wealth and caused widespread dismissal of servants. After the war the numbers rose again, at least in the more prosperous areas, but it was clear that the social origins of the domestic servants were changing. In the bigger towns they tended to come less from the vicinity than from the countryside, sons and daughters of small farmers or labourers, who would, it was thought, be biddable and hard working. The habit already to be found in the previous century of using the '*Er*' (or '*Sie*') form to address one's servants, was now common; it was a form which might easily sound abusive and was always distancing, one which might be used to any stranger whom one regarded as a social inferior. In north Germany the masters spoke high German, the servants dialect, and although some tried to educate their servants to speak in their 'educated' tongue, they and others mocked at their unsuccessful efforts to do so. The result was a growing distinction between the educated and uneducated (which did not obtain in south Germany and Austria) and which was only to be gradually eroded with the reorganization of the primary schools in the late nineteenth century. Of course the degree of change in the relationship of master and servant depended on many factors, and varied according to region, degree of urbanization and religious belief. Orthodox Christians, both Protestant and Catholic, tended to retain their patriarchal way of life; in many country estates, especially in the east, household servants still lived and ate with their masters, when other parts of Germany had already experienced the industrial revolution.

The number of servants employed in a single household in the pre-industrial period could be very large: Frau Arnstein, mother-in-law of the famous Viennese hostess Fanny Arnstein, ruled over a household of some fifty people on the *Graben* in central Vienna in the 1760s and 1770s; many of the inmates were dependent relatives, providing some kind of specialist or general service for their keep. Some decades later the Prussian minister Graf Bernstdorff had fourteen male servants in his Berlin house. The number of indoor servants increased steadily, as has been said, in prosperous urban households in the late eighteenth century until about 1840. An upper middle class family had three to five or even as many as eight servants without being especially wealthy, while in the homes of the upper classes sixteen or seventeen was normal (not including the stables). The prominent families had as many as fifty. 'Everyone wants the best servants', observed Dr von Hoven, a friend of Schiller's in bygone days, in the 1830s, 'and has two, three or even several. Every rich merchant has his own carriage and gives his serving men their own livery.'[9] The increase in the number of servants among the middle ranks of society was mainly the result of increased social pretensions among the commercial classes, just before the Napoleonic wars and when trade picked up again in the 1820s and 1830s. In towns such as Kassel or Münster where there were no big trading houses the number of servants was generally small. There were other economic reasons for this: hard times for the self-employed encouraged people in the post Napoleonic era to seek the security offered by service. It was rightly observed in 1832 by one Philipp Lindemann, enquiring into the causes of pauperism, that the position of a domestic servant was far more secure and fortunate than that of someone with his own household to finance.[10] Figures from Stettin (1797), Weimar (1820), Nuremberg (1823), Bremen (1823 and 1842), and Basel as late as 1867, show servants in these towns outnumbering apprentice craftsmen by as much as two to one.[11]

Up to about 1840 the proportion of men to women servants was high.

This can be explained by the number of specialist functions such as tailoring, barbering, etc., which men executed, and also by the fact that the dividing line between household and business was elusive or non-existent. From about the middle of the century this changed. Opportunities for the employment of men increased enormously. Public services and business enterprises began to take over many of the tasks once performed by servants – from simple things like chopping wood and fetching water, to making household provisions, such as sausages, beer, soap and candles, and providing laundry facilities. Sanitation gradually became a municipal matter, as did lighting and transport. Servants were no longer needed to accompany their masters home and light the way. Changes in social attitudes diminished the demand for certain services. One such casualty was the wet nurse: in mid eighteenth century Hamburg these constituted between 4 and 5 per cent of the populace; in Berlin just before 1901 they were a mere 0·01 per cent of the population.[12] In general, however, the decline in the demand for servants affected men much more than women. With the introduction of *Reich* statistics in 1882 concrete evidence of the declining numbers of domestic servants became available. From 1882 to 1907 the number of employed rose from 41·9 to 45·5 per cent of the populace; the percentage of servants declined relatively and absolutely from 1 329 000 in 1895 to 1 265 000 in 1907.[13]

The most striking difference between the servant body before and after industrialization is the change in the ratio of men to women. By the second half of the nineteenth century the German household was primarily a female affair. Although employment opportunities for women from the labouring classes were far greater than they had been, for girls and women of bourgeois families this was not so, since girls of even petty bourgeois families could not go to work in factories or workshops. Those who had to work were still forced to accept the position in fact if not in name of servant, as companions, governesses or nursery nurses. Because of the increased pretensions of the well-off bourgeoisie, this was felt by the employees as a particular humiliation. Intelligent and forceful women, such as Fanny Lewald, the highly successful novelist, or Malwide von Meysenbug or Frau Otto-Peters, early supporters of women's rights movements, made powerful indictments of a social order which offered women without means no escape from a life of frustration and indignity. The domestic servants who performed the manual work of the household were almost all women, and despite their overall decline in numbers relative to other occupations, a steady demand for the services of at least one domestic remained. The status of 'bourgeois', in Germany as elsewhere in Europe, demanded that one delegated all menial tasks, if one was to retain one's self-respect. Even those whose financial circumstances were straitened, such as lower paid officials and struggling professional men, made economies elsewhere rather than sacrifice this status symbol. It was above all in the larger cities that the social groups were concentrated, for whom, in the words of W. Kähler, 'without regard to their incomes, their social position made it necessary for them to keep servants'.[14] The quality of the servant was less important than the fact. One thus ensured one's standing in the community, though the reality was often rather less than satisfactory. Theodor Fontane's social novels are full of eccentric and lifelike servant figures, from old retainers to insufferable concierges; his letters to his wife in Berlin from London, where he worked as a journalist, show that they owed much to their creator's practical and often bitter experience.

> Posh people like them [referring to Privy Councillor Kugler, the art historian] always get good servants; and higher wages, nice presents and good tips mean that they remain good. We may get the second or third class, either hard-working and loose-living, or virtuous and slovenly. If she is hard-working and virtuous, her temper is bad, and if it isn't that, she's careless, stupid or dirty, or greedy, guzzles jelly and gossips on the backstairs and says we don't feed her properly.[15]

Domestic servants, unlike industrial workers in the late nineteenth century, were not mobile. For one thing, anyone wishing a good place was expected to remain several years with one family. Frau Davidis, a kind of German Mrs Beeton, advised mistresses to insist on this in her manual on household management, *The Housewife: A Present for Future Housewives*, the sixteenth edition of which appeared in 1897: 'Great importance will be given to how long maids have been in their former posts'.[16] This lack of mobility meant that such people had little sense of class solidarity, even when exploited, and little contact with groups or parties representing sectional interests. Nor were the socialists interested in this old-fashioned class of the oppressed, either in the nineteenth or in the twentieth century. The domestic servants became more rather than less hierarchical as a class or social group. The younger and the less qualified, who used to be enthusiastic supporters of the church, to argue the merits of this or that preacher and to read pious tracts, began in the second half of the century to forsake such habits, and to prefer dancing and escapist novels in their spare time. Such people had nothing in common with the 'superior class' of servants, the housekeeper, valets and coachmen, who felt a vicarious share in the rank and prosperity of their master and were proud of their own position. Indeed it would not be misplaced to speak of their having a collective class honour. As Heinrich XXXVIII Prince Reuss put it in his book *Der korrekte Kutscher* (1890) when he reported the case of two coachmen who so far 'forgot themselves' as to smoke on duty, 'They thus showed that they did not possess the manners for a decent carriage, but belonged on a bus or milkcart.'[17] The term 'domestic servant' could in fact mean a very great variety of persons and functions, even if the total number of them was declining relatively to other groups. This variety and difference from other social groups was expressed in the fact that although a national ordinance was constituted at the time of the founding of the Second Empire and made valid for all workers, the domestics remained subordinate to something like sixty different servants ordinances until the revolution of 1918.

In general one can say – rather obviously – that domestics with good employers were well off, rather better off than working men and women, but that for those whose relations with their employers were unsatisfactory, life was hard and seemingly incapable of improvement. Karl Gutzkow, who knew the grimmer aspects of life in his native Berlin better than most writers, was one of the few to represent the reality of such a life in a nineteenth century German novel. In the early part of his monumental *Der Zauberer von Rom* (1858–61) he portrayed in all its wretched detail the mental anguish and physical discomfort of a young servant girl employed by an irresponsible mistress; one of the worst features of such a case was that she did not know where to turn for help, especially if, as was usual, the girl came to the town from a rural area. In fact it was the police first, and only then the law, who were responsible for disputes between master or mistress and servants, and the police were naturally predisposed in favour of the former. Punishment, even corporal punishment, of his servant was permitted a master by law, and while servants had time off, it was the employer who decided when this should be given; the servant's wishes were immaterial. Apart from the lack of time off, the living conditions of maids even in well-to-do homes were often very poor. Notorious were the 'attics' (*Hängeböden*) in Berlin flats. As Hedwig, a cheeky young Berlin servant girl in Fontane's *Der Stechlin* remarks, 'They are always in the kitchen, right beside the stove or just opposite. You climb a ladder and if you're tired, you fall off. But mostly you make it, and then you open the door and push yourself in the opening, just like an oven. They called it "sleeping quarters".... It's worst in summer. Outside it's 30°, and the stove was on all day; it's like being put on the spit.'[18] A further bitter aspect of the insecurity of a maid's life was her treatment if she got pregnant; she was virtually certain of dismissal without reference. Under these circumstances it was very hard to get alternative work, and the number of miscarriages, still births or early death of infants of such girls was extremely high.[19]

Up to the end of the war the propertied classes showed themselves successful in opposing any change in the legal status of their servants as incorporated in the *Gesinderecht* of their area. This established their authority in society and their right to count themselves among the ruling classes. It only served to confirm their worst fears of the German revolution when, on 12 December 1918, the Council of the People's Plenipotentiaries took it on themselves finally to abolish the *Gesinderecht* for rural labourers and domestic servants in the German state.

Chapter 22
The poor

The social group which most constantly occupied the minds of the authorities in state and municipality in late eighteenth and early nineteenth century Germany was that of the poor. Hamburg is one of the few areas for which a detailed study of the conditions of life of the lowest order of society in that country exists.[1] Here the *Armenordnung* (Poor Law) of 1788 proved to be the model for many European cities and in the decade following its enactment showed laudable results. Yet a variety of external factors in the years after 1800 showed that such optimism had been vain. Hamburg, like so many other communities in Germany, proved unable to deal with the masses of the needy created by war, crop failure, disease, overpopulation, and an under-developed economy.

Those responsible for the Hamburg Poor Law had set out to solve the problem of the poor by distinguishing between those capable of work and those who were utterly unfit to support themselves. To such men as they were, formed by the ideas of the Enlightenment, beggary seemed not just a vexatious social phenomenon; it was morally reprehensible. Almsgiving no longer seemed the righteous act of a Christian towards his neighbour; rather it robbed a man of his self-respect by preventing him from seeking work to support himself and his family. The city fathers therefore provided accommodation in the various institutions of the city or weekly aid in the form of money or food for the chronically sick and the aged; they were treated free by doctors engaged for that purpose. Those capable of work were sent to the various organizations connected with the poor house to earn their living by spinning, knitting, etc.; anyone reluctant to comply was made to do forced labour in prison for a wage. More effective, at least in the short term, was the provision for the children of the poor. In the decade 1789–99, 2698 were sent to learn a trade in the so-called *Industrieschule* (industry school), 4833 more in the years 1793–99 to Sunday, evening and other schools.[2] Beggary now carried a fine of 5 *taler*, a sizeable sum.

The disasters inflicted by the French occupation of Hamburg put an impossible strain on the resources of the city. Once more the problem of the poor confronted the authorities. Few now shared the optimistic belief of the eighteenth century city fathers that it could be solved by administrative measures. Yet in one respect they had been successful, and not only in Hamburg. The composition of the poorer classes had changed. The ill, the crippled and the old remained to be cared for, but the vast hordes of beggars, the children who used to be taught from an early age to beg and steal, were greatly diminished in number, for society was no longer prepared to tolerate them as had been the case in the past. They did not of course disappear, and were joined in bad years by those rendered destitute by local or individual calamity, but beggary as a way of life was much rarer in the nineteenth century than it had been in previous times. The poor in the first half of the nineteenth century were much more likely to be those whom misfortune had robbed of their livelihood or those whose economic position was not strong enough to cope with rising prices, those whom Antje Kraus calls the 'potential poor'.

What were the conditions of life of the very poor in early nineteenth century Germany? Those responsible for administering the Hamburg Poor Law were men of experience in these matters. They made careful calculations of the minimum amount of money required to keep body and soul together. For the year 1792 they estimated that one such person needed 164 marks and 2 shillings per annum; this covered 7 kg of bread per week, 14 kg of potatoes, ½ lb each of butter and sugar, with milk, tea and salt at a total cost of just under 100 marks. Heating was reckoned at 39 marks, rent at 13, and provision was also made for lighting and ½ lb soap, but for nothing else. However, the very same diet eight years later cost more than double this amount.[3] This meant that not only were the Poor Law funds placed under great strain, but that a large number of people whose wages had been considerably above the minimum were now also in need, and even destitute.

A similar state of affairs was to be found in most, though not all,

German states. From Bremen in 1820 we have some detailed records of the income of the poorest class, which illustrate how large was the gap between what they could earn and the cost of basic necessities. The first case was a woman from Bremen, with four children between four and ten to support, who had been deserted by her husband, a musician. She could, the Bremen authorities estimated, keep body and soul together on her earnings which amounted to 15 *taler* a year from spinning and weaving, but she could not support her children. The local poor relief gave her a grant of 50 *taler*. Roughly the same income was estimated to suffice for another local man and his family, a former soldier, now a stocking weaver, aged seventy, his wife and their idiot son of eighteen. He earned 12, she 6 *taler* a year (in her case in the cigar factory); he also had a military pension of 12 *taler*. The authorities made up the difference to 64 *taler*.[4] Such incomes were not the prerogative of elderly or female workers, nor even manual labourers: in Berlin the subaltern officials were in receipt of charity on a considerable scale. In 1800, after an inquiry had been instigated by King Frederick William III, it was found that between 30 000 and 40 000 (that is, some 20 per cent of the city's population) were receiving aid; this included both royal and municipal officials such as clerks and messengers.[5] In this instance again, Klöden's memoirs provide a vivid picture of what life was like at such levels; his father was regarded as a relatively senior provincial official, yet his small family had only the barest necessities of life.[6] Almost half a century later W. H. Riehl, author of some of the earliest studies on German society, wrote an essay in the *Deutsche Vierteljahresschrift* that in his opinion the economic condition of the 'intellectual proletariat', as he termed them, the school teachers and lower paid officials, the candidates for the ministry and the unpaid *Privatdozenten* (lecturers without statutory appointment), was just as perilous as that of the labourers and artisans about whom society was showing such concern.[7] In their case destitution was made even more unbearable through the loss of their self-respect: many could neither clothe themselves in a manner befitting their profession and their class, not to speak of buying the books or instruments they needed.

Food prices fell in the 1820s, but scarcely more than a decade later they rose again, until in the so-called 'Hungry Forties' people in many German states were close to starvation. Bruno Hildebrand, professor in Marburg, cited two cases of children being born on the roadside in 10° of frost for lack of accommodation or shelter.[8] The food crisis of the 1840s was almost as serious as in Ireland: in eastern Germany in particular, more and more people had come to depend on the potato for their staple diet, because more yield could be got per hectare than from corn; when the potato failed, there was no cheap substitute. Real wages had not kept pace with rising prices in the last decades, while the rapidly rising cost of housing in the towns had actually reduced the amount of money available in the family budget for food.

All over Germany in the period of which we are speaking, the late eighteenth to the mid nineteenth century, people came steadily from the rural areas to look for work in the towns. The mass exodus from the land did not occur until the 1860s, however. Tradespeople found that the demand for their goods and services in the small villages could not provide their families with a living; there were too many would-be master craftsmen pursuing too little wealth, for Germany was still a poor country. As these people could not afford the cost of citizenship, or indeed of their mastership, they worked for cheaper rates, non-union men, as it were, to the anger and frustration of the guilds. On their low wages, physical survival was a problem, and although their wives and children usually managed to find work as well, the ever-increasing scarcity and cost of accommodation made a difficult situation often perilous. Most German towns were walled and the gates closed at night until the second half of the century – Frankfurt and Hamburg are cases in point. Building was restricted primarily by lack of space, although the wealthier citizens began to move out to villas with gardens outside the city walls leaving some space for accommodation for tradespeople and labourers. In Hamburg the number of houses and so-called '*Buden*', cottage-type houses opening on to passages and courtyards, increased scarcely at all in number between 1817 and 1852; on the other hand, the cellars and shacks erected on the top of existing dwelling houses and subdivided to shelter several families increased by 750 and 3000 respectively.[9] The cellars were regularly flooded by the rising waters of the river Elbe, but their inhabitants returned to their damp and muddy dwellings as soon as the floods had subsided. The Great Fire of 1842 compounded the misery of the poor, for it was their homes which bore the brunt of the disaster. Living accommodation which in 1790 had cost a manual worker 21 marks cost 98 in 1803–4 in Hamburg; in the latter year the poorest accommodation cost as much as 35 marks. Rents dropped again after the war to reach 84 marks in the 1840s for primitive dwelling places; a single manual worker could pay 45 marks for a place to sleep, which he might share with a colleague to help meet the cost. By 1867, 50 per cent of all flats or houses in Hamburg cost more than 150 marks. The situation in other cities was probably even worse. In Vienna the population increased by 42·5 per cent between 1827 and 1847, the accommodation by only 11·4 per cent.[10] Bad sanitation, overcrowding and malnutrition made typhus a major killer, especially in the poor quarters of the Austrian capital where, at the time of Schubert's death in 1828 of that disease, the number of deaths per annum was even greater than the births. In many smaller towns with burgeoning industrial enterprises and a high rate of immigrants among the population, such as Barmen or Elberfeld, the problem was just as bad. Most families had only one place to live and work; between the machines of the domestic workers and the beds there was scarcely room to walk. A commission set up in Barmen in 1847 to house the homeless found terrible conditions. One inspector Fabri cited an example of an annexe 'der einem schlechten Stalle glich, in einem Raum von 12 Fuss Länge, 7 Fuss Breite und 6 Fuss Höhe 10 Personen beiderlei Geschlechts und verschiedenen Alters in einem Bett mit Lumpen bedeckt, in einem anderen Raum unter den Dachziegeln, 6 Fuss lang, 7 Fuss breit und 5 Fuss hoch, 4 Personen, in einem Keller, 10 Fuss lang, 6 Fuss hoch, 8 Fuss breit, 6 Personen; ['in a room like a broken-down stable some 12 feet long, 7 feet wide and 6 feet high were ten people of both sexes in one bed, covered with rags; in another right under the roof, 6 feet long, 7 feet wide and 5 feet high, were four people; in a cellar, 10 feet long, 8 feet wide and 6 feet high, six more'].[11]

In 1862 the problem was as bad as ever; 260 houses were condemned as overcrowded; in many others five, six and seven people lived in one room, but this was not regarded as overcrowding.[12] It was not until the end of the century that houses had direct water supply; the river Wupper was more like some mighty sewer, the recipient of all the waste products of industry and humanity on its banks: it was not the fact of non-existent sanitation that was injurious to life and health, but the overcrowding which made it dangerous and often fatal.[13] Thus, among the poor, infant and child mortality remained extremely high until the end of the century, and few escaped disease and ailments of some kind. Berlin had problems of a different kind: here there was no lack of terrain for building purposes and before mid century the city was already expanding to take the immigrants swarming in from all over Germany, especially the east. Speculators solved the demand for accommodation in their own way: they built the great barracks in the northern fringe of the city for which Berlin became so notorious. In the 1840s there lived some 2500 persons in 400 rooms which seven of these blocks contained. Here in the insalubrious Voigtland, as the district was known, lived the prototype of the proletariat, 'the dregs of the non-propertied classes', as the journalist Ernst Dronke described it in his book *Berlin* (1846). In Berlin as a whole rents rose from an average of 85 *taler* in 1830 to 171 in 1872.[14] The poor were frequently evicted for non-payment of rent, which is not surprising in view of the cost – even a room in the Voigtland barracks cost about 24 *taler* a year – and also because rent was paid half yearly; it required more self-discipline and more funds than the vast majority could ever possess to put money by for rent day. When this happened, whether in Vienna or Berlin, Leipzig, Bremen or Cologne, a small handcart was sufficient to move the family possessions. The contemporary name for the poor in mid century was truly an apt one: they were called '*die Eigentumslosen*', people without possessions.[15] The problem of accommodation threatened not only the lowest income groups, but those who regarded themselves as belonging to the middle classes as well. In 1855 Theodor Mundt, erstwhile Young German writer, declared that in northern Germany at least the 'mittleren und unteren Klassen ... für ihre Verhältnisse sämmtlich zu theuer wohnen' ['middle and lower classes all live in dwellings that cost them more than they can afford'].[16] The effect of rising rents was to upset a household budget in which some 70 per cent was required for food and 25 per cent for rent among the lower paid; savings could only be made from heat, light and clothes, and thereafter on food. Nothing was left for a crisis. Nor could any provisions be made in such estimates for a recurrent expense in many families: the need to seek oblivion in beer and gin.

Contemporaries were by no means insensitive to the growth of poverty around them. Far from it. 'The social question', as it was termed in mid century, was a burning issue in drawing rooms and club rooms, in the local inns and cafés, wherever men gathered. In contrast to the populace, concerned to find the cause of the problem, state governments showed a largely negative attitude. In the minds of Germany's rulers the poor still belonged to the province 'police and public order'. Many governments and town councils reiterated traditional prohibitions on marriage of the lower orders without means to support a family, or set the *beadle* on the indigent among them who were not citizens of the community.[17] Ordinary people, many of whom as tradesmen were fearful that they too might be the next victims, agitated for state action against what they alleged to be the causes of the situation: mechanization, decline in public and private morality, and uncontrolled competition from those who were not members of guilds, fraternities and professional associations. Very many Germans in responsible positions, officials and factory owners, clergymen and university professors, not only devised possible solutions but started in a practical way to organize relief funds, public works and cooperative organizations, in order to help people to help themselves. Some present-day writers like to refer to the German middle classes in the nineteenth century as apolitical, sleepy provincials in slippers and quilted dressing gowns; they ought to be made aware of the extent of public involvement in this question and the dedication which they showed in their efforts to remedy the problem. That they failed to do so was not for lack of effort or even of practical suggestion, but because of the state of the German economy, underdeveloped and undercapitalized as it was, and because they lacked institutions for bringing pressure on the governments.

Observers of the social scene in Germany in the middle of the century believed that the current poverty was on a scale never experienced previously. Historians today would not agree with them, seeing in the crisis of the 1840s a last manifestation of the type recurrent in the *ancien regime* (as for example that of 1770–1) when the prosperity of a country was still determined by the cycle of harvests and weather, and not by business cycles. Contemporaries, and not in Germany alone, were particularly deeply disturbed at what they saw because they felt the whole social order to be threatened. They tried to express their belief in a difference of kind as well as extent of impoverishment by coining a new term: they called it pauperism. As in the case of the population question or the pollution issue today, it weighed heaviest on the minds of those not or not yet directly affected by it. The Brockhaus *Real Encyklopädie*, a German *Chambers Encyclopedia*, published in 1846, defined pauperism as:

> ein neu erfundener Ausdruck für eine höchst bedeutsame und unheilvolle Erscheinung. Es handelt sich dabei nicht um die natürliche Armut ... auch nicht um die vergleichsweise Dürftigkeit ... Der Pauperismus ist da vorhanden, wo eine zahlreiche Volksklasse sich durch die angestrengteste Arbeit höchstens das notdürftigste Auskommen verdienen kann ... und dabei immer noch sich in reissender Schnelligkeit ergänzt und vermehrt.

> a newly invented term for a very significant and fateful phenomenon. It is not a question of natural poverty, nor even of comparative need ... Pauperism exists where a numerous class of people can only earn the barest necessities despite working as hard as they possibly can ... and at the same time increases and multiplies at a terrific speed.[18]

Contrary to what most people believed at the time, pauperism was not caused by industrialization, although this undoubtedly brought a great deal of human suffering and misery in its wake.

Friedrich Engels's thesis, to this effect, was expounded in *The Condition of the Working Class in England* and was applied by many to Germany. One of the few contemporary critics, already mentioned, was

Bruno Hildebrand; he pointed out in the 1840s that pauperism was at its worst in areas where there was no industry to speak of. In the region of Upper Hesse around Marburg, for example, there were neither factories nor factory workers; 'in alter patriarchalischer Form herrscht hier neben dem Ackerbau noch der alte Handwerksbetrieb' ['the old crafts continue alongside agriculture in their traditional patriarchal form'].[19] Yet all around misery was so widespread, he said, conjuring up an image that could not but horrify his readers, that 'in den Schilderungen der irischen Armut [es] Epoche machen würde' ['which even in accounts of Irish poverty would stand out'].[20] Others, citing examples 'of the direst poverty' from Württemberg, Hesse and Baden, suggest that at least one-third of the communities in Germany were in similar straits. Modern historians would regard this last estimate as too low. In a now famous essay Werner Conze suggested that in Prussia 'mindestens 50–60% der Bevölkerung ... knapp, ja dürftig und in Krisenzeiten elend und gefährdet lebten' ['at least 50–60 per cent of the populace ... lived very frugally, even in actual need, and in times of crisis theirs is a wretched and perilous existence'].[21] Antje Kraus in the conclusion of her exemplary study of the poor in Hamburg goes so far as to say that in the first half of the century 'mindestens 60% der Bevölkerung in dürftigen und weitere 20% in knappen wirtschaftlichen Verhältnissen lebten' ['at least 60 per cent of the populace were in needy circumstances, and a further 20 per cent on the bread line'].[22] The situation was so bad in Pomerania and Berlin that the quiescent lower and middle classes were prompted to unaccustomed violence, while on the Rhine draymen broke up the barges which they felt were taking away their livelihood.

Yet such economically motivated violence was rare in Germany.[23] The real cause of pauperism in Germany between the end of the Napoleonic wars and the 1850s was firstly an extraordinary increase in the population. This was unevenly distributed, and depended on such matters as to how far the countryside had been enclosed, on the trade policies of the rulers, liberal agrarian reforms, and population policies. There was an overall trend from the eighteenth to the nineteenth century for the lower classes to increase more than the middle and upper. In rural areas the landless increased at the expense of the large and smaller farmers. In Lippe-Detmold in north-west Germany, for example, the so-called *Kolonnate*, farmers on a large, medium and small scale, increased in number between 1784 and 1848 from 5700 to 7600, while the landless labourers rose from 3500 to 8000.[24] Although this is an extreme example, the trend was almost everywhere for the lower classes to increase far more rapidly than the middle and upper, especially in the so-called *Realteilungsgebieten* in western Germany and in East Prussia. Disregard of the old limitations imposed by German states on the marriage of the lower orders was partly responsible for the increase. The local élites who could bring direct pressure on individuals in the community to observe such laws and customs were largely replaced in the first decades of the nineteenth century by the distant, impersonal state official.[25] The agrarian reforms and the liberal trade policies in many states had had the undesirable social effect of increasing the number of the landless and of apprentices who were unlikely to gain their master's title and therefore to be able to afford to marry. With the prospect so slender of permission being granted, many simply married without the consent of their local authority or lived in common law marriage. Their marriages, as innumerable government reports lamented, were almost always more fruitful than those of other classes.[26] Meanwhile, the illegitimacy rate rose alarmingly too, a phenomenon common to all European countries in the century 1750–1850. Furthermore, the population of paupers rose in areas where land had been enclosed, for the lower classes had lost grazing rights and therefore a source of food and income; after the Napoleonic wars and especially in the 1840s, the decline of the domestic industries, of weaving and spinning, in the face of English competition robbed countless thousands of their livelihood, and because their customers had no longer any money to spend, many small shopkeepers were also made destitute. Pauperism was a feature of the German social scene throughout the first half of the nineteenth century but it was always localized; some years witnessed a decline in numbers, others a frightening increase. The worst years were early in the century, 1816–17, then there was a time of cattle plague and crop failure, and worst of all were the mid 1840s when both the corn and potato harvests failed. At such times people were driven to eating dogs slaughtered with rabies in the Prussian Voigtland, cats and dead horses in Silesia, and bark, thistles and nettles in central Germany. The so-called 'hunger typhus' broke out in Westphalia and Silesia during the years 1816–17. Emigration to the New World began, especially from the south-west, on a scale comparable to that of Ireland. In 1844 the starving weavers made their ineffectual but much publicized protest. Two years later J. M. Radowitz, intimate counsellor of the king of Prussia, declared 'Das Proletariat steht in riesengrosser Gestalt da und mit ihm öffnet sich die blutende Wunde der Gegenwart, der Pauperismus' ['The proletariat like some monstrous creature lies there, and with it the bleeding wound of our age, pauperism, is laid bare'].[27] The association in the minds of the authorities between mass wretchedness and mass violence struck terror into their hearts. The awful example of the Paris mob in the 1789 revolution suddenly seemed close at hand; a social revolution must be imminent. Heine grimly satirized their fears, evoking the spectre of communism:

Es gibt zwei Arten von Ratten,
Die Hungrigen und die Satten.

There are two types of rat,
The hungry and the fat.[28]

Hegel had already pointed out in his *Grundlinien der Philosophie des Rechtes* the economic facts of the problem and the injustice caused which could well provoke the lower classes to violence: 'dass bei dem Übermass des Reichtums die bürgerliche Gesellschaft nicht reich genug ist, d.h. an dem ihren eigentlichen Vermögen nicht genug besitzt, dem Übermass der Armut und der Erzeugung des Pöbels zu steuern' ['for all the excess of wealth, bourgeois society is not rich enough – that is, has not enough of its own substance – to check the excess of poverty and the proliferation of the proletariat'].[29]

Ordinary people were less exercised by the spectre of mob violence than by the social implications for themselves. By the 1840s they were becoming deeply disturbed about the effects of pauperism on society as they knew it. The Brockhaus definition quoted above expressed their most acute fear, that 'the proletariat' was breeding faster than other social classes, and must soon engulf the traditional social order – the image used by a writer in the *Deutsche Vierteljahresschrift* of 1844, 'Krebsschaden der zivilisierten Gesellschaft' ['canker of civilized society'], was thus peculiarly apt.[30] A sense of moral outrage at the fecklessness of the poor in marrying without substance or, worse still, producing illegitimate children in ever-increasing numbers for society to maintain is a common feature of contemporary reports, petitions, letters to the papers, discussions in clubs and meeting places. The 'immorality' which lay behind this behaviour was blamed on liberalism, the Enlightenment, even on the state bureaucracy which encouraged the lower orders to disregard the limitations imposed on them by their station in life and to indulge in luxury, licentiousness and aping their betters. 'Overpopulation' was a kind of slogan, which expressed widespread fears about the future in middle class circles just before the revolution. The fear of a charge on their own pockets and of change in the social structure was a source of the deepest anxiety in the small towns and rural communities, where it was feared those who left in youth would return in want in old age to be an impossible burden on the community.[31] This, the 'conservative' interpretation of the social question, was representative of German burghers living in small towns and rural areas – in other words, of the bulk of the articulate section of the population at that time. There was a further aspect of the problem in their minds which was just as distressing: countless numbers of respectable citizens were being reduced to penury through no fault of their own. For this they blamed mechanization. 'The machine', wrote a master stocking knitter from Erlangen in 1848, where three wool spinning machines had put many out of work, 'is the destroyer of households, the ruination of the youth, the inducer of luxury, the despoiler of forests, the populator of the workhouse, the exploiter of the royal treasury, and soon the companion of general upheaval.'[32] Another writer, an official from Nuremberg, put it less rhetorically but more cogently: 'If we should enter the home of a craftsman we should see at once the bitterest want, so anxiously concealed and kept secret. The lack of orders and of markets, and low prices frequently bring the most industrious man into such distress that he and his family must suffer more than a public beggar.'[33] If he advertised his want by going on public assistance, this closed sources of credit to him; it was a vicious circle which he could not break out of through his own efforts. That the facts did not wholly correspond to the convictions of such people is not important; men are not moved to demonstrate or indeed to vote by facts, but by what their inherited traditions and prejudices persuade them are the facts. Such deep-seated anxieties among ordinary people prompted many to give their support initially to the revolution in 1848, hoping, as their kind in other countries before and since have done, to achieve a restoration of an earlier reactionary social order by radical means.[34] The failure of the revolution to provide a panacea for the social evils of the time brought such people back to the traditional attitude of the German burgher: to look for protection and security from the state.

Less widespread but more articulate was the liberal view of the problem of pauperism. A typical representative was the industrialist, Friedrich Harkort from the Rhineland, a practical man, yet one who, as a man of progressive thinking and strong social conscience, felt involved in the greatest problem of his time. Author of a tract written in the 1840s called the *Bienenkorbbrief* (*Bee-Hive letter*), which was addressed to working men and read and treasured by them and their families, he distinguished between the 'proletariat', the feckless members of society, and the artisan or labourer who through no fault of his own fell on hard times:

People talk of the proletariat and do not know what they mean. I call

> someone a member of the proletariat who was neglected by his parents, unwashed, uncombed, who was never taught how to behave nor sent to church or school. He never learnt a trade, married without substance, he brings into the world others like himself, who are always ready to fall on other people's property and to act as a canker of the community.[35]

The working man struck down by accident or sickness or the periodic crises which he believed a permanent feature of society was something quite different. Such men, Harkort felt, could be helped in a number of ways, by the state, the community, and above all by self-help in the form of association. Sickness insurance, saving schemes and cooperatives were all featured in his programme for bringing the industrial workers gradually into the burgher class, a view shared by a number of optimistic and practical men of his time. There were a variety of socialist interpretations of pauperism current in the 1840s of which the Marxist was but one. They ranged from the Utopian to the pragmatic, but none received the kind of widespread support or interest given to the conservative and liberal line; radical social ideas were much discussed among certain groups of young intellectuals, many of whom had sought refuge abroad, and among the apprentice journeymen who came into contact with such circles during their travels, and who were disaffected by the society which they had left because of its lack of prospects for them. These represented only a small minority. French radicals of the time read Rousseau, Voltaire and Diderot or Helvetius, as one modern social historian has so aptly pointed out, while their German counterparts read religious tracts and books – Lamennais's *Paroles d'un croyant* enjoyed enormous success in the 1830s and 1840s among such people, and even Germany's best known communist artisan, Wilhelm Weitling, could be called a religious Utopian rather than a political thinker.[36]

The governments of Germany produced very little that was constructive to solve the problem of pauperism, unless one can see the creation of the *Zollverein* as a step in the right direction. Formed in 1834, the Prussian-inspired *Zollverein* helped encourage trade by removing some of the most intractable obstacles, the bewildering variety of customs and toll barriers. Over the next decades more and more German states joined, and the increasing volume of trade helped to generate capital, the lack of which had been one of the chief hindrances towards industry developing and employing the surplus labour force. In the 1850s and 1860s the expansion of German industrialization, already foreseen by liberals even in the worst years of the 1840s, came about. There followed the gradual introduction of farm machinery which drove the surplus rural population into the town to provide stimulus for further industrial expansion. The grim fate threatening a large proportion of German society, the proletarianization of the middle income groups, began to recede. Germany was as yet a poor country; for many years after that period from about 1850 to 1873, which economists call the 'takeoff period' of her industrial revolution, a large percentage of her populace lived a life of frugality, even of need. Poverty remained, on the land and in the new urban workers' settlements, but the spectre of pauperism and the word itself gradually ceased to haunt the authorities and those under their care.

Section 5
The other half

Chapter 23
Women in German society

From the earliest times, women in Germanic law were accorded a different status from that enjoyed by men. This distinction was based, not on religious or philosophic grounds, but on their differing military and biological functions. From the moment of her birth, when the symbolic ceremonies attributed a lesser value to her than to a male child, and in matters of law and inheritance, a girl was treated less favourably. Salic (Frankish) law, in contrast with those of Anglo-Saxon or Visigothic lands, excluded her from succession to the throne. The unmarried girl or woman remained under her father's authority, the married woman exchanged it for that of her husband. In many Germanic tribes a widow required a male guardian to act for her in court and to administer her property. The husband's right to use physical force on his wife was confirmed as late as the sixteenth century by ecclesiastical courts and in 1756 Bavarian common law pronounced that woman 'is not merely subordinate and subject in domestic matters, but has an obligation to perform customary and proper personal and household services, as may be demanded of her by her husband, who may, if need be, chastize her in moderation'.[1]

The authority of a mother over her children was very much less than that of the father. The Prussian Civil Code of 1794 recognized that a mother had some but not equal authority with the father. The German Civil Code of 1896 did not alter this, and it was not until the present

Federal Republic was instituted that the equal rights and authority of parents over their children was accepted in law. There was no married women's property act of the type introduced into England in 1872 and 1880. Although women could acquire property according to Germanic law, they required a man to administer it, apart from cases where the husband was absent or imprisoned. Only in artisan circles was a woman, in her capacity as heiress or widow of the former master, in a position to run her business. However, in line with the traditional view that 'the state recognizes a burgher but not a burgess', she could not appear on her own behalf at guild meetings, but had to send a male representative.[2] True, the social situation of women was often less disadvantageous than the strict legal position would make it seem, and custom often anticipated changes in the law by many years.[3] Yet in general the force of convention as of law gave women less freedom than in Anglo-Saxon countries, or even in France. Restrictions on women's liberty in the political, social and economic life of her country, from whatever source these derived, remained in force longer in Germany than in most Western countries.

Largely because of the predominantly political and constitutional bias of its historians, Germany has produced few historical studies dealing with women's position. It is only in the present decade that this is being remedied, though studies tend to concentrate on the period from 1865 onwards. In the general lack of interest in this subject, a number of factors were involved: major talents were uncommon among women writers in the eighteenth and nineteenth centuries; in earlier centuries, in contrast with France, they were virtually non existent. Moreover, there are few great literary works from any period of Germany's history, apart from the High Middle Ages, which deal with women's position in society. Thus the impetus to historical work of the kind offered by the wealth of Victorian novels had no counterpart in German-speaking lands. It is true that a large body of memoir literature and correspondence from the pens of women has survived, dating from the second half of the eighteenth century onwards. Such writings were used in the years immediately preceding and again just after the Great War to embellish the impressionistic and sentimental account of times past, which used to be graced with the title of *Kulturgeschichte* or 'cultural history'. Germany did not lack women of personality and talent in the modern era, but here again, as in so many other spheres, the regional diversity, poor communications and lack of a capital city prevented many intelligent and well-connected women from achieving the intellectual independence which a number of English and French women were able to enjoy. Most significant of all was the fact that

Germany's political and social backwardness allowed the consensus of opinion to continue almost unchallenged, that the education of women was not necessary, since they had no role outside the domestic sphere. Some women of talent found an outlet in creative fields: in the eighteenth century Frau Gottsched, actress and playwright, or Sophie von Laroche, grandmother of Clemens and Bettina von Brentano, in the nineteenth the best-selling novelists, Fanny Lewald or Luise Mühlbach, or the one-eyed Countess Hahn-Hahn, who intrigued Elizabeth Barrett on their meeting in London in 1846; Charlotte Birch-Pfeiffer became a password for dramatic success in the same period. But these women did not become arbiters of taste and fashion, despite a success that was both literary and financial. They were eccentrics in the eyes of society, a role some appreciated but which in others induced a feeling of guilt. Sophie Mereau, whom Schiller helped launch an *Almanach für Frauen* in 1784, and who had a number of books to her credit when she became Brentano's mistress and in 1803 his wife, promised on the latter occasion that she would thenceforth only write cookery books. In the two and a half years of their marriage, until her death giving birth to their third child, she kept her word. Fanny Lewald, who flouted convention by living with a married man, Adolf Stahr, for many years before his divorce and their marriage, assured the Grand Duke of Weimar, with whom she corresponded for nearly half a century, that she was an excellent cook and housewife. She seems to have felt that he would not otherwise take her as seriously as she felt she deserved.

It is not surprising that in Germany the movement in favour of women's rights should be slow to get off the ground and that when it did, agitation for political rights played a very small part in its programme. A sizeable proportion of those involved in women's movements actually opposed votes for women; others withdrew it early in the twentieth century on the grounds that it would favour the socialists. The main impetus towards a women's rights movement came from those concerned, as were most German reformers, with education rather than liberty.

The churches exercised a powerful influence on the accepted role of women in German society, and this influence – in the social, as against the spiritual sphere – was longer lasting than in comparable western European countries. The advent of Lutheranism in the sixteenth century had not altered the medieval view of women and marriage in any significant manner, which continued, in the tradition of Augustinian thought, to be seen primarily in its sexual aspect. The French historian J. Neveux, in his study of religious and social life in early modern Germany, concludes his remarks on women in that society with the sage observation: 'Il s'en est fallu de peu que la femme ne soit d'ailleurs écartée purement et simplement de la communauté chrétienne, du moins en tant de personne agissante' ['It wanted little for women to have been simply excluded from the Christian community, at least as an active element'].[4]

There were at that time learned doctors of theology who denied that women had a soul. The old maxim, 'Women shall be silent in church', held good still in seventeenth and eighteenth century Germany, both in the Protestant north and the Catholic south. In Hamburg about 1700 it was not thought proper for them to sing in church, though they were expected to be devout and instil piety in their children. The anti-religious influence of the Enlightenment passed them by almost totally. While their husbands had ceased to believe, or even to pretend by their outward demeanour that they did so, they expected their wives to attend church regularly and take part in the associated social functions. It would be hard to dispute the suggestion that men regarded piety as a necessary and satisfactory opium of the weaker sex. Such attitudes were especially characteristic of the middle classes; the aristocracy, particularly those with their homes in the country, remained attached to their religion much longer, partly because they identified it with the conservative hierarchical social order. For women of all social classes, religion long remained their only outlet from the home. Their only mental fare until the late eighteenth century was devotional books – even the cynical Frederick II was satisfied to leave his unfortunate queen to spend her empty days, translating pious works from the French. In 1795 a Bremen woman wrote of her early life: until her sixteenth year 'the Bible, the catechism and a few odd sermons were all I had to read, with loving care my parents shut me up in a fortified castle, where no article of the book trade could ever reach me'.[5] What we know from other sources suggests that this experience was a typical one. Klöden's mother, intelligent but self-taught, sought help from the local pastor in getting books to read, when they came to live in West Prussia in the 1790s. His reaction was one of outrage that she would thus forget herself; she did not try again.[6] The church authorities were in no doubt as to where woman's duty lay. A south German religious publication of 1760, entitled *The Obligation of Married Women to Their Spouses,* spoke eloquently of her need to practise 'that loyalty which she owes her lord and master, who alone is lord and master in the house, whom she must aid in the tasks of the house, but only in the way he deems fitting'.[7]

Despite the restrictive influence on female individuality exercised by both churches, perhaps the most important event for women in the eighteenth and early nineteenth century was a religious movement – Pietism. Not only did Pietist preachers bring women to the conventicles, but they had them speak there about their religious experiences; the stress on feeling rather than understanding as a vehicle of such experience appealed to many women, as did the intimate personal contact between souls, which was such a feature of the movement. If the relationship between pastor and congregation was bound to foster murky sentimentalism and petty jealousies, Pietism also offered to many women the opportunity of a fuller life of mind and spirit. Pietists were encouraged to pursue self-analysis and to express their emotions in diaries and in letters to fellow initiates; for many this brought a new demonstrativeness into family relationships, which benefited their children. Thus Caroline Perthes, daughter of the Lutheran poet and pastor, Mattias Claudius, could write to her husband:

> What you write of N's children is true and distressed me greatly, for I am convinced that heartfelt love, which lets itself be seen, and in a manner felt in everything, is the dew and the rain indispensable to the growth and bloom of children. I believe that the more children are loved, and the more they are conscious of being loved, the better; of course there is a time for seriousness and discipline. But I also know many people who consider it right carefully to conceal their affection from their children.[8]

The experience of Pietism contributed to the notion that women's sensibility might be different from that of men, that they might have a personality outside their families, or that a marriage might even, as in the case of the Petersens, be a partnership of equals rather than an extension of the father-daughter relationship. Petersen, a well-known Pietist clergyman in central Germany in the first half of the eighteenth century, was of humble origin; his wife came from a noble family. In the somewhat stilted style of her letters, Frau Petersen tells her husband of her intensely felt gratitude for such a rich and happy life as theirs had proved to be.[9] The Perthes couple, at the end of the century, provided another example of the beneficial influence of Pietist thinking on domestic relations within the accepted framework of the authoritarian family. Caroline, as her husband put it, was 'a pious, true-hearted and submissive creature, but her inward course she shapes for herself and pursues it with a steady hand'.[10] In the same period, classical humanism, which in its German form owed something to Pietist influences, had a similar, though more truly liberating influence on marriage, as the letters of Wilhelm and his wife Caroline von Humboldt show, or those between Schiller and his wife.

In the majority of households, as far as we can judge, the traditional paternalism described by the baroque writer von Lohenstein in his novel *Arminius* (1689) remained unchallenged: 'The father's will, as that of the gods, knows no authority over it.'[11] The stress on paternal authority, the fear he invoked, his outbursts of temper, occasionally savage, inevitably diminished the stature of his wife: 'gentle, shy, self-contained, towards her husband patient and docile, but enduring', wrote the poet Tieck of his mother, in one of the very numerous testimonies by famous Germans to the affection they felt for their mothers.[12] 'I do not want to be loved, but feared' was a favourite saying of Count Dubsky, father of the novelist, Marie von Ebner-Eschenbach; she recalled the physical paralysis of fear which overcame herself and her sister after an unconscious transgression.[13] Even royal fathers indulged in violent outbursts, as the instance of Frederick William I's attack on his son showed, and which occurred in the presence of the queen. Not all wives were docile creatures, but the shrew was the object of particular social obloquy. Her powers to involve her female relations in plaguing unhappy man are described in eloquent and pathetic detail by the egregious master barber Johann Dietz in seventeenth century Halle.[14] The censure of society for such disregard of 'the natural order of things', in the form of a nagging wife, was considerable. Johann Miller in his novel of manners about artisan life, *Gottfried Walther* (1782), paints in lurid detail the consequences of such indulgence on the husband's part. By giving in to his new wife, Gottfried's father 'lost for ever that right which appertained to him as a man'.[15] W. H. Riehl in his highly influential book on the family, *Die Familie* (1855), which lauded the patriarchal customs of former times as mandatory for the nineteenth century, cited with approval the different standards of punishment in two Hessian villages in the sixteenth century for a harridan and a wife beater. In the former case, the neighbours tied the woman to a donkey and led her through the village streets, in the latter the clergyman simply reprimanded the husband.

The subordinate position of the women in society had sound economic reasons. She was, at least until the late eighteenth century, 'the first worker in the household'.[16] 'The girl is made as a future wife for the home. Everywhere, but especially in Germany, the woman's destiny has always been: wife, mother, household', wrote Joseph Hillebrand in *Über Deutschlands National Bildung* (1818), one of the many such works on the question of education to appear about that time.[17] Even well-born women worked with their maids in the kitchen, linen room and dairy. Bettina von Brentano, married to the poet and landowner Achim von Arnim, expected her daughters to get up with the maids at 4 a.m. on washdays, working alongside them and ending the day with lentil soup around the same table. As the farmer's wife was responsible for the farm hands as well as for her own family, so in commercial towns and in the homes of master craftsmen, the housewife provided for the physical wellbeing of her husband's employees. From about the early nineteenth century it became customary for these employees to board out, and to look after their own meals and washing, but in small towns and in many rural areas the old pattern survived much longer. The variety of tasks still performed in the home until the second half of the century left women little leisure time.

Leisure was the key to the awakening interest in education for women, a vital step in the long process of her emancipation – leisure to take advantage of the ideas expressed in the eighteenth century weeklies, and the novels which became suddenly fashionable among the upper classes after 1740. Those whose family circumstances gave them the opportunity to read found the English novelist Richardson and his German imitators heady stuff. The notion of a specifically feminine sensibility, which women discovered in these works, stimulated a demand for more and more novels. The genre had an unprecedented popularity in late eighteenth century Germany: by the 1790s, for every novel published in England, eight were appearing in Germany.[18] Neither husbands nor clergymen could find anything reprehensible in Richardson's heroines, who were virtuous yet realistically portrayed. They were women of feeling and understanding, who could transform the relationship between husband and wife from that of a father–daughter, or even master–servant, to something approaching a partnership. Pastor Hermes, author of one of the most popular German novels, *Sophiens Reise,* openly admitted that he regarded the novel simply as a more effective vehicle of improvement than a sermon or tract. This, as Johanna Schopenhauer recalled in her memoirs, was, besides Gellert, the first non-religious work her own mother had read. In the works of the delightful Gellert, notably his novel *Die schwedische Gräfin von O.* (1746), virtue was made to seem thoroughly attractive, whether in the form of patience in adversity, tolerance of others (including the Jews, most sympathetically portrayed), self-control or unselfishness. Moreover, the female readers of such novels discovered that women were thought to be interesting and problematical (an irresistible mixture). The growth of a female reading public made the author dependent on their approval for his success: in the last decades of the eighteenth century they wrote novels for the female market only. Enterprising publishers, such as Unger and Cotta, were prompted to exploit the new interest and, in an age of expensive books, to produce calendars and so-called pocket books, catering for women readers. The *Damenkalendar* and the *Taschenbuch für Damen,* two of the most popular, attracted the talents of eminent writers – Goethe and Schiller, Wieland, Jean Paul and even Hölderlin.

Women began to make their debut as writers. One of the first was Sophie von Laroche, who in her fortieth year published a sentimental and highly successful novel, *Die Geschichte des Fräulein v. Sternheim.* Wieland encouraged her and allowed his name to appear on the title page. The true author was soon known, and she shrewdly exploited her success with other novels. The Leipzig book catalogues of the next decades included many books by women.[19] Schiller was generous in his help and encouragement to women writers, among them Sophie Mereau, wife of a colleague at Jena University. In his own work he contributed to an ideal type of well-bred woman, new to bourgeois circles. The recitation of his poem *Ehret die Frauen* was a never failing success in their drawing rooms for years to come. Schiller found himself playing the role of marriage counsellor as well as literary critic to Sophie; his dry comment in a letter to Goethe could have been equally well applied to her literary production and that of her fellow scribblers: 'she has recourse to rather too sentimental means in pursuit of her very realistic aims.'[20] The mothers and sisters, wives and lovers of the German Romantic writers created a new if transient image of the female personality, and added immeasurably to the excitement of life in the Romantic circles at Jena and Berlin, Munich and Vienna. Caroline Michaelis was the most scandalous and talented, and, some believed, the most beautiful. After she had left her husband, she was seduced by a French officer, imprisoned at Mainz and rescued by August Schlegel, who married her. She found him rather tedious. Caroline eventually left him for the philosopher Schelling, and they remained united until her death in 1809. She had packed more incident into her forty-six years than most of her sex, yet she also found time for a correspondence which has lost none of its freshness and geniality with the years. Other women in Romantic circles showed similar independence: Dorothea Veit, Moses Mendelssohn's daughter, who left her husband for Friedrich Schlegel, and Sophie Mereau, who left hers for Brentano. Perhaps the most intellectually talented of all was the poetess Karoline von Günderode, friend of Bettina, who published her letters in 1840. Only fragments of her work survive, but they give promise of a talent reminiscent of Hölderlin, which never fully flowered. She sought death in the Rhine, when her lover Friedrich Creuzer decided to abandon her and return to an ailing wife. Society did not see fit to ostracize these women, for, in the exceptional years between the end of Frederick

William II's reign and the defeat of Napoleon, society, in Berlin at least, was centred on the intellectuals and the Jewish salons of Henriette Herz and Rahel Levin. The marital aberrations of these ladies were perhaps less disturbing than the sheer exuberance of their personalities and the dynamism of their intellectual gifts. Their vigour and attraction gave point to an accusation voiced in Goethe's *Wilhelm Meisters Lehrjahre*: 'men claim all higher culture for themselves, they do not want to admit us to any branch of knowledge, demanding of us that we be but dolls for playing with, or housekeepers.'[21]

However, the return to more settled times in 1815 brought a sharp reaction against the mobility of wartime and the blurring of social barriers and conventions, on which Germans generally placed such store. The critic Ludwig Börne's sneer about the German burgher, 'the thinking portion of the German people will soon return to its studies; it is already lying on its stomach',[22] contained a grain of truth. Everywhere there was evidence of a desire for a return to orderly ways. Literature and painting had already anticipated the domestic values of the new age, known severally as the Restoration, Biedermeier or pre-March era. This was especially apparent in the image of women. An ideal type of woman was projected in the art of the late Romantic period, which was to persist for over a century: the perfect woman was a pretty, girlish creature, affectionate and impulsive, but submissive, practical and hard working. Example in high places, notably at the Prussian court, had helped to inspire this ideal. The profligate Frederick William II had been succeeded by his colourless and virtuous son, married to the vivacious Luise of Mecklenburg-Strelitz. Her death at the early age of thirty-seven in 1810, after she had insisted on sharing the privations of her subjects during Napoleon's occupation, helped to foster a legend about her name, which proved astonishingly long lasting. In 1900 the *Berliner Illustrierte Zeitung* organized a survey among its readers to discover the most popular public figures, soldiers and thinkers in the world. Entitled *Die Bilanz des Jahrhunderts,* an assessment of the century, one of the questions concerned the greatest woman of the age. An overwhelming majority named Luise, with Queen Victoria a poor second, Bertha von Suttner the pacifist and George Sand tying for third place.[23]

Many of the heroines of the works by Kleist and younger Romantic writers, such as Eichendorff or Chamisso, anticipate the new ideal woman, who has qualities of mother, sister and willing servant: such are the Electress, Natalie and Käthchen, in *Prinz Friedrich v. Homburg* and *Das Käthchen v. Heilbronn,* by Kleist. The ideal woman as mistress and lover is curiously absent from nineteenth century literature in

Germany, apart from Storm's sensuous lyrics of married love, Hebbel's strident and restless heroines, and one or two more. The nearest overt reference to such matters is the young girl's expressed desire to submit herself utterly, to merge her identity with that of her future husband. As Eichendorff put it, 'How often have I deeply felt it: a girl's soul is her lover's, not her own'.[24] Or Schleiermacher's bride, who wrote to him after their engagement: 'I still cannot grasp it, you so noble, so lofty, I so lowly.'[25] Adelbert von Chamisso's widely admired and recited cycle of poems, *Frauen-Liebe und -Leben* (1830), enjoyed its popularity among young women and girls for the manner in which the poet celebrated female sensibility in love and marriage. It is perhaps worth remarking that the lines chosen by Robert Schumann to set to music were those which began:

> I shall serve him, live for him,
> Belong to him utterly,
> Surrender myself to him and
> Find myself enhanced in his reflection.[26]

The common disparity in age between husband and wife in middle class circles made this kind of relationship more credible: the scarcity of job opportunities, especially before 1850, meant that marriage was frequently delayed until the man was between thirty and forty. The writers and lawyers Chamisso and Immermann are two cases in point; they waited until they were established in their careers to marry and were twenty years older than their wives. Fontane's treatment in *Effi Briest* (1895) of the theme of disparity of age, leading to the husband's using his young wife like an adolescent daughter, is critical, quite in contrast to the picture of such marriages earlier in the century. In the earlier period, the employment situation for men and the extreme difficulty for a young woman of finding a position, meant that marriage brought security as well as status. This is well illustrated in a short story from the 1850s by Fanny Lewald, herself no mean advocate of women's rights, entitled *Die Tante.* The heroine, looking back on her married life, says of her husband: 'Like a father, a loving father ... he made my task to serve him in the home a cherished duty.'[27]

The young bride was warned in books of etiquette to take her cue from her husband as regards her behaviour towards him. The *Briefsteller für Damen,* a guide to letter writing, which was published in 1837 (2nd edition) and edited by an authority on the subject, Amalia Schoppe, tells its readers to be on their guard against venturing, even in intimate letters, into the realms of passion. 'The language of passion', it was declared, 'must always have a disagreeable and repelling effect on a well-bred, sensitive man.'[28] The impression that a German male, in seeking a marriage partner, was looking for a compound of dutiful affectionate daughter and all-understanding mother, is generally corroborated in the correspondences and literature of the time. Yet the cult of family life should not be overlooked as the source of much happiness and fulfilment for many, perhaps most women. The bond between the 'stern father' and 'gentle loving mother' – to quote the stereotype phrases – was often a deep one, the affection between parents and their children very real. It was not suppressed under some misguided educational precept, but openly demonstrated and recorded in portraiture and the wealth of lyrics and *Lieder* still popular today. The imaginative and lovingly made toys and games of the time – to be seen at their best in the Nuremberg Toy Museum, and in the smaller municipal museums in many parts of the country – testify to the agreeable quality of family life for those not living below the poverty line. Even among the poor, family festivals and rituals gave an outlet to creative talents for the mother, but also the unmarried aunt or cousin, who often shared the family home. There were, at this time, very few rebellious spirits among women or their champions. To such people the epithet 'French' was applied, meaning selfish, degenerate and loose living (as by Wolfgang Menzel), while 'German' was equated, as far as women were concerned, with docility and domesticity. It became a cliché to assert that it was unpatriotic and unfeminine to be anything else, an attitude which persisted, though not without challenge, until the end of the Third Reich.

The earliest and most vociferous, if not very redoubtable champions of women's rights (social and sexual, rather than political), were the group of writers known as the Young Germans, most of whom were born towards the end of the Napoleonic wars. Critics were suspicious from the start that these young men took the French as their model in their polemics, notably the Saint Simonists. The colourful leader of the Saint Simonists was Enfantin, erstwhile prison inmate (for immorality) and later successful director of the Lyons-Rhône railway. The very idea of preaching equality of the sexes learned from such a model excited the most redoubtable among the Young Germans' critics. Their works were banned by the Frankfurt Diet, and the conservative and Christian circles made great play of the dangers to family life from French influence, whether in the guise of liberalism, revolution or the demand for women's education or freedom to marry the partner of her own choice. The popular neo-Pietist preacher from Bremen, Friedrich Krummacher, wrote with evident self-congratulation of his daughters: 'My girls have never had what they call education. They know virtually nothing of our so-called literature, cannot speak a single foreign language; they don't know how to talk high, are shy with strangers, but they love to read Menck's *Homilies* and sing all kinds of gay songs as they work.'[29] Another instance of a similar womanly ideal is to be found in the memoirs of Albrecht von Roon, later Prussian Minister of War in Bismarck's time, when he wrote of his courtship and marriage to a Silesian pastor's daughter in the 1830s.[30] When at the end of that decade a liberal movement developed within the Protestant church in Prussia and Saxony and women attended the public meetings of popular preachers, the orthodox cleric Hengstenberg thundered in moral outrage at 'the shameful spectacle of women entering the public scene'.[31] It was not only church leaders who were quoted in support of the traditional view of woman's place, but even the arch-Pagan himself, Goethe. *Herrmann und Dorothea* could be found, with due selection, to contain many a line to embellish festive addresses or to give weight to ponderous assertions of male authority: 'Dienen lerne beizeiten das Weib nach ihrer Bestimmung' ['Let women learn early to serve, as is their destiny'.][32] Dorothea is described on her first appearance as '*gretelhaft*'; her simple peasant costume, modest demeanour and subdued 'braids, twined around silver pins' are to be met in painting and literature down to the blood and soil literature of the Nazi era. In the second half of the nineteenth century this image was put across in the immensely influential family journals, such as *Die Gartenlaube,* and the popular novels of the '*Marliteratur*' (Fontane's phrase for the work of Frau Marlitt, a best selling novelist, and her imitators). It is perhaps worth remarking that the satiric journals of the later nineteenth century rarely, if ever, made the *Hausfrau* the butt of their wit.

Advocates of women's rights were few in number in the nineteenth century, the object of indifference or derision to the majority of both sexes. Apart from the Young Germans, who were taken a little more seriously by the authorities than they deserved, supporters of women's rights were to be found among educational reformers and socialists. Among the former were some impressive personalities, women of ability and courage, often well connected, who appreciated the implication of social and regional change in mid and late nineteenth century Germany for women's present problems and future role in society. Education for women was a matter which aroused sporadic interest in Germany from about the middle of the eighteenth century onwards. From the wealthy city of Hamburg, the merchant J. H. Hudtwalcker, born in 1758, recalled that his mother, who was the daughter of a cultivated man, had only been taught to read and write and as much arithmetic as she would need for her household duties. In the upper and lower classes alike, the preparation received by girls for their adult life was based on the psychologically sound precept that they would only be happy if kept busy. 'From her earliest childhood, my mother had to sit as if chained and knit', wrote Klöden of his mother, who came from a frugal artisan background. She never, according to her son, forgot the outrage of her grandmother, who had discovered her as a child of six, sitting with her hands in her lap. 'My, oh my,' exclaimed the old lady, 'if a girl does not know what to do, let her cut a hole in her pinafore and sew it up again.'[33] The household arts were certainly well taught in Germany, and at virtually all social levels. Fontane's emancipated intellectual in *Frau Jenny Treibel* (1892), suitably named Corinne Schmidt, is quick to tell her English acquaintance Mr Nelson that she could burn a hole in his suit and return it to him next day so well darned that he would never find the place.

However, in the late eighteenth century, the influence of enlightened thinking and the emergence of a female reading public persuaded a number of educated men that their daughters might profit from tuition in academic subjects. The daughters of merchants and civil servants, of Jewish bankers and university professors, young women such as Johanna Schopenhauer from Danzig, mother of the philosopher, Sophie Mereau and her sister, Henriette Schubert, whose father was a tax-collector in Thuringia, Caroline Michaelis, a Göttingen professor's daughter, or the daughters of Daniel Itzig, are all cases in point. They were all remarkable or fortunate individuals and in no way average. The idea of state regulated educational facilities for girls was scarcely conceived of till the following century, and even then encountered many obstacles. Nor was there any demand for higher education for women: the case of Professor Schlözer's daughter Dorothea at Göttingen was quite unique. She took her doctorate there at the age of seventeen in 1787, showing a truly remarkable knowledge of philosophy, history and law, botany and mining in the process, fruit of her eccentric father's teaching methods.[34] Even the fair-minded Schiller had no time for the 'farce', as he termed it in a letter to Goethe.[35] He was wrong; there was nothing farcical about Dorothea. However, there were not many fathers like Schlözer, which was a pity, because Dorothea's later life showed that a woman could combine a felicitious domestic life with intellectual pursuits, provided of course that she had the energy to do so.

From about the middle of the nineteenth century, various circumstances contributed to encouraging demand for greater educational facilities for women. Not least important in this regard was the greater mobility of life – though this was still very relative – and the need of many women, who had not married or who had lost their husbands, to earn a living. The daughters of farmers, artisans and traders could enter service, or even domestic manufacture and the factories, but a bourgeois girl could not. She could not do nursing, since prejudice opposed the idea of girls being exposed to illness outside the family circle. For a post as a governess or even a teacher, she needed preparation. In the late 1830s, the disciples of Pestalozzi, notably Fr Fröbel, had suggested the idea of kindergarten teaching as a recognized profession for women. One of his associates was Frau Otto-Peters, who began campaigning for women teachers' organizations, and even for higher education for women in 1848. She made little progress on this front, but in 1865 she became the president of the first women's organization, at Leipzig. Her colleagues included Auguste Schmidt, Lina Morgenstern and Henriette Goldschmidt, all of whom had enthusiastically supported the 1848 revolution. An account of the psychological pressures brought to bear on women who challenged their accepted social role is to be found in the memoirs of another supporter of the revolution, Malwida von Meysenbug, friend of Mazzini and affectionate admirer of Jane Carlyle. Her efforts to improve her mind and keep up with modern thought had earned her the disapproval of her family at the small courts of Lippe and Hesse, where her father was a high-ranking official. They let her overhear such remarks as the following, about a young girl they knew, 'what a delightful creature! She would never presume to have an opinion of her own.'[36] Malwida worked for a time at an experimental school near Hamburg, which was closed in the reactionary years after the revolution. She moved to England, where she lived in penury until she became governess to Alexander Herzen's daughter. The revolution undoubtedly gave stimulus to the idea of women's education, but the immediate effect was to rouse reactionaries to stern and nervous measures. Even Fröbel's kindergarten schools, which served the socially desirable purpose of helping working mothers' children to be kept off the streets, were closed by the Prussian government in 1851 as 'atheistic and democratic'. They were not reopened until 1860.

Girls' schools continued until the end of the century to offer a curriculum designed mainly for the future housewife and mother. Academic subjects were neglected or poorly taught. It was in Karlsruhe in Baden that the first grammar school for girls was opened in 1894. This had been preceded by Helene Lange's venture in Berlin in 1889, an institution offering courses for women up to university standard. Lange had been a headmistress of a girls' school since 1876; she was the author of a famous *Yellow Brochure* (1887), calling for state training facilities for women teachers. The publication had not achieved its object, but it had aroused much comment. In 1890 she joined with Auguste Schmidt, a much more charismatic personality from Leipzig,[37] in founding the General German Women Teachers Association, which concerned itself with pay and conditions, as well as pressing for scientific and technical subjects to be taught at girls' schools. However, in the 1890s, even those who had passed the required examinations could not enter university, apart from Zurich in Switzerland, which had a small but assiduous band of women students, mostly from Russia and the Baltic provinces. In Germany in 1900 there were as many as 1000 'guest' women students, but none matriculated. In 1901 the grand duke of Baden opened his two universities at Heidelberg and Freiburg to them. In the next seven years the other German states followed suit, last of all Prussia in 1908. The distinguished botanist Daisy von Wrangell recalled in her memoirs the difficulties she experienced in getting a place. Her aristocratic lineage and Baltic background made her less sensitive to the patent disapproval of society. In 1903 she wrote to a family friend and university professor W. Penzold for advice about her choice, Greifswald. In his reply he pointed out that Greifswald had not a single woman student; at other universities, such as Marburg, the students as well as the professors strenuously opposed their admission. He suggested Heidelberg: she could pass the whole thing off as a visit to a resort and thus spare general embarrassment. Eventually she chose Tübingen. Here in 1904 she and her colleagues, all dressed in white, were received by a frock-coated official, taken to the rector's study where pig-tailed professors from the eighteenth century looked down sternly from their portraits, and were solemnly immatriculated.[38]

Women's organizations in nineteenth century Germany were almost exclusively concerned with education, not with political and social emancipation. 'What we do not want, and never, even in the most distant centuries, wish or aim for', wrote Dr Lette in the prospectus of his *Lette-Vereine,* the most important of several vocational associations of women, founded in 1865, 'is emancipation and equal rights for women.'[39] The association of which Frau Otto-Peters was president had only 11 000 members in 1877 and in the next thirty-seven years gained only 30 000 more. By comparison with women's movements in England or the United States, its policies were timid and its members aware of the general lack of support for their aims.[40] Interest then and later was confined to north Germany, partly perhaps because life was more sociable, friendship and amusement easier to come by and less restrictive in the south. This is illustrated in the memoirs of Frau Braun-Artaria, daughter of a Mannheim art dealer and friend of Paul Heyse, the painters Feuerbach and Lenbach, and the popular writer

Viktor von Scheffel. She lived in Munich after she was married and describes a charade she and her circle performed in the 1870s on the subject of female emancipation. 'What Luise Otto (-Peters) and the first pioneers of women's emancipation aimed at was quite foreign to normal women in south Germany.' [What arrogance and yet self-assurance lay in this epithet 'normal'] 'We used to laugh at the neurotic and usually old and ugly women, who would sweep in from the north and give badly attended lectures on the subject of women's rights.'[41] Such women in secure, if frugal circumstances, could afford to feel superior to the champions of women's rights. Julie Vogelstein, daughter of a distinguished rabbinical scholar and second wife of the socialist Heinrich Braun, experienced the phenomenon in another way. The cultural stultification of provincial Germany – the Vogelsteins lived in Moravia, later in Stettin – prompted Julie's mother to start a study group for women. Henriette Goldschmidt came to visit and advise on one memorable occasion. Despite, or perhaps because of the success of the venture, Frau Vogelstein aroused the atavistic prejudices of the local philistines, men and women alike, whose social envy had recourse to incitement to antisemitic prejudice to put a stop to it.[42]

However indifferent society in general proved to be, the economic facts were beginning to demonstrate the pressing need for some modification of women's role. By the year 1900 there were some 28 629 931 women living in the Empire, in a majority of almost 1 million over men. Five years earlier some 5 265 393 women were in employment; by 1907 this had risen to 8 243 498, about one third of these being married women. The majority worked in agriculture or as female domestics (4 598 986 and 1 249 383 respectively), but growing numbers were employed in industry, commerce and the service industries. The disparity between these economic facts and the lack of civic rights for women became ever more apparent in the years before 1914. There was, as has been said, no married women's property act in Germany; the Civil Code of 1896 did not greatly extend the very restricted rights of women over their property and earnings. They were allowed neither to vote, to join or form political parties, nor to attend public meetings. They were discriminated against in employment – even women teachers had to resign on marriage. Yet an ever-increasing percentage of women were not in a position to enjoy that security which in Wilhelmine Germany was regarded as a fair exchange for subordination. This was particularly so in the labouring classes. Women were being forced by economic circumstances to work long hours to help support the family. In 1893 factory work was limited, it is true, by law to eleven hours a day. This did not help women on piecework or in service, and in any case was terribly onerous if they had to run a household as well.[43]

The frequency of bad times at local and national level in the course of the industrial revolution put severe pressures on mothers of families, especially on those who had moved in from rural areas. The material problems of life encouraged prostitution in German cities and began, belatedly, to attract the attention of feminists. In some states prostitution was controlled by the police in the interests of 'public morality'. However, this could itself be the cause of scandal, as happened in a much publicized incident in Cologne in 1847, when the public censor was accosted by the police while emerging from a brothel, and, after attempting to escape, got involved in a brawl. In Kiel in the following decades the police chief complained bitterly at the repeated prosecutions by the state of inmates of the police-controlled 'houses'. There is no doubt but that the numbers of young girls earning their living by prostitution increased greatly in the late nineteenth century. August Bebel in his *Die Frau und der Sozialismus* (1883) put the figure as high as 200 000; in Berlin semi-official figures for the year 1904 put the total for the city alone as between 30 000 and 50 000.[44] Prostitutes were usually recruited from domestic servants, poorly paid employees, or country girls, who came to the town after becoming pregnant, in the hope of supporting their child.[45]

These two issues, education and prostitution, formed the principal interests of feminists up the end of the century. From about the mid 1890s, interest in female emancipation grew passionate, and was reflected in public debate and articles in newspaper periodicals and journals. However, the effect of such discussion was much less than might have been supposed, even after 1900. One of the chief reasons for this was a deep ideological split between the bourgeois feminist movement and the social democratic struggle for proletarian emancipation. On the extreme left of the Social Democrat party was Klara Zetkin, who, with the Polish Rosa Luxemburg, were known as 'the only two men in the party' – who firmly opposed any cooperation with the bourgeois movements. In Zetkin's view these were exclusively concerned with women's rights over their property, an institution she wished to abolish. 'Feminist ideas', wrote a journalist in the Leipzig *Volks-Zeitung* in late 1913, 'are a great danger for the German (Social-Democratic) Women's movement ... there is no community of interest among women as a whole.'[46] Zetkin's commitment to the solidarity of the proletariat led her logically to support the cause of pacifism in the war. It is clear, however, in spite of the wide support for pacifism in certain circles before 1914, as evinced in Bertha von

Suttner's success, that once war had broken out such attitudes no longer reflected the temper of German women, either working class or bourgeois. By the middle years of the war working women, like their menfolk, had succumbed to the siege mentality characteristic of the German nation as a whole. Indeed in bourgeois circles as far back as 1908 women's rights leaders had shown themselves aware of the contradiction between the liberal individual ideas, which had inspired their work in the nineteenth century and the privileged position they hoped to preserve for their class. During and after the war, the influence of radical feminists diminished sharply, even among the socialists.

In the same way as social attitudes in the late nineteenth century seemed to ossify in face of rapid industrial change and technological progress, so too did women seem to become backward-looking in their image of themselves. This occurred at a time when they were being called upon in increasing numbers to perform men's work, especially in the war, and when their apparent independence was reflected in the rising divorce figures. This process is illustrated in the writings and speeches of many former leaders of women's movements. Thus Minna Cauer, once celebrated for her radical views, could write in 1915: 'The necessity of subordinating oneself for the sake of the generality has made it clear to women that they belong to a greater whole, that a higher and stronger power had the right to exercise compulsion over them.... This means a step forward from a purely individual egotism, which only allows validity to the individual's own needs, to a higher development as a member of the state.'[47]

The natural conservatism of women, and German women in particular, reasserted itself after the end of the war and the experience of defeat and revolution. Great resentment was felt and expressed during the Weimar Republic by women against those members of their own sex who were 'taking the bread from fathers of families' by working. Rank discrimination against women in employment, even to the point of breaching the 1919 Constitution, aroused minimal opposition in women's circles. By the end of the 1920s it was clear that Nazi propaganda was attracting considerable support from them, and few seemed aroused to anger or resentment by the discriminatory and naively idyllic image of women, which the Nazi movement's petty bourgeois leaders were enthusiastically projecting. Quite the reverse in fact; women, especially those from middle class backgrounds, seemed to find Nazism both sympathetic and reassuring, and continued to do so after Hitler's seizure of power. Nazi policies with regard to women reduced their social role, in theory at least, to a purely domestic one;

in the exclusively male order of Nazism their function was in effect solely biological. Despite the very considerable numbers of women forced back into employment during the Second World War, it was not until after 1945 that German women were finally emancipated by law. Many would claim, perhaps misguidedly, that the process is as yet far from complete.

Conclusion Germany on the eve of the Great War

Leaving Germany for France at the end of the nineteenth century, wrote Elsie Butler, one of the most colourful of Anglo-Irish Germanists, was like going home from school for the holidays. Germany was a state where the administration functioned smoothly, where the lives of its citizens were well regulated for their own good. Trains ran on time, and a network of communications by rail, road and water brought little-known rural areas into contact with the pulse of national life. In stations and post offices, on trams and coaches, in local and national administrative buildings, on street corners and in barracks, uniformed agents of a benevolent state were there to reassure its subjects. From the 1870s onwards the central government and municipal authorities had spent vast sums of money on improving and safeguarding life, by installing drainage systems and water supplies, improving schooling and transport, and embellishing the environment with public buildings, parks and national monuments, many of the last placed at points suitable for a family outing on Sunday or holiday. National holidays commemorated events in the recent and remote past, which had contributed to the unification of Germany in 1871. Parades and concerts, particularly with military bands, provided people with further reminders of the state's claims on their loyalty and gratitude. The buildings of the Second Empire, the administrative offices, the imposing primary and secondary schools all over Germany, the railway stations and town halls, favoured mock Renaissance, mock Gothic or mock classical styles, for the new nation lacked an authentic style of its own. The massive *Reichstag* building, which was finished in the 1890s, brought this home to the visitor to Berlin in a peculiarly apt way, in that the confusion of its many styles testified to the ambiguity of its function in government. But it was all very impressive, and Berlin, where in the 1850s Lagarde had heard frogs croaking near the Royal Palace and smelt ill-functioning drains, was by 1900 a cosmopolitan and modern metropolis of some 2 million inhabitants. The fact that the state could provide inspiring symbols of the national might, and an orderly society, guarded by incorrupt officials, and at the same time offer the material comforts and conveniences of modern living, was the source of considerable satisfaction to the populace at large. The authorities were generally regarded as the agents of benevolent improvement, both of Germany's position in the world and of the material environment. The great machine of capitalist enterprise which had generated, with the aid of the state, the wealth to finance these multifarious projects, was illogically ignored, or criticized on the grounds that it had destroyed familiar ways and patriarchal relationships.

Yet it was economic and technological changes, besides the growth and redistribution of the population in nineteenth century Germany, that were the really significant factors in the evolution of her society up to the outbreak of war in 1914. The two periods of rapid industrialization, 1850–73 and 1896–1913, separated by an extended period of depression and stagnation, had turned Germany from a rural country into one where the majority of the population lived in large or medium sized towns. In 1871 only 5 per cent had lived in cities of 100 000 or more, 64 per cent in communities of under 2000; by 1910 over 21 per cent lived in large cities, over 27 per cent in towns of 5000–100 000, and only 40 per cent in small communities. In 1850 there had been only five large cities (over 100 000) in German-speaking lands; in 1913 there were as many as forty-eight in the German Empire alone. It was not until the last years of the nineteenth century that the flight from the land and the vast increase in industrial output became apparent. In the 1870s the net yield from agricultural production was greater than that of industry; two decades later the position was reversed: in twenty years investment in industry had trebled, despite the very real problems of the Depression years. Population grew faster than in any other European country: from 24 800 000 in 1816, it reached a total of 67 700 000 in 1914, despite a considerable drain caused by emigration, which only eased in the 1890s. Significant factors in this increase, though not until the end of the century, were the decline in infant mortality and death in childbirth.

However, although the movement out of agriculture into industry and commerce was recorded in the *Reich* statistics, contemporaries were not, or did not choose to be, aware of the scale and the implications of the change. Friedrich Naumann, the liberal deputy and writer, compared Germany in 1909 to an old farm where factories, daily being expanded, were erected in barns and outhouses: 'under ancient beams the most up-to-date machinery was installed and iron girders supported mud walls.'

The burden of an increasing population and its redistribution in consequence of the flight from the land was not equally shared. The north experienced a major east-west movement of people, with large numbers of rural labourers and others leaving the eastern lands of Prussia to move to Berlin, central Germany and the industrial towns of the Rhine and Ruhr. In the south, by contrast, the towns, including Munich, preserved a rural character well into the twentieth century. The lower orders of society suffered the main impact of such social dislocation, and from the effects of subsequent overcrowding in the cities, from inadequate provision for the care of the old, the sick and the young. The authorities liked to refer to the rising standard of living, but for wage labourers the annual increase of wages in Germany between 1890 and 1914, at 1 per cent, was approximately one quarter of that received by workers in Britain, the United States, France and Sweden; meanwhile food prices were rising steadily and more and more married women were being forced to work full time, with consequent stress for the family. The prodigious economic expansion of Germany since the mid nineteenth century, in the same way as the political successes, did not benefit society as a whole, but only certain sections.

The inflexibility of the ruling élite, and its failure to acknowledge in word and deed the justified expectation of people for a greater share in decisions affecting themselves, was to prove very serious for the internal stability of Germany in later years. The 'new men', whose talents had generated the wealth and dynamism behind Germany's recent successes in the political, economic and other fields, had not modified the traditional values and attitudes of the ruling class, but had been assimilated into the authoritarian power structure. The result was to increase the rigid conservatism of authority and its agents and institutions, and also to increase the already highly developed sense of self-preservation of members of the establishment. Lower income and lower status groups were either alienated from the system, their potential excluded or withheld, or through resentment at their own lack of prospects they became susceptible to the arguments of leaders of irresponsible pressure groups.

Despite the success and prosperity of Germany at the beginning of the twentieth century, Germans of most social classes were highly self-conscious about their own status and about the standing of their country in the world. This was something that had not been true a hundred or even sixty years earlier. Successive governments in Imperial Germany found it expedient to divert the attention of the populace from nascent class conflicts, or the disappointments and frustrations felt by several groups, by a policy of social imperialism: foreign political antagonisms were to be used as a domestic political cement. The struggle for colonies, the naval race, the myth of English envy of Germany, and the various aggressive patriotic organizations, such as the War Veterans Associations, the Defence and Pan-German Leagues, the League for the Defence of Teutonism in the East, etc., sought to persuade the German nation and the outside world that the Empire was united in itself. The upper and middle classes – the latter including a considerable number of people living on incomes less than those of wage labourers – had come since 1848–9, and more especially since the 1870s, to identify with the interests and policies of the state and to give, in Dieter Groh's apt phrase, 'absolute primacy to the conservation of the *status quo*'. The conservatism of these strata was not based, as in Britain, on pride in past achievement, but on anxiety at loss and change, on disquiet about the future resilience of those values which they professed to hold. Social democracy as the agent of revolutionary change was the particular object of such feelings of fear, even though members of the socialist party were already obviously bourgeois in their aspirations and even life style, and were soon to prove the force of their patriotism on the outbreak of war. It was the concentration of power and influence in the hands of relatively few, and the fact that the system was so well shielded from criticism from without and self-doubt from within, which allowed the ruling élite and their supporters to overlook the economic and social factors in the domestic political crises of the pre-war years. Accordingly, each strident voice was interpreted in terms of a conspiracy against the hallowed *status quo*. It was both a measure of the intellectual sterility of the upper classes and a fundamental irresponsibility of their leaders, which persuaded them in the summer of 1914 to choose war as an adequate answer to the nation's problems at home and abroad.

Notes

INTRODUCTION TO PART I

1 Ludwig Camerarius and Lukas Friedrich Behaim, *Ein politischer Briefwechsel über den Verfall des Reiches 1636–1648*, ed. A. Ernstberger (Munich 1961), p. 36.
2 See the cases reported from Augsburg, including that of two women who cooked and ate four dead neighbours, remarking that they had particularly enjoyed the brain, heart and kidneys, reproduced from diocesan records in P. Lahnstein, *Das Leben im Barock, Zeugnisse und Berichte 1640–1740* (Stuttgart 1974), pp. 23–5.
3 Camerarius and Behaim, op. cit., p. 34.
4 G. Franz, *Der Dreissigjährige Krieg und das deutsche Volk*, 3rd edn (Stuttgart 1961), p. 45.
5 ibid., p. 2, n. 1.
6 ibid., p. 2.
7 ibid., p. 86.
8 ibid., p. 95.
9 Montesquieu, *Lettres persanes*, Lettre CXII (Paris 1960), pp. 235 f.
10 Franz, op. cit., p. 48.
11 *Cambridge Economic History of Europe*, vol. IV, ed. E. E. Rich and C. H. Wilson (Cambridge 1967), p. 86.
12 ibid., p. 556.
13 W. Hubatsch, *Das Zeitalter des Absolutismus* (Brunswick 1962), p. 46. For the issues discussed here, see H. Kamen, 'The Economic and Social Consequences of the Thirty Years War', *Past and Present*, vol. 39 (1968), pp. 44–61.

CHAPTER 1 THE HOLY ROMAN EMPIRE

1 Rudolph II in Grillparzer's *Ein Bruderzwist in Hause Habsburg* (IV, lines 2339–42) reminds his impetuous nephew, who will one day be Emperor Ferdinand II, that

An der Uhr, in der die Feder drängt,
Das Kronrad wesentlich mit seiner Hemmung,
Damit nicht abrollt eines Zugs das Werk,
Und sie in ihrem Zögern weist die Stunde.

2 G. Benecke, *Society and Politics in Germany 1500–1750* (London 1974), pp. 64 ff.
3 ibid., p. 7.
4 W. Fürnrohr, *Der immerwährende Reichstag zu Regensburg* (Munich 1963), pp. 64 ff.
5 K. O. von Aretin, *Das Heilige Römische Reich, Reichsverfassung und Reichssouveranität 1776–1806* (Wiesbaden 1967), p. 5. Benecke has some useful things to say about translations of Reichstag and other terms (op. cit., pp. 37 f.).
6 Von Aretin, op. cit.
7 In his recent book (see note 2 above) Benecke includes and comments on a number of works, both older and contemporary writings, on various aspects of imperial structure and organization. See his bibliography in ch. 3, 'The Problems of German Federalism', pp. 23–8.

CHAPTER 2 COURT LIFE

1 Quoted in Marvin O'Connell, *The Counter-Reformation* (New York 1974), p. 327.
2 Ludwig Camerarius and Lukas Friedrich Behaim, *Ein politischer Briefwechsel über den Verfall des Reiches 1636–1648,* ed. A. Ernstberger (Munich 1961), p. 17.
3 K. Wild, *Staat und Wirtschaft in den Bistümern Würzburg und Bamberg* (Heidelberg 1906), p. 191.
4 See Peter Prosch, *Leben und Ereignisse des Peter Prosch eines Tyrolers von Ried im Zillertal,* ed. K. Pörnbacher (Munich 1964).
5 H. Mikoletzky, *Oesterreich, das grosse 18. Jahrundert* (Vienna 1967), p. 87.
6 Hugo Hantsch, '*Die drei grossen Relationen St. Saphorins über die inneren Verhältnisse am Wiener Hof zur Zeit Karls VI*', *Mitteilungen des Instituts für österreichische Geschichtsforschung,* vol. 58 (1950), p. 627.
7 Mikoletzky, op. cit., p. 101.
8 ibid., p. 121.
9 ibid., p. 127.
10 W. H. Bruford, *Germany in the Eighteenth Century* (Cambridge 1971), p. 89.
11 Mikoletzky, op. cit., pp. 102 f.
12 Bruford, op. cit., p. 87.
13 M. Baur-Heinhold, *Baroque Theatre* (London 1967), p. 11.
14 E. Fähler, *Feuerwerke des Barock, Studien zum öffentlichen Fest und seiner literarischen Deutung vom 16. bis 18. Jahrhundert* (Stuttgart 1974), p. 81.
15 P. Lahnstein, *Das Leben im Barock, Zeugnisse und Berichte 1640–1740* (Stuttgart 1974), p. 103.

16 ibid., p. 201.
17 N. Henderson, *Prince Eugene of Savoy* (London 1964), p. 5.
18 W. Treue, *Kulturgeschichte des Alltags* (Frankfurt 1961), p. 103.
19 Mikoletzky, op. cit., p. 103.
20 Quoted in E. Trunz, '*Der deutsche Späthumanismus um 1600 als Standeskultur*', in R. Alewyn (ed.), *Barockforschung* (Cologne 1966), p. 147.
21 ibid.
22 Fähler, op. cit., p. 117.
23 ibid., p. 118.

CHAPTER 3 THE GERMAN NOBILITY

1 The collection of lectures delivered at Büdingen in 1964 and published under the auspices of the Ranke Gesellschaft contain much information on the social and geographical origin, the political and military role of both kinds of nobility in this period. See in this context especially N. von Preradovich, '*Der Adel in den Herrschaften der deutschen Linie des Hauses Habsburg*', in H. Rössler (ed.), *Deutscher Adel 1555–1740 (Büdinger Vorträge)* (Darmstadt 1965), p. 206.
2 H. Rössler, '*Adel und Konfession. Ein Rundgespräch*', in Rössler (ed.), op. cit., p. 106.
3 Dieter Albert, '*Staat und Politik 1314–1745*', in M. Spindler (ed.), *Handbuch der bayerischen Geschichte* (Munich 1966), vol. 2, p. 357.
4 H. H. Hofmann, *Adelige Gesellschaft und Souveräner Staat. Studien über Staat und Gesellschaft in Franken und Bayern im 18. und 19. Jahrhundert* (*Stud. z. Bayr. Verfassungs u. Sozialgesch.*, 2) (Munich 1962), p. 95.
5 Alfred von Kageneck, in Rössler (ed.), op. cit., p. 112.
6 Erwin Riedenauer, '*Reichsritter und Konfession*', in Rössler (ed.), op. cit., p. 28.
7 H.-J. Daul, in Rössler (ed.), op. cit., p. 113.
8 H. Lahrkamp, in Rössler (ed.), op. cit., p. 128. See also Alwin Hanschmidt, *Franz von Fürstenberg als Staatsmann. Die Politik des Münsterschen Ministers 1762–1780* (Münster 1969), pp. 6 ff.
9 G. von Lenthe in Rössler (ed.), op. cit., p. 137.
10 Lahrkamp, op. cit., p. 128.
11 Preradovich, op. cit., pp. 201, 206.
12 Lady Mary Wortley Montagu, *Works* (London 1805), vol. 1, pp. 224 f.
13 Quoted in W. Flemming, *Deutsche Kultur im Zeitalter des Barock*, 2nd edn (Constance 1960), p. 39.
14 ibid., many examples.
15 F. Martiny, '*Die Adelsfrage in Preussen vor 1806 als politisches und soziales Problem*', *Vierteljahrsschrift für Sozial- und Wirtschafts -geschichte*, vol. 35 (1938), p. 113.
16 See Otto Brunner's account of the Austrian nobility in this context, *Adeliges Landleben und Europäischer Geist* (Salzburg 1949).
17 Maria von Dönhoff, *Namen, die keiner mehr nennt* (Munich 1970), pp. 100 f.
18 Klaus Deppermann, *Der hallesche Pietismus und der preussische Staat unter Friedrich I* (III) (Göttingen 1961), p. 15. Rainer Wohlfeil, 'Adel und Heerwesen', in Rössler (ed.), op. cit., pp. 325 ff.
19 Hugo Hantsch, quoted in Preradovich, op. cit., p. 201.
20 N. von Preradovich, '*Die soziale Herkunft österreichischer Kirchenfürsten*

(1648–1918)', in *Festschrift für Karl Eder* (Innsbruck 1959), pp. 242 f.

21 Quoted in G. Birtsch, *'Zur sozialen und politischen Rolle des deutschen, vornehmlich preussischen Adels am Ende des 18 Jahrunderts'*, in R. Vierhaus, *Der Adel vor der Revolution* (Gottingen 1971), p. 87.

22 G. Heinrich, *'Der Adel in Brandenburg-Preussen'*, in Rössler (ed.), op. cit., pp. 274 f.

23 K. F. von Klöden, *Jugenderinnerungen,* ed. M. Jahns (Leipzig 1874), p. 2.

24 Further details in Chapter 7 on army life.

25 Heinrich, op. cit., pp. 299 f.

26 Birtsch, op. cit., p. 80.

27 ibid., p. 90.

28 Joh. Timotheus Hermes, *Sophiens Reise von Memel nach Sachsen,* 2. Teil, *Bürgertum und Adel. Die Mesalliance des Landpredigers von Haberstroh* (Leipzig 1941), pp. 94–113.

29 Martiny, op. cit., p. 111.

30 Th. Fontane, *Der Stechlin* (Munich 1969), vol. 13, p. 316.

31 H. Schlechte, *Die Staatsreform in Kursachsen 1762–3 (Quellen z. kursächs. Retablissement nach d. 7-jährigen Krieg)* (Berlin 1958), p. 15, n. 22.

32 N. von Preradovich, *Deutsche Führungsschichten in Oesterreich und Preussen 1804–1918* (Wiesbaden 1956), p. 6.

33 G. Benecke, 'Ennoblement and Privilege in Early Modern Germany', *History,* vol. 56 (1971), p. 361.

34 ibid., p. 366.

35 Birtsch, op. cit., pp. 80, 81.

CHAPTER 4 TOWN LIFE IN GERMANY

1 Otto Brunner *'Hamburg und Wien, Versuch einer sozialgeschichtlichen Konfrontierung'* in O. Brunner (ed.), *Festschrift für H. Aubin* (Wiesbaden 1965), II, pp. 479 f. See also his *'Souveranitätsproblem und soziale Struktur in den deutschen Reichsstädten der frühen Neuzeit', Vierteljahresschrift für Sozial- und Wirtschaftsgeschichte,* vol. 50 (1968), p. 329.

2 *Cambridge Economic History of Europe,* vol. IV, ed. E. E. Rich and C. H. Wilson (Cambridge 1967), p. 83.

3 G. Franz, *Der dreissigjährige Krieg und das deutsche Volk,* 3rd edn. (Stuttgart 1961), p. 7.

4 ibid., p. 7, n. 9.

5 Reproduced in W. Flemming, *Deutsche Kultur im Zeitalter des Barock,* 2nd edn. (Constance 1960), pp. 1, 205.

6 P. E. Schramm, *Neun Generationen,* vol. 1 (Göttingen 1963), pp. 355 f.

7 Arnold Soom, *'Der Kampf der baltischen Städte gegen das Fremdkapitel im 17. Jahrhundert', Vierteljahresschrift für Sozial- und Wirtschaftsgeschichte,* vol. 49 (1962), pp. 433 ff.

8 Schramm, op. cit., p. 295.

9 Gerald Strauss, *Nuremberg in the Sixteenth Century* (New York 1968), pp. 187–230.

10 I. Bog, *'Wirtschaft und Gesellschaft im Zeitalter des Merkantilismus'*, in G. Pfeiffer (ed.), *Nürnberg, Geschichte einer europäischen Stadt* (Munich 1971), pp. 315 ff.

11 Johanna Schopenhauer, *Jugendleben und Wanderbilder,* ed. W. Drost (Tubingen 1958), p. 81.

12 Dieter Koch has described this process graphically in *Das Göttinger Honoratiorentum vom 17. bis zur Mitte des 19. Jahrhunderts. Eine soz. gesch. Untersuchung mit bes. Berücksichtigung der ersten Gött. Unternehmer* (Göttingen 1958) – namely, the intervention by the prince in the affairs of the town, the gradual demotion of local notables and their exclusion from the council, imposition of princely appointees as mayors, town clerks, etc.

13 Dieter Albert, '*Staat und Gesellschaft 1500–1745*', in M. Spindler (ed.), *Handbuch der bayerischen Geschichte* (Munich 1966), vol. 2, pp. 570 ff.

14 Lady Mary Wortley Montagu, *Works* (London 1805), vol. 1, p. 220, letter of 22 August 1716.

15 S. Busch, *Hannover, Wolfenbüttel und Celle. Stadtgründungen und Stadterweiterungen in drei welfischen Residenzen, vom 16. zum 18. Jht.* (Hildesheim 1969), pp. 87 f.

16 Schramm, op. cit., p. 105.

17 H. Moeller, *Die kleinbürgerliche Familie im 18. Jahrhundert* (Berlin 1969), p. 124; see also p. 125, n. 81, for contemporary references.

18 R. A. Dorwart, *The Prussian Welfare State Before 1740* (Harvard 1971), pp. 85 ff.

19 G. Grundmann, '*Hirschberg in Niederschlesien*', in O. Brunner (ed.), *Festschrift für H. Aubin* (Wiesbaden 1965), II, pp. 495 ff.

20 Fritz Redlich, *Kaufmäannische Selbesbiographien,* in Brunner (ed.), op. cit., I, pp. 329 f.

21 ibid., p. 328.

22 See here for many other aspects of town life in early modern Germany, H. Mauersberg, *Wirtschafts- und Sozialgeschichte zentraleuropäschier städte in neuerer Zeit. Dargestellt an den Beispielen von Basel, Frankfurt a.M., Hamburg und München* (Göttingen 1960).

23 Schopenhauer, op. cit., p. 233.

24 G. Benecke, *Society and Politics in Germany 1500–1750* (London 1974), p. 174, n. 39.

25 ibid., pp. 174 f.

26 ibid., p. 48, n. 22.

27 Quoted in Flemming, op. cit., p. 47.

28 R. Stadelmann and W. Fischer, *Die Bildungswelt des deutschen Handwerkers um 1800* (Berlin 1955), pp. 105 f.

29 W. Zorn, '*Probleme der deutschen Gewerbe- und Handelsgeschichte 1650–1800*', in Brunner (ed.), op. cit., I, p. 305.

30 Stadelmann and Fischer, op. cit., p. 120.

31 K. F. von Klöden, *Jugenderinnerungen,* ed. M. Jahns (Leipzig 1874).

32 *Carl Friedrich Zelters Darstellungen seines Lebens,* ed. J. W. Schottländer, in *Schriften der Goethe Gesellschaft,* vol. 44 (Weimar 1931), pp. 9 f.

33 O. K. Roller, *Die Einwohnerschaft der Stadt Durlachs im 18. Jahrhundert in ihren wirtschaftlichen und kulturgeschichtlichen Verhältnissen dargestellt aus ihren Stammtafeln* (Karlsruhe 1907).

34 Moeller, op. cit., pp. 92 and 90 f.; see also the case of the tinsmith Flegel of Hildesheim in the 1740s which Mack Walker describes in his vivid and imaginative book *German Home Towns* (Cornell 1971), pp. 73 ff.

35 Johann Miller (Ulm 1786), p. 12.

36 Erwin Mengers, *Denkwürdigkeiten und Erinnerungen eines Arbeiters,* II, 186, quoted in Stadelmann and Fischer, op. cit., p. 60.

37 *Memoirs of Frederick Perthes: Or Literary, Religious and Political Life in Germany from 1789 to 1843,* ed. C. T. Perthes (Edinburgh 1856), I, p. 10.
38 Quoted in Peter Glotz and W. G. Langenbücher, *Versäumte Lektionen* (Frankfurt 1971), pp. 79 f.
39 Moeller, op. cit., p. 120.
40 *Meister Johann Dietz, Des Grossen Kürfürsten Feldsher: Mein Lebenslauf,* ed. Fr. Kemp (Munich 1966; English edn. London 1960).
41 J. E. Dewald, *Biedermeir auf Walze,* in G. Moeller (ed.), *Dte. Selbstbiographien* (Munich 1966). See also a very lively account of the 'free masonry' of the wandering artisan by Chr. Bechstedt, a baker, *Meine Handwerksburschenzeit 1805–1810* (Cologne 1925).
42 Stadelmann and Fischer, op. cit., p. 135.
43 ibid., p. 17; see also Moeller, op. cit., pp. 260 ff. and 270 ff.
44 A sensitive discussion of these issues is to be found in the last chapter of Mack Walker, op. cit. (see note 34 above).

CHAPTER 5 THE EDUCATED CLASSES

1 Friedrich Paulsen, *Geschichte des gelehrten Unterrichts auf den deutschen Schulen und Universitäten vom Ausgang des Mittelalters bis zur Gegenwart,* 3rd edn. (Leipzig 1919), vol. 1, pp. 212 f.
2 *Allgemeine deutsche Biographie* (Leipzig 1876), vol. 4, p. 42.
3 e.g. the figure of Superintendent Stauzius in *Sebaldus Notanker.*
4 A. Tholuck, *Das akademische Leben des 17. Jahrhunderts mit besonderer Beziehung auf die protestantisch-theologischen Fakultäten Deutschlands* (Halle 1853–4), vol. 1, pp. 23 ff.
5 Paulsen, op. cit., vol. 2, p. 127.
6 ibid.
7 ibid., vol. 2, p. 128.
8 ibid., vol. 2, p. 129.
9 ibid., vol. 1, p. 259.
10 ibid.
11 ibid., vol. 2, p. 141.
12 ibid., vol. 2, p. 161.
13 Reproduced in R. Fick, *Auf Deutschlands hohen Schulen* (Berlin 1900), pp. 40 f., 44.
14 Cited in Golo Mann, *Wallenstein* (Frankfurt 1971), p. 29.
15 ibid., p. 30.
16 Johann Miller, *Die Geschichte Gottfried Walters, eines Tischlers, und des Städtchens Erlenburg* (Ulm 1786), pp. 146 ff.
17 Magister F. Chr. Laukhard, *Leben und Schicksale,* I-III, 13th edn. (Stuttgart 1930).
18 Paulsen, op. cit., vol. 1, p. 231.
19 H. Aubin and W. Zorn (eds.), *Handbach der dt. Wirtschafts- und Sozialgeschichte* (Stuttgart 1971), p. 590.
20 H. Rössler (ed.), *Deutscher Adel 1555–1740* (Darmstadt 1965), p. 139.
21 Pütter's *Selbstbiographie,* quoted by Paulsen, op. cit., vol. 2, p. 12.
22 Paulsen, op. cit., vol. 1, p. 515.
23 ibid., p. 482.
24 ibid., p. 521.
25 ibid.

26 Arnold Hirsch, '"*Politischer*" *Roman und* "*politische*" *Lebensführung*', in R. Alewyn (ed.), *Barocke Forschung*, 2nd edn. (Berlin-Koln 1966), p. 207.
27 See C. Hinrich's *Preussentum und Pietismus* (Göttingen 1971), p. 354.
28 Alewyn (ed.), op. cit., p. 214.
29 ibid., p. 208.
30 ibid., p. 215.
31 ibid.
32 Erich Trunz, '*Das gelehrte Deutschland*', in Alewyn (ed.), op. cit., p. 151.
33 Bernard Asmuth, *C. D. von Lohenstein (Sammlung Metzler)* (Stuttgart 1971), p. 17.
34 Rössler (ed.), op. cit., p. 346.
35 Paul Ernst, *Meine Lebenserinnerungen* (Leipzig 1930), p. 13.
36 J. D. E. Preuss, *Friedrich der Grosse* (Berlin 1832–4), vol. 3, p. 116.
37 ibid., p. 115.
38 H. Moeller, *Die kleinburgerliche Familie im 18. Jahrhundert* (Berlin 1969), p. 105.
39 ibid., p. 106.
40 Jakob von Klaveren, '*Das* "*Zeitalter des Merkantilismus*"', *Vierteljahresschrift fur Sozial- und Wirtschaftsgeschichte*, vol. 50 (1963), p. 70.
41 K. F. von Klöden, *Jugenderinnerungen*, ed. M. Jahns (Leipzig 1874), p. 98.
42 ibid., p. 242.
43 Ernst, op. cit., pp. 14 f., 54.
44 Moeller, op. cit., p. 249.
45 ibid.
46 ibid., p. 252.
47 Quoted in Moeller, p. 53.
48 F. X. Bronner, *Ein Mönchsleben aus der empfindsamen Zeit (Memoiren Bibliothek IV)* (Stuttgart, no date), p. 52.
49 Klöden, op. cit., p. 14.
50 Uwe Schweikert, *Jean Paul (Sammlung Metzler)* (Stuttgart 1970), p. 14.
51 Klöden, op. cit., p. 105.
52 F. Lucae, *Schlesiens curiose Denkwürdigkeiten* (1689), quoted in Asmuth, op. cit., p. 4.
53 Kurt Schmid, '*Andreas Reyher*', in Gunther Franz (ed.), *Thüringer Erzieher* (Köln-Graz 1966), p. 45.
54 ibid., p. 51.
55 W. von Kügelgen, *Jugenderinnerungen eines alten Mannes* (Leipzig 1911), pp. 298 ff.
56 Paulsen, op. cit., vol. 2, p. 53.

CHAPTER 6 RELIGIOUS LIFE AND THE CLERGY IN GERMANY

1 J. Nevaux, *Vie spirituelle et vie sociale entre Rhin et Baltique au XVIIe siècle* (Paris 1967), p. 62.
2 Andreas Gryphius, *Menschliches Elende* (1643).
3 Erwin Riedenauer, '*Reichsritterschaft und Konfession*', in H. Rössler (ed.), *Deutscher Adel 1555–1740* (Darmstadt 1965), p. 31. See also Walter Brandmüller, '*Das Wiedererstehen katholischer Gemeinden in den Fürstentümern Ansbach-Bayreuth*', in *Münchener theologische Studien*, vol. 1 (15) (1963), pp. 1–7.

4 H. Mikoletzy, *Österreich: Das grosse 18. Jht.* (Wien 1967), p. 153.
5 Adam Wandruszka, '*Geheimprotestantismus, Josephinismus und Volksliturgie in Österreich*', *Zeitschrift für Kirchengeschichte,* vol. 78 (1967), pp. 94–101.
6 H. Watzl, *Flucht und Zuflucht. Das Tagebuch des Priesters Balthasar Kleinschroth aus dem Türkenjahr 1683* (*Forschungen zur Landeskunde von Nieder-Osterreich,* vol. 8) (Graz-Köln 1956).
7 Rudolph Reinhardt, '*Zur Kirchenreform in Österreich unter Maria Theresia*', *Zeitschrift für Kirchengeschichte,* vol. 77 (1966), pp. 107–119.
8 Quoted in Klaus Deppermann, *Der hallische Pietismus und der preussische Staat unter Friedrich III,* vol. 1 (Göttingen 1961), p. 16.
9 Deppermann, op. cit., p. 9.
10 Carl Hinrichs, *Preussentum und Pietismus* (Göttingen 1971), p. 3.
11 An example of this last is the extraordinarily interesting correspondence between L. Camerarius and his friend Lukas Behaim at Nuremberg. Apart from its importance as a contemporary commentary on religious matters in the war years (from a Calvinist point of view), it is full of incidental details on communications, etc. (see Introduction, note 1, above).
12 Quoted in Hinrichs, op. cit., p. 186.
13 P. E. Schramm, *Neun Generationen,* vol. 1 (Göttingen 1963), pp. 95 ff.
14 Hinrichs, op. cit., p. 163.
15 Martin Brecht, '*Soziale Herkunft und theologische Bildung der lutherischen Geistlichkeit in Württemberg*', *Zeitschrift für Kirchengeschichte,* vol. 80 (1969), p. 170.
16 See R. Wittram, *Drei Generationen* (Berlin 1950).
17 R. von Thadden, *Die Brandenburgisch-Preussischen Hofprediger im 17. und 18. Jahrhundert* (Berlin 1959), pp. 188 ff.
18 Thadden, op. cit., p. 37, and *Religion in Geschichte und Gegenwart,* 3rd edn. (Tübingen 1957–62), vol. 5, p. 278, and vol. 6, pp. 388–9.
19 J. Schopenhauer, *Jugendleben und Wanderbilder,* ed. W. Drost (Tübingen 1958), pp. 54 ff.
20 ibid., pp. 5 f.
21 Flemming, op. cit., p. 155.
22 W. Bruford, *Germany in the Eighteenth Century* (Cambridge 1971), p. 255.
23 Magister F. Chr. Laukhard, *Leben und Schicksale,* 13th edn. (Stuttgart 1930).
24 Gerd Eilers, *Meine Wanderungen durchs Leben* (Leipzig 1856), vol. 1, p. 32 (of his mother).
25 E. W. Zeeden in Gebhardt, *Handbuch der deutschen Geschichte,* 9th edn., vol. 2 (Stuttgart 1970), p. 216.
26 On the Jesuits in Germany in the period of 1648–1806 see B. Duhr, S.J., *Geschichte der Jesuiten in den Ländern deutscher Zunge in der zweiten Hälfte des XVII. Jahrhunderts* (Regensburg 1921).
27 Zeeden, op. cit., p. 218.
28 R. J. W. Evans, *Rudolph II and His World* (Oxford 1973), p. 34.
29 Neveux, op. cit., p. 583, n. 1.
30 E. Schubert, '*Zur Typologie gegenreformatorischer Universitätsgründungen: Jesuiten in Fulda, Würzburg, Ingolstadt und Dillingen*', in H. Rössler and G. Franz (eds.), *Universität und Gelehrtenstand 1400–1800,* vol. 4 of *Deutsche Führungsschichten in der Neuzeit* (Limburg/Lahn 1970), p. 97.
31 ibid., p. 98.
32 J. G. Oorschot, S. J., *Friedrich Spees Güldenes Tugendbuch* (Munich 1968),

pp. 705 f.

33 Duhr, op. cit., pp. 109 f., 616.

34 Neveux, op. cit., p. 722.

35 See L. A. Veit, and L. Lenhart, *Kirche und Volksfrömmigkeit im Zeitalter des Barock* (Freiburg 1956), especially section 2, pp. 58 ff. The section on popular devotions in the *Germanisches Museum* at Nuremberg gives a vivid impression of the impact of such practices.

36 See N. von Preradovich, *'Die soziale Herkunft österreichischer Kirchenfürsten (1648–1918)'*, in *Festschrift für Karl Eder* (Innsbruck 1959).

37 Reinhardt, op. cit., pp. 107 ff.; see also the chapter on the Catholic Church in Spectrum Austriae (Vienna 1956).

CHAPTER 7 ARMY LIFE

1 Deiter Albert, *'Staat und Gesellschaft 1500–1745'*, in M. Spindler (ed.), *Handbuch der bayerischen Geschichte* (Munich 1966), vol. 2, p. 591.

2 W. Flemming, *Deutsche Kultur im Zeitalter des Barock*, 2nd edn. (Constance 1960), p. 169.

3 Golo Mann, *Wallenstein* (Frankfurt 1971), contains much incidental information on military matters, presented with imagination and scholarship.

4 Quoted in Rainer Wohlfeil, *'Adel und Heerwesen'*, in H. Rössler (ed.), *Deutscher Adel 1555–1740* (Darmstadt 1965), p. 317.

5 Flemming, op. cit., p. 169.

6 L. Hammermayer, in M. Spindler (ed.), *Handbuch z. bayr. Gesch.*, vol. 2, p. 1079, n. 2.

7 Quoted in Flemming, op. cit., p. 187.

8 Wohlfeil, op. cit., p. 323.

9 ibid., p. 330.

10 C. Grimmelshausen, *Der abenteuerliche Simplicissimus* (Darmstadt 1956), p. 46; the image is elaborated over chs. 15–18 of Book 1.

11 Otto Büsch, *Militärsystem und Sozialleben im alten Preussen 1713–1807* (Berlin 1962), p. 91.

12 Karl Demeter, *Das deutsche Offizierkorps in seinen historisch- soziologischen Grundlagen* (Berlin 1930), pp. 41, 66.

13 N. von Preradovich, *'Der Adel in den Herrschaften der deutschen Linie des Hauses Habsburg'*, in H. Rössler (ed.), *Deutscher Adel 1555–1740* (Darmstadt 1965), p. 201.

14 Büsch, op. cit., p. 1.

15 Carl Hinrichs, *Preussentum und Pietismus* (Göttingen 1971), p. 129.

16 Büsch, op. cit., p. 20.

17 ibid., pp. 118 ff.

18. H. Aubin and W. Zorn (eds., *Handbuch der dt. Wirtschafts- und Sozialgeschichte* (Stuttgart 1971), p. 585.

19 K. F. von Klöden, *Jugenderinnerungen*, ed. M. Jahns (Leipzig 1874), p. 22.

20 W. H. Bruford, *Germany in the Eighteenth Century* (Cambridge 1971), p. 33.

21 See N. von Preradovich, *'Die politisch- militärische Elite in Oesterreich 1526–1918'*, *Saeculum*, vol. 15 (1964), pp. 393 ff.

22 *Patriotisches Archiv für Deutschland*, VII (1787), p. 428, quoted in J. G. Gagliardo, *From Pariah to Patriot: The Changing Image of the German*

Peasant 1770–1840 (Kentucky 1969), pp. 43 f.
23 Gagliardo, op. cit., p. 43, n. 39.

CHAPTER 8 THE PEASANTRY

1 See introduction to G. Benecke, *Society and Politics in Germany 1500–1750* (London 1974), pp. 3–9.
2 ibid., p. 6.
3 J. Blum 'The Internal Structure and Polity of the Village Community from the Fifteenth to the Nineteenth Century', *Journal of Modern History*, vol. 43 (1971), p. 549.
4 ibid., p. 558.
5 On the very different concept of 'family' and 'household' from that of modern times, see O. Brunner's essay, *'Das ganze Haus'*, in his *Neue Wege der Sozial- und Verfassungsgeschichte*, 2nd edn. (Göttingen 1968), pp. 103–27.
6 An incisive account of the servants in a peasant household is contained in Lutz K. Berkner's 'The Stem Family and the Development of the Peasant Household: An 18th Century Austrian Example', *American Historical Review*, vol. 77 (1972), pp. 398–418, esp. pp. 416 ff.
7 D. Wiarda, *Die geschichtliche Entwicklung der wirtschaftlichen Verhältnisse Ostfrieslands*, quoted in W. von Groote, *Die Entstehung d. Nationalismus in Nordwestdeutschland 1790–1830* (Göttingen 1955), p. 105.
8 See G. Franz, *Geschichte des deutschen Bauernstands vom frühen Mittelalter bis zum 19. Jahrhundert*, vol. 4 of *Deutsche Agrargeschichte* (Stuttgart 1970).
9 H. Aubin and W. Zorn (eds.), *Handbuch der dt. Wirtschafts- und Sozialgeschichte* (Stuttgart 1971), p. 501.
10 Franz, op. cit., p. 200.
11 Aubin and Zorn, op. cit., p. 501.
12 H. Kellenbenz, *'Bäuerliche Unternehmertätigkeit im Bereich der Nord- und Ostsee'*, *Vierteljahrsschrift für Sozial- und Wirtschaftsgeschichte*, vol. 49 (1962), p. 25.
13 J. Blum in a recent article, 'The Condition of the European Peasantry on the Eve of Emancipation', *Journal of Modern History*, vol. 46 (1962), takes a different view: 'Distinctions among the servile lands in the condition of the peasantry would only be gradations in a scale of poverty and misery' (p. 424). Such generalizations can only be upheld when they are substantiated by a great deal more work on local conditions in the future.
14 Aubin and Zorn, op. cit., p. 393.
15 Quoted in J. Gagliardo, *From Pariah to Patriot: The Changing Image of the German Peasant 1770–1840* (Kentucky 1969).
16 I. Bog, *Die bäuerliche Wirtschaft im Zeitalter des 30 jährigen Krieges* (Coburg 1952), pp. 142 ff. Also G. Benecke, 'Labour Relations and Peasant Society in Northwest Germany', *History*, vol. 58 (1973), p. 351, and his 'The Problem of Death and Destruction in Germany during the Thirty Years War', *European Studies Review*, vol. 2 (1972), pp. 239–53.
17 G. Franz, *Quellen zur Geschichte des deutschen Bauernstandes* (Stuttgart 1963), vol. 2, pp. 117 ff.
18 See table in Aubin and Zorn, op. cit., p. 394.
19 J. V. von Eckhard, *Vollständige Experimentalökonomie*, quoted in Aubin and Zorn, op. cit., p. 395.
20 Aubin and Zorn, op. cit., p. 395.

21 Franz, *Geschichte*, p. 233.
22 T. C. W. Blanning, *Reform and Revolution in Mainz 1743–1803* (Cambridge 1974), p. 87.
23 See Gebhardt, *Handbuch der deutschen Geschichte*, 9th edn. (Stuttgart 1970), vol. 2, pp. 514 ff.
24 Otto Büsch, *Militärysystem und Sozialleben im alten Preussen 1713–1807* (Berlin 1962), p. 16.
25 ibid., p. 17.
26 ibid., p. 21.
27 ibid., p. 71.
28 See Peter Blickle, '*Bäuerliche Landschaft und Standschaft*', in Franz, *Geschichte*, pp. 151 f. The conclusions of Blickle's recent and well-reviewed works, *Landschaften im alten Reich, Die staatliche Funktion des gemeinen Mannes in Oberdeutschland* (Munich 1973), and his authoritative work on the mechanisms of the 1525 Peasants War, *Die Revolution von 1525* (Munich 1975), relevant for the whole early modern period in Germany, reached me too late to be incorporated into the text, as did also the work of the East German scholar K. M. Blaschke.
29 See G. Grüll, *Bauern, Herr und Landesfürst. Sozialrevolutionäre Bestrebungen der oberösterreichischen Bauern von 1650–1848* (Graz-Cologne 1963); see also Franz, *Quellen*, pp. 113 ff.
30 Franz, *Geschichte*, pp. 237 ff.
31 Aubin and Zorn, op. cit., pp. 499 f.
32 Blum, *Village Community*, p. 571.
33 Kellenbenz, op. cit., p. 35.

CHAPTER 9 THE FRINGES OF SOCIETY

1 R. A. Dorwart, *The Prussian Welfare State Before 1740* (Harvard 1971), p. 16.
2 H. Kellenbenz, '*Sephardim an der unteren Elbe*', *Vierteljahrsschrift für Sozial- und Wirtschaftsgeschichte*, vol. 40 (1957).
3 See 'The Shtadlan and Intercessor', in Selma Stern, *The Court Jew* (Philadelphia 1950), pp. 177–88.
4 Hilde Spiel, *Fanny Arnstein, oder Die Emanzipation* (Berlin 1962), pp. 64 f.
5 Selma Stern-Taubler, 'The First Generation of Emancipated Jews', *Leo Baeck Yearbook*, vol. 15 (1970), p. 3.
6 K. F. von Klöden, *Jugenderinnerungen*, ed. M. Jahns (Leipzig 1874), p. 91.
7 Spiel, op. cit., p. 25.
8 Char. Wm. von Dohm, *Uber die bürgerliche Verbesserung der Juden* (Berlin 1781), p. 10.
9 Dorwart, op. cit., p. 74.
10 Karl Wild, *Staat und Wirtschaft in den Bistümern Würzburg und Bamberg* (Heidelberg 1906), pp. 193 f.
11 J. Blum, 'The Condition of the European Peasantry on the Eve of Emancipation', *Journal of Modern History*, vol. 46 (1974), p. 420.
12 J. Neveux, *Vie spirituelle et vie sociale entre Rhin et Baltique au XVIIe siècle* (Paris 1967), p. 745.
13 Thus described by the Italian friar Samuele de Cassinis in the sixteenth century, the first known protester against the practice; see Henry Kamen, *The Iron Age* (London 1971), p. 241.

14 Keith Thomas, 'The Relevance of Social Anthropology to a Historical Study of English Witchcraft', pp. 47–79 in Mary Douglas (ed.), *Witchcraft, Confessions and Accusations* (London 1970).
15 H. C. Erik Midelfort, *Witch Hunting in Southwest Germany 1562–1684: The Social and Intellectual Foundations* (Stanford 1972).
16 See *The Journal of Master Franz Schmidt, Public Executioner of Nuremberg,* with introduction by A. Keller (English trans., London 1928).
17 See tables in Midelfort, op. cit., pp. 180–2.
18 ibid., pp. 183 ff. and bibliography.
19 S. Riezler, *Geschichte der Hexenprozesse in Bayern* (Stuttgart 1896), pp. 273 ff.

INTRODUCTION TO PART II

1 Quoted in R. Koselleck, '*Staat und Gesellschaft in Preussen 1815–1848*', in H.-U. Wehler (ed.), *Moderne deutsche Sozialgeschichte* (Cologne 1966), p. 58.
2 See Hans H. Gerth, *Bürgerliche Intelligenz um 1800. Zur Soziologie des dt. Frühliberalismus* (Göttingen 1976).
3 The 1965 and 1966 issues of *Jahrbuch für Wirtschaftsgeschichte* contain a number of articles by H.-H. Muller and others on this area of research.
4 W. Zorn, in *Handbuch der bayerischen Geschichte,* vol. 4 (2) (Munich 1975), p. 866.
5 See J. J. Sheehan, 'Liberalism and the city in nineteenth-century Germany', *Past and Present,* vol. 51 (1971), pp. 116–37, and his 'Liberalism and society in Germany 1815–48', *Journal of Modern History,* vol. 49 (1973), pp. 582–604.
6 As in the contributions by Fehn, Fried and Zorn in the *Handbuch der bayerischen Geschichte,* mentioned in note 4 above.
7 L. Gall, '*Liberalismus und bürgerliche Gesselschaft. Zu Charakter und Entwicklung der liberalen Bewegung in Deutschl.*', *Historische Zeitschrift,* vol. 220 (1975), especially pp. 354 f.
8 H.-J. Henning treats this theme at some length for north-west Germany in *Das westeutsche Bürgertum in der Epoche der Hochindustrialisierung 1860–1914: soziales Verhalten und soziale Struktur* (Wiesbaden 1972).

CHAPTER 10 THE COURTS AND THE NOBILITY

1 H. Gollwitzer, *Die Standesherren,* 2nd edn. (Gottingen 1964), p. 54.
2 R. Vierhaus (ed.), *Das Tagebuch der Baronin Spitzemberg* (Göttingen 1963), vol. 43 of *Dte. Geschichtsquellen des 19. u. 20. Jahrunderts,* p. 131.
3 Gollwitzer, op. cit., p. 237.
4 Th. Hamerow, *The Social Foundations of German Unification,* vol. 1 (Princeton 1969), p. 60.
5 H.-U. Wehler, *Das Deutsche Kaiserreich 1871–1918* (Göttingen 1973), p. 161.
6 N. von Preradovich, *Deutsche Führungsschichten in Oesterreich und Preussen 1804–1918* (Wiesbaden 1956), p. 6.
7 ibid., pp. 44 and 61.
8 ibid., p. 127.
9 ibid., p. 166.
10 See Johanna Schultze, *Die Auseinandersetzung zwischen Adel und Bürgertum in den deutschen Zeitschriften der letzten drei Jahrzehnte des 18. Jahrhunderts 1773–1806* (Berlin 1925).

11 W. Conze, article on '*Adel*' in Brunner, Conze and Koselleck (eds.), *Geschichtliche Grundbegriffe,* vol. 1 (Stuttgart 1972), p. 29.
12 E. Shorter, 'Middle Class Anxiety in the German Revolution of 1848', *Journal of Social History,* vol. 2 (1968–9), p. 207.
13 H. Rosenberg, '*Die Pseudodemokratisierung der Rittergutsbesitzerklasse*', in *Probleme der deutschen Sozialgeschichte* (Frankfurt 1969), p. 18.
14 See Chapter 19 on the peasantry, pp. 339–355.
15 R. Berdahl, 'Conservative Policies and Aristocratic Landholders in Bismarck's Germany', *Journal of Modern History,* vol. 44 (1972), p. 10.
16 H.-U. Wehler, *Bisharck und der Imperialismus*, 3rd edn. (Cologne 1972), p. 90.
17 Quoted in Berdahl, op. cit., p. 20.
18 Rosenberg, '*Zur sozialen Funktion der Agrarpolitik im Kaiserreich*', in op. cit., p. 66.
19 Wehler, *Bismarck und der Imperialismus,* p. 92.
20 W. Abel, *Agrarkrisen und Agrarkonjunktur,* 2nd edn. (Berlin 1966), p. 259.
21 See Fr. Sengle, '*Wunschbild Land und Schreckbild Stadt*', *Studium Generale,* vol. 166 (1963), pp. 619–31.
22 See P. Zimmermann, *Der Bauernroman* (Stuttgart 1975).
23 Wehler, op. cit., p. 94.
24 Rosenberg, op. cit., p. 78.
25 Among a number of recent works on the the subject, see especially H.-J. Puhle's *Agrarische Interessenpolitik und preussischer Konservatismus im Wilhelminischen Deutschland 1893–1914* (Hanover 1966); also his article, '*Parlament, Parteien und Interessenverbände 1890–1914*', in M. Stürmer (ed.), *Das kaiserliche Deutschland* (Düsseldorf 1970), pp. 340–77.
26 See Marie von Bunsen, *Die Welt von Gestern 1860–1912* (Leipzig, no date); Eng. trans. *The World I Used to Know* (London 1930).
27 R. Vierhaus (ed.), op. cit., Introduction, p. 16.
28 Robert Michels, *Probleme der Sozialphilosophie* (Leipzig 1914), quoted in Rosenberg, op. cit., p. 8.
29 H. Kraft Graf Strachwitz, *Eines Priesters Weg durch die Zeitenwende* (Dresden 1935), p. 14.
30 Vierhaus, op. cit., p. 17.
31 G. von Hertling, *Erinnerungen aus meinen Leben,* vol. 1 (Munich 1919), pp. 15 ff. and pp. 38 f.
32 Chlodwig von Hohenlohe-Schillingsfürst, *Denkwürdigkeiten* (Stuttgart 1907), vol. 1, pp. 73 ff.
33 Prinz Kraft zu Hohenlohe-Ingelfingen, *Aus meinem Leben,* 2nd edn. (Berlin 1915), p. 53.
34 Strachwitz, op. cit., pp. 12 f.
35 Preradovich, op. cit., p. 185.
36 Bertha von Suttner, *Memoiren* (Bremen 1965), pp. 107 ff.
37 K. von Stutterheim, *Zwischen den Zeiten* (Berlin 1938), p. 49.
38 Helene Marie von Kügelen, *Ein Leben in Briefen* (Stuttgart 1918), pp. 28 ff.
39 Conze, op. cit., p. 29.
40 Th. Fontane, *Briefe an seine Familie,* 2nd series, vol. III, p. 141.
41 Rosenberg, op. cit., p. 41.
42 Th. Fontane, *Der Stechlin* (Munich 1969), vol. 2, p. 61.
43 C. Brinkmann, entry under '*Adel*' in *Handbuch der Sozialwissenschaften*

(Stuttgart 1956), p. 26.

44 Rosenberg, op. cit., p. 25, n. 25.

45 Otto Büsch, *Militärsystem und Sozialleben im alten Preussen 1713–1807* (Berlin 1962), ch. 2, pp. 21–50.

46 Quoted in Conze, op. cit., p. 47, n. 194.

CHAPTER II THE CHURCHES AND RELIGIOUS LIFE IN THE NINETEENTH CENTURY

General references

Ernst Troeltsch, '*Zur religiösen Lage, Religionsphilosophie und Ethik*', pp. 1–182 in H. Baron (ed.), *Aufsätze zur Geistesgeschichte und Religionssoziologie* (Tübingen 1925, reprint 1966).

E. R. and W. Huber, *Staat u. Kirche im 19. u. 20 Jahrhundert,* vol. 1 (Berlin 1973).

The best general account of the Catholic church during this period is still to be found in Fr. Schnabel, *Deutsche Geschichte im 19. Jahrhundert,* vol. IV of *Die religiösen Kräfte,* 3rd edn. (Freiburg 1955).

Text references

1 Annette Kuhn, '*Der Herrschaftsanspruch der Gesellschaft und die Kirche*', *Historische Zeitschrift,* vol. 201 (1965), pp. 334 ff.

2 R. M. Bigler, *The Politics of German Protestantism: The Rise of the Protestant Church Elite in Prussia 1815–48* (California 1972), pp. 1 ff. A most informative study.

3 K. Epstein, *The Genesis of German Conservatism* (Princeton 1966), p. 114.

4 Kuhn, op. cit., p. 344.

5 W. Köllmann, *Sozialgeschichte der Stadt Barmen* (Tübingen 1960), p. 195.

6 The memoirs of Ernst Ludwig Gerlach are essential reading on the subject of neo-Pietism, especially interesting on the sociological aspect: *Aufzeichnungen aus seinem Leben und Werken 1795–1877,* 2 vols (Schwerin 1903).

7 Bigler, op. cit., p. 64, n. 28.

8 ibid., p. 67, n. 38.

9 ibid., pp. 80 ff.

10 ibid., p. 55.

11 ibid., p. 60.

12 ibid., p. 187.

13 ibid., p. 140.

14 ibid., p. 218.

15 Fritz Fischer, '*Der deutsche Protestantismus und die Politik im 19. Jahrhundert*', *Historische Zeitschrift,* vol. 170 (1951), p. 485.

16 See Karl Kupisch's imaginative article, '*Der Deutsche zwischen 1850 und 1865*', *Zeitschrift für Religionsgeschichte,* vol. 19 (1966), pp. 108–42, with many useful references.

17 H. Lehmann, '*Friedrich v. Bodelschwingh und das Sedanfest*', *Historische Zeitschrift,* vol. 202 (1966), p. 570. See also K. Kupisch, *Quellen zur Geschichte des deutschen Protestantismus 1871–1945,* vol. 11 of *Kulturgesch.,* ed. W. Treue (Göttingen 1960).

18 Th. Fontane, *Effi Briest* (Munich 1969), p. 97.

19 Paul Göhre, *Drei Monate Fabrikarbeiter und Handwerksbursche* (Leipzig 1891), pp. 14 f.

20 H. Rothfels (ed.), *Facsimile durch den Kladderadatsch* (Munich 1965), p. 154.
21 Köllmann, op. cit., p. 207.
22 See W. O. Shanahan, *German Protestants Face the Social Question* (Notre Dame 1954).
23 H. Lehmann, *'Fr. Bodelschwingh u. Bismarck. Christlichkonservative Sozialpolitik im Kaiserreich'*, *Historische Zeitschrift*, vol. 208 (1969), pp. 607 ff.
24 Fischer, op. cit., p. 509.
25 H. Kaelble, *'Sozialer Aufstieg in Deutschland 1850–1914'*, *Vierteljahresschrift für Sozial- und Wirtschaftsgeschichte*, vol. 60 (1973), p. 56.
26 See here H. Kraft Graf Strachwitz, *Eines Priesters Weg durch die Zeitenwende* (Dresden 1935), pp. 15 ff.
27 On this aspect see Karl Buchheim, *Ultramontanismus und Demokratie* (Munich 1963).
28 Alexander Dru, *The Church in the Nineteenth Century: Germany 1800–1918* (London 1963).
29 ibid., pp. 35–6.
30 *Denkwürdigkeiten aus dem Leben der Fürstin Amalia von Galitzin* (Berlin 1971, reprint of 1828 edn.), p. 7.
31 M. Spindler (ed.), *Handbuch der bayerischen Geschichte* (Munich 1966), p. 994.
32 Dru, op. cit., p. 41.
33 Dru is especially good on this aspect. See also F. Heyer, *The Catholic Church from 1648 to 1870* (London 1969), ch. VI, pp. 119–50.
34 E. Benz, *'Franz von Baader's Gedanken über den "Proletair"'*, *Zeitschrift für Religions- und Geistesgeschichte*, vol. 1 (1948), p. 97–123.
35 E. Gatz, *Kirche und Krankenpflege im 19. Jahrhundert* (Munich 1971).
36 On Ketteler see L. Lenhart, *Bischof Ketteler*, 3 vols. (Mainz 1966–8).
37 Quoted in K. Buchheim, *Deutsche Kultur 1830–70*-(Frankfurt 1966), p. 61.
38 Dru, op. cit., p. 111. See also Hertling's memoirs, *Erinnerungen aus meine Leben*, 2 vols (Munich 1919).
39 Dru, op. cit., p. 111.
40 Th. Eschenburg, *'Carl Sonnenschein'*, *VfZG* vol. 11 (1963) p. 333.
41 Th. Eschenburg, *Ämterpatronage* (Stuttgart 1961).
42 J. Röhl, *'Beamtenpolitik'*, in M. Stürmer (ed.), *Das kaiserliche Deutschland* (Düsseldorf 1970), p. 295.

CHAPTER 12 THE GERMAN ARMY

1 K. Demeter, *The German Officer Corps in Society and State 1650–1945* (London 1965), p. 12.
2 ibid., p. 19.
3 A. von Sydow (ed.), *Gabriele von Humboldt's Töchter* (Leipzig 1928), p. 143.
4 *Denkwürdigkeiten aus dem Leben des Generalfeldmarschalls Kriegsministers Gffiafen Albrecht von Roon*, 4th edn. (Breslau 1897), vol. 1, pp. 118 ff.
5 C. Barnett, 'The Education of Military Elites', *Journal of Contemporary History*, vol. 2 (3) (1967), p. 25.
6 W. Diest. *'Die Armee in Statt und Gessellschaft 1890–1914'*, in M. Stürmer (ed.), *Das kaiserliche Deutschland* (Düsseldorf 1970), p. 321.
7 *Handbuch zur deutschen Militärgeschichte*, V, ed. W. Schill-Rehberg and E. von Matuschka (Frankfurt 1969), p. 84.
8 Von Sydow (ed.), op. cit., p. 119.

9 M. Howard, 'William II and the Reform of the Prussian Army', in *A Century of Conflict 1850–1950: Essays Presented to A. J. P. Taylor* (London 1966), p. 94.
10 ibid.
11 ibid., p. 98.
12 Roon, op. cit., pp. 167 and 136.
13 M. Messerschmidt, '*Die Armee in Staat und Gesellschaft – die Bismarck zeit*', in M. Stürmer (ed.), op. cit., p. 94.
14 Diest, op. cit., pp. 315 f.
15 G. A. Craig, *The Politics of the Prussian Army* (Oxford 1955), p. 240.
16 H. Rumschöttel, '*Bildung und Herkunft der bayerischen Offiziere 1886 bis 1914: Zur Geschichte von Mentalität und Ideologie des bayerischen Offizierkorps*', *Militärgeschichtliche Mitteilungen*, vol. 2 (1970), pp. 81 ff.
17 Demeter, op. cit., p. 24.
18 E. Kessel, *Helmut von Moltke* (Stuttgart 1957), p. 347.
19 Demeter, op. cit., pp. 28–9.
20 Schill-Rehberg and Matuschka, op. cit., p. 85.
21 ibid., p. 86.
22 Marie von Bunsen, *Die Welt von Gestern 1860–1912* (Leipzig, no date); English trans., *The World I Used to Know* (London 1930), p. 71.
23 G. A. Ritter and J. Kocka, *Deutsche Sozialgeschichte 1870–1918* (Munich 1974), p. 224.
24 Carl Zuckmayer, '*Der Hauptmann von Köpenick*', *Meisterdramen* (Frankfurt 1970), p. 236.
25 See the article by K. Saul, '*Der "Deutsche Kriegerbund": Zur innenpolitischen Funktion eines nationalpolitischen Verbandes im kaiserlichen Deutschland*', *Militärgeschichtliche Mitteilungen*, vol. 1 (1970), pp. 95–159.
25a H.-U. Wehler, *Das Deutsche Kaiserreich 1871–1918* (Göttingen 1973).
25b ibid., p. 151.
26 See the pioneering article, much quoted nowadays, by Eckhart Kehr, '*Der deutsche Reserveoffizier*', in H.-U. Wehler (ed.), *Der Primat der Innenpolitik: Gesamt Aufsatze zur preussisch-deutschen Sozialgeschichte im 19. und 20. Jahrhundert* (Berlin 1965).
27 *Der Infanterie-Einjährige und Offizier des Beurlaubtenstandes*, quoted in Ritter and Kocka, op. cit., p. 235.
28 Schill-Rehberg and Matuschka, op. cit., p. 104.
29 ibid., p. 93.
30 See some brilliant caricatures in Golo Mann (ed.), *Facsimile Querschnitt durch den Simplicissimus* (Bern, etc., 1963), pp. 47, 59, 98, 114.
31 Diest, op. cit., p. 323.
32 Messerschmidt, op. cit., p. 104.
33 Spindler (ed.), *Handbuch der bayerischen Geschichte*, vol. V (Munich 1974), pp. 289–90. For the earlier period see N. von Preradovich, '*Die Führer der deutschen Heere 1866 in sozialer Sicht*', *Vierteljahresschrift für Sozial- und Wirtschaftsgeschichte*, vol. 53 (1966), pp. 370–6.
34 Demeter, op. cit., p. 43.
35 Rumschöttel, op. cit.
36 *Handbuch der bayerischen Geschichte*, vol. IV, p. 364.
37 K. Höfele, *Geist und Gesellschaft der Bismarckzeit 1870–1890*, vol. 18 of *Quellensammlung zur Kulturgeschichte* (Göttingen 1967), pp. 84 ff.,

especially p. 87 and 81 ff.

38 *Handbuch*, p. 100.

39 Quoted by Hans Herzfeld in *Geschichte Berlins und der Provinz Brandenburgs*, vol. 25 (*Historische Kommission* series 1971), p. 74.

40 Jonathan Steinberg, 'The Kaiser's Navy and German Society', *Past and Present*, vol. 28 (1964), pp. 105–7.

CHAPTER 13 THE BOURGEOISIE

1 Th. Zeldin, *France 1848–1945*, vol. 1, *Ambition, Love and Politics* (Oxford 1973), p. 11.

2 *Allgemeine deutsche Biographie* (Leipzig 1880), Hoffmann, vol. XII, pp. 575 ff.

3 Lenore O'Boyle, 'The Excess of Educated Men in Western Europe 1800–1850', *Journal of Modern History*, vol. 42 (1970), pp. 471 ff.

4 Mack Walker, *German Home Towns* (Cornell 1971), esp. ch. XI.

5 L. Beutin, *'Das Bürgertum als Gesellschaftsstand im 19. Jahrhundert'*, in H. Kellenbenz (ed.), *Ges. Schriften* (Cologne 1963), p. 285.

6 R. Koselleck, *'Staat und Gesellschaft in Preussen 1815–1848'*, in H.-U. Wehler (ed.), *Moderne deutsche Sozialgeschichte* (Cologne 1966), p. 81.

7 Quoted in K. Buchheim, *Deutsche Kultur zwischen 1830 u. 1870* (Frankfurt 1966), p. 71.

8 Koselleck, op. cit., p. 77.

9 Th. Hamerow, *The Social Foundations of German Unification*, vol. 1 (Princeton 1969), p. 136. See also E. Shorter, 'Middle Class Anxiety in the German Revolution of 1848', *Journal of Social History*, vol. 2 (1968–9), p. 207.

10 See two important recent articles on liberalism and bourgeois society with many references: J. J. Sheehan, 'Liberalism and Society in Germany 1815–1848', *Journal of Modern History*, vol. 45 (1973), pp. 583–604 (especially interesting with reference to municipal administration); L. Gall, *'Liberalismus und bürgerliche Gesellschaft. Zu Charakter und Entwicklung der liberalen Bewegung in Deutschland'*, *Historische Zeitschrift*, vol. 220 (1975), pp. 324–56.

11 H.-U. Wehler, *Das Deutsche Kaiserreich 1871–1918* (Göttingen 1973), p. 100 (see pp. 46 f. and 100 f. for the economic and political issues briefly discussed here).

12 For a full treatment see H. Rosenberg, *Grosse Depression und Bismarckzeit* (Berlin 1967), and also A. Gerschenkron's review in *Continuity in History and other Essays* (Cambridge, Mass., 1968), pp. 405–8.

CHAPTER 14 THE BUREAUCRATS

1 R. Koselleck, *Preussen zwischen Reform und Revolution* (Stuttgart 1967), p. 434.

2 ibid., n. 155.

3 Koselleck, op. cit., p. 435.

4 See Th. Fontane's *Mathilde Möhring* (1896) for a subtle portrait of the social milieu of a provincial Prussian official in the late nineteenth century.

5 W. Pöls (ed.), *Deutsche Sozialgeschichte. Dokument und Skizzen*, I (Munich 1973), p. 89.

6 W. Abel, '*Der Pauperismus in Deutschland*', in *Wirtschaft, Geschichte und Wirtschaftsgesch. Festschrift für Fr. Lütge* (Stuttgart 1966), pp. 293 ff.
7 W. Abel, *Massenarmut und Hungerkrisen im vorindustriellen Deutschland* (Göttingen 1972).
8 Koselleck, op. cit., p. 439.
9 Abel, '*Pauperismus*', pp. 294 f.
10 J. R. Gillis, *The Prussian Bureaucracy in Crisis 1840–60: Origins of an Administrative Ethos* (California 1971), p. 168.
11 ibid., p. 174.
12 Quoted in Gillis, op. cit., p. 179.
13 H. Kaelble, '*Sozialer Aufstieg in Deutschland 1850–1914*', *Vierteljahresschrift für Sozial- und Wirtschaftsgeschichte*, vol. 60 (1973), p. 46.
14 ibid., p. 50.
15 J. Röhl, '*Beamtenpolitik im Wilhelminischen Deutschland*', in M. Stürmer (ed.), *Das kaiserliche Deutschland* (Düsseldorf 1970), p. 289.
16 ibid.
17 J. Röhl, 'Higher Civil Servants in Germany 1890–1900', *Journal of Contemporary History*, vol. 2 (1967), p. 104 (substantially but not wholly the same as the work cited in note 15 above).
18 ibid., p. 105.
19 J. J. Sheehan, 'Conflict and Cohesion Among German Elites in the Nineteenth Century', in R. Bezucha (ed.), *Modern European Social History* (London 1972), p. 11.
20 Röhl, '*Beamtenpolitik*', p. 297.
21 Shennan, op. cit., p. 12.
22 Röhl, '*Beamtenpolitik*', p. 306.
23 ibid., p. 307.

CHAPTER 15 EDUCATION AND ELITES

1 Hajo Holborn, '*Der deutsche Idealismus in seiner sozialgeschichtlichen Beleuchtung*', *Historische Zeitschrift*, vol. 174 (1952), p. 365.
2 Quoted in L. O'Boyle, 'The Excess of Educated Men in Western Europe 1800–1850', *Journal of Modern History*, vol. 42 (1970).
3 L. O'Boyle, '*Klassische Bildung und soziale Struktur in Deutschland zwischen 1800 und 1848*', *Historische Zeitschrift*, vol. 207 (1968), p. 598.
4 ibid., pp. 598 f.
5 Fritz Ringer, 'Higher Education in Germany', *Journal of Contemporary History*, vol. 2 (1967), p. 133.
6 W. Zorn, '*Hochschule und höhere Schule in der deutschen Sozialgeschichte der Neuzeit*', in S. Skalweit and K. Repgen (eds.), *Festschrift für Max Braubach* (Münster, 1964), pp. 321–39.
7 Ringer, op. cit., p. 135.
8 ibid., p. 125.
9 G. Kotowski, *Berlin und die Mark Brandenburg im 19. u. 20. Jahrhundert* (Berlin 1968), p. 551.
10 See P. W. Lougee, *Paul de Lagarde 1827–91: A Study of Radical Conservatism in Germany* (Cambridge, Mass., 1962).
11 W. Abel, '*Der Pauperismus in Deutschland*', in *Festschrift für Fr. Lütge* (Stuttgart 1966), p. 294.
12 W. Fischer, '*Der Volksschullehrer: Zur Sozialgeschichte eines Berufsstandes*',

Soziale Welt, vol. 12 (1961), p. 41.
13 See E. N. Anderson, 'The Prussian *Volksschule* in the Nineteenth Century', in *Entstehung und Wandel der modernen Gesellschaft: Festschrift für H. Rosenberg* (Berlin 1970), pp. 261–79.
14 Fischer, op. cit., p. 44.
15 Th. Fontane and W. Herz, *Briefwechsel* (Berlin 1970), pp. 427–8.
16 Jenny Gustedt-Pappenheim, *Memoiren um die Titanen* (Berlin 1920), vol. 1, p. 86.
17 Kotowski, op. cit., p. 552.
18 H.-U. Wehler, *Das Deutsche Kaiserreich 1871–1918* (Göttingen 1973), esp. section 3.5, '*Die Matrix der autoritären Gesellschaft*', pp. 124–31, though the emotive vocabulary occasionally tends towards oversimplification.
19 Quoted in Fritz Stern, *The Failure of Illiberalism* (London 1972), p. 18.
20 ibid., pp. 3–25.
21 '*Beamtete Stellvertveter des deutschen Geistes*'.
22 Hans Schwerte, '*Deutsche Literatur im wilhelminischen Zeitaller*', *Wirkendes Wort*, vol. 14 (1964), pp. 254–70.
23 R. Engelsing, '*Das häusliche Personal in der Epoche der Industrialisierung*', in *Sozial- und Wirtschaftsgeschichte Deutschlands* (Göttingen 1973), p. 240.
24 '*Die gesellschaftliche Stellung des Schriftstellers*', in H. H. Reuter (ed.), *Sinn und Form*, vol. 13 (1961), pp. 723 f.; see also in *Hermathena* (Trinity College, Dublin, 1976) my article 'Bread, Butter and the Muses: Some Economic and Social Aspects of the German Writer's Life in the Nineteenth Century'.

CHAPTER 16 THE INDUSTRIAL ENTREPRENEURS

1 Fr. Zunkel, *Der Rheinisch-Westfälische Unternehmer 1834–79* (Cologne 1962), p. 20.
2 ibid., p. 26.
3 H. Kaelble, '*Sozialer Aufstieg in Deutschland 1850–1914*', *Vierteljahresschrift fur Sozial- und Wirtschaftsgeschichte*, vol. 60 (1973), p. 52.
4 H. Kaelble, *Berliner Unternehmer während der frühen Industrialisieru ng. Herkunft, sozialer Status und politischer Einfluss* (Berlin 1972), p. 30.
5 ibid., p. 46.
6 ibid., p. 29.
7 R. Stadelmann and W. Fischer, *Die Bildungswelt des deutschen Handwerkers um 1800* (Berlin 1955), pp. 164 ff.
8 R. Braun, '*Zur Entstehung eines ländlichen "Fabrikherren" Standes*', in Braun (ed.), *Industrielle Revolution* (Cologne 1972), p. 100.
9 ibid., p. 101.
10 See Werner Siemens, *Lebenserinnerungen*, 7th edn. (Berlin 1904).
11 Zunkel, op. cit., p. 64.
12 ibid., p. 95.
13 Kaelble, *Berliner Unternehmer*, p. 84.
14 ibid., p. 186.
15 Helene von Racowitza, *An Autobiography* (London 1910), p. 2.
16 R. A. Meyer, *Aus einem alten Berliner Bürgerhaus* (Berlin 1919), pp. 169 f.
17 Zunkel, op. cit., p. 87.
19 W. Kollmann, *Sozialgeschichte der Stadt Barhen im 19. Jahrhundert* (vol. 21 of *Soziale Praxis und Forschung)* (Tübingen 1960), p. 110.
20 Zunkel, op. cit., p. 70.

21 Fr. Engels, '*Briefe aus dem Wuppertal II*', in Karl Marx and Fr. Engels, *Werke*, vol. 1 (Berlin 1964), p. 428.
22 Zunkel, op. cit., pp. 248 f.
23 ibid., pp. 102 f.
24 ibid., p. 117.
25 ibid., p. 113, nn. 59 and 60.
26 Kaelble, *Berliner Unternehmer*, pp. 140 ff.
27 Golo Mann (ed.), *Facsimile Querschnitt durch den Simplicissimus* (Bern 1963), p. 49.
28 Karl Fischer, *Denkwürdigkeiten und Erinnerungen eines Arbeiters* (Leipzig 1903), pp. 291 ff.
29 Braun, op. cit., p. 104.
30 N. von Preradovich, *Deutsche Führungsschichten in Oesterreich und Preussen 1804–1918* (Wiesbaden 1956), p. 249.
31 H. Matis, *Österreichische Wirtschaft 1848–1913* (Berlin 1972).
32 H. Jaeger, *Unternehmer in der dt. Politik 1890–1918* (Bonn 1967), p. 275.
33 ibid., pp. 273 f.; see also Dirk Stegmann, *Die Erben Bismarks, Parteien und Verbände in der Spätphase des wilhelminischen Deutschlands* (Cologne 1970), pp. 32 ff., 146 ff.
34 H.-J. Puhle, '*Parlament, Parteien und Interessenverbände 1890–1914*', in M. Stürmer (ed.), *Das kaiserliche Deutschland* (Düsseldorf 1970), pp. 340–77.
35 Quoted in P. J. Pulzer, *Germany: A Companion to German Studies* (London 1972), p. 280.

CHAPTER 17 THE JEWS

1 R. Rürup, 'Emancipation and Bourgeois Society', *Leo Baeck Yearbook*, vol. 14 (1969), p. 70.
2 S. Dubnow, *Weltgeschichte des jüdischen Volkes* (Berlin 1922), vol. 8, p. 145.
3 There were at that time some 80 000 Jews in France, as against some 500 000 in the Empire.
4 Wanda Kampmann, *Deutsche und Juden* (Heidelberg 1963), p. 190.
5 ibid., p. 164.
6 Rürup, op. cit., p. 75.
7 Alexander Bein, 'Modern Anti-Semitism and its Place in the History of the Jewish Question', in *Between East and West: Essays Dedicated to the Memory of Bela Horovitz* (London 1958), pp. 164–93.
8 Quoted in Peter Pulzer, *The Rise of Political Antisemitism in Germany and Austria* (London 1964), p. 197.
9 C. E. Schorske, 'Politics in a New Key: Georg von Schonerer', in L. Krieger and F. Stern (eds.), *The Responsibility of Power* (London 1968), p. 237.
10 See E. Kohn-Bramsted, *Aristocracy and the Middle Classes in Germany: Social Types in German Literature 1830–1890* (London 1937), pp. 200 ff.
11 See Koppel Pinson, *Essays in Antisemitism* (New York 1942).
12 See James Parker, *Antisemitism* (London 1963).
13 Ernst Newman, *The Life of Richard Wagner* (New York 1942), vol. 4, pp. 638 f.
14 ibid., p. 643.
15 Quoted in V. Poliakov, *Le dévéloppement de l'Antisemitisme en Europe aux temps modernes 1700–1850* (Paris 1968), pp. 541 ff.

16 I. Maybaum, 'Franz Rosenzweig's Life and Work', in *Essays Presented to J. H. Hertz* (London 1942), p. 314.
17 From *Staat und Judentum. Ges. Schriften* (Berlin 1918), vol. 1, pp. 188 f.
18 Gustav Mayer, *Erinnerungen* (Zurich 1949), p. 34.
19 ibid., p. 36.
20 See J. R. P. Theobald, *Jewish Intellectuals and Modern Antisemitism* (Dissertation, Southampton 1975).
21 Samual Hugo Berman, 'Hermann Cohen', in *Between East and West: Essays Dedicated to the Memory of Bela Horovitz* (London 1958), p. 24.
22 See Edmund Silberner, *Juden und Sozialismus* (Tel Aviv 1965).
23 *Tagebücher*, quoted in Theobald, op. cit., p. 102.
24 ibid., p. 115.
25 Salcia Landmann, *Jüdische Witze* (Munich 1963).
26 Hermann Schwab, *Jewish Rural Communities in Germany* (London 1956), p. 16.
27 ibid., p. 56, and Mayer, who corrects him on a number of details.
28 Werner Sombart, *Die Juden und die deutsche Wirtschaft* (Leipzig 1911), pp. 134 f., 281 ff.
29 E. Hamburger, 'Jews in the Public Service Under the German Monarchy', *Leo Baeck Yearbook*, vol. 9 (1964), pp. 206–81; also *Juden im öffentlichen Leben Deutschlands: Regierungsmitglieder, Beamte und Parlamentarier in der monarchischen Zeit 1848–1918* (Tübingen 1968).
30 W. Pöls (ed.), *Deutsche Sozialgeschichte: Dokument und Skizzen* (Munich 1973), vol. 1, p. 89.
31 See H. E. Riessner, *Eduard Gans: ein Leben im Vormärz* (Tübingen 1965).
32 Carl Cohn, 'The Road to Conversion', *Leo Baeck Yearbook*, vol. 6 (1961), pp. 259–79.
33 Letter of 30 August 1812, in Heinz Becker, *Giacomo Mayerbeer: Briefe und Tagebücher*, vol. 1 (Berlin 1960), p. 207.
34 ibid., p. 24.
35 ibid., p. 25.
36 H. Kaelble, *Berliner Unternehmer während der frühen Industrialisierung Herkunft, sozialer Status und politischer Einfluss* (Berlin 1972), pp. 24, 39.
37 F. Stern, 'Gold and Iron: The Collaboration and Friendship of Gerson Bleichröder and Otto von Bismarck', in *The Failure of Illiberalism* (London 1972), pp. 58–73.
38 Marie von Bunsen, *Die Welt von Gestern 1860–1912* (Leipzig, no date); English trans. *The World I Used to Know* (London 1930).
39 Mordecai Yaffe, '*Das Lebensbild eines jüdischen Lehrers in der Provinz Posen*', *Bulletin of the Leo Baeck Institute*, vol. 31 (1965), pp. 207–26.
40 ibid., p. 217.
41 H. Schnee, '*Heines Väterliche Ahnen als Lippische Hoffaktoren*', *Zeitschrift für Religions- und Geistesgeschichte*, vol. 5 (1953), p. 61.
42 Mayer, op. cit., p. 150.
43 Cecil Roth, *The Jewish Contribution to Civilization* (London 1943), pp. 212 ff.

CHAPTER 18 ARTISANS AND SMALL TRADERS

1 R. Stadelmann, '*Soziale Ursachen der Revolution von 1848*', in H.-U. Wehler (ed.), *Der Primat der Innenpolitik: Gesamt Aufsätze zur preussich- deutschen Sozialgeschichte im 19. u. 20. Jahrhundert* (Berlin 1965), pp. 145 f.

2 H. A. Winkler, *Mittelstand, Demokratie und Nationalsozialismus* (Berlin 1972), has many such examples in his text, though he is probably unaware of Tieck's work.
3 L. Tieck, *Romane,* ed. Marianne Thalmann (Munich 1964), p. 244.
4 See *Der Wirt zum grünen Baum,* in the *Maximiliansmuseum,* Augsburg. Many south German municipal museums as the *Maximiliansmuseum* contain portraits of local masters and tradesmen in the early nineteenth century, often with their families, whose dress attests their status in the community.
5 Quoted by Antje Kraus, *Die Unterschichten Hamburgs in der 1. Hälfte des 19. Jahrhunderts* (Stuttgart 1965), p. 4.
6 Winkler, op. cit., p. 22.
7 ibid.
8 J. Gagliardo, *From Pariah to Patriot: The Changing Image of the German Peasant 1770–1840* (Kentucky 1969), pp. 248 f.
9 See many examples in C. Jantke and D. Hilger, *Die Eigentumslosen* (Munich 1965).
10 E. Shorter, 'Middle Class Anxiety in the Germany Revolution of 1848', *Journal of Social History,* vol. 2 (1968–9), p. 207.
11 P. H. Noyes, *Organization and Revolution: Working Class Associations in the German Revolutions of 1848–9* (Princetown 1966), p. 26.
12 ibid., p. 68.
13 ibid., p. 377.
14 See H. Moeller, *Die kleinbürgerliche Familie im 18. Jahrhundert* (Berlin 1969).
15 R. Engelsing, *Sozial- und Wirtschaftsgeschichte Deutschlands* (Göttingen 1973), p. 145.
16 W. Fischer, '*Die rechtliche und wirtschaftliche Lage des dt. Handwerks um 1800*', in *Wirtschaft und Gesellschaft im Zeitalter der Industrialisierung* (Göttingen 1972), p. 303.
17 ibid., p. 303.
18 Mack Walker, *German Home Towns* (Cornell 1971), p. 86.
19 Karl Fischer, *Denkwürdigkeiten und Erinnerungen eines Arbeiters* (Leipzig 1903).
20 W. Fischer, op. cit., p. 306.
21 ibid.
22 W. Fischer, '*Das dte. Handwerk in der Frühphase der Industrialisierung*', in *Wirtschaft und Gesellschaft* (see note 16 above), p. 326.
23 Jantke and Hilger, op. cit., p. 294.
24 W. Treue in Gebhardt, *Handbuch der deutschen Geschichte,* 9th edn., vol. 3 (Stuttgart 1971), pp. 503 f.
25 Paul Ernst, *Meine Lebenserinnerungen* (Leipzig 1930), p. 70.
26 R. Engelsing, op. cit., p. 149.
27 Fischer, *Handwerk,* op. cit., p. 335.
28 August Bebel, *Aus meinem Leben* (Berlin 1964), pp. 38 ff.
29 R. Engelsing, '*Das häusliche Personal in der Epoche der Industrialisierung*', in *Sozial und Wirtschaftsgeschichte Deutschlands* (Göttingen 1973), p. 258.
30 W. Wernet, *Handwerksindustrie und Industriegeschichte* (Stuttgart 1963), pp. 5, 14 ff.
31 Winkler, op. cit., p. 37.
32 ibid.
33 Wanda Kampmann, *Deutsche und Juden* (Heidelberg 1963), p. 251.

CHAPTER 19 THE PEASANTRY AND RURAL LABOURERS

1 See J. G. Gagliardo, *From Pariah to Patriot: The Changing Image of the German Peasant* (Kentucky 1969).
2 ibid., p. 82.
3 W. Abel, *Die drei Epochen der deutschen Agrargeschichte,* 2nd edn. (Hanover 1964), p. 62.
4 Mack Walker, *German Home Towns* (Cornell 1971), p. 187.
5 W. Henderson, *The State and the Industrial Revolution in Prussia 1740–1870* (Liverpool 1958), p. 38, n. 1.
6 See Pankraz Fried, '*Die Sozialentwicklung im Bauerntum und Landvolk*', in *Handbuch der bayerischen Geschichte,* vol. 4, pt 2 (Munich 1975).
7 P. Steinmann, *Bauer und Ritter in Mecklenburg* (Schwerin 1960), p. 234.
8 Fr. Lütge, *Geschichte der deutschen Agrarverfassung,* 2nd edn. (Stuttgart 1967), p. 289.
9 W. Conze, 'The Effects of Nineteenth Century Liberal Agrarian Reforms on Social Structure in Central Europe', in Crouzet, Chaloner and Stern (eds.), *Essays in Economic History* (London 1969), p. 59.
10 Th. Hamerow, *The Social Foundations of German Unification,* vol. 1 (Princeton 1969), p. 38.
11 Ritter and Kocka, op. cit., p. 178.
12 Lütge, op. cit., p. 280, R. Engelsing, *Zur Sozial -und Wirtschaftsgeschichte Deutschlands* (Göttingen 1973), p. 111.
13 H.-U. Wehler, *Das Deutsche Kaiserreich 1871–1918* (Göttingen 1973), p. 21.
14 Gagliardo, op. cit., p. 248.
15 G. Ipsen, '*Die preussischen Bauernbefreiung als Landesausbau*', in M. Kollmann and P. Marschalck (eds.), *Bevölkerungsgeschichte* (Cologne 1972), p. 158.
16 Abel, op. cit., p. 100.
17 Lütge, op. cit., p. 286.
18 Schnabel, op. cit., 2nd ed., vol. 2, p. 293.
19 H. Linde, '*Masurische Agrargesellschaft*', in H.-U. Wehler (ed.), *Der Primat der Innenpolitik: Gesamt Aufsätze zur preussisch-deutschen Sozialgeschichte im 19. und 20. Jahrhundert* (Berlin 1965), p. 463.
20 Quoted in H. W. Finckenstein, *Die Entwicklung der Landwirtschaft in Preussen und Deutschland 1800–1930* (Würzburg 1960), p. 9. See also Salomon Philipp Gans, *Von der Verarmung des Landmanns* (Brunswick 1831), in C. Jantke and D. Hilger, *Die Eigentumslosen* (Munich 1965), pp. 83–92.
21 K. Riha, *Die Beschreibung der 'Grossen Stadt'* (Bad Homburg 1970).
22 P. Zimmermann, *Der Bauernroman, Antifeudalismus, Konservatismus, Faschismus* (Stuttgart 1975).
23 W. Treue, in Gebhardt, *Handbuch der deutschen Geschichte,* 9th edn., vol. 3 (Stuttgart 1971), p. 400.
24 Karl Renner, *An der Wende zweier Zeiten, Lebenserinnerungen,* 2nd edn. (Vienna 1946), p. 65; see also pp. 16, 25, 56, 64, ff.
25 Ritter and Kocka, op. cit., p. 177.
26 ibid., p. 188.
27 ibid., p. 175.
28 D. Petzina, '*Materialien zum sozialen und wirtschaftlichen Wandel in Deutschland seit dem Ende des. 19. Jahrhunderts*', *Vierteljahreshefte fur Zeitgeschichte,* vol. 17 (1969), p. 323.

29 Treue, op. cit., p. 405, and Petzina, op. cit.
30 L. Gall, *Liberalismus, Historische Zeitschrift,* vol. 220 (1975), p. 355, n. 46.
31 Franz Rehbein, *Das Leben eines Landarbeiters* (*Arbeiterbiographien,* 4), ed. Paul Göhre (Jena 1911).
32 F. Fischer, *War Without Illusions* (London 1975), p. 281.

CHAPTER 20 THE INDUSTRIAL LABOUR FORCE

1 Herbert Matis, '*Über die sozialen und wirtschaftlichen Verhältnisse oesterreichischer Fabrik- und Manufakturarbeiter um die Wende vom 18. zum 19. Jahrhundert*', *Vierteljahresschrift fur Sozial- und Wirtschaftsgeschichte,* vol. 53 (1966), pp. 472–3.
2 ibid., p. 445.
3 G. V. Rimlinger, '*Die Legitimierung des Protestes: Eine vergleichende Untersuchung der Bergarbeiterbewegung in England und Deutschland*', in W. Fischer and G. Bajor (eds.), *Die Soziale Frage* (Stuttgart 1967), p. 295.
4 ibid., p. 296.
5 W. Fischer, '*Soziale Unterschichten im Zeitalter der Frühindustrialisierung*', in *Wirtschaft und Gesellschaft im Zeitalter der Industrialisierung,* vol. 1 of *Kritische Studien zur Geschichtswissenschaft* (Göttingen 1972), p. 251.
6 W. Fischer, '*Innerbetrieblicher und sozialer Status der frühen Fabrikarbeiterschaft*', in *Wirtschaft und Gesellschaft,* p. 267.
7 ibid., p. 260.
8 Fischer, '*Soziale Unterschichten*', p. 253.
8a H. Linde, '*Masuriche Agrargesellschaft*', in H.-U. Wehler (ed.), *Der Primat der Innenpolitik: Gesamt Aufsätze zur preussisch-deutschen Sozialgeschichte im 19. und 20. Jahrhundert* (Berlin 1965), p. 463.
9 Wolfgang Köllmann, *Sozialgeschichte der Stadt Barmen im 19. Jahrhundert,* vol. 21 of *Soziale Praxis und Forschung* (Tübingen 1960), p. 93.
10 Fischer, '*Innerbetrieblicher Status*', p. 270.
11 ibid., pp. 282–3.
12 W. Köllmann, '*Die Anfänge der staatlichen Sozialpolitik im Preussen bis 1869*', *Vierteljahresschrift fur Sozial- und Wirtschaftsgeschichte,* vol. 53 (1966), p. 40.
13 Matis, op. cit., p. 459.
14 ibid., p. 459.
15 Köllmann, *Sozialgeschichte der Stadt Barmen,* p. 135.
16 ibid., p. 133.
17 G. Otruba, '*Wirtschaftliche und soziale Lage Oesterreichs im Vormärz*', *Oesterreich in Geschichte und Literatur,* vol. 10 (1966), p. 174.
18 Matis, op. cit., p. 443.
19 Theodor Hamerow, *The Social Foundations of German Unification 1858–71: Ideas and Institutions,* vol. 1 (Princeton 1969), p. 73.
20 R. Engelsing, '*Zur politischen Bildung der deutschen Unterschichten 1789 bis 1863*', in *Zur Sozialgeschichte der deutschen Mittel- und Unterschichten,* vol. 4 of *Kritische Studien zur Geschichteswissenschaft* (Göttingen 1973), p. 169.
21 Hartmut Kaelble, *Berliner Unternehmer während der frühen Industrialisierung,* vol. 40 of *Veröffentlichungen der Historischen Kommission* (Berlin 1972), p. 143.
22 Wolfgang Schieder, '*Wilhelm Weitling und die deutsche politische Handwerkerlyrik im Vormärz*', *International Review of Social History,* vol. 5 (1960), pp. 265 ff.

23 Werner Conze and Dieter Groh, *Die Arbeiterbewegung in der nationalen Bewegung: Die Sozialdemokratie vor, während und nach der Reichsgründung*, vol. 6 of *Industrielle Welt* (Stuttgart 1966), p. 43.
24 ibid., p. 36.
25 ibid., p. 69.
26 ibid., p. 70.
27 On the impact of the Commune on German society, see James J. Sheehan, *The Career of Lujo Brentano: A Study of Liberalism and Social Reform in Imperial Germany* (London 1966), pp. 46 ff.
28 R. Vierhaus (ed.), *Das Tagebuch der Baronin Spitzemberg*, vol. 43 of *Deutsche Geschichtsquellen des 19. und 20. Jahrhunderts* (Göttingen 1964), entry for 1 May 1890, p. 281.
29 Lili Braun, *Memoiren einer Sozialistin* (Munich 1910), p. 601.
30 G. A. Ritter, *Die Arbeiterbewegung im wilhelminischen Reich* (Berlin 1959), pp. 281 ff.
31 C. Landauer, *European Socialism* (California 1959), p. 314.
32 W. Köllmann, '*Politische und soziale Entwicklung der deutschen Arbeiterschaft 1850–1914*', *Vierteljahresschrift fur Sozial- und Wirtschaftsgeschichte*, vol. 50 (1963), pp. 482 ff.
33 Karl Fischer, *Denkwürdigkeiten und Erinnerungen eines Arbeiters*, vol. 2 of *Leben und Wissen*, ed. Paul Göhre (Leipzig 1903).
34 Köllmann, *Politische und soziale Entwicklung*, p. 486.
35 V. D. Lidtke, *The Outlawed Party: Social Democracy in Germany 1870–90* (Princeton 1966), p. 301.
36 P. von Oertzen, *Betriebsräte in der Novemberrevolution* (Düsseldorf 1963), p. 45.
37 Lidtke, op. cit., p. 301.
38 Oertzen, op. cit., p. 38.
39 Peter Pulzer, 'German History from Bismarck to the Present', in M. Pasley (ed.), *Germany: A Companion to German Studies* (London 1972), p. 291.
40 Susanne Miller, '*Rezensionen: Arbeiten zur Geschichte der Arbeiterbewegung*', *Archiv für Sozialforschung*, vol. 10 (1970), pp. 397 ff., esp. p. 399.
41 Oertzen, op. cit., p. 40.
42 ibid., p. 42, n. 3.
43 Edward Shorter, 'Sexual Change and Illegitimacy: The European Experience', in R. Bezucha (ed.), *Modern European Social History* (London 1974), p. 253.
44 R. P. Neumann, 'Industrialization and Sexual Behaviour: Some Aspects of Working Class Life in Imperial Germany', in Bezucha, op. cit., p. 283.
45 J. M. Phayer, 'Lower Class Morality: The Case of Bavaria', *Journal of Social History* (1974), pp. 79–95.
46 Neumann, op. cit., p. 290.

CHAPTER 21 DOMESTIC SERVANTS

1 See illustrations from Hohberg's *Georgica curiosa* in W. Flemming, *Deutsche Kultur im Zeitalter des Barock*, 2nd edn. (Constance 1960), pp. 41 f., 221.
2 R. Engelsing, '*Das häusliche Personal in der Epoche der Industrialisierung*', in *Sozial- und Wirtschaftsgeschichte Deutschlands* (Göttingen 1973), p. 228.
3 Quoted in W. Pöls (ed.), *Deutsche Sozialgeschichte: Dokument und Skizzen* (Munich 1973), vol. 1, p. 340.

4 See also Engelsing's '*Dienstobotenlektüre im 18. u. 19. Jahrhundert*', in *Zur Sozialgeschichte der deutschen Mittel- und Unterschichten*, vol. 4 of *Kritsche Studien zur Geschichtswissenschaft* (Göttingen 1973), pp. 180–224.
5 ibid., p. 212.
6 Otto Brunner, *Neu Wege der Sozial- und Verfassungsgeschichte*, 2nd edn. (Göttingen 1968).
7 W. von Groote, *Die Entstehung des Nationalismus in Nordwestdeutschland 1790–1830* (Göttingen 1955), pp. 105 f.
8 Engelsing, '*Dienstbotenlektüre*', pp. 191 ff.
9 Engelsing, '*Das häusliche Personal*', p. 250.
10 C. Jantke and D. Hilger, *Die Eigentumslosen* (Munich 1965), p. 59.
11 Engelsing, '*Das häusliche Personal*', p. 254.
12 Engelsing, '*Dienstbotenlektüre*', p. 234.
13 ibid., pp. 235 f.
14 ibid., p. 240.
15 Th. Fontane, *Gesammelte Briefe* (Berlin 1920), vol. 4, p. 171.
16 Quoted in Põls, op. cit., p. 333.
17 Engelsing, '*Das häusliche Personal*', p. 233.
18 Th. Fontane, *Der Stechlin* (Munich 1969), p. 152.
19 I. Weber-Kellermann, *Die deutsche Familie* (Frankfurt 1974), p. 124.

CHAPTER 22 THE POOR

1 Antje Kraus, *Die Untersohichten Hamburgs in der ersten Hälfte des 19. Jahrhunderts, Entstehung, Struktur und Lebensverhältnisse* (Stuttgart 1965).
2 ibid., p. 48.
3 See table on p. 58.
4 Rolf Engelsing, '*Hanseatische Lebenshaltungen und Lebenshaltungskosten im 18. und 19. Jahrhundert*', in *Zur Sozialgeschichte der deutschen Mittel- und Unterschichten*, vol. 4 of *Kritische Studien zur Geschichtswissenschaft* (Göttingen 1973), p. 27.
5 Wilhelm Abel, '*Pauperismus in Deutschland*', in *Festschrift für Friederich Lütge* (Stuttgart 1966), p. 290.
6 K. F. von Klöden, *Jugenderinnerungen*, ed. M. Jahns (Leipzig 1874).
7 Wilhelm Abel, *Massenarmut und Hungerkrisen im vorindustriellen Deutschland* (Göttingen 1972), p. 12.
8 ibid., p. 8.
9 Kraus, op. cit., p. 69.
10 Herbert Matis, '*Über die sozialen und wirtschaftlichen Verhältnisse oesterreichischer Fabrik- und Manufakturarbeiter um die Wende vom 18. zum 19. Jahrhundert*', *Vierteljahresschrift für Sozial -und Wirtschaftsgeschichte*, vol. 53 (1966), p. 459.
11 Wolfgang Köllmann, *Sozialgeschichte der Stadt Barmen im 19. Jahrhundert*, vol. 21 of *Soziale Forschung und Praxis* (Tübingen 1960), p. 143.
12 ibid.
13 Lewis Mumford, *The City in History: Its Origins, Its Transformations and Its Prospects* (London 1966), pp. 292, 458 ff.
14 Kraus, op. cit., p. 72.
15 C. Jantke and D. Hilger, *Die Eigentumslosen* (Munich 1965), p. 7.
16 Kraus, op. cit., p. 72.
17 Jantke and Hilger, op. cit., pp. 16 ff.

18 Abel, *Massenarmut,* pp. 60–1.
19 ibid., p. 19.
20 ibid., p. 20.
21 Werner Conze, '*Vom "Pöbel" zum "Proletariat": Sozialgeschichtliche Voraussetzungen für den Sozialismus in Deutschland*', in Fischer and Bajor (eds.), *Die Soziale Frage* (Stuttgart 1967), p. 31.
22 Kraus, op. cit., p. 76.
23 Abel, *Massenarmut,* op. cit., p. 55. See also Richard Tilly, 'Popular Disorders in Nineteenth Century Germany', *Journal of Social History,* vol. 4 (1970–1), pp. 1–41.
24 Conze, op. cit., p. 24.
25 See Mack Walker, *German Home Towns* (Cornell 1971), and Edward Shorter, 'Middle Class Anxiety in the German Revolution of 1848', *Journal of Social History,* vol. 2 (1968–9).
26 Conze, op. cit., p. 24.
27 ibid., p. 27.
28 Heinrich Heine, *Werke* (Frankfurt 1968), p. 278.
29 Conze, op. cit., p. 22.
30 Jantke and Hilger, op. cit., p. 49.
31 Shorter, op. cit. p. 208.
32 ibid., p. 206.
33 ibid., p. 196.
34 ibid.
35 Conze, op. cit., pp. 28–9.
36 R. Engelsing, '*Zur politischen Bildung der deutschen Unterschichten 1789 bis 1863*', in *Zur Sozialgeschichte*, pp. 163–4.

CHAPTER 23 WOMEN IN GERMAN SOCIETY

1 Hans Thieme, *Die Rechtsstellung der Frau in Deutschland, Receuils de la société Jean Bodin pour l'histoire comparatives des Institutions* (Brussels 1962), p. 365.
2 K. F. Uden, *Uber die Erziehung der Töchter des Mittelstandes* (Stendal 1783), quoted in W. Rössler, *Die Entstehung des modernen Erziehungswesens in Deutschland* (Stuttgart 1961), p. 85.
3 Thieme, op. cit., p. 275.
4 J. Neveux, *Vie spirituelle et vie sociale entre Rhin et Baltique au XVIIe siècle* (Paris 1967), p. 735.
5 R. Engelsing, '*Die Bildung der Frau*', in *Der Bürger als Leser* (Göttingen 1973), pp. 302 f.
6 K. F. von Klöden, *Jugenderinnerungen,* ed. M. Jahns (Leipzig 1874), p. 14.
7 *Christliche Sitten-Lehr über die evangelischen Wahrheiten*, quoted in Rössler, op. cit., p. 372.
8 *Memoirs of Frederick Perthes: Or Literary, Religious and Political Life in Germany from 1789 to 1843*, ed. C. T. Perthes (Edinburgh 1856), vol. 2, p. 5.
9 G. Freytag, *Bilder aus deutscher Vergangenheit*, vol. 4, ed. K. Breul (Cambridge 1924), pp. 71 ff.
10 Perthes, op. cit., vol. 1, p. 95.
11 Quoted in W. Flemming, *Deutsche Kultur im Zeitalter des Barock,* 2nd edn. (Constance 1960), p. 222.
12 R. Köpke, *Ludwig Tieck, Erinnerungen aus dem Leben des Dichters* (Leipzig 1855), p. 19.

13 *Meine Kinderjahre* (Weimar, no date), p. 28.
14 *Meister Johann Dietz, Des Grossen Kürfürsten Feldscher: Mein Lebenslauf*, ed. Fr. Kemp (Munich 1966; English edn. London 1960), pp. 191 ff.
15 Johann Miller, *Die Geschichte Gottfried Walthers, eines Tischlers, und des Städtchens Erlerburg* (Ulm 1786), p. 186.
16 Engelsing, op. cit., p. 302.
17 Rössler, op. cit., p. 372, n. 1.
18 A. Ward, *Book Production, Fiction and the German Reading Public 1740–1800* (Oxford 1974), p. 55.
19 ibid., pp. 135 ff., 144 ff.
20 Sophie Merau, *Kalathiskos,* reprint of 1801–2 edn. (Heidelberg 1968), p. 11.
21 Goethe, *Wilhelm Meisters Lehrjahre,* VII.6, *Weimarer Ausgabe*, vol. xxlii, p. 54.
22 L. Börne, *Kritische Schriften* (Zurich 1964), pp. 324 f.
23 *Facsimile Querschnitt durch die Berliner Illustrierte Zeitung* (Munich 1965), p. 48.
24 J. von Eichendorff, *Werke* (Leipzig 1931), vol. 1, p. 1129.
25 Quoted in E. Heilborn, *Zwischen zwei Revolutionen, Der Geist der Schinkelzeit* (Berlin 1927), p. 142.
26 A. von Chamisso, *Werke* (Berlin 1967), p. 60.
27 Fanny Lewald, *Deutsche Lebensbilder* (Brunswick 1856), pp. 105 f.
28 Quoted in K. Buchheim, *Deutsche Kultur zwischen 1830 u. 1870* (Frankfurt 1966), p. 98.
29 Engelsing, op. cit., p. 304.
30 A. von Roon, *Denkwürdigkeiten,* op. cit., vol. 1, p. 74.
31 Quoted in R. M. Bigler, *The Politics of German Protestantism: The Rise of the Protestant Church Elite in Prussia 1815–48* (California 1972), p. 218.
32 Goethe, *Herrmann und Dorothea,* VII *Gesang.*
33 Klöden, op. cit., p. 14.
34 Dorothea von Schlözer, *Ein deutsches Frauenleben um die Jahrhundertwende 1770–1825,* ed. Leopold von Schlözer (Stuttgart 1923), esp. pp. 121 ff., 132 ff.
35 Quoted in Engelsing, op. cit., p. 297.
36 Malwida von Meysenbug, *Memoiren einer Idealistin* (Stuttgart 1922), vol. 1, p. 172.
37 Julie Braun-Vogelstein, *Was niemals stirbt, Gestaltungen und Erinnerungen* (Stuttgart 1966), pp. 30 f. By contrast Helene Lange would never let it be forgotten that she knew Greek.
38 Margarethe von Wrangell, *Das Leben einer Frau 1876–1932* (Munich 1936), pp. 132 f., 141 f.
39 R. J. Evans, *The Women's Movement in Germany 1890–1919* (Oxford D.Phil. 1972, to be published 1976).
40 Amy Hackett, 'The German Women's Movement and Suffrage 1890–1914', in R. Bezucha (ed.), *Modern European Social History* (London 1974), pp. 354 ff.
41 R. Braun-Artaria, *Von berühmten Zeitgenossen* (Munich 1918), p. 88.
42 Braun-Vogelstein, op. cit., pp. 75 f.
43 Evans, op. cit., pp. 1 f.
44 ibid., p. 34.

45 E. Shorter, 'Sexual Change and Illegitimacy: The European Experience', in R. Bezucha (ed.), *Modern European Social History* (London 1974).
46 Evans, op. cit.
47 ibid.

Note on currency values (1977)

1 taler = c. 15p
1 gulden = c. 7½p (Austria)
1 florin = c. 7½p (actually French name for gulden)
1 groschen = c. ½p

The (Prussian) taler was widely used in North German states from the time of the Customs Union (1834) onwards. In 1857 the 'unified taler' was accepted by the states of the Customs Union and Austria at the rate of 1 taler = 2 gulden (Austrian) = 1¾ gulden (South German states).

Suggestions for further reading

The following, necessarily brief, selection includes reference books, bibliographical aids, general studies, collections of essays and monographs which a student of German social history in the period or a librarian wishing to build up this section of his holdings will find useful. It does not include articles in periodicals, but reference to these will be found in the works cited below (cf. list of such periodicals on pp. 11–14 of Wehler, *Bibliographie*). The imbalance in favour of works dealing with the period 1840 onwards reflects the bias of research to date. It is a most interesting development in current German studies that this is beginning to be rectified, a process already recorded in two important new periodicals: *Geschichte und Gesellschaft* (1975 ff.) and *Internationales Archiv für Sozialgeschichte der dt. Literatur* (1976 f.), the one mainly, though not exclusively, of interest to the historian and sociologist, the other similarly for the Germanist and sociologist.

H.-U. WEHLER, *Bibliographie zur modernen deutschen Sozialgeschichte (18.–20, Jahrhundert)*, Göttingen 1976.

W. ABEL, *Agrarkrisen und Agrarkonkunktur*, Hamburg-Berlin 1966.

W. ABEL, *Massenarmut und Hungerkrisen im vorindustriellen Deutschland*, Göttingen 1972.

W. ABENDROTH, *Sozialgeschichte der europäischen Arbeiterbewegung,* Frankfurt 1965.

E. N. and P. R. ANDERSON, *Political institutions and social change on continental Europe in the 19th century,* Berkeley 1967.

K. O. VON ARETIN, *Das Heilige Römische Reich 1776–1806,* Wiesbaden 1967.

H. AUBIN *Festschrift,* ed. O. Brunner, H. Kellenbenz, E. Maschke, W. Zorn, 2 vols., Wiesbaden 1965.

H. AUBIN and W. ZORN ed., *Handbuch der deutschen Wirtschafts- und Sozialgeschichte,* 2 vols., Stuttgart 1971/76.

K. S. BADER, *Der deutsche Südwesten,* Stuttgart 1950.

FROLINDE BALSER, *Sozialdemokratie 1848/9–1863,* Stuttgart 1963.

G. BENECKE, *Politics and society in early modern Germany,* London 1974.

L. BEUTIN, *Gesammelte Schriften,* ed. H. Kellenbenz, Cologne etc. 1963.

ROBERT J. BEZUCHA, *Modern European social history* (esp. contributions by J. J. Sheehan, E. Shorter, R. Neumann and Amy Hackett), London 1974.

K. BIEDERMANN, *Deutschland im 18. Jahrhundert,* 2 vols. in 4, Leipzig 1854–80 (Aalen reprint 1969).

H. BÖHME ed. *Probleme der Reichsgründung 1848–1879,* 2. ed., Cologne 1973.

H. BÖHME, *Prologomena zu einer Sozial und Wirtschaftsgeschichte Deutschlands im 19. u. 20. Jahrhundert,* 2 ed., Frankfurt 1976.

K. BORCHARDT, *The industrial revolution in Germany,* London 1972.

E. K. BRAMSTEDT, *Aristocracy and the middle classes in Germany,* 2 ed., Chicago 1964.

P. BRAUDEL and F. SPOONER, *Prices in Europe 1450–1750,* vol. 4 of Cambridge Economic History 1967 (esp. pp. 374 ff.).

R. BRAUN, ed., *Industrielle Revolution,* Cologne 1972.

W. H. BRUFORD, *Germany in the 18th century,* Cambridge 1965.

O. BRUNNER, *Adeliges Landleben und europäischer Geist,* Salzburg 1949.

O. BRUNNER, *Land und Herrschaft,* 5 ed., Vienna 1965.

O. BRUNNER, *Neue Wege der Sozialgeschichte,* 2 ed., Göttingen 1968.

G. BRY, *Wages in Germany 1871–1945,* Princeton 1965.

O. BÜSCH, *Militärsystem und Sozialleben im alten Preussen 1713–1807,* Berlin 1962.

F. L. CARSTEN, Germany from Scharnhorst to Schleicher: the Prussian Officer Corps etc., in: *Soldiers and Governments. Nine Studies in Civil-Military Relations,* ed. M. Howard, London 1957.

F. L. CARSTEN, *Princes and Parliaments,* London 1959.

W. CONZE, *Staat und Gesellschaft im deutschen Vormärz 1815–1848,* 2 ed., Stuttgart 1970.

W. CONZE and D. GROH, *Die Arbeiterbewegung in der Nationalbewegung,* Stuttgart 1966.

DAHLMANN-WAITZ, *Quellenkunde der deutschen Geschichte. Bibliographie zur deutschen Geschichte,* 10 ed., ed. H. Heimpel and H. Geuss, Stuttgart 1969 ff.

Geschichtliche Grundbegriffe. Historisches Lexikon zur politischsozialen Sprache in Deutschland, ed. O. Brunner, W. Conze, R. Koselleck, 2 vols. (A-D, E-G), Stuttgart 1972/75.

R. DAHRENDORF, *Gesellschaft und Demokratie in Deutschland,* Munich 1965.

K. DEMETER, *The German Officer Corps,* London 1965.

K. DEPPERMANN, *Der hallische Pietismus u. der preussische Staat,* Göttingen 1961.

A. V. DESAI, *Real wages in Germany 1871–1913*, Oxford 1968.
A. DRU, *The Church in the 19th century: Germany 1800–1918*, London 1963.
D. EICHHOLTZ, *Beiträge zur dt. Wirtschafts- und Sozialgeschichte des 19. u. 20. Jahrhunderts*, Berlin (East) 1962.
L. C. EISENBART, *Kleiderordnungen deutscher Städte zwischen 1300 und 1700*, Göttingen 1962.
M. J. ELSASS, *Umriss einer Geschichte der Preise und Löhne in Deutschland*, Leiden 1936–49.
W. EMMERICH ed., *Proletarische Lebensläufe. Autobiographische Dokumente, Anfang bis 1914*, Hamburg 1974.
R. ENGELSING, *Der Bürger als Leser*, Stuttgart 1974.
R. ENGELSING, *Sozial- und Wirtschaftsgeschichte Deutschlands*, 2 ed., Göttingen 1976.
R. ENGELSING, *Zur Sozialgeschichte deutscher Mittel- und Unterschichten*, Göttingen 1972.
W. FISCHER, *Wirtschaft und Gesellschaft im Zeitalter der Industrialisierung*, Göttingen 1972.
W. FISCHER ed., *Wirtschafts- und sozialgeschichtliche Probleme der frühen Industrialisierung*, Berlin 1968.
W. FLEMMING, *Deutsche Kultur im Zeitalter des Barock*, Frankfurt 1937.
G. FRANZ, *Der dreissigjährige Krieg und das deutsche Volk*, Stuttgart 1961.
E. VON FRAUENHOLZ, *Entwicklungsgeschichte des dt. Heerwesens*, 5 vols., Munich 1935–41.
K. FUGGER, *Geschichte der dt. Gewerkschaftsbewegung*, Berlin (East) 1949 (reprint 1971).
J. G. GAGLIARDO, *From Pariah to Patriot. The Changing Image of the German Peasant*, Kentucky 1969.
A. GERSCHENKRON, *Bread and democracy in Germany*, 2 ed., New York 1966.
H. G. GEERTH, *Bürgerliche Intelligenz um 1800. Zur Soziologie d. frühen Liberalismus*, Göttingen 1976 (useful bibliography, particularly for the Germanist).
J. R. GILLIS, *The Prussian Bureaucracy in Crisis 1840–1860*, Stanford 1971.
H. GOLLWITZER, *Die Standesherrn*, 2 ed., Göttingen 1964.
D. GROH, *Negative Integration und revolutionärer Attentismus 1909–1914*, Berlin 1973.
E. HAMBURGER, *Juden im öffentlichen Leben Deutschlands 1848–1918*, Tübingen 1968.
Handbuch zur deutschen Militärgeschichte 1648–1939 (Publication of the Militärgeschichtliches Forschungsamt), Frankfurt 1964.
H. J. HAFERKORN, *Zur Entstehung der bürgerlich-literarischen Intelligenz und des Schriftstellers in Deutschland zwischen 1750- und 1800*, in: Literaturwissenschaft und Sozialwissensch, ed. B. Lutz, Stuttgart 1974.
TH. HAMEROW, *Restoration, Revolution, Reaction. Economics and Politics in Germany 1815–1871*, 2 ed., Princeton 1972.
TH. HAMEROW, *The social foundations of German unification*, 2 vols., Princeton 1969-1973.
W. HENDERSON, *The industrial revolution in Germany*, London 1974.
H.-J. HENNIG, *Das westdeutsche Bürgertum in der Epoche der Hochindustrialisierung 1860–1914*, Wiesbaden 1972.
FR.-WM HENNING, *Die Industrialisierung Deutschlands*, Paderborn 1973.

C. Hermann, *Deutsche Militärgeschichte,* Frankfurt 1966.

H. Herzfeld and G. Heinrich eds., *Berlin und die Provinz Brandenburg im 19 u. 20. Jahrhundert,* Berlin 1968.

C. Hinrichs, *Preussentum und Pietismus,* Göttingen 1971.

W. G. Hoffmann et. al., *Das deutsche Volkseinkommen 1851–1957,* Tübingen 1959.

H. H. Hofmann, *Adelige Herrschaft und souveräner Staat,* Munich 1962.

R. Höhn, *Sozialismus und Heer,* Bad Homburg 1959.

C. Jantke and D. Hilger, *Die Eigentumslosen,* Freiburg 1965.

H. Kaelble, *Berliner Unternehmer während der frühen Industrialisierung,* Berlin 1972.

E. Kehr, *Der Primat der Innenpolitik. Ges. Aufsätze zur preussisch-deutschen Sozialgeschichte,* ed. H.-U. Wehler, 3 ed., Berlin 1976.

M. Kitchen, *A military history of Germany from the 18th century to the present day,* London 1975.

E. Klein, *Geschichte der deutschen Landwirtschaft im Industriezeitalter,* Wiesbaden 1973.

D. Koch, *Das Göttinger Honoratiorentum vom 17. bis zur Mitte d. 19. Jahrhunderts,* Göttingen 1958.

J. Kocka, *Klassengesellschaft im Krieg. Dte. Sozialgeschichte 1914–1918,* Göttingen 1973.

W. Köllmann, *Bevölkerung in der industriellen Revolution,* Göttingen 1974.

W. Köllmann, *Sozialgeschichte der Stadt Barmen im 19 Jahrhundert,* Tübingen 1960.

W. Köllmann, and P. Marschalck, *Bevölkerungsgeschichte,* Cologne 1972.

R. Koselleck, *Preussen zwischen Reform und Revolution,* 2 ed, Stuttgart 1975.

R. Koselleck, *Der Beginn der Neuzeit,* Stuttgart 1976.

Antje Kraus, *Die Unterschichten Hamburgs in d. 1. Hälfte d. 19 Jahrhunderts,* Stuttgart 1965.

J. Kuczynski, *Die Geschichte der Lage der Arbeiter in Deutschland von 1789 bis zur Gegenwart,* 4 vols., Berlin (East) 1962/67.

J. Lampe, *Aristokratie, Hofadel und Staatspatriziat in Kurhannover,* 2 vols., Göttingen 1963.

D. S. Landes, *The Unbound Prometheus,* London 1969.

F. Lütge, *Deutsche Sozial- und Wirtschaftsgeschichte,* Berlin 1960.

F. Lütge, *Geschichte der deutschen Agrarverfassung,* 2 ed., Stuttgart 1967.

F. Martiny, *Die Adelsfrage vor 1806,* Stuttgart 1938.

H. Mauersberg, *Wirtschafts- und Sozialgeschichte zentraleurop. Städte in neuerer Zeit,* Göttingen 1960.

H. Mitgau, *Gemeinsames Leben. Der Familienpapiere älterer Teil 1555–1770,* Brunswick 1955.

H. Moeller, *Die kleinbürgerliche Familie im 18. Jahrhundert,* Berlin 1969 (has an excellent bibliography of literary and memoir sources in addition to sociological and historical works).

T. Nipperdey, *Gesellschaft, Kultur, Theorie,* Göttingen 1976.

J. Neveux, *Vie spirituelle et vie sociale entre Rhin et Baltique au 17e siècle,* Paris 1967.

P. H. Noyes, *Organization und Revolution: Working-class Associations in the German Revolutions of 1848–1849,* Princeton 1966.

A. Oberschall, *Empirical social research in Germany 1848–1918,* Hague 1965.

G. OESTREICH, Soldatenbild, Heeresreform und Heeresgestaltung im Zeitalter des Absolutismus in: *Schicksalsfragen d. Gegenwart,* Tübingen 1958.

T. PARSONS, *Democracy and social structure in pre-Nazi Germany,* Princeton 1942.

F. PAULSEN *Geschichte des gelehrten Unterrichts in Deutschland,* 3 ed., Berlin etc. 1919.

M. PIENDL, *Thurn und Taxis 1517–1867. Zur Geschichte d. fürstlichen Hauses in der Thurn und Taxis Post,* Regensburg 1967.

L. POLIAKOV, *Le dévélopement de l'antisemitisme en Europe au temps moderne 1700–1850,* Paris 1967 (includes 2. Empire).

W. PÖLS, *Deutsche Sozialgeschichte 1815–1870* (vol. 1), Munich 1973.

N. v. PRERADOVICH, *Die Führungsschichten Oesterreichs und Preussens 1804–1918,* Wiesbaden 1955.

H.-J. PUHLE, *Agrarische Interessenpolitik und preussischer Konservatismus (1893–1914),* Hanover 1966.

R. M. and G. RADBRUCH, *Der deutsche Bauernstand zwischen Mittelatler und Neuzeit,* Göttingen 1961.

Religion in Geschichte und Gegenwart, 3 ed., Tübingen 1957–62.

MONIKA RICHARZ ed., *Jüdisches Leben in Deutschland- Selbstzeugnisse zur Sozialgeschichte 1780–1871,* Stuttgart 1976.

S. RIEZLER, *Die Geschichte der Hexenprozesse in Bayern,* Munich 1896.

F. RINGER, *The decline of the German mandarins,* Camb./Mass. 1969.

G. A. RITTER, *Das deutsche Kaiserreich 1871–1914. Ein historisches Lesebuch,* Göttingen 1975.

G. A. RITTER, *Die Arbeiterbewegung im Wilhelminischen Reich,* 2 ed., Berlin 1963.

G. A. RITTER and J. KOCKA, *Deutsche Sozialgeschichte 1871–1914,* vol. 2., Munich 1976.

G. A. RITTER et al., *Sozialgeschichtliches Arbeitsbuch,* Munich 1976 (useful brief coll. of statistics for Germany 1871–1918).

H. RÖSSLER ed., *Deutscher Adel 155–1740,* Darmstadt 1965.

H. RÖSSLER ed., *Deutsches Patriziat 1430–1740,* Limburg 1968.

H. RÖSSLER ed., *Universität und Gelehrtenstand 1400–1800,* Limburg 1970.

W. RÖSSLER, *Die Entstehung des modernen Erziehungswesens in Deutschland,* Stuttgart 1961.

H. ROSENBERG, *Bureaucracy, Absolutism and Autocracy — The Prussian Experience 1660–1815,* Camb./Mass. 1958.

H. ROSENBERG, *Grosse Depression und Bismarckzeit,* Berlin (West) 1 1967.

H. ROSENBERG, *Probleme der deutschen Sozialgeschichte,* Frankfurt 1969.

H. ROSENBERG, FESTSCHRIFT ed. H.-U. Wehler, Göttingen 1974.

R. RÜRUP, *Emancipation und Antisemitismus,* Göttingen 1975.

O. SCHEEL, *Die dt. Universität von ihren Anfängen bis zur Gegenwart,* Berlin 1930.

R. SCHENDA, *Volk ohne Buch. Studien zur Sozialgeschichte der populären Lesestoffe 1770–1910,* Frankfurt 1970 (with wide ranging bibliography pp. 495–560, covering i.a. censorship in Germany).

TH. SCHIEDER ed., *Sozialstruktur und Organisationen europäischer Nationalbewegungen,* Munich 1971.

F. SCHNABEL, *Deutschland im 19. Jahrhundert,* 3 ed., Freiburg 1954.

A. SCHÖNE ed., *Stadt, Schule, Universität, Buchwesen und die dte Literatur im 17. Jahrhundert,* Munich 1976. (This coll. of papers given at the Wolfenbüttel Baroque Congress in 1974 indicates the growing importance of the work done under the auspices of the Herzog August Library at Wolfenbüttel in the field of early modern German social history.)

P. E. SCHRAMM, *Neun Generationen,* 2 vols., Göttingen 1963/1965.

JOHANNA SCHULTZE, *Die Auseinandersetzung zwischen Adel und Bürgertum in den dt. Zeitschriften der letzten drei Jahrzehnte d. 18 Jahrhunderts,* Berlin 1925.

E. SHORTER, *The making of the modern family,* New York 1975.

W. SOMBARTH, *Der Bourgeois,* Munich 1913.

MAX SPINDLER ed., *Handbuch der bayerischen Geschichte,* esp. vol. 2 (1966) and 4/ii (1975), Munich.

R. STADELMANN and W. FISCHER, *Die Bildungswelt des dt. Handwerkers um 1800,* Berlin 1955.

P. N. STEARNS, *European Society in Upheaval. Social History since 1800,* New York 1967.

F. STERN, *Gold and Iron*, London 1977.

MICHAEL STÜRMER ed., *Das kaiserliche Deutschland,* Düsseldorf 1970 (a useful collection of essays on German elites 1871–1918).

H. J. TEUTEBERG and G. WIEGELMANN, *Der Wandel der Nahrungsgewohnheiten unter dem Einfluss der Industrialisierung,* Göttingen 1971.

R. v. THADDEN, *Die brandenburgisch-preussischen Hofprediger im 17. und 18. Jahrhundert,* Berlin 1959.

CHARLES, LOUISE and RICHARD TILLY, *The rebellious century 1830–1930,* Harvard 1975.

F. TÖNNIES, Deutscher Adel im 19. Jahrhundert, *Neue Rundschau* 23 (1912) pp. 1041–63 (a pioneering essay).

V. VALENTIN, *Geschichte der deutschen Revolutionen von 1848–49,* Berlin 1930.

L. A. VEIT and L. LENHART, *Kirche und Volksfrömmigkeit im Zeitalter des Barock,* Freiburg 1956.

R. VIERHAUS *Der europ. Adel vor der Revolution,* Göttingen 1971.

H.-U. WEHLER, *Bibliographie zur modernen deutschen Socialgeschichte (18–20, Jahrhundert),* Göttingen 1976.

H.-U. WEHLER, *Das deutsche Kaiserreich 1871–1918,* 2 ed., Göttingen 1975.

H.-U. WEHLER, *Moderne deutsche Sozialgeschichte,* 5 ed., Cologne 1975 (a pioneering collection of essays by leading German and American social historians).

MAX WEBER, *Wirtschaft und Gesellschaft,* 2 vols., 4 ed., Tübingen 1956.

H. A. WINKLER, Bürgertum in: *Sowjetsystem und Demokratische Gesellschaft,* ed. C. D. Kernig, vol. 1, Freiburg 1966, pp. 934–53.

W. ZORN, *Handels- und Industriegeschichte Bayern-Schwabens 1648–1870,* Augsburg 1961.

Index